THE

FOUR DRAGONS

GUIDEBOOK

A Comprehensive Guide to

HONG KONG
THAILAND
SINGAPORE
TAIWAN

THE AUTHOR

FREDRIC M. KAPLAN is founder and publisher of Eurasia Press. A specialist on contemporary Asia, he is co-author of the award-winning *Encyclopedia of China Today*, *The Thailand Guidebook*, and *The China Guidebook*, and is Vice-Chairman of the China Orient Tourism Council, a member of the National Committee on US-China Relations, the New York-Beijing Friendship City Committee, and former member of the National Board of Directors of US-China Peoples Friendship Association. Mr. Kaplan is director of the China Book Club and president of Asia Passage, which organizes specialized and adventure tours to Asia. During the past three decades, Mr. Kaplan has been a resident of both Hong Kong and Thailand and has visited Singapore and Taiwan on over 20 occasions.

CONTRIBUTORS

SYBIL WONG (Hong Kong Section) was a Hong Kong resident for more than 20 years. She is a prolific writer on women's issues and on Asian topics. **ALYSSA JOYCE** (Thailand Section) is currently on the television news staff of the American Broadcasting Company in Beijing. She has authored books and articles on travel in various parts of Asia. **ED LITTLE** (Taiwan Section) is public relations director for a major hotel in Taipei. **RITA FREUD** (Singapore Section) is a writer who has taught English at two universities in China and has lived and travelled extensively in Asia. **ROBERT FREUD** (Singapore Section) is Assistant Professor in the American Language Program at Bergen Community College in New Jersey. He has lived and worked throughout East Asia.

THE

FOUR DRAGONS

GUIDEBOOK

HONG KONG • THAILAND
SINGAPORE • TAIWAN

Fredric M. Kaplan

with

Sybil Wong, Alyssa Joyce,
Ed Little, Rita Freud, and Robert Freud

EURASIA
TRAVEL
GUIDES

HOUGHTON MIFFLIN COMPANY
Boston   London   Melbourne

Distributed by
Houghton Mifflin Company, 2 Park Street, Boston, MA 02108

FIRST EDITION, 1991

Typography by Logic Communications, Inc.
Text set in Goudy Old Style. Book design by Kathie Brown
and Marci Barris; cover design by Clifford Stoltze Design;
front cover photograph © Dallas and John Heaton/
Tony Stone Worldwide. Maps by Marci Barris,
Logic Communications, Inc.

Library of Congress Cataloging in publication data available
CIP 91-55165
ISBN O-395-58577-5
ISSN 1055-8853

Printed in the United States of America
00 10 9 8 7 6 5 4 3 2 1

INTRODUCTION

IN Asia, the dragon is a mythical symbol of good tidings. For the Eurasia Travel Guides, our "four dragons" – Hong Kong, Thailand, Singapore, and Taiwan – have been emerging as great tourist destinations along the southeast corridor of the Pacific Rim.

Long established as great travel destinations within their own region, each of these countries has for more than two decades now been offering visitors enriching, reliable, and memorable holiday experiences — along with appreciable value for tourist dollars spent.

Entering the 1990s, these four dragons of tourism had all built formidable infrastructures – each with it's own brilliant swath of new hotels, ease of international access, modern internal transportation, studious site development, and high-level training of tourist sector staff and administration.

Eurasia Travel Guides is happy to welcome you to these four magnificent destinations. Trends for the 1990s show that more and more travelers from America and Europe will be responding to the allure of the four East Asia dragons. And many tourists and groups are likely to be planning visits to two or more of these countries on the same trip – capturing the dramatic contrasts offered by four places that have evolved quite separately despite close proximity to each other.

Welcome to the Four Dragons.

Fredric M. Kaplan
April 4, 1991

ACKNOWLEDGMENTS

GREAT thanks are owed to Patricia M. Godfrey, general editor for *The Four Dragons*, whose skill and persistence brought this complex work to final fruition. The book was further helped by the contributions of Della McEneaney, copy editor; Rose Bernal, indexer; and especially Marci Barris for her beautiful design work and creation of the maps, as well as to Chris Yarusi, typesetting coordinator, of Logic Communications, Inc. Contributing staff at Eurasia Press included Ellen Tormey-Smith, Jacqueline A. Rhodes, Deborah J. Kaufman, and Lita Reyes.

In addition, we would like to thank the following for help and information supplied:

Tracy Tsui Hung Chiu, of the Hong Kong Economic and Trade Office, New York City, and Edith Wei, Public Relations Officer, New York office, Hong Kong Tourist Association, for assistance with the section on Hong Kong.

Mr. Aswin, of the New York office, Tourism Authority of Thailand, and Mr. Sart Sirisinha, of the New York branch, Thailand Economic Office, for assistance with the section on Thailand.

Mahani Mohamad, of the New York office, Singapore Tourist Promotion Board, for assistance with the section on Singapore.

Mr. Paisan, Wangsai, Director, Tourism Authority of Thailand, North America East Coast; The Tourism Bureau, Republic of China (Taiwan); Government Information Office, Republic of China (Taiwan); and China (Taiwan) External Trade Development Council, for assistance with the section on Taiwan.

The New York office of the U.S. Fish and Wildlife Service, for information about restricted by-products from endangered species.

AT&T, for their *International Telecommunications Guide*, which proved invaluable in verifying phone numbers.

CONTENTS

Authors / 2
Acknowledgments / 6

HONG KONG

Hong Kong at a Glance / 23
   History of Hong Kong / 23
   Politics and Government / 27
   Economy / 30
   People and Language of Hong Kong / 35
Planning a Trip to Hong Kong / 38
   Tourist Information / 38
      Table: Hong Kong Tourist Association Offices / 38
   Costs / 39
   When to Go / 40
      Climate / 40
      Festivals and Holidays / 40
   What to Take / 44
      Clothing / 44
Getting to Hong Kong / 45
   Visas and Health Certificates / 45
   International Routings to Hong Kong / 45
      By Air / 45
       Table: Flight Time from Major Cities / 46
       Table: Airlines with Offices in Hong Kong / 48
   Entrance and Exit Procedures / 50
      Customs / 50
Traveling in Hong Kong / 52
   Know Before You Go / 52
      Weights and Measures / 52
      Electricity and Water / 52
      Health and Safety / 52
      Time Around the World / 52
      Religious Services / 54
      Everyday Amenities / 54
      Legal Protection and Precautions / 54
   Money, Currency, and Banking / 55
      Currency and Exchange Rates / 55
      Banking for Tourists / 55
      Credit Cards and Traveler's Checks / 57

Communications and the Media / 57
    Postal Service / 57
    Telecommunications / 57
Local Transportation / 60
    Sightseeing Tours / 66
Tour Packages / 69
    Hong Kong Tour Operators / 71

The Hong Kong Tour / 74
Hong Kong Island / 74
    The Central District / 74
    Wan Chai / 82
    Happy Valley / 83
    Causeway Bay / 84
    North Point, Quarry Bay, Shau Kei Wan, and Chai Wan / 85
    Big Wave Bay and Shek O / 85
    Stanley / 86
    Repulse Bay / 87
    Deep Water Bay / 88
    Aberdeen / 88
    Western District / 88
    The Peak / 89 ·
Kowloon / 89
    Tsim Sha Tsui / 89
    Yau Ma Tei / 93
    Sham Shui Po / 93
    Lai Chi Kok / 94
    Mong Kok and Hung Hom / 84
    Kowloon Tong / 94
    Wong Tai Sin / 94
    Kwun Tong / 95
The New Territories / 95
The Outlying Islands / 96
Hong Kong for Children / 99

Hotels and Lodging / 101
Hong Kong Island / 102
Kowloon / 106
    Hostels and Guest Houses / 114
New Territories / 115
The Outlying Islands / 115

Dining Out in Hong Kong / 116
Hotel Dining / 116
Restaurants / 116
    Chinese Cuisine / 116
    Western Cuisine / 122
    Grill Rooms / 126

9

CONTENTS

Asian / 126
Vegetarian Restaurants / 129
Floating Restaurants / 129
Revolving Restaurants / 130
Nightclub Restaurants / 130
Coffee Shops / 130
Afternoon Tea / 131
Pubs / 131
Street Stalls / 132
Fast Food / 132
Out-of-the-way Dining / 133

Cultural Activities, Recreation, and Entertainment / 134
Culture and Entertainment / 134
Chinese Opera / 134
Dance / 134
Theater / 136
Music—Chinese, Western, Jazz, and Folk / 136
Movies / 137
Museums / 137
Discos and Bars / 138
Sports / 139

Shopping / 143
What to Buy / 144
Antiques / 144
Arts and Crafts / 145
Jewelry / 146
Carpets and Rugs / 147
Clothing and Textiles / 147
High-Tech Products / 150
Furniture / 151
Shopping Areas /151
Hong Kong Central / 151
Causeway Bay / 153
Tsim Sha Tsui / 154
Tsim Sha Tsui East / 155

Doing Business in Hong Kong / 156
Establishing Your Business in Hong Kong / 156
Identity Card / 156
Business Registration and Incorporation / 157
Work Permits and Visas / 157
Business Practices and Conditions / 158
Accounting Requirements / 158
Arbitration / 158
Business Centers / 159
Certificates of Origin / 159

Industrial and Intellectual Property Rights / 159
Insurance / 160
Labor Market / 160
Land and Premises / 161
Legal System / 162
Trade Publications / 162
Trade Shows and Exhibitions / 163
Taxation / 163
Income Taxes / 163
Customs Duties and Excise Tax / 163
Banking and Finance / 163
Banking / 163
Stock Markets and Other Financial Markets / 164
Important Bodies Related to Business / 165
Table: Government and Quasi-Government Industry and
Trade Departments / 165
Table: Chambers of Commerce / 166
Table: Hong Kong Representatives (Trade and Industrial
Promotion) Overseas / 168
Table: Consulates and Overseas Representatives in Hong Kong
(selected list) / 171
Useful Telephone Numbers / 173

Travel Outside of Hong Kong / 175
Macao / 175
To China / 183

Appendix / 187
Language / 187
Future Status of Hong Kong / 195

THAILAND

Thailand at a Glance / 201
Geography / 202
History of Thailand / 203
Table: Chronology of Thai Dynasties and Kingdoms / 211
Politics and Government / 211
Economy / 212
People and Language / 214
People / 214
Language / 219

Planning a Trip to Thailand / 221
Tourist Information / 221
Table: TAT Offices / 222

11
CONTENTS

Travel Options / 224
    Group Tours / 224
        Table: Tour Companies / 225
    Independent Travel / 226
        Table: Tour Agencies / 227
Costs / 227
    Group Tours / 227
    Independent Travel / 228
    Intercity Travel / 228
When to Go / 229
    Climate / 229
    Festivals / 229

Getting to Thailand / 233
Visas and Health Certificates / 233
    Table: Thai Diplomatic Missions Abroad / 234
    Visa Applications / 233
    Visa Extensions / 233
    Health Certificates / 233
International Routings to Thailand / 235
    By Air / 235
        Table: Airline Offices in Bangkok / 236
    By Land / 236
    By Sea / 237
Entrance and Exit Procedures / 237
    Customs / 237
    Exit Formalities / 238

Traveling in Thailand / 239
Know Before You Go / 239
    Electricity and Water / 239
    Health and Safety / 239
        Table: Hospitals in Bangkok and Chiang Mai / 240
    Time Around the World / 241
    Religious Services / 242
    Tipping / 242
    Mores and Manners / 242
Money, Currency, and Banking / 243
    Currency / 243
        Table: Exchange Rates for the Thai Baht / 244
    Traveler's Checks and Credit Cards / 243
Communications and News Media / 245
    Postal Service / 245
    Telecommunications / 245
Local Transportation / 247
    Thai Domestic Flight Service / 247
    Rail Services / 247

Long-distance Bus Services / 248
Taxis / 249
Tuk Tuks / 249
Local Buses / 249
Sightseeing Tours / 251

The Thailand Tour / 252
Bangkok / 252
Major Attractions / 256
Other Sites / 261
Canals and Rivers / 262
Central Region / 263
Ayutthaya / 263
Kanchanaburi / 264
Khao Yai National Park / 265
Nakhom Pathom / 265
Pattaya / 265
Koh Samet / 267
Northern Region / 269
Chiang Mai / 269
Chiang Rai / 272
Sukhothai / 273
Northeastern Region / 273
Southern Region / 273
Hua Hin / 276
Koh Samui / 277
Phuket / 279

Hotels and Lodging / 282
Hotel Reservations / 283
Bangkok Hotels / 283
Superior Hotels / 283
First-Class Hotels / 286
Economy-Class Hotels / 288
Guesthouses and Apartments / 289
Central Region Hotels / 289
Pattaya / 289
Jomtien Beach / 291
Northern Region Hotels / 291
Southern Region Hotels / 292
Koh Samui / 292
Phuket / 293

Dining Out in Thailand / 297
Table: Popular Thai Dishes / 298
Table: List of Cooking Schools / 299
Hotel Dining / 299

13

CONTENTS

Restaurant Dining / 299
Restaurants in Bangkok and Environs / 300
    Thai Cuisine / 300
    Other Eastern Cuisines / 301
    Western Cuisines / 301
    Theater Restaurants / 302

Cultural Activities, Recreation, and Entertainment / 303
Culture and Entertainment / 303
    Performing Arts / 303
    Film / 304
    Cultural Societies / 304
    Nightlife / 304
Sports / 305
    Thai Boxing / 305
    Kite Flying / 306
    Other Thai Sports / 306

Shopping / 308
How to Shop / 308
What to Buy / 309
    Antiques / 309
    Metalcrafts / 309
    Ceramics / 309
    Lacquerware / 309
    Gems and Jewelry / 310
    Handicrafts / 311
    Temple Rubbings / 311
    Textiles and Clothing / 312
What Not to Buy / 313
Major Shopping Areas / 313

Doing Business in Thailand / 315
Establishing Your Business in Thailand / 315
Business Operations in Thailand / 318
Taxation / 320
Banking and Finance / 322
        Table: Thai Banking / 323
Government Bodies and Private Organizations / 328
Useful Telephone Numbers / 359

Annotated Reading List / 361

Appendix: The Thai Language / 362

SINGAPORE

Singapore at a Glance / 367
    History of Singapore: Sea Town and Lion City / 367
    Politics and Government / 372
    Economy / 373
    People and Language / 375
        People of Singapore / 375
        Languages /376

Planning a Trip to Singapore / 377
    Tourist Information / 377
        Table: Singapore Tourist Promotion Board / 377
    Travel Options / 379
    When to Go / 379
        Climate / 379
        Festivals / 380
    What to Take—and What Not To / 384
        Clothing / 384

Getting to Singapore / 385
    Visas and Health Certificates / 385
    International Routings to Singapore / 388
    Entrance and Exit Procedures / 389

Traveling in Singapore / 391
    Know Before You Go / 391
        Weights and Measures / 391
        Electricity and Water / 391
        Health and Safety / 391
            Table: Government Hospitals / 392
        Time Around the World / 392
        Religious Services / 393
            Table: Religious Services and Places of Worship / 393
        Legal Prohibitions / 395
        Social and Cultural Mores / 396
    Money, Currency, and Banking / 398
        Currency and Exchange Rate / 398
    Communications and News Media / 399
        Postal Service / 399
        Telecommunications / 400
    Local Transportation / 401
        Public Transportation / 401
        Sightseeing Tours / 406

The Singapore Tour / 409
    A City of Neighborhoods / 409
        Arab Street / 409

15
CONTENTS

Chinatown and the Singapore River / 410
Little India / 414
Colonial Heart / 416
Sights Worth Seeing / 417
Major Monuments and Landmarks / 417
Places of Worship / 419
Parks and Gardens / 420
Bird and Animal Sanctuaries / 422
Singapore for Children / 423
The Islands of Singapore / 425
Sentosa / 425
Kusu / 426
Pulau Hantu, Pulau Seking, Sisters Island /427

Hotels and Lodging / 428
Hotels with More Than 400 Rooms / 428
Hotels with 200–400 Rooms / 438
Hotels with 50–200 Rooms /447

Dining Out in Singapore / 453
Chinese Restaurants / 456
Cantonese / 456
Peking / 457
Shanghainese / 457
Teochew / 458
Other Asian Restaurants / 461
Western Restaurants / 465

Cultural Activities, Recreation, and Entertainment / 469
Culture and Entertainment / 469
Chinese Opera (Wayang) / 469
Theater / 470
Music and Concerts / 470
Cabarets and Night Clubs / 471
Special Cultural Performances / 471
Discos / 472
Cocktail Lounges and Pubs / 473
Movies / 474
Sports / 474

Shopping in Singapore / 478
Shopping Tips / 478
What to Buy / 480
Antiques and Curios / 480
Arts and Crafts / 480
Fabrics and Clothing / 482
Cosmetics and Perfumes / 483
High-Tech Products / 484
Where to Shop / 484

Orchard Road / 484
Tanglin Road / 485
Scotts Road / 485
Chinatown / 485
Arab Street / 486

Doing Business in Singapore / 489
Establishing Your Business in Singapore / 489
Residence Permits / 490
Business Registration / 491
Trademarks and Patents / 493
Copyright / 493
Taxation / 493
Banking, Finance, and Securities / 497
Business-Related Bodies and Organizations / 499
Government Bodies / 499
Useful Telephone Numbers / 515

Touring Outside of Singapore / 516
To Malaysia / 516
To China / 518
To Other Countries / 520

Singapore Reading List / 522
Articles / 522
Books / 522

TAIWAN

Taiwan at a Glance / 527
Geography / 527
History / 527
Politics and Government / 529
Economy / 531
People and Language / 532
People of Taiwan / 532
Language / 533

Planning a Trip to Taiwan / 535
Tourist Information / 535
Table: Taiwan Tourism Representatives Abroad / 535
Taiwan Travel Options / 536
Group Tours to Taiwan / 537
Touring Taiwan on Your Own / 538
Costs / 539
Air Fares / 540
When to Go / 540
Climate / 540

17
CONTENTS

Festivals / 541
What to Take—and What Not to Take / 542
 Clothing / 542
 Medicines, Personal Hygiene, and Grooming Items / 543
 Prohibited Items / 543

Getting to Taiwan / 544
Visas and Health Certificates / 544
 Table: Taiwan Government Representatives Abroad / 544
 Single-Entry Visa / 546
 Resident Visa / 547
 Group Tourist Permits / 547
 Health Certificates / 547
International Routings to Taiwan / 547
 By Air / 548
  Table: Airlines Serving Taipei / 548
 By Sea / 550
Entrance and Exit Procedures / 550
 Plant and Animal Quarantine / 550
 Customs / 551
 Exit Formalities and Airport Tax / 551

Traveling in Taiwan / 552
Know Before You Go / 552
 Weights and Measures / 552
 Electricity and Water / 552
 Safety and Health / 552
  Table: Hospitals in Taiwan / 553
 Time Around the World / 555
 Religious Services / 555
  Table: Houses of Worship / 556
 Tipping / 559
 Local Mores and Sensibilities / 559
Money, Currency, and Banking / 560
Communications and the News Media / 562
 Postal Service / 562
 Telecommunications / 562
Local Transportation / 565
 Public Transportation / 565
 Rental Cars / 566
Sightseeing Tours / 566
 Taipei City / 567
 Wulai Aborigine Village / 568
 North Coast / 568
 Leofoo Safari Park and Window on China / 568
 Penghu (Pescadores) / 569
 Taroko Gorge / 569
 Sun Moon Lake / 570

East-West Cross-Island Highway and Sun Moon Lake / 570
Sun Moon Lake and Alishan / 570
Kenting National Park / 571
Kenting National Park and Kaohsiung / 571
Round-the-Island Tours / 571

The Taiwan Tour / 573
Taipei City / 573
    Sights Worth Seeing / 576
Keelung / 579
Tamsui / 580
Wulai / 580
Eastern Taiwan / 580
    Hualien / 580
Eastern Islands / 581
    Lanyu / 581
    Lutao / 581
Central Taiwan / 582
    Taichung / 582
    Lukang / 583
    Sun Moon Lake / 583
    Alishan / 583
    Peikang / 583
Southern Taiwan / 586
    Tainan / 586
    Tsengwen Reservoir / 590
    Coral Lake / 590
    Kaohsiung / 590
    Kenting / 595
Western Islands / 595
    Penghu / 595
    Hsiao Liuchiu / 596

Hotels and Lodging / 597
Hotels in Taipei / 597
    Leading Hotels / 597
    Other Taipei Hotels / 604
Hotels in Central Taiwan / 607
    Chiayi / 607
Hualien / 608
Ilan / 610
Kaohsiung / 610
Kenting Area / 613
Taichung / 614
Taitung / 616
Taoyuan / 617
Yunlin / 618

Youth Activity Centers / 618
Youth Hostels / 619

Dining Out in Taiwan / 621
Hotel Chinese Restaurants / 622
Recommended Chinese Restaurants / 623
Cantonese Cuisine / 623
Chaochow Cuisine / 623
Hunan Cuisine / 623
Mongolian Barbecue / 624
Peking Cuisine / 624
Seafood Restaurants / 625
Shanghainese Restaurants / 625
Szechuan Cuisine / 625
Taiwanese Cuisine / 626
Vegetarian Restaurants / 626
Chinese Dining Etiquette / 626
Other Eastern Cuisines / 628
Western Cuisines / 629
Bars and Pubs / 630
Teahouses / 631
Business Clubs / 632

Cultural Activities, Recreation, and Entertainment / 633
Culture and Entertainment / 633
Chinese Opera / 633
Music / 634
Movies / 635
MTV / 635
Disco / 636
Nightclubs / 636
Sports / 637

Shopping / 640
What to Buy / 640
Precious and Semiprecious Stones / 640
Porcelain / 641
Marble / 641
Brass / 641
Cloisonné / 642
Wood Carvings / 642
Electrical and Electronic Items / 642
Tea / 642
Garments and Fashions / 643
Where to Buy / 644
Department Stores / 644
Night Markets and Bazaars / 644
Business Center / 645

Doing Business in Taiwan / 646
 Establishing Your Business in Taiwan / 646
 Business Practices and Conditions / 648
 Taxation / 649
 Banking, Finance, and Securities / 651
 Business Customs / 655
 Conventions and Exhibitions / 656
 Bureaus and Organizations / 656
  Table: Foreign Diplomatic and Consular Offices
   in Taipei / 658
  Table: China (Taiwan) External Trade Development
   Council/FETS/U.S. Branches / 659
  Business and Trade Associations / 665
  Table: U.S. Foreign Trade Associations in Taiwan / 667
 Useful Telephone Numbers / 668

Appendix: The Chinese Language in Taiwan / 669

MAPS

HONG KONG
 Hong Kong's location
  in East Asia / 24
 Hong Kong Island, Kowloon
  & The New Territories / 32
 Hong Kong Mass Transit
  Railway Route Map / 64
 Hong Kong Kowloon
  Peninsula / 76
 Hong Kong Wanchai &
  Cause Bay / 80
 Hong Kong Island
  Central District / 90

THAILAND
 Map of Thailand / 205
 Map of Bangkok / 254
 Pattaya / 266
 Koh Samet Island / 268
 Chiang Mai / 270
 Phuket Island / 280

SINGAPORE
 Island Map / 370
 Singapore MRT Route Map / 402
 Marina Centre / 407
 Arab Street / 411
 Chinatown / 412
 Little India / 414
 Orchard Road East / 424
 Orchard Road West / 430
 Geylang Serai—Shopping / 449
 East Coast Map / 474
 Orchard Road—Shopping / 479

TAIWAN
 Taiwan: Island Province Map / 530
 Taipei / 574
 Taichung / 584
 Tainan / 588
 Kaohsiung / 592

Index / 672

Photographic Credits / 688

I
Hong Kong

Hong Kong harbor

I
Hong Kong at a Glance

Hong Kong is situated just south of the Tropic of Cancer. It lies at the southeastern tip of China, adjoining the province of Guangdong, and is some 1,240 mi (2,000 km) south of Beijing (Peking). The geopolitical entity of Hong Kong has a total area of 413 sq mi (1,069 km²), of which Hong Kong Island, along with the immediately adjacent small islands, makes up 31 sq mi (79 km²), Kowloon 4 sq mi (10 km²), and the New Territories and the 200-odd islands 378 sq mi (979 km²). The biggest island is Lantau, twice the size of Hong Kong Island. The highest mountain is Tai Mo Shan in the New Territories, which is 3,140 ft (957 m) tall; Victoria Peak on Hong Kong Island is 1,811 ft (552 m). For administrative purposes, the territory is divided into 19 districts.

HISTORY OF HONG KONG

HONG KONG consists of Hong Kong Island, the Kowloon Peninsula, the New Territories, and 235 islands and islets, making a total land mass of about 400 sq mi (1,070 km²); through reclamation, the land area is being extended. Victoria, on Hong Kong Island, is the main city and commercial center. The island of Hong Kong (a name that means "fragrant harbor" in Chinese) lies at the southeastern tip of the People's Republic of China. A deep-water harbor separates it from the Kowloon Peninsula, which adjoins the province of Guangdong (Kwangtung) at the mouth of the Pearl River. The name *Kowloon* means "nine dragons," and the area is said to have been named after the eight hills in the peninsula and after the young Song Emperor who fled from the Mongols at the end of the Song Dynasty (960–1279 AD).

Hong Kong was a small, mountainous, and sparsely populated island, a part of China, when it entered history in the middle of the 19th century. During the 18th century, trading between the Manchu Emperors of China and the foreign powers, particularly Great Britain, was a one-way affair. The Chinese wanted none of the products of the West except silver bullion, and this created a balance-of-payments crisis for the British. The imbalance was righted when opium was introduced to China in huge quantities, and eventually the widespread use of opium among the Chinese caused so much silver to flow out of China

HONG KONG'S LOCATION

Hong Kong in East Asia

into the purses of the foreign traders that China outlawed the trade in 1799. However, opium continued to be smuggled in by the British from India.

Finally, in 1839 the Manchu Emperor sent an Imperial Commissioner to Canton (Guangzhou) to stamp out the illegal opium trade. The British merchants were forced to surrender all their opium in storage and, after six weeks of intense confrontation, retreated to safer sanctuary in Macao and on ships anchored in Hong Kong Harbor. In the summer of 1840, a British naval force attacked Canton in retaliation against the Chinese. A temporary peace plan, the Convention of Chuenpi, gave Britain the island of Hong Kong, which on January 26, 1841, was proclaimed a British colony. However, the Chuenpi peace plan was repudiated by both the Chinese and the British governments and fighting resumed. Shanghai fell and Nanjing was threatened, and in the end the Chinese were overwhelmed by the British in this, the first of the Opium Wars. The Manchus were forced to sign a succession of treaties that opened China's doors to Western economic, political, and religious penetration.

The Treaty of Nanking (signed in 1842 and ratified in 1843) ceded Hong Kong Island to Britain "in perpetuity." The Convention of Peking (1860) ceded the southern part of the Kowloon Peninsula (to Boundary St.) and Stonecutter's Island, also in perpetuity. The Convention of 1898 leased to Britain the New Territories (to the Shenzhen River — the border with China) and 235 outlying islands and islets for 99 years (July 1, 1898, to June 30, 1997).

Hong Kong was inhabited by a few thousand fishing people, farmers, pirates, and smugglers when it was ceded to Britain. Archaeological finds give evidence of human activities in Hong Kong from the Neolithic Age. The earliest known structure to be found is the Han Tomb in Kowloon, built within the Eastern Han Dynasty (25–220 AD). Walled villages, built in the 17th century, are still standing in the New Territories.

Under the direction of Sir Henry Pottinger, the first British governor of Hong Kong, the island's population and commerce grew steadily. The sheltered harbor, strategically located on the Far East trade routes, enabled Hong Kong to become the center of a burgeoning entrepot trade with China, and in 1910 the Kowloon Railway to the Chinese border was completed. By 1940 the population had grown to 1.6 million.

During World War II, Japanese armed forces took Hong Kong on Christmas Day, 1941. The Japanese occupation of the colony lasted for three years and eight months. After Japan's defeat and surrender on August 14, 1945, a provisional government was set up in Hong Kong, and on May 1, 1946, civil government was restored. Postwar Hong Kong struggled for its survival, and gradual progress was made both economically and socially.

The civil war between the Chinese Nationalists and Communists in the period 1948–49 drove hundreds of thousands of people to Hong Kong, swelling the population to an estimated 2.2 million. The Chinese refugees from Shanghai and other commercial centers brought with them skills and industrial know-how, and Hong Kong benefitted, particularly in textile manufacturing and other light industries. With the influx of capital, skills, and energy, Hong Kong prospered.

Then, in 1967, the Cultural Revolution in China spilled over to the colony. Riots and strikes temporarily paralyzed the economy, but Hong Kong soon returned to normal and continued its rapid development in trade, manufacturing, and tourism.

In March 1972, the Chinese Government reiterated to the United

Nations Special Committee on the Granting of Independence to Colonial Countries and Peoples that the question of Hong Kong was a matter of China's sovereign right and that the area should not be included in the UN's list of colonial territories. China has consistently held that the whole of Hong Kong is Chinese territory and that the question of Hong Kong should be settled through negotiations with Britain when conditions should be ripe.

The 500-year-old Ping Shan pagoda in Hong Kong's New Territories. Originally built with five floors, it lost the top two in a typhoon in 1954.

As the lease on the New Territories neared its expiration, concerns were expressed in the late 1970s on the future of Hong Kong. (Leased land makes up nine-tenths of the territory, including the airport, the container port, and other vital facilities, and Hong Kong cannot function without the leased land.) The British Government concluded that confidence within the territory would quickly erode if the future of Hong Kong after the 1997 deadline were not resolved. A series of informal talks between British officials and Chinese leaders were conducted in Beijing, and both governments decided the time was ripe to begin negotiations on the question of Hong Kong. In September 1982 the British Prime Minister, Margaret Thatcher, visited China, and Sino-British negotiations on the future of Hong Kong began. Following extensive talks, it became clear that China would not accept British administration in any form after 1997.

But how then were Hong Kong's stability and prosperity to be maintained after Britain's withdrawal? In June 1984, a working group was set up to consider documents proposed by both sides, and later that year a Sino-British Joint Liaison Group was established. By September 26, 1984, a draft Joint Declaration and three Annexes were initialed by both governments. Ratification took place in 1985, making it a formal international agreement, legally binding in all its parts.

The people of Hong Kong accepted as inevitable that China would resume sovereignty over Hong Kong on July 1, 1997. According to the agreement, "Hong Kong, China" will have the right of internal self-government under the "One Country, Two Systems" policy proclaimed by China. As a Special Administrative Region, Hong Kong will also have autonomy over its economic, social, and legal affairs for another 50 years after 1997.

POLITICS AND GOVERNMENT

HONG KONG was created as a British Crown Colony, with a governor nominated by Whitehall, an Executive Council, and a Legislative Council, with official majorities. The governor is the representative of the Queen in Hong Kong and he has the ultimate direction of the administration of the territory. He is also the titular commander-in-chief.

The Letters Patent, issued under the Great Seal of the United Kingdom, establish the basic framework of the administration of Hong Kong, and, together with the Royal Instructions, form the written constitution. The 14-member Executive Council advises the governor on all important policy matters. On January 2, 1988, 10 of its members were nominated (appointed) members and four ex-officio, and the governor presided over meetings. The Legislative Council enacts legislation, including acts for the appropriation of public funds. It has a maximum membership of 57, comprising the governor (who acts as president of the Council), 3 ex-officio members (the chief secretary, the financial secretary, and the attorney general), 27 nominated (appointed) members, and 26 elected members. The elected members are chosen, some by nine "functional constituencies" (occupational or professional groups, such as commercial, health care, finance and accounting) and some by an electoral college representing geographical areas.

Additionally, there are two Municipal Councils— the Urban Council, a statutory body that provides municipal services to almost 4 million people living in the urban areas; and the Regional Council, established in April 1986, as the statutory municipal authority for areas outside the jurisdiction of the Urban Council. There are also 19 district boards throughout the territory, established in 1982, to provide a forum for public consultation and participation in administration at the district level. Some members of these three bodies are elected from constituencies at large and some from each district.

As 1997 approaches, political reform leading to a more representative government in Hong Kong has attracted interest among the local populace. The government has also made plans to prepare the territory for a more self-governing role as Hong Kong becomes a Special Administrative Region of China in 1997. The Green Paper of July 1984 ("The Further Development of Representative Government in Hong Kong") contained provisions for elections to the Legislative Council, the district boards, and the Regional Council. It also called for a progressive replacement of the members in the Executive Council by members of the Legislative Council. However, these arrangements were not to be introduced until 1988 and 1991. But in 1985, a system of indirect election to the Legislative Council was introduced. And in May 1987, another Green Paper ("The 1987 Review of Developments in Representative Government") was issued, and the public was asked to respond. The purpose of this review was to consider whether the systems of representative government in Hong Kong should be further developed in 1988 and in what manner. The most controversial point contained in this document was that there would be no direct elections to the Legislative Council in 1988—a provision perceived as the result of direct pressure from the Chinese government to delay any political reform until the Basic Law (constitution) for the future Hong Kong Special Administrative Region should be written.

In February 1988 a White Paper entitled "The Development of Representative Government: The Way Forward" was issued by the government. It basically called for gradual and prudent development of a more representative government to preserve Hong Kong's stability and prosperity and permit a smooth transition in 1997. Even though a segment of the community demanded direct elections in 1988, their voice was in the minority. Political reform moves forward slowly; the prevailing wisdom is that any dramatic reform should conform with the Basic Law finalized in 1989.

In late April 1988, a draft of the Basic Law was issued by China. It granted considerable autonomy in economic, trade, cultural, and political affairs to Hong Kong for a further 50 years after the end of British rule in 1997. A provision of the draft law states that "the region shall not practice the socialist system and policies, and will maintain the current capitalist system and lifestyle for 50 years."

In the meanwhile Hong Kong has taken on another title—that of a British "dependent territory." Soon, Hong Kong will simply be "Hong Kong, China."

LEGAL SYSTEM

Hong Kong's legal system is based on English Common Law and rules of equity, so far as they are applicable to local circumstances. Statutory laws are created by Hong Kong ordinances, which generally follow the principles of British Acts of Parliament. The locally enacted laws are consolidated and revised periodically.

The courts of justice in Hong Kong are the Supreme Court (which consists of the Court of Appeal and the High Court), the District Court, the Magistrates' Court, the Coroner's Court, and the Juvenile Court. Additionally, there are the Lands, Labor, and Small Claims Tribunals.

The Government Legal Department, also known as the Attorney General's Chambers, is headed by the attorney general; it consists of four divisions—Policy and Administration, Civil, Drafting, and Prosecutions.

There is a Legal Aid Department that offers legal aid for civil and criminal cases as long as the applicants satisfy both the "means test" and the "merits test."

ECONOMY

THE economy of Hong Kong depends almost entirely on import and export trade. Hong Kong has limited natural resources, and it has to import virtually everything — raw materials and semi-manufactures, consumer goods, capital goods, foodstuffs, fuels, and even water. Its exports, therefore, have to generate enough foreign exchange earnings to pay for the imports. Over the years, Hong Kong has developed into one of the world's largest trading entities.

From the very beginning, some 150 years ago, Hong Kong has been a free port. Now, with its free trade policy and modern backup services (communications, commercial links, and international finances), its economy is among the fastest-growing ones in the newly industrializing countries (NICs). In the period from 1977 to 1987, the annual growth of domestic exports averaged 9% in real terms, almost twice the growth rate of world trade. Total trade (exports plus imports plus re-exports) was near HK$752 billion (US$96.4 billion) for 1987. China, Japan, the United States, and Taiwan are the top four importers, accounting for about 68% of the total import trade. Again, China and the United States, together with United Kingdom and Germany, are the top four domestic exporters, accounting for some 69% of the total export trade.

In the past trading was dominated by the British-controlled merchant houses, or *hong*; the main ones have been Jardine Matheson, Hutchison Whampoa, Wheelock Marden, and the Swire Group. Recently, Chinese groups have emerged and have taken over some of the old British trading houses, among them Hutchinson Whampoa.

Virtually 90% of Hong Kong's manufacturing output is exported. Domestic exports in 1987 consisted principally of apparel and clothing accessories (valued at HK$65.321 billion or US$8.375 billion)—making Hong Kong the world's largest exporter of these items. Other export items include electronics, plastic products, watches and clocks, textiles, household electrical appliances, and metal products.

Because of the increasing pressure of protectionism and external competition, Hong Kong manufacturers are diversifying their export products and at the same time are constantly searching for new markets. Since Hong Kong's manufacturing industries are small, light industries, they can be readily shifted to produce different products to meet new market needs. Industrial development has been limited to relatively labor-intensive light industry because of the shortage of land. There is hardly any heavy industry in Hong Kong. In recent years, a few industrial estates in the New Territories have been developed to accommodate industries that cannot be located in the typical multistory factory buildings in urban areas.

Gross domestic product (GDP) grew from 0.6% in 1985 (estimated at US$39.6 billion) to nearly 8.7% in 1986, and the Consumer Price Index increased by 2.5% in 1986 over the previous year. Even in the grossly inflationary years of 1979 and 1980, consumer price indexes rose only between 12 and 16% a year. Manufacturing contributes most to the GDP (some 22%), followed by the service sector (wholesale, retail, and import-export trade, restaurants and hotels, transportation, financial, insurance, real estate, and business services).

Hong Kong is the third-largest international financial and banking center, after London and New York. There are more than 150 licensed banks in Hong Kong—over 130 of them foreign—and their total deposit liabilities at the end of 1988 were HK$779 billion (US$99.9 billion). Hong Kong has an active foreign exchange market, with no exchange controls, and international banks trade through Hong Kong while the markets are closed in Europe and North America.

Hong Kong has no central bank. Key interest rates are set by the Hong Kong Association of Banks, which is a statutory body to which all licensed banks must belong. Banknotes are issued by two leading local banks—The Hong Kong and Shanghai Banking Corporation and the Standard Chartered Bank, and coins are issued by the government. The Hong Kong dollar is freely convertible into other currencies. In 1983, because of uncertainty over Hong Kong's future, the dollar dropped in value and the government pegged the currency to the U.S. dollar at HK$7.8 = U.S.$1 to shore up confidence. Currently, the Hong Kong dollar is still linked at the same exchange rate even though the U.S. government has frequently hinted that Hong Kong should revalue its dollar. Over the years the Hong Kong dollar has depreciated, along with the U.S. dollar, against the Japanese yen and the European currencies—a development that has helped boost Hong Kong's exports in those markets.

The total figure for foreign investments is not known, because there is no control of the free flow of funds and capital into and out of the territory. Manufacturing investments were put at US$6 million at the end of 1987. In general, Hong Kong businessmen expect to get investment capital and profit back within five years or less. Long-term investments hardly exist. The largest proportion of overseas investment comes from America and Japan; they see Hong Kong as a relatively cheap high-tech manufacturing base and a financial jumping-off point for the vast China market.

Hong Kong is China's fourth-largest export market, worth about

THE BRITISH CROWN COLONY OF HONG KONG
(Includes Hong Kong Island, Kowloon & the New Territories)

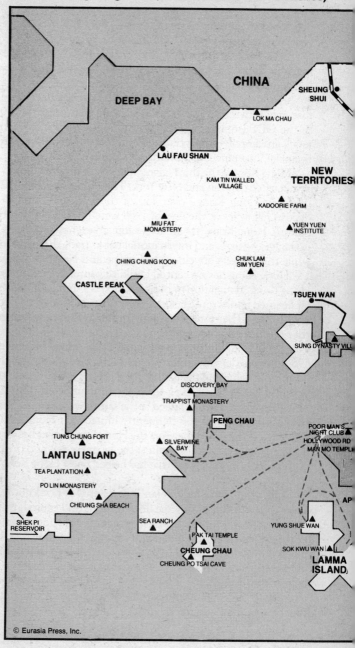

CHINA

DEEP BAY

SHEUNG SHUI

LOK MA CHAU

LAU FAU SHAN

NEW TERRITORIES

KAM TIN WALLED VILLAGE

KADOORIE FARM

MIU FAT MONASTERY

YUEN YUEN INSTITUTE

CHING CHUNG KOON

CHUK LAM SIM YUEN

CASTLE PEAK

TSUEN WAN

SUNG DYNASTY VILL

DISCOVERY BAY

TRAPPIST MONASTERY

PENG CHAU

POOR MAN'S NIGHT CLUB

HOLLYWOOD RD

MAIN MO TEMPLE

TUNG CHUNG FORT

SILVERMINE BAY

LANTAU ISLAND

TEA PLANTATION

PO LIN MONASTERY

CHEUNG SHA BEACH

SHEK PI RESERVOIR

SEA RANCH

AP

YUNG SHUE WAN

PAK TAI TEMPLE

CHEUNG CHAU

SOK KWU WAN

LAMMA ISLAND

CHEUNG PO TSAI CAVE

© Eurasia Press, Inc.

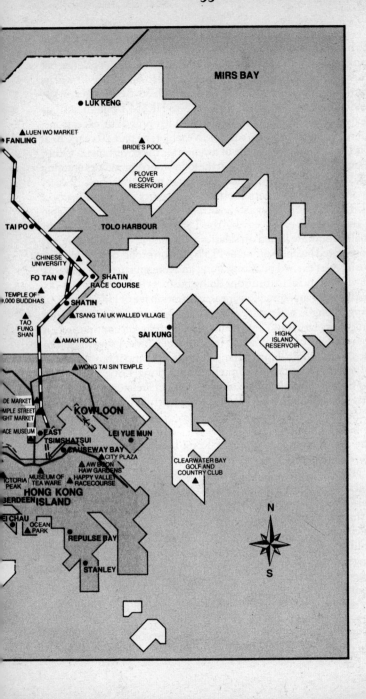

US$1.6 billion a year, not including real estate, foreign exchange funds, and banking. In 1987, more than three-quarters of Hong Kong's entrepôt trade was related to China. Beijing is estimated to earn some 40% of its total foreign exchange in Hong Kong (about US$6–8 billion a year).

Total government revenue for 1987 was HK$54.1 billion, and its total expenditure was HK$47.9 billion. With only four exceptions, general revenue has shown a surplus in each of the past 20 years. Real estate is the largest single source of revenue for the government. Other revenue comes from general tariff on the following commodities entering Hong Kong: hydrocarbon oil, alcoholic liquor, methyl alcohol, tobacco, nonalcoholic beverages, and cosmetics. Property tax is charged on occupied landed property at a standard percentage of the assessed ratable value, determined each year by the Legislative Council. Taxes on personal income are levied on salaries according to a sliding scale, on unincorporated business profits at 15.5%, and on profits of corporations at 17%. Interest earned on Hong Kong and foreign currency deposits placed with financial institutions doing business in Hong Kong is tax exempt. There is an annual business registration fee of HK$550.

Hong Kong is a separate contracting party to GATT (General Agreement on Tariffs and Trade), and that relation will continue when it becomes a Special Administrative Region of China. Its textile quota is guided by the Multi-Fibre Arrangement (MFA) and it has a bilateral textile agreement with the United States. Hong Kong benefits in varying degrees from the Generalized System of Preferences (GSP); its external trade is assisted by many governmental and quasi-governmental organizations (see Chapter X, "Doing Business in Hong Kong" below).

The Stock Exchange of Hong Kong Limited (representing the merging of four separate exchanges) started trading in April 1986. The total market capitalization by the end of 1986 was HK$419 billion and the total turnover amounted to HK$123 billion. Unfortunately, during the market crash in late 1987 it was the only stock exchange in the world that closed its floor for trading. The Hong Kong Commodity Exchange Limited, trading in futures contracts, was established in 1977. The gold bullion market operated by the Chinese Gold and Silver Exchange Society is among the most active in the world.

In general, Hong Kong's economy is run with minimal government intervention; the government's primary role is to provide the necessary infrastructure, a stable administration, and a legal framework conducive to economic growth and prosperity. This basically free-enterprise and market-disciplined system is the reason for Hong Kong's economic success.

PEOPLE AND LANGUAGE OF HONG KONG

ABOUT 5.5 million people live in Hong Kong. It is a very crowded place, with a population density of some 13,470 people per square mile (5,200 people per square kilometer). But this does not give a true picture of the real density, since only 30% of the land area is inhabited; the other 70% consists of mountains and uninhabited islands. Mongkok, in Kowloon, is believed to be the most densely populated area in the world, having some 427,350 people per square mile (165,000 people per square kilometer)!

Hong Kong's population is 98% Chinese: mainly Cantonese, a small number of Tanka (the fisherfolk who are believed to be the original inhabitants of Hong Kong), some Hoklo (Hakka) from Fukien, and many Shanghainese. The 1986 by-census showed that 59.3% of the population were born in Hong Kong, the children of immigrants from China. The largest non-Chinese population is Filipino (37,000), many of whom are brought in as domestic workers in the territory. The rest consisted of British (16,000, not including the Armed Forces), Indian (15,300), American (14,000), Malaysian and Thai (about 10,000 each), Australian, Japanese, and Portuguese (about 8,000 each), Korean (2,600), and German, French, and Dutch (about 1,500 each). A large number of boat refugees from Vietnam live in confined refugee camps and are not included in the census.

A traditional sailing junk

There are good business relations between the Chinese and the foreigners, but otherwise there is limited socializing between the two groups. However, interracial marriage is on the rise and is being accepted by the Chinese.

The Chinese on the whole are hardworking, in perpetual search of opportunities to get rich. There is almost full employment in Hong Kong; the unemployment rate stood below 2% in 1987. The labor market operates very much on free-market principles. Even though there are no strong labor unions for collective bargaining, real wages have increased by some 40% in the last two decades. Nearly 1 million people work in the service sector, while over 800,000 work in manufacturing.

There are many local entrepreneurs with a "Chinese gambler's instinct" who venture to start their own small-scale enterprises. Many have failed, but many have made it big. There are a few very rich and a lot of poor people, with an increasingly large middle class in between.

The government provides nine years of free education — over 1.5 million students are enrolled in primary and secondary schools. The seven technical institutes have approximately 50,000 full-time and part-time students. Enrollments at the Hong Kong Polytechnic and the City Polytechnic of Hong Kong are around 12,000 full-time and 19,000 part-time students. Hong Kong has three universities—Hong Kong University, the Chinese University of Hong Kong, and the Hong Kong University of Science and Technology, incorporated in April 1988, with a campus being built by the Hong Kong Jockey Club on Clear Water Bay and student enrollment slated for 1994.

There are only 25,000 hospital beds and 5,800 medical doctors serving the population of 5.5 million. However, government medical and health services are offered at little or no cost.

More than half of the population lives in public housing. These tightly packed highrise housing complexes can be found all over the territory. On the whole, the people live in crowded spaces, with a constant struggle for places in the overcrowded public transportation, restaurants, and sidewalks. Yet Hong Kong is alive with human vitality, and the rhythm is fast and restless. The one fact common to all is 1997—how to get out before Hong Kong comes under Chinese rule or how to make the best of it if one must stay. "Enjoy life now and let everything else take care of itself later" has become the motto of almost everyone in Hong Kong.

There is complete freedom of religion in Hong Kong, and all of the world's major faiths are present, not merely in places of worship, but in schools and, in varying degrees, social services. Temples to tradi-

tional Chinese Buddhist and Taoist divinities are abundant; the Roman Catholic Church has had an official jurisdiction since 1841, and a diocese was established in 1946; Protestants number some 215,000, in 52 denominations; and there are small but active communities of Muslims, Hindus, Sikhs (who came as part of the British Army in the 19th century and stayed in the police forces), and Jews.

LANGUAGES

English and Chinese are Hong Kong's official languages; most of the Chinese speak the Cantonese dialect of Chinese. But because of increasing contacts between the Hong Kong Chinese and the mainland Chinese in trade and cultural exchanges, Mandarin (or *putonghua*) is widely spoken as well. However, English is generally used in commerce and tourism. Most Chinese engaged in serving the tourist industry speak English. "Chinglish" (a mixture of Chinese and English) is often heard—a result of the cross-cultural phenomenon in Hong Kong.

II Planning a Trip to Hong Kong

TOURIST INFORMATION

THE Hong Kong Tourist Association (HKTA) is an enormously helpful and efficient organization with offices scattered around the world. For more information, contact the office nearest you.

HONG KONG TOURIST ASSOCIATION OFFICES

HONG KONG

35/F, Connaught Centre, Central; Telephone (5) 244–191; Telex 74720 LUYU HX; Fax (5) 810–4877

OFFICES ABROAD

Australia and New Zealand ▣ National Australia Bank House, 20/F, 255 George St., Sydney, NSW 2000; Telephone 251-2855; Fax (02) 221–8425; Telex: 071 24668 HKTASYD AA

France ▣ 38 Ave. George V (53 Rue François Ier, 7/F), 75008 Paris; Telephone (4) 720–3954; Telex: 042 650055 ANI F

Germany ▣ Wiesenau 1, D-6000 Frankfurt 1, Germany; Telephone (69) 722–841; Fax (69) 721–244; Telex: 041 412402 HKTAF D

Italy ▣ c/o Sergat Italia, s.r.l., Piazza Dei Cenci 7/A, 00186 Rome; Telephone 656–91–12; Telex: 623033 SERGAT I

Japan ▣ 4/F, Toho Twin Tower Bldg., 1–5–2 Yurakucho, Chiyoda-ku, Tokyo 100; Telephone (03) 503–0731; Fax (03) 503–0736

cont...

TOURIST ASSOCIATION OFFICES *(cont.)*

▣ Hong Kong & Shanghai Bank Bldg., 4/F, 45, Awaji-machi 4-chome, Higashi-ku, Osaka 541; Telephone (06) 229-9240; Fax (06) 229-9648

Singapore ▣ 13-08 Ocean Bldg., 10 Collyer Quay, Singapore 0104; Telephone 532-3668; Fax (65) 534-3592; Telex 087 28515 LUYUSN RS

United Kingdom ▣ 125 Pall Mall, London SW1Y 5EA; Telephone (71) 930-4775; Telex: 051 8950160 LUYULO G

United States ▣ 333 N. Michigan Ave., Suite 1212, Chicago, IL 60601; Telephone (312) 782-1960; Telex 023 4330404 DITTRENDDDCGO
▣ 548 Fifth Ave., New York, NY 10036; Telephone (212) 869-5008/9; Telex: 023 425817 LUYU UI
▣ 421 Powell St., Suite 200, San Francisco, CA 94102; Telephone (415) 781-4582; Fax (415) 781-5619; Telex 023 470247 LUYU UI

COSTS

THE cost of your Hong Kong trip depends on the length of your stay and how much shopping you plan to do. Specific hotel, dining, and local transporation costs are given in the appropriate sections below. Meanwhile, the following list of typical prices, in Hong Kong dollars (US$1 = HK$7.79), will give you a general idea.

Lodging: Hotel, double occupancy per day, $400–1,200; hostel and guesthouse, single occupancy per day, $150–350.

Transportation: Airport bus to Kowloon, $3; to Hong Kong $5; taxi to Tsim Sha Tsui in Kowloon, $15–20; to Hong Kong $45–55. Metered taxi $5.50 for the first kilometer, 70 cents for each additional 250 m, and $20 for crossing the harbor tunnel. Buses and minibuses, $1–5 per ride. Trams, 60 cents per ride. Peak trams, $5 one way or $9 round trip. Ferries: crossing the harbor, 50–70 cents; to outlying islands, $9–12. Mass Transit Railway, $2–5 per ride or a tourist ticket for $15. Car Rental, $200–300 per day.

Food: Lunch $50–150 per person; dinner $150–300 per person (without wine).

Drinks: Beer $10–15, soft drinks $7–10, wine $40 per carafe, hard liquor $20 and up per drink.

WHEN TO GO

HONG KONG offers year-round shopping, except for about four days during the Chinese New Year holiday (late January or early February), when most of the shops are closed. Summer months are hot and humid, with heavy rainfall, and can be uncomfortable. Typhoon (hurricane) season (April to September) can be vicious: winds may reach 64 knots or more, and almost everything shuts down. And if you are a gourmet, certain foods (Shanghai hairy crabs, rice birds, etc.) and fruits (lychee, custard apple, etc.) are seasonal. Otherwise, Hong Kong is a fun place throughout the year.

CLIMATE

Hong Kong is subtropical (latitude 22°), situated just below the Tropic of Cancer (south of Havana, Cuba, and north of Honolulu, Hawaii). Spring temperatures range from 15 to 21°C (59–70°F) with high humidity (84%) and heavy fog and rain. Summer is steamy: humidity rises to 90%, temperatures stay around 22–28°C (72–82°F), and typhoons blow at this time of year. When the Number 3 signal is up, boats go into typhoon shelters, and ferries to the outlying islands may be cancelled. When the Number 8 signal is up, all offices must be closed, public transport stops running, all the shops are shut, and planes may not be able to land in Hong Kong. Autumn (late September to December) is sunny, and the temperature stays about 17–25°C (63–77°F). It is by far the most pleasant season to visit Hong Kong. Winter is a coolish 15°C (59°F) and moderately humid.

FESTIVALS AND HOLIDAYS

Hong Kong is filled with festivals and special events. Traditional Chinese festivals and holidays are still celebrated annually, along with Western holidays. Many of the Chinese festivals are religious, some commemorate Chinese historical events, and some are rooted in legend and lore.

January
Chinese New Year, Hong Kong Arts Festival

February
Chinese New Year, Hong Kong Arts Festival, HK Open Golf
 Championships
March
International Seven-A-Side Rugby
April
Qing Ming Festival, HK International Film Festival, Birthday of Tin
Hau
May
Birthday of the Lord Buddha, Tam Kung Festival, Dragon Boat Festival,
Cheung Chau Bun Festival
June
HK Dragon Boat Festival International Race, Birthday of Her Majesty
the Queen
July
Birthday of Lu Pan
August
Hong Kong Food Festival, Maidens' Festival
September
HK Food Festival (cont'd), Hungry Ghost Festival
October
Mid-Autumn Festival, Birthday of Confucius, Chung Yeung Festival,
Super Tennis Tournament
November
HK International Kart Grand Prix, Macao Grand Prix
December
Christmas

   Chinese New Year (1st day of the 1st moon) is the most important festival and holiday for the Chinese. Family members visit each
other especially to pay respect to their elders. Children and unmar-
ried family members receive *lai see* (red envelopes of lucky money), and
special foods are served to visitors. Homes and offices are decorated
with peach and plum blossoms, tangerine fruit trees, and
chrysanthemums—symbols of luck and prosperity. In the old days
when firecrackers were legal, they exploded loudly everywhere. Shops
and restaurants close for two or three days or longer. Debts must be
settled, and barbershops and beauty parlors charge double during this
holiday.
   The most colorful of the Chinese festivals are the birthday of Tin
Hau (Queen of Heaven and Patroness of Seafaring People), which falls
on the 23rd day of the 3rd moon, and the Dragon Boat Festival (fifth

day of the fifth moon). On **Tin Hau's Birthday**, boat people make pilgrimages to Tin Hau's temples in junks bedecked with brilliant banners, paper shrines, and lanterns. The main temple is in Joss House Bay, and many guided tours offer boat rides to join the celebrations. Lion dances, with spirited drumming, are held on the temple grounds, while sacrificial offerings are laid inside.

The **Dragon Boat Festival** commemorates Qu Yuan, a fourth-century BC statesman-poet, who was removed from the court by corrupt officials after losing the emperor's trust. As a final protest, he drowned himself in the river. The local fishermen tried but failed to save him. To prevent the fish and sea serpents from devouring his body, they beat the water with their paddles and threw rice dumplings into the sea to distract them. Every year on this date, races for dragon boats (long boats with dragons' head and tail) are held all over the territory and rice dumplings (*chun*), wrapped in bamboo leaves, are eaten to celebrate this festival. Since 1976, International Races have become a part of the Dragon Boat Festival. Teams from all over the world participate in this colorful water carnival.

Qing Ming (in late spring) is observed by "sweeping" the graves of ancestors. It is not uncommon to have a picnic on the gravesites.

The **Buddha's Birthday** falls on the ninth day of the fourth moon. The statues of the Buddha in every Buddhist temple throughout the territory are washed for the occasion. Worshippers flock to the temples to receive blessings. The Po Lin Monastery on Lantau Island is the most celebrated one.

The **Tam Kung Festival** (eighth day of the fourth moon) takes place in the temple of this patron of the fishermen in Shau Kei Wan, an old fishing village. Decorated junks crowd the bay near the temple, and Chinese operas are performed during the festival.

The **Cheung Chau Bun Festival** (movable date during the fourth moon) is held on the island of Cheung Chau, with one week of festivities including religious ceremonies, street processions, Chinese opera performances, lion dances, martial arts displays, and the distribution of "blessed buns." The hundreds of round, flat pink-tinted buns are hung on three 64-foot-tall (19.5-m) towers, representing Heaven, Earth, and Man. The celebrations are meant to appease restless spirits of people who were murdered by pirates on the island hundreds of years ago. Ferries to Cheung Chau are very crowded during the festival, but special sightseeing tours are offered by many local tour agents.

The **Birthday of Lu Pan** (13th day of the sixth moon). Lu Pan, patron of the building trade, is honored at the Lu Pan Temple in Kennedy Town.

The **Maidens' Festival** (seventh day of the seventh moon) is observed traditionally by young girls praying for good husbands and happy marriages. According to legend, two young lovers were condemned by the gods to live in different stars. The birds of heaven took pity on them, and each year on this date they form a Great Heavenly Bridge with their outstretched wings so that the lovers can meet. In centuries past, young girls celebrated the festival at home with offerings to the gods of food, ornaments, money, and paper flowers.

The **Festival of the Hungry Ghosts** (14th day of the seventh moon) is also known as Yue Lan. The "hungry" ghosts are allowed to make their annual visitation to earth when the gates of the underworld are opened. The festival is observed with religious ceremonies and the burning of paper goods; street operas and public entertainments are staged to keep the wandering ghosts happy and to prevent them from venting their vengefulness on the living.

The **Mid-Autumn Festival** falls on the 15th day of the eighth moon; it is also known as the Lantern Festival or the Moon Festival. It is celebrated with colorful lanterns and mooncakes, stuffed with rich red bean or lotus seed paste, with or without a salted duck-egg yolk. Traditionally, to appreciate the full moon, people travel to high places or to open spaces and parks to view the moon. The Hong Kong Tourist Association and the Society for the Advancement of Chinese Folklore organize a Lantern Carnival at the various parks.

According to one legend, I, the Divine Archer, was rewarded for shooting down nine of the ten suns that were plaguing the world by being given an herb that bestowed immortality. His wife, Chang O, found the herb and swallowed it; then, fearing the wrath of her husband, she fled to the moon. Arriving breathless, she coughed and inadvertently spat out the herb, which turned into the Jade Rabbit, an important Chinese mythological character. Today, celebrants still look for the Rabbit and Chang O in the moon!

Confucius' Birthday (27th day of the eighth moon) is celebrated by the Confucian Society at the Confucius Temple in Causeway Bay.

Chung Yeung (ninth day of the ninth moon) is a day to go up to the mountaintops and visit ancestral graves. It is said that during the Han Dynasty a soothsayer told a man to take his family to a high place for two days. He did so, and when they returned, they found all the farm animals dead. So, even today the more superstitious Chinese journey to high places on this day to prevent misfortune and disaster.

Since all of the Chinese holidays and festivals are based on the lunar calendar and thus fall on different dates every year, check with the Hong Kong Tourist Association, 35/F, Connaught Centre, Connaught Rd., Hong Kong; Telephone (852) (5) 244–191; Fax (852) (5) 810–4877; Telex 74720 LUYU HX, for details of which festivals are being celebrated during your stay.

WHAT TO TAKE

CLOTHING

You need an overcoat and light wool suits for spring and winter. In summer, short sleeves and cotton dresses for women will do, but bring a sweater along because indoors can be air-conditioned to icy cold temperatures. You may also need a lightweight raincoat and even an umbrella. Autumn wear ranges from short sleeves to sweaters to light jackets.

Casual clothing will be acceptable everywhere except some restaurants, especially those in the hotels, and on business calls. In the evening, men are required to wear a jacket and tie, and women are requested to wear dresses in most first-class restaurants and nightclubs.

Wear comfortable shoes because you are going to do a lot of walking up and down the steep streets of Hong Kong Island.

At Christmas and the New Year, many of the big hotels feature formal dinners and dances in the ballrooms, and evening wear is expected. In fact, Hong Kong people like to dress up for those occasions. Even fur coats make their appearance.

III

Getting to Hong Kong

VISAS AND HEALTH CERTIFICATES

VALID passports and travel documents are required. Visitors from most countries can enter Hong Kong without a visa for seven days to six months. Citizens of some 26 countries, including the United States and certain Western European and South American countries, can stay for one month without a visa. Citizens of the Commonwealth and Britain's dependent territories are allowed three-month visa-free visits. Passports issued in the U.K. do not require visas at all for a stay of six months, and an extension is normally granted.

For further information on visa requirements, contact the British Consulate or High Commission in your country or call the Department of Immigration (Telephone 3–733–3111) in Hong Kong.

All visitors are required to carry sufficient funds for their stay in Hong Kong and an onward, or return, ticket.

International Certificates of Vaccination against typhoid and cholera are not required unless you have been in an infected area within the preceding 24 days. In such cases a valid certificate is needed. However, health requirements can change; check with your travel agent or with the British Consulate abroad, especially if you are visiting other parts of Asia.

INTERNATIONAL ROUTINGS TO HONG KONG

BY AIR

Almost all international airline carriers make regularly scheduled stops at Hong Kong's Kai Tak International Airport; additionally, charter and cargo planes make frequent flights to Hong Kong. There are also numerous package tours that go to Hong Kong from New York and London.

FLIGHT TIME FROM MAJOR CITIES
(in hours and minutes)

City	Time	City	Time
Amsterdam	15:35	Manila	1:50
Athens	11:40	Miami	21:50
Auckland	11:30	New York	18:50
Bahrain	7:05	Paris	15
Bangkok	2:30	Rome	12
Beijing	2:50	San Francisco	14:45
Bombay	5	Seattle	15:20
Buenos Aires	24:10	Seoul	3:30
Chicago	17	Shanghai	2:20
Delhi	4:40	Singapore	3:30
Frankfurt	12:06	Sydney	7:40
Hawaii	11:30	Taipei	1:35
Houston	18	Tokyo	4:50
Kuala Lumpur	3:30	Toronto	18:30
London	13:35	Vancouver	13
Los Angeles	16:25	Washington D.C.	20

The approach to Kai Tak International Airport is breathtaking—you come in over rocky islands washed in the South China Sea and skirt rooftops of highrise buildings with laundry drying in the sun. The runway juts out into the harbor on reclaimed land surrounded by nearby highrises.

Kai Tak Airport is one of the busiest airports in the world; more than 13 million passengers arrive and depart from it every year. However, it is also one of the most efficient—the more than a dozen immigration lines, located within comfortable walking distance of the tarmac, process passengers at a fairly rapid pace.

AIRPORT ARRIVAL

Free public phones, washrooms, and baggage carts are located beyond immigration. Porters are available, for a tip of HK$5 per piece of baggage. In the arrival hall are currency exchange windows, the Hong Kong Hotel Association's reservation desk, the information counter of the Hong Kong Tourist Association, and car rental agents.

There are well-marked signs to guide you to taxis and special airport buses, and there are several possible ways of getting from the airport to your hotel.

Hotel Buses. Hotel representatives, in colorful costumes and holding large posters, will take you to the respective hotel buses.

Local Buses. These can be boarded across from the terminal, but are not recommended, because it is almost impossible to cross the multi-lane heavy traffic to get to them.

Taxis. Taxis are metered, and charge HK$5.50 for the first kilometer and 70 cents for each additional 0.25 km. There is a surcharge of HK$20 when you go through the Cross-Harbour Tunnel to reach the Hong Kong side, and a HK$3 fee for the Aberdeen Tunnel if you continue to the other side of the island. The charge for each piece of baggage is HK$2.

Special Airport Buses. These run between the airport and Kowloon's Tsim Sha Tsui district and Hong Kong Island every 15 to 20 minutes. Route 201 (Tsim Sha Tsui) costs $2.50, and Route 200 (Hong Kong) costs $5; exact fare is required. Both routes stop at all major hotels and shopping malls. The operating hours are normally from 7:25 AM to 10:40 PM and are posted at the bus terminals. It takes about half an hour from the airport to Tsim Sha Tsui District and an hour to Central, Hong Kong side, during rush hours; otherwise, the journey normally takes about 20 minutes.

AIRLINES WITH OFFICES IN HONG KONG
(locations are Hong Kong Island unless otherwise specified)

Aer Lingus, Caxton House, 1 Duddell St.; Telephone (5) 265–877

Air Canada, 1026 Prince's Bldg.; Telephone (5) 221–001

Air France, 2110 Alexandra House; Telephone (5) 248–145

Air India, Rm. 1002 Gloucester Tower; Telephone (5) 214–321

Air Lanka, 505 Bank of America Tower; Telephone (5) 252–171

Air New Zealand, Swire House and Lee Gardens Hotel, and Ocean Centre, Kowloon; Telephone (5) 884–1488

Alitalia, 2101 Hutchison House; (5) 237–047

American Airlines, Caxton House, 1 Duddell St.; Telephone (5) 257–081

British Airways, Alexandra House and 112 Royal Gardens Hotel, Kowloon; Telephone (5) 775–023

British Caledonian, BCC House, 10 Queen's Rd.; Telephone (5) 260–062

Canadian Pacific Airlines, Swire House, and Peninsula Hotel Arcade, Kowloon; Telephone (5) 227–001

Cathay Pacific Airways, Swire House and Lee Gardens Hotel, and Peninsula Hotel Arcade and Ocean Centre, Kowloon; Telephone (5) 884–1488

China Airlines, Saint George's Bldg., and Tsim Sha Tsui Centre, Kowloon; Telephone (5) 218–431

Civil Aviation Administration of China, Gloucester Tower; Telephone (5) 216–416

Continental, 1533 Star House, Kowloon; Telephone (3) 693–339

Delta, 900 Chartered Bank Bldg., and 1005 Silvercord, Kowloon; Telephone (5) 265–875

Eastern Airlines, 7 D'Aguilar St.; Telephone (5) 237–065

Flying Tigers, 223 New Cargo Complex, Kai Tak Airport, Kowloon; Telephone (3) 769–7564

Garuda Indonesia Airways, Fu House, 7 Ice House St.; Telephone (5) 235–181/2

cont...

AIRLINES WITH OFFICES IN HONG KONG *(cont.)*

Japan Airlines, Gloucester Tower, and Harbour View Holiday Inn Lobby, Kowloon; Telephone (5) 230–081

Jardine Airways, Alexandra House, and Royal Garden Hotel, Kowloon; Telephone (5) 775–023 and (5) 774–626

KLM Royal Dutch Airlines, Fu House, 7 Ice House St.; Telephone (5) 251–255

Korean Airlines, Saint George's Bldg., and Tsim Sha Tsui Centre, Kowloon; Telephone (3) 786–221

Lufthansa German Airlines, Landmark East, and Empire Centre, Tsim Sha Tsui East, Kowloon; Telephone (5) 212–311

Malaysian Airline System, Prince's Bldg.; Telephone (5) 218–181

Northwest, Saint George's Bldg.; Telephone (5) 217–477

Pakistan International Airlines, 1104 Houston Centre, Kowloon; Telephone (3) 664–770

Pan American World Airways, Alexandra House, Central; Telephone (5) 231–1111

Philippine Airlines, 305 East Ocean Centre, Tsim Sha Tsui East, Kowloon; Telephone (3) 694–521

Qantas Airways, Swire House, and Sheraton Hotel Lobby, Kowloon; Telephone (5) 242–101

Royal Brunei Airlines, 1406 Central Bldg.; Telephone (5) 223–799

Royal Nepal Airlines, Star House, Kowloon; Telephone (3) 699–151

Sabena, 7 D'Aguilar St.; Telephone (5) 237–065

SAS, Edinburgh Tower; Telephone (5) 265–978

Singapore Airlines, Landmark, and Royal Garden Hotel, Kowloon; Telephone (5) 202–233

Swissair, Admiralty Centre, and Peninsula Hotel, Kowloon; Telephone (5) 293–670

Thai Airways International, World-Wide Plaza, and Peninsula Hotel Arcade, Kowloon; Telephone (5) 295–601

Trans World Airlines, Yardley Commercial Bldg.; Telephone (5) 413–117

United Airlines, Gloucester Tower; Telephone (5) 810–488/8

Western Airlines, 1005 Silvercord, Kowloon; Telephone (3) 724–067/8

BY SEA

Passenger ships (cruise ships) of half a dozen cruise lines make regular port stops in Hong Kong. They normally dock at Ocean Terminal (Kowloon), a huge multi-level passenger wharf complex, with hundreds of shops, coffee houses, and restaurants. The famous Star Ferry, which crosses the harbor, is only yards away.

Ferries to and from China depart and arrive near the Yau Ma Tei typhoon shelter in Kowloon. Ferries, jetfoils, and hydrofoils to and from Macao depart from the Macao Ferry Pier on Hong Kong Island. (See Chapter XI, "Travel Outside Hong Kong.")

BY LAND

Overland travel from Europe, China, and the rest of Asia is possible but rough. Trains arrive daily from Guangzhou and other cities in China. (See Chapter XI, "Travel Outside Hong Kong.")

ENTRANCE AND EXIT PROCEDURES

ANIMAL QUARANTINE

Dogs and cats will be put in quarantine unless they have resided for at least six months in the United Kingdom, Ireland, New Zealand, or Australia, and have health certificates dated within 14 days prior to arriving in Hong Kong. The Agriculture and Fisheries Department, situated at 393 Canton Rd., Kowloon (Telephone 3-688-111), can provide further information.

CUSTOMS

Hong Kong allows most items to enter duty-free. The only dutiable items are alcohol, tobacco, and petroleum products. However, you may bring in duty-free one liter of liquor; 200 cigarettes (or 50 cigars, or 250 g tobacco); 60 ml of perfume and 250 ml of toilet water. Firearms (rifles and handguns) must be declared and handed into custody until departure. Visitors may also bring in their cars for personal use free of duty.

EXIT FORMALITIES

An airport departure tax of HK$120 (adults) or HK$60 (children

2–12 years old) is required and may be paid in Hong Kong dollars only. Make sure you have enough HK dollars left to pay these taxes.

In the departure hall you will find money-changers, banks, a post office, a cable and wireless office, shops, newsstands, restaurants, bars and snack bars, pay phones, a police station, private reception rooms, and luggage storage service for your convenience.

The departure lounge, after immigration checks, is always congested because of the ever-increasing numbers of air travelers. This area is being expanded, but in the meantime every seat is taken up and both restaurant and bar space are also crowded. Last-minute shopping can be done at duty-free shops in this area. Stay outside as long as you can before clearing through immigration.

IV
Traveling in Hong Kong

KNOW BEFORE YOU GO

WEIGHTS AND MEASURES

The government's goal is the eventual exclusive use of the metric system, but provision is made, realistically, for the continued use of British imperial units (feet, pounds, gallons, and the like) and of traditional Chinese units of length and weight.

ELECTRICITY AND WATER

The local current is 200V, 50 cycles. Most hotels provide plugs and voltage conversion adaptors for any electrical appliances.

Water from the mains is drinkable; it is purified enough to satisy the World Health Organization's standards. However, in some parts of the New Territories and outlying islands, the water is from wells and is not reliable. Bottled water is available in hotels and most supermarkets.

HEALTH AND SAFETY

Pharmaceuticals are available from drugstores in shopping centers, in supermarkets, and in department stores. Public washrooms are generally free of charge except in hotels, restaurants, and major shopping malls, where the attendants expect a tip of HK$2. Very simple facilities are also provided inside the Star Ferry Concourses and at train stations; toilet paper is not normally supplied in these. The few off-the-street public toilets are so filthy as to be recommended only in case of extreme urgency.

TIME AROUND THE WORLD

Hong Kong Standard Time, which is constant all year round, is eight hours later than Greenwich Mean Time: when it is noon GMT, it is 8 PM in Hong Kong. Hong Kong is 13 hours ahead of New York and other East Coast cities in the United States, 16 hours ahead of San Francisco and other West Coast cities, and 7 hours ahead of most European cities.

When it's 12 noon in Hong Kong, the standard time in the following cities is

Amsterdam	5 AM
Bangkok	11 AM
Beirut	6 AM
Cairo	6 AM
Chicago	10 PM previous day
Dallas	10 PM previous day
Frankfurt	5 AM
Honolulu	6 PM previous day
London	4 AM
Los Angeles	8 PM previous day
Montreal	11 PM previous day
Nairobi	7 AM
New York	11 PM previous day
Paris	5 AM
Rio de Janeiro	1 AM
Rome	5 AM
San Francisco	8 PM previous day
Singapore	12 noon
Sydney	2 PM
Tokyo	1 PM
Vancouver	8 PM previous day
Zurich	5 AM

Normal office hours are from 9 AM to 5 PM Monday through Friday, and many offices stay open for half a day on Saturdays. Most banks stay open from 9 AM to 3 PM on weekdays, and some are open for half a day on Saturdays. Money changers transact business all day, and some are open seven days a week, especially in the tourist areas.

Generally, shops are open from 10 AM to 6 PM in Central Hong Kong; 10 AM to 10 PM in Causeway Bay, Hong Kong, and in Tsim Sha Tsui and Tsim Sha Tsui East in Kowloon. Most shops stay open on Sundays and public holidays, except around Chinese New Year (late January or early February), when they close for two to three days.

Most restaurants stay open until 11 PM, and some coffee shops in major hotels stay open 24 hours a day.

RELIGIOUS SERVICES

Besides the indigenous Oriental religions, Christian, Jewish, and Muslim believers are present in Hong Kong, and their services are available to travelers. For details, inquire at your hotel or call HKTA.

EVERYDAY AMENITIES

Babysitting services are available in most hotels. Hairdressing salons for men and women are found in most major hotels, and some of them have top hair stylists. The cost of a haircut, shampoo, and blow-dry is about HK$90 for women and about HK$45 for men. Neighborhood hairdressing salons are recognizable by the presence of a twirling blue, red, and white barberpole.

Laundry and dry cleaning are best done in the hotels, all of which offer same-day service. The average cost for a shirt is $20, and for a dry-cleaned suit, $50. There are neighborhood places, but they are few and far between. The Yellow Pages lists local facilities.

TIPPING

Tipping is expected everywhere, even in most restaurants where a 10% service charge has already been added to the bill. A tip of HK$2 is expected by washroom attendants.

LEGAL PROTECTION AND PRECAUTIONS

Visitors are recommended to carry some form of identification with a photograph—driver's license, passport, etc.—particularly when traveling in the New Territories and to the outlying islands.

The Consumer Council (Telephone 5–200–511) helps with fraudulent purchases. Call the Hong Kong Tourist Association's Hotlines (5–244–191 or 3–722–5555) for any problem with its member shops and restaurants. Any policeman can help you; those with a red slash under their shoulder number speak English.

If you lose anything, get your hotel clerks to help you or call the Police Station near you. Found items should also be turned in to these authorities.

MONEY, CURRENCY, AND BANKING

CURRENCY AND EXCHANGE RATE

The local currency is the Hong Kong dollar, issued either by the Hong Kong and Shanghai Banking Corporation or by the UK-based Chartered Bank. The banknotes are in different colors and in denominations of $1,000, $500, $100, $50, $20, and $10; additionally, there are $5, $2, $1, 50-cent, 20-cent, and 10-cent coins.

U.S. dollars, English pound notes, and other hard currencies are readily accepted at most shops catering to tourists.

Since 1983, the Hong Kong dollar has been linked to the U.S. dollar at a fixed rate of exchange of HK$7.80 to U.S. $1.

EFFECTIVE EXCHANGE RATES FOR THE HONG KONG DOLLAR

Country	Denomination	Hong Kong Dollars*	Country	Denomination	Hong Kong Dollars*
Australia	A$	6.0351	Mexico	P	0.0026
Belgium	BF	0.2535	Netherlands	G	4.6422
Brazil	Cz$	0.0484	New Zealand	NZ$	4.6181
Canada	CND	6.7428	Norway	Kr	1.3344
China	Yuan	1.4903	Pakistan	R	0.3578
Denmark	KR	1.3593	Philippines	Peso	0.2866
France	FF	1.5386	Portugal	E	0.0586
Germany	DM	5.2377	Singapore	S$	4.4848
India	R	0.4309	Spain	P	0.0820
Indonesia	Rp	0.0042	Sweden	Kr	1.3928
Italy	L	0.0070	Taiwan	NT$	0.2927
Japan	Yen	0.0580	Thailand	Baht	0.3099
Korea	W	0.0109	United Kingdom	£	15.1481
Malaysia	M$	2.8815	United States	US$	7.7942

*Rates cited are for reference only; rates fluctuate daily

Most banks and all the hotels will change foreign currencies, and there are money changers in business and shopping districts. The exchange rate may vary slightly from money changer to money changer, but shopping around is not worth the effort.

BANKING FOR TOURISTS

Over 100 international banking establishments have licensed banks in Hong Kong, among them Bank of America, Banque

The "Duk-Ling", a traditional Chinese sailing junk, with Asia's tallest building, the Bank of China Tower, in the background.

Nationale de Paris, Barclays International, Bank of Tokyo, Citibank, and Bank of China. In addition, hundreds of local banks are found all over the territory; the larger ones—Bank of East Asia, Hang Seng, Hong Kong and Shanghai Bank—have foreign exchange facilities.

CREDIT CARDS AND TRAVELER'S CHECKS

Major credit cards (American Express, VISA, Carte Blanche, Diners Club, JCB, MasterCard) are widely accepted, except in many local Chinese restaurants. Many shops prefer cash payment, but no surcharge is added for credit cards. Traveler's checks are as convertible as hard currencies, and all tourist shops accept them.

COMMUNICATIONS AND THE MEDIA

POSTAL SERVICE

Hong Kong has dependable mail service. Letters by air usually take four to five days to Europe and about a week to the United States and Canada. Surface mail and packages can take up to three months.

The main General Post Office on Hong Kong Island is in front of the Star Ferry Concourse, across from the Connaught Building. It has full services, including a general delivery counter and a philatelic window. Office hours are 8 AM to 6 PM daily; it is closed on Sundays and public holidays. Hotels can handle most of your letter and postcard mailings.

Following are some typical rates; a full list of other costs can be obtained at the General Post Office.

First class airmail (letter and postcard)—to elsewhere in Asia, HK$1.30 for the first 10 g, 80 cents each additional 10 g; to the rest of the world, HK$1.70 for the first 10 g, 90 cents each additional 10 g.

Air parcels—to the United States, HK$37 for the first 500 g, HK$26 each additional 500 g; to the United Kingdom, HK$63 for the first 500 g, HK$21 each additional 500 g.

Surface parcels—to the United States, 1 kg HK$30, 3 kg HK$65, 5 kg HK$105, 10 kg HK$190; to the United Kingdom, 1 kg HK$55, 3 kg HK$75, 5 kg HK$100, 10 kg HK$140.

TELECOMMUNICATIONS

Hong Kong Telephone Company Limited and Cable and Wireless (Hong Kong) Limited are the two franchised companies that provide telecommunication services. These services include telephone, telex, and telegram.

TELEPHONE

Hong Kong Telephone Company Limited is the only franchised company providing both private and business phone services. For a monthly rental charge—relatively cheap compared to what is charged in other major cities—one is allowed an unlimited number of calls within Hong Kong. For this reason, calls by patrons in most shops and restaurants are not charged. Calls from public phone booths require a HK$1 coin for the first three minutes.

Local Phone Calls. Hong Kong's country access code is 852. From within Hong Kong, three area codes are in use—(5) for Hong Kong, (3) for Kowloon, and (0) for the New Territories. The outlying islands use the (5) area code plus (981) for Cheung Chau, (982) for Lamma, and (984) or (987) for Lantau. Remember to drop the area code when calling from the same area code. For local directory assistance dial 108 or use the English-language phonebooks (residential, commercial, and Yellow Pages). For emergencies (police, fire, ambulance), dial 999; no coins are needed for a call to 999 from public phones.

International Calls. Hong Kong's international telephone service is operated jointly by Hong Kong Telephone Company Limited and Cable and Wireless (Hong Kong) Limited, which provide International Direct Dialing to more than 180 overseas destinations in addition to operator-assisted service. Long-distance phone calls can be made in your hotel through its switchboard, or you can place your calls at the following Cable and Wireless offices:
Central: Exchange Square, open 24 hours; Telephone (5) 237–939.
Tsim Sha Tsui: Ocean Terminal, open 8 AM to midnight.
Tsim Sha Tsui: Hermes House, 10 Middle Rd., open 24 hours.
Kai Tak Airport: Passenger Terminal Building.

CABLE AND TELEX

Cables and telexes can be placed with your hotel or at any of the Cable and Wireless offices: In Hong Kong at Exchange Square, 8 Connaught Place; in Kowloon at the Ocean Terminal and at Hermes House, on Middle Rd. (across from the Sheraton Hotel); or at the General Post Office.

RADIO AND TELEVISION

There are three radio stations broadcasting over 10 channels to civilians and military personnel in Hong Kong. The government-operated Radio-Television Hong Kong (RTHK) broadcasts through over channels: Radio 1 (Chinese service), Radio 2 (popular music and magazine programs appealing to young people), Radio 3 (news and information for the English-speaking population), Radio 4 (classical music and arts), and Radio 5 (bilingual, offering the BBC's World Service and Chinese programs).

The privately owned Hong Kong Commercial Broadcasting Company operates three channels in both FM and AM, one in Cantonese and one in English.

The British Forces Broadcasting Service has two radio stations. One is specifically provided for the Gurkha brigade and offers 90 hours a week of music, news, and entertainment in Nepali. The English-language station broadcasts 24 hours a day, with locally produced and imported British shows and satellite pickup of BBC news and sports programs.

Watching television is the prime leisure pastime of almost everyone in Hong Kong. Nearly 98% of households own at least one television set, and antennas grow like trees in a forest on the rooftops. There are four channels operated by two franchised commercial stations owned by Asia Television Ltd. and Hong Kong Television Broadcasts Ltd. Each station has an English-language and a Chinese-language (Cantonese) channel. All four channels carry daily news broadcasts; international news is mostly picked up by satellite. English-language channels carry many reruns from American and British television.

Radio Television Hong Kong also transmits its public affairs programs through these two commercial stations.

Television & Entertainment Times, a weekly guide to local radio and television programs, gives complete listings and other tidbits of news about Hong Kong. It costs HK$6 per issue.

THE PRINT MEDIA

NEWSPAPERS AND MAGAZINES

Hong Kong has about 45 Chinese-language dailies, two English-language dailies (*South China Morning Post* and *Hong Kong Standard*) and some 20 news agency bulletins in Chinese, English, and Japanese. *The Wall Street Journal*'s Asian Edition and *The International Herald Tribune* are also printed in the territory. Newsstands in major hotels carry newspapers and magazines from overseas, which are air-freighted in daily.

Nearly 500 magazines, in Chinese and English, are printed in Hong Kong, including the Asian editions of *Time* magazine, *Newsweek*, and the *Reader's Digest*. Locally produced magazines of regional interest are the *Far Eastern Economic Review*, *Asiaweek*, and *Asia Business*.

BOOKSTORES AND NEWSSTANDS

Books published abroad cost a little more in Hong Kong. Some of the well-stocked bookstores where you can find even the latest bestsellers are the Hong Kong Book Centre (Des Voeux Rd., Central), Kelly & Walsh Ltd. (on Ice House St.), and the Central and South China Morning Post Ltd. (Star Ferry Concourses and Ocean Galleries), which also carries its own publications. Swindon Book Co. Ltd. (13 Lock Rd., Tsim Sha Tsui and Ocean Centre) has a wide choice of English-language and picture books.

Chinese-language books can be found at Joint Publishing Co., 9 Queen Victoria St., Central, and Chung Hwa Book Co., 740 Nathan Rd., Mongkok.

Every major hotel has its own newsstand, where local and overseas magazines and newspapers are on sale. Street newsstands carrying English-language newspapers and magazines can be found only in central business districts and near the Star Ferry concourses.

LOCAL TRANSPORTATION

MORE More than 9 million rides are made on the public transport system every day. Many forms of local public transport are available: three railways (the underground Mass Transitport Railway or MTR, the Kowloon–Canton Railway, and the Light Rail Transit system), buses, minibuses, ferries and boats, trams, and taxis. The most convenient and fastest one is the MTR (see below); taxis are cheap by any international standard, and buses are numerous.

PUBLIC TRANSPORTATION

TAXIS

The metered taxis, red with silver roofs, operate in the urban area and charge HK$5.50 to start and HK 70 cents for each additional

At night, on Hong Kong Island's 85-year-old tram system.

quarter kilometer. There are taxi stands in most business and commercial areas. Taxis can stop almost anywhere to pick up customers except along yellow curbs and some restricted areas. A HK$20 surcharge is added for going through the Cross-Harbour Tunnel and HK$3 for going through the Aberdeen Tunnel. There is also a charge of HK$1–2 for each piece of luggage or large parcel.

The green and white taxis operate only in the New Territories and the fare is a little cheaper.

If you have any problem call the police hotline, (5) 277–177.

RICKSHAWS

A few "antiquated" rickshaws with red bodies and green awnings still wait around the Star Ferry concourses for tourists to hire them. The ride is symbolic, just around the concourse area, and costs about HK$20 for a few minutes, but be sure to agree upon the price before you step into one.

BUSES

Three franchised bus companies operate blue-and-white and red-and-white double-decker and single-decker buses throughout the territory. Fixed prices for each route are visible when passengers board the bus. The main depots in Kowloon are the Star Ferry Bus Terminal (outside the Star Ferry Concourse) and the Jordan Rd. Bus Terminal (next to the Jordan Rd. Ferry pier). In Hong Kong, the Central Bus Terminal is located next to Exchange Square on the waterfront in Central.

The Hong Kong Tourist Association has put out four flyers giving detailed information on how to get about Hong Kong Island and the New Territories by bus, and showing other routes to some major attractions in the territory. A very popular route (Bus No. 260) goes to Repulse Bay; it costs HK$4.80 and you can catch it outside the Star Ferry Concourse, Hong Kong side.

Bus fares range from HK$1 to HK$5.50, and exact change is required. For more information, call China Motor Bus, (5) 658–556 for Hong Kong routes and (3) 745–4466 for Kowloon and New Territories routes.

MINIBUSES

These "public light buses" seat 14 or 16. The cream and green ones run on scheduled routes, and the cream and red one on nonscheduled routes. The bus number and fares are posted on the windshield, and exact change is required. They make non-scheduled stops, and are very convenient and popular. The minibus terminal in Central is by the Star Ferry carpark and on the far side of City Hall. Route No. 1 goes to The Peak for HK$3.

TRAMS

Double-decker trams run from Kennedy Town at the western end of Hong Kong Island to Shau Kei Wan, near the eastern end, passing slowly through the Western District, Central, Wan Chai, Causeway Bay, North Point, and Quarry Bay. There is another loop that goes to Happy Valley and the racecourse. Tram stations are either narrow platforms in the middle of the road or areas marked on the ground. The entire ride costs only HK 60 cents for adults and 20 cents for children. You get on the trams from the rear entrance and exit from the front, where you deposit your fare. They run from 5:40 AM to 1:00 AM.

PEAK TRAM

The Peak Tram is really a cable car or a funicular railway. From the Garden Rd. terminus, a short walk from Hong Kong Hilton Hotel, it climbs slowly up 1,309 ft (399 m) to the Peak terminus. The fare to the top is HK$5, and a roundtrip ticket costs HK$9; children ride for HK$2 each way. The tram operates from 7 AM to 11 PM. A free shuttle bus runs between the Star Ferry, via the MTR Admiralty station, to the Garden Rd. terminus at 20-minute intervals from 9 AM to 7 PM daily.

MASS TRANSIT RAILWAY (MTR)

The MTR is an underground railway. The system consists of three interconnected lines: one goes from one end of Hong Kong Island to the other end, one runs under the harbor from Hong Kong to Kowloon and on to Tsuen Wan, and the third connects Yau Ma Tei in Kowloon (where one may change to the under-harbor line) with Kwun Tong to the east. Some 40 stations along the lines are all very clearly marked. The Tsim Sha Tsui station is right in the middle of Kowloon's commercial area, and from it you can reach Central Hong Kong in just two station stops.

The fare is from HK$1.50 to $4.50; a fare chart is above each ticket machine. The machines accept exact change only, but there are coin change machines all around. Special Tourist Tickets of HK$15 are available from HKTA or any MTR station. MTR's free booklet contains information on its routes and on connecting buses as well as places of interest in and around the stations.

As the MTR is much used by the inhabitants of Hong Kong, visitors will be well advised to avoid taking it at rush hours, when it can be uncomfortably crowded.

TRAINS

The British section of the Kowloon–Canton Railway runs from its terminus on the east coast of Kowloon to the Chinese border at Lo Wu, from which the trains continue into China and beyond. Local stops are made in Kowloon (Mong Kok and Kowloon Tong) and in the New Territories (Tai Wai, Sha Tin, Fo Tan, Sha Tin Racecourse, University, Tai Po Market, Tai Wo, Fanling, and Sheung Shui). The Sheung Shui stop is as far as you can go unless you have a visa to China, because Lo Wu is a restricted area. The one-way fare is HK$10 second class and HK$20 first class. Children under 12 pay half fare. Call Kowloon–Canton Railway, (0) 606–9600, for schedules and fares to the various stops.

In 1988 the Kowloon–Canton Railway Corporation began service on a light rail line crossing the northwestern portion of the New Territories, between Tuen Mun and Yuen Long. More than 14 mi (23 km)

HONG KONG MASS TRANSIT RAILWAY (MTR—Subway)

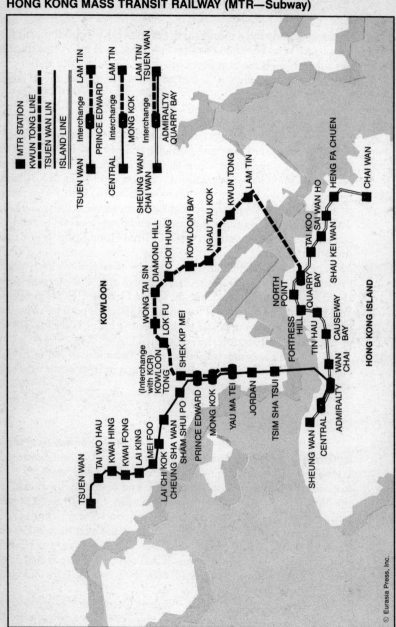

© Eurasia Press, Inc.

of double track in five routes serves 41 stops from 5:30 AM to 12:30 AM daily. Further light rail construction is under way in this area.

FERRIES

The Star Ferries, operated by the Star Ferry Company Limited, offer two passenger services between Hong Kong and Kowloon. The green and white vessels, running between Hong Kong Central and Kowloon's Tsim Sha Tsui, are still very convenient, popular, and cheap. Trips operate at frequent intervals and take from 7 to 12 minutes; the fare is only HK70 cents first class (upper deck) and 50 cents second class (lower deck). For children, it's even cheaper. This service starts at 6:30 AM, and the last run is at 11:30 PM.

The other route, between Hong Kong Central and Hung Hom in Kowloon, takes about 15 minutes. The Kowloon pier is within walking distance of the Kowloon–Canton Railway terminus.

Hong Kong and Yaumati Ferries, operated by the Hongkong & Yaumati Ferry Company Limited, offer ferry services across the harbor and to the outlying districts and islands. These ferries can carry motorcycles, private cars, and trucks. The cross-harbor passenger and vehicular pier in Hong Kong is situated to the left of the Star Ferry terminal as you face the harbor; on the other side, these ferries dock at the Yaumati Pier in Kowloon.

Ferries to the outlying islands leave from the Outlying Districts Ferry Pier just a few yards to the west of the Star Ferry Concourse. The main routes are to Lantau, Cheung Chau, and Lamma islands.

For fares and schedules to the outlying islands, call the ferry company at (5) 244-191.

There are other ferries that cross the harbor from Wan Chai and North Point, but they are too out of the way to be of much interest to tourists.

VEHICLES FOR HIRE

If you would prefer to hire a vehicle, cars, boats, and helicopters are available.

CAR RENTAL

Self-drive cars can be hired from Avis, Hertz, Budget, and other local firms at HK$200–300 a day or HK$1,300–1,800 a week, plus HK$20–25 for collision and damage waiver. All visitors with a valid overseas driving license can drive in Hong Kong for one year without a local license. American drivers should remember that the flow of traffic in Hong Kong is different from what they are used to. It is also very difficult to find parking spaces, especially during the day.

Chauffeur-driven cars are available from most of the major hotels.

BOATS

Small motorboats, called *walla-wallas*, can be hired for going across the harbor. On the Hong Kong side you can catch a *walla-walla* at Queen's Pier (to the right of the Star Ferry Concourse facing the harbor), and on Kowloon side at the Kowloon Public Pier (on the left of the Star Ferry Concourse as you face the harbor). The fare is HK$4.50 per person or HK$45 for the whole boat.

HELICOPTERS

Sightseeing helicopters can be hired from Heliservices (HK) Limited, Telephone (5) 202-200. The "Squirrel" sits five passengers and you must charter the whole craft. A short ride over Hong Kong harbor is about HK$480, around Hong Kong Island is HK$1,400, and over the New Territories is HK$3,960. Fares may change; check with Heliservices or the transportation services at your hotel.

SIGHTSEEING TOURS

There are hundreds of tours operated by tour operators. Reservations can be made at your hotel tour desk or you can book directly with the tour operators (listed at the end of this section). The Hong Kong Tourist Association has many leaflets giving detailed information on the various tours it conducts. A few are mentioned here:

HONG KONG ISLAND TOURS

Round-the-Island Tour. Prices range from HK$80 (adult) and HK$64 (child) for half-day tours to HK$120 (adult) and HK$80 (child), for a full-day tour with lunch. The tours usually include Victoria Peak, Tiger Balm (Aw Boon Haw) Gardens, Stanley Market, Repulse Bay, and Deep Water Bay. A lunch of dim sum is served on board the world-famous Jumbo Floating Restaurant in Aberdeen. Many stops are made for shopping and photo-taking.

Ocean Park Tour. Priced at HK$145-170 per adult and

HK$120–130 per child, this tour is devoted to Ocean Park, one of the world's largest aquariums. The visit includes a scenic cable car ride, covered escalator, Wave Cove, Ocean Theatre, and other rides.

WATER TOURS

Harbor Tour. A two-hour cruise around the harbor, costing HK$90 (adult) and HK$55 (child), takes you along the Kowloon waterfront (Ocean Terminal wharves, Yau Ma Tei Typhoon Shelter, and Kai Tak Airport runway) and Hong Kong waterfront (Western District, Central, Wan Chai, Causeway Bay, and North Point).

Grand Tour. For HK$245 (adult) and HK$150 (child) you are taken on a five-hour cruise around the harbor and to Aberdeen, with a Chinese lunch on board.

Sunset Cruise. A four-hour tour round the harbor for HK$175 (adult) and HK$105 (child) includes a Chinese dinner at a floating restaurant in Aberdeen and free drinks on board.

Wan Fu Cruises. At a price of HK$210–320 (adult) and HK$190–250 (child), a two-masted schooner sails you through the harbor either to Aberdeen or to both Aberdeen and Repulse Bay, with either hot or cold hors d'oeuvres or a lavish barbecue and seafood dinner served on board.

Star Ferry Harbour Cruises. The ferry company offers a variety of one-hour cruises, costing HK$50 (adult) and HK$40 (child): the Noonday Gun Cruise, Seafarers' Cruise, Sea Breezes Cruise, Afternoon Tea Cruise, Sundowner Cruise, and Harbour Lights Cruise. Some include complimentary high tea and unlimited free drinks.

NEW TERRITORIES TOURS

The Land Between. A six-hour tour for HK$180 (adult) and HK$140 (child) takes you through bustling Kowloon to the tranquil countryside and includes a Buddhist temple, Tai Mo Shan (the highest mountain in the territory), Luen Wo Market, a bird sanctuary, Tai Po, the Sha Tin Racecourse, and a Chinese lunch.

Kowloon and New Territories Tour. Costing HK$70 (adult) and HK$56 (child), this tour takes you through the resettlement estates in North Kowloon, passes the industrial town of Tsun Wan and to the satellite town of Tuen Mun, then out into the countryside to Yuen Long, Lok Ma Chau, Fanling, Tai Po, and the Sha Tin Racecourse in less than four hours.

OUTLYING ISLAND TOURS

The Buddhist Monastery Tour. Takes you to Lantau Island by ferry (afternoon departure) or by Chinese junk (morning departure) from Hong Kong and by coach to the Po Lin Monastery, where you are served a vegetarian luncheon in the grounds of the monastery. Sights includes Silvermine Bay, Tai O fishing village, and some of the loveliest beaches on the island. The morning tour costs HK$250 (adult) and HK$150 (child). For reservations, call Lantau Tours Limited, (5) 984–8255, or book through your hotel or travel agent.

NIGHT TOURS

Hong Kong Night Tour. Includes the Peak, a Western dinner at the Peak Tower Restaurant, a stroll along the open-air Night Market downtown, and a nightclub with a floor show. The HK$260 (adult) and HK$235 (child) price includes a peak tram ride, dinner, and the floor show, cover charge, and a drink at the nightclub.

Hong Kong's "Star" ferries traverse busy Victoria Harbor.

Peak-Harbor by Night Tour. This almost six-hour affair costs HK$300 (adult) and HK$265 (child) and includes a ride on the Peak Tram to the top, a Western dinner at the Peak Tower Restaurant, a stroll in the open-air Night Market, and finally, a harbor cruise on a Chinese junk with unlimited free drinks.

Tour 70. For adults only at HK$395–495, this is a junket into the red-light district of Hong Kong and Kowloon, offering visits to many nightclubs with floor shows, and lots of drinks.

Yum Sing Tours. Offers two packages, the Grand Tour and the De Luxe Tour, in which you purchase coupons at the HKTA to pubs and bars, discos, nightclubs, and hostess clubs. HKTA has a brochure "Yum Sing Night on the Town Tour" describing in detail how these coupons work.

TRAM TOURS

Hong Kong Tramways' Dim Sum Tour, for HK$80 (adult) and HK$60 (child), offers a two-hour slow ride in an open-deck 1920s antique tram through some of the busiest streets on the island, with free dim sum and unlimited drinks. It is also possible to hire the entire tram for private functions. Call Hong Kong Tramways, (5) 891-8765 or (3) 722-5555, for details.

TOUR PACKAGES

THE Hong Kong Tourist Association's Tour Development Department (Telephone 5-244-191 or 3-722-5555) offers many interesting tours. The following 10-day itinerary is highly recommended by them:

Day One
Morning—Hong Kong Island Tour: Visit the floating population in Aberdeen and the splendid beach at Repulse Bay, enjoy the panoramic view from Victoria Peak, and make a stop at Stanley Market or Aw Boon Haw Gardens.
Lunch: Dim sum at a Chinese restaurant.
Evening: Tram tour with cocktails. Ride one of Hong Kong's historic trams through the bustling, colorful streets. Dine at a revolving restaurant with an ever-changing view of the magical scene that is Hong Kong harbor by night.

Day Two
Morning—The Land Between: A full-day tour of the New Territories, the land that lies between urban Hong Kong and the Chinese border. Chinese lunch included.
Evening: Chinese cultural show and dinner in a Chinese nightclub.

Day Three
Morning: A water tour of Victoria Harbour, affording scenes of ceaseless activity as you pass busy waterfronts, the airport runway, docks, and wharves.
Afternoon: Shopping in Kowloon along the Golden Mile of Nathan Road, and at shopping complexes in Tsim Sha Tsui East.
Evening: Night tour on an open-top double-decker bus. Western-style dinner, with music and dancing to follow.

Day Four
Morning and Noon: Song Dynasty Village tour, a trip back to the China of 1,000 years ago, followed by lunch.
Afternoon: Explore the attractions along the Mass Transit Railway (underground railway), such as Ladies' Market, Jade Market, and Wong Tai Sin Temple, in a convenient and comfortable way.
Evening: A sunset cruise with dinner at a famous Aberdeen floating restaurant.

Day Five
Morning and Afternoon: Cross the Pearl River Estuary by jetfoil to the ancient Portuguese city of Macao, the first European settlement in the Far East. Or cross the border for a fascinating day trip into China.
Evening: Dinner at one of the excellent restaurants in Causeway Bay. All the regional cuisines of China are yours to discover. After dinner, shop around in Causeway Bay area, where numerous boutiques, department stores, and China Products stores are located.

Day Six
Morning and Afternoon: Explore the island of Lantau for the day; vegetarian lunch served at Po Lin Monastery.
Evening: Space Museum sky show. Then select your favorite Chinese cuisine—Beijing, Shanghai, Sichuan, Chiu Chow, Hakka, or Cantonese. Try some Chinese wine. If there's still time, join the night bustle of Causeway Bay, a popular local shopping area.

Day Seven

Morning and Afternoon: Visit Ocean Park, one of the world's largest aquariums, and Waterworld, with the world's longest escalator, a roller coaster, and other thrill rides.

Evening: Night horse racing at Happy Valley or Sha Tin. If it is not the racing season, have a Western dinner at Victoria Peak.

Day Eight

Morning and Noon: Take a cruise to Cheung Chau Island, site of the Bun Festival, and have lunch in a restaurant by the beach.

Evening: Sample various Asian cuisines from the many restaurants—Korean, Japanese, Malaysian, Indonesian, Indian, or Vietnamese. Try delicious hot snacks at street-side *dai pai dong*, the open-air food stalls in back streets all over Hong Kong.

Day Nine

Morning and Afternoon: Take the Sports and Recreation Tour to Clearwater Bay Golf and Country Club, situated in the unspoiled greenery of Sai Kung Peninsula, where many sports facilities are available.

Evening: Dance the night away to the latest beat from Europe and the U.S.A. at one of Hong Kong's many sophisticated discotheques or videotheques. Relax in a jazz bar or hotel lounge with a pianist, or join in the fun at a singalong club.

Day Ten

Morning: Take an early morning stroll into a city park and see locals practicing *tai chi*, the slow-motion exercises from which kung fu is derived. For your shopping delight, visit the factory outlets in the Hung Hom District.

Afternoon: Take a train ride to the Sha Tin area and explore this satellite town and an impressive shopping mall and music fountain.

Evening: See the harbor lights on a barbecue dinner cruise aboard the Wan Fu.

HONG KONG TOUR OPERATORS

The following tour operators are members of the Hong Kong Tourist Association:

Alliesan Travel and Tours Ltd; Telephone (5) 734–223
Anta Express Ltd; Telephone (5) 251–085
Associated Tours (HK) Ltd; Telephone (3) 7221–216

HONG KONG TOUR OPERATORS *(cont.)*

Bao Shinn Express Co. Ltd; Telephone (3) 697–111
Blue Sea Travel Service Ltd; Telephone (3) 721–1127
Cascade Tourist Service (HK) Ltd; Telephone (3) 694–971
Cherry Tourist Service Corp Ltd; Telephone (3) 694–251
Chung Yi Travel Service Ltd; Telephone (3) 697–335
EBM Tours Ltd; Telephone (3) 721–2259
ETE Tours Ltd; Telephone (5) 765–942
Eurasia Travel Service Ltd; Telephone (3) 699–481
Fiesta Tours Ltd; Telephone (3) 721–3354
Forever Travel Services Co. Ltd; Telephone (3) 722–1683
Friendly International Tours Ltd; Telephone (5) 450–388
Gemini Travel Service (HK) Ltd; Telephone (3) 669–316
Goodway Express Tours Ltd; Telephone (3) 721–8088
Holiday World Tours Ltd; Telephone (3) 723–3771
Hong Kong Meitetsu Co. Ltd; Telephone (3) 669–795
Japan Travel Agency Ltd; Telephone (3) 689–151
Japan Travel Bureau Inc (HK) Ltd; Telephone (3) 723–5884
Jecking Tour Ltd; Telephone (5) 769–282
Jetour Holiday Ltd; Telephone (3) 723–4111
Jetrade Tours Ltd; Telephone (3) 663–131
Joe Grace's Travel Centre of Hong Kong Ltd; Telephone
    (3) 722–0608
King's World Travel & Mercantile Ltd; Telephone (3) 678–041
Landtours Ltd; Telephone (3) 722–7755
Marco Polo Travel; Telephone (3) 699–311
Mayfair Tour & Travel Service Ltd; Telephone (3) 721–5445
New World Creative Tour (HK) Ltd; Telephone (3) 684–206
NJT (Overseas) Ltd; Telephone (3) 696–883
North South Travel Service Ltd; Telephone (3) 683–912
NTA Travel (HK) Co. Ltd; Telephone (3) 721–1348
Ootomo Travel Ltd; Telephone (3) 669–662
Orient Dynamic Co. Ltd; Telephone (5) 265–725
Pacific Delight Tours of Hong Kong Ltd; Telephone (3) 722–1216
Pak Shing Travel Co. Ltd; Telephone (3) 723–0288
Pan Asia Travel Service Ltd; Telephone (3) 666–423
Pearl Star Tours Ltd; Telephone (5) 434–441
President Tours & Travel Service Ltd; Telephone (3) 666–166 or
    (3) 694–808/9
Prince Travel Ltd; Telephone (3) 739–0668
Quality Travel Ltd; Telephone (5) 216–625

cont...

HONG KONG TOUR OPERATORS *(cont.)*

R.S. Travel (HK) Ltd; Telephone (5) 832–2026
Reliance Travel (HK) Ltd; Telephone (3) 723–3369
Silkway Travel Ltd; Telephone (3) 724–1661 or (3) 724–3322
Sinyo Travel Service Ltd; Telephone (5) 769–788
Star Express Ltd; Telephone (3) 699–481
T.F.C. Tours (Far East) Ltd; Telephone (3) 673–018
Tak Jin Travel Services Co. Ltd; Telephone (3) 721–1366
Top Travel Centre (HK) Ltd; Telephone (3) 723–7272
Tour East (HK) Ltd; Telephone (3) 663–311
Tourist Enterprises Ltd; Telephone (3) 674–243
Towa Travel Service Ltd; Telephone (3) 697–167
Travelscope Ltd; Telephone (5) 790–7936
Treasure Tours Ltd; Telephone (3) 680–844
Trinity Express Ltd; Telephone (3) 683–207, (3) 723–3098, or
    (3) 723–2657
Wah Sun Travel Service Ltd; Telephone (3) 694–371
Watertours of Hong Kong Ltd; Telephone (5) 254–808 or
    (3) 686–171
Windsor Tour Agency Ltd; Telephone (5) 779–031
Winston Tours Ltd; Telephone (3) 664–440

V The Hong Kong Tour

About three-quarters of Hong Kong is scenic countryside, which is conserved and protected in more than 20 country parks. The sparkling blue-green water of the South China Sea is in sight almost everywhere. On the other hand, tall buildings cut into mountains, and crowded tenement houses rise up everywhere.

HONG KONG ISLAND

THE CENTRAL DISTRICT

Also simply known as Central, this area is located in the center of the north side of Hong Kong Island, directly opposite Kowloon's Tsim Sha Tsui District, across the harbor.

Soon after Hong Kong was ceded to Britain in 1842, roads were laid along the seafront and two-story buildings were erected by the British merchant houses. At present, hardly any colonial architecture can be found, except for the old Supreme Court Building (it now houses the Legislative Council). Tall office building, hotels, and banks line the major streets. It is the center of Hong Kong's commercial life and exclusive shops.

To get to Central from Kowloon, take the Star Ferry to the Hong Kong side or the MTR to Central Station. You can also take a taxi or public bus (one with yellow and red numbers) through the Cross Harbour Tunnel. From hotels in Causeway Bay, take the tram, the MTR, or the minibuses.

Starting from the Star Ferry Concourse, walking westward, you will run into the **General Post Office** and the **Government Information Service Bookshop. Connaught Centre,** a tall building with rounded windows built on reclaimed land, is on your left. The head office of the **Hong Kong Tourist Association** (HKTA) occupies a few floors and will provide you with maps and fact sheets on interesting places to visit if you still require more information.

Take the overpass to the glass towers of **Exchange Square,** which houses Hong Kong's stock market, the **Unified Stock Exchange**; exhibits of artworks by local and other artists are regularly displayed

Des Voeux Road Central, Victoria, Hong Kong

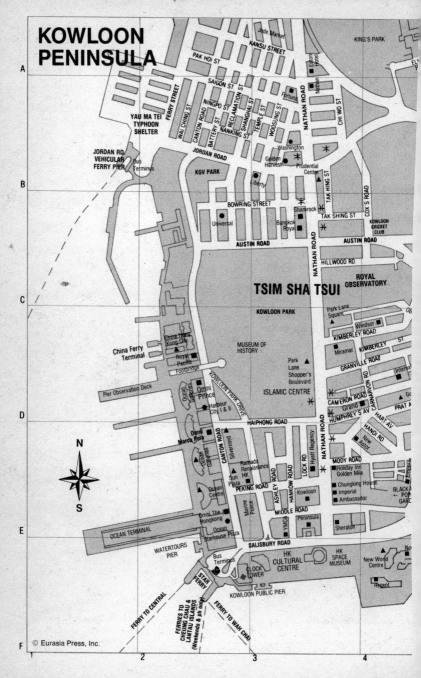

KOWLOON PENINSULA

TSIM SHA TSUI

KING'S PARK

Jade Market

KANSU STREET

PAK HOI ST

SAIGON ST

Egerton Hotel

Fortuna

YAU MA TEI TYPHOON SHELTER

NINGPO ST

RECLAMATION ST

SHANGHAI ST

TEMPLE ST

WOOSUNG ST

NATHAN ROAD

CHI WO ST

FERRY STREET

WAI CHING ST

CANTON ROAD

BATTERY ST

NANKING ST

Washington

JORDAN ROAD

JORDAN RD. VEHICULAR FERRY PIER

Bus Terminus

Golden Harvest

Prudential Centre

KGV PARK

Liberty

BOWRING STREET

Shamrock

TAK HING ST

COX'S ROAD

TAK SHING ST

KOWLOON CRICKET CLUB

Universal

Bangkok Royal

AUSTIN ROAD

AUSTIN ROAD

NATHAN ROAD

HILLWOOD RD.

ROYAL OBSERVATORY

KOWLOON PARK

Park Lane Square

Windsor

MUSEUM OF HISTORY

KIMBERLEY ROAD

Miramar

KIMBERLEY ST.

China Ferry Terminal

China Hong Kong City

Royal Pacific

Footbridge

GRANVILLE ROAD

International

Pier Observation Deck

KOWLOON PARK DRIVE

Park Lane Shopper's Boulevard

ISLAMIC CENTRE

CAMERON ROAD

CARNARVON RD.

PRAT AV

Grand

Omni Prince

Grand Stanford

Harbour City I & II

HAIPHONG ROAD

HUMPHREY'S AV

HART AV

HANOI RD

New Astor

Omni Marco Polo

CANTON ROAD

Hyatt Regency

MODY ROAD

Ocean Galleries

Silvercord

Ramada Renaissance

Sun Plaza

HK

LOCK RD.

ASHLEY ROAD

HANKOW ROAD

NATHAN ROAD

Holiday Inn Golden Mile

Chungking House

BLACK...

Ocean Centre

PEKING ROAD

Marine Police

Imperial

Ambassador

GARD...

Omni The Hongkong

Ocean Starhouse Plaza

MIDDLE ROAD

Kowloon

YMCA

Peninsula

Sheraton

OCEAN TERMINAL

WATERTOURS PIER

SALISBURY ROAD

New...

Bus Terminus

CLOCK TOWER

HK CULTURAL CENTRE

HK SPACE MUSEUM

New World Centre

STAR FERRY

KOWLOON PUBLIC PIER

Regent

N S

FERRY TO CENTRAL

FERRIES TO CHEUNG CHAU & LANTAU ISLANDS (Weekends & ph only)

FERRY TO WAN CHAI

© Eurasia Press, Inc.

2 3 4

A B C D E F

Kowloon City

TSIM SHA TSUI

■ Hotels
Ambassador	E3
Bangkok Royal	C3
Eaton Hotel	A3
Empress	E4
Fortuna	B3
Guangdong	D4
Holiday Inn Golden Mile	E3
Holiday Inn Harbour View	D5
Hyatt Regency	E3
Imperial	E3
International	D4
Kowloon	E3
Kowloon Shangri-La	E5
Miramar	D3
Nathan	B3
New Astor	E3
New World	F4
Nikko	D5
Omni The Hongkong	E2
Omni Marco Polo	E2
Omni Prince	D2
Park	D4
Peninsula	E3
Ramada Inn Kowloon	D4
Ramada Renaissance	E2
Regal Meridien HK	D5
Regent	F4
Royal Garden	D5
Royal Pacific	D2
Shamrock	C3
Sheraton	E3
Windsor	D4

■ Hostels
Chungking House	E3
Y.M.C.A.	E3

▲ Shopping Centres
Auto Plaza	D5
Chinachem Golden Plaza	D5
China Hong Kong City	D2
Empire Centre	E5
Energy Plaza	D4/5
Harbour Crystal Centre	D5
Houston Centre	E5
Intercontinental Plaza	D4
New Mandarin Plaza	D5
New World Centre	F4
Ocean Centre	E2
Ocean Galleries	D/E2
Ocean Terminal	E/F 1/2
Park Lane Shopper's Boulevard	D3
Park Lane Square	D3
Peninsula Centre	D5
Prudential Centre	B/C3
Silvercord	E2
South Seas Centre	D5
Starhouse Plaza	E/F2
Sun Plaza	E2
Tsim Sha Tsui Centre	E5
Wing On Plaza	E4

● **Cinemas/Theatres**

✳ **MTR Entrances**

⚓ **HKTA Information and Gift Centres**   F2

⚓ **Arrivals only**   B6

Kowloon City

■ Hotels
Regal Airport

in the lobby. From the overpass you have a good view of the harbor and **Blake Pier.** At the end of the pier there is an open-air snack bar and benches to enjoy the busy water traffic around the pier. The elevated overpass continues westerly along the waterfront toward the **Central Bus Terminus** below, the **Vehicular Ferry Pier,** and the **Outlying Districts Ferry Pier.** Further west, the **Macao Ferry Terminal** is visible. (Further information on taking ferries to the outlying islands and Macao can be found later.)

Use the overpass to cross the busy traffic of **Connaught Rd.,** come down from the pass, walk inland on either **Pottinger St.** or **Queen Victoria St.,** cross **Des Voeux Rd.** (watch out for the trams), and you will arrive at the **Central Market,** a three-story off-white building with over 300 stalls selling vegetables, poultry, fish, snakes, and other fresh produce. If you are curious about how to dress an eel or a frog for cooking, this is the place to learn. A warning, though: the Central Market is not the cleanest place to visit; in fact, it is permeated with the smell of slaughtering!

Further west, turn left on **Jubilee St.,** where food stalls, or *dai pai dongs,* do business under awnings. These street stalls are the equivalent of Western fast-food places, where bowls of steaming hot congee, noodles, deep-fried dough sticks, and dumplings are served from early morning until dusk.

Queen's Rd. is a busy thoroughfare that, under several names (Queen's Rd. West, Queen's Rd. Central, Queensway, and Queen's Rd. East) runs from the western end of the island to the Sports Ground. Any of the narrow paths uphill will lead you to **Hollywood Rd.** and **Cat St.** A historic one is **Ladder St.;** it consists of stone steps up which riders were carried up the hill in sedan chairs in the early days. This area has the highest concentration of antique shops—filled with Chinese porcelain, curios, and chinoise blackwood and rosewood furniture—and galleries of ancient and modern paintings.

Near the junction of Ladder St. and Hollywood Rd. is **Man Mo Temple** (Temple of Intellectual and Military Prowess), one of Hong Kong's oldest temples, where joss sticks and incense coils burn day and night.

Go back east on Hollywood Rd. and walk downhill on **Lyndhurst Terrace,** a short street lined with shops selling Chinese opera costumes and other embroidered items. It runs into **Wellington St.,** whereskillful mahjong makers, picture-framers, and ivory carvers work at their trades. Wellington St. crosses **D'Aguilar St.** and ends at **Wyndham St.** Between these two streets is an area known as **Lan Kwai Fong;** it has the most trendy restaurants and discos in Hong

Kong. Across Wyndham St. is an old, flatiron-shaped building that was an ice storage building (circa 1911) and now it houses the **Foreign Correspondents Club** and the **Fringe Club**. Walk down Wyndham St. to Queen's Rd. Central and turn left—the famous luxury department store **Lane Crawford** and some of the most glittering jewelry shops, with huge jade and gold pieces on display in the windows, line the street. Walk back on the other side of Queen's Rd. and you will find two narrow lanes, **Li Yuen St. East** and **Li Yuen St. West**, running north from it, where you can find more bargains from stalls and shops that sell undergarments, stockings, handbags, silk shirts, and other fashion accessories.

Queen's Theatre, one of the oldest movie houses in Hong Kong, stands on the corner of Queen's Rd. Central and Theatre Lane. The **Pedder Building**, on **Pedder St.**, is one of the few prewar buildings still in existence in the colony. **The Landmark**, with a rotunda-shaped lobby, is opened to exclusive boutiques on all sides and has a fountain in the center. Shops extend to the floors above and below, with four different escalators to the various levels. Take the one to **Alexandra House** and walk toward **Prince's Building,** where you will find bookshops, toy shops, and some good tailor shops.

Across Chater Rd. is the **Mandarin Hotel,** whose mezzanine contains more antique shops and boutiques.

Statue Square has bubbling water fountains, clusters of trees and shrubs, the statue of Sir Thomas Jackson (chief manager of the Hong Kong and Shanghai Bank, 1876–1902), and a simple cenotaph, which commemorates the dead of both world wars. The highly exclusive **Hong Kong Club** occupies a modern building at one side of the square. Further inland is the only remaining piece of colonial architecture, the **Legislative Building** (the old **Supreme Court House**). Across from it is the new grey and steel structure of the **Hong Kong and Shanghai Bank**, guarded by the pair of famous lions. Beside it stand the **Chartered Bank** and the **Bank of China**, also guarded by a pair of lions.

City Hall, a cultural center with a very popular Chinese restaurant, a concert hall, and a museum, is on the harbor front to the left of the Star Ferry Concourse as you look up at the Peak. And beyond that is **HMS Tamar**, the British naval shore base in Hong Kong. The funnel-shaped **Prince of Wales Building** houses British naval and army headquarters.

WAN CHAI

■ **Hotels**

China Harbour View	D3
Grand Hyatt	C1
Harbour	D2
Harbour View International House	D1
Luk Kwok	D1
New Harbour	D1
New World Harbour View	C1
Ramada Inn HK	D1

● **Cinemas/Theatres**

Cathay	E2
Cine Art 1 & 2	D2
Columbia Classics	C/D2
Imperial	E2

✳ **MTR Entrances**

╫╫╫ **Tramline**

WAN CHAI & CAUSEWAY BAY

N
S

0   0.1   0.2   0.3   km
      0.1   0.2   miles

FERRY TO TSIM SHA TSUI

FERRY TO HUNG HOM (Mon to Sat only)

WAN CHAI FERRY PIER

WAN CHAI

CONVENTION AVE.

WAN CHAI SPORTS GROUND

HK Academy for Performing Arts

Grand Hyatt ■   HK Convention & Exhibition Centre

New World Harbour View

Columbia Classics   Museum of Chinese Historical Relics

Hong Kong Exhibition Centre

HARBOUR ROAD

Harbour View International House

Cine Art 1 & 2

China Harbour View

HK Arts Centre

WAN CHAI

TelecomHouse

GLOUCESTER ROAD

Luk Kwok ■   Harbour ■

JAFFE ROAD

Ramada Inn HK ■

LOCKHART RD.

FENWICK ST

LUARD ROAD

New Harbour ■

HENNESSY ROAD

WAN CHAI ROAD

STEWART RD.

TONNOCHY RD.

MARSH RD.

HENNESSY RD.

O'BRIEN RD.

FLEMING RD.

SOUTHORN PLAYGROUND

● Cathay

WOOD RD.

MORRIS HILL SWIMMING POOL

O'KWAN RD.

JOHNSTON ROAD

Imperial ●

CROSS ST.

RUTTONJEE T.B. SANATORIUM

Tang Shiu Kin Hospital

Q.E. Stadium

HOPEWELL CENTRE

QUEEN'S ROAD EAST

QUEEN'S RD. EAST

MORRISON

© Eurasia Press, Inc.

A   B   C   D   E   F

1   2   3

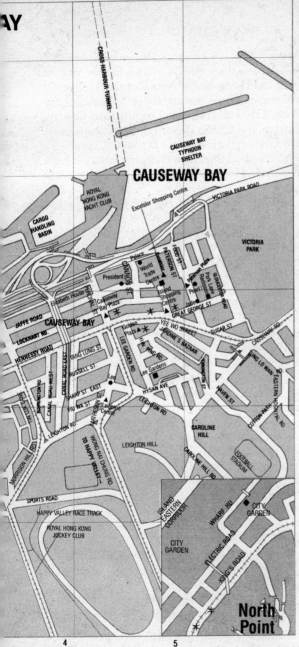

CAUSEWAY BAY

■ *Hotels*
Excelsior	C4
Lee Gardens	D4
Park Lane Radisson	C/D5

▲ *Shopping Centres*
Causeway Bay Plaza	D4
Excelsior Shopping Centre	C4
Golden Plaza	D4
Island Shopping Centre	D4
Leighton Centre	D4
Paterson Plaza	C5

● *Cinemas/Theatres*
Jade	D5
Lee	D4
Palace	C4
Pearl	C5
President	C4

✳ *MTR Entrances*

╫╫╫ *Tramline*

North Point

■ *Hotels*
City Garden

WAN CHAI

To the east of Central is Wan Chai District, known for its bars and nightclubs. Now it is more than that. On the harbor side of **Gloucester Rd.** stand the **Hong Kong Arts Centre** (15 floors of auditoriums, rehearsal studios, stages, restaurants, etc.), the **Academy for Performing Arts, HK International Exhibition Centre, HK Exhibition Centre,** and **China Resource Building** (regular exhibits of Chinese products and a good place to shop). Additionally, a cluster of multistory office buildings with shopping malls has been added: **Great Eagle Centre, Harbour Centre,** and **Sun Hung Kai Centre.**

On the harbor side is the **Wan Chai Ferry Pier,** where passenger ferries go to and from Kowloon.

Between Gloucester Rd. and Queen's Rd. East run four main parallel streets—**Jaffe Rd., Lockhart Rd., Hennessy Rd.,** and **Johnston Rd.** This is the old Wan Chai and the so-called "red light district." Large neon signs extend far out into the streets advertising topless bars, hostess clubs, and discos, but the frenzied pace has slowed down since the Vietnam R & R era. There are also some good and reasonably priced restaurants serving both Chinese and European food (see Chapter VII, "Dining Out in Hong Kong").

The old **China Fleet Club** is located at the beginning of Gloucester Rd.; two blocks down, you will find the infamous **Luk Kwok Hotel** of Suzie Wong legend. Within these four streets are some of the oldest buildings dating from colonial days—three- and four-story tenements, with open storefronts selling fruits, hardware, furniture, and construction materials. Tucked in the middle are some 24-hour mahjong parlors. The tallest building in Hong Kong, **Hopewell Centre,** 64 floors of offices, shops, restaurants, and a revolving restaurant on the top, sits on the crowded section of Queen's Rd. East. Nearby is the tiny **Hung Shing Temple,** dating back to 1860, dedicated to a seafaring god. Another 19th-century temple, **Sui Pak Temple,** up on a terrace reachable by climbing up Tik Loong Lane, is popular with people needing medical help; offerings of mirrors with auspicious inscriptions crowd the interior.

Further east is the **Wan Chai Market,** where fresh produce from China and the New Territories arrives each morning. The narrow lanes crisscrossing this area are filled with little shops selling birds, snakes, paper offerings, camphor chests, vegetables, fruits, and flowers. On any pavement you will find food stands selling noodles, congee, roast duck, and other savories.

HAPPY VALLEY

Away from the harbor, nestled in a valley, is the Royal Hong Kong Jockey Club's **Happy Valley Racecourse** (see Chapter VIII, "Cultural Activities, Recreation, and Entertainment"). Across from the racecourse, amidst flowering trees, is the terraced burial ground of some of the oldest settlers: the **Muslim Cemetery,** the **Catholic Cemetery,** and the **Colonial Cemetery**. Beyond are the **Parsee Cemetery** and the **Jewish Cemetery**. And by the side runs the **Aberdeen Tunnel** crossing under the Peak to the south side of the island.

Wong Nai Chung Rd., on the other side of the racecourse, has some of the best and most fashionable shops, selling locally made shoes and handbags. Up the hill, on Tai Hang Rd., sits a most bizarre "garden"—the **Tiger Balm Garden**, now renamed **Aw Boon Haw Gardens**. The Aw Boon brothers made a fortune from their invention, a medicinal ointment called Tiger Balm, which is a popular household item. This 150,000-square-ft (13,845-m²) garish and bizarre Chinese "Disneyland" contains terraced grottoes with stone sculptures and reliefs of weird and fearsome Chinese mythological figures. On the other hand, the estate also houses one of the finest jade collections. (Permission for a visit can be arranged by the HKTA.)

On the surrounding hillsides, hundreds of squatter shacks exist among modern highrise apartment buildings.

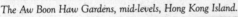

The Aw Boon Haw Gardens, mid-levels, Hong Kong Island.

CAUSEWAY BAY

Causeway Bay borders on Wan Chai, Happy Valley, and North Point. On the harbor side is the Cross-Harbour Tunnel to Kowloon and the **Causeway Bay Typhoon Shelter**. The **Royal Hong Kong Yacht Club** operates its marina on Kellett Island, adjacent to the shelter. In the evening, "dining" sampans of various sizes ply the waters of the shelter. A ride costs $60–100, for about 2–3 hours. The sampans, paddled by hand, move among fishing junks, pleasure motor launches, and sailing yachts, on narrow lanes. Kitchen sampans, bar sampans, and music sampans pull alongside for business. You can have a good meal of seafood, noodles, and congee, cooked before you in these floating kitchens. The bar sampans offer soft drinks, cold beer, and hard liquor at prices slightly higher than onshore. However, you can bring your own wine with no corkage charge. Live bands on sampans offer a song list at $25 per tune; it is not well played, but it is fun to be serenaded at sea! These "dining" sampans provide plastic tablecloths, simple rattan tables and chairs, and poor toilet facilities.

Down a few yards on the waterfront is Jardine's **Noon-Day Gun**, which is still being fired at noon every day. Legend has it that one day in the mid-1800s the merchant house of Jardine fired its gun in a 21-gun salute to welcome the return of one of its opium boats sailing into the harbor. The governor was so incensed that a mere merchant of "foreign mud" should receive the same greeting as high government officials, that as punishment, he ordered Jardine's to fire its gun at noon every day in perpetuity.

Across the shelter is the 19-acre (7.7-ha) **Victoria Park,** with swimming pools, soccer field, and tennis and basketball courts. In early mornings people of all ages do their *tai chi ch'uan* and *kung fu* exercises while joggers run around the park. Some deluxe hotels are located in this area. The five-block square west of Victoria Park has some of the best shopping and department stores (Daimaru, Matsuzakaya, Sogo, China Products, and Lane Crawford's).

Food St., two blocks long of over 20 eating places and diverse international menus, offers fun and good food under canopied lanes and fountains. At night, Food St. comes to life with people milling about, going in and out of restaurants, dining on Indian curry, Cantonese noodles, Peking Duck, American steak, Japanese teppanyaki, and Singapore sati—among the 2,000 dishes available. It is not gourmet food, but it is satisfying.

Away from the harbor and across Hennessy Rd.—Yee Woo St., the main drag where the trams run, is a maze of short streets

(Pennington, Irving, Fuk Hing, etc.) where you will find shops selling thousand-year-old eggs, dried abalone, ginseng, bird nests, rice wine, Chinese herbs, and medicine. Fruit stands and herbal teahouses spill onto the sidewalks. For a dollar you can enjoy a bowl of herbal tea or sugarcane juice, which quench thirst and are purported to have medicinal value.

Nearby, on **Hysan Ave.**, is the Lee Gardens Hotel and **Lee Theatre**—a movie house and a performing stage. The surrounding area has many small, reasonably priced ethnic restaurants—Vietnamese, Indonesian, Malaysian, Indian, Korean, Japanese, Russian, Italian, Western-style coffee shops, and, of course, purveyors of regional Chinese food.

On the south side of Victoria Park is **Tin Hau Temple**, on Tin Hau Temple Rd., one of the many temples devoted to the Queen of Heaven.

NORTH POINT, QUARRY BAY, SHAU KEI WAN, AND CHAI WAN

North Point, Quarry Bay, and Chai Wan are not really tourist spots except for the shopping complex in Taikoo Shing, in quarry Bay. Low- and middle-income highrises and small factories occupy these areas. **King's Road** runs through these sections. On the harbor side there is a ferry service to **Kwun Tong** on the Kowloon side, and nearby is the largest mortuary on the island, the **Hong Kong Funeral Home**. Further east is Quarry Bay, where the most famous site is **Taikoo Shing**, built on the Taikoo Dock of colonial fame. It is a huge complex of shops, ice and roller skating rinks, bowling alleys, and cinemas, called **City Plaza**. Continuing east, and slightly up the hill, is Chai Wan, a jungle of tall housing estates, and on the hillside is the huge Chinese cemetery.

Shau Kei Wan is an old fishing village. Near the tram terminal you can still find some shabby but good seafood restaurants. By the harbor is the **Tam Kung Temple,** and a small fleet of fishing junks still moor in the harbor.

BIG WAVE BAY AND SHEK O

The road to Shek O passes some lovely and quiet spots in the territory with mountains on one side and the many little coves below.

If you branch off Shek O Road, you will come to Big Wave Bay. This is a rather isolated beach, because no public transportation goes

Summer at Shek O Beach, Hong Kong Island.

there and no refreshment stands operate in the area, but it is a clean and lovely beach. In the valley some farmers still till the land as they did before the British came.

Shek O is a picturesque village of many small summer cottages in the native style, and winding lanes leading to numerous luxury villas. The exclusive 18-hole golf club (**Shek O Country Club**) nestles in the rolling hills. **Shek O Beach** is very popular with younger set.

STANLEY

Continuing on to the south side of the island, passing **Tai Tam Reservoir**—there is good fishing and many hiking trails around the reservoir—you enter **Stanley**. The road branches: the lower one is **Stanley Beach Rd.,** which runs along **Stanley Beach,** and the upper one is **Stanley Village Rd.,** which leads to **Stanley Village** and **Stanley Market**. Stanley was once a flourishing fishing village, but nowadays only a few fishing junks moor off the bay from the market.

On both sides of the narrow and congested main street are 50-odd shops selling mostly overrun fashions at very reasonable prices, ceramics, rattan products, and tourist bric-a-brac. This little area is known as **Stanley Market**.

On the other end of Stanley Market you will find an elegant three-story restaurant, **Stanley's Restaurant**, serving good French and continental food. The terrace on the top floor affords a view of the little harbor and **Stanley Fort**. Nearby there are two typical British pubs and an oh-so-British tea shop. Farther away stands an old temple, **Tin Hau Temple**, which serves the fishing folk and the village people.

REPULSE BAY

Repulse Bay Beach is one of Hong Kong's most popular beaches, and is very crowded on weekends and during summer school vacations. On the beachfront are open-air restaurants and food stands selling Chinese noodles and hot dogs. Adequate public facilities are provided for swimmers.

Above the beach, nestling on the foothills, is the world-famous **Repulse Bay Hotel**, rebuilt with its grand balcony and garden. Having tea or dinner on the balcony is a delightful experience. On the surrounding hills are some very luxurious highrise apartment buildings, and some grand private homes are still there, dwarfed by the tall modern highrises.

Hong Kong's Repulse Bay.

DEEP WATER BAY

North of Repulse Bay, the road forks: Repulse Bay Rd. itself goes north past the Peak and through the gap, back to Happy Valley and Central; Island Rd. continues along the coast, to **Deep Water Bay,** past the **Royal Hong Kong Golf Club**. The golf club is open to tourists on weekdays, and its restaurant serves superb seafood. Further on is the **Hong Kong Country Club**, strictly private, with tennis courts, a swimming pool, and other sporting facilities.

Nearby are **Ocean Park** and its more recent addition, **Water World,** one of Asia's largest aquariums and amusement parks. The complex, part of which is carved into a hill overlooking the South China Sea, offers water slides and other water activities from May through October. Near the more inland section is the exit—or entrance—to the **Aberdeen Tunnel** which takes you under the mountain to Happy Valley on the other side of the island.

ABERDEEN

Known as **Hueng Kong Tsai** ("Little Hong Kong") to the local inhabitants, Aberdeen is one of the oldest fishing villages and typhoon anchorages in Hong Kong. Some 5,000 boat people make their home on 3,000-odd junks and sampans on the narrow Aberdeen Harbour. This is where the famous floating restaurants are anchored and is the site of the **Aberdeen Yacht Club,** frequented by the rich and famous.

Water taxis (motorized sampans), driven mostly by women, will take you for a ride in the congested harbor or across to the island of **Ap Lei Chau,** where some of the colony's oldest boatyards are still producing classic Chinese junks.

WESTERN DISTRICT

Rounding the southwest corner of the island you will pass **Pok Fu Lam**, a quiet residential area, and the old **Queen Mary Hospital**. The low road takes you to the **Western District,** where some of the oldest shops sell salted and dried seafood, and to the waterfront, which runs into Central. The high road takes you to "mid-level" and a rather congested residential area along **Bonham Rd.** and **Caine Rd.,** where some of the upper-income Chinese live. The road then takes you back to Central, passing **Government House** and the **Botanical Garden**.

THE PEAK

Take the Peak Tram, a funicular railway, up to the Peak, 1,302 ft (397 m) above sea level. The **Lower Peak Tram Station** is up the hill on **Garden Rd.**, above and behind the **Hong Kong Hilton**, within walking distance of Central. Or you can take a free ride outside the Star Ferry Concourse, Hong Kong side. The open-air double-decker bus runs between Star Ferry Terminal and the tram station, about a 15-minute ride. Public buses and minibuses go up to the Peak regularly.

From the Peak you have a magnificent panoramic view of the harbor, Kowloon, most of Hong Kong, and some of the outlying islands. The **Upper Peak Tram Station** gives access to a revolving restaurant, souvenir shops, and an observation pavilian. Across from the terminal is the lovely, quiet **Peak Cafe,** where you can have tea and sandwiches outdoors, with a view of **Pok Fu Lam Reservoir** and **Aberdeen**. One of the nicest walks is along **Lugard Rd.,** which takes you spirally around the peak and offers a view of all sides of Hong Kong.

KOWLOON

TSIM SHA TSUI

Tsim Sha Tsui (meaning "sharp, sandy point") and Tsim Sha Tsui East are the two most popular tourist areas in Kowloon. They occupy the southern tip of the Kowloon Peninsula across from Hong Kong Central District. This area is packed with luxurious hotels, department stores, commercial complexes, nightclubs, and restaurants. The famous "Golden Mile," Nathan Rd., is the main artery.

To get there from Hong Kong, take the Star Ferry from Central or take the MTR to Tsim Sha Tsui station. The No. 1 minibus (HK$1) takes you from Kowloon Star Ferry Concourse directly to Tsim Sha Tsui East. **Kowloon Star Ferry Bus Terminal**, outside the Star Ferry Concourse, is a main bus depot to most points in Kowloon and the New Territories. **Clock Tower**, built in 1916, opposite the Star Ferry, is all that remains of the old Hong Kong Kowloon Railway terminus. **Ocean Terminal, Ocean Centre,** and **Harbour City** are an interconnected maze of shopping malls, hotels, and gourmet restaurants. There are moving walkways that deliver you to the thousands of shops.

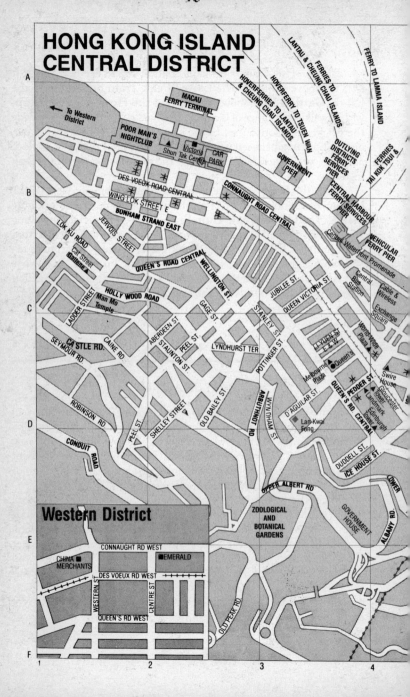

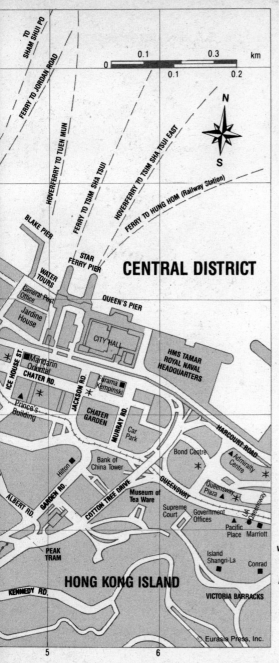

CENTRAL

■ **Hotels**
Conrad	F6
Furama Kempinski	D5
Hilton	E5
Island Shangri-La	F6
Mandarin Oriental	D4
Marriott	E6
Victoria	B2

▲ **Shopping Centres**
Admiralty Centre	E6
Cat Street Galleries	C1
Edinburgh Tower	D4
Gloucester Tower	D4
Melbourne Plaza	D3
Pacific Place	E6
Prince's Building	D4
Queensway Plaza	E6
Shun Tak Centre	B2
Swire House	D4
The Landmark	D4
World-Wide Plaza	D4

● **Cinemas/Theatres**
Queen's	D3
UA Queensway	E6

◆ **Lan Kwai Fong restaurant and shopping area** D3

✴ **MTR Entrances**

⚜ **HKTA Information and Gift Centre** D4

╫ **Tramline**

••• **Peak Tramway** F4

Western District

■ **Hotels**
China Merchants
Emerald

The clock tower of the old Kowloon-Canton Railway Station — behind the
Hong Kong Cultural Center on the Tsim Tsui Waterfront.

The dome-shaped **Space Museum**, on Salisbury Rd. opposite the Peninsula Hotel, contains a hall of solar sciences, an exhibition hall, and a space theater. Regular exhibits and sky shows are open to the public. Call (3) 721–2361 for show times.

A waterfront promenade linking the **New World Centre** with **Tsim Sha Tsui East** is a delightful way to see the harbor.

Kowloon Park has a Chinese Garden with a lotus pond and waterfall, an aviary, a rose garden, children's playground, jogging trail, and other sports facilities. The **Hong Kong Museum of History**, in Kowloon Park, contains exhibits of the natural and social history of Hong Kong. Admission is free. The **Jamia Masjid and Islamic Centre**, with four minarets and a marble dome, stands impressively along Nathan Rd.

YAU MA TEI

Just beyond Tsim Sha Tsui, Yau Ma Tei—its name literally means "oil sesame place"—is known for its **Jade Market**, underneath the Gascoigne Rd. overpass along Kansu and Battery streets, where over 400 stalls display and sell jade pieces. (Tips on buying jade can be found in Chapter IX, "Shopping.") You could get to Yau Ma Tei by taking the MTR to Jordan Station or buses 1, 2, 6, 7, 8, or 9 from the Kowloon Star Ferry Bus Terminal along Nathan Rd. You could also take a ferry from the Central Vehicular Ferry Pier in Hong Kong to the Jordan Rd. Ferry Pier in Kowloon. The Yau Ma Tei typhoon shelter is still home to many fishing junks—colorful and congested. At night the nearby area is transformed into a "Poor Man's Nightclub," with fortune-tellers, food sellers, and vendors of herbal medicines and magical cures. Street singers, singing Cantonese pop songs and excerpts from Cantonese operas, bring noise and entertainment. **Shanghai St.** and **Canton Rd.** are jammed with small shops selling Chinese wedding gowns, embroidered items, bamboo baskets, electrical appliances, and hardware. **Tin Hau Temple,** dedicated to the Taoist Queen of Heaven, is open from 8:30 AM to 5:30 PM. **Temple St. Market**, also known as "Men's St.," is where you can find various products for men. The best time to go is after 8 PM when all the bargain-hunters are out looking for a bargain and a good time.

SHAM SHUI PO

This area is the site of the **Golden Shopping Centre** where locally assembled computers and word processors, and pirated software packages, are on sale for about a third of the prices paid in the United States and Europe. Nearby is the **Han Dynasty Tomb** in Lei Cheng Uk, with a domed vault and chambers; an adjacent gallery exhibits the artifacts and shows an audiovisual program on the history of the tomb.

LAI CHI KOK

Lai Chi Kok Amusement Park is small and tacky, but the only one in town. The **Song Dynasty Village**, beside it, is a re-creation of a typical Song village with traditional pavilions, temples, and street scenes. A wedding parade is performed with period costumes. There is an entrance fee of HK$25 for adults and $5 for children.

MONG KOK AND HUNG HOM

These two industrial areas are filled with multistory factories, one next to the other. **Hung Hom,** on Kowloon's east coast, offers the best factory-outlet shopping. It is also the site of **Kai Tak International Airport** and the **Kowloon Railway Station,** where one gets the direct rail line to China; both are situated by the waterfront in Hung Hom. A 12,000–seat **Coliseum**, which houses sports events and concerts, is next to the station. The **Kowloon Walled City,** near the airport, was a seedy and criminal-filled subterranean urban area outside the jurisdiction of the local authorities; it was recognized from the earliest days as part of China. The wall no longer exists, but narrow staircases still lead down into the dark world below.

KOWLOON TONG

A quiet residential area that has seen better days, Kowloon Tong still contains some of the pre-war villas, but many of them have been converted to schools, old-age homes, and "motels" that can be rented by the hour.

WONG TAI SIN

The **Wong Tai Sin Temple,** named after a miraculous healer, is the most visited temple in the territory. It is a complex of temples with red pillars, a gilded, tilted roof, and multicolored carvings. Year round, worshippers place bundles of burning incense (joss sticks) in the huge metal urns in the smoke-filled courtyard to curry favor with the gods and pray for good health and fortune. It is the place to have your fortune read.

KWUN TONG

At the eastern end of the MTR line, this unattractive but amazing area is filled with many small factories and tall housing estates. Beyond it, at the harbor entrance, is **Lei Yue Mun,** known for its seafood restaurants.

THE NEW TERRITORIES

THE most direct way to the New Territories is by the Kowloon–Canton Railway from Hung Hom or from the Kowloon Tong station. It transverses the heart of the New Territories.

Sha Tin is the first major town along the railway line. The **Monastery of 10,000 Buddhas** is in a steep valley above Shatin. Follow the sign, and a flight of 431 stone steps takes you to a complex of temples and pagodas. The main altar contains gilded statues of the Goddess of Mercy, the Healing Buddha, and other gods and heroes; 12,800 carved Buddha statues of different sizes line the temple walls. On the other side of the valley, perched high up on the mountain, is the **Amah Rock**, which resembles a woman carrying a child on her back. It is also known as "Husband-Watching Mountain"—a widow's watch. The Royal Hong Kong Jockey Club's **Sha Tin Racecourse** is laid out in the valley. **The Jubilee Sports Centre**, one of the best sporting facilities in Asia, is practically next door. Sha Tin is one of the "new towns" housing nearly a quarter of a million people; **New Town Plaza** is its centerpiece—an extensive complex of shops and restaurants.

Beyond, on a hill, is the campus of the **Chinese University of Hong Kong**. Nearby are ferry services that take you across **Tolo Harbour** to points along the coast of the eastern peninsula, which is still virgin parkland.

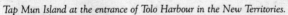

Tap Mun Island at the entrance of Tolo Harbour in the New Territories.

The next stop on the railway is **Tai Po,** a marketplace of local farm produce and the day's catch from the surrounding seas. **Fan Ling** is the home of the Royal Hong Kong Golf Club, where visitors can tee off. Then **Luen Wo Market,** a mecca for the hunter of fresh food! Shueng Shui is the last stop unless you are crossing into China, since **Lo Wu,** the actual last stop in Hong Kong territory, is in a restricted zone.

The other parts of the New Territories can best be visited by car or by public buses from the Jordan Rd. Bus Terminal.

By car, take the **Tuen Mun Highway** (or take No. 68X bus to Lam Tei in Tuen Mun), bypass Tuen Mun, another "new town" housing over 200,000 people, most of whom work in the surrounding industrial areas, and investigate the **Miu Fat Monastery,** which is on Castle Peak Rd., off Tuen Mun Highway; it offers a vegetarian lunch prepared by Buddhist monks. Nearby is the **Kam Tin Walled Village** (take the MTR to Tsuen Wan Station and change to bus No. 51), built in the 1600s by the Tang clan, who still live there.

Travel along the waterfront and you come to **Lau Fau Shan,** the oyster paradise. You buy your seafood from an open-air market and have them cooked in a dozen or so restaurants there. You can also reach Lau Fau Shan by taking No. 68X bus from the Jordan Rd. Bus Terminal to Yuen Long and changing there to No. 55 bus.

Lok Ma Chau stands on a hill overlooking the Shenzhen (Sham Chun) River, the border with China. Take the No. 68X bus from the Jordan Rd. Bus Terminal to Yuen Long, change to No. 76K, and get off at the junction of Castle Peak Rd. and Lok Ma Chau Rd.

Return on Clear Water Bay Rd., which takes you past mountains dotted with Spanish-style villas and the **Clear Water Bay Beach. Shaw's Movie Town,** Asia's Hollywood, sits on a hill overlooking **Sai Kung.** Take Hiram's Highway down to Sai Kung, where the new Marina Cove resort, yacht clubs, and a marina are located on the water's edge. The road takes you back to Kowloon by the airport.

THE OUTLYING ISLANDS

MANY of the 235 outlying islands can be reached by ferries operated by the Hongkong & Yaumati Ferry Company from the Outlying Districts Services Pier and Government Pier, Connaught Rd., on Hong Kong's waterfront west of Central. The three main islands of interest are Lantau, Cheung Chau, and Lamma. Roundtrip fares range from HK$9 to HK$22, and travel time is about an hour or two. The ferries are extremely crowded on summer weekends and holidays; get your tickets in advance to beat the crowd. Call the ferry company at (5) 423–081 or the HKTA at (3) 722–5555 for ferry schedules.

LANTAU ISLAND

Lantau Island is the largest island, even larger than Hong Kong Island, but it is not developed to the same degree. **Silvermine Bay (or Mui Wo)**, the major township, is within walking distance of the ferry landing. The beach is clean, and on the beachfront is the **Silvermine Bay Hotel**, which offers Cantonese and Western food, and facilities for water sports. Take a bus, across from the pier, to **Po Lin Monastery** (or "Precious Lotus" Monastery), high up on the Ngong Ping plateau, passing the 2-mi-long (3.2-km) **Cheung Sha Beach**, the **Shek Pik Reservoir**, and **tea gardens** and plantations where air-conditioned bungalows are available for overnight stays. At the monastery, you can lunch on a vegetarian feast for a small sum; the three huge bronze statues of the Buddha are bathed ceremoniously every year about May, on the Lord Buddha's birthday.

Above the Po Lin Monastery on Hong Kong's Lantau Island is Asia's largest outdoor bronze Buddha.

Return by bus on Tai O Rd. to **Tai O**, a fishing village where most of the houses are built on stilts. Take a hand-pulled cable boat over a small stretch of water to **Tai O Island** to visit **Kwan Ti Temple** and **Hung Shing Ye Temple**. You can lunch at one of the restaurants in the marketplace. Take the Tai O bus back to Silvermine Bay. There are a few decent restaurants near the ferry pier, among them the Roma Restaurant serving both simple Chinese and Western food. A side trip by local "ferry junk," next to the ferry pier, takes you to **Peng Chau Island**. There isn't much on this island, but the ride is very pleasant and cheap. The return ferry ride back to Hong Kong is most pleasant and relaxing in the evening when you can sit on the open deck and enjoy the sunset.

CHEUNG CHAU ISLAND

This dumbbell-shaped "Long Island" is only 7.5 mi (12 km) west of Hong Kong. Many junks, with fishing folk living on them, anchor in the sheltered waters off the narrow isthmus. There is no public transportation on this tiny island. The waterfront (*praya*) off the ferry dock is a lively place, with street stalls selling fresh vegetables and fruit, fresh and dried seafood, and the famous local pungent shrimp paste, and people milling outside the many cafés and restaurants. The narrow streets wind up and down the gently sloping hills and lead to many simple summer cottages and small shops. Visit the **Pak Tai Temple**, built in 1783 to the "Spirit of the North." The dominant building on the island is the **Warwick Hotel**, surrounded on both sides by **Tung Wan Beach** and the tiny **Kwun Yum Wan**. The hotel's terrace café offers a beautiful view of the South China Sea and a relaxing place to have a snack. If you have time, walk or take a local ferry to **Sai Wan** (western end of the island) to visit **Tin Hau Temple,** dedicated to the Queen of Heaven and goddess of the sea, and the cave of the notorious pirate Cheung Po Tsai. Motorized sampans or *kai do* leave from next to the ferry pier at a cost of HK$1–5 depending on the number of passengers for the ride.

The **Bun Festival** on Cheung Chau Island is an annual extravaganza in late April or early May to appease the dead and celebrate the gods of the earth. Huge bamboo towers, covered with pink and white buns, stand outside the Pak Tai Temple. The whole island, which attracts thousands of spectators from Hong Kong and all over, is festive—colorful floats, dancing children, bands, noise, and burning incense.

LAMMA ISLAND

This is the closest of the outlying islands, only a 40-minute ferry ride from Central to **Yung Shue Wan** or **Sok Kwu Wan,** the two main villages. Sok Kwu Wan can also be reached from Aberdeen by motorized sampan. There are a few lovely beaches and a **Temple to Tin Hau,** the Queen of Heaven and goddess of the sea. The footpath and trail to **Mount Stenhouse** (or Mount Lamma), 1,148 ft (350 m) high, is a good climb. The island has good, popular seafood restaurants.

HONG KONG FOR CHILDREN

THERE are various sights and activities to be found in Hong Kong that should please the children in your party.

ASIAN CULTURE

Free shows of indigenous music and dance are given regularly in the Ocean Terminal lobby in Kowloon and in the atrium of the Landmark in Central, Hong Kong. **Puppet shows** (glove puppets, string puppets, and rod puppets) by the Han Hau-nien Troupe are given frequently in the open-air spaces. Background music and sound effects accompany the play. Check with HKTA for presentations.

Acrobatics, magic shows, and martial arts (Chineseboxing, sword plays, and mock combats with antique weapons) are presented jointly by the Hong Kong Tourist Association and local sponsors in the Landmark (Central, Hong Kong) and the Ocean Terminal lobby (Kowloon).

Children might also find the **Song Dynasty Village** of interest.

FUN AND GAMES

Next to the Song Dynasty Village is the **Lai Chi Kok Amusement Park,** which has limited rides but can be fun.

Video games and other games can be found at Chuck E. Cheese (Tsim Sha Tsui East) and at McDonald's (Star House, Kowloon).

Ocean Park, on Hong Kong Island, has some of the world's newest and most exciting thrill rides — Dragon roller coaster, Spider, Space Wheel, Crazy Galleon, etc. Sea lions, dolphins, and a killer whale perform in the Ocean Theatre. The cable-car ride takes you up to the headland, and the world's longest outdoor escalator winds through the park. It is open every day and admission for adults is HK$70 and children HK$35, including all rides. Call (5) 550-947 for information on special Ocean Park City bus tours.

Water World, next to Ocean Park, is an amusement park with giant waves, slides, and pools. Admission depends on the time of day — from HK$15 to HK$40. Call (5) 556-055 for information.

MUSEUMS AND LIBRARIES

The **Hong Kong Space Museum** (Salisbury Rd; Telephone 3-721-2361) features a planetarium and two exhibition halls. The Hall of Solar Sciences has an automatic Solar Telescope, which offers the public "live" information about the sun, and microcomputers are available for visitors to test what they have learned from the exhibits. Open every day except Tuesday. Admission to the Space Theatre show is HK$15 for adults and HK$10 for children under 15.

The **Museum of Chinese Historical Relics** (28 Harbour Rd., in Causeway Centre, Wan Chai; Telephone 5-832-0411) provides a permanent exhibition site for cultural treasures from China. Open daily, 10 AM to 6 PM. Admission HK$12.

Hong Kong Museum of History (Haiphong Rd., Tsim Sha Tsui, Kowloon; Telephone 3-671-124) is open daily except Fridays, from 10 AM to 6 PM. Admission is free.

The most conveniently located **public library** is in the High Block, City Hall, next to the Star Ferry Concourse, Hong Kong. There are more than 20 public libraries in the urban area.

The **Botanical and Zoological Gardens** in mid-level, Hong Kong, have many species of birds and plants.

SPORTS

Roller-skating and ice-skating rinks are located at City Plaza in Taikoo Shing on Hong Kong Island. Tennis, windsurfing, and other sporting facilities are described in the section on sports in Chapter VIII, "Cultural Activities, Recreation, and Entertainment." Horseback riding is offered by the Royal Hong Kong Jockey Club at its Pok Fu Lam Riding School (Telephone 5-501-359).

The **Jubilee Sports Centre,** in Sha Tin, offers many sporting events, including international tournaments and workshops. Contact the HKTA to arrange play time.

VI

Hotels and Lodging

H ong Kong has some of the best hotels in the world, offering first-class comfort, fine restaurants, coffee shops, and lounge bars. Many of these restaurants are listed in the Chapter VII, "Dining Out in Hong Kong." Most hotels have swimming pools, sauna and fitness rooms, hairdressing salons for both men and women, florists, shopping arcades, tailors, and other essential services. Many major hotels have an in-house business service center providing a secretary, word processor, photocopy machine, facsimile transmission machine, etc. at a reasonable rate. Some also offer babysitting services.

By the middle of 1988, a total of 29,000 hotel rooms were available for occupancy. The occupancy rate was nearly 90% in 1987, and the peak months of October and November usually bring full houses to all hotels.

A 10% service charge and a 5% government room tax are added to the hotel bill.

The lobby of the Grand Hyatt Hong Kong Hotel, modelled after the salon of a 1930's passenger liner.

Many hotels offer winter packages at Christmas time and into the Chinese New Year. For example, Furama Inter-Continental has a "Super Shopping Safari Package"; the Hong Kong Hilton, "Hong Kong Hilton Advantage"; and the Hyatt Regency, "Festively Hyatt" holiday. Check with your travel agent for more information.

The Hong Kong Hotels Association (Suite 622, Peninsula Centre, 67 Mody Rd., Tsim Sha Tsui East, Kowloon) publishes an annual *Hong Kong Hotels Directory*, which gives detailed descriptions of every hotel in town.

HONG KONG ISLAND

HOTELS on Hong Kong island are concentrated in two main areas: Central (along the harbor front) and Causeway Bay (near the Cross Harbor Tunnel). The **Mandarin** hotel is by far the most elegant and the **Hong Kong Hilton** the most popular.

Asia (111 rooms)
Address: 1A Wang Tak St., Happy Valley
Telephone: (5) 749-922
Fax: (5) 838-1622
Telex: HX 84323 EAHTL
Rates: Twin—$440-680

Tucked away in an old residential area in Happy Valley, this moderately priced hotel has a casual Western restaurant that is popular with local people.

Caravelle (102 rooms)
Address: 84 Morrison Hill Rd.
Telephone: (5) 754-455
Fax: (5) 832-5881
Telex: HX 65793 CARAV
Rates: Twin/double—$360-400

Another moderately priced hotel in the Happy Valley area, close to Wan Chai nightlife and Causeway Bay shopping.

China Harbour View (211 rooms)
Address: 189 Gloucester Rd.
Telephone: (5) 838-2222
Telex: HX 81088 CNTEL
Rates: Twin/double—$600-700

Opened in early 1988 with such up-to-date facilities as in-room safes and wheelchair service, this hotel is near a complex of shopping malls and office buildings in the Wan Chai–Causeway Bay area.

China Merchants (285 rooms)

Address: 160 Connaught Rd. West
Telephone: (5) 596–888
Fax: 590–038
Telex: HX 66701 CMHTL
Rates: Twin/double—$460–620

This hotel is affiliated with the China Merchants Group, which has ticketing and reservations for hotel accommodations in the PRC; some rooms have a view of the harbor, and both Chinese and Western cuisine are available.

Emerald (288 rooms)

Address: 152 Connaught Rd. West
Telephone: (5) 468–111
Fax: (5) 590–255
Telex: HX 84847 EMERA
Rates: Twin—$380–420

An out-of-the-way hotel in the Western district.

Excelsior (925 rooms)

Address: 281 Gloucester Rd.
Telephone: (5) 767–365
Fax: (5) 895–6459
Telex: HX 74550 EXCON
Rates: Twin/double—$800–1,250

Situated near the Cross-Harbour Tunnel exit and across from the Royal Hong Kong Yacht Club, the Excelsior features tennis courts and a golf practice green. It is within walking distance of all the major department stores in the Causeway Bay area.

Furama Inter-Continental (521 rooms)

Address: 1 Connaught Rd., Central
Telephone: (5) 255–111
Fax: (5) 297–405
Telex: HX 73081 FURAM
Rates: Twin/double—$1,000–1,350

On the eastern end of Central, the Furama has a front that overlooks the harbor, and the rooftop revolving restaurant, La Ronda, serves an international buffet. The lobby is upstairs, and there are some good Japanese restaurants in the basement. The pastry shop on the ground floor is a favorite of the locals.

Grand Hyatt (575 rooms)
Address: 1 Harbour Road, Wan Chai
Telephone: (5) 861–1234
Fax: (5) 861–1677
Telex: 68434 GH HK
Rates: Twin/double from $230

   The splendid new Hyatt (opened late 1989) dominates Hong Kong harbor from Wan Chai, one of the colony's most colorful shopping and entertainment areas. The Grand Hyatt, (distinguished from its sister Hyatt in Kowloon), is enveloped in the new Hong Kong Convention and Exhibition Centre.

Grand Plaza (336 rooms)
Address: 2 Kornhill Rd., Quarry Bay
Telephone: (5) 886–0011
Fax: (5) 886–1738
Telex: HX 3–67645 GPH
Rates: Twin/double—$520–920

   The Grand Plaza, all the way out in Quarry Bay, opened in spring 1988; its features include outdoor tennis courts, a jogging track, and an indoor swimming pool.

Harbour (200 rooms)
Address: 116 Gloucester Rd., Wan Chai
Telephone: (5) 748–211
Fax: (5) 722–185
Telex: HX 73947 HABOH
Rates: Twin/double—$420–550

   The lobby and rooms of the harbour are small but functional, and its special facilities include assistance in visa applications to China and onward booking of China Travel Service.

Harbour View (320 rooms)
Address: 4 Harbour Rd., Wan Chai
Telephone: (5) 201–111
Fax: (5) 865–6063
Telex: HX 61073 CYMCA
Rates: Twin/double—$385–560

Affiliated with the Chinese YMCA, the Harbour View is next door to the two performing arts centers in Wan Chai waterfront and offers spartan rooms and simple dining facilities.

Hong Kong Hilton (780 rooms)
Address: 2 Queen's Rd., Central
Telephone: (5) 233–111
Fax: (5) 845–2590
Telex: HX 73355
Rates: Twin/double—$1,100–1,600

Its renovated rooms can compete with those of any newly opened hotel; the Dragon Boat Bar, on the second floor lobby, is a favorite meeting place; the Grill is a popular luncheon site for business clientele; and the rooftop Eagle's Nest has a good view of the city. The heated outdoor swimming pool with the adjacent health club provides good services.

Hong Kong Marriott (609 rooms)
Address: 15 Queen's Rd., Central
Telephone: (5) 810–8366
Fax: (5) 845–0737
Telex: 66899 MARTT HX

One of Hong Kong's newer hotels, the Marriott opened in the latter part of 1988.

Lee Gardens (800 rooms)
Address: Hysan Ave., Causeway Bay
Telephone: (5) 895–3311
Fax: (5) 769–775
Telex: HX 75601 LEGAR
Rates: Twin/double—$800–1,100

Accessible to Causeway Bay shops, the Lee Gardens has a lobby a little tight for the large numbers of guests, but the top-floor Rainbow Room serves good dimsum.

Mandarin Oriental (544 rooms)
Address: 5 Connaught Rd., Central
Telephone: (5) 220–111
Fax: (5) 297–978
Telex: HX 73653 MANDA
Rates: Single/double—$1,050–1,750

Centrally situated in the business and commercial centers of Hong Kong, the Mandarin Oriental was once adjudged the "best hotel in the world" by an international survey. All the rooms facing the harbor have balconies and a view of the water. Top-grade services and the variety of cuisine offered by the many restaurants make it a choice place to stay. An unusual feature is the Greco-Roman "bath" on the roof, with health club facilities nearby.

New Harbour (173 rooms)
Address: 41 Hennessy Rd., Wan Chai
Telephone: (5) 861–1166
Fax: (5) 865–6111
Telex: HX 65641 HTLNH
Rates: Twin/double—$450–630

Situated in the middle of Wan Chai, the New Harbour is a simple hotel with moderate facilities.

Park Lane (837 rooms)
Address: 310 Gloucester Rd., Causeway Bay
Telephone: (5) 890–3355
Fax: (5) 767–853
Telex: HX 75343 PLH
Rates: Twin/double—$900–1,400

Located on one side of Victoria Park in Causeway Bay, the Park Lane is accessible to the major shopping areas.

Ramada Inn (284 rooms)
Address: 61 Lockhart Rd., Wan Chai
Telephone: (5) 861–1000
Fax: (5) 476–912
Telex: HX 86608 HTLVT
Rates: Twin/double—$450–630

On top of the Macao Ferry Terminal in Central, the Ramada also offers fully furnished efficiency apartments for short-term rental. Other amenities include an open-air pool and tennis courts.

KOWLOON

MOST of the luxury hotels are found in Tsim Sha Tsui East and on the tip of Kowloon Peninsula. The two outstanding hotels are The Peninsula and The Regent; the more moderate ones include the Bangkok, Chung Hing, King's, Ritz, and the Shamrock. The rest are in the first-class luxury category.

Ambassador (315 rooms)
Address: The beginning of Nathan and Middle roads.
Telephone: (3) 666–321
Fax: (3) 690–663
Telex: HX 43840 AMHOC
Rates: Twin/double—$680–880
   Recently renovated, the Ambassador offers two restaurants serving Western and Chinese cuisine, a good coffee shop, and a lobby bar.

Bangkok Royal (70 rooms)
Address: 2–12 Pilkem St.
Telephone: (3) 679–181
Fax: (3) 692–209
Telex: HX 52999 BKKRH
Rates: Twin/double—$440–680
   A small hotel on a back street mostly serving visitors from Thailand, it has a good Thai restaurant.

Chung Hing (90 rooms)
Address: 380 Nathan Rd.
Telephone: (3) 887–001
Telex: HX 51463 CHHTL
Rates: Twin/double—$260–310
   A simple place with spacious rooms and a Chinese restaurant.

Empress (189 rooms)
Address: 17–19 Chatham Rd.
Telephone: (3) 660–211
Fax: (3) 721–8168
Telex: HX 44871 EMPTL
Rates: Twin/double—$600–900
   Popular with tour groups, this is a hotel with balconies and adequate service.

Fortuna (186 rooms)
Address: 351 Nathan Rd. (Mong Kok area)
Telephone: 851–011
Fax: (3) 780–0011
Telex: HX 44897 HOFOR
Rates: Twin/double—$560–760
   Not in the fancy Tsim Sha Tsui area, the Fortuna mainly caters to groups from Southeast Asia.

Grand (194 rooms)
Address: 14 Carnarvon Rd.
Telephone: (3) 669–331
Fax: (3) 723–7840
Telex: HX 44838 GRAND
Rates: Twin/double—$660–820
   An old and reliable hotel with modern facilities.

Grand Tower (545 rooms)
Address: 627 Nathan Rd.
Telephone: (3) 789–0011
Fax: (3) 789–0945
Telex: HX 31602 GNT
Rates: Twin/double—$500–800
   Clean, bright rooms and good examples of such Asian cuisines as Chiu Chow and Japanese.

Guangdong (245 rooms)
Address: 18 Prat Ave.
Telephone: (3) 739–3311
Fax: (3) 721–1137
Telex: HX 49067 GDHCL
Rates: Twin/double—$450–680
   Chinese and Western decor with all-modern facilities.

Holiday Inn (597 rooms)
Address: 70 Mody Rd.
Telephone: (3) 721–5161
Fax: (3) 695–672
Telex: HX 38670 HIHV
Rates: Twin/double—$980–1,450
   Most rooms have a harbor view, and there is an Executive Club floor for businessmen. The hotel has many restaurants, including a snack bar by the rooftop pool.

Holiday Inn Golden Mile (598 rooms)
Address: 50 Nathan Rd.
Telephone: (3) 693–111
Fax: (3) 698–016
Telex: HX 56332 HOLIN
Rates: Twin/double—$920–1,120
   As dependable as any Holiday Inn worldwide this hotel offers a

popular lobby bar, a delicatessen corner, a rooftop swimming pool, and the Baron's Table, a German restaurant.

Hong Kong (789 rooms)
Address: 2 Canton Rd., Harbour City, Tsim Sha Tsui
Telephone: (3) 676–011
Fax: (3) 723–4850
Telex: HX 43838 HONHO
Rates: Twin/double—$900–1,500

Because of its convenient location, this recently renovated hotel is nearly always fully occupied. It has an outdoor swimming pool and some good restaurants—The Belvedire and The Mistral among them.

Hyatt Regency (723 rooms)
Address: 67 Nathan Rd.
Telephone: (3) 311–1234
Fax: (3) 739–8701
Telex: HX 43127 HYATT
Rates: Twin/double—$770–1,400

Business travelers enjoy the Regency Club accommodations, which include a top-quality restaurant, Hugo's, and a popular bar and nightclub, Polaris.

Imperial (221 rooms)
Address: 30 Nathan Rd.
Telephone: (3) 662–201
Fax: (3) 311–2360
Telex: HX 55893 IMPHO
Rates: Twin/double—$500–750

A no-nonsense, comfortable hotel geared to visitors on the go.

International (89 rooms)
Address: 33 Cameron Rd.
Telephone: (3) 663–381
Fax: (3) 695–381
Telex: HX 34749 INTLH
Rates: Twin/double—$400–780

Another small and comfortable hotel in the center of commerce and shopping.

King's (72 rooms)
Address: 473 Nathan Rd. (Mong Kok–Yau Ma Tei)
Telephone: (3) 780–1281
Rates: Twin/double—$260–290
  A little out of the way, and more popular with regional travelers.

Kowloon (708 rooms)
Address: 19 Nathan Rd.
Telephone: (3) 698–698
Fax: (3) 698–698
Telex: HX 47604 KLNHL
Rates: Twin/double—$570–660
  Part of the Peninsula Group, the Kowloon is billed as a "business hotel" with reasonable room prices and adequate facilities.

Marco Polo (441 rooms)
Address: Harbour City
Telephone: (3) 721–5111
Fax: (3) 721–7049
Telex: HX 40077 MPHK
Rates: Twin/double—$750–950
  Managed by the Peninsula Group, the Marco Polo has a small lobby and small rooms but is well run and economical. Guests have the use of the swimming pool in the Hong Kong Hotel. The Brasserie, a French provincial restaurant, is popular.

Miramar (542 rooms)
Address: 130 Nathan Rd.
Telephone: (3) 681–111
Fax: (3) 691–788
Telex: HX 44661 MIRHO
Rates: Twin/double—$790–1090
  A multi-wing building in the center of commercial activities; electronic cards for added security.

Nathan (186 rooms)
Address: 378 Nathan Rd.
Telephone: (3) 885–141
Telex: HX 31037 NATHO
Rates: Twin/double—$370–540
  Further up in the "Golden Mile"; small but adequate.

New Astor (151 rooms)
Address: 11 Carnarvon Rd.
Telephone: (3) 667–261
Fax: (3) 722–7122
Telex: HX 52222 NAHTL
Rates: Twin/double—$600–800
   A well-situated corner hotel, popular with tour groups.

New World (729 rooms)
Address: 22 Salisbury Rd. (New World Centre)
Telephone: (3) 694–111
Fax: (3) 699–387
Telex: HX 35860 NWHTL
Rates: Single/twin—$460–1040
   On the harbor front, the New World has some small economy rooms and a gourmet restaurant, the Park Lane; it is surrounded by a huge shopping mall and boasts an outdoor swimming pool.

Nikko Hong Kong (461 rooms)
Address: 72 Mody Rd.
Telephone: (3) 739–1111
Fax: (3) 331–3122
Telex: HX 31302 NIKHO
Rates: Twin—$950–1450
   Brand-new and on spacious grounds in Tsim Sha Tsui East, this hotel is part of Nikko Hotels International; all-day dining is available in the Café Serena.

Park (900 rooms)
Address: 61 Chatham Rd. South
Telephone: (3) 661–371
Fax: (3) 739–7259
Telex: HX 45740 PARKH
Rates: Twin/double—$600–900
   Though not outstanding, this is an old favorite, conveniently located and with adequate room facilities.

Peninsula (210 rooms)
Address: Salisbury Rd.
Telephone: (3) 666–251
Fax: (3) 722–4170
Telex: HX 43821 PEN
Rates: Single—$1,450–2,100

One of the world's top ten, the Peninsula has a grand baroque lobby where tea is served with elegance and style. The large rooms have high ceilings in the old-fashioned way. Gaddi's, one of the best restaurants in town, and Chesa, serving Swiss food, are among the many top-quality dining facilities in the hotel. There is no health club or swimming pool, but other good services compensate for this shortcoming.

Prince (401 rooms)

Address: Canton Rd., Harbour City
Telephone: (3) 723-7788
Fax: (3) 721-5545
Telex: HX 50950 PRN
Rates: Twin/double—$750-950

Another Peninsula Group hotel, the Prince shares many facilities with the Hong Kong Hotel.

Ramada Renaissance (498 rooms)

Address: 8 Peking Rd.
Telephone: (5) 215-571
Fax: (5) 845-0461
Telex: HX 81252 RAMDA
Rates: Double—$1,100-1,900

Affiliated with Ramada International Hotels, this hotel opened in early 1989. It features many conference and banquet rooms and a Continental-Italian restaurant.

Regal Airport Hotel (384 rooms)

Address: 30 Sa Po Rd.
Telephone: (3) 718-0333
Fax: (3) 799-2503
Telex: HX 40950 HOMRA
Rates: Twin/double—$750-1,050

An indoor walkway connects the Regal to the airport. The rooms are comfortable and sound-proofed, and there are many restaurants serving Asian and Western food; a favorite place for airline passengers.

Regal Meridien (590 rooms)

Address: 71 Mody Rd.
Telephone: (3) 722-1818
Fax: (3) 723-6413
Telex: HX 40955 HOMRO
Rates: Single—$840-1,240

Part of the Air France–Meridien chain. Le Restaurant de France serves *haute cuisine*, and the basement disco Hollywood East is one of the best.

Regent (602 rooms)
Address: Salisbury Rd.
Telephone: (3) 721–1211
Fax: (3) 739–4546
Telex: HX 37134
Rates: Twin/double—$1,150–1,700

As contemporarily elegant as the Peninsula is Old-World charming. The shiny granite floor leads to a multi-level lobby lounge where a ceiling-high glass window allows a full view of the harbor. Having tea at the Regent is as chic as having it in the Peninsula. The Plume is a deluxe restaurant. Some suites have balconies, and all rooms have marbled bathrooms with the bath and shower separated from the toilet.

Ritz (60 rooms)
Address: 122 Austin Rd.
Telephone: (3) 692–282
Fax: (3) 724–4993
Telex: HX 49794 HRITZ
Rates: Twin/double—$360–500

An economical bed space, reachable by MTR (Jordan Rd. station).

Royal Garden (433 rooms)
Address: 69 Mody Rd.
Telephone: (3) 721–5215
Fax: (3) 699–976
Telex: HX 39539 RGHTL
Rates: Single/double—$800–1,250

The floors open onto an atrium with a triangular pool and potted plants; the rooms are fine and The Flower Lounge serves very good Cantonese food.

Shamrock (150 rooms)
Address: 223 Nathan Rd.
Telephone: (3) 662–271
Fax: (3) 739–7354
Telex: HX 50561 SHAMH
Rates: Twin/double—$350–450

A budget hotel with Chinese decor, situated near the Jordan St. MTR station.

Shangri-La (719 rooms)
Address: 64 Mody Rd.
Telephone: (3) 721–2111
Fax: (3) 723–8686
Telex: HX 36718 SHALA
Rates: Twin/double—$1,125–1,800

Sitting on a harbor-front property, the Shangri-La has a good view of the harbor and the promenade. The lobby, where coffee, tea, and snacks are served, is big and comfortable; there is also bar service. The rooms are well equipped, with 24-hour TV programs and information bulletins. Outstanding restaurants include Nadaman (Japanese), Shang Palace (Chinese), and Margaux (French).

Sheraton Hong Kong (922 rooms)
Address: 20 Nathan Rd.
Telephone: (3) 691–111
Fax: (3) 739–8707
Telex: HX 45813 HKSHR
Rates: Double—$880–1,700

Still a favorite, this hotel boasts Hong Kong's first external glass elevators; the Pink Giraffe supper club on the roof offers international cabaret acts, and the Japanese restaurant Unkai is one of the best.

HOSTELS AND GUESTHOUSES

The choice is limited, but in Kowloon you will find:

Booth Lodge (The Salvation Army), 11 Wing Sing Lane, Yau Ma Tei; Telephone: (3) 771–9266
Caritas Bianchi Lodge, 4 Cliff Rd., Yau Ma Tei; Telephone: (3) 881–111
Chungking House, 4/F, Block A, Chungking Mansions, 40 Nathan Rd.; Telephone: (3) 665–362
First Hotel, 206 Portland St.; Telephone: (3) 780–5211
STB Hostel (HK) Ltd, 2/F, Great Eastern Mansion, 255–261 Reclamation St.; Telephone: (3) 321–073
YMCA International House, 23 Waterloo Rd.; Telephone: (3) 771–9111
YMCA of HK (English-speaking), Salisbury Rd.; Telephone: (3) 692–211
YWCA Guest House, 5 Man Fuk Rd., Waterloo Hill; Telephone: (3) 713–9211

NEW TERRITORIES

Carlton (60 rooms)
Address: Tai Po Rd., Kowloon
Telephone: (3) 866–222
Telex: HX 501655 CARHO
Rates: Twin/double–$360–450

An old three-story hotel, the Carleton features terrace dining and "country" atmosphere. A little out-of-the-way in North Kowloon.

Riverside Plaza (830 rooms)
Address: Tai Chung Kiu Rd., Sha Tin
Telephone: (0) 649–7878
Fax: (0) 649–7791
Telex: HX 30013 HORPA
Rates: Twin/double—$700–900

From this hotel, in the developed new town of Sha Tin, one can easily take the MTR and the railway to Kowloon and points north.

THE OUTLYING ISLANDS

CHEUNG CHAU

Warwick (70 rooms)
Address: East Bay
Telephone: (5) 981–0081
Fax: (3) 785–3342
Telex: HX 74369 FEORG
Rates: Twin/double—$420–520

A first-class seaside hotel with private pier and terrace dining.

LANTAU ISLAND

Discovery Bay Village Resort
Telephone: (5) 984–8295.

Mostly for local families on extended vacation; sports facilities include tennis, water sports, and a golf course.

Silvermine Beach Hotel
Telephone: (5) 987–6080.

Near the ferry pier and on the edge of Silvermine Beach, this hotel offers moderate room services and simple dining. It has a children's pool and barbecue facilities.

VII

Dining Out in Hong Kong

H ong Kong has more than 40,000 eating places and over 4,000 restaurants serving local and international cuisine. There are bars aplenty, and pubs are becoming very popular. Service in most hotel restaurants is essentially very good, but the waiters can be very rude in Chinese restaurants. In general, dining out in Hong Kong is cheaper than in the West: you can get by nicely with HK$500 (US$65) for two in a first-class restaurant serving Western food, or with much less in a Chinese restaurant. A 10% service charge is normally added to the bill, except in the smaller restaurants, which expect a tip equivalent to 10%. Most restaurants accept credit cards, except again in the smaller restaurants, particularly the Chinese restaurants.

HOTEL DINING

MOST of the hotels have good to excellent dining facilities, and some of them have the best Chinese and Western cuisine in Hong Kong. All hotels has well-stocked wine cellars with both vintage and nonvintage wines. Generally the prices are more expensive and the atmosphere more formal than in restaurants not in hotels. Hotel restaurants are popular with the local people, and reservations are recommended. All of them take a variety of credit cards. Many require a jacket for men, so be prepared. Lunch hours are normally from 11 AM to 3 PM, and dinners are served between 6 and 11 PM. The hotel restaurants are listed under regional cuisine.

RESTAURANTS

CHINESE CUISINE

Cantonese cuisine predominates, with Peking, Shanghainese, Szechuan, and Chiu Chow dishes close favorites. Most of the Chinese restaurants are plain and perhaps even drab, except those in the hotels, but Chinese go to restaurants to eat, not for the ambiance. Prices generally range from HK$35 to HK$200 a dish. Of course, some high-quality shark's fin and abalone dishes can cost up to HK$500–1,000. Some restaurants do serve a set dinner for 4–6, ranging from HK$250 to 1,500. Most of the menus are in Chinese only, so bring along someone who can read and speak Chinese. All non-hotel Chinese restaurants have limited wine lists of both Chinese and European wines; they also serve Chinese and imported beer. A few words on Chinese wines here: they are distilled from rice, millet, and other grains, with herbs and flowers to give them medicinal value and aromas. The most popular wines are Siu Hing ("Yellow Wine"), which is distilled from rice and served warm; Go Leung and Maotai, strong—70% alcohol—liquors distilled from millet or sorghum; and Ng Ka Pay, a bittersweet herbal wine.

CANTONESE

Cantonese dishes are generally light, with not too much oil and not too much hot spice; most dishes are delicately sautéed or steamed. Some popular dishes include poached shrimps, stir-fried minced quail and bamboo shoots served with fresh lettuce, sliced grouper with Chinese ham and bamboo shoots, shark's fin soup with shredded chicken, diced winter melon with mixed meat and seafood, steamed fish, and sautéed crab with ginger and scallion.

Almost all Cantonese restaurants serve dimsum for lunch. These are small dishes or baskets of steamed or fried delicacies. A typical dimsum parlor has trays of dimsum loaded on carts, pushed by a waiter or waitress who shouts the names of the dishes. Just stop them and point to what you want. The fancier restaurants offer a dimsum menu. Each dish costs from HK$5 to 16. The classic is *har kau*, a shrimp dumpling; other favorites include *shiu mai* (pork dumpling), *cha siu bau* (steamed barbecued pork bun), *chun kuen* (spring roll), *woo kok* (deep-fried taro stuffed with meat and vegetables). Sweet dimsum include *daan* tart (egg custard tart), *tsin chan go* (steamed layered cake), and *ma lai go* (steamed spongy cake).

Boil and Boil Wonderful, Food St., Causeway Bay, HK (Telephone: 5-779-788), serves "home cooking" in earthen casserole pots.

The Bloom, Basement, Pedder Bldg., 12 Pedder St., Central, HK (Telephone 5-218-421), offers dainty dishes well served. House specialties are shark's fin wrapped in sliced fresh lobster, roast suckling pig, and steamed *lung kong* chicken.

The Chinese Restaurant, Hyatt Hotel, 67 Nathan Rd., Tsim Sha Tsui, Kowloon (Telephone 3–662–321 ext. 881), serves Cantonese cuisine. The specialties are braised shark's fin with brown sauce, steamed grouper, and fried lobster balls.

City Hall Restaurant, 2/F, City Hall Low Block, Central, HK (Telephone 5–211–303), has a huge variety of dimsum and other simple tasty dishes.

Eagle's Nest, Hong Kong Hilton, 2 Queen's Rd. Central, HK (Telephone 5–233–111 ext. 2501), is on the top floor with a good view of the city. It also serves Northern Chinese dishes. Try the Vagabond Chicken, Lotus Vegetables, and the Baked Stuffed Sea Whelk. It serves dimsum at lunch hour. It also has a cocktail lounge.

Fook Lam Moon, 459 Lockhart Rd., HK (Telephone 5–772–567) and 31 Mody Rd., Tsim Sha Tsui, Kowloon (Telephone 3–660–286), is known for its sautéed frog's legs and crispy chicken.

Golden Unicorn, Hong Kong Hotel, Canton Rd., Tsim Sha Tsui, Kowloon (Telephone 3–722–6565), offers the well-known Drunken Prawns and Unicorn Chicken.

Guangzhou Garden, Exchange Square, Connaught Rd., Central, HK (Telephone 5–251–163), is a gourmet delight with modern decor and a full view of the harbor. House specialties are Braised Bird's Nest with Pigeon Egg (order in advance), Double-Boiled Whole Chicken Stuffed with Shark's Fin (order in advance), and Sautéed Milk.

Jade Garden Restaurant, Swire House, Central, HK (Telephone 5–239–966); Entertainment Bldg., 30 Queen's Rd. Central, HK (Telephone 5–234–071); and Star House, Salisbury Rd., Kowloon (Telephone 5–661–326): a restaurant chain serving reliable food.

Lai Ching Heen, The Regent, Salisbury Rd., Kowloon (Telephone 3–721–1211) offers some very good and typical Cantonese dishes, such as Stewed Winter Melon Soup and Sautéed Diced Chicken. Also try its Deep-Fried Pear with Scallops.

Loong Yuen, Holiday Inn Golden Mile, 50 Nathan Rd., Tsim Sha Tsui, Kowloon (Telephone 3–739–6268), offers top-quality Cantonese dishes.

Luk Yu Tea House, 24 Stanley St., Central, HK (Telephone 5–235–463/5), is the oldest original teahouse, and serves very delicate dimsum and some very good traditional dishes for dinner. It still has ceiling fans and brass spittoons. Famous for its wide variety of good-quality Chinese tea.

Man Wah, Mandarin Hotel, 5 Connaught Rd., Central, HK (Telephone 5–220–111 ext. 4025), on top of the hotel, serves gourmet Cantonese food in a lush setting. House specialties are Shark's Fin Soup, Deep-Fried Loong Kwong Chicken, and the Man Wah Fried Rice.

Rainbow Room, Lee Gardens Hotel, Hysan Ave., Causeway Bay, HK (Telephone 5–895–3311), a quiet restaurant on the top floor that serves very good Cantonese dishes. Its small selection of dimsum is about the best in town. Other specialties are seafood dishes and Peking Duck.

Regal Seafood Restaurant, Regal Meridien Hotel, 71 Mody Rd., Tsim Sha Tsui East, Kowloon (Telephone 3–723–8881), serves a variety of seafood such as Alaskan clams, abalone, local scallops, and fish à la Cantonaise.

Shang Palace, Shangri-La Hotel, 64 Mody Rd., Tsim Sha Tsui East, Kowloon (Telephone 3–721–2111 or 3–721–8524), has a traditional Chinese decor of gold and red-lacquered wood. It serves good suckling pig and baked chicken in salt. Its dimsum are legendary.

Spring Moon, The Peninsula, Salisbury Rd., Kowloon (Telephone 3–666–251). Try the crisp and succulent *Kar Luen Lau* Chicken and Shark's Fin Soup; the abalone dishes are superb. Desserts include sweet cashew nut cream and sweet lotus seed broth with bamboo fungus. Its dimsum menu is limited but very delicately done.

Sun Tung Lok Shark's Fin Restaurant, Harbour City, Canton Rd., Kowloon (Telephone 3–722–0288); and 137 Connaught Rd. West, Hong Kong (Telephone 5–462–718), specializes in seafood—shark's fin of different qualities, many kinds of snakes with chrysanthemum petals, sea moss, and swimming local fish.

West Villa, 313 Des Voeux Rd., Central, HK (Telephone 5–437–388), a very popular place that includes in its menu roast pigeon and dishes cooked in earthen pots.

Yung Kee, 32 Wellington St., Central, HK (Telephone 5–231–562), is a place known for its succulent roast goose and other barbecued meats. It is a very crowded place, especially during the lunch hour.

CHIU CHOW

Chiu Chow (Swatow, or Shantou), in the eastern part of Guangdong province, is famous for its shellfish dishes: deep-fried shrimp balls and crabmeat balls, steamed lobster, and sautéed slices of whelk. The slices of cold duck are classic, and the famous "Iron Buddha" (*tit koon yam*) tea is automatically served in small cups as an aperitif.

Chiu Chow Garden, Basement, Connaught Centre, Central, HK (Telephone 5–258–246); and Hennessy Centre, 500 Hennessy Rd., Causeway Bay, HK (Telephone 5–773–391). House specialties are sliced soy goose, shrimp and crabmeat balls, and double-boiled shark's fin soup. The famous "Iron Buddha" tea, strong and bitter, is served in little cups before and after dinner. Also try the fried *e-fu* noodles with sugar and vinegar.

Manning Chiu Chow, Asian House, 1 Hennessy Rd., Wan Chai, HK (Telephone 5–861–2882), serves typical Chiu Chow dishes such as sliced cold goose with garlic and vinegar sauce, steamed crab, shark's fin Chiu Chow-style, and of course, "Iron Buddha" tea.

PEKING

Peking Duck, with crisp golden skin and succulent meat, served with steamed buns and savory sauce, is the favorite. Beggar's Chicken is a spectacular and delicious dish, composed of chicken stuffed with vegetables and herbs, and wrapped in lotus leaves, sealed in clay, and baked. Instead of rice, wheat noodles or steamed or fried buns accompany the dishes. Hotpots, with your own mix of sauces, are very popular in winter months.

Chung Chuk Lau (Pine and Bamboo Restaurant), 30 Leighton Rd., Happy Valley, HK (Telephone 5–774–919), serves good Peking Duck and Yellow Fish in Wine Sauce; in the winter it has Mongolian Hotpot (you cook you own meat in a steaming pot with your own mix of a variety sauces).

Peking Garden, Basement, Alexandra House, Chater Rd., Central, HK (Telephone 5-266-456); and Excelsior Shopping Arcade, Causeway Bay, HK (Telephone 5-777231), has an extensive menu that includes Beggar's Chicken (order in advance), Peking Duck, and Prawns in Chili Sauce. An expert noodle-maker demonstrates how noodles are made.

Spring Deer, 42 Mody Rd., Tsim Sha Tsui, Kowloon (Telephone 3-664-012), is a popular place for Peking Duck; it has good noodles and steamed meat buns.

SHANGHAINESE

Shanghainese food is oilier and heavier than Cantonese cooking. Eels, crisply fried or sautéed in heavy garlic, are a Shanghainese specialty. Another "Shanghainese only" item are the "hairy" crabs imported from a lake near Shanghai between October and December. They are expensive but a delicacy. Other popular dishes include "Drunken Chicken" (chicken marinated in Chinese wine), Sweet and Sour Yellow Croaker, and Sautéed Shrimps with Peas. This cuisine has some of the best pan-fried and steamed dumplings, for example, pan-fried dumplings with pork or vegetable fillings.

Great Shanghai, Prat Mansion, 26 Prat Ave., Tsim Sha Tsui, Kowloon (Telephone 3-668-158), is an old establishment that still serves very good food. Try the Fried Yellow Fish with Sweet and Sour Sauce and the Fried "Crystal" Shrimps.

Shanghai Garden, Hutchinson House, Central, HK (Telephone 5-238-322), serves food from Shanghai and surrounding areas, including sautéed eels in garlic sauce, braised mixed fresh vegetables, river shrimps, and Sichuan eggplant and garlic sauce. The steamed or fried onion bread is top grade.

Yat Pan Hong, 38 Kimberley New St., Tsim Sha Tsui, Kowloon (Telephone 3-678452), is a casual place serving good spiced smoked fish and steamed vegetable buns.

SICHUAN

Sichuanese dishes are known for their fiery taste, the result of heavy use of chili, spices, and other "hot" ingredients. Some popular dishes are hot and sour soup, fried yellow croaker with soybean and chili sauce, smoked duck in camphor and tea, sautéed diced chicken in chili bean paste, sautéed eggplant in spicy fish-flavored sauce, and dry-fried string beans.

Lotus Pond, Harbour City, Canton Rd., Tsim Sha Tsui, Kowloon (Telephone 3-724-1088), is a fancy place with good smoked pigeon and spicy shrimps and chicken.

Pep 'n Chili, 12 Blue Pool Rd., Happy Valley, HK (Telephone 5-738-251/4), is a very popular up-market restaurant housed in a small, charming building. Its specialties are Spiced Cold Cuts, Sichuan Smoked Duck and Diced Chicken in Chili Sauce.

Prince Court Sichuan, Sutton Court, Harbour City, Canton Rd., Kowloon (Telephone 3-663-100). House specialties are Drunken Prawns, Fish Maw, Smoked Duck, and Smoked Pigeon, assorted cold cuts, and abalone dishes.

Sichuan Garden, Gloucester Tower, The Landmark, Central, HK (Telephone 5-214-433), the Prawns in Chili and Garlic Sauce, and the Smoked Duck are exceptionally good.

Sze Chuen Lau, 446 Lockhart Rd., Causeway Bay, HK (Telephone: 5-981-9027). Its specialty is smoked duck. Other dishes worth trying are Prawns in Chili, and Eggplant in Garlic Sauce.

WESTERN CUISINE

Restaurants serving Western cooking range from simple bistros to the most fancy hotel dining rooms, and the cuisines from American to Continental.

AMERICAN

Beverly Hills Deli, 2 Lan Kwai Fong, Central, HK (Telephone 5-265-809), offers over-sized corned beef and pastrami sandwiches. Other specialties include Texas chiliburgers and huge hot dogs. Sodas and Kosher wines are available.

California, Lan Kwai Fong, Central, HK (Telephone 5-211-345), has guacamole dip, Golden Gate Grilled Chicken, hamburgers, a salad bar, and American cocktails. It also has some good California wines.

San Francisco Steak House, 101 Barnton Court, Harbour City, Kowloon (Telephone 3-722-7576), is known for its American steaks and prime ribs, with French fries and onion rings, and baked potato with sour cream and chives. It also has a good salad bar. The California wine menu is extensive.

BRITISH

Bentley's Oyster Bar and Seafood Restaurant, Basement, Prince's Bldg., Central, HK (Telephone: 5-868-0881), offers good fresh Dover sole and oysters on the half-shell or cooked in many different ways. The dressed crab is also good. There is an extensive wine list, but try the Black Velvet (champagne mixed with Guinness).

FRENCH

Au Trou Norman, 6 Carnarvon Rd., Tsim Sha Tsui, Kowloon (Telephone 3-668-754), a small bistro that offers solid dishes such as Mignon d'Agneau à la Moutarde and Langue de Veau Vallée d'Auge. A complimentary glass of Calvados and a full listing of French wines are available.

La Brasserie, The Marco Polo, 13 Canton Rd., Harbour City, Kowloon (Telephone 3-721-5111 ext. 148), serves French provincial dishes such as Escargots Provençale, French onion soup, Bouillabaisse, and good desserts in a casual setting. The wine list includes plenty of Burgundies and Bordeaux.

Le Restaurant de France, Regal Meridien, 71 Mody Rd., Tsim Sha Tsui East (Telephone 3-722-1818), offers high-standard French nouvelle cuisine.

Gaddi's, The Peninsula, Salisbury Rd., Kowloon (Telephone 3-666-251), has perhaps the grandest French cuisine in town. The Crèpes Farcies au Crabe is superb, the Mignon de Veau Champenoise and the Carrée d'Agneau aux Gousses d'Ail et au Thym are excellent. The Grand Marnier Soufflé is irresistible.

Margaux, Shangri-La Hotel, 64 Mody Rd., Tsim Sha Tsui East, Kowloon (Telephone 3-721-2111), serves high-quality Continental and

French food. House specialties are Filet of Sole with Salmon Mousse, Deep-Fried Turbot Filet Wrapped in Noodles with Black Bean Sauce, and Crabmeat Crèpes.

Stanley's French Restaurant, 86 Stanley Main St., Stanley, HK (Telephone 5–813–8873), housed in a small multi-story building on the edge of a beach, serves gourmet food that includes Escargots Bourguignonne, Rack of Lamb Provençale, and Creole and Cajun dishes. A lovely place to enjoy your food and wine.

ITALIAN

Bologna Ristorante Italiano, Elizabeth House, 250 Gloucester Rd., Causeway Bay, HK (Telephone 5–747–282), has some nice dishes such as Cartoccio di Scaloppine con Asparagi and Ossobuco alla Milanese.

La Taverna, 1 On Hing Terrace (off Wyndham St.) Central, HK (Telephone 5–228–904), has an open-air terrace where diners can enjoy some genuine Italian food such as Ravioli alla Bresciana, Tagliata, and Gamberoni all'Anice. Good selection of Italian wines.

The Pizzeria, Kowloon Hotel, 19 Nathan Rd., Tsim Sha Tsui, Kowloon (Telephone 3–698–698 ext. 3322), has good pizza and many pasta dishes. The pasta buffet includes cannelloni, fettucine, lasagna, spaghetti, and salads.

CONTINENTAL

Baron's Table, Holiday Inn Golden Mile, 50 Nathan Rd., Tsim Sha Tsui, Kowloon (Telephone 3–693–111), serves Austrian, German, and Swiss food. The salad bar is ample, and the cheesecake is delicious.

The Belvidere, Holiday Inn Harbour View Hotel, 70 Mody Rd., Tsim Sha Tsui, Kowloon (Telephone 3–721–5161), serves gourmet European food. Its specialties are Burgundy Snails, Grilled Escalopes of Salmon, and Lobster Bisque with chunks of lobster meat.

Chesa, The Peninsula, Salisbury Rd., Kowloon (Telephone 3–666–251), is a Swiss restaurant serving fondues, choices of veal, and roasted potatoes. Lots of Swiss wines.

Hugo's, Hyatt Hotel, 67 Nathan Rd., Tsim Sha Tsui, Kowloon (Telephone 3–662–321), serves good European food and innovative seafood dishes such as Poached Lobster Tail in Vanilla Sauce. The U.S. Prime Beef Roast and the Baked Rack of Lamb are house specialties.

Jimmy's Kitchen, South China Building, 1 Wyndham St., Central, HK (Telephone 5-265-293); and Kowloon Centre, 29 Ashley Rd., Tsim Sha Tsui, Kowloon (Telephone 3-684-027/29), is an old standby serving Chinese, French, and Indian cuisines. Its specialties are Chicken Madras, Grilled or Spiced Grouper, and Deep-Fried Ice Cream.

Market St., 19 Wyndham St., Wilson House, Central, HK (Telephone 5-810-7566), serves a variety of foods that you pick from a center stall—tiger prawns, lobster, mussels, salmon, Cornish hen, all cuts of steak, fresh vegetables, and other viands and are cooked as you like them in any style or form.

Park Lane, New World Hotel, 22 Salisbury Rd., Tsim Sha Tsui, Kowloon (Telephone 3-694-111), offers good value in Continental cuisine, including King Prawns with Green Peppercorn Sauce and Rack of Lamb.

Pierrot, 25/F, Mandarin Hotel, 5 Connaught Rd., Central, HK (Telephone 5-220-111 ext. 4028), is known for its guest chefs of international repute and the ever-changing menus. It is basically a French restaurant with superb cuisine.

The Plume, The Regent, Salisbury Rd., Kowloon (Telephone 3-721-1211), has a most luxurious setting with a full view of the harbor and the Peak. It serves the best-quality Continental and French food. House specialties include Scallop Salad with Basil, Red Crab Bisque with Tarragon, and Filet of Fresh Salmon. A glass of Kir is on the house, and Beluga caviar is always on the menu. Its cellar has about 10,000 bottles of the best vintage wines.

The Rotisserie, Furama Inter-Continental, 1 Connaught Rd., Central, HK (Telephone 5-255-111), prides itself on monthly promotions of European specialties. The eight-course "Gourmet Dinner" is a very good buy. The cheese and dessert trolleys offer ample choices.

Tai Pan, Hong Kong Hotel, Canton Rd., Tsim Sha Tsui, Kowloon (Telephone 3-676-011 ext. 3901), offers Continental cuisine: lobster is cooked in various ways, and the Dover sole is also very good. Prime cuts of steak from the United States are excellent but expensive.

The Verandah, 109 Repulse Bay Rd., Repulse Bay, HK (Telephone 5–812–7353 or 5–812–2722), is a close re-creation of the old place in the Repulse Bay Hotel, and diners still can see the bay beyond. The Continental and French dishes on the menu are not superb, but still of good quality. Try the Seafood Crèpes and the Flamed Pepper Steak. Grand Marnier Soufflé is still on the menu.

GRILL ROOMS

All the grill rooms also serve Continental food.

Bocarino's Grill, Hotel Victoria, Shun Tak Centre, Connaught Rd., Central, HK (Telephone 5–407–228 ext. 7422/23), offers Continental cuisine. The meats are grilled on a mesquite broiler; the seafood is also good. Wines from Europe, Australia, and New Zealand are available.

Excelsior Grill, Excelsior Hotel, Causeway Bay, HK (Telephone 5–767–365), offers, besides grilled meat, Boston lobster, Alaskan King Crab, and King Prawns. An extensive menu and a good wine selection.

Hilton Grill, 2/F, Hong Kong Hilton, 2 Queen's Rd. Central, HK (Telephone 5–233–111 ext. 647), serves American, English, and European food. It is known for the Roast Beef on the Wagon and seasonal game dishes. Seafood dishes—grilled King Prawns and Macao sole—are fresh and nicely done.

Mandarin Grill, Mandarin Hotel, 5 Connaught Rd., Central, HK (Telephone 5–220–111 ext. 4020), is a very popular place for business people and locals. Its U.S. Prime Rib on the Wagon is superb, as are its wide range of appetizers and seafood dishes. Extensive wine list.

Verandah Grill, The Peninsula, Salisbury Rd., Kowloon (Telephone 3–666–251 ext. 1190), offers a huge selection of grilled meats and seafood. Wines come from the extensive Peninsula wine cellar.

ASIAN

Spices, 109 Repulse Bay Rd., Repulse Bay, HK (Telephone 5–812–22711), presents dishes from all over Asia—Indian, Indonesian, Filipino, Malaysian, and Thai—cooked with authentic indigenous spices. The setting is lovely. A wide selection of Asian beers.

RESTAURANTS

INDIAN

Ashoka, G/F, 57 Wyndham St., Central, HK (Telephone 5–249–623), offers typical northern Indian cuisine. Try the Tandoori Mixed Grill and Chicken Bhurtha.

Bombay Palace, Far East Finance Centre, 16 Harcourt Rd., Admiralty, HK (Telephone 5–270–115), is part of an international chain serving mild curry dishes and good kebab. It offers a variety of North Indian breads and sweets.

Gaylord, Hody Commercial Bldg., 6 Hart Ave., Tsim Sha Tsui, Kowloon (Telephone 3–724–3222), has good lamb curry.

INDONESIAN

Indonesian, 26 Leighton Rd., HK (Telephone 5–779–981); and 66 Granville Rd., Tsim Sha Tsui, Kowloon (Telephone 3–673–287), has good *satay* and *gado gado* salad. It also serves *rijstaffel* (a lunch consisting of almost every dish on the menu) on Sunday.

Java Rijstaffel, 38 Hankow Rd., Tsim Sha Tsui, Kowloon (Telephone 3–671–239), serves *rijstaffel* regularly; its *nasi goreng* (fried rice) and *sambals* (little dishes) are good.

Ramayana, Houston Centre, Mody Rd., Tsim Sha Tsui East, Kowloon (Telephone 3–721–7029), has some good *satays* and set meals.

JAPANESE

Most of the Japanese restaurants serve *saki* and Japanese beers, and have a sushi bar.

Benkay, Basement, The Landmark, Central, HK (Telephone 5–213–344), has a sushi bar and a teppanyaki bar.

Inagiku, The Peninsula, Salisbury Rd., Kowloon (Telephone 3–666–251 or 3–739–1898), serves good sushi and sashimi. The tempura and charcoal-grilled beef are done just right.

Nadaman, Shangri-La Hotel, 64 Mody Rd., Tsim Sha Tsui East, Kowloon (Telephone 3–721–2111), has high-quality tempura, Kobe beef sukiyaki, and other traditional dishes.

Unkai, Sheraton Hong Kong Hotel and Towers, 20 Nathan Rd., Kowloon (Telephone 3-691-111 ext. 2), has house specialties of Kaisaki course, tempura, sushi, and teppanyaki. Try their lunchbox, a miniature black lacquered box with each drawer filled with delicacies.

KOREAN

You go to a Korean restaurant for its open-grilled barbecue of assorted meats with six or seven side dishes of vegetables, beancurd, and dried fish. Also try the hot fish soup.

Arirang Restaurant, 76 Morrison Hill Rd., Happy Valley, HK (Telephone 5-723-027).

Arirang Korean Restaurant, Sutton Court, Harbour City, Tsim Sha Tsui, Kowloon (Telephone 3-692-667).

Koreana Restaurant, 1 Paterson St., Causeway Bay, HK (Telephone 5-775-145).

MALAYSIAN-SINGAPOREAN

Malaya Restaurant, 158 Wellington St., Central, HK (Telephone 5-251-580), has a big selection of *satays* and curries. It also serves Chinese and Western dishes.

Satay Hut, Mody Rd., Kowloon (Telephone 3-723-3628), serves a variety of *satay* and other dishes from Malaysia.

Singapore Restaurant, 143 Des Voeux Rd. West, Hong Kong (Telephone 5-402-991).

THAI

Chili Club, 68 Lockhart Rd., Wan Chai, HK (Telephone 5-272-872, has good *tom yum gung* (spicy and sour soup) and chili beef salad.

Golden Elephant Thai Restaurant, Bamton Court, Harbour City, Tsim Sha Tsui, Kowloon (Telephone 3-692-733), serves good-quality Thai food.

Royal Thai, Elizabeth House, 250 Gloucester Rd., HK (Telephone 5-832-2111), has some of the finest Thai dishes prepared by chefs from

Bangkok. Many of the Thai curry dishes are cooked with coconut cream. The set dinners (HK$110–$220) offer 10 different dishes. A limited wine selection is available.

Sawadee Thai Restaurant, 1 Hillwood Rd., Kowloon (Telephone 3–722–5577), offers Thai curries and a variety of seafood dishes. Try the Steamed Fish in Plum and Ginger Sauce. Singha beer is available.

VIETNAMESE

Golden Bull, New World Centre, Tsim Sha Tsui, Kowloon (Telephone 3–694–617), has a good Hot and Sour Prawn Soup and Vietnamese beer. Its house specialties are Seven-Style Beef and Roast Suckling Pig.

Vietnam City, 92 Granville Rd., Kowloon (Telephone 3–667–880).

VEGETARIAN RESTAURANTS

Bodhi Vegetarian Restaurant, 56 Cameron Rd., Tsim Sha Tsui, Kowloon (Telephone 3–739–2222); and 338 Lockhart Rd., Causeway Bay, HK (Telephone 5–732–155), serves both Chinese and Western dishes.

Vegi Food Kitchen, 8 Cleveland St., Causeway Bay, HK (Telephone 5–890–6660).

Wishful Cottage Vegetarian Restaurant, 336 Lockhart Rd., Causeway Bay, HK (Telephone 5–735–645).

Woodlands International Restaurant, 8 Mindon Ave., Tsim Sha Tsui, Kowloon (Telephone 3–693–718), serves very good Indian vegetarian dishes. Try the Madras *hali* (a combination of various dishes).

Y. Yuen General Restaurant, Yuen Yuen Institute, Sam Dip Tam, Tsuen Wan, New Territories (Telephone 0–490–9882).

FLOATING RESTAURANTS

The Jumbo (Telephone 5–539–111), **Sea Palace** (Telephone 5–527–340) and **Tai Pak** (Telephone 5–525–953) are moored in Deep Bay, Aberdeen, Hong Kong. They all serve sea-caught fish that you can pick from a swimming tank, and other Cantonese dishes. It's fun to take a sampan ride out to the restaurants.

REVOLVING RESTAURANTS

Juno Revolving Restaurant, 655 Nathan Rd., Mong Kok, Kowloon (Telephone 3–915–403).

La Rondo, Furama Inter-Continental, 1 Connaught Rd., Central, HK (Telephone 5–255–111 ext. 502-3), revolving slowly on top of the hotel, offers the "Four Nations" buffet of Chinese, Japanese, Indian, and European cuisine and breathtaking views while you dine. There is a cocktail lounge and live music for dancing in the evening.

Revolving 66, 62/F, Hopewell Centre, 183 Queen's Rd. East, Wan Chai, HK (Telephone 5–286–231), serves Western food.

NIGHTCLUB RESTAURANTS

Pink Giraffe, 18/F, Sheraton Hong Kong Hotel and Towers, 20 Nathan Rd., Kowloon (Telephone 3–691–111 ext. 4) is a restaurant-nightclub high up in the sky, reached by a glass-bubble elevator. It serves high-quality nouvelle Continental cuisine, and has an extensive champagne selection and wine list.

Some of the large Chinese restaurants have nightclub acts.

COFFEE SHOPS

All major hotels have decent to very good coffee shops; they will not be listed here. A cup of coffee in a hotel coffee shop, however, usually costs twice what it does in a coffee shop outside a hotel.

California, 30 D'Aguilar St., Central, HK (Telephone 5–211–345).

Maxim's, Connaught Centre, Central, HK (Telephone 5–257–977); 36A Queen's Rd., Central, HK (Telephone 5–257–552) and Tsim Sha Tsui Centre, Tsim Sha Tsui East, Kowloon (Telephone 3–668–635).

Peak Tower Coffee Shop, Upper Peak Tram Terminal, The Peak, HK (Telephone 5–972–62), has a view of Hong Kong.

Terrazza, The Landmark, Des Voeux Rd.,, Central, HK (Telephone 5–264–200), a good place to rest your feet while shopping.

AFTERNOON TEA

Hong Kong still has a few places that serve afternoon tea, a tradition adopted from the British. Finger sandwiches, toasted scones with fresh cream, and sweet pastries are served with a pot of tea with hot milk or lemon. Many hotels have a tea in the lobby in the afternoons, but the grandest of them are served by **The Peninsula** and **The Regent** in their grand lobbies.

The Verandah in Repulse Bay and the **Westminister** in Stanley also offer afternoon tea.

PUBS

These eating establishments are becoming so popular that there is a long list of them, with savory and without, with an adequate lunch menu and without. Pub food is simple and hearty, but some pubs go fancy and charge for it, too. Yes, you can get steak-and-kidney pie, shepherd's pie, fish and chips, and Scotch eggs in many of these pubs.

Beefy's Tavern, 76 Canton Rd., Tsim Sha Tsui, Kowloon (Telephone 3–674–697).

The Blacksmith's Arms, 16 Minden Ave., Tsim Sha Tsui, Kowloon (Telephone 3–696–696).

Bull and Bear, Hutchinson House, 10 Harcourt Rd., Central, HK (Telephone 5–257–436). Very crowded during lunch hours.

Dickens' Bar, The Excelsior Hotel, Gloucester Rd., Causeway Bay, HK (Telephone 5–767–365), serves a good buffet of curry and all the other pub food.

Friar Tuck, Harbour City, Kowloon (Telephone 3–723–3298); and Edko Tower, Ice House St., Central, HK (Telephone 5–242–332), with an Olde English ambiance and large menu.

Grammy's Lounge, Supreme House, 2A Hart Ave., Tsim Sha Tsui, Kowloon (Telephone 3–683–833).

Jockey, Shopping Arcade, Swire House, Central, HK (Telephone 5–261–478), offers a full lunch menu.

Kangaroo Pub and Windjammer Restaurant, 11 Chatham Rd., Tsim Sha Tsui, Kowloon (Telephone 3–723–9439).

Mad Dogs, 33 Wyndham St., Central, HK (Telephone 5–252–383), is a Scottish pub with good pub food.

Ned Kelly's Last Stand, 11A Ashley Rd., Tsim Sha Tsui (Telephone 3–660–562), serves Australian food and Aussie lager.

Waltzing Matilda, 9 Cornwall Ave., Tsim Sha Tsui (Telephone 3–676–874), also serves Aussie lager and hearty Aussie food.

STREET STALLS

Also known as *dai pai dong,* these eating places are scattered all over Hong Kong Island, Kowloon, and the New Territories. Many of them consist of only a few tables and benches serving noodles and congees. These are the very popular local equivalent of outdoor cafés.

FAST FOOD

To the Chinese, "fast food" means a bowl of noodles or a plate of rice with slivers of meat and sauce from any of the small eating places. This form of eating is very traditional and has existed for centuries. But Western fast food is catching on and is particularly popular with the younger generation.

Kentucky Fried Chicken, 6 D'Aguilar St., Central, HK; 40 Yee Wo St., Causeway Bay, HK; Everest Arcade, 241 Nathan Rd., Yau Ma Tai, Kowloon.

Lindy's Restaurant, 15 Watson Rd., North Point, HK.

McDonald's Restaurants, 5 Queen's Rd., Central, HK; Yu To Sang Bldg., 37 Queen's Rd., Central, HK; Sanwa Bldg., 30 Connaught Rd., Central, HK; 23-29 Jordan Rd., Yau Ma Tai, Kowloon; 21 Granville Rd., Tsim Sha Tsui, Kowloon; 2 Cameron Rd., Tsim Sha Tsui, Kowloon; 12 Peking Rd., Tsim Sha Tsui, Kowloon; Star House, Tsim Sha Tsui, Kowloon; Ritz Bldg., 625 Nathan Rd., Mong Kok, Kowloon; and many other locations.

OUT-OF-THE-WAY DINING

Popular places, but not gourmet food, can be found in the outlying areas. These include **Lau Fau Shan** in the New Territories (near Yuen Long), where oysters are produced locally. Restaurants cook them the way you want—sautéed, steamed, deep-fried, poached, in soup, or how ever.

Lei Yue Mun (Lyemum) is a small fishing village at the eastern end of Kowloon, where you choose live seafood from the market and have it cooked up by the many restaurants in the area. To get to Lei Yue Mun take the MTR to Kwung Tong and a taxi to the market.

If you want to have really good pigeon, go to Sha Tin. One of the best restaurants is **Lung Wah,** near the railway station. Any restaurant inside the shopping mall also does it up well.

Sham Tseng (Deep Well), on the Tuen Mun Rd., about 12 mi. (19 km) out from Kowloon, has tiny pigeonhole restaurants that serve golden roast goose upstairs, downstairs, and everywhere. Some of the seafood dishes are very fresh and nicely done. "Valet parking" is nearly mandatory, since the only street to these restaurants is extremely narrow and congested.

"Dining sampans" in the Causeway Bay Typhoon Shelter provide a leisurely ride about the Shelter while food is ordered from the "floating kitchens" serving seafood in black bean or oyster sauce, noodles, congees, and vegetables. Beer and hard liquor are available from the "floating bar" sampans.

On Repulse Bay Beach you will find an indoor-outdoor restaurant, **Sea View Restaurant,** serving ordinary Chinese food. But you can eat in your bathing suits under sun umbrellas! They also serve sandwiches and beer.

Buddhist vegetarian food is offered by **Po Lin Monastery** on Lantau Island, which also offers spartan lodgings for overnight guests.

All the other outlying islands are known for their simple but good seafood restaurants, generally located near the ferry pier.

VIII
Cultural Activities, Recreation, and Entertainment

An enormous variety of pastimes are available within the small area of Hong Kong, from serious drama and music, both Western and Oriental, through hiking and sports to nightclubbing. Herewith, a brief listing.

CULTURE AND ENTERTAINMENT

CHINESE OPERA

There is no regular opera season, but there are many special performances by both the local groups (Cantonese companies and Soochow lyrical groups) and visiting troupes from China and Taiwan. Check with the HKTA for performance schedules. The Asian Arts Festival in October also features Chinese opera presentations.

Chinese opera combines singing, acting, recitation, acrobatics, and dancing in exaggerated form. The costumes and makeup are very colorful—both realistic and surrealistic.

DANCE

The 30-member **Hong Kong Dance Company** performs regularly throughout the territory. They do Chinese classical and folkdance numbers and newly choreographed works on Chinese historical themes. The **Hong Kong Academy of Ballet** is both a professional ballet company and a vocational ballet school. It gives performances of classical Western ballets. The **Modern Dance Theatre** of Hong Kong is more avant-garde, combining modern dance, Chinese dance, and innovative music.

Chinese folksongs and dances are presented jointly by the HKTA and local business sponsors; many of the dances are based on themes of minority cultures such as the mountain tribes of Tibet and Xinjiang. These performances include the popular ribbon dance.

The highly specialized and stylized Pi Husi and Unicorn dances are also presented by the HKTA.

Cantonese Opera

THEATER

The **Hong Kong Repertory Theatre** is a professional group doing Chinese plays and translated Western plays in Cantonese. The **Chung Ying Theatre Company,** a professional company with Chinese and British actors, presents plays in Cantonese and English. **Actors Rep** is a group of professional actors performing in City Hall and the Hong Kong Arts Centre.

Two local amateur groups, the **Garrison Players** and the **Hong Kong Stage Club,** offer a few performances a year. The **Fringe Club** does a variety of plays, both musical and dramatic.

The Arts Centre, Wan Chai (Telephone 5-823-0230), presents regular performances by both local groups and visiting companies, especially during the annual Hong Kong Arts Festival held every January and February. City Hall (Telephone 5-739-595) is a regular venue for many of the drama events in Hong Kong.

MUSIC—CHINESE, WESTERN, JAZZ, AND FOLK

The Hong Kong Chinese Orchestra mostly plays traditional Chinese music. It gives regular concerts around town. Telephone (3) 721-3283 for information.

Free concerts of Chinese instrumental music are regularly given by the HKTA in the major shopping malls. Instruments such as the 26-string *pipa*, the *er-hu*, the bamboo flute, and a seven-string lute produce sounds that are quite unusual.

The **Hong Kong Philharmonic Orchestra,** with 100 musicians from all over the world, offers a series of concerts. Telephone (5) 832-7121.

Jazz is played at Rick's Café, 4 Hart Ave., Tsim Sha Tsui, Kowloon (Telephone 3-672-939), three and four nights a week. Jazz can also be heard at Dickens' Bar in the Excelsior Hotel, Causeway Bay, HK (Telephone 5-767-365); Ned Kelly's Last Stand, 11A Ashley Ave., Tsim Sha Tsui, Kowloon (Telephone 3-660-562); and the **Godown,** Sutherland House, Central (Telephone 5-221-608), every Wednesday night.

Folk music can be heard in The Fringe Club, Dairy Farm Bldg., Wyndham St., Central. Frequent concerts and vocal recitals are presented by visiting orchestras and artists in City Hall or in the Hong Kong Arts Centre.

CULTURE AND ENTERTAINMENT

MOVIES

There are many movie houses showing Chinese, British, and American films. All seats are numbered and reserved, and can be bought in advance. Five showings a day are the norm: 12:30, 2:30, 5:50, 7:30, and 9:30 PM. The theatre is cleared after each showing, so you cannot stay over for the next show. Some Chinese movies have English subtitles.

The major cinema houses in Hong Kong include Columbia Classics, Great Eagle Centre, 23 Harbour Rd. (Telephone 5-738-291); Pearl, Paterson St., Causeway Bay (Telephone 5-776-352); Park, 180 Tung Lo Wan Rd., Causeway Bay (Telephone 5-702-412); Lee, 27 Percival St., Causeway Bay (Telephone 5-895-4433); Palace, 280 Gloucester Rd., Causeway Bay (Telephone 5-895-1500); Empress, 10 Nullah St., Mong Kok (Telephone 3-809-570; London, 219 Nathan Rd. (Telephone 3-661-056); and Ocean, Harbour Centre, Tsim Sha Tsui (Telephone 3-724-5444).

The local newspapers have listings of all movie houses and show times. Studio One is a film society that shows artistic and award-winning international films.

MUSEUMS

The **Flagstaff House Museum of Tea Ware** (Victoria Barracks, Queensway, Hong Kong) displays more than 500 pieces of tea ware, including Yi Xing tea ware from Jiangsu Province and other exquisite tea sets. Admission is free.

Fung Ping Shan Museum, Hong Kong University (94 Bonham Rd., Hong Kong), has a good collection of Tang and Qing Dynasty paintings, Shang and Zhou ritual vessels, 3d-millennium BC ceramics and painted pottery. Admission is free.

Hong Kong Museum of Art (High Block of City Hall, 10th and 11th Floor, Hong Kong) contains collections of Chinese art and antiquities, including painting, calligraphy, rubbings, ceramics, bronze, lacquerware, jade, papercuts, and embroidery. Admission is free.

Hong Kong Museum of History (inside Kowloon Park, Haiphong Rd., Tsim Sha Tsui, Kowloon) has one of the most comprehensive collections of late 19th- and early 20th-century photographs of Hong Kong.

Hong Kong Space Museum (Salisbury Rd., Tsim Sha Tsui, Kowloon; Telephone 3-721-2361). Admission is HK$15.

Jade Museum (inside Tiger Balm Gardens; Telephone 5-616-211) contains a great collection of jade. Admission is free but must be arranged in advance.

Museum of Chinese Historical Relics 2/F, Causeway Centre, 28 Harbour Rd., Wan Chai, Hong Kong) regularly exhibits treasures from China.

DISCOS AND BARS

These establishments are still popular and alive in Hong Kong, and some very sophisticated ones have appeared on the scene in recent years. Generally, an entrance fee of HK$50–100 is charged, which includes two drinks.

Many of the popular discos are in the hotels: **Faces** in the New World Hotel, **Hollywood East** in the Regal Meridien Hotel, **Polaris Club** in the Hyatt Regency Hotel, and **Talk of the Town** in the Excelsior.

Other favorites in Kowloon include the Apollo 18, Silvercord, Tsim Sha Tsui; **Canton,** Harbour City; and **Hot Gossip,** World Finance Centre, Harbour City, Tsim Sha Tsui. In Hong Kong there are the **California,** D'Aguilar St., Lan Kwai Fong; **Casablanca,** Aberdeen Marina Carpark, Aberdeen; **Disco Disco,** 40 D'Aguilar St., Central; and **The Godown,** Basement, Sutherland House, Central.

COCKTAIL AND PIANO BARS

All the major hotels provide instrumental music in at least one of the bars, lobbies, or restaurants. The Captain's Bar in the Mandarin has light and contemporary jazz; there is a string quartet in the lobby of the Shangri-La Hotel, and The Peninsula Hotel's L'Aperitif features piano music.

CABARET

At the Hong Kong Hilton Hotel, Central (Telephone 5-233-111), entertainments accompany dinner irregularly. Some of the large Chinese restaurants in Tsim Sha Tsui and Yau Ma Tei have elaborate floorshows, among them the Golden Crown Restaurant on Nathan Rd., the Ocean Palace Restaurant and Nightclub in Ocean Centre, and the Ocean City Restaurant and Nightclub in the New World Centre.

GIRLY BARS AND HOSTESS CLUBS

The golden era of R & R during the Vietnam War is long gone, but there are still girly bars and hostess clubs catering to a different clientele. The charges (cover, minimum, hostess, escort, etc.) and different drink prices for customers and companionable young women vary greatly from club to club. Check before you go!

In Kowloon: **China City Night Club,** Peninsula Centre, Tsim Sha Tsui East (Telephone 3-723-278); **Club Bottoms Up,** 14 Hankow Rd., Tsim Sha Tsui (Telephone 3-721-4509); **Club Cabaret,** New World Centre, Tsim Sha Tsui (Telephone 3-698-431); **Club Deluxe,** New World Centre Office Bldg., Tsim Sha Tsui (Telephone 3-721-0277); **Club Kokusai,** 81 Nathan Rd., Tsim Sha Tsui (Telephone 3-676-546); **Club New Lido,** 36B Hankow Rd., Tsim Sha Tsui (Telephone 3-683-479); **Club New World,** Hotel Miramar, Tsim Sha Tsui (Telephone 3-668-687); **Club Volvo,** Mandarin Plaza, 14 Science Museum Rd., Tsim Sha Tsui East (Telephone 3-692-883), the biggest and the loudest in town; **The Players Club and Topless Bar,** 69 Peking Rd., Tsim Sha Tsui (Telephone 3-676-802).

In Hong Kong: **Club Celebrity,** 175 Lockhart Rd., Wan Chai (Telephone 5-755-601); **Club Dai-Chi,** 257 Gloucester Rd., Causeway Bay (Telephone 5-831-935); **Mandarin Palace Night Club,** 24 March Rd., Wan Chai (Telephone 5-756-551); **New Tonnochy Night Club,** 1 Tonnochy Rd., Wan Chai (Telephone 5-754-376); and **Pussycat Bar,** 36 Lockhart Rd., Wan Chai.

SPORTS

BOATING AND SAILING

There are several boat clubs and yacht clubs that offer boating and sailing facilities: the Royal Hong Kong Yacht Club on Kellett Island, the Aberdeen Boat Club, the Hebe Haven Yacht Club, and the Stanley Services Boat Club. You must have reciprocal club rights from abroad in order to use their boats or be taken there by a member.

Pleasure junks can be rented from the Boating Centre (Telephone 5-223-527) or Charter Boats Ltd. (Telephone 5-557-349), which has many types of boats.

GOLF

There are a few golf courses that admit overseas visitors. The Royal Hong Kong Golf Club has a nine-hole course at Deep Water Bay

(Telephone 5-812-0088) on Hong Kong Island and two 18-hole courses at Fanling (Telephone 0-901-211) in the New Territories; visitors can only play on weekdays unless they have reciprocal club rights. The green fees at Fanling are HK$360 for a single round or HK$480 for the day; at Deep Water Bay, HK$100 for a single round.

The Clearwater Bay Golf and Country Club on Sai Kung Peninsula has an 18-hole golf course. The fee is HK$300, which includes cart hire. The Hong Kong Tourist Association organizes a special tour to the Club for a discount price.

Visitors can play seven days a week at the Discover Bay Golf Club on Lantau Island. A hovercraft ferry leaves from Blake Pier in Central regularly. Call (5) 987-7271 for more information.

Clubs can be rented at all the courses.

HORSE RACING

The Hong Kong Jockey Club operates two racecourses—one in Happy Valley on Hong Kong Island and the other in Sha Tin, New Territories. Betting on horses is the only legalized form of gambling in Hong Kong and therefore is very popular. The season is from September to May. The Hong Kong Tourist Association arranges special trips for overseas visitors which include a badge to the Members' Enclosure, with lunch or dinner and transportation. The price is HK$220. Call the HKTA (5-244-191) for bookings and detailed information. The Jockey Club also lets in overseas visitors—show up at the Badge Enquiry Office at the track, show your passport, pay HK$50 for a badge, and you can punt freely in the Members' Stand. The Jockey Club's number is 5-790-4827.

ROLLER SKATING AND ICE-SKATING

City Plaza, Taikoo Shing, on Hong Kong Island, has a first-class roller-skating rink (Telephone 5-670-391) and an ice-skating rink (Telephone 5-675-388). There is also a roller-skating rink at Lai Chi Kok Amusement Park in Kowloon (Telephone 3-744-2942). Skates can be rented at all these places.

RUNNING AND JOGGING

You can actually run or jog in the many pocket parks in the territory or on the official jogging track in Victoria Park, Causeway Bay, across from the Park Lane Hotel, or Kowloon Park's 700-metre Fitness Trail, which adjoins the "Golden Mile" of Nathan Rd. in Tsim Sha Tsui.

The Bowen Rd. path in mid-peak on Hong Kong Island is very popular with joggers. The most spectacular track is up on the Peak. It starts from behind the Peak tram station near Lugard Rd.

The Hong Kong Running Clinic (Telephone 5-746-211) welcomes visitors to join its regular jog every Sunday morning (7:30 AM) from the Adventist Hospital at 40 Stubbs Rd., Hong Kong, or its evening jogs on Tuesdays and Thursdays.

SWIMMING

Hong Kong has hundreds of beaches, but only about 30 of them have services provided by the government. These public beaches have changing rooms, showers, toilets, lifeguards, swimming floats, swimming-zone safety markers, barbecue pits, and picnic areas. The four popular beaches on Hong Kong Island that can be reached easily by public transportation are Repulse Bay, Deep Water Bay, Stanley Beach, and Shek O Beach. They are very crowded in the summer months and on public holidays. It's also not unusual for the beaches to be so polluted that swimmers are not allowed to go in.

The popular beaches in the New Territories are located along Castle Peak Rd.—Ting Kau, Lido, Hoi Mei, Gemini, Dragon, and New and Old Cafeteria. But some of these don't have changing rooms or showers.

There are also some very lovely beaches on Sai Kung Peninsula and on the outlying islands.

Public swimming pools are located at Victoria Park, Causeway Bay (Telephone 5-704-682), and on Oi Kwan Rd., Wan Chai (the Morrison Hill Swimming Pool; Telephone 5-753-028). Check the times available for public use.

Most big hotels have swimming pools on the premises.

TENNIS

A limited number of public tennis courts are available to visitors, but they are hard to book. The court fee is HK$15 per daytime hour or HK$30 per hour after 7 PM. The courts on Hong Kong Island are at Bowen Rd. (Telephone 5-282-983), Victoria Park (Telephone 5-706-186), and Wong Nai Chung Gap (Telephone 5-749-122). In Kowloon there is the Kowloon Tsai Park Court (Telephone 3-367-878). Many private clubs in Hong Kong have tennis courts, but you must be taken there by a club member.

WALKING AND HIKING

There are more than 20 country parks in Hong Kong. Some of them provide picnic areas with barbecue pits, campsites, way-marked walks, nature trails, rain shelters, refreshment stands, and public toilets.

On Hong Kong Island are the Aberdeen Country Park, the Pok Fu Lam Country Park, and the Tai Tam Country Park. A recommended walk would start at the Peak and go down to the Pok Fu Lam Country Park, and then back up to the Peak.

Tai Mo Shan Country Park, Sai Kung Country Park, and Plover Cove Country Park are in the New Territories. On Lantau Island is the Lantau Country Park.

The government pamphlet "How to Get to Hong Kong's Country Parks" can be picked up from the HKTA.

If you are ambitious, the MacLehose Trail is for you. It is Hong Kong's first long-distance hiking route, stretching for over 62 mi (100 km) from Tuen Mun to Tai Long Wan at the other end of the New Territories.

WATER SKIING

The Hong Kong Water-skiing Association (Telephone 0–431–2290) supplies skiing equipment for an hourly fee. The sport can be enjoyed in Deep Water Bay, Repulse Bay, and Stanley on the southern side of Hong-Kong Island, and off Lamma Island.

WINDSURFING

This is becoming a very popular sport in the territory. Windsurfing facilities are available at Stanley Beach (Telephone 5–660–320 or –660–425); at Tung Wan Beach on Cheung Chau Island (Telephone 5–981–8316); at Tolo Harbour, near Tai Po in the New Territories (Telephone 0–658–2888), and at Sha Ha Beach (Telephone 3–281–5605). Most of them offer lessons.

Also call the Hong Kong Windsurfing Association (Telephone 5–223–316) for more information.

IX   Shopping

Hong Kong is full of shopping centers, shopping malls, department stores, hotel·arcades, special markets, bazaars, and alleys of shops.

The main shopping areas are located in Central and Causeway Bay on Hong Kong Island, and Tsim Sha Tsui and Tsim Sha Tsui East in Kowloon. You may venture out to Stanley Market for clothes, to Happy Valley for custom-made shoes and handbags, or to Hung Hom for factory outlets, but generally you can find everything in these four shopping areas. As a rule, shops in Central are open from 10 AM to 6 PM and in the Causeway Bay area to 10 PM ; shops in Tsim Sha Tsui are open from 10 AM to 7:30 PM or later. The only days shops are closed is during the Chinese New Year (late January or early February) and when the No. 8 typhoon signal is hoisted.

A fixed-price policy is observed by practically all stores except some smaller shops. To be sure, do some comparison shopping before you buy. You should also know that shops displaying a Hong Kong Tourist Association (HKTA) red and white sign (a red junk) are members of the association and reputable shops. (The HKTA's free pamphlet "The Official Guide to Shopping, Eating Out and Services in Hong Kong" gives a comprehensive list of member shops and restaurants). Some shops do give a discount if you pay cash or buy more than one item, or both. Most shops will take credit cards, but they prefer cash or traveler's checks.

You do need detailed receipts and warranties for expensive purchases. Sometimes, customs officials require a list of serial numbers, model numbers, gold content, etc. on high-value items such as jewelry, watches, and electrical and photographic equipment.

Many shops will pack your purchases and ship them directly to their destination; there is a reasonable surcharge for this service, which normally includes insurance covering loss in transit. You may also want to take out insurance covering damage in transit.

Fraudulent sales are not uncommon. If you have a complaint about goods purchased at a HKTA membership shop, call its hotline (5) 244–191, ext. 278. Direct other complaints to the Royal Hong Kong Police Force Fraud Squad, Criminal Investigations Department (Telephone 5-284-511, ext. 25) or to the Consumer Council at (5) 748–297.

WHAT TO BUY

HONG KONG still offers comparatively good prices on almost everything, from Oriental antiques to the latest high-tech products.

ANTIQUES

In Central, the **Hollywood Rd.** area is still the place to go for antiques and works of art. Many of the old family-owned shops have gone, replaced by European entrepreneurs bringing with them sophisticated displays and an air of elegance. You will find Ming vases, old and new engraved screens, antique silverware, rare maps, antique and reproduction furniture, lacquer chests, and much more.

Try the following: **Art City** (195 Hollywood Rd.), **Eastern Dreams** (corner of Hollywood Rd. and Lyndhurst Terrace), **Altfield Gallery** (1 Hollywood Rd.), **Everlasting Chinese Arts Studio** (172A Hollywood Rd.), **Helene Bennett Antiques** (35 Hollywood Rd.), **Luen Chai Curios Store** (22 Upper Lascar Row), **Tang's Fine Antiques & Arts** (161 Hollywood Rd.), and **Yue Po Chai Antique Co.** (132 Hollywood Rd.).

The **Cat St. Galleries,** 38 Lok Ku Rd., houses a few dealers under one roof and may be worth visiting.

Other shops in Central include **Banyan Tree Ltd** (213 Prince's Bldg.), **Craig's Ltd.** (St. George Bldg.), **Gallery 69 Ltd.** (123 Edinburgh Tower), **Ian McLean Antiques** (73 Wyndham St.), and **P. C. Lu & Sons Ltd.** (Mandarin Hotel arcade).

In Kowloon try **Amazing Grace Elephant Co., Banyan Tree Ltd., Charlotte Horstmann and Gerald Godfrey Ltd., Hung Kee Arts Centre, Oriental House of Decor Ltd., Treasure House,** and **Y. F. Yang & Co.**—all located in the Harbour City complex in Tsim Sha Tsui. Others worth visiting in the Tsim Sha Tsui area are **The Collectors Shop** (Hongkong Hotel arcade), **Eileen Kershaw Ltd.** (West Wing, Peninsula Hotel), **Gallery 69 Ltd.** (Regent Hotel lobby), **John K. Fong** (40 Cameron Rd.), **The Oriental Arts Co.** (Sheraton Hotel shopping mall), **P. C. Lu & Sons Ltd.** (Peninsula Hotel arcade), and **Sovereign Co.** (New World Centre).

Annual auctions of private collections are held in Hong Kong by **Christie's** (in late January) and **Sotheby's** (in May and October) in a major hotel, attracting an international crowd.

ARTS AND CRAFTS

On **Hong Kong Island** the shops and galleries on Hollywood Rd. have decent selections of "arts and crafts" in addition to Ming and Qing vases. A few shops in Stanley Market and inside the Peak Tower Village (upper terminal) also sell handicrafts and artsy curios.

Chinese Arts & Crafts (Queen's Rd., in Central, and on Wyndham St.) has many scroll paintings and embroidered silk squares and rounds, and small carved ivory and jade items. **The Asian Collector Gallery** (19 Wyndham St., HK) stocks Japanese prints and old maps and engravings. The **Hong Kong Museum of Art** (City Hall High Block, Central) and the **Arts Centre** (Wan Chai) have on sale modern and old prints. **Rain Field Folkcraft** (Admiralty Centre) has a nice range of items. **Tsi Ku Chai** (Hong Kong Diamond Exchange Bldg., 8 Duddell St., Central) and **Oriental Arts Gallery Centre** (Silvercord, 30 Canton Rd., Tsim Sha Tsui) have Oriental and Western paintings on sale. **The Welfare Handicrafts Shop** (Connaught Centre, in Hong Kong, and Ocean Terminal, Kowloon) has a small collection of items, and all proceeds go to local charity. In **Kowloon's** Ocean Terminal you will find many shops, among them the **Indonesian Shop, Kon Tiki, Mountain Folkcraft,** and **Tai Shan Gallery.**

Chinese Arts & Crafts (Star House, Tsim Sha Tsui) has a good selection. **Regalia Art Treasures** (New World Shopping Centre, Tsim Sha Tsui) carries handicrafts.

Amazing Grace Elephant. (2/F, Yeu Shing Industrial Bldg., Kin Fung St., Tuen Mun, NT) offers ceramic elephants, teapots, and the like. **Artistic Furniture Co.** (39 Chatham Rd.) sells camphorwood chests and carved furniture. **Artland Ivory Factory Ltd.** (Houston Centre, 64 Mody Rd., Tsim Sha Tsui East) has all kinds of ivory cavings. **Chu's Jade Manufacturer** (1A Kimberley St., Tsim Sha Tsui) sells jade carvings. **Hai Feng Wood Arts Ltd.** (8 Luk Hop St., San Po Kong) makes birds, especially ducks, and other items of carved wood.

"Museums & Arts & Crafts," a pamphlet put out by the HKTA, gives fuller listings.

IVORY

Ivory objects are widely available in the territory, which has a long-standing tradition of ivory carving. However, if you are a national of a country that has subscribed to the Convention on International Trade in Endangered Species (CITES), you should be aware that you will not be allowed to bring back ivory objects purchased abroad. While it is permitted to import antique ivory, stringent documentary proof of antiquity is required, of a kind that can usually be obtained only by institutions or companies, not by private individuals. If you are not sure about your country's policy, call its consulate or the Hong Kong Trade Department (3–722–2491).

That said, you can find ivory carvings in antique shops on Hollywood Rd., arts and crafts shops on Wyndham St. and on Wellington St. on the Hong Kong side. In Kowloon many of the antique and arts and crafts shops in Harbour City and in Tsim Sha Tsui East stock ivory pieces. You should get a Certificate of Origin from the shop where you purchase the ivory pieces.

JEWELRY

Hong Kong has thousands of jewelry shops—in shopping malls, shopping centers, hotel shopping arcades, along Canton Rd., Nathan Rd., Queen's Rd. Central, Hennessy Rd., Hollywood Rd., and even in some department stores. For reliable places to shop consult the HKTA's "Official Guide to Shopping, Eating Out and Services in Hong Kong."

Some of the most prestigious international jewelers have shops in Hong Kong: **Asprey** (Prince's Bldg., Central), **Cartier** (Peninsula Hotel and Swire House), and **Van Cleef & Arpels** (Landmark and Peninsula Hotel). The two biggest local stores are **King Fook Gold & Jewelery Co.** (30 Des Voeux Rd. Central) and **Chow Tai Fook Jewelery Co.** (44 Queen's Rd., Central).

For jade, you may take a stroll down **Jade Market** in Kansu St., Kowloon, where jade pieces in all shapes and colors are displayed by hundreds of jade merchants. Jade comes in different shades of green, brown, orange, purple, and white; and in different qualities and prices. Practically every jewelry shop carries jade items—rings, brooches, necklaces, and other trinkets.

WATCHES

Watches are everywhere. Street stalls hawk locally made watches for as low as HK$10 a piece! **Seiko** has a large showroom in Star House (Tsim Sha Tsui), **Rolex (HK) Ltd.** is located in Connaught Centre, and **Cartier** has its own shop in Prince's Bldg., Central. Again, all the shopping malls and hotel shopping arcades have shops selling moderately priced to expensive watches.

CARPETS AND RUGS

You can buy Tianjin carpets, locally made carpets, Persian carpets, and Turkish and Afghan rugs in Hong Kong. **Chinese Arts & Crafts** and all the **China Products** stores have good stocks of Tianjin carpets and carpets made in Xinjiang and Shanghai. **Tai Ping Carpets,** a local manufacturer, also does custom-made carpets; its showroom is in Hutchison House, Central. Other stores selling Oriental and occidental carpets and rugs are **Oriental Carpet Trading House** (42 Wyndham St., Central), **Persian Carpets Ltd.** (118 Hollywood Rd., Central), **Tribal Rugs Ltd.** (Admiralty Centre, Central), **Carpet World** (Elizabeth House, 250 Gloucester Rd., Causeway Bay), **Aristocrat Rug Co.** (Star House, Tsim Sha Tsui), **Carpet House** (Ocean Terminal, Tsim Sha Tsui), **Chinese Carpet Centre** (Ocean Centre, Tsim Sha Tsui), **Chinese Rugs Co.** (New World Centre, Tsim Sha Tsui), and **Sultan Persian Rugs** (33 Chatham Rd., Tsim Sha Tsui).

CLOTHING AND TEXTILES

EMBROIDERY, LINEN, AND SILK

A large selection of hand-embroidered tablecloths, napkins, placemats, and handkerchiefs in linen and lace can be found at **Asia Trading Co.** (Ocean Terminal), **Chinese Arts & Crafts,** all the **China Products** stores, **Swatow Drawn Work** (Worldwide House, Central), and in the shops on Wyndham St. and On Lan St. in Central.

CLOTHING

Children. For Chinese-style babywear, try any of the **China Products** shops. For Western-style children's clothing **Charade** (Landmark in HK; Regent Hotel in Kowloon), **Children's Clothing Company** and **Circles** (Landmark and City Plaza in Hong Kong; Ocean Centre in Kowloon), **Crocodile** and **Crystal** (City Plaza and Harbour City in Kowloon), and **Mothercare** in Windsor House (311 Gloucester Rd., Causeway Bay).

"Baby Lane" (Fat Hing St., Western, HK) and the two alleyways in Central (Li Yuen St. East and West) have many shops selling Chinese padded jackets and windbreakers.

Men. Thousands of tailors do business in hotel shopping arcades and along Nathan Rd., Peking Rd., and other side streets in Tsim Sha Tsui. Some of the most reputable tailors are **A. Man Hing Cheong**

Ltd. and **British Textile Co.** (Mandarin Hotel Arcade, Central), **Art's Tailors Ltd.** (Swire House, Central), **Ascot Chang** (Prince's Bldg., Central, and the Peninsula and Regent hotels in Kowloon), **Charley Chang Tailor** (Hong Kong Hilton Hotel Arcade, Central), and **Mee Yee & Company** (28 Stanley St., Central), **British Tailor & Co.** (Regent Hotel Arcade, Kowloon), and **Sam's** (Burlington Arcade, 94 Nathan Rd., Kowloon).

A suit, depending on the quality of the material, costs from HK$1,000 to HK$3,500; cotton shirts cost about HK$120–250, and silk ones, over HK$500. Most tailors can copy any style, including the suit you have on, but at least two fittings are recommended. If you are satisfied, leave your measurements behind and order by mail whenever you need another suit or coat.

In addition to the hundreds of skillful tailors, many boutiques selling ready-to-wear suits, jackets, and shirts may be found throughout Hong Kong. Many of these are located in hotel shopping arcades, main shopping malls, and department stores.

Women. Dressmakers in Hong Kong are just as famous as tailors for men. Dressmakers can be found in most of the large shopping malls and shopping centers, such as Harbour City, and in hotel shopping arcades. If you want to have a silk or brocade *cheong-sam* made, go to any of the Chinese Products stores. In addition, fashion clothing of top world designers (Calvin Klein, Charlotte Ford, Ralph Lauren, Yves St. Laurent, Levi Strauss, Gloria Vanderbilt) is well represented in the many chic boutiques in Hong Kong.

Some of the major fashion stores are **Boutique Bazaar** (Landmark, Swire House, and Peninsula Hotel), **Chanel Boutique** (Peninsula Hotel), **Celine Boutique** (Landmark; Matsuzakaya department stores), **Christian Dior** (Landmark), **Diane Freis** (Connaught Centre, Prince's Bldg., and Harbour City), **D'Urban** (Landmark; Matsuzakaya, Mitsukoshi, and Daimaru department stores), **Esprit** (Prince's Bldg., in Central, and Auto Plaza, in Tsim Sha Tsui East), **Giorgio Armani** (Mandarin Hotel), **Green & Found** (Landmark and Ocean Centre), **Gucci** (Landmark and Peninsula Hotel), **Hermè**s Boutiques (Landmark and Peninsula Hotel), **Issey Miyake** (Swire House), **Jenny Lewis** (Swire House, Peninsula Hotel, and Ocean Centre), **Joyce Boutique** (Landmark and Peninsula Hotel), **Kinsan Collections** (29 Wyndham St., Central), **Loewe** (Landmark), **Michel Rene** (Landmark, Harbour City, and New World Centre), **Nina Ricci** (Regent Hotel), and **Pavlova** (Swire House).

Stanley Market in Stanley is known for its clothing stores selling garments from casual and fashion jeans to silk dresses and blouses. The stores on both sides of **Granville Rd.,** Tsim Sha Tsui, have piles of clothing—mostly casual—at very reasonable prices.

Overruns and slightly imperfect items of top-fashion clothes can be picked up at bargain prices from **factory outlets** on Man Yue St. in Hung Hom, Kowloon. Factories for top European and American fashion houses are located inside Kaiser Estate and can be reached easily by taxi. On the Hong Kong side you can find factory outlets in **Shoppers World Ltd.** (Pedder Bldg, Central), **Lim Ying Ying Ltd.** (Hong Kong Chinese Bank Bldg., 61 Des Voeux Rd., Central), and **Nova Monde Fashions Ltd.** (52 Wellington St., Central).

Ready-made silk blouses and housecoats can also be found in **Chinese Arts & Crafts** and all the **China Products** stores.

FUR

There are not many furriers in Hong Kong, but because of top workmanship and fine hand-finishing, locally produced fur garments are highly competitive. The major stores are **Broadway Fur Co.** (Houston Centre, Tsim Sha Tsui East), **East Asia Fur Co.** (Tsim Sha Tsui Centre, Tsim Sha Tsui East), **The Camay Fur Co.** (Gloucester Tower, Landmark, Central), **Fur Chiba** (New World Shopping Centre, Tsim Sha Tsui), **Jindo Fur Salon** (World Finance Center, Harbour City), **Philip Chin's Canada Fur Store** (Hilton Hotel arcade, Central), **Siberian Fur Store** (21 Chatham Rd., in Kowloon, and 29 Des Voeux Rd., Central), and **Stylette Models** (New World Shopping Centre, Kowloon, and Excelsior Hotel arcade, Hong Kong).

LEATHER GOODS

Both locally made and imported leather goods such as belts, briefcases, handbags, luggage, and shoes are available from department stores and specialty shops.

Expensive imports can be found at **Fendi** (Swire House, in Hong Kong, and Hankow Centre, Tsim Sha Tsui), **Gucci Company, Ltd.,** and **Louis Vuitton Boutique** (Landmark and Peninsula Hotel shopping arcade), **Hermès** boutiques and **Loewe** (Gloucester Tower, Landmark), and **Bruno Magli** and **Gold Pfeil** (Ocean Terminal).

Shops selling the less expensive locally made products are located in Li Yuen St. East and West, Central. Ready-made and custom-made ladies' leather handbags and shoes can be found along **Wong Nai Chung Rd.** in Happy Valley, Hong Kong.

HIGH-TECH PRODUCTS

CAMERAS AND OTHER OPTICAL GOODS

On **Hong Kong Island,** go to Hennessy Rd. in **Causeway Bay** and the hotel shopping arcades in Central. In **Kowloon,** shops selling these items are crowding each other on Lock Rd. and Nathan Rd. in Tsim Sha Tsui.

For glasses and contact lenses, the most reputable place is **The Optical Shop,** which has branches all over, including a large shop in Ocean Terminal. They are qualified to examine your eyes and make prescription glasses in less than 24 hours.

COMPUTERS

IBM-compatible personal computers, locally made or locally assembled, are available at bargain prices. Monitors, both black and white and color, and printers of various makes are also for sale at much lower prices than in Europe or the United States. You should make sure that they can be adapted easily to your local main voltage; Hong Kong uses 110 volts. The standard computer brands, such as Apple and IBM, are also sold in Hong Kong, but they are somehow more expensive than in the United States.

Software packages go for a song, but they are almost surely pirated editions. The Hong Kong authorities have been clamping down on such pirated editions, but they are still available even though not openly displayed.

The best places to look for computers are **Asia Computer Plaza** (Silvercord, 30 Canton Rd., Tsim Sha Tsui), **Penisula Centre** (Tsim Sha Tsui East), **Golden Shopping Centre** (Sham Shui Po, Kowloon), **Ocean Shopping Arcade** (140 Wan Chai Rd., HK) and **Hong Kong Computer Centre** (54 Lockhart Rd., HK).

AUDIO AND VIDEO EQUIPMENT AND ACCESSORIES

Hong Kong has always been the marketplace for getting products made in Japan or Korea or elsewhere for less. The shops may not carry the latest models, but as a whole they are well stocked and eager to do business. Whenever you buy a piece of electrical or electronic equipment, make sure that it is compatible with or can be adapted to your domestic voltage. When buying videocassette recorders, make sure they are compatible with the TV broadcasting systems in your country. If possible, contact the relevant local agents for list prices, types of guarantees, etc. The HKTA's brochure "The Official Guide to Shopping, Eating Out and Services in Hong Kong" has a listing of shops and sole agents (Telephone 5-244-191 ext. 278). In **Central** Tak Shing House (20 Des Voeux Rd.) has a couple of audio and video shops—**Bang & Olufsen Ltd.** (Telephone 5-268-800) and **The Radio People Ltd.** (Telephone 5-223-638). **Fortress Ltd.**, Yu Sung Boon Bldg., 107 Des Voeux Rd. (Telephone 5-441-665), has a large selection, and also carries other electrical appliances. **Philips Hong Kong Ltd.**, Edinburgh Tower, The Landmark (Telephone 5-249-566) is worth a look.

In **Wan Chai** and **Causeway Bay** there are many shops along Hennessay Rd. and Percival St. selling audio-video equipment and accessories at very competitive prices.

In **Kowloon,** shops selling audio-video equipment and accessories are concentrated in Harbour City, Nathan Rd., Carnarvon Rd., and Cameron Rd. in the Tsim Sha Tsui area.

FURNITURE

Custom-made furniture, contemporary and reproductions, Chinese and Western, is available in blackwood, rosewood, teak, and rattan. Antique furniture can be found in many antique shops. For modern furniture try **Interiors** (38 D'Aguilar St., Central), **Furniture Boutique** (3 Tin Hau Temple Rd., Causeway Bay, HK), **Design 2000** (Ocean Centre, Tsim Sha Tsui), and **Carlton Woodcraft Manufacturing Ltd.** (14 Canton Rd., Tsim Sha Tsui).

The antique shops on Hollywood Rd. in Central carry some Chinese blackwood and lacquer pieces. Rattan furniture shops are located on Queen's Rd. East in Hong Kong. Camphorwood chests can also be found on Queen's Rd. East and on Canton Rd. in Kowloon.

SHOPPING AREAS

HONG KONG CENTRAL

The 20-block area on either side of the Star Ferry Concourse (Connaught Rd. Central to Lyndhurst Terrace and from Admiralty to Wing On St.) contains the major shops, shopping malls, and department stores.

Mandarin Hotel Arcade (Connaught Rd. Central and Ice House St.) has elegant antique shops, tailors for both men and women, shirts, jewelers, and carpets.

Swire House (Chater Rd. and Pedder St.) contains some fancy designer clothing boutiques and shops offering beaded silk dresses and accessories, high-quality costume jewelry, and silk dresses.

Prince's Bldg. (Des Voeux Rd. Central and Ice House St.) has tailors for women's clothes, shirtmakers, optical shops, bookshops, toy shops, and camera shops.

The Landmark (Des Voeux Rd. Central and Pedder St.) has the ritziest designer boutiques, art galleries, and expensive jewelry shops, scattered all through the five-floor, four-building complex. It also has a wide selection of hi-fi equipment, records, crystal, and chinaware.

The **Central Bldg.** (Queen's Rd. Central and Pedder St.) houses shops that sell silk and woolen clothes, handbags, jewelry, and silver. The best smoke shop, **Tabaqueria Filipina,** where you can find top-quality Cuban cigars, is on the ground floor.

The **Pedder Bldg.** (12 Pedder St.) contains boutiques, factory outlets, and furriers.

Lane Crawford (Queen's Rd. Central) is a high-class department store that carries expensive and luxury goods. It has fine silver, jade, jewelry, china, and men and women's clothing.

The **Chinese Merchandise Emporium** (92–104 Queen's Rd. Central) carries a wide variety of goods from China—tablecloths, satin bedding, clothing for the whole family, furniture, dinnerware, porcelain vases, toys, shoes, and many other items.

Li Yuen St. West and East, the two alleys between Queen's Rd. Central and Des Voeux Rd., are lined with stalls selling handbags, women's underwear, silk and cotton shirts, sweaters, stockings, jackets, pants, scarves, lingerie, junk jewelry, and most of the thousand-and-one things. Behind the stalls are boutiques and shops selling needlepoint, fabrics, shoes, leather goods, and the like.

Wing On St. (Cloth Alley), farther down on Queen's Rd. Central, has 40-odd shops selling all kinds of fabrics—silk, cotton, linen, satin, wool, flannel, lace, synthetic fabrics.

Stores on both sides of **Queen's Rd. Central** display huge pieces of jade, gold and diamond rings, pearl necklaces, gold necklaces, diamond brooches, gold chains, and rubies and other precious stones. And in between, thousands of watches with international brand names glitter in the showcases.

Farther west are the two oldest department stores selling mostly items imported from the West: **Sincere** and **Wing On.**

Stanley St., above Queen's Rd. Central, has more boutiques selling less expensive clothes, shops selling film and slides, optical shops, stationers, and hardware stores.

Wellington St., above Stanley St., has a few shops that sell ivory items—bracelets, necklaces, carved figures, chopsticks, chops (carved seals) and mahjong sets. But remember CITES. There are also some good frame shops and more boutiques here.

Lyndhurst Terrace is known for its embroidery shops selling Chinese wedding items such as bedcovers, pillowcases, and bedspreads. It also has a shop selling Indonesian batiks and other craft items.

Hollywood Rd. is famous for its antique and furniture shops, which line both sides of the street.

Upper Lascar Row (Cat St.), north of Hollywood Rd., still has a few street stalls selling dubious antiques.

Wyndham St. has many small shops that sell handicrafts from various parts of Asia, carpets from the Middle East, and decorative arts from Japan.

On the corner of Wyndham St. and Queen's Rd. Central is the **Chinese Arts and Crafts** shop, with selected jewelry, objets d'art, and linen and silk items from China.

On **Queen's Rd. Central,** going east, are many expensive fabric shops and watch shops.

The **Hilton Hotel Arcade** (Queen's Rd. Central and Garden Rd.) has at least 10 tailors and dressmakers, camera shops, audiovisual equipment shops, shoe and handbag shops, and jewelers.

Admiralty features three large interconnected shopping complexes—**Admiralty Centre, Queensway Plaza,** and **United Centre.** The Japanese department store **Matsuzakaya** has a branch here, and hundreds of other shops sell shoes, optical goods, men's and women's clothing, audiovisual equipment, toys, knitting supplies, children's items, paintings, and prints.

CAUSEWAY BAY

Four large Japanese department stores are located in Causeway Bay—**Daimaru** and **Matsuzakaya** on Paterson St., **Mitsukoshi** in Hennessy Centre, and **Sogo** on Hennessy Rd. **Land Crawford** has a branch store nearby in Windsor House. **China Products Company** also has a branch in the area. On both sides of **Hennessy Rd.** and **Percival St.** are camera, stereo, and audiovisual equipment shops with very competitive prices. **Jardine's Bazaar,** tucked away in a narrow street, is jammed with stalls selling low-priced clothing and accessories. There are also hundreds of shops selling items from jogging shoes to gold watches in the area.

TSIM SHA TSUI

The largest complex of shopping centers is **Harbour City,** which consists of three separate but connected buildings—**Ocean Terminal, Ocean Centre,** and **Ocean Galleries.** Over 500 shops, more than 50 coffee shops, bars, and restaurants, and a supermarket are located in this complex. A few major hotels are also attached to it. Brochures on monthly events and shopping maps are handed out freely by Harbour City staff. **Ocean Terminal** is where the ocean liners moor; over 200 shops are housed in this long, two-deck building. The Y-shaped **Ocean Centre** is connected to the front of Ocean Terminal, and on the other side is **Ocean Galleries,** which has a moving walkway in the middle of the maze of shops. You should be able to find everything here, from Chinese antiques to imported leather goods, from silk dresses to top men's fashions.

Across from Harbour City, on Canton Rd., is **Silvercord,** another shopping mall. **Canton Rd.** has a few furniture stores selling teak, rosewood, and rattan furniture.

Lock Rd., Haiphong Rd., and **Hankow Rd.** are lined with shops that sell cameras, calculators, binoculars, ivory figurines, porcelain and bronze lamp bases, jewelry, handbags and luggage, silk and linen dresses, jackets, stereo equipment, and more.

Among the many shops in **Star House** (Salisbury and Canton Roads) is **Chinese Arts & Crafts,** a good place to buy high-quality made-in-China merchandise.

The **Peninsula Hotel** (Salisbury Rd.) has a most elegant shopping arcade with designer fashions and accessories from Dior, Gucci, Hermès, Chanel, Jenny Lewis, Joyce, and other famous designers; there are also some fine jewelry stores.

Duty-Free Shoppers (Hankow Centre, 5 Hankow Rd.) is a department store with items not necessarily cheaper than those in other stores.

Isetan of Japan Ltd. (Sheraton Hotel arcade) is an upscale department store carrying merchandise made in Japan.

Nathan Rd., the "Golden Mile" of shopping, has hundreds of shops selling cameras, cosmetics, stereo equipment, optical goods, shirts, dresses, jewelry, watches, and souvenirs. The Chinese department store **Yue Hwa Chinese Products Emporium** (54 Nathan Rd.) has a big selection of goods from China, and **Shui Hing,** another department store (23 Nathan Rd.), carries large selections of imported Western goods.

TSIM SHA TSUI EAST

The **New World Shopping Centre** (Salisbury Rd.) has lots of shops selling merchandise from Japan, especially electronic equipment and high-fashion men's and children's clothes. The large Japanese department store **Tokyu** is housed here. **The Regent Hotel,** connected to it, has an elegant shopping arcade with good antique and jewelry shops and tailors.

The side streets to the east of Nathan Rd. (**Mody Rd., Carnarvon Rd., Cameron Rd.,** and **Granville Rd.**) are a continuous bazaar. **Empire Centre, Energy Plaza, Houston Centre, Peninsula Centre, South Seas Centre, Tsim Sha Tsui Centre, Wing On Plaza,** and many more are crowded from the harborfront to Chatham Rd. and beyond.

X   Doing Business in Hong Kong

Hong Kong's economy is based on export and import trade, with a growing financial sector servicing international financial markets. Since Hong Kong is a free-trade port, it has no exchange controls, and tariffs are virtually nonexistent. The overall tax structure is simple, and tax rates are lower than those in other industrialized countries of the world. Hong Kong's manufacturers are skilled and its labor force hardworking, both of which give Hong Kong distinct advantages as a manufacturing base. In general, Hong Kong is run with minimal government intervention, and its basically free-enterprise and market-discipline system is attractive to overseas investments.

Because of its proximity to China, Hong Kong serves as a base for trade with that country. Its container port, the second busiest in the world, and its efficient air cargo operations enhance its attractiveness as a base for business.

Establishing a business in Hong Kong is easy and simple. In fact, the government encourages foreign businesses to set up offices in Hong Kong. There is no minimum capital requirement for a company and no limit to the percentage of foreign business participation in the ownership or capital structure of the company. At the same time, there are no special incentives offered to foreign investors and no tax holidays, but Hong Kong's other advantages compensate for these factors.

ESTABLISHING YOUR BUSINESS IN HONG KONG

IDENTITY CARD

Everyone who enters Hong Kong and intends to stay for more than 180 days must register for an identity card; exceptions are children of consuls and of consular staff under 18 years of age, children under 11 years of age, those serving in Britain's military services, and special cases approved by the Commissioner of Registration.

The office that issues Hong Kong identity cards is located in the basement of the National Mutual Centre, 151 Gloucester Rd., Hong Kong (Telephone 5–890–9393).

Application forms are also available from the Registration of Persons Office of the Immigration Department, whose Hong Kong office is located in the Park Commercial Centre, 6–10 Shelter St., Hong Kong (Telephone 5–839–3222), and whose headquarters is in Kowloon, 2/F, Mirror Tower, 61 Mody Rd., Tsim Sha Tsui East (Telephone 3–733–111 or 3–732–8333). The forms are free of charge for new applicants.

A Hong Kong identity card is required for the registration of a business in Hong Kong.

BUSINESS REGISTRATION AND INCORPORATION

Any company (sole proprietorship, partnership, or limited company or corporation) doing business or carrying on other activity "for the purpose of gain" in Hong Kong is required to register with the Companies Registry (Queensway Government Office Bldg., 66 Queensway, Hong Kong; Telephone 5–862–2600 or 5–862–2604). Details for registration can be obtained from the Business Registration Office, 3/F, Windsor House, 311 Gloucester Rd., Causeway Bay, Hong Kong (Telephone 5–894–3149).

Registering is a simple process: the annual business registration fee is HK$600 (HK$550 plus HK$6 for every HK$1,000 of nominal capital). If a business has branches, each branch is required to get a branch registration certificate for an annual registration fee of HK$15 and a levy of HK$100.

If you wish to form a limited liability company, a lawyer or an accountant can get you a "shelf" company for around HK$5,000. Particular requirements, including company name, can be easily adjusted to your specifications.

Companies incorporated overseas are also required to register certain documents with the Companies Registry for a fee of HK$500 and some small filing fees, within one month of establishing a place of business in Hong Kong.

Certain businesses—restaurants, medical and legal practitioners, and public accountants among them—must apply for appropriate types of licences in addition to registering the business.

WORK PERMITS AND VISAS

Any foreigner, other than a holder of a British (U.K.) passport, who wants to work in Hong Kong must obtain a Hong Kong employment (work) visa. Those with a firm commitment (in writing) from an established local firm can get one from any British embassy or consulate.

The employment (investment) visa is required for those foreigners who wish to set up business in Hong Kong. Application forms can be obtained at the British embassy or consulate, and the normal processing period is between eight weeks and three months, depending on whether you are opening an overseas branch office in Hong Kong or setting up a totally new business in Hong Kong. In the first case, you must provide details of your business in the country where it is registered, including financial statements, how long the business has been in operation, the type of business, and the number employed. In the latter case, you must provide detailed information about the kind of business you wish to establish in Hong Kong, the estimated capital investment, the number of those to be employed, financial statements, and the like.

In either case the applicant must nominate two referees (sponsors) in Hong Kong; these must provide the Hong Kong Immigration Department with supporting documentation for the person or persons sponsored.

The wife and family of a male applicant must apply for dependent visas. A wife with dependent status can work in Hong Kong. However, a married woman applicant cannot sponsor her husband for a dependent visa. The Hong Kong Immigration Department will not grant dependent status to an accompanying husband. However, the husband can enter Hong Kong with his wife as a visitor and then apply for an extension to his visitor status, but normally only one or two three-day extensions are granted. Get a local law firm to help you.

BUSINESS PRACTICES AND CONDITIONS

ACCOUNTING REQUIREMENTS

The Hong Kong Companies Ordinance requires all companies doing business in Hong Kong to keep proper records. The Hong Kong Society of Accountants is responsible for accounting and auditing standards, based on the British system; it also registers professional accountants. For further information, contact the Society at 17/F, Belgian House, 77–79 Gloucester Rd., Hong Kong (Telephone 5–299–271).

ARBITRATION

The Hong Kong International Arbitration Centre was established in 1985 to meet a growing need for arbitral services in Asia and for the speedy and reliable resolution of commercial disputes in the territory. The Centre has adopted the UNCITRAL Rules for International Arbitrations and has its own Rules for Domestic Arbitrations. It is located at 1 Arbuthnot Rd., Central (Telephone 5-252-381; Telex 65354 RSI HX).

BUSINESS CENTERS

If you need temporary office space, there are many business centers located on both the Hong Kong and Kowloon sides. These business centers offer both personnel (secretaries, messengers, translators, and interpreters) and equipment and services (telex, copiers, fascimile, word processors, phones). They also provide meeting facilities and consultancy on China trade.

CERTIFICATES OF ORIGIN

Factories producing items that require Certificates of Origin must register with the Factory Registration Office of the Certification Section of the Trade Department (1st Floor, Ocean Centre, Canton Rd., Kowloon; Telephone 3-722-2477 or 3-722-2479).

Organizations that issue Certificates of Hong Kong Origin include the Federation of Hong Kong Industries and Hong Kong General Chamber of Commerce. Certificates can only be issued to manufacturers registered with the Trade Department. A fee of HK$45 is charged upon submission of application. All enquiries should be directed to the Certification of Origin Office, Certification Section, Trade Department, Ocean Centre, Canton Rd., Kowloon (Telephone 3-722-2475 or 3-722-2517.

INDUSTRIAL AND INTELLECTUAL
PROPERTY RIGHTS

Hong Kong adheres to the Paris Convention for the Protection of Industrial Property, the Berne International Copyright Convention, and the Geneva and Paris Universal Copyright Conventions.

COPYRIGHT

Copyright is protected "by registration under the United Kingdom Copyright Act and the Hong Kong Copyright Ordinance." The government has extensive powers to investigate any infringement, and the owner of the copyright can take action against the offender. Copyright infringement is a criminal offense.

For further information contact the "One-Stop" Unit of the Industry Department, 14/F, Ocean Centre, 5 Canton Rd., Kowloon (Telephone 3-722-2434).

TRADEMARKS AND PATENTS

Trademarks are registered under the Trademarks Ordinance at the Trademarks Registry, Queensway Government Office Bldg., 66 Queensway, Hong Kong (Telephone 5-862-2628). The Patents Registry, a subdivision of the Commercial Division, is also located in the Queensway Government Office Bldg. Hong Kong patents and trademarks enjoy the same rights as those granted in the United Kingdom. The Design Council of Hong Kong, located at 4/F, Hankow Centre, Hankow Road, Tsim Sha Tsui, Kowloon (Telephone 3-723-0818), provides design registration. It is part of the Federation of Hong Kong Industries. However, despite legal protection for copyrights and registered patents, Hong Kong "pirates" almost everything—from computer software to designer clothes and handbags.

The Customs and Excise Department has a special task force to investigate complaints, and has extensive powers of search, seizure, and forfeiture. It collaborates with international enforcement authorities and owners of trademarks to fight any infringement.

INSURANCE

Setting up a business in Hong Kong requires that you have the normal types of insurance (employee compensation, fire, burglary, and public liability). Premiums vary according to the size and type of business. There are plenty of insurance providers in Hong Kong—U.S. companies, European companies, and others.

LABOR MARKET

Hong Kong has a total workforce of 2.7 million—63% men and 37% women. The overall average daily wage in 1987 was HK$149 for men and HK$109 for women. However, almost all salaried workers do receive "double pay" at year-end—usually paid out during the Chinese New Year. There is no statutory minimum wage in Hong Kong, rates being determined purely by supply and demand. Overall, the workers are motivated and expect to work long hours. Unemployment rates in the late 1980s were about 4%, and in 1987 fell to under 2%. In fact, there was a shortage of workers in certain sectors. In general, manufacturing employs nearly 35% of the workforce, while over 23% work in wholesale and retail trade and hotels and restaurants. The monthly salary for a secretary ranges from HK$2,500 to $13,000; a receptionist makes between HK$3,000 and $5,000; a word processing operator earns from HK$3,500 to $6,000; and a company chauffeur, HK$3,500–$4,500. The standard employment contract is based on a three-month probation period, and normal benefits include two weeks' annual leave, in addition to 11 public holidays. Most of the 400 local trade unions are ineffectual; however, wages have increased over the years because of a continuous full employment rate and a high demand for skilled workers. Even at that, workers are very mobile; they will leave and work for the highest wages offered. Additionally, there are no regulations governing the relative proportion of local to overseas staff that may be employed by a company. For more information contact the Hong Kong Labour Department, 16/F, 30A Pier Road, Harbour Bldg., Central.

LAND AND PREMISES

All land in Hong Kong belongs to the Crown (the government), and no one is allowed to own it, except for a few historical exceptions. The government does, however, sell or grant long and short leaseholds at regular auctions. A wide range of office premises are for rent on either side of the harbor. After the collapse of the property industry in the early 1980s, the rents stabilized, but they are still high by any international standard. You can find expensive floor space (at HK$30 per square foot per month, not including management fees and utilities) in the marble and glass office buildings in Hong Kong's Central District or premises costing half that a short distance away in Wan Chai or Causeway Bay. Prime office space in Kowloon's Tsim Sha Tsui area rents for HK$20 per square foot per month. The expense of outfitting an office is up to the tenant. The cost varies roughly from HK$1,800 to $5,380 per square yard. Factory space is very much in demand. It is usually in multistory buildings in the urban areas, but industrial estates are being built in the New Territories, and New Towns such as Sha Tin, Fo Tan, and Tai Po offer floor space at about HK$2.50 per square foot per month for high-tech industries that require large space. On top of rent, the government charges "rates" (a tax) at 5.5% of the annual rent. Other costs include stamp duties and legal fees, which are usually shared between landlord and tenant. A deposit of up to three months' rent is expected.

LEGAL SYSTEM

Hong Kong's legal system is based on English Common Law and rules of equity, as applicable to local circumstances. Hong Kong also make its own ordinances and has its own interpretations. English is the language of the law, and it will probably remain so even after 1997. However, interpreters are available at all proceedings. Hong Kong follows the British system of having solicitors and barristers—solicitors advise clients and barristers argue cases in court. For more information contact The Law Society of Hong Kong, Room 1230, Swire House, Central (Telephone 5–221121)

TRADE PUBLICATIONS

There are hundreds of trade newspapers and magazines published in Hong Kong in both Chinese and English. Contact any HKTA or Hong Kong Government Industrial Promotion Office overseas. The Hong Kong Trade Development Council produces two product magazines: *Hong Kong Enterprise* and *Hong Kong Toys*. Its *Hong Kong Trader*, a bi-monthly newspaper, is airmailed free to overseas subscribers. It also publishes an annual guidebook, *Hong Kong for the Business Visitor*, in seven languages. Other specialized trade magazines are *Hong Kong Apparel, Hong Kong Jewelry Annual, Hong Kong Watches and Clocks, Hong Kong Household, Hong Kong Gifts and Premiums*, and *Hong Kong Electronics*. The following publications may be of use to you:

- *Business Guide to Hong Kong*, Citibank, Citicorp Centre, 18 Whitfield Rd., Causeway Bay, Hong Kong: A free 56-page guide to Hong Kong's business climate.
- *Directory of Hong Kong Industries*, Hong Kong Productivity Council: HK$350, contains information on manufacturers.
- *Doing Business in Hong Kong*, Price, Waterhouse, Prince's Bldg., 22/F, Central: An 111-page guide to taxes and the business climate.
- *Investment in Hong Kong*, Peat, Marwick, Mitchell & Co., Prince's Bldg., Central; They also publish *Banking in Hong Kong* and *Taxation in Hong Kong*.

Other sources of information are on sale in the Hong Kong Publications Centre, General Post Office Bldg., Central, and the various bookstores and newsstands.

TRADE SHOWS AND EXHIBITIONS

These are held regularly at the new Hong Kong Convention and Exhibition Centre in Wan Chai. Chinese product fairs are usually housed in the China Resource Bldg. in Wan Chai. The Hong Kong Trade Development Council (Great Eagle Centre, 23 Harbour Rd., Hong Kong; Telephone 5-833-4333) publishes a monthly "Businessmen's Calendar: A List of Trade Conferences & Exhibitions in Hong Kong."

TAXATION

INCOME TAXES

Any person doing business in Hong Kong is required to register with the Inland Revenue Department (Windsor House, 311 Gloucester Rd., Causeway Bay, Hong Kong; Telephone 5-894-5098 or 5-894-5001). Taxes may be assessed on four separate and distinct sources of income: business profits tax, salaries tax, property tax, and interest tax. Profits tax is levied only on profits arising from a trade, profession, or business carried on in Hong Kong. Profits of unincorporated businesses are taxed at 16.5%; profits of corporations are taxed at 17%. Salaries tax is limited by a ceiling of 15.5% before deductions and other allowances. Property tax is at the standard rate of 16.5%; property owned by a corportion carrying on a business in Hong Kong is exempt from property tax, but the profits derived from the ownership are taxed as profits tax. Taxable interest is taxed at a rate of 16.5%.

CUSTOMS DUTIES AND EXCISE TAX

Customs duties and excise taxes are levied on certain commodities such as alcohol, perfume, cigarettes, and cigars. Contact the Customs and Excise Department for information, 8/F, Harbour Bldg., 38 Pier Rd., Central (Telephone 5-852-3324). Stamp duties are confined to transactions in shares and marketable securities.

BANKING AND FINANCE

BANKING

Hong Kong does not have a central bank, and bank notes are issued by the Hong Kong and Shanghai Banking Corporation and the Standard Chartered Bank. Hong Kong's deposit-taking institutions are legally classified into three types: licensed banks, licensed deposit-taking institutions, and registered deposit-taking companies. Banking licenses are granted at the discretion of the Governor in Council in accordance with the Banking Ordinance. Licensed banks must meet stringent criteria of capital and time in business; they are required to belong to the Hong Kong Association of Banks, which set the maximum interest rates they may pay. At the end of 1988, there were 158 licensed banks in Hong Kong, 35 of which were locally incorporated, and total deposits in these institutions amounted to HK$779 billion.

Licensed deposit-taking company status is granted at the discretion of the Financial Secretary. Licensed deposit-taking companies are allowed to have smaller issued share capital, and to have been in business for less time than licensed banks, but they are not allowed to offer as many services. At the end of 1988 there were 35 such institutions, holding total depositary liabilities to customers of HK$31 billion.

Registered deposit-taking companies are registered by the Commissioner of Banking; they need meet even less stringent criteria, and are more limited in the amount and term of the deposits they may accept. At the end of 1988, there were 216 registered deposit-taking companies in Hong Kong, which had total deposit liabilities to customers of HK$36 billion.

Normal banking hours are from 9 AM to 3 PM weekdays, but some banks stay open later and stay open to noon on Saturdays. Money can be transferred easily and quickly within Hong Kong and overseas. Local checks can generally be cleared overnight, but foreign checks may take up to three weeks to clear. For further inquiries on banking, contact the Commissioner of Banking, 9/F, Queensway Government Offices, 66 Queensway, Hong Kong (Telephone 5–862–2671).

STOCK MARKETS
AND OTHER FINANCIAL MARKETS

The Stock Exchange of Hong Kong Limited is an amalgam of four separate exchanges. Since its inception in mid-1986 the daily average turnover has been US$108 million. The total capital raised through new issues and rights issues from April 2, 1986, to June 30, 1987, was US$3 billion. Only members of the Stock Exchange of Hong Kong Limited are permitted to trade as stockbrokers. At the end of 1987, there were 773 corporate and individual members. Following a week of setbacks on Wall Street in mid-1987, the Hong Kong Stock Exchange closed its floor for trading. A Securities Review Committee was set up to overhaul the exchange, and its recommendations were published in June 1988. The recommendations were well received by the financial community, and the Hong Kong Government also welcomed them.

The Hong Kong Commodity Exchange Limited operates markets in cotton, sugar, soybeans, and gold, and the Hang Seng Index futures. Gold traded through the Chinese Gold and Silver Exchange Society is of 99% fineness, and its weight is measured in taels (one tael equals approximately 1.2 troy oz). The prices are quoted in Hong Kong dollars and usually closely follow the major markets in London, New York, and Zurich. The other gold market, commonly known as the loco-London gold market, is also very active in Hong Kong. Prices are quoted in US dollars and weight is measured in troy ounces of 99.95% fineness.

The foreign exchange market, an integral part of the global market, has a 24-hour trading day because of Hong Kong's time zone location. The major currencies traded on the local market include the Hong Kong dollar, the US dollar, the deutsch mark, pound sterling, yen, Swiss franc, and Australian dollar. Because of the time-zone advantage, an advanced telecommunications system, and the absence of exchange controls, Hong Kong handles a large volume of world trade.

IMPORTANT BODIES RELATED TO BUSINESS

GOVERNMENT AND QUASI-GOVERNMENT INDUSTRY AND TRADE DEPARTMENTS

The Industry Department (14/F & 15/F, Ocean Centre, 5 Canton Rd., Tsim Sha Tsui, Kowloon; Telephone 3-722-2434 and 3-722-2573) is responsible for the implementation of the government's industrial policies; its One-Stop Unit provides quick and comprehensive services on manufacturing in the territory.

The Trade Department (Telephone 3-722-2333) is responsible for Hong Kong's commercial relations with foreign governments and has information on international quotas for Hong Kong products.

The Customs and Excise Department enforces the laws of Hong Kong that govern dutiable commodities, dangerous drugs, import and export controls, and intellectual and industrial property rights, and carries out trade-related inspections and investigations.

cont...

TRADE DEPARTMENTS *(cont'd)*

The Federation of Hong Kong Industries (408 Hankow Centre, 5–15 Hankow Rd., Tsim Sha Tsui, Kowloon; Telephone 3–723–0818; Telex 84652 HKIND HX; Cable: FEDINDUSTR HONGKONG), represents industry's interests in the territory and has a testing and standards unit.

The Hong Kong Export Credit Insurance Corporation (2/F, South Seas Centre, Tower 1, 75 Mody Rd., Tsim Sha Tsui, Kowloon; Telephone 3–723–3883) extends credit to exporters selling products overseas.

The Hong Kong Industrial Estates Corporation develops and manages fully serviced industrial estates.

The Hong Kong Productivity Council (12/F, World Commerce Centre, Harbour City, 11 Canton Rd., Tsim Sha Tsui, Kowloon; Telephone 3–723–5656; Telex 32842 HX; Cable PROCENTRE HONGKONG) promotes industrial productivity in Hong Kong.

The Hong Kong Trade Development Council (31/F, Great Eagle Centre, 23 Harbour Rd., Hong Kong; Telephone 5–833–4333; Telex 73595 CONHK HX; Cable CONOTRAD HONGKONG) promotes and develops Hong Kong's overseas trade; it has more than 20 offices overseas. Its Hong Kong headquarters provide computerized trade enquiries service; its economic research section and library are a wealth of resource.

The Industry Development Board is the government's advisory body on all major industry-related matters.

CHAMBERS OF COMMERCE

American Chamber of Commerce, 10/F, 1030 Swire House, Connaught Rd., Central; Telephone (5) 260–165; Telex 83664 HX; Cable AMCHAM HONGKONG.

British Chamber of Commerce in Hong Kong, 6/F, 8 Queen's Rd., Central; Telephone (5) 810–8118.

Canadian Chamber of Commerce, 11/F, 1 Exchange Square, Central; Telephone (5) 244–711.

cont...

CHAMBERS OF COMMERCE *(cont'd)*

Chinese General Chamber of Commerce, 7-F, Chinese General Chamber of Commerce Bldg., 24–25 Connaught Rd., Central; Telephone (5) 256–385.

Chinese Manufacturers' Association, 3/F, Chinese Manufacturers' Association Bldg., 64–66 Connaught Rd., Central; Telephone (5) 456–166; Telex 63526 HX; Cable MAFTS HONGKONG.

Hong Kong General Chamber of Commerce, United Centre, 22/F, 95 Queensway, Hong Kong; Telephone (5) 299–229; Telex 83535 HX; Cable CHAMBERCOM HONGKONG; comprises more than 2,700 companies.

Hong Kong Japanese Chamber of Commerce and Industry, 38/F, Hennessy Centre, 500 Hennessy Rd., Causeway Bay, Hong Kong; Telephone (5) 776–129 or (5) 776–252.

Hong Kong Management Association, 14/F, Fairmont House, 8 Cotton Tree Drive, Central; Telephone (5) 266–519.

Indian Chamber of Commerce, 2/F, Hoseinee House, 69 Wyndham St., Hong Kong; Telephone (5) 233–877; Telex 64993 HX; Cable INDCHAMBER HONGKONG.

Korean Society of Commerce in Hong Kong, Korean Centre Bldg., 119–121 Connaught Rd., Central; Telephone (5) 439–387.

Kowloon Chamber of Commerce, 2/F, 2 Liberty Ave., Ho Man Tin, Kowloon; Telephone (3) 760–0393.

Swedish Chamber of Commerce, 3607 Gloucester Tower, The Landmark, Central; Telephone (5) 250–349.

Hong Kong Representatives
(Trade and Industrial Promotion) Overseas

Australia
Hong Kong Trade Development Council, 71 York St., Sydney, NSW 2000; Telephone (02) 298–343/6; Fax (02) 290–1889; Cable HONGKONREP SYDNEY; Telex AA121313 CONSYD

Austria
Hong Kong Trade Development Council, Rotenturmstrasse 1–3/8/24, A-1010 Vienna; Telephone (222) 533–9818; Cable CONOTRADREP WIEN; Telex 115079 HKTDC A; Fax (222) 535–3156

Belgium
Hong Kong Government Industrial Promotion Office, Ave. Louise 228, 1050 Brussels; Telephone (2) 648–3966; Telex 04661750 HONREP B; Telecopier: (2) 640–6655

Canada
Hong Kong Trade Development Council, Suite 1100, National Bldg., 347 Bay St., Toronto, Ontario M5H 2R7; Telephone (416) 366–3594; Fax (416) 366–1569; Cable CONOTRAD TORONTO; Telex 06218056 HKTDC TOR

China
Hong Kong Trade Development Council, 19 Jianguomenwai Dajie, Beijing; Telephone (1) 500–2255 ext. 2860/1; Fax (1) 500–3285; Telex 22927 HKTDC CN

France
Hong Kong Trade Development Council, 18 Rue D'Aguesseau, 75008 Paris; Telephone (1) 4742–4150; Fax (1) 4 742–7744; Telex 641098 HKTDC F

Germany
Hong Kong Trade Development Council, Bockenheimer Landstrasse 93, D-6000 Frankfurt/Main; Telephone (069) 740–161; Fax (069) 745–124; Cable CONOTRAD FRANKFURT; Telex 414705 COFRA

Hong Kong Trade Development Council, Hansastrasse 1, D-2000 Hamburg 13; Telephone (040) 417–422/442, 444–579, 445–674; Facsimile: (040) 459–436; Cable CONOTRAD HAMBURG; Telex 214352 CONHA D

cont...

HONG KONG REPRESENTATIVES OVERSEAS *(cont.)*

Italy
Hong Kong Trade Development Council, 2 Piazzetta Pattari, 20122 Milan; Telephone (02) 865–405/715; Fax (02) 860–304; Cable KONGTRAD MILAN; Telex 333508 HKTDC I

Japan
Hong Kong Government Industrial Promotion Office, No. 32, Kowa Bldg., 2–32 Minami Azabu 5-chome, Minato-ku, Tokyo; Telephone (03) 446–8111; Telecopier (03) 446–8126

Hong Kong Trade Development Council, Osaka Ekimae Dai-San Bldg., 6/F, 1–1–3 Umeda, Kita-ku, Osaka 530; Telephone (06) 344–5211/4; Fax (06) 347–0791; Cable CONNOTRADD OSAKA; Telex J26917 HKTDCT

Hong Kong Trade Development Council, Toho Twin Tower Bldg., 4/G, 1–5–2 Yurakucho, Chiyoda-ku, Tokyo 100; Telephone (03) 502–3251/5; Fax (03) 591–6468; Cable CONNOTRADD TOKYO; Telex J26917 HKTDCT

Netherlands
Hong Kong Trade Development Council, Prinsengracht 771–773 g/f, 1017 JZ Amsterdam; Telephone (020) 277–101; Cable CONOTRAD AMSTERDAM; Telex 15081 HKTDC NL;

Sweden
Hong Kong Trade Development Council, Kungsgatan 6, S–111 43 Stockholm; Telephone (08) 100–677 or 115–690; Fax (08) 723–1630; Cable CONOTRAD STOCKHOLM; Telex 11993 TDC S

Switzerland
AA Hong Kong Economic and Trade Office, 37–39 Rue de Vermont (1/F) 1211 Geneva 20, Switzerland; Telephone (022) 344–351; Fax (022) 339–904; Cable PRODROME GENEVA; Telex 04528880 HKGV CH

Hong Kong Trade Development Council, Bellerivestrasse 3, 8008 Zurich; Telephone (01) 251–0185; Fax (01) 251–0814; Cable CONOTRAD ZURICH; Telex 58550 CONZH CH

United Kingdom
Hong Kong Government Industrial Promotion Office, 6 Grafton St., London W1X 3LB; Telephone (71) 499–9821; Cable HONGAID LONDON; Telex 05128404 HKGOVT G Telecopier (71) 493–1964

Hong Kong Trade Development Council, 8 St. James Square, London SW1Y 4JZ; Telephone (71) 930–7955; Fax (71) 930–4742; Cable CONOTRAD LONDON SW1; Telex 916923 CONLON G

cont...

HONG KONG REPRESENTATIVES OVERSEAS *(cont.)*

United States

Hong Kong Trade Development Council, 333 North Michigan Ave., Suite 2028, Chicago, IL 60601; Telephone (312) 726–4515; Fax (312) 726–2441; Cable CONOTRAD CHICAGO; Telex 728335 HONG KONG CGO

Hong Kong Trade Development Council, 154–2 World Trade Center, 2050 Stemmons Freeway, Dallas, TX 75258; Telephone (214) 748– 8162; Fax (214) 742–6701; Cable HONGTRADS DALLAS; Telex 791719 HKTDC DAL

Hong Kong Trade Development Council, 350 South Figueroa St., Suite #282, Los Angeles, CA 90071; Telephone (213) 622–3194/5, 622–0082; Fax (213) 613–1490; Cable CONOTRAD LOS ANGELES; Telex 194288 HKTDC LA LSA

Hong Kong Economic and Trade Office, British Consulate General, Tower 56, 14/F, 126 East 56th St., New York, NY 10022; Telephone (212) 355–4060; Fax (212) 308–7827; Telex 023420086 NY HKO

Hong Kong Government Industrial Promotion Office, Tower 56, 14/F, 126 East 56th St., New York, NY 10022; Telephone (212) 752–3650 or 752–3658; Telex 025420086 NYHKO; Telecopier (212) 308–7827

Hong Kong Trade Development Council, 548 Fifth Ave., 6/F, New York, NY 10036; Telephone (212) 730–0777; Fax (212) 398–0530; Telex 710 581 6402 HKTDC NYK

Hong Kong Economic and Trade Office, British Consulate General, 180 Sutter St., 4/F, San Francisco, CA 94104; Telephone (415) 397–2215; Fax (415) 421–0646; Telex 0230171611 HKIND SFO

Hong Kong Government Industrial Promotion Office, 180 Sutter St., San Francisco, CA 94104; Telephone (415) 956–4560; Telex 025171611 HKIND SFO; Telecopier (415) 421–0646

Hong Kong Economic and Trade Office, British Embassy, 1233 20 St. NW, Suite 504, Washington, DC 20036; Telephone (202) 331–8947; Fax (202) 331–8958; Cable PRODROME WASHINGTON; Telex 023440484 HK WSH UI

Consulates and Overseas Representatives in Hong Kong (Selected List)

Australia, Harbour Centre, 25 Harbour Rd., Wan Chai, HK, Telephone (5) 731–881

Austria, Wang Kee Bldg., 34–37 Connaught Rd., Central, HK, Telephone (5) 228–086

Bangladesh, 3807 China Resources Bldg., 26 Harbour Rd., Wan Chai, HK, Telephone (5) 728–278

Belgium, St. John's Bldg., 33 Garden Rd., HK, Telephone (5) 243–111

Bhutan, Kowloon Centre, 29–43 Ashley Rd., Kowloon, Telephone (3) 692–112

Brazil, Shell House, 28 Queen's Rd., Central, HK, Telephone (5) 157–002

Burma, Sung Hung Kai Centre, 30 Harbour Rd., Wan Chai, HK, Telephone (5) 891–3329

Canada, Exchange Square, Tower 1, 8 Connaught Pl., HK, Telephone (5) 810–4321

People's Republic of China, China Travel Service (HK) Ltd., CTS House, 78–83 Connaught Rd., Central, HK, Telephone (5) 259–121

Colombia, C. M. A. Bldg., 64–66 Connaught Rd., Central, HK, Telephone (5) 458–547

Denmark, Great Eagle Centre, 23 Harbour Rd., Wan Chai, HK, Telephone (5) 893–6265

Egypt, Woodland Garden, 10 MacDonnell Rd., HK, Telephone (5) 244–174

France, Admiralty Centre, Tower 2, 18 Harcourt Rd., HK, Telephone (5) 294–351

Federal Republic of Germany, United Centre, 95 Queensway, HK, Telephone (5) 298–855

Greece, Kam Chung Bldg., 54 Jaffe Rd., HK, Telephone (5) 200–860

India, United Centre, 95 Queensway, HK, Telephone (5) 284–029

Indonesia, 6–8 Keswick St., Causeway Bay, HK, Telephone (5) 790–4421

Israel, Prince's Bldg., Central, HK, Telephone (5) 296–091

cont...

CONSULATES AND OVERSEAS REPRESENTATIVES *(cont.)*

Italy, Hutchison House, Central, HK, Telephone (5) 220–033

Japan, Bank of America Tower, 12 Harbour Rd., Central, HK, Telephone (5) 221–184

Jordan, World Shipping Centre, Harbour City, Kowloon, Telephone (3) 696–399

Republic of Korea, Korea Centre Bldg., 119–120 Connaught Rd., Central, HK, Telephone (5) 437–562

Malaysia, Malaysia Bldg., 47–50 Gloucester Rd., Wan Chai, HK, Telephone (5) 270–921

Mexico, World-Wide House, 19 Des Voeux Rd., Central, HK, Telephone (5) 214–365

Netherlands, Central Bldg., Central, HK, Telephone (5) 225–127

New Zealand, Connaught Centre, Central, HK, Telephone (5) 255–044

Norway, AIA Bldg., 1 Stubbs Rd., HK, Telephone (5) 749–253

Pakistan, Asian House, 1 Hennessy Rd., Wan Chai, HK, Telephone (5) 274–622

Panama, Wing On Centre, 111 Connaught Rd., Central, HK, Telephone (5) 452–166

Peru, Golden Plaza, 745–747 Nathan Rd., Kowloon, Telephone (3) 803–698

Philippines, Hang Lung Bank Bldg., 8 Hysan Ave., Causeway Bay, HK, Telephone (5) 890–8823

Portugal, Exchange Square, Tower 2, 8 Connaught Pl., HK, Telephone (5) 225–789

Singapore, United Centre, 95 Causeway, HK, Telephone (5) 272–212/4

Spain, Melbourne Plaza, Central, HK, Telephone (5) 253–041

Sweden, Hong Kong Club Bldg., 3A Chater Rd., Central, HK, Telephone (5) 211–212

Switzerland, Gloucester Tower, 11 Pedder St., Central, HK, Telephone (5) 227–147

Thailand, Hyde Centre, 221–226 Gloucester Rd., Causeway Bay, HK, Telephone (5) 742–201

United States, 26 Garden Rd., HK, Telephone (5) 239–011

Uruguay, 7 Bowen Rd., HK, Telephone (5) 440–066

Venezuela, Star House, Kowloon, Telephone (3) 678–099

USEFUL TELEPHONE NUMBERS

Ambulance Service, St. John's (free):
  Hong Kong, (5) 766–555
  Kowloon, (3) 713–5555
  New Territories, (0) 437–543

Box Offices:
  Arts Centre Box Office, (5) 823–0230
  City Hall Box Office, (5) 739–595

Emergency Services (Ambulance, Fire, Police): 999

General Post Office:
  Hong Kong, (5) 231–071
  Kowloon, (3) 884–111

Hong Kong Tourist Association:
  General Office and Information Service, (5) 244–191
    and (3) 722–5555
  Japanese Information Service, (5) 233–996

Hospitals (with 24-hour casualty wards):
  Hong Kong Adventist Hospital, 40 Stubbs Rd.,
    Hong Kong, (5) 746–211
  Queen Elizabeth Hospital, Wylie Rd., Kowloon,
    (3) 710–2111
  Queen Mary Hospital, Pokfulam Rd., HK, (5) 819–2111

Immigration Department: (3) 733–3111

Medical Services:
  Call the hotel doctor or dial 999 in case of emergency

Police:
  General Enquiries, (5) 284–284, ext 231
  Crime Hotline, (5) 277–177

Telephone Services:
Information, 108
Problems, 109
Calls to China, 012
IDD Code Enquiries, 013
Overseas, 010, 011, 012
Time, 1152

Transportation:
China Motor Bus, (5) 658–556
Hongkong & Yaumati Ferry Co., (5) 423–081
Hong Kong International (Kai Tak) Airport,
   (3) 769–7531
Hong Kong Tramways, (5) 891–8765
Kowloon–Canton Railway, (0) 606–9606
Kowloon Motor Bus, (3) 745–4466
Mass Transit Railway, (3) 750–0170
Peak Tramways Co. Ltd., (5) 220–922

The Chek Lam Sim Yuen temple in the New Territories.

XI   Travel Outside of Hong Hong

MACAO

The Portuguese enclave of Macao lies 40 nautical miles to the west of Hong Kong; it is connected to China by a narrow isthmus demarcated by the historic Barrier Gate (Portas do Cerco). Now it is a thoroughfare with trucks and pushcarts carrying goods to and from China.

Macao was founded by the Portuguese in 1557 as a base for the lucrative China trade; it is thus the oldest European settlement in Asia. It has remained a Portuguese dominion until now, but in 1974 it was officially declared a Chinese territory under Portuguese administration, and will come under Chinese rule in 1997 after Hong Kong's status changes.

The main attractions in Macao are legalized gambling, good Portuguese cuisine and wine, and the relaxed "Mediterranean" atmosphere of outdoor cafés and a tree-lined harborfront.

Macao consists of a peninsula and two islands—Taipa and Colôane—and has a total land area of about 6 sq mi (15.5 km). Less than 5% of the 300,000-odd population are Portuguese and Macanese (people of mixed Portuguese and Chinese ancestry); the rest are Chinese, with a few European professionals working in major hotels and casinos.

TOURIST INFORMATION

In Hong Kong, the Macao Tourist Information Bureau is located at 305 Shun Tak Centre (Macao Ferry Terminal), Connaught Rd., Central. Most of the major hotels and local travel agents provide free brochures, maps, and hotel and restaurant information.

In Macao, the Department of Tourism (Telephone 77218) is located at Travessa do Pavia; it also has an information counter at the arrival pier.

GETTING TO MACAO

VISAS

Visas are not required by most nationals for up to a six-month stay. Upon arrival, tourist visas are issued for carriers of valid passports at HK$50 for an individual, HK$75 for a family, and HK$25 for group members. Nationals of countries that do not have diplomatic relations with Portugal must apply in advance for a visa from a Portuguese consulate.

TRANSPORTATION

A variety of convenient sea links connect Hong Kong and Macao. Most vessels leave from the Macao Ferry Pier on Hong Kong Island, about 1 mi (1.6 km) west of the Star Ferry Terminal.

Jetfoil. Operated by the Far East Hydrofoil Company (Telephone: HK 5–455–566 and 5–859–3288; Macao 3474). Each craft carries about 250 passengers and makes the trip in about 50 minutes. They leave every half hour from 7 AM to sundown and every hour between 7 PM and 1:30 AM. Roundtrip fares are first class (upper deck)—from HK$66 weekdays to HK$88 night trips; economy fares (lower deck)—from HK$57 weekdays to HK$77 night trips. Beer, soft drinks, and snacks are available on board.

Hydrofoil. Operated by Hong Kong Macao Hydrofoil (the same booking agent, and therefore the same phone numbers as the jetfoil). These are smaller and slower craft, which make the trip in an hour and 15 minutes, with half-hourly departures during daylight hours. The roundtrip fares are HK$46 on weekdays and HK$58 on weekends and holidays.

Jetcat. Also operated by Hong Kong Macao Hydrofoil. Each craft carries 215 passengers, and the trip takes about 70 minutes. They run 10 roundtrips a day and the fares are HK$46 weekdays and HK$58 on weekends and holidays.

Ferry. Shun Tak Shipping Co. (Telephone: HK 5–457–021; Macao 3586) runs three ferries to and from Macao. These vintage vessels provide leisurely, scenic voyages, which take about three hours each way. Three roundtrips are offered daily—morning, afternoon, and night—with extra trips on holidays and special weekends. Saloon seats cost about HK$30 and private cabins about HK$150. Hot and cold food, beer, and soft drinks are available on board.

TICKETS AND TOURS

Tickets and package tours can be booked at virtually any hotel or from local travel agents. On a weekday you can buy tickets from the ticket counters at the Macao Ferry Pier. On weekends and holidays, thousands of Hong Kong residents travel to Macao to gamble, and it is virtually impossible to obtain tickets unless you have booked in advance. Jetfoil tickets can be bought from Ticketmate outlets in the pier and major stations. A departure tax of HK$15 is levied by the Hong Kong government.

GETTING ABOUT IN MACAO

CURRENCY

The local currency is called the *pataca* (M$), and consists of 100 *avos*. The pataca is roughly on a par with the Hong Kong dollar, which is used freely in Macao.

LANGUAGE

Portuguese is the official language, Cantonese is the spoken language, and English is widely understood in casinos, hotels, and restaurants.

TELEPHONES

There is no charge for local calls. The area code for Taipa and Colôane islands is (2). Directory assistance is 73001 and police is 76464. Direct dialing to Hong Kong is available from most hotels and casinos.

LOCAL TRANSPORTATION

Buses. Macao has a few public buses that also go to the islands of Taipa and Colôane. Fares are M$1 to Taipa and M$1.50 to Colôane.

Mini-buses. Seating 14 persons, these charge about HK$200 for 3–4 hours; the driver also acts as a tour guide.

Pedicabs. These are two-passenger, three-wheeled "rickshaws," pedalled by a driver. With the top down the pedicab is the most leisurely way to see Macao. A ride from the pier to the end of the Praia Grande costs about M$20 (for two) or about HK$30 an hour.

Taxis. Taxis are very cheap: about M$4 when the meter starts running, and about M$80 an hour. Many of these taxi drivers also conduct sightseeing tours. There are surcharges for going over the bridge to Taipa and Colôane.

Bicycle and Mini-moke. Bicycles can be rented from shops around Rua do Campo near the Praia Grande and from the Hyatt-Regency and Oriental Hotels. However, bicycles are not allowed to cross the bridge to Taipa. Mini-mokes seat four and can be rented at the Macao Ferry Pier for HK$230–280 per day.

HOTELS AND POUSADAS

Hotels in Macao range from deluxe international first-class standard to seedy, rundown places for the gambling commuters. *Pousadas* are inns with a distinctive Portuguese-Macanese flavor. Addresses for these hotels and inns are not listed here because Macao is such a small place that practically everywhere can be reached by foot, pedicab, or taxi.

Bela Vista, a charming old place with a lovely terrace that serves good Portuguese food.

Estoril has the Paris Nightclub on the ground floor and a good Chinese restaurant.

Hyatt Regency and Taipa Island Resort, on Taipa Island at the end of the Macao-Taipa bridge, has a coffee shop, a lounge (The Greenhouse), a restaurant (O Pescador) serving Continental food, and a Japanese teppanyaki grill. A free shuttle bus goes from the pier and the Lisboa Hotel casino.

Lisboa houses two floors of casinos, with many restaurants and bars, and the Crazy Paris Show.

Pousada de São Tiago, built into the ruins of the 17th-century Barra Fort, with a fountain and the restored chapel of St. James, is charming and unique. The luxurious Fortaleza Restaurant serves top-quality Portuguese and European cuisine. The terrace, with a view of the inner harbor, is a lovely place for light snacks and Portuguese wine.

Pousada de Colôane, on Colôane Island overlooking a sandy beach, has a superb restaurant serving some of the best Portuguese food in town. The Sunday buffet, at M$45 per person, is very popular.

RESTAURANTS

Good Macanese food is spicy and interesting. The most popular dishes are African Chicken, or Chicken Biri-Biri (Chicken Piri-Piri)—charcoal-grilled chicken marinated in spices—and grilled garlic prawns. Most menus in the Macanese-Portuguese restaurants are in Portuguese; Portuguese wines include *vinho tinto* (red wine), *vinho bianco* (white wine), *vinho rose* (rosé wine), and *vinho verde* (young white wine of a greenish tint).

Delicious Chinese food, especially the roast pigeon and baked local crabs, is served in many Chinese restaurants. Continental restaurants can be found in all the major hotels and casinos. There are also a few restaurants that serve Italian and Japanese cuisine.

MACANESE-PORTUGUESE

Beira Mar, 63 Rua de Praia Grande (Telephone 73499), serves excellent Macanese and Portuguese food.

Bela Vista, Rua Comendador Kou Ho Neng (Telephone 73821). The dining terrace has a view of the harbor.

Belo Restaurant, 43 Avenida Almeida Ribeiro (Telephone 73989). Reasonable home-cooking.

Caseiro, 27E Rua Abreu Nunes (Telephone 573323). Home-cooking, a home-style bakery, and good seafood dishes.

Fortaleza Restaurant, in the Pousada de São Tiago (Telephone 78111). Luxurious dining and superb cuisine.

O Pescador, in the Hyatt-Regency Hotel, Taipa Island (Telephone 2-7000).

Pousada de Colôane, on Colôane Island (Telephone 2-8143). Dining by the seaside.

Solmar, 11 Rua da Praia Grande (Telephone 74391). A local favorite.

Vasco da Gama, in the Royal Hotel (Telephone 552222).

CHINESE

Chiu Chow, in the Lisboa Hotel (Telephone 77666), serves top-quality food.

Fat Siu Lau, 64 Rua da Felicidada (Telephone 73585). The roast pigeon is still very good.

Long Kei, 7 Largo do Senado (Telephone 573970). Considered the best Chinese restaurant in town.

Tong Kong, 32 Rua da Caldeira (Telephone 77364). Serves Hakka cuisine.

CONTINENTAL

A Galera, Hotel Lisboa (Telephone 77666). A grill room.

A Pousada, Hyatt-Regency Hotel, Taipa Island (Telephone 2–7000). More than a café, it has good buffets.

Caesar's Palace, Hotel Lisboa (Telephone 76996). Open 24 hours.

Grill, Oriental Hotel (Telephone 567888). Grilled food and some Portuguese dishes.

Portas do Sol, Hotel Lisboa (Telephone 77666). Floor shows and dancing.

CASINOS

The casinos are very casual and noisy, crowded with keen gamblers, especially on weekends and holidays. They are run by a syndicate under a five-year franchise granted by the government, which receives a tax of over HK$700 million plus 25–30% of gross income and other emoluments. Children under 18 are not allowed, but apart from that, rules are few and identity checks are slack.

Palacio de Macau, the floating casino moored in the inner harbor, is gaudy and loud. Those in the **Oriental Hotel** and the **Jai Alai Stadium** are smaller and more intimate. The most popular one is the two-story casino in the **Lisboa Hotel.** Bar service is available in most of these casinos. The usual games of blackjack, roulette, baccarat, craps, and the Chinese games *fan tan* and Big and Small (*dai siu*) pack the floors. Slot machines are everywhere.

SIGHTSEEING

Historic buildings and ruins of the golden era of Portuguese domain in Asia in the 16th and 17th centuries stand as reminders of past glory. The chief landmark is the ornate stone facade of **São Paulo** (St. Paul), the only remains of the church built between 1602 and 1627. It was once the greatest church in Asia. Below it is **São Domingos,** a church with a beautiful altar. Nearby, surrounding a big square with a fountain, you will find some of the most historic and impressive European architecture in Asia. The **Leal Senado** (Royal Senate), seat of the municipal government, occupies the southeast side of the square and across from it is the **Santa Casa de Misericordia** (Holy House of Mercy). The imposing **Central Post Office** occupies one corner, and on the far side are ancient commercial buildings with open-air arcades and handsome columns.

In Macau, the Ruins of St. Paul is all that remains of the old
Church of the Mother of God, built during the 17th Century.

The walls and cannons of **Monte Fort,** built by the Jesuits in the 1600s, stand on a hill overlooking the harbor. From **Guia Fort** and the **Lighthouse** the entire panorama of Macao is in sight.

The **Camões Museum** (the building and grounds were once owned by the British East India Company for its *taipan*) houses paintings by George Chinnery, Chinese antiques, and pieces of 19th-century European furniture and artifacts. Next to it is the **Old Protestant Cemetery,** where more than 150 Americans and British subjects were buried a few hundred years ago.

The pink **Palacio** (government offices) and a few other charming old villas line the Praia Grande, a tree-shaded avenue along the harbor.

The Chinese also left some historic sites in Macao, the oldest being **A-Ma Temple,** near Barra Point. Macao was named after this area, which was known as A-Ma-Gao (A-Ma Bay) in honor of the Taoist goddess A-Ma. Other temples erected on the penisula include **Lin Fung Mui** (Temple of the Lotus) and **Kun Iam,** a temple of many Buddha statues.

The memorial house of Dr. Sun Yatsen, founder of the Chinese Republic, is frequented by most Chinese visitors to Macao. The **Lou Lim Ieoc** garden is peaceful, with running water under arched bridges, fish ponds, and pagodas.

SPECTATOR SPORTS

Harness racing is held on Taipa Island at the Macao Trotting Club throughout the year. **Greyhound racing,** at the open-air Canidrome, is held on weekends and special days. **Jai Alai** games are on every night in the Jai Alai stadium across from the ferry pier. The annual **Macao Grand Prix** is run on the third weekend in November, and top international drivers race regularly in this event.

SHOPPING

Though Macao is also a duty-free port, the selection of merchandise is limited compared to Hong Kong. Shops run along both sides of the main street, Avenida Almeida Ribeiro, and around the Central Hotel near the inner harbor. Some shops selling antiques and other chinoiserie are tucked away in the small alleys. The best buy is Portuguese wine, Madeira or Port, one bottle per person of which may be brought into Hong Kong duty-free.

THE ISLANDS

Taipa is connected to the mainland by bridge, and Colôane is connected to Taipa by another bridge. Taipa is now dominated by the Hyatt Regency Hotel, the University of East Asia, and the Macao Trotting Club. Duck farming and firecracker manufacturing, the traditional base of the local economy, still exist.

Colôane is still undeveloped except for the Pousade de Colôane. It has two lovely beaches and the Chapel of St. Francis Xavier where holy relics, including an armbone of the saint, are kept.

TO CHINA

THE proximity of Hong Kong to China makes it a major port of entry for travelers to China. It is now simple to make trips across the border.

DAY TRIPS

The most popular one-day excursions into China are to **Shenzhen** and **Zhongshan. Shenzhen** is a Chinese Special Economic Zone (SEZ) on Hong Kong's northern border, reachable by train, car, and tour buses. The tour includes lunch, a trip to the Shenzhen Reservoir, and visits to industrial and commercial areas. The **Zhongshan** trip begins with a hydrofoil ride to Macao, where you enter China through the Barrier Gate. A long bus ride, passing through a countryside with rice paddies, water buffaloes, and farmhouses, takes you to Cuiheng Village, the birthplace of Dr. Sun Yatsen, the founder of modern China. Have lunch in Shiqi, a small town nearby, do some sightseeing, and visit a commune before riding back to Macao.

The Hong Kong Tourist Association arranges the following day trips:

To Shenzhen (HK$350–450) — nine-hour trip by coach or train: cross the border to Shenzhen; visit an art gallery, a kindergarten, and the Shenzhen Reservoir; have a Chinese lunch and spend time shopping.

To Zhongshan (HK$380 – 540) — 12-hour journey by hydrofoil to Macao, then by bus to Dr. Sun Yatsen's birthplace; visit a school and a commune, enjoy a Chinese lunch and some shopping, then back to Hong Kong by hydrofoil.

To Shekou and Guangzhou (HK$790–800) — a 14-hour journey, which includes a hovercraft ride to Shekou; a visit to an exhibition of the Terracotta Warriors, a school, and the free market; then by bus to Guangzhou, where you will see the Guangzhou Zoo, Yuexiu Park, and other historic sites. The trip includes a Chinese lunch and time for shopping before returning to Hong Kong in a through train.

It is also possible to go to China on your own, but it takes time to arrange the trip and it costs more than group tours.

MORE THAN A DAY TRIP

China Travel Service (HK), Ltd., a representative of China International Travel Service (CITS), offers group tours lasting from 1 to 14 days. The Hong Kong Head Office is located at 4/F, CTS House, 78-83 Connaught Rd., Central (Telephone 5-853-3533; Fax 5-419-777; Telex 85222 HCTSF HX; Cable CHITRAFORN). The Central Branch Office in Hong Kong is at 2/F, China Travel Bldg., 77 Queen's Rd., Central (Telephone 5-252-284), and the Kowloon Branch Office is at 1/F, Alpha House, 27 Nathan Rd. (Telephone 3-721-1311; Fax: 3-721-7757; Telex 40536 CTSKL HX.

Your hotel tour desk or local travel agents can also arrange a wide variety of tours to China

BY AIR

CAAC (Gloucester Tower, HK; Telephone 5-211-314) operates three to four daily flights to Guangzhou and twice-daily nonstop service to Beijing, as well as direct flights to Shanghai, Tianjin, Nanjing, Hangzhou, Guilin, and many other cities. Cathay Pacific has services to Shanghai, and Dragonair flies to many southern Chinese cities.

BY RAIL

Daily nonstop service and express trains between Kowloon and Guangzhou leave from the Hung Hom station. A single journey to Guangzhou costs HK$135–215. One piece of luggage (44 lbs or 20 kg) per person is allowed; each extra piece costs HK$40.

There is a change of trains at the Hong Kong–PRC border, where passengers board a PRC train to Guangzhou. The entire journey, including a lunch stop in Shenzhen, takes about four hours.

BY HOVERCRAFT

The journey from Kowloon (Tai Kok Tsui Ferry Pier) in the

morning to Zhoutonzha Pier on the outskirts of Guangzhou takes about three hours. The return trip is in the afternoon. A single trip costs HK$145.

BY SHIP

These are modern steamers that sail from Hong Kong to the various ports in China.

Hong Kong–Guangzhou. The *Xinghu* and the *Tianhu* sail on alternate nights (9 PM) from Hong Kong on the 80–mi (129–km) journey up the Pearl River, and return from Guangzhou every morning at 9 AM. Dining and recreation facilities are available on board. Double-occupancy first-class cabins cost HK$130 per passenger.

Hong Kong–Xiamen. The ships make the 300-mi (483-km) journey between Hong Kong and Xiamen Island in about 22 hours.

Hong Kong–Shantou. The *Dinghu* sails on alternate days to Shantou along the 191-mi (307-km) South China coast route in about 14 hours.

Hong Kong–Shanghai. Weekly sailings by the *Shanghai* and the *Haixing* to Shanghai take about 60 hours. Deluxe cabins cost about HK$845 and economy class, HK$260. Both ships provide gourmet food and swimming pools.

CTS/CITS TOURS

Guangzhou 3-Day Excursion. Departs Tuesdays, Thursdays, and Saturdays by hovercraft. Roundtrip fare is US$220 per person.

Guangzhou–Guilin 4-Day Excursion. Roundtrip by hovercraft and train. Departs every Wednesday; fare US$390 per person.

Beijing, Xian, Chongqing, Yangtse River Cruise, Wuhan, and Shanghai 13-Day Excursion. Roundtrip by air at US$1,440 per person. Departures in April and from July to October (contact CTS for dates).

ENTRANCE AND EXIT FORMALITIES

VISAS

Visas can be issued in less than 72 hours; an "urgent" request will get you one in about 24 hours for a surcharge of around UK$120.

Individual visas are not required in a group tour; the guide carries one group visa for all, but every passport is inspected (though not stamped).

CUSTOMS

Liberal quotas on cigarettes (30 packages), liquor (four bottles), and film but not on reading material, radio transmitters, and other items. Get the latest regulations from CITS. A simple customs form has to be filled out, and the duplicate must be returned to Customs when leaving China.

Appendix

LANGUAGE

CANTONESE, for most non-Chinese, is the most difficult Chinese dialect to speak since every word is pronounced with one of ten tones—level, rising, falling, etc. The following is the common romanization for some useful Cantonese words and phrases.

NUMBERS

0	ling	11	sup-yat
1	yat	12	sup-yee
2	yee	13	sup-saam
3	saam	14	sup-sai
4	sai	15	sup-ng
5	ng	16	sup-lok
6	lok	17	sup-chat
7	chat	18	sup-baat
8	baat	19	sup-gau
9	gau	20	yee-sup
10	sup	30	saam-sup

31	saam-sup-yat
32	saam-sup-yee, etc.
41	sai-sup-yat
42	sai-sup-yee, etc.

100	yat baak
1000	yat chin
10,000	yat maan
100,000	sup maan
1,000,000	yat baak maan

WEEK AND DAYS OF WEEK

The word for "week" (*lie by* or *sing kay*) is followed by a number from one to six to denote any of the first six days of the week, i.e.:

lie by yat or sing kay yat	Monday
lie by yee or sing kay yee	Tuesday
lie by saam or sing kay saam	Wednesday
lie by sai or sing kay sai	Thursday
lie by ng or sing kay ng	Friday
lie by lok or sing kay lok	Saturday
lie by yaat or sing kay yaat	Sunday

MONTHS OF THE YEAR

The word for "month" (*yuet*) is preceded by a number from one to twelve to denote any of the twelve months of the year, i.e.:

yat yuet	January
yee yuet	February
saam yuet	March
sai yuet	April
ng yuet	May
lok yuet	June
chat yuet	July
baat yuet	August
gau yuet	September
sup yuet	October
sup-yat yuet	November
sup-yee yuet	December

YEAR

The word for "year" is *nien*; for example, 1988 is *yat-gau-baat-baat nien* and 1989 is *yat-gau-baat-gau nien*. You simply put the numbers in front of the word *nien*.

GENERAL PHRASES

English	Cantonese
I, Me; My, Mine	*ngoh; ngoh di or ngoh ge*
You; Your, Yours	*nei; nei di or nei ge*
He, It/She	*tab or kui*
His, Its/Hers	*tah di or kui ge*
We, Us; Our	*ngoh; ngoh di*
They, Them	*kui di*
Their, Theirs	*kui di ge*
I am	*ngoh hai*
We are	*ngoh di hai*
You are	*nei hai*
He/she/it is	*kui hai*
They are	*kui di hai*
Who, Whom?	*ben goh, ben wai?*
When	*gei see*
What	*mat yeh*
Where	*ben do*
Why	*dim gaai*
How	*dim yeung*
Hello, how are you?	*nei ho ma?*
Very well, Very good	*ho ho*
Not well, Not good	*m'ho*
Quite well, Quite good	*gei ho*
Good morning	*jou san*
Good night	*madn, ngan*

Goodbye, See you again	*joy geen*
Thank you (gift)	*deu je*
Thank you (service)	*m'goi*
Please	*tcheng*
Would you please	*m'goi nei, tcheng nei*
Excuse me, I'm sorry	*dui m'jyu*
Yes	*hai*
Yes, it is	*hai ah*
No	*m'gai*
No, it isn't	*m'hai ah*

TRAVEL AND TRANSPORTATION

Turn right	*jyun yau*
Turn left	*jyun choh*
Stop the car	*ting che*
Quickly, hurry up	*faai di*
Slowly, slow down	*maan di*
Careful, take care	*sui sum*
Front	*chin*
Back	*hou*
Luggage	*haan lei*
Airport	*fei gay cheung*
Bicycle	*daan che*
Bus	*ba si*
Car	*hey che*
Mini-bus	*siu ba*
Motor boat	*din syun*
Motorcycle	*din daan che*
MTR (underground)	*dai har tit*
Taxi	*dik si*
Ferry	*goh hoi syun*

Plane	*fei gay*
Rickshaw	*che dzai*
Train	*fou che*
Train station	*fou zhaam*
Tram	*din che*

PLACE NAMES

Hong Kong	*Heung Gong*
Kowloon	*Gau Lung*
New Territories	*San Gaai*
Central District	*Ghung Waan*
Wan Chai	*Waan Chai*
Causeway Bay	*Tung Lo Wan*
The Peak	*Saan Deng*
Repulse Bay	*Chin Sui Waan*
Stanley	*Chik Chue*
Aberdeen	*Heung Gong Chai*
Ocean Park	*Hoi Yeung King Yuep*
Star Ferry, Hong Kong	*Tin Sing Ma Tau*
Star Ferry, Kowloon	*Tsim Sha Tui Ma Tau*
Outlying Districts, Services Pier	*Gong Noy Sin Ma Tau*
Macau Ferry Pier	*O Moon Ma Tau*
Kai Tak Airport	*Kai Tak Kay Cheung*

RESTAURANT

Menu	*choy bai*
Bill, please	*mai daan, m'goi*
Breakfast	*jou chaan*
Lunch	*ng tchaan*
Dinner	*maan chan*
Chinese food	*tong choy, chang tsaan choy*
Western food	*sai tsaan choy*
Dim sum	*dim sum*

Tea	*cha*
Chinese tea	*ching cha*
Tea with milk	*nai cha*
Tea with lemon	*ling mong cha*
Coffee	*gar fey*
Milk	*njou nai*
Fruit juice	*gwoh tchap*
Water	*seui*
Soda	*hey seui*
Beer	*bai jau*
Wine or liquor	*jau*

Rice	*faan*
Plain steamed rice	*baak faan*
Fried rice	*tchau faan*
Noodle	*mein*
Fried noodle	*tchau mein*
Soup noodle	*tong mein*

Bread	*mein bao*
Toast	*dou, see*
Sandwich	*saam, men jee*

Ice cream	*suet go*
Ice cream soda	*suet go saw da*

Sugar	*tong*
Salt	*yim*
Pepper	*woo cjiu fun*
Butter	*ngau yau*

Beef	*ngau yuk*
Beef steak	*ngau bai*
Chicken	*gaai*
Duck	*gaai*
Goose	*ngoh*
Lamb, mutton	*yueng, yuk*

Pork	*jyue yuk*
Pork chop	*lyue bani*

Seafood	*hoi sin*

| Fruit | *shaan kwoh* |
| Dessert | *tim ban* |

Sour	*syuun*
Sweet	*timm*
Bitter	*fou*
Hot (spicy)	*laat*

SHOPPING

Antique	*goo tung*
Artworks,	*kung jai ban*
Arts and crafts	

| Book | *syu* |
| Bookstore | *syue gok* |

| Department store | *baak foh kung see* |

| How much (money)? | *gay dou chin?* |

Ten dollars	*sup maan*
One dollar	*yat maan*
Ten cents	*yat ho*
Bank note	*ngan jih*
Check	*jih piu*
Traveler's check	*leui hang piu*
U.S. dollar	*mei kam*
English pound	*ying bong*

POSTAGE AND TELECOMMUNICATIONS

Cable, telegraph	*din bou*
Cable, telegraph office	*din bou gok*
Post office	*yau jing gok*
Stamp	*yau piu*
Telephone	*din wah*

POLICE

Inspector	*bong baan*
Policeman	*chaai yan*
Police station	*chaai gok*

BUSINESS (COMMERCIAL TERMS)

Accountant	*wui gai see*
Advertisement	*gong go*
Agent	*doi lei yan*
Broker	*ging gei*
Businessmen	*seung yan*
Capital	*buin in ch*
Capital loss	*seit buin*
Cash	*yin gam*
Commission	*yung*
Company	*gung see*
Deposit	*deng gam*
Discount	*jit kau*
Expenditure	*fai yung*
Factory	*gung chong*
Goods	*foh*
Insurance	*bo him*
Invoice	*faat piu*
Lawyer	*lou see*
Manager	*ging lei*
Office	*sai sze lau*
Price	*ga chin*
Profit	*lei yiak*
Receipt	*sau tiu*
Retail	*ling sau*
Signature	*chim ji*
Wages	*yan gung*
Wholesale	*pai faat*

OTHER IMPORTANT WORDS

Bank	*ngan hong*
Bar	*au bar*

Church	*lei baai tong*
Hospital	*yee yun*
Hotel	*jau dim*
Movie houses	*hei yun*
Restaurant	*jau lau*
Toilet	*chiso*

FUTURE STATUS OF HONG KONG

THE following is the official text of the agreement between Britain and China on the future status of Hong Kong.

JOINT DECLARATION
OF THE GOVERNMENT OF THE UNITED KINGDOM OF
GREAT BRITAIN AND NORTHERN IRELAND
AND
THE GOVERNMENT OF THE PEOPLE'S REPUBLIC OF
CHINA ON THE QUESTION OF HONG KONG

The Government of the United Kingdom of Great Britain and Northern Ireland and the Government of the People's Republic of China have reviewed with satisfaction the friendly relations existing between the two Governments and peoples in recent years and agreed that a proper negotiated settlement of the question of Hong Kong, which is left over from the past, is conducive to the maintenance and stability of Hong Kong and to the further strengthening and development of the relations between the two countries on a new basis. To this end, they have, after talks between the delegations of the two Governments, agreed to declare as follows:

1. The Government of the People's Republic of China declares that to recover the Hong Kong area (including Hong Kong Island, Kowloon, and the New Territories, hereinafter referred to as Hong Kong) is the common aspiration of the entire Chinese people, and that it has decided to resume the exercise of sovereignty over Hong Kong with effect from 1 July 1997.

2. The Government of the United Kingdom declares that it will restore Hong Kong to the People's Republic of China with effect from 1 July 1997.

3. The Government of the People's Republic of China declares that the basic policies of the People's Republic of China regarding Hong Kong are as follows:

(1) Upholding national unity and territorial integrity and taking account of the history of Hong Kong and its realities, the People's Republic of China has decided to establish, in accordance with the provisions of Article 31 of the Constitution of the People's Republic of China, a Hong Kong Special Administrative Region upon resuming the exercise of sovereignty over Hong Kong.

(2) The Hong Kong Special Administrative Region will be directly under the authority of the Central People's Government of the People's Republic of China. The Hong Kong Special Administrative Region will enjoy a high degree of autonomy, except in foreign and defence affairs which are the responsibilities of the Central People's Government.

(3) The Hong Kong Special Administrative Region will be vested with executive, legislative and independent judicial power, including that of final adjudication. The laws currently in force in Hong Kong will remain basically unchanged.

(4) The Government of the Hong Kong Special Administrative Region will be composed of local inhabitants. The chief executive will be appointed by the Central People's Government on the basis of the results of elections or consultations to be held locally. Principal officials will be nominated by the chief executive of the Hong Kong Special Administrative Region for appointment by the Central People's Government. Chinese and foreign nationals previously working in the public and police services in the government departments of Hong Kong may remain in employment. British and other foreign nationals may also be employed to serve as advisers or hold certain public posts in government departments of the Hong Kong special Administrative Region.

(5) The current social and economic systems in Hong Kong will remain unchanged, and so will the life-style. Rights and

freedoms, including those of the person, of speech, of the press, of assembly, of association, of travel, of movement, of correspondence, of strike, of choice of occupation, of academic research and of religious belief will be ensured by law in the Hong Kong Special Administrative Region. Private property, ownership of enterprises, legitimate right of inheritance and foreign investment will be protected by law.

(6) The Hong Kong Special Administrative Region will retain the status of a free port and a separate customs territory.

(7) The Hong Kong Special Administrative Region will retain the status of an international financial centre, and its markets for foreign exchange, gold, securities and futures will continue. There will be free flow of capital. The Hong Kong dollar will continue to circulate and remain freely convertible.

(8) The Hong Kong Special Administrative Region will have independent finances. The Central People's Government will not levy taxes on the Hong Kong Special Administrative Region.

(9) The Hong Kong Special Administrative Region may establish mutually beneficial economic relations with the United Kingdom and other countries, whose economic interests in Hong Kong will be given due regard.

(10) Using the name of "Hong Kong, China", the Hong Kong Special Administrative Region may on its own maintain and develop economic and cultural relations and conclude relevant agreements with states, regions and relevant international organisations.

The Government of the Hong Kong Special Administrative Region may on its own issue travel documents for entry into and exit from Hong Kong.

(11) The maintenance of public order in the Hong Kong Special Administrative Region will be the responsibility of the Government of the Hong Kong Special Administrative Region.

(12) The above-stated basic policies of the People's Republic of China regarding Hong Kong and the elaboration of them in Annex I to this Joint Declaration will be stipulated, in a Basic Law of the Hong Kong Special Administrative Region of the People's Republic of China, by the National People's Congress of the People's Republic of China, and they will remain unchanged for 50 years.

4. The Government of the United Kingdom and the Government of the People's Republic of China declare that, during the transitional period between the date of the entry into force of this Joint Declaration and 30 June 1997, the Government of the United Kingdom will be responsible for the administration of Hong Kong with the object of maintaining and preserving its economic prosperity and social stability; and that the Government of the People's Republic of China will give its cooperation in this connection.

5. The Government of the United Kingdom and the Government of the People's Republic of China declare that, in order to ensure a smooth transfer of government in 1997, and with a view to the effective implementation of this Joint Declaration, a Sino-British Joint Liaison Group will be set up when this Joint Declaration enters into force; and that it will be established and will function in accordance with the provisions of Annex II to this Joint Declaration.

6. The Government of the United Kingdom and the Government of the People's Republic of China declare that land leases in Hong Kong and other related matters will be dealt with in accordance with the provisions of Annex III to this Joint Declaration.

7. The Government of the United Kingdom and the Government of the People's Republic of China agree to implement the preceding declarations and the Annexes to this Joint Declaration.

8. This Joint Declaration is subject to ratification and shall enter into force on the date of the exchange of instruments of ratification, which shall take place in Beijing before 30 June 1985. This Joint Declaration and its Annexes shall be equally binding.

Done in duplicate at Beijing on 26 September 1984 in the English and Chinese languages, both texts being equally authentic.

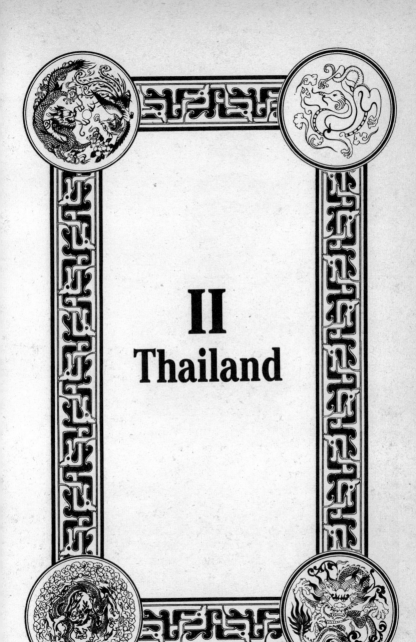

II
Thailand

The Grand Palace, Bangkok

I Thailand at a Glance

The Kingdom of Thailand contrives to offer a combination of old and new Asia that is both charming and accessible. It is a beautiful, friendly, and inexpensive place, blessed with a stable and growing economy and 30 years' experience in the tourist industry. From glorious and crazed Bangkok in the central plains, to lovely Chiang Mai city in the north and the splendid beach resorts in the south, Thailand offers both the exotic complexity of Asia and the comforts of home. A well-developed transportation and accommodation system satisfies the whims and worries of all varieties of travelers and tourists to Asia.

Landscapes, culture, people, handicrafts, food, and entertainment all conspire in Thailand to make it one of the world's most alluring vacation and travel destinations. As its formerly inaccessible neighbors — Laos, Cambodia (or Kampuchea, depending on your factional affiliation), Vietnam, and, perhaps, Burma (now officially known as the Union of Myanmar) — open up to Western tourists and entrepreneurs, Thailand will grow ever more important as a cultural and commercial center in the region.

Thailand first boomed for a certain variety of Western tourists during the Vietnam War, when American GIs hit Bangkok for "R-and-R." Since then this beautiful country has been criticized for running a "consumer-dictated" tourist industry, i.e. one that caters to some of the lower instincts among male tourists. Bawdy jokes abound about travel to Thailand, and Bangkok in particular. "Oh, you're going to Thailand, are you?" Or "I didn't think Western women were interested in visiting Bangkok." Thailand's notorious sex-tourist industry is still thriving, but in recent years the country has sought to downgrade the emphasis on single male travelers. The year 1988, for instance, was the Year of Arts and Handicrafts in Thailand, a promotional campaign to draw attention to the country's more gentile appeals. Over five million tourists visited the Kingdom during that year, and the large majority were interested in far more than the bare-bosomed beauties of Bangkok.

GEOGRAPHY

UNTIL very recently, one of Thailand's greatest allures was its location smack in the midst of the otherwise impenetrable Indochinese landmass. It is bordered by Burma on the east, by the Democratic People's Republic of Laos in the north and east, and by Cambodia (Democratic Kampuchea) in the southeast. Far to the south, Malaysia has traditionally furnished Thailand's only open border.

Strangely shaped like a bulbous balloon squeezed up from the narrow bottom, Thailand has often been said to resemble an elephant's head. The head proper is composed of three of Thailand's distinct geographic regions: the mountainous north; the semiarid and poor plateau in the northeast where, according to some historians, the world's first civilization flourished nearly 6,000 years ago; and the fertile, highly populated central plains around the Chao Phraya River and Bangkok. The narrow isthmus of southern Thailand is the elephant's trunk, stretching south from Bangkok to the Malaysian border, with gorgeous seas on either side.

From its northern border with Burma and Laos to the very southern Malaysian border, Thailand measures over 1,000 mi (1,600 km). At its broadest point, the country extends only 485 mi (786 km) from the Burmese border on the west to the Kampuchean border on the east. The total area of the country is about 198,500 sq. mi (514,000 km^2) — about the same size as France.

Most Thais live and work in the wide, low-lying plains of the delta of the Chao Phraya in central Thailand. It is this fertile heartland, around the modern capital of Bangkok, that nurtured ancient Thai kingdoms and continues to be the richest and most developed part of the nation. Ayutthaya, the golden capital of a powerful and independent Thai kingdom in the 14th and 15th centuries, is located just 45 miles (72 km) north of Bangkok. To the west of this region, high hills stretch toward the border of isolationist Burma. To the east and south, the coastal plain curves around the Gulf of Thailand to meet the refugee-crowded border with Cambodia.

Thailand's poorest and least-developed region is in the northeast, where a sandstone plain stretches up to the banks of the Mekong River. The Mekong forms part of Thailand's long border with Laos. Just west, Thailand's second city, Chiang Mai, lies in the only important level area in the hilly northwest, a region populated by colorful, and sometimes illicitly commercial hill tribes. This area is known in the West as the "Golden Triangle" of opium cultivation and heroin production.

HISTORY OF THAILAND

PRIOR to the 13th century AD, when the first independent Thai kingdom appeared, the history of this region is obscure and largely undocumented. Up until that time, the area currently known as Thailand is thought to have been controlled by different princes, ruling separate but loosely linked agricultural communities across a broad stretch of fertile land from southern Burma through south-central Thailand and Cambodia. Historians call this era the Dvaravati period, from a Sanskrit term meaning "place having gates." Little is known about this period, other than that the people practiced Theravada Buddhism and produced a great many pieces of beautiful Buddhist art.

By the 11th century AD, the dominant cultural group in the region were the Khmers of modern-day Cambodia. The Dvaravati culture declined then, and Khmer influences in art, language, and religion took over. Indigenous Thais were called *Syams* by the Khmers, a Sanskrit word meaning "dark." *Syam* is the origin of *Siam*, the name by which Thais and Thailand were known for many centuries.

Far to the north of the Khmer empire, however, a kingdom of Thais was flourishing in the southeast of China. The Nanzhao Kingdom of the Bai people, as they are called in China, dominated much of modern-day Yunnan Province in China's southeast. From the 7th through the 13th century AD, they rivaled Chinese dynasties in power and influence. Then the Mongol chieftain Kublai Khan conquered all of China and eventually Nanzhao in the mid-13th century. Historians believe that this precipitated a gradual immigration of Thai peoples to the south, to the jungles of southern Yunnan Province, northern Laos, and eventually to northern Thailand.

The first independent Thai kingdom in what is now Thailand began when a group of Thai princelings united and conquered a Khmer garrison at Sukhothai in north-central Thailand, founding the first capital on Thai soil there in 1238. King Ramkamheng (1283-1317), Sukhothai's second king, was a powerful leader who both held off the constantly threatening Khmers to the east and extended Thai domination south of Sukhothai to the central plains and the Chao Phraya delta area around modern-day Bangkok. The king also brought scholars together to create a written script of the Thai language and encouraged the development of trade between Thailand and the powerful northern empire in China. Although the Sukhothai Kingdom, plagued by rival Thai factions in the fertile southern part of the land, was relatively short-lived, it is remembered by historians

ROAD DISTANCES FROM BANGKOK (KM.)

Km.

	Km.		Km.
Ayutthaya By Rail 1.20 hrs. By Road 45 mins	76	**Nakhon Ratchasima** By Rail 5 hrs. By Road 4 hrs.	259
Bang Saen By Road 1.15 hrs.	104	**Nakhon Si Thammarat** By Rail 15 hrs. By Road 13 hrs.	780
Chanthaburi By Road 3.30 hrs.	245	**Nan** By Air 1.30 hrs. By Road 10.30 hrs.	668
Chiang Mai By Rail 14 hrs. By Air 1 hr. By Road 10 hrs.	696	**Pattaya** By Road 1.45 hrs.	147
Chiang Rai By Air 1.15 hrs. By Road 12 hrs.	785	**Phetchaburi** By Rail 2.30 hrs. By Road 2 hrs.	123
Chumphon By Raii 8.30 hrs. By Road 5.15 hrs.	463	**Phitsanulok** By Rail 6.10 hrs. By Air 45 mins. By Road 5.30 hrs.	377
Hat Yai By Rail 17 hrs. By Air 1.15 hrs. By Road 15 hrs.	933	**Phuket** By Air 1 hr. By Road 10 hrs.	862
Hua Hin By Rail 4 hrs. By Road 2.45 hrs.	240	**Rayong** By Road 2.30 hrs.	179
Kanchanaburi By Rail 2.30 hrs. By Road 1.30 hrs.	128	**Sakon Nakhon** By Air 1 hr. By Road 8 hrs.	647
Khon Kaen By Rail 8 hrs. By Air 1 hr. By Road 5.15 hrs.	449	**Songkhla** By Road 15 hrs.	950
Lampang By Rail 11 hrs. By Air 1.30 hrs. By Road 7.30 hrs.	599	**Sukhothai** By Road 5 hrs.	427
Lamphun By Rail 13 hrs. By Road 8 hrs.	670	**Trat** By Road 4.15 hrs.	315
Lop Buri By Rail 2.15 hrs. By Road 1.55 hrs.	153	**Ubon Ratchathani** By Rail 10 hrs. By Air 1.30 hrs. By Road 8 hrs.	629
Nakhon Pathom By Rail 1.25 hrs. By Road 40 mins.	56	**Udon Thani** By Rail 10 hrs. By Air 1.30 hrs. By Road 6.45 hrs.	564
Nakhon Phanom By Road 10.30 hrs.	740	**Yala** By Rail 18 hrs. By Road 16.30 hrs.	1084

as a golden age of Thai culture and art. It laid the groundwork for the next Thai kingdom, Ayutthaya, a much more sophisticated and politically powerful stage in the cultural development of Thailand.

Sukhothai power began to decline soon after the death of its mighty King Ramkamheng. By the middle of the 14th century, the more southern city of Ayutthaya had become the most powerful city-state in the region, and in 1376, Sukhothai itself was annexed by Ayutthaya kings. For the next four centuries Ayutthaya was an immensely powerful regional force. Ayutthaya kings extended Thai control into the southern part of modern-day Burma, and south into

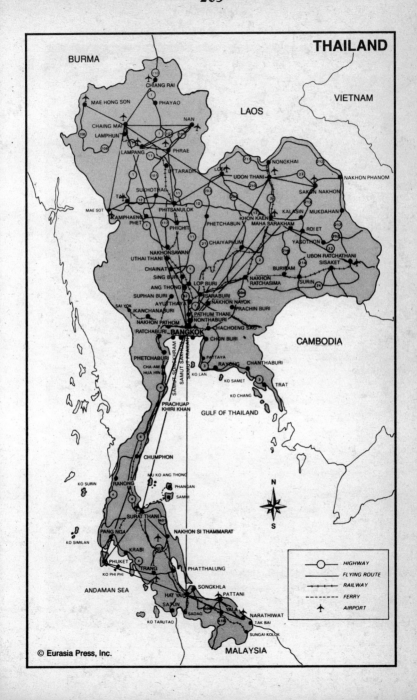

Photo by John A. McCullough

the Malay Peninsula. This period marked the first real contact between Thais and Europeans. Those traders, missionaries, and diplomats who made their way to Siam heralded Ayutthaya as one of the greatest and most beautiful cities in Asia. At this point Thai leaders began to practice an artful diplomacy in dealing with European powers. They allowed the establishment of embassies and trading companies — a Portuguese embassy was established in 1511, a Dutch embassy in 1605, an English embassy in 1612, a Danish embassy in 1621, and a French embassy in 1662.

Burma, to the west, was always a thorn in the side of Thai kingdoms and became a serious threat to Ayutthaya in the 16th century. Finally, in 1569, Burma attacked Ayutthaya and forced the Thais into submission. During the sack of the kingdom they captured a young Thai prince named Naresuan and later, when he was in his teens, sent him back to Thailand to assist in an ongoing struggle against the Khmers of Cambodia. He formed his own Thai army and repelled the Cambodians and, eventually, the Burmese themselves. Understandably, the Thais made him king, at the ripe age of 16, and he is known in history as King Naresuan, the Black Prince. He is one of the most glorious of historical heroes for the Thais, and one of the most notorious for the Burmese and the Cambodians: in the struggle to secure Ayutthaya for the Thais, he killed the heir to the Burmese throne in a single combat, and also beheaded the Cambodian king in public.

In the 17th century, the wealth and power of the Ayutthaya court were tempting not just to Thailand's near neighbors, but also to the increasingly greedy European colonial powers, who were gobbling up pieces of Asia as fast as their boats could enter ports. At first, Thai rulers signed treaties allowing these foreign powers trading and missionary rights, but then, as the foreigners became more aggressive in their demands and in their involvement in the country's internal politics, the court became more conservative.

King Nerai (ruled 1656–1688), another much-loved and well-respected Thai monarch, tried to play one power off against the other and to enlist British, and then French, help to fend off aggressive Dutch trading forays. At this point a Greek merchant and official with the British East India Company, Constantine Paulkon, was appointed by the king as an adviser on foreign affairs. As King Nerai grew old and feeble, the Greek was made Minister in Charge of Trade and then Chief Minister. The Thai court was not pleased with this intrusion and eventually, after French warships arrived in Bangkok with Paulkon's blessing, Thai officials took action. In 1688 they arrested and executed

Paulkon, as well as a number of French missionaries. That marked the end, for a time, of Thai relations with the outside world. To this day, the word meaning "foreigner" in Thailand is *farang,* derived from the word *farangset,* which means "French."

Beset by domestic conflicts and threatened on both sides by strong regimes in Burma and Cambodia, Thailand was a weak and declining power in the 18th century. In 1767 the Burmese invaded once again and completely destroyed Ayutthaya. As the kingdom disintegrated, the provinces went off on their own and were ruled separately by members of the Thai nobility or taken over by foreign powers. The country was soon after reunified, however, by an extraordinary warrior-king of Chinese descent named Taksin. At the time of the Burmese siege, he had escaped from Ayutthaya with 500 men, and built a new army in Cambodia. Though he recaptured Ayutthaya, he established his capital at Thonburi, a fishing village on the western side of the Chao Phraya south of the old capital, and declared himself king in 1769.

In 1781, a palace coup led by General Chakri deposed and beheaded Taksin. The next year, Chakri assumed the kingship, taking the title Rama I and founding the dynasty that was to rule Thailand as an absolute monarchy until 1932, and establishing the Thai capital in what is now Bangkok.

For the next century, a series of by turns inspired and mediocre Ramas (II through the present IX) ruled Thailand and dealt with the ever more serious threats of foreign encroachment upon their sovereignty. One of Thailand's more famous monarchs was Rama IV, or King Mongkut, who ruled from 1851 through 1868. (He was the king of *The King and I.*) While his half-brother, Rama III, took the throne, he waited out his turn for kingship in a Buddhist monastery and is remembered as a scholar-king. He was not only adept in Sanskrit, Pali, and Latin, but he also learned to read and write English from visiting American missionaries. He was a great reformer and studied the scientific and technological developments in the West with great interest.

In part because of his openmindedness, but also because he sensed that, after the British defeated the Chinese empire in the Opium Wars of the mid-nineteenth century, accommodation with the European powers was the only way to save Thailand from foreign intervention, he encouraged European involvement in the country. In 1855 he concluded the Bowring Treaty with the British. Along with later treaties with the United States and Japan, it allowed foreigners easy trading access to Thailand and greatly reduced import duties on their goods. With such favorable terms, the colonial powers did not feel the need to move on Thailand in the way they had taken over other Asian nations, and they also viewed the country as an important buffer state between the English in Burma and Malaya and the French in Indochina. Thus Thailand managed to avoid the colonization that plagued every other nation in this part of the world during the 19th century.

King Mongkut's son, Chulalongkorn, or Rama V, ruled from 1868 to 1910. He continued his father's reformist tradition and constructed railways throughout the country, established a civil service, and implemented a legal code. By this time, however, the French were moving more aggressively into Cambodia, Vietnam, and Laos, and they precipitated what is now known as the Paknam Incident to demand concessions from the Thai government. After insisting that Thailand give up its claims on all land east of the Mekong River (modern-day Laos), the French government sent warships up the Chao Phraya. Repeating the same mistake made by the Chinese a half-century earlier, a Thai fortress at Paknam fired on the warships. The French fired back, and then issued a list of demands to which the Thai government was forced to accede in reparation for its supposed "aggression" against the French.

In 1896 the British and French agreed to allow Thailand its independence, but in turn Thailand had to give up its claim to Laos to the French and to four states in the south to the British.

The absolute monarchy of the Chakri Dynasty came to an end in 1932. A group of Thai students inspired and mounted a successful coup against the monarchy in the hope of setting up a constitutional democracy. The king at the time, Rama VII, agreed to serve as a constitutional head of state on the model of the British and Scandinavian systems. However, he abdicated in 1935, to be succeeded by his nephew, Ananda Mahidol (Rama VIII). One of the coup leaders, a commoner named Phibul Songkhram, emerged as head of government in the late 1930s. Following the old monarchial pattern of appeasing the foreigners to maintain the Thai state, Phibul made a deal with the Japanese at the beginning of World War II which allowed them into Thailand without a struggle. Obviously, had he not done so, Thailand would have fallen bloodily to the Japanese as did the rest of Asia, but popular resistance to this move caused Phibul to resign in 1944.

In 1946, Rama VIII was assassinated under mysterious circumstances and his brother Bhumipol became king as Rama IX. King Bhumipol is and remains an extremely popular monarch; his picture is displayed all over the country and he is widely considered the father of the Thai people. His reign has witnessed dozens of coups within the civilian and later military governments, but the King remains, for the people at least, the ultimate arbiter of politics.

Thailand was ruled by a succession of military governments from the early 1950s through the early 1970s. Various attempts to reinstitute democratic rule were tried, but eventually military leaders would launch a coup, repeal or suspend the constitution, and institute military rule throughout the land. In the autumn of 1973, 100,000 people demonstrated in downtown Bangkok at the Democracy Monument (a monument to the 1932 coup that overthrew absolute monarchy), demanding a return to constitutional rule. The military government reacted with strong-arm tactics, and over a hundred people were killed by riot police. The action backfired, however, and brought about the downfall of the military regime. The military leaders were forced—by the King himself, it is said—into exile, and a much-hailed "democracy period" was launched.

An elected constitutional government ruled Thailand until October 1976, when student protests once again erupted in Bangkok and precipitated a crisis that brought about the return of military rule. This "democracy period," however, is passionately remembered among Thais as a time of unprecedented freedom of the press and of great public debates about the future of Thai society and politics. After the 1976 coup many leftist intellectuals became disillusioned with the government and, when the government cracked down on dissenters, an insurgent rebel force was created in the north.

There was another coup in 1977, and then another in 1980, which installed General Prem Tinsanulon as Prime Minister. In August 1988, in Thailand's first election since 1976, Chatichai Choonhaven became prime minister, and his government seems to be slowly but surely moving away from dominance by the military. Chatichai has great popular appeal among Thais, and he is fortunate in governing the country at a time when it is enjoying one of the fastest growth rates in all of Asia. Foreign investment is rising, tourism is flourishing, and Thais, at this point, are looking forward to a stronger and more stable country that can take the lead in regional development.

CHRONOLOGY OF
THAI DYNASTIES AND KINGDOMS

Dvaravati Period: loosely linked city-states around the fertile central plain.	Approximately
Nanzhao Kingdom of the Bai minority in Yunnan Province, China.	BC 600 – AD 1200
Khmer (Cambodian) influence	1000–1200
Sukhothai Kingdom, central Thailand	1238–1376
Ayutthaya Kingdom, central Thailand	1376–1765
Chakri Dynasty	1782–Present
Rama I (General Phya Chakri), capital moved to Bangkok	1782–1809
Rama II	1809–1824
Rama III (Phra Nang Klao)	1824–1851
Rama IV (King Mongkut)	1851–1868
Rama V (King Chulalongkorn)	1868–1910
Rama VI (King Vajiravudh)	1910–1925
Rama VII (King Prajadhipok)	1925–1935
Democratic coup, constitutional monarchy, coup leader Phibul Songkhram came to power.	1932
Rama VIII (King Ananda Mahidol)	1935–1946
Rama IX (King Bhumipol)	1946–Present

POLITICS AND GOVERNMENT

THAILAND has been ruled by a constitutional monarchy since 1932. There is a constitution—actually ten different constitutions since the first one was formulated in 1932—and a parliamentary system of government with an elected lower house, the House of Representatives; an upper house, the Senate, of political appointees; and a prime minister, who heads the party or parties that form a majority in the House. The monarch, King Bhumipol, is the head of state but he actually has little more power and is chiefly a ceremonial figure.

As is apparent from the account of the history of Thailand the military has played a very important role in 20th-century Thai politics — as evidenced most recently by the latest non-violent military coup of February 1991. Until very recently, every political party had to have the support of the military if it expected to achieve anything in the political arena. The Senate is largely made up of military appointees, and a joint session of the House and the Senate is still required for any discussion of constitutional matters.

The previous administration of Chatichai Choonhaven and his ruling coalition of six main parties had begun to move away from this military domination. In the summer of 1989 a constitutional amendment was approved to make the speaker of the House of Representatives the overall president of the parliament. This move attempted to diminish the Senate's— and therefore the military's influence.

Over the years, parliamentary elections for the house have not produced any majority party. Political power is obtained through careful coalition building, bargaining, negotiating, and backdoor understandings among various party leaders and the military. The current coalition government is dominated by the Chart Thai party— like other Thai parties, the Chart Thai is clearly linked to one personality, that of Chatichai Choonhaven — and includes other major parties, such as the Social Action Party and the Democratic Party. The ruling coalition is considered a center-right government with strong pro-business ties. The main opposition parties are the Prachakorn Thai and the Solidarity Party. Thai political parties have few major ideological differences; rather, they are mainly vehicles for different political personalities.

Thailand is divided into 73 provinces, each of which is administered by a governor appointed by the central government. Each province is sub-divided into districts, sub-districts, and villages.

ECONOMY

THAILAND'S economy has boomed and diversified in the 1980s, earning the country a justifiable reputation as one of the up-and-coming dragons of Asia. The current economic plan (1987 to 1992) has a target of 5% growth per year, but in 1988 the economy grew at a rate of 11% and the 1989 rate was almost as high.

Some of the most bullish sectors of the Thai economy are those related to foreign investment and export. Exports of manufactured goods, tourism, and foreign investment have all expanded in recent years. This expansion has placed Thailand in a good position to follow the other Asian dragons, such as South Korea, Taiwan, and Singapore, into the ranks of the so-called newly industrialized countries (NIC). Foreign investment has climbed steadily since 1980 and almost doubled between 1986 and 1987, from 34,610 million baht (US$1.4 million) in 1986 to 65,998 million baht (US$2.6 million) in 1987. Japan leads other countries in its investments in Thailand, followed by Taiwan, the western European countries, and the United States.

Like other Third World nations, Thailand has traditionally depended on exports of unprocessed agricultural and mineral products for foreign exchange. Such products formerly made up half of all exports, and in the 1960s, the export of such products as rice, rubber, maize, tapioca, and sugar grew at a rate of 5%. However, by the 1970s the percentage of total exports that were agricultural products began to decline, even as total exports grew at an annual rate of 25%. In their place, processed agricultural products, such as canned seafood and fruits, and especially light industrial products, such as textiles, garments, gems and electronic components, made up a larger and larger share of total exports. In the 1980s this trend continued at increased speed: primary agricultural products declined to one-fourth of total exports, while manufactured goods, especially textiles and garments, came to make up over half of total exports. Despite this decline, Thailand remains one of the world's five net food exporters—and the only one in Asia.

The United States is Thailand's largest export market, followed by Japan, Singapore, the Netherlands, Germany, and Hong Kong.

The average per capita income in 1987 was US$900, translating to a daily minimum wage of only 78 baht or US$3 for Bangkok, and 68 baht in rural areas. Of the other member states in the Association of Southeast Asian Nations (ASEAN), only Indonesia has lower wages than Thailand. The labor force boasts a literacy rate of nearly 90%, however; a very highly educated group by Asian standards.

About 80% of Thais are still engaged in agriculture. The northeast is the poorest region of the country, with the lowest inflation rate, lowest cost of living, and very little tourism. The north produces maize, tea, rice, and is an important source of teak for the lumber industry. In central Thailand, the most fertile and well-developed region, the main agricultural products are fruit, sugarcane, and rice. In the south, fishing, tin mining, and rubber production are the predominant industries.

In the northern hills above Chiang Mai and in the notorious Golden Triangle of northern Thailand, Burma, and Laos, the cultivation of opium is still a major industry. The opium poppy is not new to these hills. It has been cultivated for thousands of years, and was not introduced, for instance, to meet the heroin cravings of addicts in the West. In recent years hill tribe economies have become dependent on the cultivation of the poppy for their livelihood. Because poppies thrive on the steep slopes and poor soils of this region, it is the hill tribes' primary cash crop.

Since the mid-1960s, the cultivation of opium poppies has been dominated by various insurgent forces operating in these remote northern areas. In northern Thailand, Kuomintang or Nationalist Army refugees who fled China after the 1949 revolution are powerful opium warlords. The trade in this area, and also across the border in northern Burma, is dominated by anti-Burmese government rebels such as the Burmese Communist Party, the Shan States Army, and the Shan United Army. The most famous and notorious of these opium warlords is a half-Shan, half-Chinese general named Khun Sa. He commands the Shan United Army, an anti-Burmese government rebel force that finances its operations through the immense profits from the opium trade.

The U.S. government has devoted great sums of money and considerable numbers of personnel to help the Thai military fight the opium warlords in the north. They have tried crop substitution in the hills, but these attempts have largely failed in the face of the enormous profits to be made on opium and the Robin Hood-like reputation of the remote warlords. The U.S.-backed Thai military forces have had some success in recent years in pushing the cultivation and trade back further into the hills of Burma, Laos and China.

PEOPLE AND LANGUAGE

PEOPLE

Among Thailand's total population of approximately 50 million, there are numerous small ethnic groups and a majority Thai population, which is an amalgamation of many races. While some scholars believe that the Thais are actually a branch of the Chinese, most agree that they are an ethnic group that derives from Mon, Khmer, Burmese, Malay, Laotian, Persian, and Indian peoples.

Even before Thais migrated south from southeastern China into northern Indochina, there was a definite Thai culture dispersed throughout the coastal areas of what is now southern China and northern Vietnam. When the Thais did finally coalesce in modern-day Thailand, they met indigenous tribes known as Mons and Lawas. Thai culture and language were imposed upon these peoples, who were rapidly assimilated, but at the same time the Thais absorbed the Buddhist religion practiced by the Mons.

About 75% of Thailand's 50 million people are ethnic Thais, about 14% are of Chinese origin, and the remaining 11% include various hill tribes in the north, southern Malay-related tribes, and a very small minority group of Westerners who total about 14,000. The dominant hill tribe groups include the Karen, Meo, Yao, Akha, Lahu, and Lisu.

Bangkok is Thailand's most populous city, with approximately 6 million people crowding its bustling streets. Chiang Mai in the north is the country's second largest city, with a total population of just over 100,000. Throughout the country the literacy rate is well above 80% and the average life expectancy is 61 years; both figures compare very favorably with other developing nations' and express the general prosperity of this small country.

THE SOCIAL ORDER

The most important feature of Thai social order is the monarchy. There are few nations in the world today that exhibit such a profound and ubiquitous reverence for their traditional royal family. The king, queen, and their royal children are considered benevolent parents of the nation, and Thais throughout the country respect them deeply. In movie theaters, for instance, a portrait of the king is shown at the beginning, in lieu of previews, and the national anthem is played while the audience stands in reverence. The king's birthday (December 5) and the queen's (August 12) are both national holidays.

It is important that visitors understand the deep respect that Thais offer to their royals. When attending any kind of public ceremony at which a member of the royal family is present, watch your neighbors carefully and follow their lead in actions and responses.

Even in dealing with commoners—their neighbors, friends, colleagues, and foreign visitors—Thais are extremely courteous and respectful. Their culture contains numerous linguistic and traditional gestures of courtesy of which Western visitors should be aware.

Bangkok is, of course, more Westernized and modern than any other area in this diverse country, and in the capital ignorance of national customs will not be regarded as a great faux pas. Yet understanding how Thais treat each other will go a long way in helping visitors ingratiate themselves with their hosts.

The handshake, for instance, is a Western custom, and traditionally Thais prefer to greet each other with a *wai*. This is a gesture somewhat like the *namasti* of Indians, in which the palms of the hands are placed together in front of the chest as if in prayer; it is accompnied by a little bow of the head, a greeting, and a smile. Generally a younger person will wai an older person. The gesture is charming, gentle, and endearing.

Courtesy and politeness are important in Thai culture, yet these are gentle formalities that mask a much more simple relationship between peoples. This is demonstrated by the fact that up until the early years of the 20th century, most Thais were known only by their personal name. During the reign of Rama VI (1910–1925), Thais were obligated to choose a surname from lists especially prepared for that purpose. In daily life, Thais still refer to each other by their personal names and even in the telephone directories people are listed by their first names. Most people are addressed by their first names, though for more polite usage it may be prefixed by the Thai courtesy title *Khun*, equivalent to *Mr.*, *Mrs.*, *Miss*, *or Ms.*

RELIGION

The second important element of Thai culture is the Buddhist religion. Thais describe their political system as a Buddhist monarchy, and their religion is more than just a belief system or social custom; it is a way of life.

Over 90% of Thais are Theravada Buddhists. Also called Hinayana or the Lesser Vehicle, the Theravada sect is prevalent in Thailand, Burma, Laos, and Cambodia, where it was introduced by missionaries from India who were dispatched in the 3rd century BC to spread the word. Theravada is the earliest and, according to believers, least corrupted form of Buddhism, a religion that in its propagation over the centuries has taken many forms and has divided into many branches. Chinese and Japanese Buddhists, for instance, follow Mahayana Buddhism, the Greater Vehicle, a sect that branched off a few centuries after the death of Buddha in the 6th century BC.

You cannot help noticing the overwhelming influence of religion on everyday Thai life. In the midst of the honking, belching, diesel-fuming cacophony of Bangkok, you will still see dozens of orange-robed monks making their rounds through the streets each morning. Towering above the low-lying city dwellings, or above the rice paddies of the countryside, a golden-spired *wat*, or temple, will rise to inspiring heights.

There are over 20,000 monasteries in Thailand, and 150,000 monks throughout the country. It is a traditional and almost universally observed custom among Thai males to spend a certain period of time as monks—usually between finishing school and beginning a career or marrying. These Buddhist retreats usually occur during the annual Rains Retreat, a three-month period during the rainy season when all

A golden-spired Wat

monks stay within their monasteries. In addition, it is not unusual for a Thai male to retire from his job and spend the remainder of his life in a Buddhist monastery.

Among the general population, there is an unquestioned reverence and respect for Buddhist monks. Early each morning in every part of the country, monks leave their temples or monasteries to go begging for food and alms. Feeding monks, giving donations to the temples, and performing regular worship are all part of a lay Buddhist's efforts to acquire merit and to prevent a reincarnation as a lesser being. In rural Thailand, the village *wat* often functions as the local hostelry, the village news and employment center, school, hospital, dispensary, and community center.

In very simple terms, Buddhism is based upon the enlightenment of Siddhartha Guatama, the Buddha, in the 6th century BC. Buddha discovered what he called the Four Noble Truths: all existence is suffering; suffering is the result of craving, or desire; to eliminate suffering you must eliminate desire; the eight-fold path is the way to eliminate desire and obtain nirvana, the end of suffering.

The overriding importance of Buddhism in Thai life is underscored by the existence of an institutionalized Buddhist hierarchy in the country which combines religious strength with political and economic power. The *Sangha* is the name of the Buddhist brotherhood and it consists of two main sects, the Mahanikai and the Thammayut. The latter, founded by King Mongkut, is more rigorous and disciplined than the former, and its monks are allowed to eat only once each day.

The two main sects have recently been challenged by an unorthodox Buddhist organization called the *Santi Asoke* or Peace Above Peace. The leader of this sect, a former television celebrity named Phra Bodhirak, refuses to follow the religious discipline of the Sangha, and in the spring of 1989 he was defrocked. Yet the Santi Asoke is popular among many Buddhists in Bangkok and among several powerful politicians. The order has more than 1,000 of its own monks, who practice an austere regime of worship and discipline which includes strict vegetarianism. Given what many claim are the overriding political and business interests of the mainstream Buddhist order, the charismatic Phra Bodhirak's efforts to revive traditional Buddhist practices in Thailand have struck a chord.

In addition to the predominant religion of Buddhism, approximately 4% of Thais are Muslim and 0.6% are Christian. Most Thai Muslims live in the south, close to the border of Islamic Malaysia. Thailand's most resplendent mosque is found in Patani in Yala Province on the Malay border.

Remnants of pre-Buddhist religions in Thailand are also apparent. Brahmanism, a school of the Indian Hindu religion, influences some traditional Thai festivals including the Songkran and the Ploughing Ceremony. In addition, small and lovely spirit houses—dollhouse-sized temples adorned with flowers and incense — can be seen everywhere. Adorning the courtyards of homes and the intersections or corners on major highways, these spirit houses are erected to attract spirits who otherwise might harm the residents of the homes or drivers on the highways.

There are certain religious taboos that Western visitors should follow. It is unlawful in Thailand to commit any insulting act to an object or a place of religious worship. If a religious ceremony is under way when you visit a temple, do not disturb it. It is unlawful to impersonate a monk or holy man, and Buddhist priests are forbidden to touch or to be touched by a woman or to accept anything from the hand of a woman. If a woman wants to give something to a Buddhist monk, she should first hand the object or food to a man and have him hand it to the monk. Alternatively, she can put it down on a piece of the monk's saffron robe or on a handkerchief in front of him. All Buddhist images, large or small, ruined or not, are sacred in Thailand. Do not climb on or do anything disrespectful to images of the Buddha, even if they sit in the midst of centuries-old ruins.

The basic rules for getting along in this very religious country are to dress neatly wherever you go, and avoid going bare-chested or wearing revealing shorts or skirts or skimpy tops. Do not wear shoes inside a chapel or temple. In Muslim mosques, men should wear hats and women long pants or skirt, a long-sleeved blouse or sweater, and a scarf over the head.

LANGUAGE

The Thai language sounds entirely foreign to the untrained Western ear. It is one of the oldest languages in southeast Asia and is similar, in some respects, to Chinese. Like the Chinese language, Thai is tonal and monosyllabic, and each sound can have numerous different meanings depending upon the tone used when it is pronounced. There are five different tones in standard, central Thai: a level or mid-tone, a high tone, a low tone, a falling tone, and a rising tone. The script, a lovely swirligig, is written from left to right. It is of Sanskrit origin and consists of 44 consonants and 48 vowel and dipthong possibilities. While there is an official Thai-English transcription system, there still does not seem to be much uniformity in the English spellings given to Thai words.

Despite the difficulties of learning the Thai language, it is surprisingly easy to communicate with your Thai hosts. For one thing, English is Thailand's second language and is widely spoken throughout Bangkok and Chiang Mai. In the countryside, where English is less well-known, people are accustomed to dealing with visitors who speak little or no Thai, and rudimentary communication is not difficult using body language.

A basic Thai greeting, plus a polite *wai*, is an excellent way to begin communication. To say hello in Thai, if you are a man, say *Sawat dii khrap*; for women, *Sawat dii kha*.

Elegant Thai temple architecture, Bangkok

II Planning a Trip to Thailand

TOURIST INFORMATION

THE Tourism Authority of Thailand, commonly known as TAT, does a better-than-respectable job of keeping tourists happy inside Thailand and promoting the country to the curious crowds outside. It provides advice; maps of the country, towns, and cities; colorful booklets on the main tourist sites; and lists of recommended tour surveyors and salespeople.

The head office in Bangkok is open every day from 8:30 AM to 4:30 PM. There is a small office in the incoming passenger lounge at the Bangkok International Airport, and their telephone number is 523-8972/3.

TAT does more than just receive the lost and the weary. It warns visitors to beware of pickpockets and of people who offer "special guided tours" around the area or to "special" shopping outlets. There are a great many hucksters in Thailand, especially in Bangkok, and if you accept the services of a stranger, be on your toes. TAT is affiliated with the Tourist Assistance Center for people who have been robbed, cheated, or otherwise endangered and who are in need of "security assistance." In Bangkok, the Tourist Assistance telephone numbers are 281–5051, 282–8129.

TOURISM AUTHORITY OF THAILAND (TAT)

TAT OFFICES IN THAILAND

TAT Head Office, 4 Ratchadamnoen Nok Ave., Bangkok 10100; Telephone 282–1143/7; Fax 280–1744; Telex 72059 TAT BKK TH

Central Region

Saeng Chuto Rd., Amphoe Muang, Kanchanaburi 71000; Telephone (034) 511–200

382/1 Beach Rd., South Pattaya; Telephone (038) 428–750, 429–113

North

135 Praisani Rd., Amphoe Muang, Chiang Mai 50000; Telephone (053) 235–334

209/7–8 Surasi Trade Center, Boromtrailokanat Rd., Amphoe Muang, Phitsanulok 65000; Telephone (055) 252–742/3

Northeast

2104–2104 Mitraphap Rd., Tambon Nai Muang, Amphoe Muang, Nakhon Ratchasima 30000; Telephone (044) 243–427/751

Sala Prachakhom, Si Narong Rd., Amphoe Muang, Ubon Rachathani 34000; Telephone (054) 255–603

South

1/1 Soi 2 Niphat Uthit 3 Rd., Hat Yai, Songkhla 90110; Telephone (074) 243–747, 245–986

73–75 Phuket Rd., Amphoe Muang, Phuket 83000; Telephone (076) 212–212, 211–036

5 Talat Mai Rd., Ban Don, Amphoe Muang, Surat Thani 84000; Telephone (077) 282–828, 281–828

TAT OFFICES ABROAD

Australia
12th Floor, Royal Exchange Building, 56 Pitt St., Sydney 2000; Telephone (02) 277-549/0; Fax (02) 251-2465; Telex 23467 THAITC AA

France
Office National du Tourisme de Thailand, 90 Avenue des Champs Élysées, 75008 Paris; Telephone 4562-0865/6, 4562-8748; Fax 4563-7888; Telex 650093 TATPARF

Germany
Thailandisches Fremdenverkehrburo, Bethmann Strasse 58/IV D-6000, Frankfurt/Main 1; Telephone (69) 295-704/804; Fax (69) 281-468; Telex 413542 TAFRAD

Hong Kong
Room 401, Fairmont House, 8 Cotton Tree Drive Central; Telephone 868-0732/0854; Fax 868-4585; Telex 63092 HKTAT HX

Italy
Ente Nazionale per il Turismo Thailandese, 50 Via Barberini, 00187 Rome; Telephone (06) 474-7410/7660; Fax (06) 474-7660; Telex 626139 TAT I

Japan
Hibiya Mitsui Bldg., 1-2 Yurakucho 1-Chome, Chiyoda-ku, Tokyo 100; Telephone (03) 580-6776/7, 508-0237; Fax (03) 508-7808; Telex J33964 TATTYO

5th Floor, Hirano-Machi Yachiyo Bldg., 2-8-1 Hirano-Machi, Higashi-ku, Osaka 541; Telephone (06) 231-4434; Fax (06) 231-4337; Telex J64675

cont...

TAT OFFICES ABROAD *(cont.)*

> **United Kingdom**
>
> 49 Albemarle St., London WIX 3FE; Telephone (71) 499–7670/9; Telex 298760 THAI TRG, TAT/LON
>
> **United States**
>
> Suite 1101, 3440 Wilshire Blvd., Los Angeles, CA 90010; Telephone (213) 382–2353; Fax (213) 380–6476; Telex 686208 TTC LSA
>
> Suite 2449, 5 World Trade Center, New York, NY 10048; Telephone (212) 432–0433; Fax (212) 912–0920; Telex 667612 TOT UW

TRAVEL OPTIONS

GROUP TOURS

There are literally dozens of good tour companies throughout the English-speaking world that offer tour options to Thailand. Many tours are of the "Oriental odyssey" variety, stopping by in Thailand en route between Hong Kong and Singapore or the South Pacific and Australia. There are shopping tours to Bangkok, Hong Kong, and Singapore; "Oriental classics," which stop off in some of China's famous cities in addition to Thailand; and "Five capitals," with visits to Tokyo, Beijing, Bangkok, Singapore, and Hong Kong. Other tours concentrate solely on the kingdom, with trips to Bangkok, Chiang Mai, and one or more of the southern seaside resorts.

Some tour companies, such as Innerasia Expeditions, Himalayan Travel, and Mountain Travel, specialize in adventure tours to the kingdom, and these can be an exciting introduction to some of the more beautiful and offbeat regions. Innerasia, for instance, offers "deluxe adventures" ranging from island hopping in the seas off the southern isthmus to trekking among the hill tribes in the north.

A selective list of some of the better and more established tour companies in the United States and Canada with Thai itineraries follows.

TOUR COMPANIES

Abercrombie & Kent International, 1420 Kensington Rd., Oak Brook, IL 60521–2106; Telephone (312) 954–2944, (800) 323–7308

Adventure Center, 5540 College Ave., Oakland, CA 94618; Telephone (415) 654–1879, (800) 228–8747

American Express, 100 Church St., New York, NY 10007; Telephone (212) 640–5130, (800) 241–1700

Amity Tours, 1219 Arguello Ave., Redwood City, CA 94063; Telephone (415) 364–5930, (800) 523–8406

Asia Passage, 168 State St., Teaneck, NJ 07666; Telephone (201) 837-1400, (800) 488-0604

ATS/Tourworld, P.O. Box 2078, Suite 201, 1101 East Broadway, Glendale, CA 91205; Telephone (818) 502–1914, (800) 423–2880

Cultural Tours, 360–2600 Granville St., Vancouver, BC V6H 3V3; Telephone (604) 736–7671, (800) 663–1751

Innerasia Expeditions, 2627 Lombard St., San Francisco, CA 94123; Telephone (415) 922–0448, (800) 551–1769

Inter/Pacific Tours International, 111 East 15 St., New York, NY 10003; Telephone (212) 953–6010, (800) 221–3594

Kuo Feng Tours, 15 Mercer St., New York, NY 10013; Telephone (212) 219–8383, (800) 233–8687

Mountain Travel, 5420 Fairmont Ave., El Serrito, CA 94530; Telephone (415) 527–8100, (800) 227–2384

Odyssey Tours, 1821 Wilshire Blvd., Santa Monica, CA 90403; Telephone (213) 453–1042, (800) 654–7975

cont...

Pacific Asia Tours, Suite 300, 8447 Wilshire Blvd., Beverly Hills, CA 90211; Telephone (213) 653-3393, (800) 843-3851

Pacific Delight Tours, 132 Madison Ave., New York, NY 10016; Telephone (212) 684-7707, (800) 221-7179

Solrep International, 2524 Nottingham, Houston, TX 77005; Telephone (713) 529-5547, (800) 213-0985

Trans National Travel, The Trans National Bldg., 2 Charlesgate West, Boston, MA 02215; Telephone (617) 262-0123

Unitours, 8 South Michigan Ave., Chicago, IL 60603; Telephone (312) 782-1590, (800) 621-0495

INDEPENDENT TRAVEL

Many of the travel companies listed above can also arrange transportation and accommodations for individuals wishing to travel on their own in Thailand. With its many years of experience in tourism, Thailand is one of the most convenient and easy travel destinations for independent travelers in Asia. In Bangkok, Chiang Mai, Phuket, and Pattaya, there are first-class hotels and restaurants with employees who speak excellent English and who can organize local sightseeing tours of their region. Flight connections between major Thai cities—on the excellent national carrier, Thai Airways—are frequent and relatively inexpensive. Trains and buses are also numerous.

If you wish to travel off the beaten track in Thailand, transportation and accommodations are less deluxe, but by no means prohibitively primitive. See the chapters that follow for information on these areas and, if you are looking for the most convenient means of getting to and staying in more remote areas, contact local Thai travel agents for specific details upon your arrival in Bangkok.

Bangkok has thousands of official and ad-hoc travel agents, many of which offer cut-rate airfares around Asia and budget sightseeing tours around the country. Some are less than completely reliable. A list of TAT-recommended Bangkok travel and tour agencies follows.

TAT — RECOMMENDED TRAVEL AGENCIES

Arlymear Travel Co., 109 Surawongse Rd., C.C.T. Bldg., Bangkok 10500; Telephone 236–0103; Telex 87361 TH; Cable ARLYMEAR

Diethelm Travel, 544 Ploenchit Rd., Bangkok 10500, Telephone 252–4041/9; Telex TH 81183 DIETRAV

East West Tours Co., 135 Soi Sanam Khli (Soi Polo), Wireless Rd., Bangkok 10500; Telephone 253–0681/5; Fax 253–6178; Telex EWTEX TH 82971

Eurothai Travel Service Co., Suite 201, Wongwaiwit Bldg., 164/14 North Sathorn Rd., Bangkok 10500; Telephone 236–6382/6266; Telex 21153 EUROT TH

Siam Express Ltd., 14th floor, 90/34–35 Sathornthani Bldg., North Sathorn Rd., Bangkok 10500; Telephone 236–9570/9; Telex 82690 SIAMEX TH

World Travel Service Co., 1053 Charoen Krung Rd., Bangkok; 10500; Telephone 233–5900/9; Telex 82680 WTX BKK TH

COSTS

GROUP TOURS

Tours to Thailand and tours that include Thailand in their Asian itineraries tend to vary widely in costs, depending on the degree of luxury offered along the way. Abercrombie & Kent, for instance, offers a 21-day tour that includes Singapore and Hong Kong and costs $3,990 per person, not including airfare to Hong Kong. The single-occupancy supplement for this tour is $1,090. They also offer a 14-day tour to Thailand and Hong Kong for $2,965 per person with a $915 single-occupancy supplement.

These prices are in the upper end of the market, and offer the highest standards of luxury and convenience during your tour.

A more reasonably priced trip is offered by Cultural Tours in Vancouver, in which a 14-day tour will cost $2,895, including airfare from Vancouver. Mountain Travel specializes in adventure tours, and its land prices for Thailand are quite low: a 7-day tour starts at $600 per person, and a 15-day one starts at $1,050, not including airfare to Thailand. Innerasia Expeditions' 15-day tours average $2,300 per person, not including airfare.

INDEPENDENT TRAVEL

As can be inferred from the above prices, you can travel in Thailand as cheaply or as expensively as your purse requires. Hotels in Bangkok, Thailand's most expensive city, run the full gamut from international-class, four-star hotels (one hotel, the Oriental, has long held the reputation of being the world's *best* hotel!) costing from US$50 to $100 per night, to cut-rate, dirt-cheap dives that can be as inexpensive as US$2 to $4 per night.

Food expenses in Thailand are equally varied. At expensive hotels and restaurants that cater to the tourist crowd, prices may run as high as US$15 to $30 per person, but an average meal in Bangkok should not be more than US$10. Outside of Bangkok, food prices are much cheaper, and TAT estimates that average living expenses outside of Bangkok can be as low as US$10 per day. Such economical traveling costs leave one with money for purchases of Thai silk, gems, handicrafts, and numerous attractive souvenirs.

INTERCITY TRAVEL

It is not expensive to travel around Thailand. Thai Airways is an excellent airline and offers frequent and convenient flights around the nation. In addition to Bangkok, there are 21 provincial airports throughout the country, and you can reach just about any destination on Thai Airways. Flights are surprisingly inexpensive: a one-way flight to Phuket from Bangkok is about US$50, and to Chiang Mai in the north about the same.

The north and the south of the nation are linked by an efficient and well-run national rail system with first-, second-, and third-class carriages. There are surcharges for express trains, for air-conditioning, and for the upper-class cabins, which are amazingly comfortable and private. Traveling to Chiang Mai from Bangkok in a first-class, air-conditioned, two-bed cabin should cost approximately US$35 for the 14-hour ride. Third-class travel on trains, with no beds or air-conditioning, is obviously the cheapest method of travel.

The final means of travel within Thailand is the ubiquitous tour bus, both government-owned and private. Government-owned tour buses are very cheap and very slow. The better bets are the numerous private charter bus companies that run charters between Bangkok and other major tourist destinations such as Chiang Mai, Surat, Hat Yai, Pattaya, Phuket, and Krabi. Private companies can be more expensive than the government-run buses, but the extra cost is usually worth it in air-conditioning, speed, and comfort. An overnight trip to Chiang Mai on a private bus should cost approximately US$10. Tickets for these buses can be booked at most hotels or at any Bangkok travel agency.

WHEN TO GO

CLIMATE

Thailand has a tropical climate with three principal seasons: cool from November through February, hot and humid from March through June, and hot and rainy from July through October. Average temperatures throughout the year are about 83°F (30°C), ranging from a high of 96°F (35°C) to lows of 62°F (17°C). The most comfortable season for Thai travel is during the cool months of the winter.

FESTIVALS

Thailand has innumerable local and national festivals that offer wonderful distractions for the foreign visitor. Check with your local TAT office for the specific annual schedule, as dates change with the lunar calendar each year.

Beginning the year in January, Thailand's most exciting festivals include the **Chaiyaphum Elephant Roundup** in Surin province in the northeast. This is a reenactment of medieval warfare and a two-day extravaganza put on largely for the benefit of tourists. In Chiang Mai at about this time of year, the **Bo Sang Umbrella Fair** celebrates the traditional northern skill of painted umbrella making with contests, exhibitions, and parades.

About February of each year, Chiang Mai also celebrates its annual **Flower Festival** with spectacular floral floats, flower displays, handicraft sales, and parades. Another northern event, in the town of Nakhon Phanom along the Mekong River, is the important

Buddhist festival called **Phra That Phanom Chedi Homage-paying Fair,** which celebrates a relic of the Buddha with an annual five-day fair. The relic, a footprint of the Buddha, has become the symbol of northeastern Thailand. The first important Buddhist holiday of the year also takes place in February, or, according to the Thai calendar, on the full moon of the third lunar month. This festival is called **Magha Puja** and is a Buddhist holy day and a national holiday, with ceremonies taking place during the day at temples throughout the country.

In March, dove lovers from across southeast Asia gather in Yala for a **Barred Ground Dove Festival**, a dove cooing contest with more than 1,400 competitors annually.

Chakri Day on April 6 each year is a national holiday celebrating the founding of the Chakri Dynasty, the current ruling family in Thailand. The **Pattaya Festival** also takes place annually in the beginning of April with food and floral floats, beauty contests, and fireworks. The most important festival of the year is **Songkran**, the Thai New Year, which begins with a national holiday on April 13. It is kept for three days throughout the country and marked by such customs as throwing water on one and all as a sign of purification. Prepare to be drenched!

In late April or early May each year a **Royal Plowing Ceremony** takes place in Bangkok to mark the official commencement of the rice planting season. This ceremony is presided over by the King and is a holdover from ancient Brahmin customs.

Coronation Day on May 5 is another national holiday, commemorating King Bhumipol's coronation in 1950. Across the nation on the first full moon of the sixth lunar month (usually in May), the **Visakha Puja** is celebrated to mark the birth, enlightenment, and death of the Buddha. This is the holiest of all Buddhist holy days, and across the country temples are crowded with worshippers.

In June, the **Thai International Swan Boat Race** is scheduled, for the benefit of tourists, with competitors from several countries racing their traditional boats on the Chao Phraya river in Bangkok. **Asanhabucha** is a national holiday that falls on the full-moon day of the eighth lunar month (usually July) and marks the Buddha's first sermon to his disciples and the beginning of **Phansa**, the annual Rains Retreat, during which monks vow to stay inside their monasteries for study and worship. In Ubon Ratchathani in the northeast, the commencement of **Phansa** is observed with a **Candle Festival** of carved beeswax candles carried spectacularly in parades.

In August, the **Rambutan Fair** is a festival in Surat Thani to

Candle Festival held at Ubon Ratchathan in July

celebrate the Rambutan tree with floats, exhibitions, and demonstrations of trained monkeys who harvest coconuts. On August 12, the **Queen's Birthday** is a national holiday, and impressive decorations are displayed on all public buildings in Bangkok.

A **Chinese Vegetarian Festival** in Phuket each September commemorates the immigrant Chinese workers who arrived in this area in the 19th century. The local residents confine themselves to a vegetarian diet for nine days, while the devout indulge in such ascetic exercises as skewered cheeks, pierced tongues, and firewalking.

Ok Phansa, which usually falls in October, marks the end of **Phansa** with various celebrations across the country. In Surat Thani, the **Chak Phra Festival** features images of the Buddha pulled in ceremonial processions in carriages and boats. In Nakhon Phanom on the bank of Mekong River intricately decorated little boats with lighted candles drift across the water. October 23 is **Chulalongkorn Day**, a national holiday to celebrate Thailand's much-loved 19th-century monarch.

A nationwide festival in November called **Loi Krathong** has been called Thailand's loveliest festival. Each year, under the full moon Thais fill their rivers, canals, lakes, and streams with small lotus-shaped banana-leaf boats, each with a lighted candle, incense, a flower, and a small coin to honor the water spirits and wash away last year's sins. This festival marks the end of the rainy season and falls on the full-moon of the 12th lunar month.

The **Surin Elephant Roundup** is one of Thailand's most internationally famous festivals and takes place on the third weekend in November. Over a hundred trained elephants are assembled in the provincial capital of Surin to demonstrate their log-pulling capabilities and to parade spectacularly around the town.

In December the **King's Birthday** on December 5 is a national holiday marked by a large military parade in Bangkok two days before the birthday. **Constitution Day** on December 10 is also a national holiday.

III   Getting to Thailand

VISAS AND HEALTH CERTIFICATES

ALL foreign nationals visiting the Kingdom of Thailand must have valid passports. The only exception are Hong Kong Chinese who carry their Certificate of Identity instead of a passport.

VISA APPLICATIONS

For stays of 15 days or less, no visas are required for visitors to Thailand who hold an on-going plane or train ticket (on-going tickets are rarely checked). A transit visa will allow you to stay in Thailand for 30 days, a regular tourist visa for 60 days, and a non-immigrant visa for 90 days. These visas are good for only one entry to Thailand and are valid for 90 days from the date of issue. Multiple-entry visas are also available.

If you stay in Thailand for 90 days or more in one year, a tax clearance will be required before you leave the country.

Visas are available at Thai diplomatic missions around the world and the cost is US$5 to $10.

VISA EXTENSIONS

You can apply for visa extensions at the Immigration Office in Bangkok (Soi Suan Phlu, Sathon Tai Rd, Bangkok 10120; Telephone 286–9230/28/31). The fee is approximately 500 baht (US$20) and an extension of more than 30 days is usually not allowed.

HEALTH CERTIFICATES

No inoculations or vaccinations are required unless you are coming from or have passed through areas with cholera or typhoid. It is advisable to have a tetanus booster and a cholera immunization before a trip to Thailand. If you are traveling outside of Bangkok, it is advisable to take malaria pills before, during, and after your travels. Contact your doctor for a prescription.

THAI DIPLOMATIC MISSIONS ABROAD (Selected)

Australia

Royal Thai Embassy, 111 Empire Circuit, Yarralumla, Canberra, ACT 2600; Telephone 273–1149/2937

Canada

Royal Thai Embassy, 180 Island Park Dr., Ottawa, Ontario K1Y OA2; Telephone (613) 722–4444

Malaysia

Royal Thai Embassy, 206 Jalan Ampang, Kuala Lumpur, Malaysia; Telephone 248–0958; Telex TATKL 31089 (MA)

Singapore

Royal Thai Embassy, 370 Orchard Rd., Singapore 0923; Telephone 235–7694/901; Telex 65 7335653

United Kingdom

Royal Thai Embassy, 29–30 Queen's Gate, London, SW7 5JB; Telephone (71) 589–2853/2857/2944/7338/0173

United States

Royal Thai Consulate-General, 801 N. La Brea Ave., Los Angeles, CA 90038; Telephone (213) 937–1899

Royal Thai Consulate-General, Suite 1834, 35 East Wacker Drive, Chicago, IL 60601; Telephone (312) 326–2447/8

Royal Thai Consulate-General, Room 505–507, 53 Park Place, New York, NY 10007; Telephone (212) 732–8166/7

Royal Thai Embassy, 2300 Kalorama Rd., NW, Washington, DC 20008; Telephone (202) 241–2542/3

INTERNATIONAL ROUTINGS TO THAILAND

BY AIR

Don Muang International Airport in Bangkok is served by 30 international airlines, including the national carrier, Thai International Airways. Thai International has frequent flights from North America to Bangkok, and their port of departure is Seattle. From Seattle, an economy class one-way ticket is US$940, and business class one-way is $1,010. Discounted fares are much cheaper, of course, but must be purchased at least two weeks ahead of time and availability is limited. Discounted Thai International round-trips from Seattle are $1,000 with no stops enroute, or $1,120 round-trip with stops allowed.

Other major airlines with connections to Bangkok include Northwest, Korean Air, China Airlines, Cathay Pacific, Finnair, British Airways, and Air Canada. If you are in Hong Kong, Singapore, or other major Asian cities, there are countless flights to and from Bangkok on dozens of different airlines. Air China, the People's Republic of China's rather spartan national carrier, will take you to and from Bangkok and Beijing, or Bangkok and Kunming (the capital of Yunnan Province in southwest China) once or twice a week.

Thai International also has connections from Bangkok to and from Penang and Kuala Lumpur in Malaysia, Vientiane in Laos, and Hanoi in Vietnam.

AIRPORT TRANSFER INFORMATION

Don Muang International Airport is 12 mi (19 km) outside of Bangkok, and it is very easy to get back and forth between the airport and the city. There is an airport bus to the City Terminal at the Asia Hotel which costs 60 baht per person. Another airport bus, run by Thai International, will also take you to various hotels in Bangkok for approximately 100 baht. A taxi should cost you approximately 300 baht.

If you are eager to head directly to the beach, an air-conditioned coach will take you from the airport to Pattaya for 180 baht. These buses leave three times a day at 9 AM, 12 noon, and 7 PM.

AIRLINE OFFICES IN BANGKOK

Aeroflot, Telephone: 233–6965/7
Air France, Telephone: 236–0157/8
Air India, Telephone: 256–9614/20
Air Lanka, Telephone: 236–0159
Alitalia, Telephone: 234–5257
British Airways, Telephone: 252–9817
Canadian International, Telephone: 251–4521
Cathay Pacific, Telephone: 233–6105/9
China Airlines, Telephone: 253–4241/4
Egypt Air, Telephone: 233–7601/3
Finnair, Telephone: 251–5012
Garuda, Telephone: 233–0918/2
Iraqi Air Lines, Telephone: 235–5733/7
Japan Air Lines, Telephone: 233–2440
KLM, Telephone: 235–5150/9
Korean Air, Telephone: 234–9283/9
Lufthansa, Telephone: 234–1350/9
Malaysian Airline, Telephone: 243–9790/4
Northwest Airlines, Telephone: 253–4822
Pakistan International, Telephone: 234–2961/4
Philippine Airlines, Telephone: 233–2359/2
Qantas, Telephone: 236–9193/6
Royal Jordanian, Telephone: 236–0030/9
Royal Nepal Airlines, Telephone: 233–3921/4
Sabena, Telephone: 233–5940/1
Scandinavian Airlines, Telephone: 253–4181/5
Saudi Arabian, Telephone: 236–9395/9
Singapore, Telephone: 236–0440
Swissair, Telephone: 233–2935/8
Thai Airways International, Telephone: 513–0120/36

BY LAND

Until very recently, the only overland access to Thailand was from northern Malaysia. This is a busy border, and there are innumerable trains, buses, and taxis that will take you across. There are direct trains to and from Thailand and Kuala Lumpur, Singapore, or smaller Malaysian cities.

You can now also travel overland between Thailand and Laos in the northeast; the usual disembarkation points are the northern cities of Chiang Mai and Chiang Rai.

BY SEA

For the adventurous at heart, there is a ferry that travels from Kuala Perlis in northern Malaysia to Satun in southern Thailand. The voyage takes approximately one and a half hours and, while not in the least deluxe, it offers an interesting entry to the kingdom.

ENTRANCE AND EXIT PROCEDURES

CUSTOMS

Thai customs officials are very strict with regard to smuggling drugs or other prohibited items, such as obscene literature and firearms.

You can bring 200 cigarettes or 250 grams of tobacco and one bottle of liquor into the country, as well as one still camera with five rolls of film, or one movie camera with three rolls of film–or both.

A visitor to Thailand is not allowed to bring more than 10,000 baht into the country, nor leave with more than 500 baht without special permission.

In order to leave Thailand with any Thai antique or art object, one must obtain an export license. It is forbidden to take out of Thailand any images of the Buddha or of a Bodhisattva, or fragments taken from such images.

An export license to export art and antiques can be obtained from the Department of Fine Arts at the National Museum. The procedure for doing so is somewhat complicated: photograph the front view of the object(s) and make two postcard-sized prints. With a copy of your passport, take the photos to the National Museums Division in Bangkok or to the Chiang Mai National Museum in Chiang Mai or the Songkhla National Museum in Songkhla. Begin these proceedings at least three to five days before the date of shipment or departure. For further information, telephone the Bangkok National Museum at either 224-1370, 224-1402, or 224-1396.

EXIT FORMALITIES

There is an airport tax of 150 baht when you leave Thailand on an international flight. A tax of 20 baht is required on domestic flights.

If you have stayed in Thailand longer than 90 days within one calendar year, or if you have received a Thai work permit or a Certificate of Residence, or have entered on a nonimmigrant visa in the business class, you are required to have a Tax Clearance Certificate before you leave the country. Applications may be made to the Tax Clearance Sub-Division, Central Operation Division, Revenue Department, 1 Chakrapongse Rd,, Phranakorn District, Bangkok.

IV

Traveling in Thailand

KNOW BEFORE YOU GO

ELECTRICITY AND WATER

Electrical current throughout Thailand is 220 volts and 50 cycles with both square and round-pegged outlets. Most international-class hotels have 110-volt outlets, however, for shavers and similar electrical devices.

Tap water in Thailand is simply not safe for drinking. Use only distilled or boiled water. Most restaurants serve bottled water with meals.

HEALTH AND SAFETY

Unlike many similar Asian countries, Thai street vendors are generally hygenic and safe. This is a great bonus because the street food in Thailand is phenomenally good and quite inexpensive. Though nibbling travelers have been known to suffer unpleasant intestinal reactions in Thailand to all the uniquely Thai bacteria in their food, basic precautions should allow you great culinary adventures on Thai streets. Avoid the water—and ice sold in soda drinks or ice-cooled refreshments on the street. Disdaining an iced drink, most travelers drink their street-side soda poured into a plastic bag.

Other than guarding against malaria with prophylactic pills and perhaps a mosquito net, and carrying along some Lomotil for the ever-possible scourge of diarrhea, your chief health concern in Thailand should be the sun. Wear sunglasses and a hat, if you can, and cover yourself well with sun block if you plan to stay outside for any length of time. The sun in Thailand is much stronger than is immediately apparent, and even a few hours in the midday sun could result in serious burns.

If you do have a more serious health problem, there are some very good hospitals in Bangkok and Chiang Mai

---

HOSPITALS IN BANGKOK AND CHIANG MAI

The Bangkok Christian Hospital, 124 Silom Rd., Bangkok; Telephone: 233–6981/9
The Seventh Day Adventist Hospital, 430 Phisanuloke Rd., Bangkok
Chiang Mai Hospital, Suanduk Rd., Chiang Mai
McCormick Hospital, Nawarat Rd., Chiang Mai

If you trek among the hill tribes in the north, you will be inundated with requests for medical help by the local people. They will suddenly appear at your lodging with cuts and gashes, boils and goiters, complaining of headaches and other illnesses. Obviously, previous foreign guests have showered them with medical attention. If you carry antiseptic, bandages, aspirin, or other mild first-aid equipment, you may find it all used up by the time you come down from the hills.

SAFETY

Thailand is not an unsafe country in which to travel. There have been incidents, however, which highlight the need for caution, especially if you are a woman traveling on your own.

Avoid the gaggles of "unofficial" taxis, especially in Bangkok and especially if you are a woman and it is nighttime. Stick with official taxis or official buses. The area around Bangkok's main train station is particularly notorious for hassles to women travelers, and all cheap hotel rooms should be carefully inspected for peepholes and sturdy locks.

Pickpockets and con men are notorious in Bangkok. Stories abound about the traveler on a crowded city bus who disembarks, only to find the back of his/her shirt or a dress sliced open and a hidden money bag mysteriously and unnoticably gone. Keep your valuables close to your body, preferably in front on a money belt, and store the rest in the hotel safe. Be wary of people who approach you with special deals, special stores, or special tours. These people are far more savvy than you about how to get around and get lost in Bangkok.

Avoid at all cost any involvement with drugs in Thailand. People may offer to sell you something, but many tourists have found that the sale was a sting: the tourist ends up in prison and the seller ends up with a hefty reward from the local police station.

A woman traveling alone may be hassled by Western and Thai men alike. The majority of tourists to Thailand continue to be single males, and many have just one thing on their minds for their vacation. You may cross their line of vision at the wrong time. Just don't make friends easily, and if you can, hook up with other travelers as you move through the more remote areas of the country. Thai men may "come on" to you, but they are easily dissuaded if you meet them with a firm and absolute refusal—of dinner, a walk along the beach, a trip to his "friend's" home, etc.

Aware of these security problems, the Thai authorities have set up a Tourist Police Department with English-speaking officers to help tourists in trouble. If you need assistance in Bangkok, call the Tourist Assistance Center at 281-5051 between 8 AM and midnight. There are bilingual Tourist Police Departments attached to TAT offices in Pattaya, Chiang Mai, Hat Yai, and Phuket as well.

TIME AROUND THE WORLD

Thailand time is Greenwich Mean Time plus 7 hours. Thus, midnight in Bangkok is 5 PM the same evening in London. Bangkok time is 12 hours ahead of U.S. Eastern Standard Time, 13 ahead of Central, 14 ahead of Mountain, and 15 ahead of Pacific.

When it is noon in Bangkok, the local time in the following cities is

Amsterdam	6 AM
Beirut	7 AM
Cairo	7 AM
Chicago	11 PM previous day
Dallas	11 PM previous day
Frankfurt	6 AM
Hong Kong	1 PM
Honolulu	7 PM previous day
London	5 AM
Los Angeles	9 PM previous day
Montreal	midnight that day
Nairobi	8 AM
New York	midnight that day
Paris	6 AM
Rio de Janeiro	2 AM
Rome	6 AM

San Francisco	9 PM previous day
Singapore	1 PM
Sydney	3 PM
Taipei	1 PM
Tokyo	2 PM
Vancouver	9 PM previous day
Zurich	6 AM

BUSINESS HOURS

Government offices are open from 8:30 AM to 4:30 PM Monday through Friday. There is usually a lunch break from noon to 1:00 PM. Banking hours are from 8:30 AM to 3:30 PM Monday through Friday. The General Post Offices keep the same schedule as government offices, but in many post offices a 24-hour cable service is available. Private shops are generally open from 8 AM to 8 PM daily, and many night markets in Bangkok keep the streets hopping far into the wee hours of the morning.

RELIGIOUS SERVICES

Thailand has always been known for religious tolerance and freedom of worship. Sizable minorities of Muslims, Hindus, and Sikhs follow their ancient religious traditions, and there are also some Thai Christians. Jewish and Christian services are available in many localities for visitors.

TIPPING

Surprisingly, given the numbers of Western tourists in the kingdom, direct tipping in hotels and visitor-oriented restaurants is not expected. Most bills come with a 10 or 15% service charge already added to the purchase costs—check carefully! If a taxi driver helps with your luggage or with special requests, he expects to be tipped. Otherwise, such tipping is optional.

MORES AND MANNERS

It is considered very rude in Thailand to point your foot at a person or especially at any kind of Buddhist image. The foot is the lowest and therefore dirtiest limb of the body. At the same time, the head is regarded as the highest part of the body, and one should never touch a Thai head. As part of this simple yet complex system of respect and propriety, young people will try to keep their heads lower than those of older people in order to avoid giving the impression of "looking down" on their elders.

As in all Asian countries, it is generally frowned upon to exhibit anger or lose your temper in public. This may seem quite a challenge in the face of the heat and crowds of Bangkok, for instance, but this overwhelming frenzy is precisely the reason native Thais avoid public passions. Keep cool, go slow, take your time, and everything will work itself out. If you expect immediate answers or cool efficiency, you run the risk of exhibiting poor manners—a bad strategy in any case—and you may drive yourself into a completely ineffective and unhealthy temper.

MONEY, CURRENCY, AND BANKING

CURRENCY

The national currency is the baht (the word is pronounced "bawt"), which is divided into 100 satang. Baht notes can be distinguished by their colors: the 500 baht note is purple, the 100 is red, the 20 is green, and the 10 is brown. Coins come in denominations of 5, 2, and 1 baht, 50 and 25 satang. The coins are difficult to distinguish, however, so study your handful of change carefully to learn the different values.

One baht equals about four U.S. cents, and one U.S. dollar is the equivalent of about 25 baht.

TRAVELERS' CHECKS AND CREDIT CARDS

Travelers' checks in U.S. dollars are the easiest to change in Thailand, and there are countless money changers and banks that will accept these checks. Hotel exchange counters generally offer a lower rate of exchange than do the banks and authorized money changers on the streets.

If you are carrying travelers' checks in a currency other than U.S. dollars, it is best to change your money in Bangkok, where you are likely to get a better rate.

Major credit cards are generally accepted all over Bangkok as well as in the better hotels and restaurants in the major tourist spots outside of Bangkok such as Chiang Mai, Phuket, and Pattaya. If you are

EFFECTIVE EXCHANGE RATES FOR THE THAI BAHT

Country	Denomination	Baht
Australia	A$	19.4743
Belgium	BF	0.8182
Brazil	Cz$	0.1562
Canada	CND	21.7580
China	Yuan	4.8090
Denmark	KR	4.3863
France	FF	4.9648
Germany	DM	16.9014
Hong Kong	HK$	3.2269
India	R	1.3903
Indonesia	Rp	0.0135
Italy	L	0.0224
Japan	Yen	0.1871
Korea	W	0.0352
Malaysia	M$	9.2983
Mexico	P	0.0085
Netherlands	G	14.9799
New Zealand	NZ$	14.9019
Norway	Kr	4.3058
Pakistan	R	1.1544
Philippines	Peso	0.9248
Portugal	E	0.1891
Singapore	S$	14.4718
Spain	P	0.2646
Sweden	Kr	4.4945
Taiwan	NT$	0.9446
United Kingdom	£	48.8808
United States	US$	25.1509

Note: To be used as guidelines only; actual rates fluctuate daily.

traveling to more remote areas, it is best to carry cash, as credit cards will not be accepted as payment. There is an American Express agent at SEA Tours, Room 414, Siam Center, 965 Rama I Rd., Bangkok.

COMMUNICATIONS AND NEWS MEDIA

ALL major hotels in Thailand provide telex, cable, and overseas telephone services.

POSTAL SERVICE

The mail service in Thailand is generally considered reliable and efficient. Post offices throughout the nation follow the same hours as other government offices. The Bangkok General Post Office is open from 8 AM to 6 PM, Monday through Friday, and from 9 AM to 1 PM on Saturday, Sunday, and public holidays. Provincial post offices generally close earlier in the day, about 4:30 PM. There is a 24-hour-a-day telegram service from the Bangkok General Post Office.

INCOMING CORRESPONDENCE

You can, of course, receive incoming correspondence at your hotel. If you are truly traveling, however, poste restante mail services seem to work fairly well at the major post offices in Thailand. Be sure to tell your friends and families to highlight (i.e. capitalize and underline) your surname, as Thai postal clerks may file your letter under the wrong name if they are unsure which is the surname.

TELECOMMUNICATIONS

TELEPHONE

Domestic long-distance calls may be dialed direct on private as well as public (blue) telephones. The public telephones tend to be unreliable, however, and it is best in any case to ask the help of a Thai speaker when you are dialing long-distance around the country.

Direct-dial international phone calls are easy from any of Bangkok's major hotels, or from Bangkok's Central General Post Office on New Rd., open 24 hours a day. Outside of Bangkok, it is best to place your calls from the town's central telephone exchange (often the Post Office), or from a major hotel, if there is one. Keep in mind that any hotel places a hefty surcharge on any international call.

Thailand's country code, used for calling from outside the kingdom, is 66. Area codes for major Thai cities are:

Ayutthaya	(035)
Bangkok	(02)
Chiang Mai	053)
Chiang Rai	(054)
Krabi	(075)
Pattaya	(038)
Phuket	(076)
Sukhothai	(055)
Surat Thani	(077)

TELEVISION AND RADIO

Your only hope for English-language radio is the Thai national public radio station at FM 97. They broadcast local, national, and international news and business throughout the day, and have music in the mornings. On FM 107, there is a thrice-daily English-language news broadcast at 7 AM, 6 PM, and 7 PM. Western classical music can be heard nightly from 9:30 PM to 11:00 PM on FM 101.5, the Chulalongkorn University station.

If you have a shortwave radio, you can also pick up the Voice of America, the BBC, or Radio Australia. Frequencies are given in the *Bangkok Post* and *The Nation*.

Television is almost entirely Thai-language. There are four television networks in Bangkok, with Channel 9 dominating the airwaves as the only national public television station, broadcasting daily from 6 AM to midnight.

NEWSPAPERS

There are three fairly decent English-language newspapers in Thailand: the *Bangkok Post*, *The World*, and *The Nation*. *The International Herald Tribune* is also available in Bangkok at major newsstands and major hotels. All of the above may be more difficult to find when you are traveling in the provinces. While the foreign news in the two Thai papers may all sound the same, the local news is often interesting and colorful, adding some depth to your vacation to these parts.

LOCAL TRANSPORTATION

THAI DOMESTIC FLIGHT SERVICE

You can fly just about anywhere in Thailand, and the domestic airline offers clean, efficient, inexpensive, and modern service. Outside of Bangkok, there are 21 airports in the country, though most are reached only by small Avro 748s instead of the usual Boeing 737s operated on the main routes. It is fairly easy to purchase tickets in Bangkok or elsewhere, though in the peak tourist season during the winter months you may want to book ahead through your travel agent at home or one in Bangkok.

It is generally easier to purchase the tickets through one of Bangkok's travel agencies, but Thai Airways offices are located throughout the country

---

THAI AIRWAYS DOMESTIC OFFICES

Bangkok, 6 Larn Luang Rd.; Telephone (domestic reservations) 280–0070/80; Telephone (international reservations) 234–3100/19
Chiang Mai, 240 Prapokklao Rd.; Telephone 211–541, 211–420/7
Phuket, 78 Ranong Rd.; Telephone 211–195
Surat Thani, 3/27–28 Karoonrat Rd.; Telephone 273–710

RAIL SERVICES

Thai railways win accolades from seasoned travelers. There are four main rail lines, all of which start up, end up, or go through Bangkok. The northern line runs from Bangkok to Chiang Mai, and the southern line goes from Bangkok along the east coast through Surat Thani to and across the Malaysian border. The northeastern line travels from Bangkok to Nong Khai on the Laotian border; the eastern line moves from Bangkok to Ubon Ratchathani.

For information on rail schedules and prices, call the Rail Travel Aids at the State Railway of Thailand in Bangkok at 223–7010 or 223–7020. You can book tickets through a travel agent or directly at Bangkok's main train station, the Hualamphong station. A reservation form (in different colors for different lines) is available at an advance booking counter; you then take it to the ticketing counter to be filled out.

There are three main classes on Thai trains, with third class the least expensive, and first a positive luxury. Many first-class cabins are air-conditioned with two beds, while second-class also offers sleeping berths with four to a room

The great advantage of train travel is the scenery—usually breathtaking—and the company. Train travel affords an excellent opportunity to get to know the country and its people a bit better.

LONG-DISTANCE BUS SERVICES

Thailand boasts excellent highways throughout the country, and one of the most interesting and cheapest ways to travel is by long-distance bus. There are both government and privately owned charter bus companies. The latter are preferable to the former, in terms of both comfort and speed.

There are three long-distance bus stations in Bangkok, one for each major direction. The Northern and Northeastern Bus Terminal, for trips to Chiang Mai, Chiang Rai, and the northeast, is located on Phahonyothin Rd. and can be telephoned at 279–4434/7 for air-conditioned buses, and 279-6222 for regular buses. The Southern Bus Terminal is located at Charansanitwong Rd., and its two telephone numbers are (air-conditioned) 411–4978/9 and (regular) 411–0511. The Eastern Bus Terminal is located at Sukhumwit Rd., telephones (air-conditioned) 391–330 and (regular) 392–2391.

For privately owned charter buses, tickets can be booked through most hotels or at any travel agency. Fares may be a bit higher than for the government-run buses, but the coaches travel at breakneck speeds (which has advantages and disadvantages), and are air-conditioned and generally more comfortable. There are at least a half-dozen companies running buses to the major tourist destinations such as Chiang Mai, Phuket, Krabi, Koh Samui, and Pattaya.

COASTAL PASSENGER SHIP SERVICES

If you are traveling to one of the many islands off the Thai mainland, there are many different classes of boats at your disposal. The most common routes are between the Ban Don pier near Surat Thani in southern Thailand and Koh Samui, or between Phuket and the various offshore islands in its area, such as Koh Phi Phi. Some of these boats are regular ferries with regular schedules, others are fishing boats privately hired for the ride, and still others are ad-hoc tourist cruises set up by local hotels and travel agencies. The most exciting ride is in a narrow Thai longboat, whose prow sticks up like a Viking ship's as you bounce across the waves. All of these boats are easy to find and easy to hire, should you need the private ride. See the chapters that follow for specific details.

TAXIS

In Bangkok, most taxis are now air-conditioned and are usually easy to find. Fares are not metered, however, and as is true throughout the kingdom, you must negotiate on a fare before you agree to take the ride. Taxis are not expensive, and are an easy and informative way to get around.

TUK TUKS

The most common form of transportation throughout Thailand is the three-wheeled, diesel-belching, open-back vehicles called *tuk tuks* (named after the knocking sound of their overtaxed engines). Cheaper than taxis, they can offer a scenic, if polluted, ride through the city. As you do with taxis, agree on a price before you start off. Most drivers can understand numbers in English, as well as the names of destinations.

SONG THAEWS

In Bangkok and in the major provincial cities, there are also *song thaews*, pickup trucks with bench-seats and roofs, which cruise along set routes and can be waved down from the side of the street. Just ask the driver if he is going in your direction,—for example, say "Phuket town?"— and pay a fare of approximately 2 baht, depending on the destination.

LOCAL BUSES

The local bus service is good, albeit slow and sometimes terrifying. One bus driver on a recent careering trip through Bangkok clipped so many cars en route that he just pulled over to the side and gave up the wheel, and all the passengers tumbled out to look for a safer taxi!

Route signs are in Thai only, which poses some difficulty for those who cannot read that language, but route maps in English are avail-

Popular Tuk-Tuk, three-wheeled taxi

able from the TAT office and at most hotels and bookshops. Fares range from 2 to 15 baht.

RENTAL CARS

Travelers with a valid international driving license can rent a car for personal adventures on the lunatic urban streets, or around the countryside. Avis is located in Bangkok on North Sathorn Rd., telephone 233–0397; Hertz can be found at 1598 New Phetburi Rd., telephone 252–4903/6. In Chiang Mai, Avis is at the Dusit Inn Hotel on 122 Chang Khlan Rd., telephone 251–034, 236–835. On Phuket, Phuket Car Center at Takuapa Rd., telephone 212–671/3, and Pure

Car Rent at 75 Ratsada Rd., telephone 211–002, offer jeeps, cars, and mopeds.

SIGHTSEEING TOURS

THERE are numerous sightseeing tours available in and around Bangkok, Chiang Mai, and other major tourist destinations. Contact one of the Thai travel agencies listed in the previous chapter, or call the Association of Thai Travel Agents in Bangkok at 252–0069 for detailed information on tour offerings.

In and around Bangkok, the most popular tours include trips to the ancient capital of Ayutthaya along the Chao Phrya River, tours to Kanchanaburi, site of the "Bridge over the River Kwai" and an Allied war cemetery, and boat tours through the canals of Thonburi and through the oft-photographed Bangkok floating market.

In the north, the most popular tours are treks into the hills to visit and stay with hill tribes living in the "Golden Triangle," travel down the Mekong River, and visits to the famous temples along the Burmese border.

In the south, sightseeing tours that originate in the most popular tourist areas such as Phuket or Koh Samui will include boat trips to neighboring islands, snorkeling and scuba diving trips, and visits to waterfalls and caves.

V

The Thailand Tour

BANGKOK

THERE is a good chance that you'll hate Bangkok on your first visit. It is not an immediately endearing metropolis. Many visitors leave the Thai capital city with relief, and only those with a special understanding and acceptance of Asian anarchy and frenzy are easily drawn to this crazed city.

But Bangkok can often weave a spell around visitors, leaving them with an amused tolerance for its chaos and a loving affection for its dissipation. Bangkok is most definitely "mad, bad, and dangerous to know," and those are the qualities that make it so alluring.

The name *Bangkok*, which means "Village of the Wild Plum," is not the name by which Thais know their principal municipality. *Bangkok* was the name of the tiny fishing village located on this spot when Rama I decided to build his capital here in the 18th century. Royal leaders bestowed imperial names on their capital, and Bangkok, in the Thai language, actually has what may well be the world's longest name. The thirteen-word title begins with *Krungthep*, meaning the "City of Angels," and winds on with tongue-twisting complexity to end, finally, with *Sakkathattiya-avisnukarmprasit*. The full name translates to Great City of Angels, Supreme Repository of Divine Jewels, the Great Land Unconquerable, the Grand and Prominent Realm, the Royal and Delightful Capital Full of Nine Noble Gems, the Highest Royal Dwelling and Grand Palace, the Divine Shelter and Living Place of the Reincarnated Spirits.

Bangkok has been the capital of Thailand since 1782, when the first Chakri king, Rama I, rejected Thonburi on the west bank of the Chao Phraya river and decided to re-create the glories of Ayutthaya on the site of a Chinese fishing village on the east bank. Ayutthaya had been protected from attack by being an island city, surrounded by river and canals, which together formed a moat around the royal palaces. Thus, as they rebuilt Bangkok on the model of Ayutthaya, the kings constructed a network of *klongs*, or canals, to hem it in.

The city is sprawled across a flat alluvial plain about 25 mi (40 km) upstream from the Gulf of Thailand. With a population of over six million, or over one-tenth of the entire Thai population, Bangkok is congested and seems barely contained within its streets and buildings. The old and the new intermix in Bangkok as they do nowhere else in the world — over 400 resplendent golden *wats*, or temples, are scattered about the city, towering above, or hiding behind, streets thronged with diesel buses, painted trucks, and scurrying pedestrians. Intermingled among the modern dress of Bangkok's urban population are monks, swathed in saffron robes, heads shaved, making their way from temple to alms.

In the early years, Bangkok's undisputed heart was the area around the Royal Palaces, on a nub of land that juts into the curve of the Chao Phraya. Over the centuries, however, modernization and development have dispersed central Bangkok over a wide area, leaving the city with no discernible center or main district. Yet for the tourist the heart remains in this older area, where temples and palaces compete to offer a spectacular vision of the exotic Far East.

Just north of this neighborhood is the new royal and modern administrative district called Dusit. The National Assembly building is here, as is the Dusit Zoo, and the Chitralada Palace, the present residence of Thailand's royal family. Chinatown, a sprawl of narrow streets and colorful shops, is just south and east of the old Royal Palace area. The original residents of Bangkok were Chinese who were transplanted to this spot when Rama I decided to build his own royal city on their village.

Bangkok's modern business and shopping districts are centered on Silom and Surawong roads, which run parellel to each other to the south, around a curve of the Chao Phraya from Chinatown. This is also the infamous nightlife district of Bangkok, especially Pathong Rd., which runs between Silom and Surawong. This whole area is full of shops, restaurants, nightclubs, go-go bars, hotels and banks. The so-called Old Farang, or foreign, Quarter is at the western end of Silom and Surawong, on New Rd., which runs along the river. Here are the old Oriental Hotel, the East Asiatic Company buildings, the Oriental Plaza, and Assumption Cathedral, all legacies of the colonial era.

The final neighborhood or high-spot to keep in mind for your visit to Bangkok is the river itself, and the canals that stretch into Thonburi. While dirty, busy, and polluted, the Chao Phraya is a welcome relief from the hot city and is easy to navigate. Countless river taxis go up and down, and then into the maze of canals in Thonburi.

HOTELS

1.	Ambassador	C4
2.	Asia	B3
3.	Bangkok Palace	B3
4.	Dusit Thani	C3
5.	Erawan	C3
6.	Hilton International	C3
7.	Hyatt Central Plaza	A4
8.	Indra Regent	B3
9.	The Landmark	C4
10.	Le Meridian President	C3
11.	Mandarin	C3
12.	Manhattan	C3
14.	Montien	C3
15.	Narai	C3
16.	New Imperial	C3
17.	The Oriental	C2
18.	The Regent Bangkok	C3
19.	Royal Orchid Sheraton	C2
20.	Shangri-La	C3
21.	Siam Intercontinental	C3
22.	Silom Plaza	C3
23.	Tawana Ramada	C3
24.	Windsor	C4

TOURIST ATTRACTIONS

1.	Grand Palace & Wat Phra Kaeo	B2
2.	Wat Pho	B2
3.	Wat Arun	C2
4.	Wat Benchamabophit	B2
5.	Wat Traimit	C2
6.	National Museum	B2
7.	National Gallery	B2
8.	Dusit Zoo	B2
9.	Suan Pakkard Palace	B3
10.	Jim Thompson's House	B3
11.	Snake Farm	C3
12.	Lumphini Park	C3
13.	Chatuchak Park	A3-4
14.	Weekend Market	A3
15.	Ratchadamnoen Boxing Stadium	B2
16.	Lumphini Boxing Stadium	C3

EMBASSIES

1.	Apostolic Nunciature	C3
2.	Argentina	C4
3.	Australia	C3
4.	Austria	C3
5.	Bangladesh	C4
6.	Belgium	C3
7.	Brazil	C4
8.	Brunei	C3
9.	Bulgaria	B5
10.	Burma	C3
11.	Canada	C3
12.	Chile	C4
13.	China	B4
14.	Czechoslovakia	C3
15.	Denmark	C3
16.	Egypt	C3
17.	Finland	C3
18.	France	C2
19.	Germany	C3
20.	Hungary	C4
21.	India	C4
22.	Indonesia	B3
23.	Iran	C3
24.	Iraq	A3
25.	Israel	C3
27.	Japan	C3
28.	Korea	C3
29.	Laos	C3
30.	Malaysia	C3
31.	Nepal	C5
32.	The Netherlands	C3
33.	New Zealand	C4
34.	Norway	C4
35.	Pakistan	C3
36.	The Philippines	C4
37.	Poland	C2
38.	Portugal	C2
39.	Romania	C3
40.	Saudi Arabia	C3
41.	Singapore	C3
42.	Spain	C3
43.	Sri Lanka	C3
44.	Sweden	C3
45.	Switzerland	C3
46.	Turkey	C3
47.	United Kingdom	C5
48.	U.S.A.	C3
49.	U.S.S.R.	C3
50.	Vietnam	C3
51.	Yugoslavia	C4

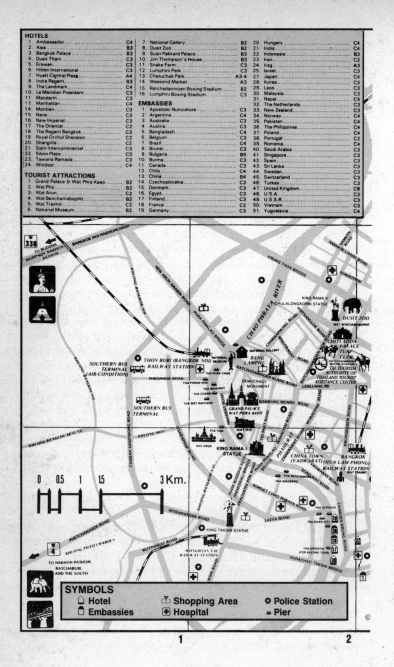

SYMBOLS

- Hotel
- Embassies
- Shopping Area
- Hospital
- Police Station
- Pier

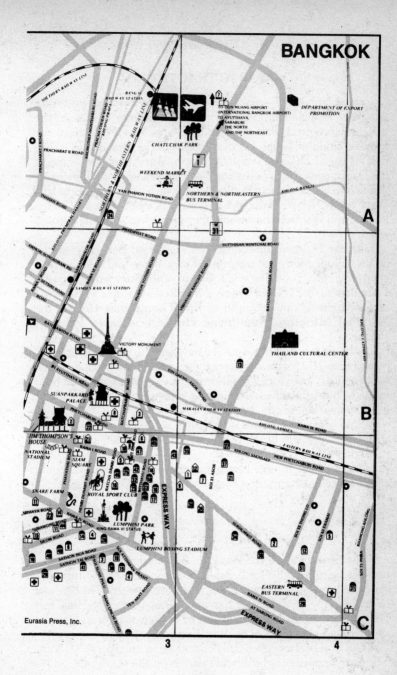

BANGKOK

DEPARTMENT OF EXPORT PROMOTION

SOUTHERN RAILWAY LINE

BANG SU RAILWAY STATION

PRACHACHUEN ROAD
PRACHA CHEUN ROAD
KHLONG PRAPA

TO DON MUANG AIRPORT
(INTERNATIONAL BANGKOK AIRPORT)
TO AYUTTHAYA,
SARABURI
THE NORTH
AND THE NORTHEAST

PRACHARAT II ROAD

CHATUCHAK PARK

WEEKEND MARKET

YAN PHAHON YOTHIN ROAD

NORTHERN & NORTHEASTERN
BUS TERMINAL

KHLONG BANGSU

A

PRADIPHAT ROAD

SUTTHISAN WINITCHAI ROAD

ANNOI SONGKHRAM RD

RAMA V ROAD
SETSIRI ROAD

SAMSEN RAILWAY STATION

PHAHON YOTHIN ROAD

VIBHAVADI RANGSIT ROAD

RATCHADAPHISEK ROAD

KHLONG LAPHRAO

RATCHAWITHI ROAD

VICTORY MONUMENT

THAILAND CULTURAL CENTER

SI AYUTTHAYA RD.

DIN DAENG ROAD

SUANPAKKARD PALACE

PHETCHABURI ROAD

MAKASAN RAILWAY STATION

B

RAMA IX ROAD

KHLONG SAMSEN

JIM THOMPSON'S HOUSE

RAMA I ROAD

EASTERN RAILWAY LINE

KHLONG SAENSAEB

NEW PHETCHABURI ROAD

NATIONAL STADIUM

SIAM SQUARE

SOI 21 ASOK

SOI 23 SUKHUMVIT ROAD

SNAKE FARM

ROYAL SPORT CLUB

EXPRESS WAY

SIPHAYA ROAD

SURAWONG ROAD

SILOM ROAD

LUMPHINI PARK

KING RAMA VI STATUE

LUMPHINI BOXING STADIUM

SOI 33 THONG LO

SOI 63 EKAMAI

SOI 55 PHRA KHANONG

KHLONG

SATHON NUA ROAD

SATHON TAI ROAD

NARATHIWAT
RATCHANAKHARIN ROAD

EASTERN BUS TERMINAL

RAMA IV ROAD

AT NARONG ROAD

YEN NAI ROAD

EXPRESS WAY

C

Eurasia Press, Inc.

3   4

255

MAJOR ATTRACTIONS

There are many—too many—attractions for the visitor to Bangkok. A sightseeing itinerary should include, of course, the spectacular **Grand Palace** compound and **Wat Phra Keo**, the Emerald Buddha Temple on the grounds of the Grand Palace. The latter is one of Thailand's most holy spots. **Wat Arun**, the Temple of the Dawn, is on the opposite bank of the river, and its tall *prang*, or steeple, is a wonderful spot from which to gain a view of the entire city. **Wat Pho**, the Temple of the Reclining Buddha, **Wat Saket**, the Golden Mount, and **Wat Benchambopit**, the Marble Temple, are all also well worth a visit.

On the Thonburi side of the river, the **Royal Barges** are stored in a warehouse and offer a glimpse of royal pomp and splendor. For shopping and browsing visit **Silom** and **Surawong roads, Chinatown,** and the old **Thieves' Market**. Museums with a sense of old Bangkok can be found at **Jim Thompson's House,** the **National Museum, Kamthieng House**, and **Suan Pakkard Palace.**

Bangkok may best be savored by travelers who use it as a jumping-off point: spend a few days in the city, then a week on a beautiful beach in the south. Come back for a few more days of shopping, then head off to the hills of northern Thailand, and then return to Bangkok for a last splurge before you depart the kingdom.

Only a few of Bangkok's hundreds of temples and sights are discussed below. For further exploring — and to facilitate your way through the mazes of Bangkok's alleys — it is best to purchase an illustrated street map at one of Bangkok's many bookstores. You could spend a week just exploring Bangkok for undiscovered temples!

ROYAL PALACES

The **Grand Palace** and **Wat Phra Keo** must be on the top of any tourist's sightseeing list for Bangkok. Once visited, this fortress, the symbolic heart of old Bangkok, will never be forgotten. The best way to arrive at the Grand Palace compound is by boat along the Chao Phraya. Arriving thus, you will be met by a vision of spires and steeples that recreate the glories of ancient Siam.

The Royal Palaces open daily at 8:30 AM; admission is 100 baht. The main entrance to the Grand Palace is on the north side, on Na Phralan Rd. There are five major buildings within the mile-square compound, all of which have been added to by different monarchs and which express a progression in architectural tastes.

As you first come in the main gate, the **Chakri Maha Prasat** lies straight ahead, beyond an entrance to the inner courtyard. This building is famous for its strange mix of architectural styles: the facade is Italian, while the roof is typically Thai.

To the right of the Chakri Maha Prasat is **Dusit Maha Prasat**, built by Rama I in 1782 and originally an audience hall for the king. It is now used as a lying-in-state compound for recently dead kings and is said to be the finest building within the compound. The coronation of King Rama I took place in this hall and, in the middle, a big stone slab, hewn in 1292 by a Sukhothai king, stands as the seat of a throne.

The **Ampon Phimok Pavilion** is just west of the Dusit, and the **Amarin Winitchai Hall** is just east of the Chakri Maha Prasat. The Amarin Winitchai Hall was used as a royal court of justice in the past and is currently the coronation room. **Borombiman Hall** occupies the southeast corner of the compound and was the receiving hall for state visitors.

The highlight of the Grand Palace is the royal chapel called **Wat Phra Keo,** or Emerald Buddha Temple. It occupies the northeast corner of the compound and enshrines Thailand's most holy object, a 2⅓-ft high (73-cm) green Buddha discovered in Chiang Rai in the 15th century. This temple was built in the 18th century as a resting place for the Emerald Buddha and is spendidly decorated with blue tiles and elaborate murals. The Emerald (actually green jasper) Buddha is enclosed in glass. Three times each year the King arrives to perform the sacred rite of changing its seasonal attire. On either side stand two additional Buddhas, said to personify the first two kings of the Chakri Dynasty. Photography is forbidden within the temple, as are shoes.

WATS (TEMPLES)

Wat Arun (Arun Amarin Rd., Thonburi). Wat Arun, the Temple of Dawn, is beautiful, but the best part about visiting this temple is its location across the river from the Royal Palaces. Taking the river ferry from Tha Tien pier on the Bangkok side is an adventure in itself.

Named after Aruna, the Indian god of dawn, Wat Arun is famous for its tower, called Phra Prang, which is one of Bangkok's most outstanding monuments. The 243-ft-high (74-m) tower is decorated with little pieces of colorful porcelain that in the early morning hours,

Bangkok's Wat Phra Keo

light up with the bright and pastel colors of the morning. A beautiful view of Bangkok and the Grand Palaces is available from this tower. Phra Prang is supported by clusters of stone animals and giants; in each of the four corners the god Indra sits on his white elephant. On the lower terrace beneath the tower, you can see four small pavilions, each with an image of the Buddha at a different stage of his life.

Also on the Thonburi side of the river are **Wat Kalayanimit**, located near the mouth of Klong (canal) Bangkok Yai, and **Wat Prayoon**, further downstream. If you can find them, **Wat Suwannaram** and **Wat Dusitaram** are both ancient temples located in Thonburi, their interiors decorated with beautiful 18th- and early 19th-century murals. Wat-searching in Thonburi can make a fascinating afternoon, as this side of the river imparts a truer sense of old, pre-colonial Thailand.

Wat Benchamabopit (Sri Ayutthaya Rd., in Dusit). Built by Rama V (King Chulalongkorn), this wat illustrates the confusion of cultures and styles that has overcome Thailand in recent centuries.

The temple is constructed with Italian Carrara marble (hence its other name, "The Marble Temple"), and is covered with a three-tiered roof of Chinese glazed tiles. The gate is Khmer-inspired, and the pavilions on either side are Javanese. In the courtyard gallery there are more than 50 Buddha images created in styles of all periods of Thai Buddhist art and of Buddhist countries.

Wat Bovornivet (Phra Sumen Rd., a block north of the Democracy Monument). This temple is not really a tourist site, but the most important temple of the Thammayut monastic sect, the stricter of the two main disciplines that make up Thai Buddhism. The Thammayut sect was established by King Mongkut after his years of monastic discipline before taking up the throne in the 19th century. It is a beautiful temple, very much in use.

Wat Mahadhatu (just west of the Pramane Ground, north of the Grand Palace on Na Phrathat Rd.). The chapel of Wat Mahadhatu, or the Temple of the Great Relic, is said to be the largest in Bangkok, and the temple is respected as an important center for meditation studies. One of Bangkok's two Buddhist Universities is located on its grounds, and there is an interesting herbal medicine market in one of the courtyards. You can study Buddhist meditation here, or just observe the monks at work.

Wat Pho (Maharaj Rd., south of the Grand Palace). Wat Pho, the Temple of the Reclining Buddha, is the oldest and largest temple in Bangkok. Its construction was begun in 1793 by Rama I. There are many structures packed into the large compound of Wat Pho, but the central and most astounding chapel, called a *bot*, is the one that contains an enormous Reclining Buddha, made out of brick and concrete and finished with gold. The image is 150 ft (46 m) long and 40 ft (12 m) high.

The bot is in the middle of a courtyard surrounded by cloisters filled with rows upon rows of seated Buddha images. The Reclining Buddha is the largest in the kingdom, and the temple contains the largest collection of Buddhist images in Thailand.

Wat Rachanada (southwest corner of the Mahachai and Ratchadamnoen Klang intersection, opposite Wat Saket). This temple is best known for its amulet market located in the first courtyard. Vendors ply their trade in the Buddhist luck charms and while their wares may be more expensive than those in other markets, the collection is fascinating.

Wat Rajapradit and Wat Rajabophit (between Sanam Chai and Ban Mo roads, southeast of Grand Palace, separated by Klong Lot). These two small temples are rarely visited by tourists, but are easily accessible to the main tourist areas. If you find yourself in the little alleys and canal-ways, they are well worth a visit. Wat Rajapradit is charming, built on a raised stone platform and flanked by Khmer-style towers. Wat Rajabophit, just across the canal, was built in the 19th century and is a bizarre but pleasing combination of Western and oriental styles. The chapel interior is Italian Gothic and there are relief carvings of European soldiers at the main entrance to the chapel.

Wat Saket (corner of Mahachai Rd. on the south side of Ratchadamnoen Ave). Wat Saket is most famous for its "Golden Mount," a 256-foot (78-m) high artificial hill topped with a gilded chedi that enshrines sacred relics of the Buddha. Fantastic views of Bangkok are available from atop the mount. The wat itself, at the base of the mount, is one of Bangkok's oldest, and is best visited during an annual November temple fair.

Wat Suthat (Bamrung Muang Rd., southwest of Wat Rachanada). Visit this 19th-century temple to see the superb murals, recently restored, which illustrate incidents in the life of the Buddha. The double roof of the long and narrow temple building is unique in Thai architecture.

MUSEUMS

Jim Thompson's House (Soi Kasemsan II, opposite National Stadium on Rama I Rd.). Jim Thompson was an American entrepreneur who settled in Bangkok after World War II and revived the Thai silk industry. Thompson himself disappeared mysteriously in 1967 in the Malaysian hill country, but he left behind a gorgeous museum-home, and a thriving silk trade. His home consists of a group of seven Thai-style houses, with one of the finest private art and antiquities collections in Thailand. The Jim Thompson Thai Silk shop is located at 9 Surawong Rd. Open Monday to Friday 9 AM–4 PM.

Kamthieng House (Siam Society, 131 Soi 21, Sukhumvit Rd.). The Kamthieng House is approximately 120 years old and is a typical northern-style Thai building. There are antique wood carvings and gorgeous folk art on display in the house and in the rice barn out back. Open 9 AM–noon, 1 PM–5 PM daily.

National Museum (opposite the northwest corner of the Pramane Ground). The National Museum features one of the largest and most comprehensive collections of art, sculpture, and folk exhibits in Southeast Asia. They are housed in beautiful old palace structures to the north of the Grand Palace. Admission charge except on Sunday. Open daily except Monday and Friday, 9 AM–noon and 1 PM–4 PM

Suan Pakkard Palace (Sri Ayutthaya Rd.). Open daily except Sunday, 9 AM–4 PM

Vimanmek Throne Hall (behind the National Assembly, opposite Dusit Zoo). The Throne Hall was the private museum of Rama V. There are exhibits of antique furniture, paintings, and jewelry belonging to the Thai Royal Family. Few tourists make it to this sight, and the four-story wooden building offers a fascinating insight into the collections of the regal Thais. Open Wednesday through Friday, 9:30 AM–4 PM

SHRINES

Erawan Shrine (corner of Ploenchit and Ratchadamri roads, next to Erawan Hotel). For some reason, this small and unpretentious shrine has become Bangkok's most popular good luck charm. It was originally built by the hotel to ward against bad luck, but is now thronged with charm seekers from throughout the city. The shrine encloses a statue of Brahma, the four-headed Hindu god, and there are often performances of classical Thai dance.

Lak Muang (opposite the Emerald Buddha Temple on Ta Phra Chan Rd.). Erected by Rama I as a symbolic foundation of the capital city, the pillar is a source of good luck and the favored abode of the city's guardian spirits.

OTHER SITES

Chinatown (off Charoen Krung and Yaowaraj roads, along the southern curve of the Chao Phraya, south of the Grand Palace). In the 18th century, Chinese traders had to move from the Grand Palace area to a section known as Sampeng, where they managed to thrive. Chinatown is like Chinatowns everywhere — a warren of colorful and bizarre shops, strange smells, loud voices, red banners, and cheap knicknacks. The gold shops are painted red and white, and the most famous shopping street is Sampeng Lane, also known as Soi Wanit I, just south of Yaowaraj Rd. An Indian Market, also called Pahurat Cloth Market, is at the western end of Sampeng Lane and is full of Indian fabrics and souvenirs. Thieves' Market, known in Thai as Nakhon Kasem, is at the northwestern corner of Chinatown between New and Yaowaraj roads. Go there for old and new antiques, Chinese porcelain, brasswork, and tacky souvenirs.

Pramane Ground (north of the Grand Palace). This wide open space in the midst of the congested city is the Royal Cremation Ground and used to be the site of a thriving weekend market (now moved, see below). The annual Plowing Ceremony in May is still held here, and there are celebratory events around the King's birthday in December.

Royal Barges (Klong Bangkok Noi, in Thonburi, just across the Phrapinklao Bridge). The Royal Barges are incredibly ornamented river boats used only for ceremonial processions on the river. They are worth a visit, if only to round out a day visiting temples in Thonburi, or to get a glimpse of how the other 1% lives. There are signposts in English just over the bridge in Thonburi to lead you to the boathouse.

Weekend Market (Chatuchak Park, off Phaholyothin Rd., near the Northern Bus Terminal). Outside of downtown Bangkok, the Saturday and Sunday Weekend market is an orgy of handicrafts, cheap food, and cheap thrills. There are over 35 acres of stalls set up in this park, with antiques—real and fake—jewelery, clothing, fruits, vegetables, and pets. If you are in Bangkok on a weekend, don't miss it.

CANALS AND RIVERS

Unlike Bangkok, where many of the canals were filled in as the city expanded, Thonburi boasts many old waterways still in use. It is quite easy to bargain for the hire of your own longtail boat for a tour from one of the piers on the Bangkok side of the river.

The trip to Thonburi most favored by tourists is the one to the Floating Market on Klong Dao Kanong. Unfortunately, the early morning tourist boats (check any local travel agency or a hotel for a tour) often outnumber the fruit and vegetable boats. For a more authentic and less-crowded floating market, join a tour from Bangkok to Damnoen Saduak, about 87 mi (140 km) southwest of the city.

River taxis ply the waterways in Thonburi and the Chao Phraya river all up and around Bangkok. There are piers on both sides, and

Fruits at Bangkok's Damnoen Saduak Floating Market

you just jump aboard, tell the ticket seller where you are going, buy a ticket, and watch carefully for your stop. It is a wonderfully scenic and relaxing way to see the city. You can take a taxi into Thonburi and just stay aboard for the ride all the way through and back to Bangkok.

Luxury river cruises are operated by the Oriental Hotel, at the end of Silom Rd., aboard its Oriental Queen barge. They run daily up the Chao Phraya to the ancient capital of Ayutthaya.

CENTRAL REGION

AYUTTHAYA

The ancient Thai capital of Ayutthaya is located about 43 mi (70 km) upstream from Bangkok, and can be reached by boat, train, bus, or car. A visit to this magnificent crumbling ruin of a city, glorious capital from 1350 to 1767, brings you back to the days when Thailand truly ruled this entire region, when palaces and temples dominated the central plains and made this a great trading entrepôt.

When the Burmese destroyed this city in the 18th century, they left behind hundreds of resplendent Buddha images and temple steeples. In modern times, many of these ancient images are still draped with orange cloth, bearing powerful testimony to the deep and enduring spirituality of the Thais. The highlights of the Ayutthaya ruins include the ruins of the old royal temple, Wat Phra Sri Sanphet, and its three pagodas; the 14th-century Wat Phra Ram; and the extensive ruins of Wat Mahathat. In the southeast corner of old Ayutthaya — a city so vast that it was surrounded by a wall more than 7 mi (12 km) long—is Wat Suwan Dhararam, built by the father of Rama I and still in use. In all there were three major palace complexes and 400 temples in ancient Ayutthaya.

There are two museums in modern Ayutthaya, and the principal one, Chao Sam Phraya Museum, is located in the center of town on Rojana Rd. It is closed on Mondays and Tuesdays. The collection of bronze and stone statues helps the meager imagination grasp the size and beauty of Ayutthaya. A smaller museum, Chan Kasem Palace, is northeast of the city and is housed in a 17th century palace building built on the site of King Naresuan's palace.

The best and most beautiful approach to Ayutthaya is aboard the Oriental Queen from Bangkok. For 850 baht, you boat up, sightsee, have lunch and refreshments, and then bus back to Bangkok. The boat departs daily at 8 AM from the Oriental Hotel.

KANCHANABURI

Kanchanaburi, better known as the location of the bridge that spans the River Kwai (i.e. "The Bridge over the River Kwai"), is located some 80 mi (130 km) west of Bangkok and is a popular day trip from the capital. Even if you are not a movie or a World War II buff, it is truly a lovely trip through the Thai countryside and offers views into Thai rural life that you might otherwise miss.

The bridge itself, which actually spans a river called Khwae Yai, was built by Allied prisoners of war pressed into labor by their Japanese overlords. Over 100,000 members of labor gangs and 16,000 Allied prisoners died from beatings, starvation, and disease while building the bridge and a railroad. The Allied War Cemetaries in the town express this historical point quite vividly.

The ruins of an old Khmer town called Muang Sing are just a few miles north of Kanchanaburi. All over this area you can find caves, waterfalls, and interesting cave temples. Get there by taking a bus, train, tour, or taxi from Bangkok.

KHAO YAI NATIONAL PARK

The 540,000-acre (218,700-ha) Khao Yai National Park is located about 124 mi (200 km) north of Bangkok. This park contains spectacular virgin jungle and forest and ample wildlife—tigers, bears, elephants, monkeys, and butterflies—wildflowers, trees, and even orchids to satisfy the nature needs of the urban refugee. Hiking trails and lodges make it easy for the first-time visitor to this mountainous region.

It is a three- to four-hour journey by car or public bus from Bangkok. To stay at the Khao Yai Motor Lodge, where there are comfortable bungalows, make reservations through TAT.

NAKHON PATHOM

One of the tallest Buddhist monuments in the world can be seen in Nakhon Pathom, only 35 mi (56 km) west of Bangkok. The 380-ft-high (116–m) Phra Pathom Chedi supposedly marks the spot where Buddhism was introduced to Thailand 2,300 years ago. Nakhon Pathom is said to be the oldest city in all of Thailand, and it was a center of the ancient and somewhat mysterious Dvaravati kingdom.

Just south of here, Damnoen Saduak, mentioned above as the sight of a great floating market, is also a famous historical and religious monument. It is believed to have been the earliest center of Buddhist learning in Thailand.

Nakhon Pathom can be reached from Bangkok by bus, car, or train.

PATTAYA

Pattaya, in the words of one longtime Bangkok resident, is "an eyesore to beat all eyesores." It takes all kinds, of course, and there are hundreds of thousands of Western visitors who enjoy this raucous beach resort each year. The Thais call it their Riviera, and they advertise Pattaya as having the best of everything: every imaginable water and land sport, nightlife Bangkok-style, shopping, luxury hotels, and great restaurants. If it's golf, tennis, scuba, go-go girls for hire, and a beach scene á la Acapulco that you are looking for, then Pattaya is where you'll find them in Thailand.

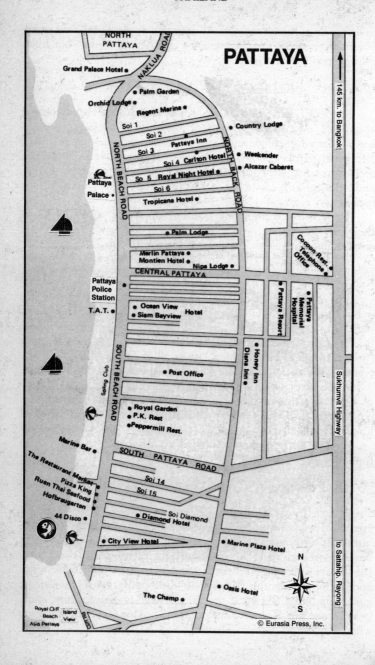

PATTAYA

145 km. to Bangkok

NORTH PATTAYA

NAKLUA ROAD

Grand Palace Hotel

Palm Garden

Orchid Lodge

Regent Marina

Soi 1

Country Lodge

Soi 2

Pattaya Inn

Soi 3

Soi 4 Carlton Hotel

Weekender

So 5 Royal Night Hotel

Alcazar Cabaret

Pattaya Palace

Soi 6

NORTH BEACH ROAD

NORTH BACK ROAD

Tropicana Hotel

Palm Lodge

Merlin Pattaya

Montien Hotel

Nipa Lodge

Cocoon Rest. / Telephone Office

CENTRAL PATTAYA

Pattaya Resort

Pattaya Memorial Hospital

Pattaya Police Station

T.A.T.

Ocean View

Siam Bayview Hotel

Honey Inn

Diana Inn

Sailing Club

SOUTH BEACH ROAD

Post Office

Royal Garden

P.K. Rest.

Peppermill Rest.

Marine Bar

SOUTH PATTAYA ROAD

The Restaurant Market

Pizza King

Ruen Thai Seafood

Hofbraugarten

Soi 14

Soi 15

44 Disco

Soi Diamond

Diamond Hotel

City View Hotel

Marine Plaza Hotel

Sukhumvit Highway

to Sattahip, Rayong

N

S

The Champ

Oasis Hotel

Royal Cliff Beach

Asia Pattaya

Island View

© Eurasia Press, Inc.

Pattaya's development and popularity stem from its easy proximity to Bangkok: it is only a two-hour drive from the capital, and there are countless buses and shuttle services from all over town which take you there with little effort or energy. Pattaya used to be a sleepy fishing village, but it has been transformed by modernity into an internationally famous beach resort. Americans have to take some credit for this development — Pattaya got its start in the water sports and sex trade business because of the placement of an American base nearby.

The southern end of Pattaya Bay, the main beach area, is known as "the strip" and is full of go-go bars, Bangkok transvestites, and a number of deluxe hotels. The northern end, by contrast, has some nicer, quieter beaches, and some relatively inexpensive bungalows for rent.

For those who wish to search beyond the obvious, there are a couple of offshore islands, Koh Larn and Koh Phai, which offer fantastic snorkeling and even basic accommodations. Boats can be hired at the main beach for these trips. Pattaya is justifiably famous for its fresh seafood, which though overpriced, is available in abundance.

KOH SAMET

For those in search of a somewhat quieter — even idyllic — beach retreat, Koh Samet is a beautiful little island only 124 mi (200 km) from Bangkok. There are 15 bays and numerous superb beaches on this

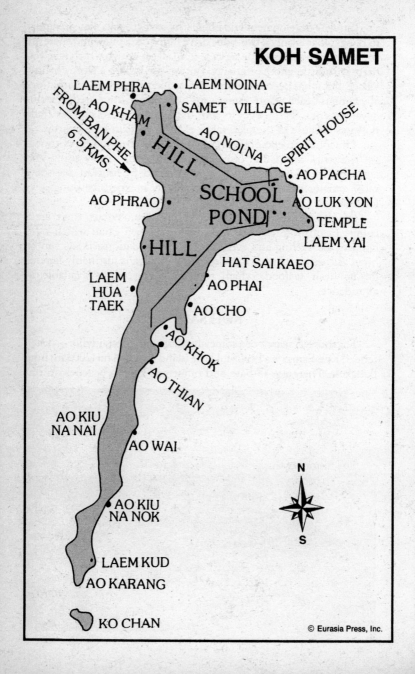

KOH SAMET

LAEM PHRA

LAEM NOINA

SAMET VILLAGE

FROM BAN PHE

6.5 KMS.

AO KHAM

AO NOI NA

SPIRIT HOUSE

HILL

AO PACHA

SCHOOL POND

AO PHRAO

AO LUK YON

TEMPLE

LAEM YAI

HILL

HAT SAI KAEO

AO PHAI

LAEM HUA TAEK

AO CHO

AO KHOK

AO THIAN

AO KIU NA NAI

AO WAI

AO KIU NA NOK

N

S

LAEM KUD

AO KARANG

KO CHAN

© Eurasia Press, Inc.

51-sq-mi (131-km²) island. Foreigners discovered Samet about a decade ago, and you may find it somewhat crowded — but nothing compared to Pattaya. If you do not have time to travel to some of the beautiful palm-fringed islands of the south, then Koh Samet is an excellent compromise. You will understand Thailand's reputation as a beach paradise. There are dozens of inexpensive beach bungalows with comfortable, but not luxurious, accommodations for as little as 30 or 40 baht a night. The beaches are lovely, the snorkeling excellent, and the nightlife very quiet. Koh Samet tends to get crowded with Thais on national holidays.

Koh Samet can be reached by taking a bus from Bangkok to either Rayong or, more conveniently, to Ban Phe. Boats leave the Ban Phe pier for Samet throughout the day. The prettiest beaches, such as Sai Kaew, Ao Thap Thim, or Ao Phai, are an easy walk from the place where the boat drops you off at the village harbor at Na Dang.

NORTHERN REGION

CHIANG MAI

Chiang Mai is Thailand's second city, and it couldn't be more different from Bangkok. Located approximately 435 mi (700 km) north of the capital, Chiang Mai sits in a fertile valley, surrounded by hills and forests. Its temperatures are generally cooler than those of Bangkok, and its atmosphere—compared with Bangkok's frenzy—is one of gentle beauty and craft. The city is full of spectacular flower gardens and wild northern orchids, which hang in baskets from many of the lovely teak homes. It is called the Rose of the North, and is especially famous, say the Thais, for the beauty of its women, temples, and gardens.

The history of this beautiful city stretches back to the earliest Thai kingdoms. A prince from the Nanzhao Kingdom in southern China founded Chiang Mai at the foot of Doi Suthep Mount in 1962. Until this century the city had its own ruling prince and its own royal family, and it continues to be distinct in dialect, costumes, dances, and cuisine. The natives of Chiang Mai — population is about 100,000 strong — are said to view themselves as culturally superior to their southern upstart cousins. Their charming city, brimming over with folk art and handicrafts from the hill tribes that live in the surrounding hills, make this claim seem legitimate.

Given its long history as a center of religion and trade, Chiang Mai is understandably full of old temples. There are over 300 wats

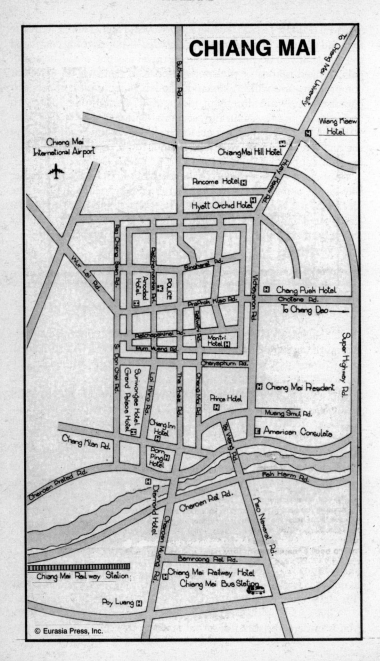

CHIANG MAI

© Eurasia Press, Inc.

scattered about the old and new parts of the city, many of which date back to the 14th century. The oldest Chiang Mai wat is called Wat Chiang Mun, and it is located within the ancient city square. Wat Chedi Luang, which dates back to 1411, is the site of the city's *lak muang*, or guardian pillar. The temple is famous for its great *chedi* or tower. One of the more interesting wats is Wat Ched Yod, located outside of town near the Chiang Mai Museum. The seven towers are modelled on Indian originals, and the grounds of this quiet temple are quite pleasant. Finally, Wat Phra Singh, built in 1345, is worth a visit to see the 1,500-year-old Buddha of mysterious origins.

The most dramatic temple in Chiang Mai, and the one offering the most spectacular views, is Wat Doi Suthep, built in the 14th century to house a relic of the Buddha. To reach the temple, on the side of Doi Suthep Mount, 10 mi (16 km) southwest of Chiang Mai city, you must climb the 300-step Dragon Staircase. If the weather is clear, the view from the top will reveal Chiang Mai spread out below as it has lain for centuries.

The original Chiang Mai was a walled and moated city, but the heart of modern Chiang Mai lies just to the east of the old city, between the east wall and the Ping River. The main street is called Ta Pae Rd. and runs through the city, out the east wall and then over the river where the name changes to Charoen Muang Rd. The TAT office, the bus stations, and the train station are all located in this general area east of town. One of Chiang Mai's charms is that it is small enough to negotiate on bicycles — they're for rent all over town.

In addition to its genial atmosphere and general beauty, two things make Chiang Mai especially popular with tourists: the abundance of cheap and distinctive folk art, and its proximity to the hills, where the villages of various hill tribes can be visited. In the old days, Chiang Mai's craftsmen lived in separate villages scattered around the edges of town. As the city has grown, however, it has absorbed the crafts into its own arteries. Thus, in modern Chiang Mai, you can find different streets and areas devoted to silver making, lacquer production, embroidery, and wood carving. Ta Pae is the main shopping center, and there is a nightly bazaar in an area between Suriwong Rd. and Ta Pae Rd. where all kinds of cheap local products are for sale. Outside of town, the village of Lamphun is famous for its silks and cotton, and Baw Sang is popular for its painted paper umbrellas.

Hill tribe treks used to be quite an adventure for the intrepid backpacker and wilderness enthusiast. These days, after literally hundreds of thousands of tourists have trekked their way up to the Akha, Karen, Meo, and Yao tribal villages, these exotic hikes are no

Work elephants being bathed at Chiang Dao's Camp

longer a unique experience. Still, a visit to the hills offers a glimpse of a kind of ancient lifestyle that has disappeared elsewhere in the world. While a trek is a rough way to travel, it can be immensely rewarding for the curious and sensitive traveler. Nearly every hotel and guesthouse in Chiang Mai can arrange a guide and tour up into the hills. These treks usually involve a bus or truck ride out of Chiang Mai, and a few days of trekking with overnights in the villages. The Tribal Research Center at the Chiang Mai University is a good place to do a little research before you set off into the hills.

Chiang Mai is easily accessible from Bangkok by overnight bus, train, or many of Thai Airways daily flights.

CHIANG RAI

Chiang Rai is the other major town in northern Thailand, but it has little to recommend it other than access to some of the most remote border and tribal regions. It is located approximately 620 mi (1,000 km) north of Bangkok and 62 mi (100 km) north of Chiang Mai, not far from the borders of Burma and Laos.

There are two major temples in the city: **Wat Prasing** and **Wat Phra Kaeo.** The latter is believed to have been the original residence of the Emerald Buddha now in Bangkok. Chiang Rai is the jumping off point for many river trips and treks into the hills. This town is considered the apex of the infamous Golden Triangle, however, and it is not an altogether safe region for Western tourists. Join a trek with a reputable company, and check around carefully for reports of robberies and holdups on the rivers and the roads before you go.

You can reach Chiang Rai by bus or plane from Chiang Mai, or by boat — a very popular route — from Tha Thon on the Burmese border north of Chiang Mai.

SUKHOTHAI

The ruins of the ancient city of this name, Thailand's first capital, are located approximately 7 mi (12 km) from new Sukhothai, 273 mi (440 km) north of Bangkok. The new city is undistinguished, but the ruins themselves, now divided into five zones and well-maintained by the Thai authorities, are an impressive site for history buffs.

An excellent museum in the new city, the Ramkhamhaeng National Museum, offers a good introduction to the extensive site. Getting to and around the site is not difficult: hire a *tuk-tuk* in town for the day, or rent a bicycle for more personal explorations. There are innumerable impressive wat ruins within the Sukhothai Historical Park, where immense guardian stone Buddhas preside over the whole ruined kingdom.

You can reach Sukhothai by bus from Chiang Mai or Bangkok.

NORTHEASTERN REGION

THE Thais call the northeastern plateau of their country Esarn, after the pre-Khmer kingdom that existed there and in Kampuchea to the south. It is a region with a rich past, but modern Thailand's poorest and least developed. Much of this vast upland plain is devoted to rice growing, but the area around Loei province, in the northwest of the region, is mountainous and heavily forested. The northeast is bordered to the north and east by the Mekong river and Laos, and to the south by Kampuchea. The northeast is chronically vulnerable to drought, and thus the people of this region are always teetering on the edge of extreme poverty.

There are few major tourist sights in the northeast, and the region remains the least Westernized and most traditional in Thailand. For this reason, many Thais and many of the foreigners who do travel to this region see it as the "real" Thailand, the heartland of traditional values and culture. A journey through the northeast can be immensely rewarding for the traveler unafraid of leaving behind modern comforts. There are infrequently visited and magnificent Khmer ruins and wats, some of the best silk in all of Thailand, and some of the country's most spectacular mountain scenery.

Nakhon Ratchasima, also called Khorat, is the first major city on the route from Bangkok through the northeast. It is only 155 mi (250 km) from Bangkok, and is host to the only TAT office in the region. Its renown as a tourist location is due to the nearby **Phimai** ruins, an 11th-century temple complex located 37 mi (60-km) to the northeast. The white and pink sandstone Khmer shrine is called Prasat Hin Phimai and is a magnificent sight in this remote countryside.

You can reach Khorat by bus, train, and sometimes plane, from Bangkok. Phimai is accessible by an hour and a half bus ride from Khorat.

Khon Kaen, located about halfway between Khorat and Udon Thani in the northeast, is a university town. This area is famous for its silk production, and notorious for the manufacture of Thai Sticks, a particularly potent form of marijuana. There are interesting night markets and fantastic food stalls in Khon Kaen, and the town is accessible by bus from Khorat, Bangkok, and Phitsanuloke in the north, by train from Bangkok and Khorat, and by plane from Bangkok.

The main reason to visit **Udon Thani,** in the far northeast, is to see the prehistoric excavations at **Ban Chiang,** or to travel onwards to Vientiene in Laos. Ban Chiang is about 31 mi (50 km) east of Udon Thani and is thought to be the sight of the world's oldest Bronze Age civilization. The excavations there reveal an agricultural society that flourished some 5,600 years ago. Udon Thani is 348 mi (560-km) northeast of Bangkok and can be reached by bus, train, or plane.

Just west of Udon, Loei Province is considered one of Thailand's most beautiful and unspoiled regions. The provincial capital is called Loei, and is located about 350 mi (560 km) from Bangkok, and some 90 mi (150 km) from Udon.

About 47 mi (75 km) outside Loei city is **Phukradung National Park,** probably the best and most spectacular example of this remote province. The park includes a 4,920-ft-high (1,500-m) mountain, the top of which is a plateau traversed by hiking trails and dotted with bungalow accommodations. There are buses to Loei from Bangkok and Udon, and buses from Loei to Phukradung.

On the eastern border between Thailand's northeast and Laos, the town of **Nakhon Panom** is famous for its **Phra That Phanom,** the region's most revered shrine. Part of the ancient Khmer empire that had its center in Angkor, That Phenom is a Lao-style wat with a great chedi. The chedi is the symbol of the Esarn and is a sacred object to Buddhists all over Thailand—it is thought to be about 150 years old.

The Northeast's most sacred shrine, Phra That Phanom, Nakhon Panom.

There are buses to Nakhon Panom from Udon Thani and Khon Kaen.

Along the southern border of this region, the town of **Surin** is worth a visit for the annual Elephant Roundup in November, and the provincial capital of **Ubon Ratchathani** is famous for its annual candle festival to mark the beginning of the Rains Retreat in mid-summer. You can reach Ubon Ratchathani by bus from Nakhon Phanom or Bangkok, by train from Khorat or Bangkok, and by plane. Surin is accessible by bus or train from Bangkok.

SOUTHERN REGION

THE south is beaches—beaches and islands so idyllic you'd think they were a movie set; vacations so cheap and beautiful and so easy to enjoy, you'd think this was a paradise dreamed up by travel agents in search of the perfect retreat.

Thailand's southern isthmus has many cultural links to Indonesia and Malaysia. The pace of life is slow, easygoing, and comfortable. Southern Thais are called *pak tai*, and you can easily see the influences of both Chinese immigration and Malaysian Islam in their culture and dress. The standard of living in the south is higher than in many other regions in Thailand, an outgrowth as much of the tourist trade as it is of the rubber, tin, and coconut industries based here. Pak tai people live close to the sea, and there is a wonderful abundance of the freshest seafood imaginable in every town, village, and bungalow hotel.

The attractions of the south are numerous and varied, though all emphasize the sea and the beach, a pure retreat from rigors of traveling and shopping. Phuket is the most famous, and most overdeveloped, beach resort. Koh Samui, a fabled "find" of the backpacking crowd in the early 1980s, is now not far behind Phuket in crowds and popularity. The most beautiful and "undiscovered" seashore paradises are in the provinces of Krabi and Trang, the Phi-Phi Islands off Phuket, and the southwest seashore just north of the Malaysian border.

HUA HIN

The first southern beach resort as you travel south from Bangkok is Hua Hin, the oldest seashore resort in Thailand and a favorite of Bangkok inhabitants and the royal family. Hua Hin is perched on the west coast of the isthmus on the Gulf of Thailand, 144 mi (232 km) south of Bangkok.

The royal family's summer residence, located here since the 1920s', is called *Klai Kangwon*, meaning "Place Far From Worries." Hua Hin is a fairly quiet town, though it bustles at times with trainloads of Thai tourists from Bangkok. There is an old golf course opposite the classic colonial-style Hua Hin Railway Hotel. The beach is also reminiscent of colonial days, with a beach promenade lined with old-fashioned deckchairs.

Proximity to Bangkok and lack of crowds make Hua Hin an ideal place for quiet family vacations. There are government buses from the Southern Bus Terminal in Thonburi, numerous private coaches, and daily trains from Bangkok.

KOH SAMUI

When the backpacking traveling crowd of Europeans, Americans, and Australians stumbled upon this 44-sq-mi (17-km²) island about 20 years ago, they thought they had discovered paradise. Overcome with wonder and lacking in forethought, these early explorers spread the word about Koh Samui: a perfect little palm-fringed, white-sanded slice of beach beauty—small villages and indescribably cheap beach bungalows, thatched-roof restaurants on the white sand, phosphorescent flitterings of light in the warm nighttime ocean, fresh seafood and tropical fruits served by smiling Mama Sunshine and her cohorts (the early entrepreneurs with a keen eye for the bahts to be made from backpackers).

The word spread: go to Koh Samui. And so they did, and this little island, like so many other places in the world, is now a happily crowded playtime beach resort for the international crowd. "You should have seen it 10 years ago," the truly enlightened say. Yet Koh Samui retains its charms and its beauties despite the relative crowds, and Thai developers in-the-know say that Samui will never become another Phuket. A newly constructed airport on the island will greatly reduce its relative inaccessibility, and more crowds will doubtless arrive. There are at least four deluxe hotels on the island, and more in the planning stages. But Samui lacks some of the basic resources necessary for full-fledged overdevelopment. Electricity and water are its main inadequa-

Tropical Seashore at Koh Samui

cies, so developers promise Samui will be saved from being totally ravaged.

Koh Samui is the third largest island in Thailand and the largest of a 20-island archipelago located off the east coast in the Gulf of Thailand. A 50-mi-long (80-km) ring road now circles the island, offering easy access to all beaches and bays, including the three best known and most developed: Lamai, Mae Nam, and Chaweng, all located on the north and east coasts. Other than the perimeter of the island, which is all palms and beach, Samui is two-thirds mountain and rolling hills, offering stunning views from a motorbike or jeep ride.

Samui's known history goes back about 1,500 years to a time when fishermen began plying the protected waters of Bophut and Mae Nam bays on the north shore. A life of coconut harvesting and fishing went on very much unchanged through the 20th century until the advent of tourism in the mid-1970s.

The main port and only real town on Koh Samui is Ban Na Thon, on the southwestern side of the island. The two main beach strips, Chaweng and Lamai, are both on the east coast, and easily accessible by the omnipresent *tuk-tuks* and taxis that meet ferries in Na Thon. There are nearly 70 bungalow operations around the island—a testimony to the entrepreneurial savvy of Samui residents—with the great majority clustered on the two main beaches. Chaweng is host to most of the first-class bungalow accommodations, all of which are clustered, quite unobtrusively, near the center of the beach. Near Lamai beach, look for the Lamai Cultural Hall, where the abbot of the local wat has gathered Samui curiosities in a room in his monastery's school. Quieter and equally beautiful beaches include Big Buddha, Bophut, and Mae Nam.

Many travelers prefer to keep moving, onward and upward to even more remote islands. Two nearby islands that have siphoned some of the superfluous tourist trade from Samui are Koh Pha Ngan and Koh Tao. Both have great snorkeling and scuba, and are quieter, less developed, and more like "what Samui was 10 years ago." There are bungalow accommodations on both islands, though electricity and running water may be in short supply at some locations. Boats travel from Na Thon to Koh Pha Ngan twice daily, and there are less frequent boat services from Na Thon to Koh Tao.

Samui is located approximately 22 mi (35 km) off the Thai mainland, south of the mainland city of Surat Thani. To reach Samui, take a bus, train (there are six daily from Bangkok), or plane to Surat Thani, and then take an express boat or ferry from Ban Pon, the nearby pier, to Samui. There are usually three express boats a day, taking two and a half to three hours to reach Samui from Surat. An airport is planned for the island; check with Thai Airways to see if it has opened.

PHUKET

Phuket is a case study of how development transforms paradise. It's not a new story—and it is not all ugly—but the changes that have taken place in Phuket in the last 20 years are an outstanding example of how Westernization and modernization have gradually encroached upon Thailand. It is said that 20, or perhaps 30 years ago, Phuket resembled the Koh Samui of today.

Phuket's name is derived from a Malay word meaning "mountain," and the island is full of hills, sandy cliffs, beautiful beaches, and wildlife. At the turn of the century a British explorer of Phuket described a wealth of animals he had found there, including wild elephants, rhinoceros, tigers, water buffaloes, monkeys, birds, and reptiles. For centuries the island, Thailand's largest, has been one of the wealthiest regions in the country. As early as the ninth century of this era, it was a prosperous trading center for Arab and Indian merchants and had a thriving tin-mining industry. By modern times it had become the country's richest province, its wealth deriving from both tourism and tin.

With an area of 313 sq mi (810-km²), the island proper measures 31 mi (50 km) north to south, and only 13 mi (21 km) at its widest. Commerce and industry are concentrated along the island's east coast, especially in and around Phuket town, a rather dull provincial city with a populatiion of about 50,000. Phuket's most interesting feature is its Sino-Portuguese architecture. The east coast is, however, a great place for catching a boat to some of Phuket's most stunning offshore sights. A total of 39 offshore islands surround Phuket, and many of them have managed to preserve themselves as beautiful little paradises. The most popular destinations from the east coast of Phuket include Koh Phi-Phi, a pair of remote but habitable and popular islands in Krabi Province, and Phang Nga Bay, on the mainland, 47 mi (75 km) from Phuket town. The bay is spectacularly beautiful, studded with limestone towers straight out of a James Bond thriller—literally; the bay was featured in *The Man With the Golden Gun*.

On the extreme southeastern corner of the island, Rawai gives promise of the type of beach to be found on the spectacular west coast. Rawai is more of an unspoiled local fishing village than a modern beach resort, but it repays exploration. Indigenous inhabitants, called Sea Gypsies, live in some settlements at the cove's northern end, and numerous boats with the distinctive local high sterns can be rented for trips to nearby Koh Bon and Koh Hai islands.

But it is as you drive up the west coast that you can see why developers targeted this island for their efforts in the late 1970s and 80s. The sea is stunning, and the beaches, fronting bays that are some large, some small, but all resplendent, seem like perfect expanses of nearly empty white. Nearly empty, that is, except for the growing

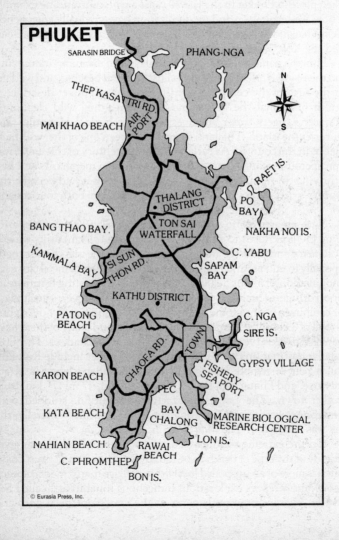

PHUKET

SARASIN BRIDGE

PHANG-NGA

N

S

THEP KASATTRI RD.

MAI KHAO BEACH

AIR PORT

RAET IS.

THALANG DISTRICT

PO BAY

TON SAI WATERFALL

NAKHA NOI IS.

BANG THAO BAY

SI SUN THON RD.

C. YABU

KAMMALA BAY

SAPAM BAY

KATHU DISTRICT

PATONG BEACH

C. NGA

SIRE IS.

TOWN

CHAOFA RD.

FISHERY SEA PORT

GYPSY VILLAGE

KARON BEACH

PEC

KATA BEACH

BAY CHALONG

MARINE BIOLOGICAL RESEARCH CENTER

NAHIAN BEACH

RAWAI BEACH

LON IS.

C. PHROMTHEP

BON IS.

© Eurasia Press, Inc.

number of high-luxury resort hotels that are now scattered along the coast.

Moving north from Promthep Cape, the southern tip of Phuket and a superb sunset spot, you come to Nai Harn, a delightful small beach, but dominated by the exclusive Phuket Yacht Club Hotel, one of many hotels in Phuket that have decided to take up an entire cove for their own use. Others needs not apply.

Next north is Kata beach, with a beautiful bay, a dozen different hotel and bungalow units, and a sprawling Club Med complex at its northern end. Karon is a dune-backed beach with many hotels and a long stretch of white sand. It could be Mexico, it might even be Florida, but it is beautiful despite the crowds. Just to the north of Karon is Karon Noi, a little indentation in the coast completely filled with a Le Méridien hotel.

Beyond Patong, which comes next, are some of the most beautiful, quiet, and still wonderful beaches on Phuket. Try Kamala and Surin, little-visited and not very accessible, with a luxurious and private hotel at the northern end of Surin. There is also a nine-hole golf course off Surin beach. Nai Yang beach is at the far north of Phuket island, close to the international airport. It is actually a national park, some 5½ mi (9 km) long and virtually undisturbed, with only one hotel. In season, many sea turtles come there to lay their eggs.

Phuket is 539 mi (867 km) south of Bangkok, is connected to the mainland by a bridge, and is easily accessible from the capital. There are numerous daily buses, both luxury air-conditioned and more plebian government, as well as six daily flights on Thai Airways. Trains from Bangkok will take you to Surat Thani, a few hours away by bus on the east coast. While on Phuket, there are private cars, jeeps, and motor bikes for rent.

There are other places to visit in southern Thailand, but most would be best if you discovered them on your own. The new stars on the enlightened travelers' itinerary are **Krabi** and **Trang** provinces, east and south of Phuket along the southwestern coast. Krabi is slowly but surely being developed by the same Euro-Thai interests that discovered Phuket two decades ago. Yet it remains stunningly beautiful, simple, and uncrowded. Trang, further to the south, is even more so.

The two major cities in southern Thailand as you make your way towards the Malaysian border are **Hat Yai** and **Songkhla**. Hat Yai, approximately 588 mi (947 km) from Bangkok, is southern Thailand's principal commercial and industrial center. Songkhla, a fishing town located on the Gulf of Thailand, is far more interesting, with a fine beach, some offshore islands, and a nearby bird sanctuary.

VI

Hotels and Lodging

Hotels, resorts, guesthouses, and bungalows—Thailand's accommodations run the full gamut of cost and style, with opulently luxurious deluxe hotels side by side with dirt-cheap dives. Yet even the most budget accommodations are likely to have a sparkle of Thai charm, and the most deluxe hostelries will pamper you beyond belief. Bangkok, as the nation's capital and the center of all business and trade activities, possesses the greatest variety and the highest class of hotels in Thailand.

The further off the beaten track you travel, the more rustic and rugged the hotels and guesthouses are likely to be. In cities and towns in the northeast, for instance, or in other cities visited infrequently by Western tourists, your accommodations will be very basic, often lacking hot water or a private bath. Yet in the most popular tourist cities — such as Pattaya, Chiang Mai, Phuket, and Koh Samui — little expense has been spared to give tourists all the comforts of home.

European, American, and Asian hotel interests discovered the tourist potential of Thailand years ago, and there is a plethora of first-class international hotels throughout the country. The Siam Lodge Group of Hotels, for instance, a European-Thai company, has a half dozen excellent hotels scattered across the country, and two more in the planning stages in the newest hot spots. There are Hiltons, Sheratons, Hyatts, and Holiday Inns, Novotels, Le Méridiens, Club Meds, and Inter-Continentals. Balancing this galaxy of internationals are more traditional and low-key Thai establishments, which offer high standards of service and comfort, as well as hundreds of low-budget bungalows and guesthouses along beaches and village streets.

Prices are reasonable throughout Thailand. In luxury hotels you will pay rates similar to international-class hotels anywhere, ranging from US$60–200 and upwards per night. Comfortable accommodations can be found in Bangkok and elsewhere in the US$20–30 range, and very cheap lodgings are available in most places for as little as US$2–10 per night. Most hotels include a 10% service charge plus an 11% tax in their charges. Room rates given below are for a double room, usually with a bath, during the high season. Expect lower rates for a single, or for travel during the summer or fall. Rates quoted are current as of 1990.

HOTEL RESERVATIONS

The most convenient way to make reservations at hotels in Thailand is to work with an experienced travel agency in the United States. The agency will cover the telex, fax, or telephone charges, and leave you well set up for your journey to the kingdom. It is advisable but not always necessary to have reservations before you embark on your journey, and bear in mind that only the better class of hotels will accept reservations from abroad.

If you are traveling beyond Bangkok without reservations, it is a good idea to have a travel agency in Bangkok set you up in the destination of choice. While advance reservations remove much of the hassle of travel, many places in Thailand are quite accustomed to travelers arriving without reservations and needing a room for that night. In places such as Koh Samui, Koh Samet, Krabi, and Chiang Mai—very popular destinations for tourists without a set itinerary— there are dozens of inexpensive bungalow hotels and guesthouses, and it is advisable to take a little walk or a taxi ride around to find the one that best suits your needs.

While the hotel listings below—covering the cities or island of Bangkok, Pattaya, Chiang Mai, Phuket, and Koh Samui only—are by no means comprehensive, they do include most of the better-class hotels and resorts. There is a great deal of room for personal improvisation in your travels through the kingdom, and this hotel listing merely gives you a good base upon which to develop your own itinerary.

BANGKOK HOTELS

SUPERIOR HOTELS

Airport Hotel
Address: 333 Choet Wutthakat Rd.
Telephone: 566–1020/1; US reservations: (800) 448–8355
Telex: 87424 AIRHOTL TH
Rates: Double—2,576 baht

Located right next to the airport, and possessing all the charm and comforts of a good airport hotel anywhere in the world, this Siam Lodge hotel is considered one of Bangkok's most convenient. There is a regular shuttle bus to downtown, a swimming pool, disco, exercise room, shopping arcade, and convention facilities.

Dusit Thani

Address: 946 Rama IV Rd.
Telephone: 233–1130/59, 236–0450/70
Telex: 8170, 81027 DUSITOTEL TH
Rates: Double—3,927–5,891 baht

The Dusit Thani is a resplendent structure at the end of Silom Rd., one of Bangkok's main shopping and entertainment arteries. Known as one of Bangkok's best hotels, it is especially renowned for the variety of its dining establishments: there are seven restaurants, featuring different cuisines.

Hilton International

Address: Nai Lert Park, 2 Wireless Rd., Ploenchit
Telephone: 253–0123, 253–6470
Telex: 72206 HILBKK TH
Rates: Double—4,641 baht

The Hilton is located somewhat out of the bustle and is famous for its extensive tropical gardens. This is an excellent, peaceful, quiet hotel; a good option for those who seek elegant respite from the crowds.

Hyatt Central Plaza

Address: 1695 Phahonyothin Rd.
Telephone: 541–1234
Telex: 20173 CENTEL TH
Rates: Double—2,805 baht

While the Hyatt is located some 9 mi (15 km) from downtown Bangkok, it is a popular hotel for conventioneers and golfers. It has over 600 rooms and is located next door to a huge department store and shopping mall. An 18-hole golf course is across the street.

The Imperial

Address: 6 Soi Ruamrudi, Wireless Rd.
Telephone: 254-0023
Telex: 82301, 84418 IMPER TH
Rates: Double—3,009 baht

The Imperial is popular with business travelers because of its business discounts and ample convention facilities. It is a comfortable hotel, with tennis courts and good service.

The Oriental

Address: 48 Oriental Ave.
Telephone: 236-0700/39
Telex: 82997 ORIENTL TH
Rates: Double—5,738–7,344 baht

Arguably the very best hotel in Bangkok, if not the world, the Oriental is a journey back into the Somerset Maugham days of colonial languor. The food and service are excellent, the rooms and lobby areas stunning, and the location, in the midst of the Old Farang quarter right alongside the river, is unsurpassed. If you can't afford to stay here, come for a cocktail at dusk.

The Regent Bangkok

Address: 155 Ratdamri Rd.
Telephone: 251–6127
Telex: 20004 REGBKK TH
Rates: Double—4,896–6,528 baht

With a good shopping location and a reputation as a popular meeting place, the Regent is a high-standard hotel renowned for its food and service.

Royal Orchid Sheraton

Address: 2 Captain Bush Lane, Siphaya Rd.
Telephone: 234–5599
Telex: 84491, 84492 ROYORCH TH
Rates: Double—3,188–3,545 baht, depending on the season

If you want to be close to the Oriental in location, but not in price, stay at the Sheraton, an impressive and comfortable hotel on the riverbank off Silom and Surawong roads.

Shangri-La

Address: 89 Soi Wat Suan Plu, Charoen Krung Rd.
Telephone: 236–777
Telex: 84265 SHANGLA TH
Rates: Double—5,483–6,044 baht, depending on the season

Certainly in the top ranks for location, service, and rates in Bangkok, the Shangri-La is a new hotel located near the Oriental on the banks of the Chao Phraya River.

Siam Inter-Continental
Address: 967 Rama I Rd.
Telephone: 253–0355/7
Telex: 81155 SIAMINT TH
Rates: Double—3,851 baht

The beautiful architecture of the Inter-Continental is a relief to the eyes after a foray in the shopping madness outside the hotel doors. Quiet gardens on the grounds further extend the atmosphere of peace and quiet in this excellent hotel.

FIRST-CLASS HOTELS

Bangkok Center
Address: 328 Rama IV Rd.
Telephone: 235–1780/99
Telex: 72067, 72068 BACENHO TH
Rates: Double—1,000–3,200 baht

A moderately priced Thai hotel with a convenient location.

The Boulevard
Address: 17 Soi 7 Sukhumvit Rd.
Telephone: 255–2930/40
Fax: 255–2950
Telex: TH 84033 BLVDHTL
Rates: Double—2,448 baht

With a prime location near the American and other embassies, the Boulevard is the Siam Lodge Group's latest Bangkok offering. All 250 rooms come with a private balcony, air-conditioning, and 24-hour room service. There is a fitness club and a well-appointed business center.

The Menam
Address: 2074 Charoen Krung Rd., Yannawa
Telephone: 289–1148/9, 289–0352/3.
Telex: 21098, 87423 MENAM TH
Rates: Double—1,734 baht

This new hotel is located on prime hotel real estate along the riverbank. It is equipped with tennis courts, a jogging track, and beautiful rooms overlooking Thonburi.

The Montien
Address: 54 Surawong Rd.
Telephone: 234–8060, 233–7060/9
Telex: 81160, 82938 TH
Rates: Double—1,352–3,188 baht, depending on season and class
of accommodations
If you want to be where it all happens, the Montien offers a location at the center of the nightlife district. It is a good hotel, but can get a bit noisy in the wee hours of the morning.

The Narai
Address: 222 Silom Rd.
Telephone: 233–3350/89
Telex: 81175 NARITEL TH
Rates: Double—1,964 baht
Also in the midst of the nightlife and shopping district, the Narai is popular with Thais for its nightclub and sky-high penthouse restaurant.

The Royal
Address: 2 Ratchadamnoen-Klang Rd.
Telephone: 222–9111/20
Telex: 84252 ROYALHO TH
Rates: Double—944 baht
A decent and moderately priced hotel located in the midst of the Grand Palace district.

Tawana Ramada
Address: 80 Surawong Rd.
Telephone: 236–0361/90
Telex: 81167 TAWARAM TH
Rates: Double—3,060 baht
A busy but comfortable hotel, located on Surawong Rd. in the central shopping district.

YMCA
Address: 27 Sathon Tai Rd.
Telephone: 287–1900
Telex: 72185 BYMCA TH
Rates: Double—600–1,400 baht
A surprisingly well-kept, clean, and comfortable bargain.

ECONOMY-CLASS HOTELS

The traditional budget backpacking crowd finds lodging in two Bangkok areas: Soi Nga Duphi, a lane that branches south off Rama IV Rd. in the embassy district, and on Khaosarn Rd., near the Democracy Monument north of the Royal Palace. The former is notorious for the **Malaysia Hotel**, a cheap dive formerly popular with international travelers, now more sleazy than adventurous. The latter is the budget area of choice these days, with dozens of small, family-run hotels with prices in the 40–100 baht range. Other inexpensive hotels and guesthouses include:

The Bangkok Youth Hostel
Address: 25/2 Phitsanulok Rd.
Telephone: 282-0950, 281-6834
Rates: 120–150 baht; 35 baht per person in dormitory

The Ramada
Address: 1169 Charoen Krung Rd.
Telephone: 234-8971/5
Telex: 84150 RAMADA TH
Rates: Double—360–600 baht

Royal Plaza
Address: 30 Naret Rd.
Telephone: 234-7019, 234-3789
Telex: 21063 ROPLAZA TH
Rates: Double—270–550 baht

The Star
Address: 36/1 Soi Kasemsan 1, Rama I Rd.
Telephone: 215-0020/1
Rates: Double—250–400 baht

The Swan
Address: 31 Custom House Lane, Charoen Krung Rd.
Telephone: 233-8444, 234-8594
Rates: Double—200–480 baht

GUESTHOUSES AND APARTMENTS

Amara Court (16 rooms)
Address: 645/44–51 Phetburi Rd.
Telephone: 251–8940/81
Rates: 450 baht/day, 5,500/month

Chusi Guesthouse (13 rooms)
Address: 61/1 Soi Rambutri, Chakkraphong Rd.
Telephone: 282–9941
Rates: 40–80 baht

Ladda Apartment (10 rooms)
Address: 3rd Floor, 85 Patpong 1 Rd.
Telephone: 233–7924
Rates: 300–550 baht

Narai Guesthouse (80 rooms)
Address: 5/7 Sukhumvit Rd., Soi 53
Telephone: 258–7173, 258–0601
Rates: 1,224 baht

CENTRAL REGION HOTELS

PATTAYA

The main beach and day and nightlife area in Pattaya is crammed with over 100 hotels, some deluxe and gleaming, others seedy and crowded. You'll find better swimming and less crowded conditions just south of Pattaya at Jomtien (also spelled Chom Thien or Thian), where there are only a dozen or so hotels as yet.

Nipa Lodge
Address: Pattaya Beach Resort 20260
Telephone: (038) 428–195, 428–321; U.S. reservations (800)
    448–8355
Fax: (038) 428–097
Telex: TH 85903 SIAMLUX
Rates: Double—1,173–1,658 baht, depending on the season
The Nipa, one of Siam Lodge's lodges, was Pattaya Beach Resort's first hotel. There are 150 rooms on the beach, an olympic-size pool,

and lovely tropical gardens. Restaurants feature French, German, and Thai cuisine, and all varieties of land and water sports are available nearby.

Novotel Tropicana

Address: 98 Mu 9, Pattaya Beach Rd.
Telephone: (038) 428–645/8, 428–566; Bangkok reservations 236–2891
Rates: Double—969 baht

With only 186 rooms, the Tropicana was one of the first luxury hotels in town. It occupies an unfortunately central position in the middle of the "strip."

Orchid Lodge

Address: Pattaya Beach Resort 20260
Telephone: (038) 428–161, 428–323; U.S. reservations (800) 448-8355
Fax: (038) 428–165
Telex: TH 85903 SIAMLUX
Rates: Double—1,403–1,887 baht

Located on the quieter northern end of the beach, the Orchid Lodge has 10 acres of landscaped gardens, an olympic-sized pool with a bar, a children's pool and playground, and two tennis courts. There are Italian, seafood, German, and British restaurants.

The Royal Cliff Beach Resort

Address: Cliff Rd.
Telephone: (038) 421–421/30; Bangkok reservations 282–0064
Rates: Double—1,938–5,177 baht

The Royal Cliff occupies an enviable position in Pattaya: on a cliff jutting out between Pattaya and Jomtien. This is the "better" part of town as far as hotel class is concerned, and the Royal Cliff is one of the best hotels, with the best location, in the area. It has two private beaches, guest-only boats, and tennis courts.

The Wong Amat Hotel

Address: 471 Pattaya Beach Rd.
Telephone: 426–999; Bangkok reservations 541–1784, 541–1234 Ext. 2285/88
Rates: Double—1,071–1,199 baht

A nice hotel located comfortably north of the crowded strip.

JOMTIEN BEACH

On Jomtien Beach, south of Pattaya, you will find fewer hotels, and more peace and quiet. Try:

Suan Nong Nooch
Telephone: 429–321; Bangkok reservations 252–1786, 251–2161
    Ext. 8.
Rates: Double—800–1,000 baht

Sugar Hut
Telephone: 421–638, 422–600
    Traditional Thai-style bungalows for about 600 baht.

Villa Navin
Telephone: 428–564, 428–786; Bangkok reservations 251–7636
Rates: Double—2,000–2,400 baht

NORTHERN REGION HOTELS

There are numerous hotels and guesthouses in Chiang Mai, many of them very charming and authentically Thai in style and design. You will find the majority of good guesthouses (in the 50- to 500-baht range) along Moon Muang Rd. and the near the Ping River. Recommended guesthouses include:

Chiang Mai Guesthouse
Address: 91 Charoen Prathat Rd.
Telephone: (053) 236–501
Rates: 200–300 baht

New Chiang Mai Hotel
Address: Chiyapoom Rd.
Telephone: (053) 236–561
Rates: 250 baht

There are also a few very nice hotels, with good amenities and rates to match. The best include:

Chiang Mai Orchid
Address: 100 Huay Kaew Rd.
Telephone: (053) 221–625; Bangkok reservations 233–8261
Rates: Double—1,224–1,581 baht

Long considered the "best" hotel in town, the Orchid is the favored hotel of state and royal guests to Chiang Mai. It has a swimming pool and lovely gardens, and is located west of the old city walls.

The Rincome Hotel
Address: Huey Kaew Rd. 50000
Telephone: (053) 221–044, 221–130; U.S. reservations
  (800) 448–8355
Fax: (053) 221–915
Telex: TH 49314 RINCOMR
Rates: Double—1,352–1,709 baht

A small and cozy hotel with good conference facilities and excellent food and wine. The dining room ceiling is charmingly decorated with a Chiang Mai hallmark: painted umbrellas. There are an Olympic-sized pool, tennis courts, a jogging track, and an 18-hole golf course nearby.

SOUTHERN REGION HOTELS

KOH SAMUI

Koh Samui is, for most travelers, an island of bungalows and thatched-roof cottages where on-the-spot exploration takes precedence over advance planning. There are close to a hundred bungalow operations to choose from on Koh Samui, the great majority of them clustered on the two most popular beaches: Chaweng and Lamai. One bungalow is much like another in style and service; most lack private bathrooms and 24-hour hot water, but they make up for these inconveniences with stunning beach-side locations and usually excellent food at the bungalow restaurant. Bungalow rates range from 100–200 baht per night at the lowest end, to 500–1,200 baht per night for those with air-conditioning, private baths, and the like.

At the upper end of the Koh Samui market there are a couple of luxury resorts that have found this paradise suitable for exclusive developments. Expect the utmost in comfort and luxury—swimming pools, water sports, air-conditioning, and pampered seclusion from the beach mobs.

The Imperial Samui Hotel
Address: Chaweng Beach, Koh Samui
Telephone: (077) 421–390; Bangkok reservations 254–0111, 254–0023; U.S. reservations (800) 448–8355
Rates: Double—3,494–4,182 baht

Tong Sai Bay Hotel
Address: Baan Plailaem, Bophut, Koh Samui
Telephone: (077) 421–450/51; Bangkok reservations 254–0111
Rates: Double—3,825–4,539 baht

PHUKET

PATONG BEACH

There are over 30 different hotels and guesthouses along the most crowded and developed stretch of beach in Phuket, called Patong Beach. If you are looking for a "scene," a less-developed but quickly maturing younger cousin to Pattaya, then Patong is Phuket's answer. Just a couple of the dozens of hotels are mentioned here:

The Coral Beach Hotel
Address: 104 Moo 4, Patong Beach, Kathu District, Phuket 83121
Telephone: (076) ?21–106/13; U.S. reservations (800) 448–8355
Telex: TH 67957 7 CORALSL
Rates: Double—1,275–2,142 baht

The Coral Beach was the first international-class hotel on Patong. Its graceful architecture and beautiful landscaping reveal its years of experience and involvement in Phuket. The hotel is secluded off to the side of the main beach on a rolling hillside, with 68 acres (28 ha) of forest and a private beach for guests. Rooms are simple but pleasant, with balconies over the sea; there are two swimming pools, plus a children's pool. This hotel is popular for family holidays. Food at the hotel is excellent and there are ample sports and touring facilities as well.

Holiday Inn Phuket
Address: 86/11 Thaweewong Rd., Patong Beach, Phuket 83121
Telephone: (076) 321–020; U.S. reservations (800) HOLIDAY
Telex: 69545 HIPHUKT TH
Rates: Double—1,173–1,403 baht

The Holiday Inn is a familiar and comfortable institution, offering predictable and good services in the middle of Patong. Tennis courts, swimming pools, health club and sauna, three bars, conference facilities, and good German food at one of the hotel's restaurants make this a popular holiday spot for families and sports buffs.

NORTH OF PATONG

Dusit Laguna
Address: 390 Srisoontorn Rd., Chergtalay District, Amphur
  Talang, Phuket 83110
Telephone: (076) 311–320/9; Bangkok reservations 236–0450/9
Fax: (076) 311–174
Telex: 69554 DLAGUNA TH
Rates: Double—1,964–2,321 baht

Located on a 1½-mi-long (2.5-km) private beach, the Dusit Laguna offers all the comforts of home and a great deal more peace, quiet, and privacy than the hotels located in Patong. Each of the 240 rooms has a minibar, a television, and a private balcony. Excellent food in seafood, Thai, and Western restaurants, a bar overlooking the sea, a disco, and ample conference and banquet facilities make this a popular hotel for all kinds of tourists. There are also good sports facilities, including tennis and golf (on a nearby putting green).

The Pansea Hotel
Address: Pansea Beach, Phuket
Telephone: (076) 212–901/4; Bangkok reservations 235–6075/6
Rates: Double—1,760–10,226 baht

The Pansea puts guests up in traditional and luxurious bungalows which overlook the sea from vantages along a steep slope. The hotel is nestled in a private bay, and rates include breakfast and dinner.

Pearl Village

Address: Nai Yang Beach and National Park, PO Box 93,
  Phuket 83000
Telephone: (076) 311–338/376/383; Bangkok reservations
  252–5245
Fax: (076) 311–304
Telex: 65539 VILLAGE TH
Rates: Double—1,581–1,964 baht

Pearl Village is a Thai resort with a prime location in the midst
of a well-managed national park. It has 185 rooms, in both separate
cottages and larger buildings, tucked away on 35 acres (14 ha) of
landscaped tropical gardens. The restaurants serve excellent Thai and
international cuisine and ample sports activity is available, including
scuba and windsurfing, tennis and golf.

SOUTH OF PATONG

Kata Thani Hotel

Address: Kata Noi Beach, Phuket 83000
Telephone: (076) 214–824/6; Bangkok reservations (02) 235–9529
Fax: (076) 214–827, 216–632
Telex: 69516 KATHANI TH
Rates: Double—1,479–2,933 baht

With a beautiful location on a truly beautiful beach, the Kata
Thani offers all the expected amenities including convention facili-
ties, a swimming pool, and in-house movies. It shares the beach with
Club Med, but that doesn't diminish the beauty of this lovely spot.

Le Meridien

Address: 8/5 Moo 1 Karon Noi, Phuket 83000
Telephone: (076) 321-480/5; U.S. or Canada reservations (800)
  543–4300
Fax: (076) 321–479
Telex: 69542 MERIHKT TH
Rates: Double—2,193–2,627 baht

This French-owned and -managed resort occupies the entire
landspace of a little cove called Karon Noi, or "Relax Bay." It is a large
resort with 470 rooms surrounded by 40-some acres (16 ha) of tropical
gardens. All rooms have sea views and private balconies, minibars,
color TV, and IDD telephones. There are four restaurants serving Thai,
European, and seafood specialties, and both lounge and poolside bars.

Sports include sailing, windsurfing, scuba, fishing, archery, tennis, and squash. What more could you want?

Phuket Island Resort
Address: 73/1 Rasda Rd., Phuket 8300
Telephone: (076) 212–676; Bangkok reservations 252–5320/1
Fax: (076) 215–956
Telex: 69555 PIR ISLAND TH
Rates: Double—1,275–1,709 baht

This large hotel complex was Phuket's first luxury resort and offers bungalows and rooms with a country view or with a sea view. The complex slopes down a hillside to the sea and has all the modern amenities as well as numerous dining establishments and sports facilities for badminton, tennis, diving, and a private beach on nearby Bon Island.

Phuket Yacht Club.
Address: Nai Harn Beach, Phuket 83130
Telephone: (076) 214–020/7; Bangkok reservations 251–4707
Telex: 69532 YACHT TH
Rates: Double—2,321–3,188 baht

Phuket's most exclusive facility is located on private Nai Harn beach near the southern tip of the island. Room facilities feature everything you might want (including "piped music"), and the 129 rooms are beautifully decorated and designed. There is a lovely swimming pool and well-maintained tennis courts.

VII   Dining Out in Thailand

One of the principal highlights of any trip to Thailand is the food. Thai food is delicious: absolutely fresh, sometimes highly—but always marvelously—spiced, and usually beautifully presented. Thai cuisine depends on the freshness of local ingredients, and then on a repertoire of spices, herbs, peppers, and sauces, to create a vast menu of delights. The cuisine has a reputation for being very spicy; sometimes this is the case, but hot food can be avoided easily, if you want, and the most potent peppers are often optional condiments.

Traditional homestyle Thai food is dominated by vegetables, fish, and seafood. Important spices for most dishes include fresh coriander (cilantro), turmeric in southern Thailand, and ginger, used in nearly everything. Other crucial ingredients include lemongrass, basil, vinegar, and cardamom. Meals are complimented by a group of basic sauces—shrimp paste, tamarind sauce, and chili sauce. Rice is the mainstay for nearly all meals, and a meal usually consists of five or six dishes including curry, soup, omelettes, vegetables, and fish. Thai chefs, like the Chinese, work with a basic repertoir of four tastes: salty, sweet, sour, and pungent.

Other common side dishes to a Thai meal include *nam plaa*, a salty fish sauce, and *nam prik*, a delicious chili and lime sauce. Salads, often served with a mildly spicy peanut sauce, are called *yam*, and after-dinner sweets, which come in all varieties, are called *kanom*. Thai food is consumed, happily, with a fork and spoon, not chopsticks. End a meal, or cool off on a hot day, with a delicious mug of Thai iced coffee, called *ka fei yan*, a wonderful concoction of coffee and sweetened condensed milk.

In addition to all the fresh vegetables, fish, and seafood, Thailand is blessed with an abundance of exotic tropical fruits. Fruits you are likely to see in the markets (though not necessarily recognize) include guavas, jackfruit, papayas, mangoes, rambutans, custard apples, pineapple, and, finally, the odorific durian.

POPULAR THAI DISHES

kaeng kari gong prawn curry
pla kho lad phrik fried grouper with chili sauce
pla phad khing fish with fresh ginger
moo grap crispy fried pork
kaeng mat sa man rich beef curry with peanuts
kaeng kai spiced chicken ragout
kaeng som fish and vegetable ragout
tom yam goong sour soup with prawns
kaeng chut a mild-flavored soup made of vegetables, shrimp,
    chicken, and pork
kaeng liang Thai vegetable soup
tom ka gai chicken and coconut milk soup
kao tom kung mild rice soup flavored with shrimp
khat yat sai omelette filled with meat, onions, and sugar peas
khao prat fried rice
priao wan sweet and sour pork with vegetables
phak bung phat Thai fried vegetables
mi klob vermicelli with bits of meat, shrimp, and egg in a sweet
    and sour sauce
po pia egg roll with bean sprouts, pork, and crabmeat
pla prieo wan sweet and sour fried fish
gai phat phrik spicy fried chicken
kung tot krob crisp fried prawns
pla tot fried fish
kuai tiao lat na noodles with meat, vegetables, and gravy
kuai tiao haeng noodles with a small amount of meat, bean
    sprouts, and spices
kuai tiao nam same as above but with broth
ba mi klob rat na kung fried noodles and shrimp
kieo haeng wonton soup with bits of vegetables and spices

If you are so smitten with Thai cooking that you would like to learn
how to replicate it at home, here are some suggested cooking schools
in Bangkok:

BANGKOK COOKING SCHOOLS

Bussaracum Restaurant, 35 Soi Phi Phat, 2 Convent Rd., Bangkok 10500; Telephone 235–8915.

Modern Housewife Center, 45/6-7 Sethsiri Rd., Bangkok 10400; Telephone 279–2831/4.

UFM Food Center Co. Ltd, 593/29-39 Sukhumvit 33/1 Bangkok 10110; Telephone 259–0620/33.

The Thai Cooking School at the Oriental, 48 Oriental Ave., Bangkok 10500; Telephone 236–0400/20, 437–6211.

HOTEL DINING

Major hotels throughout Thailand feature both Thai and European cuisines. The Thai cuisine can be very good, but chefs often water down the Thai spices in order to please what they assume to be the more sensitive palates of Western visitors. If you want to sample true Thai spices, help yourself to one of the chili sauces on the table.

In addition, usually excellent French, German, American, and British food is often available in hotel restaurants. See the restaurants listed below for some suggestions of superb hotel dining.

RESTAURANT DINING

In Bangkok you will find the most extraordinary array of cuisines, with more choice and greater quality than in perhaps any other city on the globe. In addition to dozens of good Thai restaurants, there are also excellent venues for Chinese, Korean, Italian, French, German, Indian, Middle Eastern, Japanese, and American food. There are also hundreds of noodle stalls and outdoor food stalls, offering snack food and lunch specials. These are very popular with Thais, and despite their rather unhygenic looks, are considered quite safe for Westerners. Since food is most definitely part of the Thai adventure, don't miss an occasional food stall foray.

Most major restaurants in Bangkok and in the tourist cities will have a Thai and English menu. Many restaurants outside of Bangkok don't have menus at all, however, and it is advisable to try to memorize a repertoir of favorite dishes for your off-the-beaten-track culinary cruises.

RESTAURANTS IN BANGKOK AND ENVIRONS

THAI CUISINE

Ban Chiang, 14 Soi Srivieng, off Silom Rd.; Telephone 236–7045. A beautiful old Thai mansion with good food.

Banya, Opposite the Oriental Hotel on the river; Telephone 437–7329. They will send a boat to pick you up from the pier at the Oriental. The location is special and they serve reasonably priced Thai food.

Bussaracum, 35 Soi Phi Pat, 1 Convent Rd.; Telephone 235–8915. Favorite among Thai gourmets and expatriates, lovely setting and extraordinary food. Try the fish cakes.

Laikhram, Soi 49/4, 11/1 Sukhumvit. Gourmet Thai, reasonably priced. Try the green papaya salad called *som tam*.

Lemongrass, Soi 24 off Sukhumvit Rd.; Telephone 258–8637. Famous for excellent Thai food in traditional surroundings.

Maharaj, at the Maharaj stop of the express boat on the Chao Phraya; Telephone 221–9073. Good food with Thai music from 7 to 9 PM nightly.

Tumpnakthai Garden Restaurant, Rajadapisek Rd.; Telephone 277–8833. Seats 3,000 people and the waiters roll by on skates. Good food despite the gimmicks.

The Toll Gate, 245/2 Soi 31 Sukhumvit Rd.; Telephone 258–4634. Royal cuisine and expensive.

Whole Earth, Soi Langsuan near Lumpini Pk.; Telephone 252–5574. Vegetarian and Thai food.

Yokyor Restaurant, 4 Visukasut Rd.; Telephone 281–1829. On a riverboat on the river. Good fish.

OTHER EASTERN CUISINES

CHINESE CUISINE

The Golden Dragon, 108–114 Sukhumvit Rd.; Telephone: 251–4553. Great dim sum.

JAPANESE CUISINE

Akamon, Soi 21, 223 Sukhumvit; Telephone 258–3875.

Tokugawa Japanese Restaurant, Ambassador Hotel; 8 Soi 11 Sukhumvit; Telephone 251–5140. Expensive, of course, but famous for their beef dishes.

INDIAN CUISINE

Royal India, 392/1 Chakraphet Rd. Usually an all-Indian clientele (which speaks well for the authenticity of the food), serving great food at moderate prices.

WESTERN CUISINES

BRITISH CUISINE

Bobby's Arms Pub and Restaurant, Patpong 2 Rd., Carpark Bldng.; Telephone 233–1759. Good fish and chips.

FRENCH CUISINE

Le Vendóme Restaurant, 75/5 Soi II Sukhumvit Rd.; Telephone 250–1220.

Normandie, Oriental Hotel; Telephone 236–0400. Dining room is styled after the restaurant car of the Orient Express. Expensive and world-famous. On the river.

La Brasserie, Regent Hotel, Ratdamri Rd.; Telephone 251–6127.

GERMAN CUISINE

By Otto, Sukhumvit Rd.; Telephone 252–6836. A beer garden and bakery.

ITALIAN CUISINE

L'Opera, 55 Soi 39 Sukhumvit. Great Italian food.

Pan Pan, Sukhumvit Rd. on corner of Soi 33; Telephone 258–9304. An Italian café.

THEATER RESTAURANTS

Sala Rim Nam, Thonburi side of the river; Telephone 437–6211. Thai classical dancing with great Thai food.

Baan Thai, 7 Sukhumvit Soi 32; Telephone 258–9517. Famous for their classical dance shows nightly at 9:00 PM.

Piman Thai Theater Restaurant, 46 Soi 49 Sukhumvit Rd.; Telephone 258–7866. Watch Thai classical dance and listen to Thai music while dining.

VIII

Cultural Activities, Recreation, and Entertainment

CULTURE AND ENTERTAINMENT

Thailand has its own traditions of theater and dance, which are well worth the visitor's patronage, and its own films, mostly of the martial arts variety. There are cultural societies for European expatriates, and, of course, a well-known—not to say notorious—nightclub scene.

PERFORMING ARTS

There are two main styles of Thai classical drama, both of which may be seen at the National Theater, on Na Phrathat and Chao Fa

Classical dancer in the costumes of Nora Dance

roads. In the *Iakhon* drama, unmasked actors, often women, perform plays on various themes. By contrast, the *khon* dance-drama draws its plots from the Indian epic the *Ramayana*; the players wear masks, and the action is accompanied by music and song. It is well worth seeing if you are in Bangkok on the second and fourth weekends of the month, when it is usually staged. Call the National theater at 224–1342 for information. There are also outdoor performances given every Saturday and Sunday at 4:30 PM. On the last Friday of each month a special public exhibition of Thai classical dancing is staged. Call 221–5861 for information.

There are also frequent free performances of Thai classical dancing at the Lak Muang or Erawan Hotel shrines, and several restaurants and hotels have performances for tourists. The Oriental Hotel, for instance, offers dance and martial arts performances in the riverside garden on Sundays and Thursdays at 11 AM.

FILM

You will find numerous Thai, American, and European films listed daily in the *Bangkok Post*. Although the Western films are usually dubbed into Thai, Thai films can be an interesting experience in body language—all *kung fu* and martial arts. The English-language newspapers are also a good source of news about cultural events in town.

CULTURAL SOCIETIES

Alliance Française, Next to the YMCA on Sathorn Tai Rd.; Telephone 286–3879. Shows French films each week.

British Council, 189 Surawong Rd.; Telephone 324–0247.

Goethe Institute, 102/1 Phra-Athit Rd.; Telephone 281–7211.

Siam Society (Royal Patronage), Sukhumvit Soi 21 (Soi Asoke). Frequent exhibitions of folk art and a reference library.

NIGHTLIFE

No matter how much tourism officials and government authorities try to change Bangkok's image, there is too much money to be made from the more seedy side of Bangkok's nightlife. There are an estimated 300,000 bar girls, hostesses, and masseuses at work in

Bangkok, most of them peasant girls lured by the big city lights and the hope of lucrative employment. These working women seem to enjoy their jobs, and their clients have helped to give Bangkok the raucous, rowdy, ribald reputation it now enjoys.

Most of the girly bars are concentrated in the notorious nightlife districts along Sukhumvit Rd. from Soi 21 on, and especially on Patpong I and II between Silom and Surawong roads. Another infamous and rowdy nightspot is the aptly named Soi Cowboy between Sukhumvit Sois 21 and 23.

These bars and clubs specialize in live sex shows, striptease, and erotic dancing. Drinks are in the 50–60 baht range, and nondancing girls are available for conversation and can be taken out after or, for a fee, during the show.

Massage parlors are among the most famous and infamous highlights of the female trade in Bangkok. Crowds of young women are usually found seated behind a glass wall with numbers pinned to their shirts. Pick a masseuse, and she's yours for the duration. The massage parlors are concentrated in the Patpong area and along new Petchburi Rd.

For those not in search of a commercial encounter with the opposite sex, there are also good nightclubs in most of the big hotels, many of which feature excellent music by local and Filipino bands. One of the newest and biggest discos is the Nasa Spacedrome on Suapa Rd. (Telephone 221–1685).

SPORTS

In Thailand, you can play golf or tennis or go to the races, as you can in most parts of the world. And, of course, Thailand is famous for its beach sports, dealt with in Chapter V. But Thailand also has its own fascinating sports, some fierce and exciting, others elegant and graceful.

THAI BOXING

The most famous and most popular Thai sport—popular with Thais and foreigners alike—is Thai boxing (called *muay Thai*). Thai boxing is a wild and often very violent sport in which contestants are allowed to use virtually any part of their bodies to beat—literally— their foe. Thai boxing can be seen at Lumpini Stadium on Rama IV Rd. (Telephone 363–8766) every Tuesday, Friday, and Saturday at

6 PM. It can be seen at the Ratchadamnoen Stadium on Ratchadamneon Nok Rd. (Telephone 281-8546) every Monday, Wednesday, and Thursday at 6 PM.

TAKRAW

Another popular Thai sport, though not one you are likely to see in a formal stadium, is takraw. It is usually played by boys or men who kick around a small ball of woven rattan. It is more a demonstration of skill and grace than a competitive sport, and the point of the game is to keep the ball in the air.

KITE FLYING

From February to April, especially on the Pramane Ground near Wat Phra Keo, you can see Thais of all ages practicing one of the most colorful and popular Thai pastimes, kite flying.

OTHER THAI SPORTS

Other popular, though less readily observable, Thai sports include sword fighting, cockfighting (often on display at the Weekend Market), fish fighting (also on display at the Weekend Market; the best fighter is the male Siamese fighting fish), beetle fighting, and cricket fighting.

HORSE RACING

There are horse races every Saturday at 12:15 PM at the Royal Bangkok Sports Club, Henri Dunant Rd. (Telephone 251-0181/6) and every Sunday at 12:15 PM at the Royal Turf Club of Thailand, 183 Phitsanulok Rd. (Telephone 282-3770).

GOLF

There are numerous golf courses available for your sporting pleasure:

Army Golf Course (18 holes), Ramintra Rd.; Telephone 521-1530.
Bang Phra Golf Course (18 holes); Chonburi.
Krungthep Sports Golf Course (18 holes); Telephone 374-6064.
Navatanee Golf Course (18 holes); Telephone 374-7077.
Navy Club Golf Course (9 holes), Bangona; Telephone 393-1652.
Railway Training Center Golf Course (18 holes), Phaholyothin Rd.; Telephone 271-0130.

Rose Garden Golf Course (18 holes), Booking office: 4/8 Sukhumvit Soi 3; Telephone 253–2276, 253–0295/7.

Royal Bangkok Sports Club (18 holes), Henri Dunant Rd.; Telephone 251–0181/6.

Royal Thai Air Force Golf Club (18 holes), Don Muang; Telephone 523–6103.

Siam Country Club (18 holes), Pattaya; Telephone (038) 418–002.

TENNIS

Tennis facilities can be found at:

AUA, 179 Rajadamri Rd.; Telephone 252–7067/9.

YMCA, 27 Sathorn Tai Rd.; Telephone 287–1900, 287–2727.

WATER SPORTS

See Chapter V, "The Thailand Tour," and Chapter VI, "Hotels and Lodging," for pointers to the best beaches for water sports.

IX Shopping

HOW TO SHOP IN THAILAND

The main rule for Thai shopping is to remember that bargaining is the rule, not the exception. You are expected to bargain, and to do so, of course, with subtlety and tact. If you are out of practice though, no one will mind. It probably just means that the proprietor will walk away with more money! If you bargain well, you can expect to get your item for 20% to 30% less than the first quoted price. The only places where you cannot bargain are in the large department stores and a few fixed-price shops.

In order to avoid any questions about quality, quantity, or authenticity, you should obtain receipts for everything you purchase. If you are buying jewelry or gemstones, certificates of guarantee are especially important. If you are using credit cards, make sure that the shop is not adding an extra surcharge on top of the price. It can come as a surprise when you receive your bill in a few weeks.

Remember that no image of the Buddha or genuine antique is allowed to leave the country without a special export license from the Fine Arts Department at the National Museum. This can take some time to arrange—discuss it with the store owner, and see Chapter III for details.

There are many bargains to be had when shopping in Thailand, and some of the best buys include Thai silk and cotton, gems and jewelry, silverware, bronzeware, leather goods, temple rubbings, Thai dolls, and paintings. It is, however, all too easy to pay too much for your purchase, and it is advisable to take some time when you are shopping. Compare prices, and avoid touts who receive a commission—often secretly tacked on to your purchase price—for getting you into the shop. Most of the better tourist shops accept major credit cards and can even ship your package home for you.

The Tourism Authority of Thailand publishes a bimonthly *Official Shopping Guide*, which includes shopping tips, maps of the major shopping areas, and a comprehensive list of TAT-approved shops. Shops approved by TAT display the TAT emblem, a drawing of a peasant woman sitting between baskets balanced on either end of a pole carrier.

WHAT TO BUY

ANTIQUES

There are many beautiful bronze or stone statues, woodcarvings, jade, celadon ware, and paintings to be found. Beware of fake antiques, and remember, there is a ban on exporting Thai antiques; check with the shop owner or the Fine Arts Department of the National Museum.

METALCRAFTS

Bronze has been used in Thailand for many centuries, especially for casting images of the Buddha. Bronze cutlery sets can be lovely gift items, and some are decorated with rosewood and buffalo horn handles. Some of the best handmade pewter in the world comes from Thailand. It is all lead-free. Thai silver is renowned for its detailed craftsmanship and good price. See especially the jewelry, cigarette, and cigar boxes, cutlery, bowls, and small boxes made by the hill tribes. Many have traditional patterns in high and low relief. Nielloware, or *thom*, as it is called in Thai, is a popular product: it is silver inlaid with black alloy, and the craft dates back to the 17th century.

CERAMICS

THAI CELADON

Celadon is a high-fired stoneware produced by Chinese artisans in Thailand over 800 years ago. Its manufacture was a lost art until after World War II, when it was rediscovered at Sukhothai. For fine examples of this art try the Celadon House on Silom Rd.

POTTERY

Sangkhalok stoneware was made by potters from China 700 years ago. Given the ban on exporting antiques, we can be thankful that modern factories are now producing items in this ancient type of stoneware as well.

LACQUERWARE

Lacquerware is another ancient Thai craft, and there are many different designs. The most traditional form is black with gold decoration. Typical items include ashtrays, bowls, and jewelry boxes. Like handicrafts, lacquerware is best purchased at Chiang Mai.

GEMS AND JEWELRY

One of Bangkok's many names is "The Jeweled Abode of Indra," and the kingdom is fast gaining a reputation as one of the gem and jewelry capitals of the world. Gem mining began to be organized on a large scale in the 1960s, and since that time the quality of the craftsmanship and of the gems themselves has improved immensely. There are now elegant jewelry shops all over Bangkok, particularly in luxury hotels and shopping centers. The gem and jewelry export business now ranks as Thailand's fifth largest earner of foreign exchange.

There are some dangers in jewelry shopping in Bangkok, however, as many tourist guides steer their customers to shops and lapidaries where the guides get a commission. Keep in mind that the price of a stone is based on vast variations in color, clarity, and cut as well as carat weight, and it often takes a trained eye to spot the differences. If you are planning on doing some serious gem and jewelry shopping, you would be well-advised to purchase *A Buyer's Guide to Thai Gems and Jewelry* by John Hoskins, which offers an excellent introduction to the scene and tips on how to judge stones.

As always, you should compare prices on the items you are interested in at a number of shops, particularly those in the better parts of town. The best shops are members of the Gem and Jewelry Traders Association, and TAT can provide you with a list of reputable gem stores. Bargaining is expected, and reductions of 10% to 15% are not unusual. A very low price should make you suspicious, and remember that these sellers are experienced: a good bargain should be expected, but not a steal. Also remember that "18K gold" in Thailand can be anything from 9K to 14K international. Make sure you ascertain which measuring system is used, and ask for international standards only.

Some recommended gem and jewelry traders include:

Bualadd, Peninsula Plaza, 153 Rajadamri Rd.; Telephone 253–9760.

Yves Joallier, Charn Issara Tower Building, 3d Floor, 942–83 Rama IV Rd.; Telephone 233–3292.

World Jewels Trade Center, 987 Silom Rd.

Tok Kwang, 244/6 Silom Rd.; Telephone 233–0658. Good pearls.

Cabochon, Oriental Hotel, Oriental Ave. Telephone 236–6607. Provides a certificate of guarantee.

HANDICRAFTS

The best place for handicrafts is Chiang Mai, but if you can't make it there, Bangkok has some lovely offerings. These are mostly the work of hill-tribe craftsmen and are wonderful, colorful memories of your trip to Thailand. The embroidery is gorgeous, and comes in all forms, including clothing, bags, and pillowcases. Also look for lacquerware, painted umbrellas, wood carvings, basketwork, and mobiles. Try the handicraft shops on Silom Rd., at the Siam Center Building on Rama I Rd., and Narayan Phand on Larn Luang Rd.

THAI DOLLS

Handmade Thai dolls, in the form of classical dancers, members of the hill tribes, farming folk, and animals, are lovely and popular souvenirs.

KHON MASKS

Khon masks are used in Thai classical masked plays. They are made from hardened papier-mâché, and are brightly painted to represent demons, monkeys, and other characters from the Indian epic *The Ramayana*.

WICKERWARE

Thai wickerwork is based on traditional designs, and is woven from rattan, bamboo, palm leaves, rushes, sisal fibers, and banana straw. There are baskets, handbags, mats, hats, and furniture available, all of high quality and interesting design.

WOOD CARVINGS

Another traditional Thai craft product—woodcarvings of animal figures such as elephants and water buffaloes, salad bowls, platters and trays, and fine furniture—makes good purchases. Most of the workshops are in the northern provinces around Chiang Mai.

TEMPLE RUBBINGS

Temple rubbings are an inexpensive and easy to carry gift item, available on rice paper or cloth, in charcoal, gold, or oil paint. They contain motifs from temples throughout Thailand. For a truly fancy result, try having them framed with Thai silk borders.

TEXTILES AND CLOTHING

THAI SILK

Perhaps Thailand's most famous product, Thai silk is handwoven and is considered one of the best silks in the world. A wonderful variety is available in solid colors, patterns, or brocade, light and heavy weights. You can buy it by the yard, or have it made up into dresses, shirts, neckties, and even cushion covers by a custom tailor. Mudmee (tie-dyed) silk is a special product from the northeast in which the silk threads are tied in the desired pattern before thay are dyed.

For good but expensive silk, try Jim Thompson's Shop at 9 Surawong Rd. There are countless other places to buy silk as well.

LEATHER

Suprisingly, Thailand is a great place to purchase leather items. This is a recent phenomenon, and the quality of finished products, including clothing, shoes, and bags, is rapidly improving. There are over one hundred tanneries on the outskirts of Bangkok, and most Thais have all their shoes custom-made! There are good buys in boots, and crocodile, snakeskin, and top-quality leather bags. (However, you may not be able to bring crocodile items into the United States. Several crocodiles are officially listed as endangered species, and products made from these species may not be brought in.)

CUSTOM-MADE CLOTHING AND SHOES

Tailors in Thailand are cheaper than those in Hong Kong and Singapore and usually just as good. You will have better luck with the end result if you give the tailor an item of clothing to copy.

READY-MADE CLOTHING

Inexpensive and good-quality clothing is sold in street markets all over Bangkok and Chiang Mai. The sizes may be small, but if you are lucky you'll find good casual items that will withstand the heat better, perhaps, than the clothes you brought with you.

WHAT NOT TO BUY

There are a great deal of fake designer goods, especially on the street markets in Bangkok and Chiang Mai. You can purchase these of course, but don't believe that you have actually gotten a LaCoste polo shirt or a Cartier watch. Prerecorded cassette tapes—that is, pirated recordings—are for sale everywhere. While this is a very inexpensive way to expand your music collection, the quality of these tapes is often dubious, and they violate the copyright laws.

MAJOR SHOPPING AREAS

Because of Bangkok's uneven and unplanned sprawl, there is no clearly defined downtown, and the major shopping areas are sprinkled throughout the city. No matter—half the fun of shopping in Bangkok is the adventure of getting to the store. For Thais, the best place to shop is one of the new, gleaming, often immense department stores or shopping arcades. The department stores are good for your basic necessities: toiletries, the forgotten swimsuit, a ready-made shirt or skirt, interesting food and beverage items. Shopping arcades populate the hallways of many deluxe hotels and are often stacked with excellent and expensive boutiques—a safe and uncomplicated way to purchase a bolt of Thai silk or a piece of embroidery.

The more adventurous hit the streets for bargains and souvenirs, and Bangkok gives you ample choice of where and how to shop. The **Silom and Surawong Rd.** area, where many of the better hotels, nightclubs, and restaurants are located, is also an area packed with fine and expensive tourist shops. Stroll down Silom, and then up the parallel Surawong, and cap off the afternoon with a walk down New Rd. and into the shops at the Oriental Hotel.

Along **Rama I Rd.** near the embassies and the Siam Inter-Continental Hotel, good shopping can be found in the Siam Center Shopping complex or at the Siam Square, across the street.

Near the Democracy Monument, north of the Royal Palace area in a district called **Banglampoo,** you'll find many boutiques and inexpensive souvenir stores. This is where the international travel crowd hangs out—just off Ratchadamnoen Ave. is Khao San Rd. with a plethora of budget guesthouses and hotels—and local entrepreneurs have set up shop en masse to take advantage of the tourist trade. There are nice items for sale in these shops, including handmade leather shoes, bags, jewelry, and the like, but beware of fakes and cheats.

Shopping centers dominate the shopping scene around **Rajdamre and Ploenchit roads.** The Rajdamri Arcade, the Rajprasong shopping center, and the Thai Daimaru Department Store are all fashionable hangouts for Thai teenagers—but that doesn't mean you won't be able to find some bargains or useful items here.

The Weekend Market, on Sundays at Chatuchak Park in the northern part of the city, is an event, a carnival, a spectacle, and not to be missed. If you need Christmas presents for ten nieces and nephews, or even a few special items for a few special people, it can be immensely entertaining and ultimately rewarding to wander amidst the vast array of merchandise, live and dead, for sale at this market. Everything from silks and cotton, to ready-made shirts and sarongs, bird cages, fighting fish, and lovely northern hill tribe embroidery is for sale.

The so-called **Thieves' Market** is a good excuse to visit Chinatown and is located on either side of Charoen Krung (New Rd.) and Yaowaraj. You'll find hundreds of little shops selling everything from toilets to birds' nests, Chinese paper lanterns, and medicinal herbs. There are many pawnshops and buckets of bric-a-brac. The name of this market is not without justification, and what looks like a real bargain—a "genuine" antique, for instance—is more likely to be a 20th-century fake. Still, shopping in this area can often yield great finds in bronze and brass, and Yaowaraj Rd. is especially well-known for its gold.

For a truly Thai souvenir, travel to Wat Rachanada and find the **Amulet Market.** This temple is located on Mahachai Rd. near Ratchadamnoen Ave. Religious Thais believe strongly in the protective powers of amulets, a kind of Buddhist charm worn around the neck on a gold or silver chain.

Doing Business in Thailand

As more and more foreign enterprises, trading companies, banks, and businesses are discovering, Thailand can be a very good place to do business. In recent years the Thai government has concentrated on moving the economy away from traditional commodity exports such as tapioca, tin, and lumber, and has decided to concentrate development in the manufacturing sector. Currently, manufacturing accounts for 60% of exports and fully one-quarter of Thailand's gross national product. The economy is currently growing at a rate of nearly 10% per year, establishing the country's emerging status as a newly industrialized country, one of Asia's Four Dragons.

Foreign investment in Thailand— usually but not always taking the form of joint ventures with majority Thai ownership—has accelerated in recent years. Such foreign investment is found in many sectors of the economy, predominantly manufacturing, trade, mining and quarrying, construction, the service industries, finance, and, to a lesser extent, agriculture. The Japanese are the largest investors in Thailand, followed by Taiwan, Western Europe, and the United States.

ESTABLISHING YOUR BUSINESS IN THAILAND

WORK PERMITS AND BUSINESS REGISTRATION

According to the Employment Act of 1978, all aliens must obtain work permits to work in Thailand. If an alien enters under the Investment Promotion law, an application for a work permit must be submitted within 30 days of entry. Upon entering the country, the foreigner must obtain a nonimmigrant visa, valid for periods of either 90 days or one year, and apply for a work permit.

To set up a public limited company (having a minimum of 15 promoters and 100 shareholders) or a private limited company (having a minimum of 7 promoters and 7 shareholders), an investor must first file a Memorandum of Association with the Company Registrar in the

Ministry of Commerce. Then, after all shares to be paid for have been subscribed, a statutory meeting is called. Within three months of the statutory meeting the directors must register the establishment of the company. If the company will be subject to the income tax, they must also obtain a company income tax identity card and tax number from the Revenue Department. Finally, an application is filed for business tax registration.

INCENTIVES AND REGULATIONS

INVESTMENT PROMOTION POLICY

One of the principal avenues into the Thai market is through the government's Investment Promotion Policy, originally promulgated in 1954 and reformed to its current state in 1977. In 1960 the Board of Investment (BOI) was set up to administer investment promotion and legislation, and currently the Office of the Board of Investment (OBOI), under the administration of its secretary general, is assigned the task of providing investors with assistance and advisory services in all aspects of investment in Thailand.

Projects eligible for investment promotion status may be categorized into agroindustries, minerals, metal and ceramic industries, chemicals and chemical products, mechanical and electrical equipment, and services. Priority development targets include projects that
- generate employment or are labor-intensive
- are located outside Bangkok and the surrounding six central provinces
- generate substantial foreign exchange earnings and strengthen the balance of payments, such as through export-oriented production
- utilize Thailand's own natural resources
- conserve energy or substitute indigenous energy supplies for imported fuels
- support the development of basic industries that can enhance other industrial development

Investment promotion through the BOI can provide tax incentives such as corporate income tax holidays, exemption or reduction of most duties and business taxes on imported items, and exclusion from taxable income of dividends during the income tax holiday. There are also guarantees against nationalization, state competition, and state monopolization. Permission is also given for foreign currency to be remitted abroad as well as for foreign ownership of land, and the entry and employment of foreign nationals.

Additional incentives are available for projects located in Investment Promotion Zones, a broad geographical area including every province in the country except for Bangkok and the five surrounding provinces.

Export-oriented industries are granted other incentives such as deductions on income increment derived from exports, as well as on transportation and insurance costs. While all these incentives help ease the entry to the Thai market, one does not have to receive BOI promotional privileges to invest in Thailand.

APPLYING FOR PROMOTIONAL PRIVILEGES

To apply for these privileges, a prospective business must file two copies of the application form, which is available from the Secretary's Office of the OBOI. After receiving approval, the applicant must set up the company within six months of accepting the approval and submit the following documents to the OBOI:

- the memorandum of association
- the certificate of business registration
- a certificate stating the registered capital
- a list of Directors indicating those empowered to bind the company, and the address of the company
- a list of shareholders and their nationalities
- a document showing the transfer of funds from overseas, or a certificate of investment from overseas issued by the Bank of Thailand
- a joint-venture contract, licensing agreement, technical assistance contract, or technology transfer contract, or any combination of them
- a completed Promotion Certificate application form

THE ALIEN BUSINESS LAW

The Civil and Commercial Code of Thailand governs commercial transactions and corporate matters and would permit unrestricted participation by all persons, regardless of nationality and business activities, if it weren't for the Alien Business Law of 1972. This law significantly narrows the freedom of foreigners to do business in Thailand. In effect, the Alien Business Law prevents foreign investors, as defined by the Alien Business Law, from having more than a certain fixed amount of the shares in an enterprise. An alien is defined as a natural or juristic person without Thai nationality, and an alien business is one in which half or more of the capital is owned by aliens, half or more of the shareholders or partners are aliens, or the managing partner is an alien. A business can lose its alien character if a transfer of a majority of its shares, partnership interests, or management to Thai persons takes place.

There are three categories of business, and which businesses are included in what categories may be changed by royal decree. Of the three, businesses in category A are absolutely closed to aliens. This category includes rice farming, salt extracting, internal agricultural trade, buying and selling real estate, building construction, and such service industries as law, accounting, architecture, advertising, and barbering and beauty parlor operation. Foreigners may open businesses in category B if the foreign business has BOI promotional privileges. This category includes many agricultural businesses and industrial and handicraft businesses involving local agricultural products. For a comprehensive list of restricted activities, contact the Thai Office of the Board of Investment, 555 Vipavadee Rangsit Rd., Bangkhen, Bangkok 10900; Telephone 270–1400.

Category C businesses include commercial enterprises involving wholesale trade; exporting; retailing of machinery, equipment, and tools; and some industrial and handicraft businesses. Category C businesses are theoretically open to aliens, but the authorities have a policy of not issuing new permits to new alien business in this category unless they are convinced that these businesses could not be carried out by native Thai firms.

If they wish to engage in a business activity governed by the Alien Business Law, foreigners must apply to the Ministry of Commerce for an Alien Business License, which may be valid for a fixed period, or for an unlimited time but subject to certain conditions.

BUSINESS OPERATIONS IN THAILAND

SELLING TO THAILAND

If you are interested in marketing your product in Thailand, no special license is required. There are numerous and detailed import restrictions, however, and the possibility of hefty import taxes. Contact the Thai Customs Department for specifics, and get in touch with your country's chamber of commerce for restrictions on importing to your own country or elsewhere. Thai trade centers and trade associations around the world can supply helpful advice on this issue.

BUYING FROM THAILAND

Various government-issued documents are required before items may leave the country. An export license, issued by the Ministry of Foreign Trade, is necessary, as are certificates of origin and the payment of various taxes. For some products, such as silverware, gems, and jewelry, a certificate must be obtained from the Department of Standards; art and antiques require an export license from the Deparment of Fine Arts at the National Museum; and certain items, such as textiles and garments, are restricted for resale by quota and other restrictions in the United States and other countries. Export duties may also have to be paid; see the section on the customs tax, below. For further details on buying from Thailand, and for help in contacting partners and trade agents in Thailand, consult the Thai Trade Center in your own country.

SETTING UP A FACTORY IN THAILAND

Procedures for setting up or expanding a factory in Thailand involve submitting application forms to the Investment Services Center (ISC) of the OBOI. The ISC will give notice of approval or non-approval within 90 days of the submission.

ACCOUNTING STANDARDS

Books and accounts must kept according to the provisions in the Civil and Commercial Code, the Revenue Code, and the Accounts Act. They may be kept in any language, but a Thai translation must be attached. A balance sheet must be prepared once each year, certified by the company auditor, approved by the shareholders, and filed with the departments of Revenue and Commercial Registration.

LABOR

There is a Labor Protection Law, stipulating work hours, holidays, medical leave, maternity leave, guidelines for wages and overtime, etc. Though this law is not strictly enforced, there is a growing agitation from labor groups to protect the Thai workforce from exploitation.

FOREIGN EXCHANGE CONTROLS

There are no exchange control restrictions on remittances into Thailand, though remittancees must be registered within seven days of a loan commitment, or no later than the day when the loan is converted into local currency.

Any remittance of funds into or out of Thailand requires exchange control approval, which is granted depending on a company's tax liability.

Funds imported for business purposes must be registered with the Bank of Thailand to facilitate later repatriation. The Exchange Control Authority will usually grant approval for remitting profits, and dividends derived from registered foreign investment after income tax and other taxes, as well as principal, interest on loans, and fees and royalties have been deducted.

A person operating under the Investment Promotion Act of 1977, or an investor in a business incorporated outside Thailand but operating under the act, is permitted to remit foreign currency abroad under the following conditions:

— If it represents the investment capital that the person brought into Thailand and the dividends or other benefits derived from the investment capital.

— If it represents a foreign loan and interest charged to the person investing in the activity.

— If it represents foreign obligations by the person under a contract for the use of rights and services related to the activity.

EXCHANGE RATES

Interest and exchange rates are to a great degree controlled by the Bank of Thailand. It sets the average value of the Thai baht against major currencies, establishing a flexible system that allows for gradual exchange rate adjustments on a daily basis. The baht is tied to approximately 80–85% of the U.S. dollar and to about 10% of the yen.

TAXATION

FOREIGN individuals and corporations doing business in Thailand, or otherwise deriving income from Thailand, are subject to a variety of taxes.

CUSTOMS DUTIES AND EXCISE TAX

CUSTOMS TAX

Customs taxes are governed by the Customs Law as amended, and by the Customs Tariff Decree, which covers about 2,000 items with both specific and advalorem rates. Export tariffs are imposed on only a few items including rice, rawhide, rubber, wood, raw silk, scrap iron, and powdered fish. Apart from tariff duties, certain imports and exports are also subject to business tax.

Imports arriving by air, sea, or land must undergo a clearance process. Import entry and supporting documents must have been filed and processed at any time prior to the arrival of the goods. Charges must be paid for landing and storage, along with the tariff duties and business tax.

Certain kinds of goods require an export license under the Export Standard Act of 1979. Tax incentives and exemptions can be granted to international trading companies that meet certain conditions. As a general rule, there are few exchange control restrictions on export transactions. With certain exceptions, exporters are required to obtain a Certificate of Exportation from an authorized bank in order to authorize the Customs Department to clear the goods for export.

EXCISE TAXES

Excise taxes are levied on a number of goods, including petroleum products, tobacco, liquor, soft drinks, fruit juice, matches, and cement.

INCOME TAXES

PERSONAL INCOME TAX

Income taxes must be paid by anyone who derives income from a company or post in Thailand. Rates range from 7% to 55%, and exemptions are granted to certain persons such as UN officials, diplomats, and certain visiting experts. An individual who is present in Thailand for more than 180 days in any tax year is treated as a resident of Thailand.

CORPORATION TAX

"Registered" companies listed on the Securities Exchange of Thailand pay a reduced rate of 30% of net profits. Foundations and associations engaging in business activities pay taxes at a rate of 10% of gross business income.

A company is responsible for paying income tax for all its regular employees and withholding it from their salaries. Business tax is levied on gross receipts and is usually calculated monthly. The rate depends on the nature of the business. A municipal tax of 10% of the business tax is also paid at the same time.

Profits remitted or retained abroad from a business operated in Thailand are subject to a 20% withholding tax in addition to corporate income tax. If a payment is made to a company or partnership incorporated under foreign law, 25% has to be withheld from the gross remittance. This applies to loan interest, royalties, or management fees. Thailand has treaties with 22 countries for the avoidance of double taxation and such a treaty is currently being negotiated with the United States.

TAX CLEARANCE CERTIFICATE

Before an alien who has been in the country for more than 90 days in any one calendar year may leave Thailand, he or she must obtain a tax clearance certificate from the Revenue Department showing that all taxes due have been paid or that a surety has guaranteed they will be paid.

BANKING AND FINANCE

BANKING

The finance market in Thailand is dominated by commercial banks, which account for nearly 80% of all business financing. There are approximately 15 locally incorporated banks, the largest being the Bangkok Bank. Thai banks have over 1,900 domestic branches with a market share of about 95% of total deposits and loans in the banking system. Thai commercial banks have become increasingly international, with six banks collectively having over 30 overseas branches and representative offices.

THAI BANKING

GOVERNMENT BANKS

Bank of Thailand,
273 Samsen Rd.,
Bangkok 10200;
Telephone 282–3322

Bank of Agriculture and Agricultural Cooperatives,
469 Nakon Sawan Rd., Dusit,
Bangkok 10300;
Telephone 282–5181/90, 282–5770/9

Government Housing Bank,
77 Ratchadamnoen Rd., Bangkok;
Telephone 281–7499, 281–7245

Industrial Finance Corporation of Thailand,
1770 New Petchburi Rd.,
Bangkok 10310;
Telephone 251–7181/90

COMMERCIAL BANKS

Asia Trust Bank Ltd.,
80-82 Anuwongse Rd.,
Bangkok 10500;
Telephone 222–2171/80

Bangkok Bank Ltd.,
333 Silom Rd.,
Bangkok 10500;
Telephone 234–3333

Bangkok Bank of Commerce Ltd.,
171 Surawongse Rd., Bangkok 10500;
Telephone 234–2930/8, 234–4349

cont...

COMMERCIAL BANKS *(cont.)*

Bangkok Metropolitan Bank Ltd.,
2 Chalermkhet 4 Rd., Plabplachai,
Bangkok 10100;
Telephone 223-0561

Bank of America,
2/2 Wireless Rd., Bangkok 10500;
Telephone 251-6333

Bank of Asia,
601 Charoenkrung Rd.,
Bangkok 10100;
Telephone 222-5111, 221-9123/32

Bank of Ayudhya Ltd.,
550 Ploenchit Rd., Bangkok 10500;
Telephone 252-8391, 252-8171

Bank of Canton Ltd.,
197/1 Silom Rd., Bangkok 10500;
Telephone 234-7030/9

Bank of Tokyo Ltd.,
62 Silom Rd., Bangkok 10500;
Telephone 233-0790/8

Banque Nationale de Paris
(Southeast Asia Representative),
5th Floor, Dusit Thani Office Bldg.,
Rama IV Rd., Bangkok 10500;
Telephone 233-4310, 233-1655

Bharat Overseas Bank Ltd.,
221 Rajawong Rd., Bangkok 10500;
Telephone 221-8181/2, 222-4144/5

cont...

COMMERCIAL BANKS *(cont.)*

Chase Manhattan Bank,
Siam Center, 965 Rama I Rd.,
Bangkok 10500;
Telephone 234–1141/50

**Continental Illinois National Bank
and Trust Co. of Chicago**
(Representative Office),
9th Floor, Panunee Bldg.,
518/3 Ploenchit Rd., Bangkok 10500;
Telephone 251–0623/4, 251–0644

First Bangkok City Bank Ltd.,
20 Yukol 2 Rd., Bangkok;
Telephone 233–0500/19

Four Seas Communications Bank Ltd.,
231 Rajawong Rd., Bangkok 10500;
Telephone 222–2161/5

Hong Kong and Shanghai Banking Corporation,
Hong Kong Bank Bldg.,
64 Silom Rd., Bangkok 10500;
Telephone 233–5995, 233–1904

Import-Export Bank of Japan,
10th Floor, Boon Mitr Bldg.,
138 Silom Rd., Bangkok 10500;
Telephone 234–4879, 235–7373

Indo-Suez Bank,
142 Wireless Rd., Bangkok 10500;
Telephone 252–2111/9

International Commercial Bank of China,
95 Suapa Rd., Plabplachai, Bangkok;
Telephone 221–8121/4, 221–2731

cont...

COMMERCIAL BANKS *(cont.)*

Korea Exchange Bank,
(Representative Office),
8th Floor, Kongboonma Bldg.,
699 Silom Rd., Bangkok 10500;
Telephone 234-0989

Krung Thai Bank Ltd.,
35 Sukhumwit Rd., Bangkok 10110;
Telephone 251–2111

Laem Thong Bank Ltd.,
289 Surawongse Rd., Bangkok 10500;
Telephone 233–9730/9, 234–0882/4

Manufacturers Hanover Trust Co.,
10th Floor, Dusit Thani Office Bldg.,
Rama IV Rd., Bangkok 10120;
Telephone 233–0727/8

Mitsui Bank Ltd.,
Boon Mitr Bldg., 138 Silom Rd.,
Bangkok 10500;
Telephone 234–3841/7

Mercantile Bank Ltd.,
Ngow Hock Blg., 127 Sathon Tai Rd.,
Yannawa, Bangkok 10120;
Telephone 286–3392, 286–9232

Nakornthon Bank,
1016 Rama IV Rd., Bangkok 10500;
Telephone 233–2111, 234–6415

Siam City Bank Ltd.,
1101 New Petchburi Rd.,
Bangkok 10400;
Telephone 252–4425/9

cont...

COMMERCIAL BANKS *(cont.)*

Siam Commercial Bank Ltd.,
1060 New Petchburi Rd., Bangkok 10400;
Telephone 251–3114

Société Generale,
(Representative Office),
12th Floor, Kian Gwan House,
140 Wireless Rd., Bangkok 10500;
Telephone 251–9270, 251–7121

Standard Chartered Bank,
Dusit Thani Office Bldg.,
1–3 Rama IV Rd., Bangkok 10500;
Telephone 234–0821

Thai Danu Bank Ltd.,
393 Silom Rd., Bangkok 10500;
Telephone 233–9160

Thai Farmers Bank,
400 Phahon Yothin Rd., Bangkok 10400;
Telephone 270–1122, 270–1133

Thai Military Bank,
34 Phayathai Rd., Bangkok 10400;
Telephone 282–2727, 282–7740, 282–7731/5

Union Bank of Bangkok Ltd.,
624 Jawaray St., Bangkok 10100;
Telephone 233–4740, 233–4421/9

United Malayan Banking Corporation,
U.M.B.C. Bldg., 149 Suapa Rd., Bangkok;
Telephone 221–9191/5

World Bank,
Udom Vidhy Bldg., Rama V Rd.,
Bangkok 10500;
Telephone 235–5300/7

There are 14 foreign banks licensed to operate in Thailand, and 31 foreign representative offices. The Bank of Tokyo and Mitsui Bank are ranked first and second in their share of the total assets of the 14 foreign bank branches. Chase Manhattan has a large presence in Thailand, as does Citicorp, which ranks as the third largest foreign bank in Thailand.

There are also financial institutions including finance and security companies with assets totalling 13% of the total financial system. There are 100 finance and securities firms and 25 credit financiers that offer syndicated loans and consumer finance. There are also three non-commercial banks administered by the government involved in agriculture, housing, and savings.

THE STOCK MARKET

The Securities Exchange of Thailand, established in 1974, has gradually become a center for exchange of equity and debt paper. The members of the exchange consist of licensed securities companies who trade in listed or registered securities and authorized securities.

GOVERNMENT BODIES AND PRIVATE ORGANIZATIONS

WHETHER you are visiting on business or for pleasure—or both— you may need to apply to various government bodies and agencies in the course of your stay in Thailand. In addition there are numerous private organizations that can help make your sojourn more pleasant or profitable. The following tables supply addresses and telephone numbers for contacting some of these bodies.

EXPORT-PROMOTION OFFICES AND GOVERNMENT MINISTRIES DEALING WITH FOREIGN TRADE AND INVESTMENT

Ministry of Industry
Rama VI Rd., Bangkok 10400
Telephone 245–7790, 245–8033
Telex 84375 MOIT

The Industrial Estates Authority of Thailand
628 Nikhom Makkasan Rd.
Phayathai, Bangkok 10400
Telephone 253–2965
Cable Address IEAT BANGKOK

Alien's Occupational Control Division
Labour Department
Mitmaitri Rd., Phayathai, Bangkok 10400
Telephone 245–3700, 245–3902

Board of Investment
16th Floor, Thai Farmers Bank Bldg.
400 Phahonyothin Rd., Bangkok 10400
Telephone 270–1400/20
Telex 72435 BINVEST TH

Department of Export Promotion
Ministry of Commerce
22/77 Ratchadaphisek Rd., Bangkok 10900
Telephone 511–5066/77
Fax 512–1079
Telex 82354 DEPEP TH

cont...

FOREIGN TRADE OFFICES *(cont.)*

Department of Foreign Trade
Ministry of Commerce
Sanamchai Rd., Bangkok 10200
Telephone 223–1481/5

Department of Industrial Promotion
Ministry of Commerce
Rama IV Rd., Bangkok 10400
Telephone 246–0033, 246–1155

Department of Labor
Ministry of Interior
Fuangnakhon Rd., Bangkok 10200
Telephone 221–5140/4

Department of Lands
Ministry of Interior
Phraphipit Rd., Bangkok 10400
Telephone 222–6130/40

Department of Mineral Resources
Ministry of Industry
Rama VI Rd., Bangkok 10400
Telephone 246–1161/9

Eastern Seaboard Development Committee
618 Nikhom Makkasan Rd., Phyathai, Bangkok 10400
Telephone 253–3533/75
Telex 72391 SB TH

Fiscal Policy Office
Ministry of Finance
Soi Arisamphan, Rama VI Rd., Bangkok 10400
Telephone 271–0204
Telex 82823 FISTOLO TH

cont....

FOREIGN TRADE OFFICES *(cont.)*

Immigration Division
National Police Department
Soi Suan Phlu, Yannawa, Bangkok 10500
Telephone 286–9229/30

National Economic & Social
Development Board
962 Krung Kasem Rd., Bangkok 10100
Telephone 282–1151/6

National Statistical Office
962 Lan Luang Rd., Bangkok 10100
Telephone 282–1481/5

Department of Customs
Art Narong Rd., Klong Toey, Bangkok 10110
Telephone 286–1010/9

Department of Business Economics
Ratchadamnoen Rd., Bangkok 10200
Telephone 281–7340, 281–7199, 281–7104

Export Service Center
22/77 Ratchadaphisek Rd., Bangkok 10900
Telephone 511–5066/77
Telex THC TH82354

Tourism Authority of Thailand
Ratchadamnoen Nok Ave., Bangkok 10100
Telephone 282–1143/7

Tourist Assistance Center
(Tourist Police)
Tourism Authority of Thailand
Telephone 281–0372, 281–5051

The Revenue Department
Chakkrapong Rd., Bangkok 10200
Telephone 281–5777

cont...

FOREIGN TRADE OFFICES *(cont.)*

Securities Exchange of Thailand
132 Sinthon Bldg., Wireless Rd., Bangkok 10500
Telephone 250–0001/8

Communication Authority of Thailand
1160 Charoenkrung Rd., Bangkok 10500
Telephone 233–1050

Telephone Organization of Thailand
977 Ploenchit Rd., Pathumwan, Bangkok 10500
Telephone 257–1190

Bangkok Mass Transit Authority
888 Nailert Bldg., Petchburi Rd., Phyathai,
Bangkok 10400
Telephone 252–9083, 252–3106, 251–0924/5
251–0933/4, 251–0940/1

Public Relations Department
Ratchadamnoen Klang Rd., Bangkok 10200
Telephone 281–8821

THAILAND'S TRADE AND COMMERCIAL OFFICES OVERSEAS

BONN
Office of the Commercial Counsellor
Royal Thai Embassy
Bad Godesberg,
53 Bonn-Bad, Godesberg 1

BRUSSELS
Office of the Commercial Counsellor
Royal Thai Embassy
2 Square du Val de la Cambre
1050 Brussels, Belgium
Telephone (02) 640–5950, (02) 640–6070
Telex 635 10 THAI BR B

CANBERRA
Office of the Commercial Counsellor
Royal Thai Embassy
20 Hicks Street, Red Hill, Canberra
A.C.T. 2603, AUSTRALIA
Telephone 951164
Cable THAITRADE CANBERRA

COPENHAGEN
Office of the Commercial Counsellor
Royal Thai Embassy
Vesterbrogde 1 C, 1st Floor
1620 Copenhagen V., DENMARK
Telephone (01) 135354
Cable TRADETHAI COPENHAGEN
Telex 16600 FOTEX DK
Attn. TRADETHAI CPH

cont...

THAI OVERSEAS COMMERCIAL OFFICES *(cont.)*

DAKAR
Office of Thai Trade Commissioner
12 Boulevard Pinet, Laprade
B.P. 3837, DAKAR SENEGAL
Telephone 219398

GENEVA
Office of the Commercial Counsellor
Permanent Mission of Thailand
28, Chemin Colladon
1209 Geneva, SWITZERLAND
Telephone 981363, 980576
Telex 28993 THAI CH

THE HAGUE
Office of the Commercial Counsellor
Royal Thai Embassy
Delistraat 47, The Hague
THE NETHERLANDS
Telephone 07060149
Cable THAITRADE THE HAGUE
Telex 34276 THAI NL

HONG KONG
Office of Trade Commissioner
221-226, Gloucester Rd.
2nd Floor, Hyde Centre Causeway Bay
HONG KONG
Telephone 5-742201/4
Telex 76348 THTRH HX

JAKARTA
Office of the Commercial Counsellor
Royal Thai Embassy
Bangkok Bank Bldg., 3rd Floor,
Jalan M.H. Thamarin 3, Jakarta
REPUBLIC OF INDONESIA
Telephone 353757
Cable THAITRADJAKARTA

cont...

THAI OVERSEAS COMMERCIAL OFFICES *(cont.)*

KUALA LUMPUR
Office of the Commercial Counsellor
Royal Thai Embassy
30 Parry Rd., Kuala Lumpur
MALAYSIA
Telephone 424601
Cable THAITRADE KUALA LUMPUR

LAGOS
Office of the Commercial Counsellor
Royal Thai Embassy
Ruxtor Fd, Ikoyi
P.O. Box 3095, Lagos
NIGERIA

LONDON
Office of the Commercial Counsellor
Royal Thai Embassy
41 Albermarle St.
London WIX 3 FE ENGLAND
Telephone (71) 493–5749
Cable THAITRADE LONDON
Telex 298706 THATIR G

MANILA
Office of the Commercial Counsellor
Royal Thai Embassy
4th Floor, Oledan Building,
Ayala Avenue, Makati, Metro
P.O. Box 1487 MCC, Manila
REPUBLIC OF THE PHILIPPINES
Telephone 86–75–64
Cable THAITRADE MANILA
Telex 722-2149

cont...

THAI OVERSEAS COMMERCIAL OFFICES *(cont.)*

NAIROBI
Office of the Commercial Counsellor
Royal Thai Embassy
Park Lands Road, P.O. Box 30637
Nairobi, KENYA
Telephone 582967
Cable THAITRADE NAIROBI

NEW DELHI
Office of the Commercial Counsellor
Royal Thai Embassy
E-17 Ring Road, Defence Colony
New Delhi
REPUBLIC OF INDIA
Telephone 623875
Cable THAITRADE NEW DELHI

OTTAWA
Office of the Commercial Counsellor
c/o Royal Thai Embassy
396 Cooper St., Suite 310
Ottawa, Ontario, K2P 2M7
CANADA
Telephone (613) 2384002, 2384004
Cable THAITRADE OTTAWA
Telex 0534883 THAITRADE

PARIS
Bureau du Counseiller Commercial
Ambassade Royal de Thailande
184 rue de l'Université
75007 Paris, France
Telephone 551-73-43
Telex 270837 THCOMPR

cont...

THAI OVERSEAS COMMERCIAL OFFICES *(cont.)*

BEIJING (PEKING)
Office of the Commercial Counsellor
Royal Thai Embassy
No. 40 Kuang Hua Lu, Beijing
PEOPLE'S REPUBLIC OF CHINA
Telephone 523986, 523955
Telex 22145 THAI CN

ROME
Office of the Commercial Counsellor
Royal Thai Embassy
Via del Serafico, 135
00142 Rome, ITALY
Telephone 5030804, 5035225
Telex 680418 THAII
Cable THAITRADE ROME

SEOUL
Office of the Commercial Counsellor
Royal Thai Embassy
123–26 Itaewon-Dong
Yongsan-Ku, Seoul
REPUBLIC OF KOREA
Telephone 792–4446
Cable THAITRADE SEOUL
Telex KSHAKIL F. 24491
Attn. THAITRADE SEOUL

SINGAPORE
Office of the Commercial Counsellor
Royal Thai Embassy
370 Orchard Road,
SINGAPORE 0922
Telephone 7373060
Cable THAICOMM SINGAPORE
Telex RS25168

cont...

THAI OVERSEAS COMMERCIAL OFFICES *(cont.)*

TOKYO
Office of the Commercial Counsellor
Royal Thai Embassy
14–10, Chuo-Cho
2 Chome, Meguro-Ku,
Tokyo, JAPAN
Telephone 793–5821, 793–5876
Cable THAITRADE TOKYO
Telex THAITRADE J25733

VIENTIANE
Office of the Commercial Counsellor
Royal Thai Embassy
Vientiane
LAO P.D.
P.O. Box 128
Telephone 3716

WASHINGTON, DC
Office of the Commercial Counsellor
Royal Thai Embassy
1990 M St., N.W. Suite 380
Washington, D.C. 20036
UNITED STATES OF AMERICA
Telephone (202) 467–6790/1/2/3

OVERSEAS EXPORT SERVICE INSTITUTIONS

BANGKOK
Export Service Center
22/77 Rachadapisek Rd., Bangkhen
Bangkok 10900, Thailand
Telephone 511–5066/77
Telex: 82354 THC TH

FRANKFURT
Thai Trade Center
6000 Frankfurt/Main
Bethmannstrasse 58/Kaiserstrasse/15, Germany
Telex 4189399 TTICD
Cable THAICENTER, GERMANY

LOS ANGELES
Thai Trade Center
3440 Wilshire Boulevard, Suite 1101
Los Angeles CA 90010 U.S.A.
Telephone (213) 380–5943/44, 380–9916
Telex TTC LSA 686208

NEW YORK
Thai Trade Center
5 World Trade Center
Suite 2447, New York, NY 10048
Telephone (212) 466–1777/9
Telex 645690 THAICOM NYK
Cable THAICOM NEW YORK

cont...

OVERSEAS EXPORT SERVICES *(cont.)*

ROTTERDAM
ASEAN Trade Promotion Center
CBI Bldg., 5th Floor,
Rotterdam, The Netherlands
P.O. Box 30009
Telephone (010) 13 27 06
Telex 27151 CBIBZ

SYDNEY
Thai Trade Center
12th Floor, Royal Exchange Bldg.
Sydney 2000, Australia
Telephone 241–1075/6
Telex THAITC AA 23467
Cable THAICENTER SYDNEY

TOKYO
ASEAN Promotion Center for Trade
World Import Mart Bldg. (6 Fl),
1–3 Higashi Ikebukuro
3-chome, Toshima-ku
Tokyo, Japan 170
Telephone (03) 987–1301
Cable ASEANCENTER TOKYO
Telex (0) 2722031

VIENNA
Thailaendische Handelsabteilung
Thailaendische Botschaft
Gottfried Kellergasse 2/38
A-1030 Wien, Austria
Telephone (0222) 75 41 19
Telex 135971 VTC A

FOREIGN EMBASSIES IN BANGKOK

Australia
37 Sathorn Tai Rd.
Telephone: 2860411

Canada
Boonmitr Bldg., 11th Floor
138 Silom Rd.
Telephone: 2341561

People's Republic of China
57 Ratchadaphisek Rd.
Telephone: 2457032, 2457037

France
Customs House Lane
Telephone: 2340950

Germany
9 Sathorn Tai Rd.
Telephone: 2864227

India
4–6 Soi Prasanmit, Sukhumvit Rd.
Telephone: 2580300/6

Indonesia
600–602 Phetchaburi Rd.
Telephone: 2523135

Italy
92 Sathorn Nua Rd.
Telephone: 2864844

Japan
1674 New Phetchaburi Rd.
Telephone: 2526151

cont...

FOREIGN EMBASSIES IN BANGKOK *(cont.)*

Malaysia
35 Sathorn Tai Rd.
Telephone: 2861390

Nepal
189 Sukhumvit Rd., Soi 71
Telephone: 3917240

New Zealand
93 Wireless Rd.
Telephone: 2518165

Philippines
760 Sukhumvit Rd.
Telephone: 2590140

Singapore
129 Sathorn Tai Rd.
Telephone: 2862111, 2861434

United Kingdom
Wireless and Ploenchit roads
Telephone: 2527161

United States
95 Wireless Rd.
Telephone: 2525040/9

USSR
1081 Sathorn Nua Rd.
Telephone: 2349824

PRIVATE-SECTOR BUSINESS CONTACTS IN THAILAND

Board of Trade of Thailand
150 Rajbopit Rd., Bangkok 10200
Telephone 221–0555, 221–1827, 221–9350

American Chamber of Commerce
7th Floor, Kian Gwan House,
140 Wireless Rd., Bangkok 10500
Telephone 251–9266/7, 251–1605

Australian-Thai Chamber of Commerce
Room 608, 6th Floor, Dusit Thani
Office Bldg., 946 Rama IV Rd.
Bangkok 10500
Telephone 233–1785/6

British Chamber of Commerce
9th Floor, Bangkok Insurance Bldg.
302 Silom Rd., Bangkok 10500
Telephone 234–1140/69 Ext. 335

Thai-Chinese Chamber of Commerce
233 Sathorn Tai Rd., Bangkok 10120
Telephone 234–1571/3

Chambre de Commerce Franco-Thai
9th Floor, Kian Gwan House
140 Wireless Rd., Bangkok 10500
Telephone 251–9385/6

German-Thai Chamber of Commerce
6th Floor, Kong Boonma Bldg.
699 Silom Rd., Bangkok 10500
Telephone 233–9113

cont...

PRIVATE BUSINESS CONTACTS IN THAILAND *(cont.)*

India-Thai Chamber of Commerce
13 Attakarnprasit Lane,
South Sathorn Rd., Bangkok 10120
Telephone 286–1961, 286–1506

Japanese Chamber of Commerce
4th Floor, Panunee Bldg.
518/2 Ploenchit Rd., Bangkok 10500
Telephone 252–0178/9, 251–7418

Philippine-Thai Chamber of Commerce
Room 810, 8th Floor, Dusit Thani
Office Bldg.
946 Rama IV Rd., Bangkok 10500
Telephone 233–4260/4

The Thai Chamber of Commerce
150 Rajbopit Rd., Bangkok 10200
Telephone 221–3351, 221–6532/4

Thai-Korean Chamber of Commerce
8th Floor, Kong Boonma Bldg.
699 Silom Rd., Bangkok 10500
Telephone 233–1322/3

TRADE ASSOCIATIONS IN THAILAND

Animal Health Products Association
69/26 Athens Theater Lane, Phayathai Rd., Bangkok 10400

Artificial Flower, Foliage and Plant Manufacturers Association
407 Moo 7, Teperak Road, Samrong Nua, Samuth Prakarn
Telephone 394-3998

Association of Members of the Securities Exchange
132 Sinthorn Bldg., Wireless Rd., Bangkok 10500
Telephone 252-7251/5

Association of Thai Industries
394/14 Samsen Rd., Bangkok 10300
Telephone 282-2482/3, 282-2485

Association of Thai Travel Agents
Racha Hotel, 18 Sukhumvit 4 Rd., Bangkok 10110
Telephone 252-5102/9

Auto Parts Manufacturers Association
79/1 Chueaploeng Rd., Bangkok 10120
Telephone 286-3055

Automotive Industries Association
394/14 Samsen Road, Dusit, Bangkok 10300
Telephone 282-2482/3

Bangkok Chinese Importers & Exporters Association
869-875 Songwad Rd., Bangkok 10100
Telephone 221-1594

Bangkok Ice Transporters Association
1042-4 New Petchburi Rd., Bangkok 10310
Telephone 251-7623/4

cont...

TRADE ASSOCIATIONS *(cont.)*

Bangkok Medical Traders Association
1714 Krung Kasem Rd., Bangkok 10100
Telephone 222-4339

Bangkok Motion Picture Exhibitors Association
352 Rama I Rd., Bangkok 10500
Telephone 251-1735

Bangkok Rice Millers Association,
233 Sathorn Tai Rd., Bangkok 10120
Telephone 234-0329, 234-2221

Bangkok Shipowners & Agents Association
197/1 Silom Rd., Bangkok 10500
Telephone 233-4366

Book Importers & Distributors Association
292/15-16 Luklaung Rd., Bangkok 10300
Telephone 282-0583

Canned Provisions Traders Association
114-114/1 Langsuan Lane, Ploenchit Rd., Bangkok 10500
Telephone 252-2438, 251-2533

Chalerm Loke Market Traders Association
503/4-5 Husaadin Lane, Phayathai, Bangkok 10400
Telephone 251-6739

Chemical Traders Association
104 6th Floor Panawong Bldg.
Surawongse Rd., Bangkok 10500
Telephone 235-0200/9 Ext 58

Chinese Construction Association
209 Nawarat Lane, Yannawa, Bangkok 10120
Telephone 222-4032

cont...

TRADE ASSOCIATIONS *(cont.)*

Coffee Traders Association
42 Padsai Rd., Bangkok 10100
Telephone 221–5698

Cosmetic Importers & Exporters Association
306 Silom Rd., Bangkok 10500
Telephone 233–6931/9 Ext 266

Cosmetic Manufacturers Association
292/39 Surachai Advocate & Solicitors
2nd Floor, Lan Luang Rd., Bangkok 10100
Telephone 281–5548

Credit Foncier Trade Association
48-52 Soi Phanthachit, 3rd Floor,
Maitreechit Rd., Bangkok 10100
Telephone 233–9720/9

Crops Producer & Trade Promotion Association
32/9 Soi Aree Samphan 4
Rama VI Rd.
Samsen Nai, Bangkok 10400

Electric Appliances Trade Association
Room 205, 2nd Floor, Rama Theatre
Rama IV Rd., Bangkok 10500

**Fire Extinguisher Manufacturers &
Trade Association**
103 Susarn Lane, Silom Rd., Bangkok 10500
Telephone 281–2353, 281–7310

Fish Sauce Factories Association
895/71 Bastadthong Rd., Bangkok 10500
Telephone 252–5701, 251–9238

cont...

TRADE ASSOCIATIONS *(cont.)*

Formed Glass Dealers Association
102 Chula Lane 16, Phayathai Rd., Bangkok 10500
Telephone 252–4281

General Insurance Association
233 Ruamrundee Lane, Wireless Rd., Bangkok 10500
Telephone 251–4120, 251–4132

Glassware Products Association
645/40 Soi Metro Shopping Center,
Petchburi Rd., Bangkok 10400
Telephone 251–3818

Government Lottery Dealers Association
250 Amnoey Songkram Rd., Bangkok 10400
Telephone 241–3899

Housing Business Association
6th Floor, Seri Bldg.
1053/1 Phahonyothin Rd.
Bangkok 10400
Telephone 279–8852

Ice Wholesalers Association
1042–44 Petchburi Rd., Pathunam, Bangkok 10400
Telephone 251–7623/4

Insurance Brokers Association
2nd Floor, H.L.R. Bldg. 285 Convent Rd., Bangkok 10500
Telephone 234–7680/6

Jewelers' Association
42/1 Soi Panumas, Ban Moh, Bangkok 10200
Telephone 221–4465

Jute Bag Traders Association
219-221 Songsawad Rd., Bangkok 10100
Telephone 234–5615

cont...

TRADE ASSOCIATIONS *(cont.)*

Leather Association
205 Rama IV Rd., Prakanong, Bangkok 10110
Telephone 391–3296/8

Liquor Dealers Association
44-46 Chalermkhet Rd., Suanmali, Bangkok 10110
Telephone 223–3418, 223–9959

LP-Gas Traders Association
522 Phahonyothin Rd., Saparnkwai, Bangkok 10400
Telephone 279–2341

Mekhong Whisky Provincial Dealers Association
69 Chalermkhet 1 Rd., Bangkok 10100

Oil Traders Association
603/4–6 Nakhon Chaisri Rd., Bangkok 10300
Telephone 241–0771/5

Pharmaceutical Products Association
4186 Klauy Nam Thai Lane, Rama IV Rd., Bangkok
Telephone 392–4849

Photographic Dealers Association
96–98 Chula Lane 6, Rama IV Rd., Bangkok 10500
Telephone 251–9322

**Radio, Television & Sound Systems
Traders Association**
119 Harasmaung Rd., Bangkok 10500
Telephone 251–4894, 251–8250

Rice Exporters Association,
37 Soi Ngamduplee, Rama IV Rd.
Yannawa, Bangkok 10120
Telephone 286–3258, 286–5279

cont...

TRADE ASSOCIATIONS *(cont.)*

Sawmills Association
350 Isudhikasat Rd., Bangkok 10200
Telephone 281–9345, 282–0510

Signboard Makers Association
185/2 Gangshan Lane, Nanglinchi Rd., Bangkok 10120
Telephone 286–2200, 286–0510

Small Industries Association
207/15 Petchkasem Rd., Paricharoen, Bangkok 10160
Telephone 467–1192

Society of Thai Weight & Measures Manufacturing
265/177–178 Soi Thaveevatana
Sathupradit Rd., 3rd Floor, Bangkok 10120
Telephone 284–2042

Southeast Asia Cattle Breeders & Traders Association
Chokechai Bldg., 690 Sukhumvit Rd., Bangkok 10110
Telephone 391–8011, 391–8240

Spare Parts Enterprise Association
1350-52 B.C.C. Bldg., Bantadthong Rd., Bangkok 10500
Telephone 214–1799

Sports Goods Trade Association
234 Siam Sq., Soi 2 Rama I Rd., Bangkok 10500
Telephone 233–9851

Steel Bar Industry Association,
93 Langsuan Lane, Ploenchit Rd., Bangkok 10500
Telephone 252–0636

Stevedoring Promotion Association
214 Surawongse Rd., Bangkok 10500
Telephone 233–2170/3

cont...

TRADE ASSOCIATIONS *(cont.)*

Sugar Dealers Association
305 Suanmali Rd., Bangkok 10100
Telephone 223–6923

Tanning Industry Association
4174-6 Rama IV Rd., Bangkok 10500
Telephone 395–0922

Tea Merchants Association
70 Suankwangtung Flat
Rama IV Rd., Bangkok 10100
Telephone 222–0748, 221–4511 Ext 709

Thai Agricultural Merchants Association
582–584 Anuwongse Rd., Bangkok 10100
Telephone 222–0301

Thai Aquaculture Development and Exporting Association
1575 Chareon Nakorn Rd.,
Klongsarn, Bangkok 10600
Telephone 465–5630, 466–1701

Thai Bankers Association
302 Silom Rd., Bangkok 10500
Telephone 234–1140

Thai Barge Operators Association
713//57 Liab Menam Chao Phraya Rd.,
Sathupradit, Yannawa, Bangkok 10120
Telephone 284–3070, 284–7172

Thai Battery Trade Association
3669/3-4 Rama IV Rd., Phrakanong, Bangkok 10100

Thai Coffee Exporters Association
16/1 Kasemraj Rd., Klong Toey, Bangkok 10110

cont...

TRADE ASSOCIATIONS *(cont.)*

Thai Contractors Association
110 Wireless Rd., Bangkok 10500
Telephone 251–0697, 252–2953

Thai Feed Manufacturers Association
36 Yenchit Lane, Chan Rd., Bangkok 10120
Telephone 211–0562

Thai Fertilizer and Agricultural Marketing Association
148–150 Chakrapetch Rd., Wangburapa, Bangkok 10200
Telephone 221–9241, 221–8807

Thai Fertilizer Producers Trade Association
Telephone 234–4347, 234–1956

Thai Finance & Security Association
134/2–3 Silom Rd., Bangkok 10500
Telephone 233–5856, 233–5893

Thai Fishery and Frozen Products Association
4th Floor, Warner Theatre Bldg.
119 Mahesak Rd., Bangkok 10500
Telephone 235–7793/4

Thai Fishmeal Producers Association
44/38 Soi Choduek
Mahapruetharam Rd., Bangkok 10500
Telephone 235–1590

Thai Footwear Industry Trade Association
245/40 Soi Yuthasili, Pinklao-Bangyikhan Rd.
Bangkok 10700

Thai Fruit and Vegetable Exporters Association
298/14 Pitsanuloke Rd., Bangkok 10300
Telephone 281–9268

cont...

TRADE ASSOCIATIONS *(cont.)*

Thai Furniture Industry Association
Industrial Service Division
Kluaynamthai Lane, Rama IV Rd., Bangkok 10110
Telephone 391–5176

Thai Glass Traders Association
1 Paniang Rd., Bangkok 10200
Telephone 281–3310

Thai Handicraft Promotion Association
4th Floor, Room 423, Ministry of Industry Bldg.
Rama VI Rd., Bangkok 10400
Telephone 282–4149, 282–4202 Ext 220

Thai Hardware Association
132/37–9 Tanuratana Lane 2, Yannawa, Bangkok 10120
Telephone 286–8590, 286–2667

Thai Hotels Association
1035/2 Ploenchit Rd., Bangkok 10500
Telephone 252–9850/9 Ext 233

Thai Jute Association
52/3 Thai Laithong Bldg.
Surawongse Rd. Bangkok 10500
Telephone 234–2623, 234–9024, 233–0871

Thai Jute Mill Association
283 Sriboonruang Bldg., Silom Rd., Bangkok 10500
Telephone 234–1438/9, 233–7000 Ext 14

Thai Lac Association
66 Chalermkhet 1 Rd., Bangkok 10100
Telephone 223–8331

cont...

TRADE ASSOCIATIONS *(cont.)*

Thai Life Assurance Association
36/1 Saphanku Lane, Rama IV Rd., Bangkok 10120
Telephone 286–0897

Thai Maize & Produce Traders Association
52/17–18 Thai Laithong Bldg.
Surawongse Rd., Bangkok 10500
Telephone 233–7560, 233–3042, 234–4387

Thai Merchant Association
150 Rajbopit Rd., Bangkok 10200
Telephone 221–3300, 221–2228/9

Thai Niello & Silver Ware Association
Department of Industrial Promotion
Rama VI Rd., Bangkok 10400
Telephone 282–6885

Thai Orchid Exporters Association
245/23 Soi Yuthasil, Pinklao-Bangyikhan Rd.
Bangkok 10700
Telephone 467–4955, 420–1419, 420–2021

Thai Orchid Growers and Traders Association
35/1 Moo 3 Kweang Langsong
Nongkham, Bangkok 10160
Telephone 420–1005, 420–1334

Thai Packing Association
Industrial Service Division
Klauynamthai Lane, Rama IV Rd., Bangkok 10110
Telephone 391–5722, 391–5081

Thai Pesticides Association
9th Floor, Yada Bldg., 56 Silom Rd., Bangkok 10500
Telephone: 235–0110/9

cont...

TRADE ASSOCIATIONS *(cont.)*

Thai Pharmacies Association
Room No. 401 Choon Bldg.
195–201 Charumuang Rd., Bangkok 10500
Telephone 214–2516/7 Ext 261, 262

Thai Plastic Industries Association
215-217, 3rd Floor, Mahatun Bldg.
Rajawongse Rd., Bangkok 10100
Telephone 223–6183/6

Thai Plywood & Veneer Association
289 Laemthong Bank Bldg.
Surawongse Rd., Bangkok 10500
Telephone 234–4123

Thai Printing Association
2 Nang Linchee Rd., Yannawa, Bangkok 10120
Telephone: 254-5568

Thai Pulp & Paper Industry Association
1426/8–10 4th Floor, Unison Bldg.
Krungkasem Rd., Bangkok 10100
Telephone 223–2184

Thai Rice Mill Association
81–81/1 New Rd., Talad Noi, Bangkok 10100
Telephone 235–8449, 235–7863

Thai Rubber Traders Association
57 Rongmuang Lane 5,
Pathumwan, Bangkok 10500
Telephone 214–3420

cont...

TRADE ASSOCIATIONS *(cont.)*

Thai Shipbuilders and Repairers Association
239/9 Surasak Rd., Bangkok 10500
Telephone 235-0310/9

Thai Shipowners Association
c/o Ministry of Communication
5 Ratchadamnoen Rd., Bangkok 10200
Telephone 281-1172

Thai Silk Association
Industrial Service Division
Klauynamthai Lane, Rama IV Rd., Bangkok 10110
Telephone 390-0684

Thai Soap Manufacturers Association
189 Sukhumvit 21 Rd., Bangkok 10110
Telephone 392-1036, 391-5177 Ext 43

Thai Stationery Traders Association
1173/5 New Rd., Bangkok 10100

Thai Steel Furniture Association
357-363 Mahachai Rd., Bangkok 10200
Telephone 221-0362, 221-6998

Thai Sugar Manufacturing Association
78 Kiatnakin Bldg., Bush Lane, New Rd., Bangkok 10500
Telephone 233-4156, 233-5858

Thai Sugar Producers Association
49 Sukhumvit 60 Rd., Bangkok 10110
Telephone 311-1518, 311-1450

Thai Synthetic Fiber Manufacturers Association
Dusit Thani Bldg., 4th Floor
1-3 Rama IV Rd., Bangkok 10500
Telephone 233-0750, 233-1701/3

cont...

TRADE ASSOCIATIONS *(cont.)*

Thai Tape and Photograph Record Traders Association
2000/45 Watvorajanyawas Lane, New Rd.
Yannawa, Bangkok 10120
Telephone 289–1370

Thai Tapioca Flour Industries Trade Association
Thaniya Bldg., 9th Floor, 62 Silom Rd.
Bangkok 10500
Telephone 234–9055/6

Thai Tapioca Trade Association
120 Sathorn Nua Rd., Bangkok 10500
Telephone 234–0620, 234–4724

Thai Textile Manufacturing Association
454–460 Sukhumvit 51 Rd.
Near Washington Theatre, Bangkok 10110
Telephone 392–9056, 392–8236

Thai Timber Exporters Association
462/1–5 Union Insurance Co. Ltd., Bldg.
4th Floor, Room 403, Siphaya Rd., Bangkok 10500
Telephone 233–6773

Thai Tourism Industry Association
Narai Hotel, 222 Silom Rd., Bangkok 10500
Telephone 233–3350, 233–6503/4

Thai Transporters Association
485/1 Sri Ayudhaya Road, Bangkok 10400
Telephone 252–4131, 252–4955 Ext 294

Thai Video Tape & Disc Traders Association
120/26 Indra Trade Center Room,
3019 Rajprarop Rd., Bangkok 10400
Telephone 251–111 Ext 719

cont...

TRADE ASSOCIATIONS *(cont.)*

Thailand Shipping Association
137–141 Tarau Road, Klong Toey, Bangkok 10110
Telephone 286–2195

Timber Exporters & Importers Association
144/16–7 Silom Rd., Bangkok 10500
Telephone 235–4135/8

Timber Merchants Association
4 Yen-Agas Rd., Bangkok 10120
Telephone 286–5565

Tinplate Container Manufacture Association
251 Sukhumvit 21 Rd., Prakanong, Bangkok 10110
Telephone 391–7547

Trade & Contracting Promotion Association
6/1 Kasem Sophon Lane, Samsen Rd.
Bangkok 10300
Telephone 585–9210

Transport Association
1570 Krungkasem Rd., Bangkok 10100
Telephone 222–6185

Union Textile Merchants Association
252–4 Mahachak Rd., Bangkok 10100
Telephone 222–3559, 222–6220

Warehouse Trade Association
150 Rajbopit Rd., Bangkok 10200
Telephone 221–3300

Weaving Association
12/14–15 Chula Lane 20, Bantadthong Rd.
Bangkok 10500
Telephone 214–2572, 255–8372

cont...

TRADE ASSOCIATIONS *(cont.)*

Wheat Consumers & Traders Association
6/1 Napasup Yak Sam Lane, Sukhumvit Rd.
Bangkok 10110
Telephone 391–3964

USEFUL TELEPHONE NUMBERS

Immigration Office, Soi Suanphlu, Sathorn Tai Rd., Bangkok 10120;
Telephone 286–9028, 286–9230, 286–4231

Revenue Department, Chakkapog Rd., Bangkok 10200; Telephone
281–5777, 280–0140

The Fine Arts Department, Na-Phrathat Rd., Bangkok 10200;
Telephone 221–4817, 224–1370

Tourism Authority of Thailand, Ratchadamnoen Nok Ave.,
Bangkok 10100; Telephone 282–1143/7

Tourist Assistance Center c/o TAT, Telephone 281–5051

The State Railway of Thailand, Hnua Lam Phog (Bangkok)
Station, Rama IV Rd., Bangkok 10500; Telephone 223–7010, 223–7020

Northern and Northeastern Bus Terminal, Phahonyothin Rd.,
Bangkok 10900; Telephone 271–0101/5, 279–4484/7

Southern Bus Terminal, Charansanitwong Rd., Bangkok 10700;
Telephone 411–0112, 411–4978/9

Eastern Bus Terminal, Sukhumvit Rd. (Ekamai), Bangkok
10110; Telephone 391–2504, 392–2521

POLICE

    Metropolitan Mobile Police, Telephone 511–1753
    Highway Patrol Division, Telephone 245–5206, 245–8882
    Crime Suppression Division, Telephone 221–9111, 222–5151
    Tourist Police, Telephone 221–6206/10, 281–5051

Tourism Authority of Thailand (TAT), Telephone 281–0372, 282–1143/7

Fire Department, Sri Ayutthaya 199; Telephone 245–5352, 246–0199

Ambulance, Telephone 252–2171/5

Immigration, Telephone 286–7003

International Calls, Teleplhone 235–0030/5

Bangkok Airport, Telephone 531–0022, 523–6201

Domestic Airlines, Telephone 280–0090, 280–0070

State Railway of Thailand, Telephone 223–0341/8

XI

Annotated Reading List

BLC Publishing Co. *Setting Up in Thailand: A Guide for Investors*, BLC Publishing Co., Ltd., 1988.

Cooper, Robert and Nanthapa, *Culture Shock: Thailand*, Singapore: Times Books International, 1982. A Guide to the pitfalls awaiting the uninformed foreigner blundering in Thailand.

Keys, Charles F., *Thailand: Buddhist Kingdom as Modern Nation-State*, Boulder, Colorado, and London: Westview Press, 1987. Recent Thai history in readable style. Especially good on relations between Thais and hill tribes.

Silapakorn University, *Art in Thailand: A Brief History*, Bangkok: Silapakorn University, 1970. A useful guide to the arts.

Smith, Malcolm, *A Physician at the Court of Siam*, Oxford: Oxford University Press, 1982. Memoirs of an English court doctor in the early 20th century. Palace life during reigns of kings Mongkut and Chulalongkorn.

Warren, William, *Jim Thompson: The Legendary American of Thailand*, New York: Houghton, 1970. Bangkok's most famous expatriate, who revived the silk trade and disappeared in Malaysia in 1967.

Wyatt, David, *Thailand: A Short History*, New Haven: Yale University Press, 1984. Good general history.

Appendix: The Thai Language

Though modern Thai has 21 consonant sounds, the Thai script, first developed in the 13th century, contains 44 consonants, along with 15 vowel symbols. The extra consonant symbols are used to indicate the tonal value of a word. There are five different tones in Thai, and they are essential in determining the meaning of a word. The five tones are level or mid, low, falling, rising, and high. There is no agreed-upon system of romanization for Thai, with the result that variant spellings of the same word can be found even within one book in a Western language.

Following is a very brief list of some helpful phrases in Thai. For a more in-depth study, buy the *Thailand Phrasebook*, published by Lonely Planet and available in Bangkok bookstores.

SOME USEFUL THAI PHRASES

English	Thai
Good morning, Good evening Good afternoon, Good night Hello, Good-bye	Sawat dii (to be polite, a man would say "Sawat dii khrap"; a woman would say "Sawat dii kha").
Mr., Miss, Ms., Mrs.	Khun
Yes	Chai
No	Mai or Plao
How are you?	Khun sa bai di ru?
Very well, thank you	Sa bai di, khopkhun
I am going to	Chan cha pai
How much do you want?	Khun tong kan tao rai?
Too much	Mak pai
Too expensive	Phaeng pai
Any discount?	Lot ra-kha noi dai mai?
Understand?	Kao Chai mai?
I don't understand	Chan mai kao chai
Please speak slowly	Prot put cha-cha
Not expensive	Mai phaeng
No, I won't go	Chan mai pai
Please drive slowly	Prot khap cha-cha

cont...

USEFUL THAI PHRASES *(cont.)*

English	Thai
Please be careful	Prot, ra-wang
Turn to the right	Leio khwa
Turn to the left	Leio sai
Drive straight on	Khap trong pai
Slow down	Cha-Cha
Stop	Yut
How much is this?	Ra-kha tao rai?
Please wrap it for me	Ho hai duai
I'm sorry	Chan sia chai
Excuse me, pardon me	Kho thot
Very good	Di mak
No good	Mai di
Good Luck	Chok Di
Please	Karuna or Prot

NUMBERS IN THAI

English	Thai	English	Thai
1 , 2	Nung, Song	25	Yi-sip-ha
3 , 4	Sam, Si	30	Sam-sip
5 , 6	Ha, Hok	40	Si-sip
7 , 8	Chet, Paet	50	Ha-sip
9 , 10	Kao, Sip	60	Hok-sip
11	Sip-et	70	Chet-sip
12	Sip-song	80	Paet-sip
13	Sip-sam	90	Kao-sip
14	Sip-si	100	Nung Roi
19	Sip-kao	400	Si Roi
20	Yi-sip	600	Hok Roi
21	Yi-sip-et	1,000	Nung Phan
22	Yi-sip-song	10,000	Nung Mun

cont...

III
Singapore

I

Singapore at a Glance

HISTORY OF SINGAPORE:
SEA TOWN AND LION CITY

EARLY historical records ascribe two nicknames to Singapore: Sea Town and Lion City. Like the two sides of a coin, each nickname represents much of what Singapore is today — both a major trading port and a fiercely independent survivor of colonial rule and occupation.

Singapore occupies an island, some 26 by 14 mi (42 by 23 km) in extent, with an area of approximately 220 sq mi (570 km²), along with a number of adjacent islets. A ⅔-mi (1-km) causeway connects the city-state to the Malay Peninsula to the north. Strategically situated at the western entrance to the South China Sea, Singapore has always played a major role in the ambitions of the region's superpowers. In the 7th century AD, when Singapore was known as Temasek, or "Sea Town," it was a trading center within Sumatra's Srivijaya Empire. "Sea Town" changed to "Lion City" in the 13th century. Legend has it that Sang Nila Utama, a Malay prince, landed on the island during a storm and saw an unusual animal, "very swift and beautiful, its body bright red, its head jet black." Although what he saw was probably a tiger, when he established the island as his own base he named it Singa Pura or "Lion City."

At the end of the 14th century, Java and Siam (now Thailand) struggled for regional control of the Malay Peninsula. Shortly after 1390, it is believed, the Malay ruler of the island was driven off by Javanese forces of the Majapahit Empire. After that time, as historical records of Singapore diminished, the great "Lion City" was eventually reclaimed by the jungle and by the *orang laut*, sea gypsies known for fishing and piracy.

Though Indians, Thais, and Javanese had invaded and fought over ancient Singapore, it was the British who reclaimed it from the jungle and established a modern city-state. In 1819, Sir Stamford Raffles of the British East India Company concluded a treaty with Sultan Hussein of Johore and the Temenggong, or local ruler, of the Malay Penin-

Sir Stamford Raffles

sula and Singapore, by which the Company was granted the right to set up a trading post at the mouth of the Singapore River.

Raffles spent only nine months in Singapore, but his initial efforts accomplished much. A stable government and successful trading base attracted many Chinese and Indian immigrants. In 1824 the Dutch acknowledged British rule over the area, and later in that year the Sultan granted Singapore to the Company in perpetuity. In 1826, Singapore became part of the Straits Settlements, along with Penang and Malacca, and was governed by the British East India Company as a residency of India. In 1858 its rule was transferred from the Company to the India Office of the British Government, and in 1867 it became a crown colony under the British Colonial Office.

Singapore thrived under British rule: by 1830 it had surpassed Penang and Malacca in population and economic growth, and it eventually became the world's main sorting and exporting center for rubber. A truly prestigious "Sea Town," it served ships traveling the seas between Europe and East Asia for 110 years.

This golden age of Singapore ended abruptly in December of 1941 when Japanese aircraft bombed the city. After resistance by British forces and local volunteers, the city fell to the Japanese on February 15, 1942. During the three and a half years of Japanese occupation, Singapore, renamed Syonan, or "Light of the South," by the Japanese, suffered greatly. Its economy deteriorated and inflation increased. Malnutrition and starvation plagued the inhabitants of Singapore. In 1945, British warships returned to Singapore and on August 21 the Japanese surrendered.

British administration continued until 1946. When the colonial administration came to an end, the Straits Settlements was dissolved and, on April 1, 1946, Singapore became a separate Crown colony.

The People's Action Party (PAP) won the first general election, in May 1959, and Lee Kuan Yew, a Cambridge-educated lawyer, became the first prime minister. Internal self-government was achieved in June of the same year. In 1963 Singapore became part of the Malaysian Federation, but two years later, on August 9, 1965, it became a sovereign, democratic, and independent nation.

The new government implemented an intensive industrialization program. Education was made compulsory with an emphasis on technology and computer education. In addition to a government-sponsored "productivity movement," financial incentives were offered for industrial enterprises.

By 1970 the population surpassed two million. Prime Minister Lee and the PAP strove to instill cohesiveness along with a sense of

SINGAPORE: Main Roads and Places of Interest

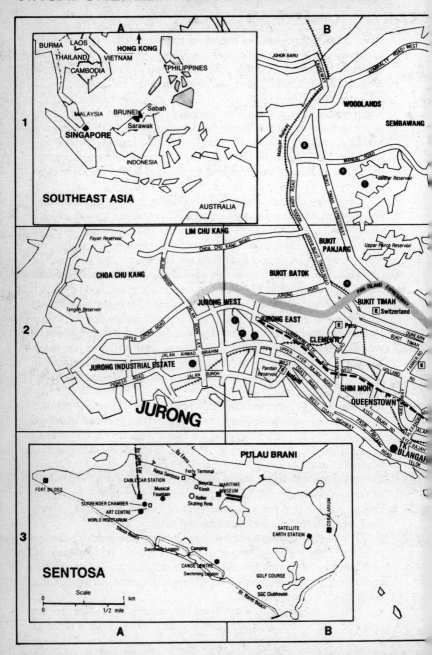

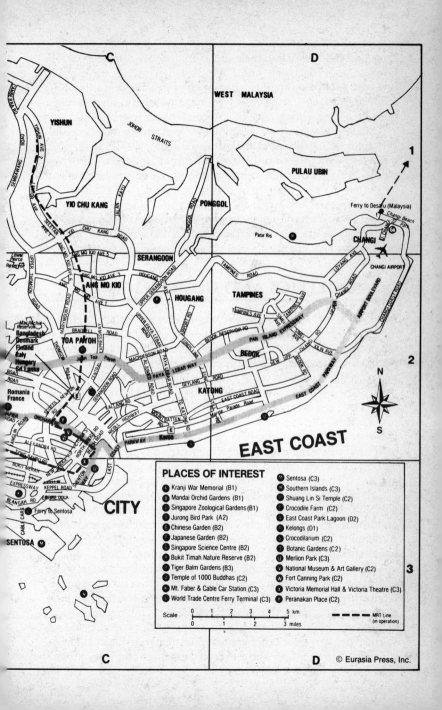

PLACES OF INTEREST

- ⒶKranji War Memorial (B1)
- ⒷMandai Orchid Gardens (B1)
- ⒸSingapore Zoological Gardens (B1)
- ⒹJurong Bird Park (A2)
- ⒺChinese Garden (B2)
- ⒻJapanese Garden (B2)
- ⒼSingapore Science Centre (B2)
- ⒽBukit Timah Nature Reserve (B2)
- ⒤Tiger Balm Gardens (B3)
- ⒥Temple of 1000 Buddhas (C2)
- ⓀMt. Faber & Cable Car Station (C3)
- ⓁWorld Trade Centre Ferry Terminal (C3)
- ⓂSentosa (C3)
- ⓃSouthern Islands (C3)
- ⓄShuang Lin Si Temple (C2)
- ⓅCrocodile Farm (C2)
- ⓆEast Coast Park Lagoon (D2)
- ⓇKelongs (D1)
- ⓈCrocodilarium (C2)
- ⓉBotanic Gardens (C2)
- ⓊMerlion Park (C3)
- ⓋNational Museum & Art Gallery (C2)
- ⓌFort Canning Park (C2)
- ⓍVictoria Memorial Hall & Victoria Theatre (C3)
- ⓎPeranakan Place (C2)

Scale

| 0 | 1 | 2 | 3 | 4 | 5 km |

| 0 | 1 | 2 | 3 miles |

- - - MRT Line
(in operation)

© Eurasia Press, Inc.

Singaporean identity into the multi-ethnic society composed of 75% Chinese, 15% Malaysian, and 8% Indian. Top priority was given to low-cost public housing for which all had equal opportunity. New schools, apartments, and houses were made available to all; today eight out of ten Singaporeans live in government apartments.

Progress towards modernization has been remarkably successful. Per capita annual income is now estimated at S$15,000 (U.S. S$7,500), a seven-fold increase since 1970, making this island the third richest nation in Asia. Singapore's strategic location is now fully exploited: its port is used by more than 600 shipping lines. The nation has emerged as a primary center for commerce and industry, and as one of the world's major oil-refining and -distribution centers. Singapore's immaculate streets, streamlined skyscrapers, and multi-ethnic variety of sights and sounds attract over three million visitors a year.

POLITICS AND GOVERNMENT

SINGAPORE is a parliamentary democracy. Parliament is elected for a five-year term by a majority of the people; voting is compulsory for all citizens 21 years of age and over. There are 79 members of parliament (elected from single-member constituencies), 20 political parties, and a president who serves as constitutional head of state.

The People's Action Party (PAP), led by Prime Minister Lee Kuan Yew, has held a monopoly on power since 1959. In fact, in the five parliamentary elections held since 1959, the PAP has lost a total of only two seats, and those in the 1984 election. In its economic and social policies, the government advocates higher education, with incentives and financial aid offered to this end, and encourages individual ambition, on the principle that contribution should be rewarded.

At the same time, it keeps a very tight rein on social order. There are moral campaigns, slogans, and steep fines for spitting, jaywalking, and littering. The overall plan is to strive for excellence and social conformity. The "Three-S Productivity Plan," promoted by the government, stresses Social Responsibility, Social Attitude, and Skill.

To an almost frightening degree, the government attempts to orchestrate the social, educational, and political future of Singaporeans. Concerned over the falling birth rates of the better-educated Chinese majority in Singapore, the Social Development Unit organizes social gatherings such as boat trips and dinner parties for college graduates so that they can meet other graduates of similar intellectual levels.

Prime Minister Lee, who is expected to retire within the next few years, has stressed the importance of training young leaders for the next political phase. In his 1982 Eve of National Day address, Lee stated: "My deepest concern is how to make the young more conscious of security. By security I mean defense against threats to our survival, whether the threats are external or internal."

Consistent with his stated concern for internal security, Prime Minister Lee's attitude toward political opposition in Singapore has been less than tolerant. Significant opposition to his rule has emerged in recent years, and many younger professionals who disagree with a system they feel to be autocratic have left Singapore to seek employment abroad. Using the Internal Security Act to silence opposition, the PAP has jailed numerous dissidents without trial in recent years. The government has come under strong criticism by international human rights organizations and, in some cases, by the governments of both Great Britain and the United States. News organizations considered too provocative in their criticism of and reporting on the Lee Kuan Yew government — such as the highly respected *Asian Wall Street Journal* and the *Far Eastern Economic Review* — have been denied visas for their correspondents, and sales of their publications have been restricted in Singapore.

Fueling further criticism of his regime is speculation that Lee is planning to establish a family dynasty by passing on the premiership to his eldest son, Lee Hsien Loong, while Lee himself takes over the presidency.

ECONOMY

SINGAPORE'S economic boom of the 1970s derived primarily from its strategic trade situation and from its hardworking people. Industry and tourism were also key factors.

The main industries that developed throughout the 1950s were lumber and rubber, fishing, shipbuilding, tin smelting, and brick manufacturing. Rural areas produced vegetables, pigs, poultry, and fruit.

In 1959, when the PAP came to power, it concentrated on industrialization and on diversifying Singapore's economic base through entrepôt trade. The Economic Development Board, established in 1961, developed industrial sites in Jurong, Kallang Basin, Tanghi Halt, Kampong Ampat, Kallang Park, Tanjong Rhu, Tiong Bahru, Redhill, and Kranji. With the establishment of the Development Bank of Singapore in 1968, loans were provided for new industries

Singapore Skyline

and for the expansion of existing industries. Also established in 1968, the International Trading Company Ltd., a part-government, part-private organization, served the expansion of exports. Foreign investors were attracted by well-educated cheap labor and tax incentives.

Suitable tourist attractions and sustained visitor growth have been promoted through the Singapore Tourist Promotion Board, established in 1964. Its functions include organizing conventions, exhibitions, travel groups, festivals, and sporting events, as well as devising programs to redevelop and preserve ethnic and historical areas of the island.

In 1986 the export of manufactured goods increased, and industries such as electronics, transportation, equipment, and petroleum expanded. Transportation and communications also improved the economy, in part because of more competitive charges.

Today most Singaporeans enjoy a high standard of living, and about 80% of the population own homes. After Brunei and Japan, the per capita income is the highest in Asia. Within the last two years, the economy has faltered slightly because of a decrease in the demand for Asian exports. To counter this situation President Lee has expanded trade with China, held down wages, and continued to emphasize higher education.

Government strategies for the 1990s include maintaining a high savings rate, allocating resources for their most effective use in production, depending on the private sector, promoting offshore activities, and creating a favorable business environment.

PEOPLE AND LANGUAGE

PEOPLE OF SINGAPORE

We think of New York as a "melting pot." Singapore, which is comparable in size to New York, is sometimes referred to as "instant Asia" because of its multi-ethnic mix of Chinese, Indian, Malay, and Eurasian.

The Malays were the original residents of Singapore. When Raffles arrived, Singapore was basically a Malay fishing village. The present population differs from that of the past in being more stable and less transient. Early immigrants from China and India came to the island without intending a permanent stay. At that time (pre-Raffles), there was a surplus of males, and the population increased by migration rather than natural increase. The early settlers were poor and illiterate.

In 1821 the first junk arrived from Amoy (Xiamen), bringing Chinese from Fukien (Fujian) province; in their own dialect they called themselves Hokkiens, a name by which they are still known. They were followed by other groups from various parts of China: Hakkas, a people that had originally migrated to Canton (Guangdong, or Kwangtung) from the north and long maintained their own language there; Cantonese; Hainanese, from Hainan Island; Kuongsais (Kwongsais), from the middle reaches of Guangxi (Kwangsi); and Hokchius, as their native dialect names them, from Fuzhou (Foochow). Each group specialized in certain trades and lived together in certain districts. The Cantonese and the Hakkas worked as blacksmiths, shoemakers, carpenters, and tailors. The Hokchius were barbers and ran the coffee shops. The Hokkiens dominated trade and industry, and they continue to do so today. Most came to Singapore hoping to become wealthy and then return home.

In contrast to the Chinese, the Malays had a more conservative outlook on commerce and wealth, perhaps because of their Islamic practice and traditional lifestyle. In general, this has carried over into modern society; religion and family may be considered more important than material gain. Some Malays have combined traditional values with mainstream professions.

Indians are the third ethnic group of Singapore. The first Indians, from the south, included both Hindus and Muslims. Bengalis, Ceylonese, Sikhs, Parsis, Sindhis, and Gujeratis followed. Large numbers of Indian laborers were brought in by the British in 1825. These laborers built public buildings such as Government House and Saint Andrew's Cathedral, and they also constructed roads and bridges. Some became clerks, merchants, teachers, and retail traders. Others worked as servants and messengers. Today many Punjabis and Sikhs are watchmen or policemen. In modern Singapore, Indians also work in journalism and various sectors of business.

Rounding out Singapore's "instant Asia melting bowl" are Eurasians and Europeans. The Eurasians can be traced back to the Portuguese colonies of Malacca and Goa. There are currently about 20,000 Eurasians in Singapore. The Europeans, primarily French, Portuguese, Dutch, and Belgian, derive from the early pioneers who came to the island to take up professions. Most modern Europeans working in Singapore have become citizens or work as "expatriate" professionals on contract.

LANGUAGES

Malay, Chinese, Tamil, and English are the official languages of Singapore. English is used for commerce and administration. Many residents speak several languages and dialects, and almost all educated Singaporeans speak English. In recent years, the government has initiated a "Use Mandarin" campaign to encourage the Chinese community to speak Mandarin rather than the numerous Chinese dialects. The pinyin romanization is likewise being adopted for the English transciption of Chinese names and terms in official publications. However, some private businesses and organizations continue to use the traditional spellings. Thus, government tourist pamphlets may recommend the Sichuan cuisine of a restaurant that calls itself, say, The Szechwan Kitchen. Traditional romanizations are also commonly used for names and terms that represent local dialect pronunciations, rather than Mandarin, for example, *Hokkien* for Mandarin Fujian, traditionally *Fukien*.

II Planning a Trip to Singapore

TOURIST INFORMATION

THE Singapore Tourist Promotion Board, with a head office in the Raffles City Tower and regional offices in major cities throughout the world, can supply maps, brochures, and information to help the prospective visitor plan a trip.

SINGAPORE TOURIST PROMOTION BOARD

HEAD OFFICE

Singapore Tourist Promotion Board, Raffles City Tower, 250 North Bridge Rd. #36-04, Singapore 0617; Telephone 339-6622; Fax 339-9423; Telex STBSIN RS 33375

REGIONAL OFFICES

AUSTRALIA

Singapore Tourist Promotion Board, c/o Forum Organisation, 55 Saint George's Terrace, Perth WA 6001; Telephone (09) 325-8033; Fax (09) 221-3135; Telex AA 92110

Singapore Tourist Promotion Board, Suite 1604, Level 16, Westpac Plaza, 60 Margaret St., Sydney NSW 2000; Telephone (02) 241-3771/2; Fax (02) 232-3658; Telex STBSYD AA 127775

CANADA

Singapore Tourist Promotion Board, 175 Bloor St. East, Suite 1112 North Tower, Toronto, Ontario M4W 3R8; Telephone (416) 323-9139; Fax (416) 323-3514; Telex (06) 217510 SINGA POR TOR

FRANCE

L'Office National du Tourisme de Singapour, Centre d'Affaires Le Louvre, 2 Place du Palais-Royal, 75044 Paris; Telephone (01) 4297-1616; Fax (01) 4297-1617; Telex SINGPAR 213593F

GERMANY

Fremdenverkehrsburo von Singapur, Postrasse 2-4, D-6000 Frankfurt/Main; Telephone (69) 231-456/7; Fax (69) 233-924

HONG KONG

Singapore Tourist Promotion Board, Suite 1402, Century Square, 1-13 D'Aguilar St., Central; Telephone (5) 224—052/3; Fax (5) 810-6694; Telex 86630 ETBHK HX

JAPAN

Singapore Tourist Promotion Board, 1st Floor, Yamato Seimei Bldg., 1-Chome, 1-7 Uchaisaiwai-cho, Chiyoda-ku, Tokyo 100; Telephone (03) 593-3388; Fax (03) 591-1480; Telex STBTYO J25591

KOREA

Singapore Tourist Promotion Board, c/o Nara Corporation, Dongsan Bldg. 28-1, Jamwan-dong, Seocho-ku, Seoul 137-030, CPO Box 1894, Seoul; Telephone (02) 549-0691; Fax (02) 549-0690; Telex K29956 NARAD

NEW ZEALAND

Singapore Tourist Promotion Board, c/o Walshes World, 2nd Floor, Dingwall Bldg., 87 Queen St., P.O. Box 279, Auckland 1; Telephone (9) 793-708; Fax (9) 390-725; Telex WALWOR NZ21437

SWITZERLAND

Fremdenverkehrsburo von Singapur, c/o Schellenberg, Ogilvy & Mather AG, Werbeangentur BSW, Bergstrasse 50, 8932 Zurich; Telephone (01) 252-5365; Telex 816464 SOMZ CH

TAIWAN

Singapore Tourist Promotion Board, 9th Floor, TFIT Tower, 85 Jenai Rd., Sec. 4, Taipei; Telephone (2) 721–0664; Fax (2) 781–7648; Telex 24974 STPBTPE

UNITED KINGDOM

Singapore Tourist Promotion Board, 1st Floor, Carrington House, 126–130 Regent St., London W1R 5FE; Telephone (71) 437–0033; Fax (71) 734–2191; Telex STBLON G893491

UNITED STATES

Singapore Tourist Promotion Board, 333 North Michigan Ave., Suite 818, Chicago, IL 60601; Telephone (312) 704–4200; Fax (312) 704–4204; Telex 798975 SINGPOR TB CGO

Singapore Tourist Promotion Board, 8484 Wilshire Blvd., Suite 510, Beverly Hills, CA 90211; Telephone (213) 852–1901; Fax (213) 852–0129; Telex SING-UR 278141

Singapore Tourist Promotion Board, 590 Fifth Ave., NBR 12th Floor, New York, NY 10036; Telephone (212) 302–4861; Fax (212) 302–4801; Telex 220843 SING-UR

TRAVEL OPTIONS

BECAUSE of its small size, Singapore is rarely the sole destination of vacationers. For most tourists, whether they are traveling on their own or in a package tour, Singapore is a stopover or extension of a trip to one or more other destinations.

WHEN TO GO

CLIMATE

Singapore is little more than 1° north of the equator and, not surprisingly, has a tropical climate ideal for those who enjoy swimming, sailing, and other water sports. Year-round temperatures range from 87°F (30.6°C) at noon to 75°F (23.8°C) at night.

February to October is mostly sunny with cooling sea breezes and only occasional showers. From November through January there is frequent rain due to the northeast monsoon.

FESTIVALS

No matter when you visit Singapore, you'll almost certainly be able to take in a festival. It's a great way to learn more about the cultural and religious traditions of each ethnic group, or if you're a Westerner, to celebrate a familiar holiday such as the New Year in an exotic location. The dates of many religious festivals vary from year to year, since like the Christian Easter and the feasts whose dates depend on it, they are determined by a lunar calendar. The Chinese and Hindu calendars, like the Jewish and Christian, are lunisolar; that is, the months are determined by the phases of the moon, but various devices are used to bring them into correlation with the solar year of approximately 365 days. Hence these feasts fall at the same general time of the year each year; months are therefore given for them. The Muslim religious calendar is completely lunar, and since a year of 12 lunar months is shorter than the solar year, Muslim feasts progress through the seasons in a cycle of 33 years. It is therefore impossible to state even approximately when they will occur and have that statement hold true for more than a year or two. For the specific dates of festivals and locations of events, contact the Singapore Tourist Promotion Board.

January 1: New Year's Day. Banks and businesses are closed. Nightclubs and hotels offer parties and foreign entertainment. Some churches have midnight services.

January: Ponggal, The Harvest Festival. A four-day festival celebrated by the South Indians. Food offerings of rice, curries, spices, and sugarcane are made in thanksgiving to the gods. Evening prayers are sung with bells, clarinets, conch shells, and drums. The best place to view the festival is Perumal Temple on Serangoon Road.

January-February: Thaipusam. Hindu penitants and well-wishers march in a five-mile procession from Perumal Temple on Serangoon Rd. to Chettiar Temple on Tank Rd., chanting prayers. The penitents pierce their bodies (foreheads, tongues, and cheeks) with skewers and weighted hooks. No pain or blood is apparent; however, this festival is not for the squeamish.

Thaipusam, a Hindu festival

February and September: Birthday of the Monkey God. A Chinese celebration with more amazing feats: cheeks and tongues are pierced with spears by some devotees and others, possessed by spirits, perform acrobatics, puppet shows, and Chinese opera. The best locations to view all this are the two large temples at Eng Hoon and Cumming streets.

January-February: Chinese Lunar New Year. A 15-day celebration marked by family gatherings of filial piety, good luck money packets for younger family members, and bright red banners and paper cuttings outside spotless homes and shops. Special foods are followed by sumptuous banquets. It is the luckiest time of the year to marry. Among the annual processions are the Chingay Parade, the dragon dance, floats, stilt walkers, and much more.

March-April: Good Friday. Christian services are offered in churches throughout the city. A candlelit procession begins at Saint Joseph's Catholic Church on Victoria St.

Qing Ming. In a commemoration similar to All Soul's Day, the Chinese pay respect to their ancestors by placing offerings of food and incense at burial sites.

Songkran. A Thai water festival marking the beginning of the year's solar cycle. In Thai Buddhist temples, images of the Buddha are bathed with holy water, visitors and worshippers are blessed by being splashed with water, and caged birds are set free.

Vesak. This festival commemorates the birth, enlightenment, and death of the Buddha with day-long celebrations in Singapore's Buddhist temples. Vegetarian feasts, candlelit processions, special exhibitions, lectures on Buddhist doctrine, and notable festivities at the Kong Meng San Phor Kark See temple complex on Bright Hill Drive and at the Temple of One Thousand Lights on Race Course Rd. are just some of the events around town.

June 4: Festival of the Arts. Local artists, theatrical groups, and international entertainers participate in recitals, cultural programs, plays, ballets, Chinese opera, and orchestral performances during this festival.

May-June: Dragon Boat Festival. Competitors come from all over Asia, the United States, Europe, Australia, and New Zealand to participate in this colorful regatta of 12-meter-long boats, painted with scales and decorated with dragon heads. For a less athletic and more

Chinese New Year

gustatory delight, try this festival's delicacy: a glutinous rice dumpling stuffed with meat and wrapped in bamboo leaves and called a *zongzi*.

August 9: National Day. On this anniversary of the nation's independence, witness the processions of floats, fireworks, parades, and cultural performances. Admissions to events at the parade grounds is by ticket only.

August-September: Market Festival and Festival of the Hungry Ghosts. During the seventh lunar month, Chinese tradition holds that spirits are allowed to wander the earth for one month. Joss sticks and paper money are burned, feasts are prepared as offerings to honor the spirits, and lavish celebrations are held by holders of market stalls. Market Festival is the best time of the year to see a Chinese opera.

September-October: Mooncake Festival. The ingredients of this festival are mooncakes, delicious circles of dough filled with a sweet paste of lotus seeds, nuts, and red beans, family dinners, exquisite lantern processions, and exhibitions under a full autumn moon.

September-October: Thimithi. A Hindu firewalking festival honoring the goddess Dtaupadai offers a spectacular ceremony which includes devotees walking across pits of burning embers. The best location to watch the spectacle is Sri Mariamman Temple at South Bridge Rd.

October-November: Deepavali. This festival commemorates the triumph of light over darkness and good over evil with rows of lighted oil lamps, temple bells with evening prayer, and a magnificent procession.

Merlion Week. A week-long carnival of fireworks, food fairs, and masquerade balls ending with the Singapore Powerboat Grand Prix.

December 25: Christmas. Yuletide celebrations take place everywhere. Shoppers along Orchard Rd. are treated to glittering light displays. Many shopping centers stage choir performances and pageants.

Muslim Festivals. Among the colorful observances of Singapore's Muslims are **Ramadan** and **Hari Raya Puasa**. The former is a month of daylight fasting and evening prayers at the mosques. Special stalls at Bussoran Stand near the Sultan Mosque sell Malay delicacies for breaking the fast at sundown. Hari Raya Puasa is the festival, known as Id al-Fitr in other parts of the Muslim world, marking the end of the Ramadan fast. It is marked by prayers at the mosques, family celebrations, and lively festivities in Geyland at night. In the late 1980s and early 1990s these observances fell in April and May.

WHAT TO TAKE—AND WHAT NOT TO

CLOTHING

In general, dress is informal. Light, casual clothing suitable to the tropical climate is acceptable. In most restaurants and nightclubs, except for the very exclusive, evening dress—and even suits—and ties, are not obligatory. It is important to note, though, that shirts and ties should be worn for business meetings, and that in general blue jeans and tee-shirts are frowned upon in most discos. Running suits, shorts, and thongs are also considered too informal at most restaurants, deluxe hotels, and coffee houses.

MEDICINES

Singapore has excellent medical facilities, and legitimate pharmaceuticals are easily available with a proper prescription. If you bring with you any medicines that would require a prescription in Singapore, be sure to bring along a copy of the prescription form, signed by your physician, testifying that the preparations are indicated by your condition. Singapore has extremely strict laws against the use and possession of controlled substances.

OTHER

Singapore is thoroughly modernized, and personal grooming and hygiene products are readily available and of a quality that Westerners are used to. Eyeglass wearers who bring a copy of their prescription will be able to obtain replacements with no difficulty and at a reasonable cost.

III

Getting to Singapore

VISAS AND HEALTH CERTIFICATES

NATIONALS of member-states of the Commonwealth of Nations, the Republic of Ireland, Liechtenstein, Monaco, the Netherlands, San Marino, and Switzerland do not need visas, nor do holders of UN laissez-passers and U.S. citizens who are not planning to work or take up residence in Singapore. Nationals of most western European nations and of Japan, South Korea, and Pakistan do not need visas if they will be staying for up to 90 days and will not be seeking employment. Nationals of most other countries outside central and eastern Europe do not require visas for stays of up to 14 days if not seeking employment. Nationals of Afghanistan, India, Kampuchea, Laos, the People's Republic of China, the USSR, and Vietnam must have a visa regardless of the length and purpose of their stay, except that holders of valid Soviet or Chinese passports may visit for less than 24 hours without a visa if they have confirmed exit travel bookings.

Singapore maintains diplomatic and consular offices in leading cities throughout the world, at which one may apply for a visa if necessary.

SELECTED SINGAPORE DIPLOMATIC OFFICES ABROAD

Australia ◙ Singapore High Commission, 17 Forster Crescent, Yarralumla ACT 2600, Canberra; Telephone (61) (6) 273-3944; Fax (61) (6) 273-3260; Telex AB SINGAWA AA 62192

Belgium ◙ Singapore Embassy, 198 Avenue Franklin Roosevelt, 1050 Brussels; Telephone (32) (2) 660-3098/9; Fax (32) (2) 660-8685; Telex AB 26731 SINGEM B

Canada ◙ Contact Singapore UN Mission or Singapore Consulate, c/o Roberts & Muir, Suite 901, 840 Howe St.,

cont...

Vancouver, BC V6Z 2L2; Telephone (1) (604) 682–9766; Fax (1) (604) 682–6746

Denmark ◙ Contact Singapore High Commission, United Kingdom

France ◙ Singapore Embassy, 12 Square de l'Avenue Foch (entry by 80 Avenue Foch), 75116 Paris; Telephone (33) (1) 4500–3361; Fax (33) (1) 4500–6179; Telex AB SINGEMP 630994F

Germany ◙ Singapore Embassy, Sudstrasse 133, 5300 Bonn 2; Telephone (49) (228) 312–007/8/9; Fax (49) (228) 310–527; Telex AB 885642 SING D

Hong Kong ◙ Singapore Commission, 9th Floor, Units 901-2, Admiralty Centre Tower I, 18 Harcourt Rd.; Telephone (852) (5) 272–212; Fax (852) (5) 861–3595; Telex AB 73194 SCIHK HX

India ◙ Singapore High Commission, E 6 Chandragupta Marg, Chanakyapuri, New Delhi 110021; Telephone (91) (11) 604–162, 608–149; Fax (91) (11) 677–798; Telex AB 3172169 SING IN; or Singapore Consulate, 9th Floor, 94 Sakhar Bhawan, 230 Nariman Pt., Bombay 400–021; Telephone (91) (22) 204–3205/09/11; Telex AB 114026 SINB IN

Indonesia ◙ Singapore Embassy, Block X/4 KAV No. 2, Jalan H. R. Rasuna Said, Kuningan, Jakarta 12950; Telephone (62) (21) 520–1489/90/91/92; Fax (62) (21) 520–1486; Telex AB 62213 SINGA IA; or Singapore Consulate, 3 Jalan Tengku Daud, Medan, North Sumatra; Telephone (62) (61) 513-366; Fax (62) (61) 513–134

Italy ◙ Contact the Singapore Embassy in Germany

Japan ◙ Singapore Embassy, 12–3 Roppongi, 5-Chome, Minato-ku, Tokyo 106; Mailing address P.O. Box 32, Azabu Post Office. Minato-ku, Tokyo 106; Telephone (81) (3) 586–9111/2/3/4; Fax (81) (3) 582–1085; Telex AB SPOREMB J 22404

Korea ◙ Singapore Embassy, c/o Room 2128, Seoul Hilton International, 395 5-ka, Namdaemun-ro, Chung-ku, Seoul 100-095; Mailing address CPO Box 7692; Telephone (82) (2) 753-7788; Fax (82) (2) 754–2510; Telex AB R26695 HILTON SEOUL; or Singapore Consulate, c/o Ashin Shipping Co., Ltd., 16th Floor, New KAL Building, 51 Sokong-dong, Chung-ku, Seoul; Telephone (82) (2) 753–1211; Fax (82) (2) 757–4919; Telex AB ASHINCO K 24722

Mexico ◙ Contact the Singapore UN mission

cont...

Netherlands ◙ Contact Singapore Embassy in Belgium or Singapore Consulate, Grindweg 88, 3055 VD Rotterdam; Telephone (31) (10) 461–5899; Fax (31) (10) 418–2390

New Zealand ◙ Singapore High Commission, 17 Kabul St., Khandallah, Wellington, P.O. Box 29023; Telephone (64) (4) 792–0767; Fax (64) (4) 792–315; Telex AB SINGAWAKIL NZ 3593

Norway ◙ Contact Singapore High Comission in the United Kingdom or Singapore Consulate, Middelthunsgt 17, Oslo; Mailing address P.O. Box 1166 Sentrum 0107, Oslo 1; Telephone (47) (2) 485–000, 484–367; Fax (47) (2) 568–664; Telex AB 19784 XIAIFN

Pakistan ◙ Contact Singapore Embassy, 40 Babel St., Dokki 11511 Cairo, Egypt; Mailing address ATABA P.O. Box 356, Cairo; Telephone (20) (2) 704–744, 703–772; Fax (20) (2) 348–1682; or Singapore Consulate, Lakson Square Building, 2 Sarwar Shaheed Rd., Karachi 1; Telephone (92) (21) 526–419; Fax (92) (21) 513–410; Telex AB LAKSN PK

Portugal ◙ Contact the Singapore Embassy in France or Singapore Consulate, Lusograin, Rua dos Fanqueiros 135–1, 1100 Lisbon; Telephone (351) (1) 878–647; Fax (351) (1) 870–937; Telex AB 16173 LUGRAN P

Spain ◙ Contact the Singapore Embassy in France or Singapore Consulate, Huertas 13, Madrid 28012; Telephone (34) (1) 429-3193; Fax (34) (1) 276–9194; Telex AB 1FEMA E

Sweden ◙ Contact the Singapore Embassy in Germany or Singapore Consulate-General, Storgatan 42, 11455 Stockholm; Telephone (46) (8) 663-7488; Fax (46) (8) 662–2035; Telex SINGAWAKIL SWEDEN

Taiwan ◙ Office of the Singapore Trade Representative, Taipei, 9/F., 85 Jenai Rd., Sec. 4, Taipei; Telephone (886) (2) 772-1940

Thailand ◙ Singapore Embassy, 129 South Sathorn Rd., Bangkok; Telephone (66) (2) 286–2111/1434/9971; Fax (66) (2) 287–2578; Telex AB SINGEMB TH 82930

United Kingdom ◙ Singapore High Commission, 2 Wilton Crescent, London SW1X 8RW; Telephone (44) (71) 235-8315/6/7; Fax (44) (71) 245-6583 (ID 583), (44) (71) 235-9792 (TDB); Telex AB 262564 SHCIUK G

United Nations ◙ Permanent Mission of Singapore, 25th Floor, 2 UN Plaza, New York, NY 10017; Telephone (1) (212)

cont...

826–0840/1/2/3/4; Fax (1) (212) 826–2964; Telex AB 421283
SGWU U1

United States ◼ Singapore Embassy, 1824 R St. NW,
Washington, DC 20009–1691; Telephone (1) (202) 667–7555; Fax
(1) (202) 265–7915; Telex AB SINGEMB 440024

Proof of smallpox and cholera vaccination is not required unless
travelers are arriving from a cholera-infected area; smallpox is considered to have been eradicated. Yellow fever vaccination is required of
any person above the age of one who has passed through an infected
area (Africa, South America) within the preceding six days.

ASEAN VISA-FREE FACILITY

Citizens with valid passports from ASEAN countries can visit
Malaysia and Thailand for 14 days without a visa.

For the Philippines a visa is required for a stay of more than 21 days.
Indonesia offers two months without a visa to bona fide tourists,
provided that they have onward tickets and use designated points of
entry and exit.

INTERNATIONAL ROUTINGS
TO SINGAPORE

BY AIR

A number of international airlines provide direct flights to Sin-
gapore. Among them are Aeroflot, Alitalia, British Airways, KLM,
Lufthansa, Sabena, SAS, and Swissair from Europe; Air Canada,
Northwest, and United from North America; Quantas and Air New
Zealand from Australia and New Zealand; and Air India, China
Airlines, Garuda Indonesian Airways, Indian Airlines, Japan Air
Lines, Pakistan Airlines, Philippine Airlines, and Singapore's own Sin-
gapore Airlines from elsewhere in Asia. It is also possible to reach Sing-
apore by connecting flights on other airlines, and many lines that do
not offer direct flights nonetheless have offices in Singapore.

When you arrive in Singapore's Changi Airport, a moving side-
walk takes you to the luggage-claiming area and then to an area where

banking, postal, currency exchange, hotel reservation, and car rental services are available. A short tunnel leads to the Arrival Crescent, where you can get a taxi for the 20–minute ride on the East Coast Parkway to the center of the city. The fare from the airport includes a S$3 surcharge. Buses can be taken from the basement passenger terminal, or you may hire a car.

BY SEA

Passenger lines serve Singapore from North America, Europe, Australia, India, and Hong Kong. P. and O. Cruises Ltd. departs from the United States, Australia, and the United Kingdom. Pearl Cruises departs from Bangkok, Singapore, and Hong Kong. Standard immigration laws are followed regarding entry. Upon arrival, the Tourist Promotion Board offers an information service.

BY LAND

The Malay Peninsula is connected to Singapore via the Causeway by road or rail. International express rail services serve Singapore from Bangkok with stops en route in Haadyai, Butterworth, and Kuala Lumpur. Departure times from Bangkok are Monday, Wednesday, and Saturday at 4:10 PM. Express Rakyat provides service from Butterworth and Kuala Lumpur to Singapore. Fares and schedules for six additional daily services can be obtained by calling the railway station on Keppel Rd. (Tel. 222–5165).

ENTRANCE AND EXIT PROCEDURES

ANIMAL QUARANTINE

Because of the strict rabies control measures in effect in these countries, dogs and cats brought in from the United Kingdom, the Republic of Ireland, Australia, and New Zealand need not be quarantined if certain procedures are carried out. Any other animals—including birds—brought in must be accompanied by an import permit. The permit, which much be applied for at least two weeks before arriving, can be obtained from the Director of Primary Production, c/o City Veterinary Centre, 40 Kampong Java Rd., Singapore 0922 (Tel. 251–1203).

CUSTOMS

Duty-free Customs Allowances (except for incoming travelers from Malaysia): 1 bottle (1 liter) spirits, wine, or beer; 50 cigars, 200 cigarettes, 8 oz (250g) tobacco; and chocolates, cookies, or other confections of not more than S$50 value. These items can be purchased by travelers who are over 18 years of age at the duty-free emporium in the airport arrival hall. These items are for your own personal use, and must not be sold or given away. Spirits, wines, beer, tobacco, and sweets beyond this allowance, as well as leather bags and wallets, garments, and imitation jewelry beyond those needed for your personal use must be declared on entering the country and may be liable to duties.

Import permits are required for weapons, arms, ammunition, live or stuffed animals, raw or cooked meat products, plants, seeds, poisons, vaccines, controlled drugs, and prerecorded cartridges, cassettes, videotapes, or disks. Customs strictly restricts pornography, and any dangerous weapon must be declared and turned in at customs. It will be returned upon departure.

EXIT FORMALITIES

There is no export duty. Export permits are required for arms, ammunition, explosives, animals, gold in any form, platinum, precious stones in jewelery (except personal effects within limits). Any goods in excess of reasonable personal effects are to be declared at exit points and an Outward Declaration prepared, if necessary.

Passengers going to Brunei and Malaysia pay an airport tax of S$5; all others pay S$12. Airport tax coupons can be purchased at most hotels, TAS, and airline offices in town.

IV

Traveling in Singapore

KNOW BEFORE YOU GO

WEIGHTS AND MEASURES

The metric system of measures has been in effect in Singapore since 1971.

ELECTRICITY AND WATER

Voltage is 220–240 volts AC, 50 cycles. If necessary, most hotels have adapters or transformers. Tapwater is clean and safe. You should try to drink six glasses of water a day to counterbalance the tropical climate and avoid dehydration.

HEALTH AND SAFETY

In general, Singapore is a safe city day or night, as standards of security are quite high. Commonsense precautions are advised.

Singapore has high-quality medical facilities. Well-qualified doctors are on 24–hour call at most hotels. Also, if you consult the Yellow Pages of the Singapore phone book, you can find doctors listed under "Medical Practitioners" and dentists under "Dental Surgeons." Your embassy can recommend a specialist or private practitioner.

There are many well-equipped government hospitals in Singapore. Service is available to noncitizens at a slightly higher rate than citizens.

Pharmaceuticals are available at various outlets such as hotels, supermarkets, department stores, and shopping centers. Registered pharmacists may be consulted from 9:00 AM to 6:00 PM. Some outlets are open until 10:00 PM.

GOVERNMENT HOSPITALS

Alexandra Hospital (General), Alexander Rd. Telephone 473—5222

Kandang Kerbau Hospital (Maternity), Hampshire Rd. Telephone 293—4044

Singapore General Hospital, Outram Rd. Telephone 222–3322

Tan Tock Seng Hospital (General), Moulmein Rd. Telephone 256–6011

Toa Payoh Hospital (General), Tao Payoh Rise Telephone 256–0411

MEDICAL PHONE NUMBERS AND SERVICES

Ambulance–995

Pharmacies

    Medical Hall—Straits Building, Wellington Building, Scotts Shopping Centre;

    Robinson's Chemist—Specialist's Shopping Centre;

    Marican's Drug Stores—branches at The Arcade, Tanglin Shopping Centre;

    Guardian Pharmacy—Cold Storage Centerpoint, Katong Shopping Centre, Parkway Parade.

    See your Yellow Pages for additional pharmacies.

TIME AROUND THE WORLD

When it's 12 noon in Singapore, the standard time in the following cities is

Amsterdam	5 AM
Bangkok	11 AM
Beirut	6 AM
Cairo	6 AM
Chicago	10 PM previous day
Dallas	10 PM previous day
Frankfurt	5 AM
Hong Kong	12 NOON
Honolulu	6 PM previous day
London	4 AM

cont...

Los Angeles	8 PM previous day
Montreal	11 PM previous day
Nairobi	7 AM
New York	11 PM previous day
Paris	5 AM
Rio de Janeiro	1 AM
Rome	5 AM
San Francisco	8 PM previous day
Sydney	2 PM
Tokyo	1 PM
Vancouver	8 PM previous day
Zurich	5 AM

RELIGIOUS SERVICES

Because of its history as a British colony, and the presence of the Dutch in the area as well, the Western religions are well-represented in Singapore, and travelers should have no difficulty finding services of their own denomination. But Singapore's diversity is nowhere more evident than in its religious makeup. Confucian and Taoist, Buddhist and Hindu temples, Islamic mosques, Jewish synagogues, and Anglican, Roman Catholic, and Protestant churches, and even an Armenian one, can be found. Westerners visiting Eastern places of worship should respect the sensibilities of the worshippers.

Temples and Mosques. It is customary to remove one's shoes before entering a mosque or Indian temple. Mini-skirts or shorts would not be appropriate dress for a visit.

RELIGIOUS SERVICES AND PLACES OF WORSHIP

CHRISTIAN

ANGLICAN

Saint Andrew's Cathedral
Coleman St.
Telephone: 337–6104

cont...

METHODIST
Wesley Methodist Church
5 Fort Canning Rd.
Telephone: 336–1433

PRESBYTERIAN
Orchard Road Presbyterian Church
3 Orchard Rd.
Telephone: 337–6681

ROMAN CATHOLIC
Cathedral of the Good Shepherd
Queen St.
Telephone: 337–2036

JEWISH
Jewish Synagogue
Waterloo St.
Telephone: 336–0692

Reuben Manasseh Mayer Synagogue
Oxley Rise

MUSLIM
Hajjah Fatimah Mosque
Java Rd.

Sultan Mosque
North Bridge Rd.
Telephone: 293–4405

BUDDHIST
Shuang Lin Si Temple
184 E Jalan Toa Payoh
Telephone: 251–1836

Temple of 1000 Lights
366 Race Course Rd.
Telephone: 294–0714

cont...

HINDU

Sri Mariamman Temple
242 South Bridge Rd.
Telephone: 221–0413

TAOIST

Tian Fu Gong Temple
158 Telok Ayer St.
Telephone: 222–2651

WHEN IN SINGAPORE:

LEGAL PROHIBITIONS

In a Car. If you do not put on your seatbelt, you may be subject to a S$50 fine. This includes front seat passengers of private cars and taxis.

Smoking. Smoking in public is discouraged. Watch for signs that serve as reminders in the following locations: public buses, elevators, movie theaters, theaters, and government offices. Offenders may be fined up to S$500. It is also advisable not to smoke in taxis.

Littering. Singapore is one of the world's cleanest cities for a reason: the government has worked hard to promote social consciousness. The maximum fine for littering is S$500.

Drug Abuse. The maximum penalty for possession or consumption of drugs is 10 years in jail or a fine of S$20,000 or both.

Gambling. Charity Draws, Toto, Big Sweep, Singapore Sweep Lotteries, and horse-racing bets placed through the Singapore Turf Club are legalized; all other forms of gambling are prohibited.

Jaywalking. You will risk a S$50 fine if you cross a street within 50 meters of a pedestrian crossing, overhead bridge, or underpass. When there is no special pedestrian route, cross at traffic lights.

In sum, if you jaywalk across a street, toss a ticket stub on the corner, or get into your car and forget to put on your seatbelt, you could end up with very little money for side trips.

SOCIAL AND CULTURAL MORES

Imagine arriving at the airport or a hotel lobby and waving to a porter or bellboy to help you with your luggage. You wonder momentarily why he looks a bit askance. In Asian culture, you signal someone to come to you by holding the palm extended and facing downward, and moving in toward the body. Signaling someone to you with a waving forefinger is considered bad taste, comparable to calling a dog.

It takes a long time to assimilate what is appropriate or inappropriate in any culture; nonetheless there are certain guidelines you can follow regarding Asian culture which will prevent misunderstandings.

Tipping. Most hotels include a 10% service charge with every bill. Porters and bellboys can receive a S$1 tip. In most other places, such as snack stalls, local restaurants, and taxis, it is customary not to tip.

Tone of Voice. In Asian culture, the more important the subject, the quieter the voice. This may be helpful to remember for business meetings or important social gatherings.

Non-Verbal Communication. Pointing with the forefinger is not appropriate. Use your thumb with the palm slightly closed. Pounding a fist into an open palm is considered an obscene gesture.

Greetings. "Have you eaten?" or "Where are you going?" is more common than "How are you?" or "How's it going?"

Forms of Address. Asians are fairly formal about using first names. If you don't want to be thought somewhat forward, it is a good idea to wait for the other person to suggest doing so.

Formality. Business meetings or important social events may seem as if they take longer to get going. In some ways this indicates how imporant the event is, and though the process may seem drawn out, it is greatly respected.

Asian Face. At Chinese banquets, rice is usually served at the end of the meal or not at all. Asking for rice during the banquet might cause the host to "lose face" because he hadn't given his guest enough to eat. Any kind of embarrassment or direct confrontation is considered a loss of face. Western teachers may feel frustrated if they ask their Asian students a question and no one responds. It is safer to keep silent than to give an incorrect answer and lose face. In the business community, although Singaporeans are more aware of Western-style business relationships, an employee may not openly disagree with a superior. This is not "two-faced" but rather consideration that his superior may "save face."

Topics for Discussion. It's not unusual for Asians to ask about your salary or how much you paid for something. Finding the best bargain is a national pastime and it often comes up in conversation. On the other hand, sharing personal or private concerns is frowned upon. It is said that those who are open and direct should not be trusted because they will reveal confidences.

Modesty, Reserve, Compliments. Being frank and direct, particularly about achievements or possessions, is not common in Asian culture. Humility, modesty, and consensus are considered admirable traits. It may seem as though compliments are fended off more than acknowledged. It's not unusual for a Chinese host to prepare a ten-course meal and when told how wonderful the food is, to say: "Oh, it's just an ordinary family dinner."

Touching. Asians are more reserved about displays of affection and physical contact, particularly between members of the opposite sex. Even greeting an acquaintance with a hug or a kiss, or touching a shoulder while talking with an associate, may raise some eyebrows if it is between a man and woman. Also it is common for men to walk arm in arm or for women to hold hands.

Visiting a Home. It may not be expected, but most people remove their shoes when entering a home. Guests often bring fruit or cake as a small gift for the host. Although punctuality is often important for a business meeting, you should plan on arriving about 15 minutes late for a visit to a private home.

Gifts. Malays, Chinese, and Indians usually don't open gifts until after a guest has left. Fruit, food baskets, and candy are appropriate gifts for Chinese. Inappropriate gifts for Chinese would be clocks, handkerchiefs, flowers, and anything white, blue, or black, as these have negative connotations. It is customary to give gifts in pairs. It is not unusual for a Malay woman to give a guest something from her own wardrobe. This is a special compliment and shows that she is very fond of her guest. Perfume for women, cotton shirts for men, or something for the home are appropriate gifts for Malays. Inappropriate gifts would be food containing pork or lard, liquor, ashtrays, or anything relating to dogs, such as a Snoopy tee-shirt or toy dog. Always give a gift to an Indian with the right hand. Something for the home, fruit, or candy are appropriate gifts. Anything white or black is inappropriate.

EXCHANGE RATES FOR THE SINGAPORE DOLLAR

Country	Denomination	Singapore Dollars*	Country	Denomination	Singapore Dollars*
Australia	A$	1.3457	Malaysia	M$	0.6425
Belgium	BF	0.0565	Mexico	P	0.0006
Brazil	Cz$	0.0108	Netherlands	G	1.0351
Canada	CND	1.5035	New Zealand	NZ$	1.0297
China	Yuan	0.3323	Norway	Kr	0.2975
Denmark	KR	0.3031	Pakistan	R	0.0798
France	FF	0.3431	Philippines	Peso	0.0639
Germany	DM	1.1679	Portugal	E	0.0131
Hong Kong	HK$	0.2230	Spain	P	0.0183
India	R	0.0961	Sweden	Kr	0.3106
Indonesia	Rp	0.0009	Taiwan	NT$	0.0653
Italy	L	0.0016	Thailand	Baht	0.0691
Japan	Yen	0.0129	United Kingdom	£	3.3777
Korea	W	0.0024	United States	US$	1.7379

*For reference only. Obtain effective rates at time of exchange.

MONEY, CURRENCY AND BANKING

CURRENCY AND EXCHANGE RATE

The Singapore dollar is divided into 100 cents. Bank notes are denominated as S$1, S$5, S$10, S$20, S$50, S$100, S$500, S$1,000, and S$10,000. Coins are 1 cent, 5 cents, 10 cents, 20 cents, 50 cents, and 1 dollar. The exchange rate: US$1 = S$1.74, UK£1 = S$3.38, Australia A$1 = S$1.35. Travelers' checks usually get a better rate of exchange then cash.

There are no restrictions or limitations on the amount of foreign currency notes, cash, checks, and other instruments of payment imported to or exported from Singapore. Imports and exports of gold must be declared to the Trade Development Board.

BANKING FOR TOURISTS

Banking hours are 10:30 AM – 3:00 PM Monday through Friday, and 9:30 AM – 11:30 AM Saturday. (Branches of the Development Bank of Singapore are open until 3:00 PM on Saturday.) Not all banks handle transactions for traveler's checks and foreign currency on Saturday. Some banks conduct these transactions in small amounts, based on Friday's rate.

In addition to banks and hotels, money can be changed wherever a "Licensed Money-Changer" sign is displayed. Licensed money-changers may be found at most shopping complexes. The rate is slightly better than bank rates. It is best not to change money through anyone not licensed.

CREDIT CARDS

American Express, Visa, Asiacard, Diners Club, Carte Blanche, JCB, MasterCard, and Air Travel Card are all commonly accepted as well as credit cards from international hotel chains and airlines. Note: In most shops, if you pay in cash, a 3% – 5% discount is available.

COMMUNICATIONS AND NEWS MEDIA

POSTAL SERVICE

Postal service is available at the front desks of most hotels. Postal service hours are usually 8:30 AM– 5:00 PM on weekdays and 8:30 AM– 1:00 PM on Saturdays.

The General Post Office and the Customer Services Centre at Exeter Rd. are both open 24 hours daily.

The postal rate for local letters is 10 cents; airmail postcards to Hong Kong are 20 cents; to Japan and Australia 25 cents; to the United Kingdom, Europe, and the Middle East 40 cents; and to the United States 55 cents. Aerogrammes to all parts of the world are 35 cents.

Speedpost is an international express service. For information call 448-7733.

TELECOMMUNICATIONS

TELEPHONE

Direct-dialing service from hotels is available to most principal cities in the world. Local calls made from most hotel rooms are free. Calls from public pay phones cost 10 cents.

CABLE AND TELEX

The International Country Code for Singapore is 65. Telex messages may be sent at Telecoms offices and at most hotels.

FAX

Facsimiles can be sent from computers to 40 countries by IDD and to an additional 41 destinations with operator assistance. There is also a Telepac service, through which you can access databases in 28 destinations both local and foreign.

RADIO AND TV

RADIO

Daily services are in English and Chinese from 6:00 AM to midnight. For English-language broadcasting try Radio One (90.5 MHz);Radio Five (92.4 MHz), and British Broadcasting World Service (88.9 MHz). Check daily newspaper listings for program schedules.

TELEVISION

Most hotels offer a teletext service which provides up-to-date information on entertainment, special events, news, financial reports, and airline schedules. Daily programming in four languages includes Channel 5: daily from 3:00 PM to midnight, Saturday 1:00 PM to 1:00 AM, Sunday 9:00 AM to midnight; Channel 8: daily from 6:00 PM to 11:00 PM, Saturday and Sunday 3:00 PM to 11:30 PM; Channel 12: daily from 8:00 PM to 10:30 PM (educational and cultural programming).

PRINT MEDIA

NEWSPAPERS AND MAGAZINES

The *Straits Times* is an English-language daily. There are also

Chinese, Malay, and Tamil newspapers. *Business Times*, a business daily, also provides information on ship schedules. For information on cultural events, look for the *Arts Daily*, a monthly publication available at most hotels. International editions of foreign newspapers and magazines such as *Newsweek*, the *International Herald Tribune*, *Asiaweek*, and the *Far Eastern Economic Review* can be purchased in major hotels. Long-term residents should visit MPH Bookstores for a larger selection of English-language magazines and newspapers. Newsstands are found in shopping centers and along Change Alley and Orchard Rd.

BOOKSTORES AND NEWSSTANDS

Singapore has a thriving book publishing industry, with local branches of such major Western publishers as Addison-Wesley, Harcourt, Harper, Heinemann, Longman, Macmillan, Prentice Hall, Simon & Schuster, and the Oxford University Press, as well as many local firms supplying books in many languages. Bookstores likewise offer both new and second-hand books on a variety of subjects in English and the other official languages of Singapore. Many bookstores also serve as lending libraries.

LOCAL TRANSPORTATION

PUBLIC TRANSPORTATION

TAXIS

Taxis are identifiable by a taxi sign on the roof. Dial-a-taxi service is available 24 hours a day by calling 452-5555 or 250-0707. The fare starts at S$1.60 for the first 1.5 km for up to two pa~~engers. For each additional 300 m, an additional S$.10 is charged, and a S$0.05 surcharge is levied for each passenger above two. There are other additional charges: S$3 for a trip from the airport; S$1 for each piece of luggage stowed in the trunk (hand luggage is exempt); and a 50% surcharge for travel between midnight and 6 AM. A scheme of charges to discourage cars in the central business district (CBD) during rush hours has also been instituted: a S$1 surcharge is levied on all taxi trips leaving the CBD between 4 and 7 PM on weekdays, and noon and 3 PM on Saturdays. Furthermore, any car—including a taxi—carrying fewer than four persons, counting the driver, that enters the CBD from

SINGAPORE SUBWAY (MRT) ROUTE MAP

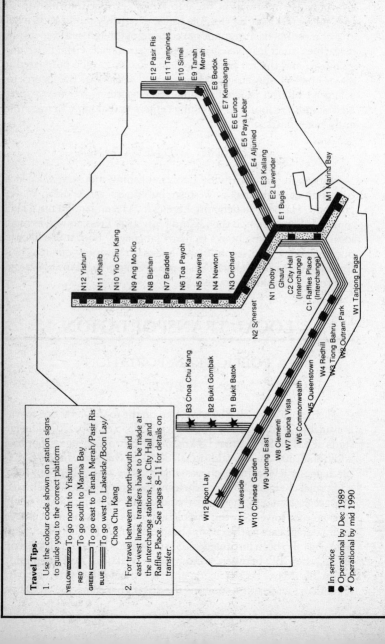

Travel Tips.

1. Use the colour code shown on station signs to guide you to the correct platform

   YELLOW ▨▨▨▨ To go north to Yishun

   RED ▬▬▬▬ To go south to Marina Bay

   GREEN ═══ To go east to Tanah Merah/Pasir Ris

   BLUE ≡≡≡ To go west to Lakeside/Boon Lay/ Choa Chu Kang

2. For travel between the north-south and east-west lines, transfers have to be made at the interchange stations, i.e. City Hall and Raffles Place. See pages 8–11 for details on transfer.

In service
■ Operational by Dec 1989
● Operational by mid 1990
★

N12 Yishun
N11 Khatib
N10 Yio Chu Kang
N9 Ang Mo Kio
N8 Bishan
N7 Braddell
N6 Toa Payoh
N5 Novena
N4 Newton
N3 Orchard
N2 Somerset
N1 Dhoby Ghaut

E12 Pasir Ris
E11 Tampines
E10 Simei
E9 Tanah Merah
E8 Bedok
E7 Kembangan
E6 Eunos
E5 Paya Lebar
E4 Aljunied
E3 Kallang
E2 Lavender
E1 Bugis

M1 Marina Bay

C2 City Hall (Interchange)
C1 Raffles Place (Interchange)

W1 Tanjong Pagar
W2 Outram Park
W3 Tiong Bahru
W4 Redhill
W5 Queenstown
W6 Commonwealth
W7 Buona Vista
W8 Clementi
W9 Jurong East
W10 Chinese Garden
W11 Lakeside
W12 Boon Lay

B3 Choa Chu Kang
B2 Bukit Gombak
B1 Bukit Batok

TRANSFER INFORMATION

You can transfer between the north-south and east-west lines only at the two interchange stations, City Hall and Raffles Place.

If you stop at the right interchange station, all you have to do is to cross from one side of the platform to the other. There will be colour-coded signs in the interchange stations to help you.

The right interchange station is shown in the transfer guide below:—

C1 RAFFLES PLACE (Interchange)

		NORTHBOUND YELLOW
EASTBOUND GREEN	• For passengers on eastbound trains from Lakeside/Boon Lay/Choa Chu Kang and heading north towards Yishun • For passengers on northbound trains from Marina Bay and heading east towards Tanah Merah/Pasir Ris	
	UPPER PLATFORM	
WESTBOUND BLUE	• For passengers on westbound trains from Tanah Merah/Pasir Ris and heading south towards Marina Bay • For passengers on southbound trains from Yishun and heading west towards Lakeside/Boon Lay/Choa Chu Kang	**SOUTHBOUND** RED
	LOWER PLATFORM	

Example

To travel from **Lakeside to Orchard**, do the following:—
• Board the eastbound train at Lakeside station
• Alight at Raffles Place station
• Cross the upper platform to board the northbound train to Orchard station

Note:

If you stop at the wrong interchange station, all you have to do is to *change platform level*. For example, if you are travelling from Lakeside to Orchard station and has stopped at City Hall instead of Raffles Place for the transfer, all you have to do is to take the escalator from the lower to the upper platform at City Hall station to board the northbound train.

C2 CITY HALL (Interchange)

		NORTHBOUND YELLOW
EASTBOUND GREEN	• For passengers on northbound trains from Marina Bay and heading west towards Lakeside/Boon Lay/Choa Chu Kang • For passengers on westbound trains from Tanah Merah/Pasir Ris and heading north towards Yishun	
	UPPER PLATFORM	
WESTBOUND BLUE	• For passengers on southbound trains from Yishun and heading east towards Tanah Merah/Pasir Ris • For passengers on eastbound trains from Lakeside/Boon Lay/Choa Chu Kang and heading south towards Marina Bay	**SOUTHBOUND** RED
	LOWER PLATFORM	

Example

To travel from **Ang Mo Kio to Bedok**, do the following:—
• Board the southbound train at Ang Mo Kio station
• Alight at City Hall station
• Cross the lower platform to board the eastbound train to Bedok station

7:30 AM to 10:15 AM, Monday to Saturday, must pay a fee to obtain a special sticker on any day that it does so. The fee for a taxi is S$2, paid by the passenger at any of several kiosks on the outskirts of the CBD. Only one such sticker must be bought each day, so if you can get a cab that has already taken a fare to the CBD and obtained a sticker that day, you will not have to pay for another one.

BUSES

Buses run from 6:00 AM to 11:30 PM, with fares ranging from S$0.40 to S$0.80. You can buy a special "Explorer Ticket" from the Singapore Bus Service (red and white buses) and travel anywhere on the island for a daily fare of S$5, or S$12 for three days. This ticket entitles you to unlimited service, and you can break up the trip whenever you wish. You will receive a bus map with your ticket (with six routes for major points of interest) and a coupon booklet for free gifts and discounts at various tourist spots. These tickets are available from major hotels and travel agents. Bus service charts and bus guides are available at most bookstores and newsstands.

MASS RAPID TRANSIT (SUBWAY)

Construction of the Singapore MRT began in 1983. The system has two lines, one running north-south and the other east-west. Of 42 stations 15 are underground, 26 are elevated, and one is at ground level. The Yio Chu Kang to Toa Payoh line opened in November 1987, and the Novena to Outram Park line opened in December 1987. Completion of the system is expected by 1990. Fares range from S$0.50 to S$1.10, depending on the length of the journey.

FERRIES

Service from the World Trade Centre in Singapore to Sentosa Island is available every 15 minutes from 7:30 AM to 11:00 PM from Monday through Thursday and to midnight Friday through Sunday and on public holidays and their eve.

RENTAL CARS

Car rental rates for an air-conditioned vehicle vary from company to company. A rented car can cost from S$60 to S$200 per day, with a weekly charge ranging from S$360 to S$1,200. Mileage charges start at S$.60 per km. A chauffer-driven car's hourly rate starts at S$40 for a minimum of three hours. Daily rates are S$212 to $420 for eight hours.

To drive in Singapore you must have a valid International Driver's License, or a current valid license. Speed limits are 50 km per hour on all roads and 80 km per hour on expressways unless otherwise indicated by signs. As in the United Kingdom, drivers travel on the left-hand side of the road. When approachng a roundabout, or traffic circle, always yield to the right. Car rental companies can explain the coupon parking system.

CAR RENTAL COMPANIES

Ace Tours and Car Rentals Pte., Ltd.
Hotel Asia, 37 Scotts Rd.
Telephone: 235–3755/235–4433

Sintat Thrifty Rent-A-Car
1 Maritime Square,
#13–06/World Trade Center
Telephone: 273–2211/Cable: SINTACAR/Telex: RS 26740

For additional information about car rentals, check the Yellow Pages in the Singapore telephone book under "Motorcar Renting and Leasing."

VEHICULAR TOURS

TRISHAWS

Trishaws are bicycles with sidecars attached, and are another popular way of getting about Singapore. Trishaw tours are available daily from 7:00 PM to 9:00 PM. Some include a ride through various neighborhoods with dinner (S$65) or a ride with a drink (S$36). For information call Association Tours Pte., Ltd., at 235-7222. It is best to arrange for a trishaw tour only through a hotel or travel agent, since there is no standard fare structure.

BOATS

Boats can be rented at Jardine Steps or Clifford Pier on the waterfront. The fare is S$50 (up to ten people) for a one-hour cruise to the southern islands.

HELICOPTERS

You can take a 40-minute tour of the island for S$750 (charge for one flight in one helicopter) with a maximum of five passengers. The flight begins at the Seletar Secondary Airport, proceeds to the waterfront, then travels around Sentosa Island, to Jurong, and returns to Seletar. For more information, call Helicopter Services at 481-5711.

SIGHTSEEING TOURS

There are a great variety of tours in Singapore geared toward a range of interests and budgets. The most expedient way to choose a tour that appeals to you is to inquire at your hotel desk (most hotels have tour services) or to call the Singapore Tourist Promotion Board (235-6611). A 3-4-hour coach tour with hotel pick-up will cost about S$20-S$35. Should you have special interests, the STB can arrange a three-hour itinerary tailored to your interest, with a guide who speaks English or another language of your choice. The fee for this service is S$36 to S$76. Below are some of the more popular tours.

COACH TOURS

City Tour—3½ hours.
Rates: S$21 adult, S$11 child.
Tour Operator: Tour East, RMG, Siakson, Singapore Sightseeing.
Itinerary: Elizabeth Walk, Supreme Court, City Hall, Singapore River and Merlion Park, Chinatown, Sri Mariamman Temple, Haw Par Villa, "Instant Asia" Cultural Show, Botanic Gardens.

Round Island Tour—8½ hours.
Rates: S$56 adult, S$28 child.
Tour Operator: Tour East.
Itinerary: Haw Par Villa, Jurong lookout point, Lim Chu Kang (vegetable and poultry farms), orchid farm, lunch at Admiralty House, public housing apartment, Bright Hill Temple, Changi Point boat ride, Crocodilarium.

Heritage Tour—3½ hours.
Rates: S$19 adult, S$9 child.
Tour Operator: RMG.
Itinerary: Arab Street, Sultan Mosque, Little India, Raffles Landing Site, Thian Hock Keng Temple, National Museum.

Footsteps of Raffles—3¾ hours.
Rates: S$25 adult, S$12 child.

Tour Operator: Tour East.
Itinerary: National Museum, Little India, Raffles Hotel, Raffles Landing Site, Thian Hock Keng Temple, Mount Faber, Botanic Gardens.

Shopping Tour—3½ hours.
Rates: S$17 adult, S$8 child.
Tour Operator: Tour East.
Itinerary: Arab Street, Change Alley, Lim's Handicraft in Holland Village.

Singapore by Night—3½ hours.
Rates: S$39 adult, S$29 child.
Tour Operator: Singapore Sightseeing.
Itinerary: Dinner at Newton Circus Hawker Centre, drive through city, Mount Faber, Raffles Hotel.

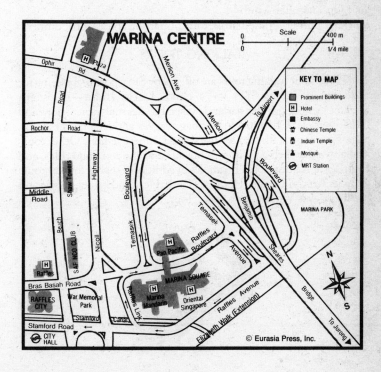

BOAT TOURS

Island Picnic— 7½ hours.
Rates: S$45 adult, S$25 child.
Tour Operator: Tour East.
Itinerary: Coach to Clifford Pier, bumboat to Pulau Seking to visit Malay village, shrines on Kusu Island, picnic lunch, fishing, snorkeling on Sisters Island.

Twilight/Dinner Cruise
Rates: S$33 adult, S$17 child.
Tour Operator: Tour East, RMG.
Itinerary: Coach to Clifford Pier, harbor cruise in Chinese junk around Kasu, Pulau Terkukor, and Sentosa islands, buffet dinner.

Starlite Dinner Cruise—3 hours.
Rates: S$36 adult, S$18 child.
Tour Operator: Eastwind.
Itinerary: Sunset Chinese junk tour of harbor and islands, dinner.

WALKING TOURS

Three-hour walking tours are offered by Singapore Sightseeing for S$28 for an adult, S$14 for a child. **Little India**—goldsmith workroom, flour grinder, garland maker, hawker stalls, spice shops and Indian temple. **Chinatown** — image carver and clog maker shops, Sago Lane food stalls, coffee shops and Chinese temple. Other tours available offer such activities as breakfast at the zoo, tram rides, and High Tea at Raffles Hotel. Examples of additional special interest tours include: Arts and Crafts, Houses of Faith, Flora and Fauna, People and Heritage, and Violet Oon's Food Tour.

V The Singapore Tour

A CITY OF NEIGHBORHOODS

ALTHOUGH Singapore is very much a modern city, it's a modern city with something extra. The ethnic neighborhoods of old Singapore, considered unsightly during the country's thrust towards modernization, are now being spruced up. Present government policy considers these neighborhoods assets to its tourist trade, and renovation is now preferred to demolition. The Singapore Urban Redevelopment Authority is drawing up a plan for conserving historic Singapore; it oversees government projects and encourages the private sector to undertake restorations too. As a result, some of the newest sights in Singapore are some of the oldest.

Visitors to Singapore can enjoy not only all the amenities of this clean, efficient city with its lavish shopping complexes and streamlined transportation system, but also a sense of Singapore's heritage as the sights and sounds of Arab Street, Chinatown, and Little India entice the visitor to meander through the countless side streets, alleys, and secret corners of each neighborhood. Where else can you buy a Benares sari, visit a Chinese temple, and sip Arabic coffee, all in one day? Little India, Arab Street, and Chinatown are essential parts of Singapore's charm, and sightseeing in these districts is truly fascinating. There are lots of narrow lanes and alleyways to wander through and all kinds of unique shops for browsing.

ARAB STREET

Some say your nose will tell you when you've come to the district called Arab Street. That is because of the many flower essences to be found there. This area, also known as Kampong Glam, is among those slated for restoration and renewal. Wandering along Arab St. proper and Beach Rd., you will see a number of shops selling traditional items such as batiks, silks, basketware, carpets, and jewelry. Dates from Oman, brassware, and tablecloths can also be found here. There are more shops on Baghdad St. On North Bridge Rd. and nearby are many Muslim restaurants and shops selling loose semiprecious stones, floral

The Sultan Mosque—Arab Street

Further on at Jalan Sultan, you can stop at Sultan Plaza to see Arab, Indonesian, Malay, and Muslim Indian cloth traders. A colorful array of brocades, velvets, batiks, tapestries, tulle, and sequined fabrics are on display. You may also want to explore the "religious supermarket" or pick up some Filipino handicrafts.

The Jama-Ath Mosque is on the corner of Victoria St. Behind the mosque, within Jalan Sultan, Rocher Canal Rd., and Jalan Kubor St., there are Muslim burial grounds. A white cloth tied to a headstone indicates that a relative has recently visited.

You may want to walk along Victoria St. to see the last of the barrelmakers or return to North Bridge Rd. to take a break at one of the many Muslim restaurants opposite the Sultan Mosque.

CHINATOWN AND THE SINGAPORE RIVER

Elgin Bridge, over the Singapore River, was Singapore's first bridge. Crossing it and walking toward South Bridge Rd. will bring you to Boat Quay, a good starting point for exploring Chinatown. It was here that the bumboats arrived and departed with spices, cotton, silk, and tea. Here are old riverside shrines where sailors prayed to Chinese water gods, and offices of transport and trading companies surmounted by distinctive Chinese balconies with green ceramic balustrades. Here too, in innumerable shops and stalls, traditional craftsmen still ply their trades and proffer their wares. This is one of the areas that have recently benefitted from Singapore's commitment to preserving its past.

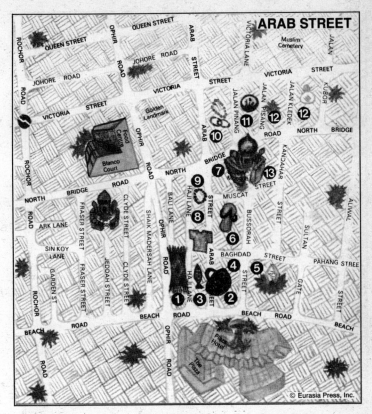

ARAB STREET

1. Textiles (batik, fabric, prayer rugs)
2. Cane and Basketware
3. Fishing Tackle
4. Sarabat Stall (ginger drink tea, coffee)
5. Muslim Gravemakers
6. Indian Leather Sandals & Bags
7. Indian Herbal Medicines, Spices
8. Batik, Textiles, Clothing
9. Jewellers
10. Goldsmiths
11. Dancers' and Brides' Jewellery & Accessories
12. Perfume Essences
13. Sultan Mosque

essences, "James Bond" walking sticks, incense burners, worry beads, and much more. Over the shopfronts towers the dazzling golden dome of the Sultan Mosque, which lies between the road and Muscat St. If you plan your walk ahead, you can hear the call to prayer at dawn, 12:30 and 4:00 PM, sunset, and 8:15 PM. Sultan Gate is a short distance from the mosque. Here you can see Istana Kampong Glam, a majestic building that dates from the 1840s and was once the residence of the sultan. At the opposite end of the street, there are Chinese foundries, and nearby traditional stonemasons carve headstones.

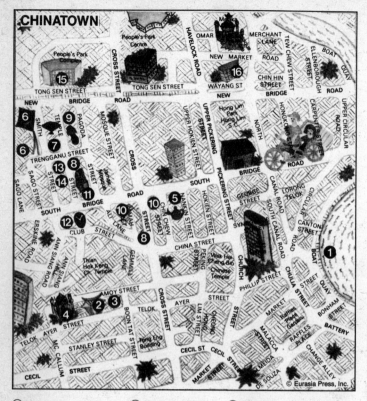

① Boat Quay	⑥ Chinatown Complex	⑪ Sri Mariamman Temple
② Thian Hock Keng Temple	⑦ Kites, Fans	⑫ Masks, Lion Dance Heads
③ Nagore Durgha Shrine	⑧ Dried Mushrooms	⑬ Porcelain, Woks, Housewares
④ Al-Abrar Mosque	⑨ Dishes, Clogs	⑭ Temple Shops, tinsmiths
⑤ Shop Selling Chinese Tea	⑩ Goldsmiths	⑮ People's Park Shopping Complex
		⑯ Thong Chai Medical Institution

The Temple of the Calm Sea (Wak Hai Cheng Bio), located on Phillip St., was built from 1852 to 1855 by people from Canton; its roof is decorated with scenes from Chinese opera. Continue on to Telok Ayer St., which once ran parallel and close to the original seashore. That made it an excellent location for merchants and traders—of many sorts: between 1850 and 1870, the street was notorious for its slave trade. Here you can visit the Temple of Prosperity and Virtue (Fuk Tak Chi), have your palm read by a street calligrapher, browse in Meow Choon Foh Yit Kee (Number 134), a traditional Chinese medicine hall, visit the paper merchants, buy some Chinese teacakes or herbal teas, or stop at #123, an old-fashioned barber shop.

Across Boon Tat St. are three national monuments: Al Abrar Mosque; Durgha (Nagora) Shrine; and the Thian Hock Keng, or Temple of Heavenly Happiness, the oldest Chinese temple in Singapore, built by Chinese immigrants as a thank-offering for safe passage.

On Amoy St., nestled amidst the Hokkien shops and clubs, is one of Chinatown's secret corners. A tree grows on the roof of one of the shophouses. The Tien Chor Keng Temple is also on this street. If you go left along Cross St. you will come to a small square at the foot of Club St. On Club St. itself you can see image carvers at work and a traditional walled Chinese house. Further on, at Ann Siang Hill, traditional theater masks are displayed for sale.

The jinriksha station on the corner of Tanjong Pagar and Neil Rd. dates back to 1903 and was once the central point for over 9,000 rickshaws. It has recently been restored, along with the whole area between Tanjong Pagar, Neil Rd., and Duxton Rd., as part of Singapore's new commitment to preserving the memorials of its history. Restaurants and teashops, antique dealers and kite makers, occupy newly restored and freshly painted shophouses.

If you cross Neil Rd. and take Sago St., you can visit the shops where paper cars and houses are made to be used for funeral offerings. Trengganu St. offers a colorful display of local fruit and fresh flowers.

Try out your bargaining skills on Mosque St. where many of the shops sell secondhand goods. There is a teahouse on this street which serves Chinese snacks (dimsum, or *dianxin*) from 8:00 to 11:00 AM.

From Mosque St., take South Bridge Rd. The Chung Hua Bookshop, which specializes in traditional and modern paintings, calligraphy, and artifacts, is at #71. Chan Pui Kee and Co., established in 1913, is at #86 Neil Rd. (as South Bridge becomes Neil Rd). Here you can find lacquerwood furniture and traditional Chinese, Indonesian, and Peranakan furniture. Taking South Bridge toward the river, you will see goldsmiths, shops which sell medicinal crushed pearls, and wholesale jewelers.

Strolling along Gross St. (near South Bridge Rd.), you can find instruments and books for geomancy. Further on look for glass containers of all shapes and sizes on display, a floral oil shop, and a "frog shop!"

Toward the end of South Bridge Rd., on Upper Circular, before returning to the river, you might like to visit Yeo Swe Huat, where traditional hand-painted bamboo and rice paper lanterns and festival masks are on display.

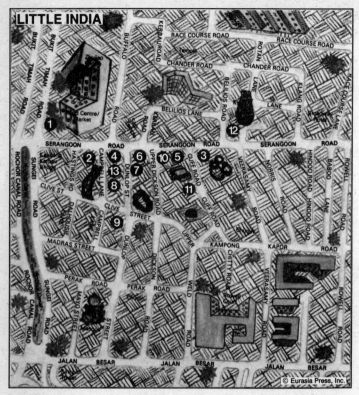

1. Zhu Jiao Market
2. Sari Shops
3. Goldsmiths
4. Spices & Dry Goods
5. Luggage, Trunks
6. Poster Seller
7. Komala Vilas Vegetarian Restaurant
8. Provision Shops
9. Traditional Kitchen Utensils
10. Spice & Lentil Mill
11. Fish Head Curry Restaurants
12. Sri Veeramakaliaman Temple
13. Garlands

LITTLE INDIA

The area around Serangoon Rd. is known as Little India, and it offers a panorama of terrace houses, colorful saris, glittering glass bangles, brocades, spices, fruit, and incense. Along the maze of streets you'll see fortune-tellers, open-air barbershops, and the famous dhoby shops, where clothes are laundered in huge cauldrons and then beaten on stone slabs.

Start at Buffalo Rd. which specializes in saris, flower garlands, and audio equipment. Look above the doorways for strings of dried mango.

This traditional Indian symbol represents blessings and good fortune.

The Arasu Emporium at #10 Buffalo Rd. features ornaments for dances and weddings. Number 16 (Ganapathi) offers garlands and ear piercing.

Traveling along Serangoon Rd., you will find shops for incense (#68) and traditional musical instruments (#73) as well as goldsmiths and Indian necklace shops (#75).

Further on is the Sri Veramakaliamman Temple, built in 1881 by indentured Bengali workers. This temple is dedicated to Kali the Courageous, and the black statue of Kali inside the temple represents a ferocious incarnation of Siva's wife. Thre is also a shrine to Ganesh, the elephant god of wisdom.

A memorial hall to Mahatma Gandhi is located on Race Course Lane. From Race Course Lane to Race Course Rd. you can see the site of Singapore's first racetrack at Farrer Park.

Nearby on Kinta Rd., there is a Burmese Buddhist temple which dates back to 1878. At this temple there is an 11-ft (3.3-meter) statue of the Buddha. The white marble for this statue came from a 10-ton block of Mandalay marble.

In this area are a Chinese medical hall, a mill for spices, shops offering birds and birdcages and also, on Roberts Lane, a beautiful row of houses. Watch for the giant dragon joss sticks on Birch Rd. and more unique shophouses on Owen Rd. At the Perumal Temple (Serangoon Rd.), there is a beautiful 66-ft-high (20-m) gateway with elaborate carvings.

Strolling back to Norris Rd., you will see cooks at work preparing flat Indian bread (*chapatis*) and an open field for the dhoby shops, traditional Indian laundries. Another picturesque old house is at #26 Veersamy Rd. Down the road you will also find a tin trunk shop and a shop where corn and beans are ground.

Walking towards Clive St., look for astrologers and sellers of silver charms. There is a fantastic display of fish and prawn crackers, beans, nuts, rice, sparkling bangles, garlands, and pots and pans at the corner of Clive St. and Campbell Lane.

A few must-see places in Little India are the Zhu Jiao Centre, in the Buffalo Rd. area, which includes one of the largest wet markets in Singapore, the well-known block of old houses in Petain St. (in front of #12 you can see curry puffs being prepared), and the Abdul Gafoor Mosque with its lovely courtyard setting (41 Dunlop St.).

COLONIAL HEART

Begin your walk at the General Post Office. This was originally Fort Fullerton, which was built in 1830 to guard the entrance to the Singapore River. Cross the river by way of Cavanaugh Bridge, made in Glasgow and assembled in Singapore in 1869. At Empress Place there is a line of impressive colonial-style government buildings dating back to 1864. You can walk across the square and see what's playing at the Victoria Theatre and compare programs at the Victoria Memorial Hall on the right. Outside the Victoria Theatre is the famous bronze statue of Raffles. Continuing on to North Boat Quay, you are greeted by the noble Raffles again: a replica of the bronze statue marks the spot where Raffles is believed to have stepped ashore in 1819. Parliament House, the oldest government building in Singapore, stands beside the replica.

At the entrance to Parliament House, the bronze statue of an elephant commemorates the visit in 1871 of Siamese King Chulalongkorn. The main part of Parliament House was originally an elegant two-story mansion, built by the architect George Coleman in 1827.

Supreme Court and City Hall are across from Parliament House. The Supreme Court was completed in 1939. Its classical Italian murals and high, vaulted archways and columns contrast with the stately steps of City Hall, the site of the formal surrender of the Japanese forces on September 12, 1945.

Further on, the Padang provides yet another impressive view. The Padang ("field" or "plain" in Malay) was the only spot on the island not covered with mangrove swamp when Raffles first arrived.

Saint Andrew's Cathedral is on Coleman St. The site for this church was chosen by Raffles, and the present Gothic-style Anglican building was built between 1856 and 1863. Inside this church are the Coventry Cross and the Canterbury Stone. Singapore's oldest church, the Armenian Church of Saint Gregory the Illumintor, can be found on the corner of Coleman and Hill streets. Its square plan with projecting porticoes recalls the Greek cross design traditional in Armenian churches, but its elevation is in a classic Western style, and its steeple could grace a New England village church.

Behind the church, climb Fort Canning Rise, once known as Forbidden Hill, the ancient fortress of Malay kings. The white stone gothic gates of Fort Canning Park lead to an old Christian cemetery. The gravestones of Singapore's first European settlers date back to 1820. Here, you can also wander through the ruins of Fort Canning and see what remains of the old guardhouse, earthworks, and metal gates.

SIGHTS WORTH SEEING

MAJOR MONUMENTS AND LANDMARKS

Armenian Church (Hill St.). Saint Gregory the Illuminator was built in 1835 from funds contributed by Singapore's Armenian community. It is the oldest church in Singapore though no longer used for regular services.

Empress Place Museum (Empress Place). A building originally constructed in 1854 to serve as the New Court House, and later expanded to serve various other government departments, it was closed for restoration in 1986 and reopened in April 1989 as a museum. Its first exhibition, the Treasures of Qing, was one of a series, to be jointly sponsored by Singapore and the People's Republic of China, illustrating Chinese archaeology, history, and culture. From April 1990 to April 1991, a similar exhibition of Han Dynasty treasures was held, and more such exhibitions are scheduled. Open 9:30 AM– 9:30 PM.

House of Tan Yeok Nee (corner of Clemenceau Ave. and Penang Rd.). Of interest to architects and Sinophiles, this residence of Tan Yeok Nee, a wealthy merchant, was built in 1885. Its keyhole gables, terracotta tiles, and granite pillars exemplify an architectural style then popular in South China. At present it is the headquarters of the Salvation Army. Open Monday – Friday 8:30 AM – 4:30 PM and all day Sunday. Closed Saturday.

Merlion Park, Singapore River. For a relaxing stroll away from the hustle of the city center, take a walk along the edge of the harbor. Bring your camera to capture the Merlion, the symbol of Singapore. Half lion, half fish, and 26 ft (8 m) high, the Merlion stands guard at the mouth of the Singapore River.

National Museum and Art Gallery (Stamford Rd.). Originally known as the Raffles Museum (opened in 1887), the National Museum and Art Gallery houses a wealth of information on the ethnology, history, and art of Singapore and Southeast Asia. Prominent exhibits include: History of Singapore, which consists of 20 dioramas depicting social, economic, and political development; Haw Par Jade Collection, displaying 380 pieces of jade, one of the largest collections in the world; Straits Chinese Gallery, a collection of ornate

Merlion Park, Singapore River

furniture and artifacts; and local contemporary art and changing exhibitions. Open Tuesday – Sunday 9:00 AM – 4:30 PM. Art Gallery: 9:00 AM–5:30 PM. Closed on Monday. Admission S$1.00 adult, S$0.50 child.

Raffles Hotel (Beach Rd.). The Armenian Sarkie brothers opened this hotel in 1887. Its French Renaissance architecture with palm-shaded courtyards and verandas lured princes, authors, and film stars to the reception desk. Raffles' Long Bar is the home of the Singapore Sling. The Writers' Bar is a tribute to such former literary guests as Rudyard Kipling, Somerset Maugham, Noel Coward, and Joseph Conrad, all of whom are reputed to have spent long hours here, literarily musing over potent Singapore Slings.

Sir Stamford Raffles Landing Site (behind Parliament House). From 1989 to mid-1991, the Raffles was closed for extensive restoration. A bronze statue of Sir Stamford Raffles marks the spot on the bank of the Singapore River where it is believed Raffles first stepped ashore in 1819. (This statue is a copy of the original bronze statue, which now stands in front of the Victoria Theatre.)

Supreme Court and City Hall (Saint Andrew's Rd.). These neoclassical buildings with Corinthian columns overlook the Padang. The Supreme Court was completed in 1939 and City Hall was completed in 1929.

Thong Chai Medical Institution (Tong Ji Yi Yuan Wayang St.). Originally, in 1892, this building served as a free hospital. Today it is a handicraft emporium where you can buy jade, ivory, scrolls, porcelain, bonsai trees, and many other handicrafts. Open Monday–Saturday 9:40 AM–5:30 PM.

War Memorial (Memorial Park, Beach Rd.). Four white columns almost 230 ft (70 m) high, representing the four cultures of Singapore, stand in memory of civilians who lost their lives during the Japanese occupation of World War II.

PLACES OF WORSHIP

Al Abrar Mosque (Telok Ayer St.). Also known as Koochoo Pally ("small mosque" in Tamil), Al Abrar Mosque was built from 1850 to 1855 by Indian Muslims.

Cathedral of the Good Shepherd (Queen St.). This Roman Catholic cathedral was completed in 1846.

Chettiar Hindu Temple (Tank Rd.). Some of the impressive features of this temple—which was completed in 1984—are a 75-ft-high (23-meter) gateway, a ceiling decorated with lotus flowers, chandeliers and 48 glass panels (angled to reflect the sunrise and sunset). The original temple on this site was built by Chettiar Indians who settled in the area in the 1850s. Opportune times to visit this ornate temple are during the nine-day Navarathri Festival and during Thaipusam (see festival calendar). Open 8:00 AM–noon and 5:30 PM–8:30 PM

Saint Andrew's Cathedral (Coleman St.). This Gothic-style Anglican cathedral was built between 1856 and 1863, and houses many historic memorials. Among them are a window whose dedication reads: "To the memory of Sir Stamford Raffles, Kt., the illustrious founder of the settlement of Singapore. This window is dedicated by the citizens AD 1861."

Siong Lim Temple (184 East Jalan Toa Payoh). One of the largest Buddhist temples in Singapore, Siong Lim Temple was built between 1898 and 1908. It has many ornate and decorative features, notably its carved marble Siamese Buddhas.

Sri Mariamman Temple (242 South Bridge Rd.). Although this temple is located in the middle of Chinatown, it is the oldest Hindu temple in Singapore. Built between 1827 and 1843, it has been refaced and redecorated many times. The most recent restoration was completed in 1984. Its spectacular decoration includes many polychromed gods and goddesses. There is an annual fire-walking ceremony on this site.

Sultan Mosque (North Bridge Rd.). The first mosque built on this site was completed in the 1820s. Sultan Mosque, completed in 1928, is the largest mosque in Singapore. The mosque is decorated with oriental rugs and a crystal chandelier. At midday on Fridays, large crowds of Muslims congregate for prayer.

Tan Si Chong Su Temple (Magazine Rd.). Located on the banks of the Singapore River is this Chinese Palace–style ancestral temple and hall built for the Tan clan in 1876.

Temple of 1,000 Lights (Race Course Rd.). A 49-ft-high (15-meter) statue of the Buddah is surrounded by glittering lights. There are also many Buddhist relics in this temple.

Thian Hock Keng Temple (Telok Ayer St.). Singapore's oldest Chinese temple was built in 1840 and its name means "Temple of Heavenly Happiness." It was here that newly arrived immigrants offered prayers of thanks for their safe passage. The temple features granite pillars, carvings, stonework, a statue dedicated to the goddess of the sea, and many ancestral tablets.

PARKS AND GARDENS

Botanic Gardens (Napier and Cluny roads). Originally a collection of tropical trees and plants, the Botanic Gardens now cover 79 acres

(32 ha) of parklands and primary jungle. Highlights include palms; tropical and subtropical trees; an extensive variety of shrubs and flowers; ornamental lakes and islands complete with tortoises, Peking ducks, and swans; and an orchid enclosure with 2,500 plants. There are free open-air concerts every Sunday at 5:30 PM. Open 5:00 AM–11:00 PM Monday – Friday, 5:00 PM–midnight weekends and public holidays.

Bukit Timah Nature Reserve (Upper Bukit Timah Rd.). On this 2- to 3-hour jungle trek, well-marked trails guide you to the top of the highest hill in Singapore. Exotic birds, butterflies, and monkeys can be seen amidst vegetation of the same kind that covered Singapore when Raffles arrived. Good walking shoes are advised.

Chinese and Japanese Gardens (off Yuan Ching Rd., Jurong). Open 9 AM–7 PM Monday–Saturday, 8:30 AM–7 PM Sunday and public holidays. Combined admission to both gardens, S$2.50 adult, S$1.20 child, S$0.50 for each still or movie camera.

◼ *Chinese Garden, or Yu Hwa Yuan.* Designed in the Song Dynasty style and reminiscent of the Summer Palace in Beijing, this 13.5-acre (5.5-ha) garden is on its own island. A classical garden atmosphere is created by curved bridges, lotus, willows, bamboo, and twin pagodas. Paddling and rowing boats are available. Admission S$2.00 adult, S$1.00 child, S$0.50 for each still or movie camera.

◼ *Japanese Garden, or Seiwaen.* This "Garden of Tranquility" is linked to the Chinese Garden by a white bridge. It employs traditional Japanese landscaping and architecture, and is one of the largest classical gardens outside Japan. Admission S$1.00 adult, S$0.50 child, S$0.50 for each still or movie camera.

Fort Canning Park (Fort Canning Rise and Clemenceau Ave.). This hilltop park was once the ancient fortress of Malay kings. It makes an interesting half-hour afternoon stroll rich in history. Highlights include the Old Christian Cemetery; Sacred Malay Grave; Forbidden Hill; and Ruins of Fort Canning.

MacRitchie Reservoir (Lornie Rd.). This jungle park surrounds a tranquil reservoir and is a popular spot for jogging and picnicking.

Seletar Reservoir (Mandai Rd.). Contemplate the vast scenic views from an observation tower.

Mandai Orchid Garden (Mandai Lake Rd.). In addition to a spectacular hillside covered with exotic orchids, you can also visit the Water Garden of rare tropical plants. Open daily 9:00 AM–5:30 PM. Admission S$1.00 adult, S$.50 child.

Mount Faber (off Kampang Bahru Rd.). Telescopes provide views of the city, harbor, and southern islands from the highest point on this part of the island. You can also take a cable car to Sentosa from this point.

BIRD AND ANIMAL SANCTUARIES

Jurong Bird Park (Jalan Ahmad Ibrahim, Jurong). There are 3,500 birds in this scenically landscaped garden. Highlights include a fascinating bird show; the world's largest walk-in aviary; and a nocturnal birdhouse. Open 9 AM – 6 PM daily; extra show 1:30 PM Sunday and public holidays. Free flight show 10:30 AM; parrot circus 3:30 PM. Buffet breakfast at the Song Bird Terrace every morning between 9 and 11 AM. Admission S$3.50 adult, S$1.50 child; S$.50 per still and cine camera; tramcar S$1.00 adult; S$.50 child.

Singapore Crocodilarium (730 East Coast Parkway). A crocodile farm, where you can see live crocodiles or buy products made from their skins. Open daily 9 AM–5:30 PM . Admission S$2.00 adult, S$1.00 child under 12; crocodile wrestling exhibition daily (except Mondays and rainy days) at 11:45 AM and 4:15 PM.

Singapore Zoological Gardens (Mandai Lake Rd.). This open zoo, located near the Seletar Reservoir, has over 1,600 animals. Whenever possible the animals are confined behind natural barriers. Among the exhibits are such exotic animals as rare Bawean hog deer, cheetahs, iguanas, Komodo dragons, and the world's smallest hoofed animal, the mousedeer. Monday to Saturday (except public holidays) at 9 AM an American or Japanese breakfast is served, complete with an orangutan as your companion. You can also have tea at 3 PM. For breakfast and tea tours, inquire at your hotel desk. Other daily attractions include animal showtime at 10:30 AM, 11:30 AM, 2:30 PM, and 3:30 PM and elephant baths at 9:30 AM.

The most convenient way to get to the zoo from downtown is by the regular coach service, which has 11 pickup points. For schedule information, inquire at your hotel desk.

Open daily 8:30 AM–6:30 PM. Admission S$4.00 adult, S$1.50 child, S$0.50 for still cameras, S$2.00 for movie cameras.

Bird Concert (Tiong Bahru and Seng Poh roads). Sunday mornings at 8 AM, bird owners bring their feathered friends for an informal concert outside a coffee shop.

Van Kleef Aquarium (River Valley Rd.). This aquarium has 4,600 different kinds of fish.

SINGAPORE FOR CHILDREN

Singapore has a wide variety of indoor and outdoor amusements for children. Two of the most prominent are

Water Sports. Big Splash, at East Coast Parkway, and CN West Leisure Park in Jurong. For S$5.00 you can visit the Wet 'N Wild Sports Complex in the East Coast Lagoon. This complex is noted for its water tunnels.

Mini Car Racing. On weekends the East Coast Recreation Centre has a Grand Prix of remote-controlled mini racing cars.

OTHER PLACES OF INTEREST

Haw Par Villa (Tiger Balm Gardens, Pasir Panjang Rd.). The original core of this attraction was a garden, built in the 1930s by the Aw Boon brothers, manufacturers of the skin cream Tiger Balm (the gardens were also known as Tiger Balm Gardens). The groves and plantings were decorated with statues, fountains, and tableaux depicting scenes from Chinese legends and myths, which had weathered and were beginning to crumble by 1989. In July of that year, the gardens were closed and work began on their restoration and expansion into a modern theme park centered on the same myths and legends. On reopening in late 1990, it will feature water rides, multimedia presentations, puppet shows, and other attractions, along with the original statues and grounds, carefully restored. Open 9 AM–6 PM every day. Admission about S$15

New Ming Village (32 Pandar Rd.). Master craftsmen demonstrate the art of Chinese pottery making. Hundreds of Ming and Qing reproductions are displayed for sale. Open 9 AM–5:30 PM daily.

Singapore Mint Coin Gallery (249 Jalan Boon Lay, Jurong). Coins, medals, and medallions from around the world are displayed here.

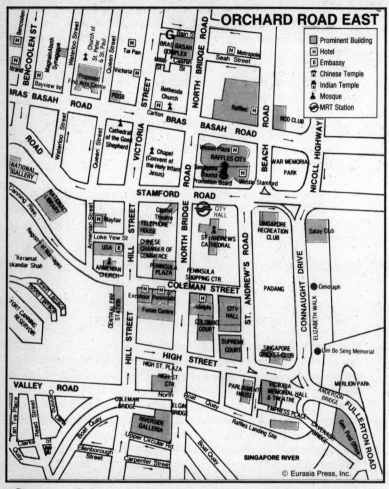

Singapore Science Centre (off Jurong Town Hall Rd.). Five hundred exhibits in four special theme galleries explore subjects such as life sciences, physical sciences, and aviation. The exhibits are geared to a hands-on experience. Multimedia shows, lectures, and films are also presented. The Science Centre also features an Omnitheater complex which houses a planetarium, three exhibition halls, a restaurant, and a bookshop. Highlights include the Aviation Gallery (largest in the Asia-Pacific region), the Discovery Centre Gallery, a Walk-in Forest, and the Omnimax Movie. Open Tuesday–Sunday 10 AM–6 PM. Admission S\$2.00 adult, S\$0.50 children under 16.

ODDS AND ENDS

Fortune Telling. If you see people using bamboo sticks and divining blocks before a Chinese temple altar, they are seeking their fortune through a 5,000-year-old system of divination known as the *I Ching*.

Something Old, Something New. You may have everything you need for a Western wedding, but why not stop in at Mawar Puteh at #02–09, a bridal specialty shop in Katong People's Park Complex. Mawar Puteh sells bridal jewelry, and on request will embroider cushions and dresses in gold or silver thread.

Paper flowers on bamboo sticks are part of Malay weddings. Red double-happiness papercuts in the window of a Chinese home signify a marriage in the family.

The Wet Market. Outdoor markets where you can buy fruit, vegetables, meat, and flowers are known as wet markets. Most Singaporeans still prefer to shop at the wet market rather than at modern supermarkets. You should experience this array of colors, textures, and aromas at least once in a while in Singapore. Try the Cuppage Centre on Cuppage Rd. or the recently restored Kreta Ayer Complex in Chinatown.

THE ISLANDS OF SINGAPORE

SENTOSA

Whether you spend a day or a weekend at Sentosa (Tranquility) Island, you won't want for activities. A variety of recreational pastimes, such as swimming, boating, golfing, and roller-skating, are only some of the attractions of this island. Others are The Maritime Museum, Gun Museum, Wax Museum, Art Centre, World Insectarium, Rare Stones Museum, Coralarium (display of over 3,000 exotic shells and living corals), and Nature Walk (hundred-year-old trees and ferns).

Near the Sentosa Ferry Terminal are the Musical Fountain (computer-controlled sprays of colored water), Monorail (spectacular views of the island), Rasa Sentosa Food Centre (food stalls), and Pasar Malam night bazaar, which is open 6:00 — 10:00 PM, Friday, Saturday, and Sunday.

PACKAGE TOURS TO SENTOSA

Sentosa Tour. A 3½-hour daily trip on coach and ferry. Rates S$30 adult, S$15 child. Tour Operators are Tour East, RMG, Siakson, and Singapore Sightseeing. The itinerary includes transportation by coach to the ferry terminal, ferry to Sentosa, monorail to Coralarium, with visits to the Pioneers of Singapore exhibit, Surrender Chambers, Fort Siloso, Maritime Museum, and then a cable car ride to Mount Faber.

Sentosa Discovery. Daily 3½-hour itinerary by coach and ferry. Rates S$19 adult, S$14 child. The tour operators are Elpin Tours and Limousine Services. Their itinerary includes transportation to the Mount Faber Cable Car Station, cable car ride to Sentosa, monorail ride, Coralarium, and visits to the Wax Museum, Fort Siloso, Maritime Museum, Musical Fountain, and return by ferry.

KUSU

Legend has it that Kusu, or "Turtle Island," was formed when a turtle transformed itself into an island to save the lives of two shipwrecked sailors. The island is 30 minutes by ferry from the World Trade Centre and is a convenient retreat from the bustle of city life.

Kusu has two well-known landmarks: a Chinese temple and a Malay keramat. Thousands of Chinese devotees make an annual pilgrimage to the Tua Pekong Temple. The keramat is a hilltop shrine where Muslims come to pray. Other attractions on the island are a tortoise sanctuary, rock garden, and two lagoons. Kusu is also an ideal location for swimming, fishing, skin diving, and picnicking.

Haw Par Villa

The hills and lagoons of this shady island make for a pleasant day of swimming, lazing, or walking on the island's many trails. There are regular ferries from the World Trade Centre to Kusu or Saint John's. Round-trip is S$5.00 for adults, S$2.50 for children. There are two ferries daily, and eight ferries on Sundays and public holidays.

PULAU HANTU, PULAU SEKING, SISTERS ISLAND

These islands provide a relaxing antidote to sightseer burnout. Both Pulau Hantu and Sisters Island are popular for fishing and snorkeling. Pulau Seking has a picturesque Malay-inhabited island village with stilt houses built out over the sea.

Although there are no ferry services to these islands, boats can be chartered from Jardine Steps or Clifford Pier.

VI

Hotels and Lodging

Singapore has a great many hotels, of varying sizes, styles, and rates, and more are being built. Because of fluctuations in seasonal demand, the world and local economy, and the international exchange rates, hotel rates are subject to change and all figures given here should be verified before making reservations. Hotels in the following sections are listed in alphabetical order, disregarding the word *Hotel*; thus "Hotel Acme" would come before "Grande Deluxe Hotel."

HOTELS WITH MORE THAN 400 ROOMS

ANA (456 rooms)
Address: 16 Nassim Hill, Singapore 1025
Telephone: 732-1222
Fax: 732-2222
Telex: RS 21817
Rates: Standard—Single S$120, Double S$130; Deluxe—Single
 S$125–130, Double S$150
 Located on Nassim Hill, the ANA is close to the Botanic Gardens, the Singapore Handicraft Centre, and the Tourist Information Centre. Room facilities include air-conditioning, a fully stocked minibar, refrigerator, International Direct Dial (IDD) telephones, color television, and radio. Continental and Japanese cuisines are served. There is a business center as well as medical services, swimming pools, and a shopping arcade.

Boulevard Hotel Singapore (528 rooms)
Address: 200 Orchard Blvd., Singapore 1024
Telephone: 737–2911; US telephone: 800–877–2227
Fax: 737-8449
Telex: RS 21771 BOUTEL
Rates: Standard—Single/Double S$225/S$305; Deluxe—
 Single/Double S$335
 The Boulevard is located in the Orchard Rd. district within walking distance of the Singapore Handicraft Centre. The air-

conditioned rooms have minibars, kitchenettes, tea- and coffee-making facilities, lounge sets, desks, and IDD telephones. There are business class rooms and a business center and lounge. Dining facilities include American, Japanese, and Indian cuisines and a coffee house featuring local food. Additional facilities include a discotheque, two pools, and a fitness club as well as a drugstore, tour desk, and hotel shops.

Carlton Hotel (420 rooms)

Address: 76 Bras Basah Rd., Singapore 0718
Telephone: 338–8333
Fax: 339–6866
Telex: RS 42076 CARLHO
Rates: Standard/Single S$240, Double S$260; Deluxe/Single S$260, Double S$280.

One of Singapore's newer hotels, the Swiss International Carlton is conveniently situated between Marina Square and the National Museum and Art Gallery, within easy walking distance of many of the major shopping centers and tourist attractions. The rooms' bay windows afford views of the harbor or the city skyline.

The air-conditioned rooms, with thermostat controls, feature tea- and coffee-making facilities, minibars, writing desks, IDD telephones with bathroom extensions, and radio and television sets, the latter offering the latest movies and flight information. A business center offers a private office and several boardrooms. Concierge and room service are available round the clock, and on-premises restaurants include the Cafe Victoria, serving international cuisine; a French brasserie; a Cantonese restaurant; a wine bar offering vintage wines by the glass; and the Pool Grill. A swimming pool, jacuzzi, health center with sauna, and a hair salon are also available.

The Glass Hotel Singapore (509 rooms)

Address: 317 Outram Rd., Singapore 0316
Telephone: 733–0188
Fax: 733–0989
Telex: RS 50141 GLHTL
Rates: Standard—Single/Double S$160; Deluxe—Single/Double S$190

The Glass Hotel is near the Singapore River, and entrance to the hotel is from the southeast to comply with the Chinese belief that this is the best direction for good luck.

The contemporary air-conditioned rooms are equipped with

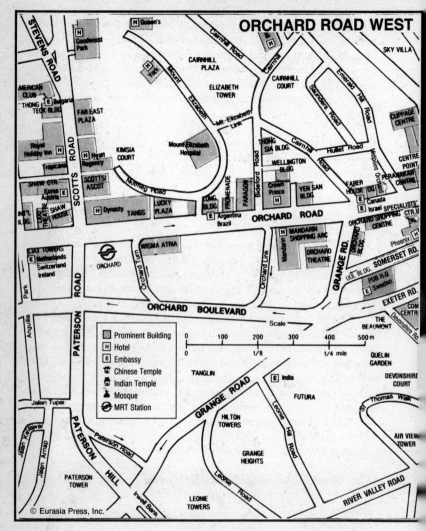

IDD telephones, built-in hair driers, radio, color television, refrigerators, and minibars. Dining facilities feature a Chinese theater restaurant and a French restaurant.

On the landscaped rooftop of the hotel annex, there is a large swimming pool and a smaller pool for children. A comprehensive business center is available. Other facilities include a shopping arcade, health center, and tennis courts.

Harbour View Dai-Ichi Hotel (420 rooms)
Address: 81 Anson Rd., Singapore 0207
Telephone: 224-1133
Fax: 222-0749
Telex: RS 40163 DAISIN
Rates: Standard—Single S$180, Double S$200; Deluxe—Single
  S$220, Double S$240.

The Dai-Ichi Hotel Harbour View is strategically located in the
heart of the business district, 10 minutes from the World Trade Centre
and 15 minutes from the Orchard Rd. shopping district. The air-
conditioned rooms with piped-in music have refrigerators, minibars,
and IDD telephones. Restaurant cuisine is Continental and Japanese.
There are also meeting and banquet facilities, hotel shops, a pool, and
free shuttle service to other districts on the island.

Hilton International Singapore (435 rooms)
Address: 581 Orchard Rd., Singapore 0923
Telephone: 737-2233; US telephone: 800-HILTONS
Fax: 732-2917
Telex: RS 21491 HILTELS
Rates: Standard—Single S$280, Double S$300;
  Deluxe—Single S$300, Double S$320

The recently renovated Hilton is in a convenient location for
business travelers and tourists. Rooms feature executive writing desks,
IDD telephones, television, refrigerators, and hair-driers, along with
standard deluxe amenities. Twelve executive suites are available,
featuring personal butler service, whirlpool baths, and steam rooms.
In addition to the extensive range of services at the business center,
there are 11 function rooms which can be used for exhibits, meetings,
and banquets.

French and Cantonese cuisines are served in the main dining room
which features a market-style display of fresh fish, vegetables, herbs,
and meat. Recreation and entertainment facilities are provided by a
rooftop swimming pool with food stalls, backgammon, and a music
room which serves an English-style afternoon tea. The hotel also has
a shopping arcade, a health club, and exclusive boutiques.

Hyatt Regency Singapore (1,108 rooms and suites)
Address: 10-12 Scotts Rd., Singapore 0922
Telephone: 733-1188; US telephone: 800-228-9000
Fax: 732-1696
Telex: RS 24415 HYATT

Rates: Standard—Single/Double S$310; Deluxe—Single/Double S$350.

The Hyatt is within walking distance of the Orchard Rd. shopping district. Its newly upgraded rooms in the main tower have IDD telephones, color television, and minibars. Guests on the 19th-21st floors receive complimentary breakfasts and cocktails as well as butler service.

Cuisine is French, Italian, and Continental. The hotel offers a fitness center, swimming pool, tennis and squash courts, along with a business center and convention and exhibition facilities.

Mandarin Singapore (1,200 rooms)
Address: 333 Orchard Rd., Singapore 0923
Telephone: 737-4411; US telephone: 800-663-0787
Fax: 732-2361
Telex: RS 21528 MANOTEL
Rates: Standard—Single S$280, Double S$320; Deluxe—Single S$300, Double S$340

This elegant hotel is conveniently located near the financial district. Rooms have air conditioning, color television, IDD telephones, tea- and coffee-making facilities, and refrigerators. Sewing kits, bathroom scales, and hair driers are also provided.

The Mandarin's wide selection of dining and entertainment includes five restaurants, five bars, a nightclub, and a disco. Japanese, English, French, Chinese, and Continental cuisines are served. Recreational facilities include a gym, mini-golf course, swimming pool, tennis and squash courts, massage, sauna, and steam baths. Business travelers are offered a comprehensive executive center.

Marina Mandarin Singapore (640 rooms)
Address: 6 Raffles Blvd., Marina Square, Singapore 0103
Telephone: 338-3388
Fax: 339-4977
Telex: RS22299 MARINA
Rates: Deluxe—Single/Double S$300

This hotel's Marina Square location provides easy access to and from the airport and to the main tourist spots in the city. The Square houses the largest shopping complex in Southeast Asia.

Rooms have air conditioning, color television, IDD telephones, radios, minibars, and tea- and coffee-making facilities. Italian, French, and Chinese cuisines are served. Additional services are a medical clinic, health club and gym, valet, butler, babysitting, and a business center.

New Otani (408 rooms)
Address: 177A River Valley Rd., Singapore 0617
*Telephone:*338–3333; US telephone: 800–421–8795
Fax: 339–2854
Telex: RS 20299 SINOTA
Rates: Standard—Single S$210, Double S$230; Deluxe—Single S$250, Double S$270

The Hotel New Otani, situated on the banks of the Singapore River, is within easy access of the shopping and financial districts.

Rooms have air conditioning, color television, IDD telephones, minibars, refrigerators, and tea- and coffee-making facilities. Japanese, Chinese, and Western cuisines are served. Facilities include a swimming pool, a ballroom, a business center, and a shopping arcade.

New Park Hotel (555 rooms)
Address: 181 Kitchener Rd., Singapore 0820
Telephone: 291–5533
Fax: 297–2827
Telex: RS 33190
Rates: Standard—Single S$180; Double S$200; Deluxe—Single
S$230, Double S$270

Formerly called the President Merlin, this modern hotel is situated close to Singapore's Little India, with its temples, mosques, and old houses.

All rooms have baths, TVs, IDD phones, and refrigerators, and those on the penthouse level also have tea- and coffee-making facilities, hair driers, and private cafes. The hotel's restaurants offer Chinese, Thai, and other cuisines, and the cafe is open 24 hours. There are banquet rooms for up to 400 people, and well-equipped conference rooms.

Novotel Orchid Inn (457 rooms).
Address: 214 Dunearn Rd., Singapore 1129
Telephone: 250–3322; US telephone: 800–221–4542
Fax: 250–9292
Telex: RS 21756 NOVSIN
Rates: Standard—Single/Double S$130; Deluxe—Single/Double S$150

Rooms have IDD telephones, air conditioning, color television, refrigerators, minibars, and tea- and coffee-making facilities. Special services for business travelers are provided in the Plymouth Executive Wing, which has eight large function rooms. Guests in this wing are provided with express checkout, nonsmoking floors, separate lobby and reception areas, and private balconies.

The restaurants in the Novotel feature French Provincial and Chinese food. The 24-hour coffee house serves local and international food. Other facilities are a health center, swimming pool, and nine hole golf putting green. Free daily shuttle service to Orchard Rd. is available.

Omni Marco Polo Singapore (603 rooms)

Address: Tanglin Rd., Singapore 1024
Telephone: 474–7141; US telephone: 223–5652
Fax: 471–0521
Telex: RS 21476 OMPS
Rates: Standard—Single/Double S$300; Deluxe—Single/Double S$350

The Marco Polo is close to the Botanic Gardens and the Singapore Handicraft Centre. The hotel has been highly rated by international business travelers. Rooms have IDD telephones, air conditioning, color television, executive-style desks, minibars, and 24-hour room service. There is an extensive business center as well as several function rooms. A swimming pool, fitness center and a shopping arcade are available. The restaurants serve Continental and French cuisines. There is also a Spanish-style coffee house, and local food is served on the hotel patio.

Oriental Singapore (527 rooms)

Address: 5 Raffles Ave., Marina Square, Singapore 0103
Telephone: 338–0066
Fax: 339–9537
Telex: RS 29117 ORSIN
Rates: Deluxe—Single, S$295–S$350; Double, S$330–S$390

The Oriental is is another hotel in the Marina Centre complex, and has a superb view of the harbor.

Rooms have air conditioning, color television, IDD telephones, and hair driers. Sichuan, Continental, and local cuisines are featured in the hotel restaurants, and light snacks and barbecue are available at the hotel café and poolside bar. The hotel has a swimming pool, health center, and squash and tennis courts. Additional facilities and services include an executive center, conference facilities, a ballroom, and 24-hour car rental.

Pan Pacific Singapore (800 rooms)
Address: 7 Raffles Blvd., Marina Square, Singapore 0103
Telephone: 336–8111; US telephone: 800–538–4040
Fax: 339–8111
Telex: RS 38821 PPSH
Rates: Standard—Single S$260, Double S$300; Deluxe—Single
  S$300, Double S$340

The Pan Pacific, situated in Marina Square, is within easy access by expressway of all main areas of the city.

Rooms have air conditioning, color television, separate shower rooms, and hair driers. Executive suites are equipped with personal computers. Dining facilities include a rooftop Chinese restaurant and a Japanese restaurant with a traditional garden. There is also a grill room, a cocktail lounge, a café, and a poolside snack bar. Additional facilities include a swimming pool, tennis courts, health center, executive center, and conference rooms.

The Regent (441 rooms)
Address: 1 Cuscaden Rd., Singapore 1024
Telephone: 733–8888; US telephone: 800–327–0200
Fax: 732–888
Telex: RS 37248 REGSIN
Rates: Standard—Single/Double S$275; Deluxe—Single/Double
  S$325

Rooms are supplied with the amenities of a deluxe hotel, such as air conditioning, color television, IDD telephones, refrigerators, and hair driers. Other features include a shopping arcade, fitness center, business center, and 24-hour communication and limousine services. Continental, Cantonese, and French cuisines are served.

River View Hotel (476 rooms).
Address: 382 Havelock Rd., Singapore 0316
Telephone: 732–9922
Fax: 732–1034
Telex: RS 55454 RVHTEL
Rates: Standard—Single S$140, Double S$160; Deluxe—Single S$180,
Double S$200

The River View faces the Singapore River and is easily accessible from the shopping and commercial areas.

Rooms have air conditioning, color television, IDD telephones, and minibars. Continental, Japanese, and local cuisines are served. Recreational facilities include a fitness center, swimming pool, and disco. Conference rooms with audiovisual equipment, secretarial service, telex, and facsimile facilities are available for business guests.

Royal Holiday Inn Crowne Plaza (495 rooms).
Address: 25 Scotts Rd., Singapore 0922
Telephone: 737-7966; US telephone: 212-355-2660
Fax: 737-6646
Telex: RS 21818 HOLIDAY
Rates: Standard—Single S$260, Double, S$300; Deluxe—Single S$300, Double S$340

Rooms have air conditioning, color television, refrigerators, and minibars. The hotel is conveniently located in the main shopping and entertainment areas. Dining attractions include a continental gourmet restaurant, a Chinese restaurant with Sichuan cuisine, a Malay-Indonesian restaurant, a deli-restaurant, and a Viennese café. Other facilities include a business center and pool.

Seaview Hotel (435 rooms).
Address: 26 Amber Close, Singapore 1543
Telephone: 345-2222
Fax: 345-1741
Telex: RS 21555 SEAVIEW
Rates: Standard—Single S$120, Double S$140; Deluxe—Single S$150, Double S$180

The Seaview Hotel is 10 minutes from the airport and connected to the city center by the East Coast Parkway.

Rooms have air conditioning, color television, and radios. Chinese and Western cuisines are served. The cocktail lounge features live entertainment. Recreational facilities include a swimming pool and disco. Golf, tennis, and water sports can be enjoyed at nearby East Coast Park. The Katong district is also nearby and is notable for its department stores and restaurants.

Shangri-La Singapore (810 rooms).
Address: 22 Orange Grove Rd., Singapore 1025
Telephone: 737-3644; US telephone: 800-457-5050
Fax: 733-7220, 733-1029
Telex: RS 21505 SHANGLA
Rates: Standard—Single S$300, Double S$330; Deluxe—Single S$425, Double S$455

Shangri-La Singapore is within walking distance of Orchard Rd. Rooms have air conditioning, color television, IDD telephones, minibars, and refrigerators. The specialty restaurants serve Japanese, Chinese, and international fare. Recreational facilities include a health club, swimming pools, tennis courts, and a golf putting green. In 1988 it was voted the "Best Business Hotel in the World."

Sheraton Towers Singapore (407 rooms).
Address: 39 Scotts Rd., Singapore 0922
Telephone: 737-6888; US telephone: 800-325-3535
Fax: 737-1072
Telex: RS 37750 SHNSIN
Rates: Deluxe—Single/Double S$160

Sheraton Towers is within easy access of the Orchard Rd. shopping district. Rooms have air conditioning, color television, and IDD telephones. Additional amenities include 24-hour butler service, complimentary valet service, wake-up tea, coffee, newspapers, individual check-in desks, and express checkout. Elegant dining facilities feature European, Chinese, and local specialities. In addition to the hotel's three restaurants, there is a coffee house, a bar, a disco, and lounges. Business travelers will appreciate the comprehensive business center which includes word-processing and secretarial services, private offices, and meeting rooms.

Additional facilities are a swimming pool, health club, gym, ballroom, and function rooms.

Tai-Pan Ramada Hotel (500 rooms)
Address: 101 Victoria St., Singapore 0718
Telephone: 336-0811; US telephone: 800-228-9898
Fax: 339-7019
Telex: RS 21151 TAIPAN
Rates: Standard—Single S$180, Double S$200;
Deluxe — Single S$200, Double S$220

Situated in the heart of the business district, the Tai-Pan Ramada is close to Raffles City and a short drive from Orchard Rd.

Rooms have oversized beds, extra work desks, air conditioning, color television, minibars, refrigerators, tea- and coffee-makers, and IDD telephones. Chinese, Japanese, and Thai food is served. Other hotel facilities include a discotheque, pool, fitness center, shopping arcade, business center, and multipurpose rooms. A shuttle to key business and shopping areas is provided four times daily on weekdays.

Westin Plaza and Westin Stamford (Westin Plaza 796 rooms;
Westin Stamford 1,253 rooms and 80 suites).
Address: 2 Stamford Rd., Singapore 0617
Telephone: 338–8585; US telephone: 800–228–3000
Fax: 338–2862
Telex: RS 22206 RCHTLS
Rates: (Westin Plaza) Standard—Single S$290, Double S$300;
Deluxe—Single S$320, Double S$360.
Rates: (Westin Stamford) Standard—Single S$250, Double S$290;
Deluxe—Single $300, Double $340

Rooms in the Westin Plaza and the Westin Stamford have air
conditioning, color television, writing-dining tables, minibars, and
refrigerators. Restaurants in the Raffles City complex offer a wide
variety of cuisines including French, Italian, Chinese, and Japanese.

Recreational facilities include a health club, pools, and tennis and
squash courts. The Westin Stamford is designed primarily for large
convention groups. Spacious convention rooms are equipped with
extensive facilities such as the latest in audiovisual equipment and
simultaneous translation. The business center is open 24 hours a day.
The Raffles City complex also features a 75-store shopping arcade.

HOTELS WITH 200–400 ROOMS

Amara Hotel Singapore (350 rooms)
Address: 165 Tanjong Pagar Rd., Singapore 0208
Telephone: 224–4488
Fax: 224–3910
Telex: RS 55887 AMARA
Rates: Standard—Single S$170, Double S$180; Deluxe—Single
S$200, Double S$210

The Amara Hotel is conveniently located near Singapore's
commercial district, close to a MRT station, the harbor, and the World
Trade Centre. It is also part of a shopping, entertainment, and hotel
complex.

Rooms have color television, air conditioning, IDD telephones,
radios, refrigerators, minibars, and guest safes. Chinese and
Continental cuisines are served. Facilities include squash and tennis
courts, children's roof deck play area, coffee house, music room, and
lobby bar. A business center, multipurpose function rooms, daily
newspapers, and complimentary toiletries are also available.

Apollo Singapore (317 rooms).
Address: 405 Havelock Rd., Singapore 0316
Telephone: 733-2081
Fax: 733-1588
Telex: RS 21077 APPOLLO
Rates: Standard—Single/Double S$145; Deluxe—Single/Double
    S$165

Located on the outskirts of Chinatown, the Apollo overlooks the old warehouses along the Singapore River.

Rooms have air conditioning, color television, and IDD telephones. Chinese, Japanese, and Indonesian cuisines are served. Facilities include convention rooms, a Japanese department store, and disco lounge.

Best Western Garden Hotel (216 rooms)
Address: 14 Balmoral Rd., Singapore 1025
Telephone: 235–3344
Fax: 235–9730
Telex: RS 50999 GARTEL
Rates: Standard—Single S$140, Double S$160; Deluxe—Single
    S$170; Double S$190

Rooms have air conditioning, color television, IDD telephones, radios, and refrigerators. Continental cuisine is served in the hotel's restaurant, and cocktail lounge and poolside service are offered for lunch and dinner. Facilities include two swimming pools, an exercise and sauna room, a small shopping arcade, and banquet and convention rooms.

Cairnhill Hotel (220 rooms)
Address: 19 Cairnhill Circle, Singapore 0922
Telephone: 734-6622
Fax: 235–5598
Telex: RS 26742 CANHIL
Rates: Standard—Single S$144, Double S$162; Deluxe—Single
    S$162, Double S$180

The Cairnhill is situated in a residential area and is a short walk from Orchard Rd. Rooms have air conditioning, color television, IDD telephones, minibars, and refrigerators. The Cairn Court restaurant serves Peking and Sichuan cuisine. Local food and western snacks are served in the 24-hour coffee shop, and the cocktail lounge features live entertainment. Other facilities are a shopping arcade, and a function room which can be used for receptions and seminars.

Crown Prince Hotel (303 rooms)
Address: 270 Orchard Rd., Singapore 0923
Telephone: 732–1111
Fax: 732–7018
Telex: RS 22819 HCROWN
Rates: Standard/Deluxe—Single S$195, Double S$225

The Crown Prince, which opened in 1984, is located in the main shopping and tourist area of the city. Rooms are equipped with air conditioning, color television, telex, IDD telephones, minibars, and refrigerators. Suites have steam and whirlpool baths. Chinese and Japanese cuisines are served. Additional facilities are a two-level department store, and meeting and banquet rooms.

Dynasty Singapore (400 rooms)
Address: 320 Orchard Rd., Singapore 0923
Telephone: 734–9900
Fax: 733–5251
Telex: RS 36633 DYNTEL
Rates: Standard—Single S$205, Double S$230;
Deluxe—Single S$235; Double S$260

The pagoda-style design of the Dynasty Singapore is an impressive addition to the Singapore skyline. The Dynasty is located in the hotel, entertainment, and shopping district at the Orchard and Scotts roads intersection.

Rooms have air conditioning, color television, IDD telephones, radios, and minibars. Continental and Chinese cuisines are served. Facilities include meeting rooms with audiovisual equipment, swimming pool with a poolside snack bar, coffee house, lounges, and a traditional Chinese garden.

Hotel Equatorial (224 rooms)
Address: 429 Bukit Timah Rd., Singapore 1025
Telephone: 732–0431
Fax: 737–9426
Telex: RS 21578 EQUATOR
Rates: Standard—Single S$160, Double S$180; Deluxe—Single
S$180,
Double S$200

Located in a residential area, the Hotel Equatorial provides shuttle service to the nearby Orchard Rd. shopping district and Chinatown. Rooms are furnished with air conditioning, color television, IDD telephones, minibars, and refrigerators. Swiss, Continental, Chinese, and Japanese cuisines are served. Refreshments and cocktails are also available in the coffee house, poolside patio, and lobby bar.

Excelsior Hotel (300 rooms)
Address: 5 Coleman St., Singapore 0617
Telephone: 338–7733
Fax: 339–3847
Telex: RS 20678 EXCELH
Rates: Standard—Single S$160, Double S$175; Deluxe—Single
     S$175, Double S$190
     Centrally located, the Excelsior is connected by an underground walkway to the Peninsula Hotel and to Peninsula Plaza.

Guest rooms are furnished with air conditioning, color television, radios, IDD telephones, and refrigerators. Japanese, Chinese, Indian, and Western food are served in the hotel's restaurants, and the 24-hour coffee shop is noted for its local food. The hotel also features four floors of shopping and recreational facilities.

Furama Hotel Singapore. (352 rooms)
Address: 10 Eu Tong Sen St., Singapore 0105
Telephone: 533–3888
Fax: 534–1489
Telex: RS 28592 FURAMA
Rates: Standard—Single S$65, Double S$75; Deluxe—Single S$75,
     Double S$85
     The Furama is located on the periphery of Chinatown, within walking distance of the commercial district and convenient to City Hall and the Singapore River.

Its air-conditioned rooms offer color TV, refrigerators, and minibars. Japanese and various Chinese cuisines are offered in the restaurants, which also include a poolside snack bar and a bar in the lobby. A pharmacy, beauty parlor, florist, and several boutiques are within the hotel, which also includes a gym and swimming pools. Business travelers have available a business center and private office, along with audiovisual-equipped function rooms.

Goodwood Park Hotel (231 rooms).
Address: 22 Scotts Rd., Singapore 0922
Telephone: 737–7411; US telephone: 800–877–2227
Fax: 732–7411
Telex: RS 24377 GOODTEL
Rates: Deluxe—Single S$355, Double S$400

Goodwood Park Hotel

The Goodwood Park Hotel is conveniently accessible to the Orchard Rd. district. Its air-conditioned rooms are equipped with radio, color television, IDD telephones, minibars, and refrigerators. Suites are furnished with kitchenettes, dining-drawing rooms, lounge, sauna, steambath, and private elevators.

The hotel offers four restaurants serving Chinese, Japanese, Continental, and Western specialties. Additional facilities and services include a coffee lounge, lobby bar, two swimming pools, business center, gift shop, and medical, secretarial, convention, and tourist services.

Hotel Grand Central (365 rooms).

Address: 22 Cavenagh Rd., Singapore 0922
Telephone: 737–9944
Fax: 733–3175
Telex: RS 24389 GRAND
Rates: Standard—Single S$91, Double S$105; Deluxe—Single S$104, Double S$119

Conveniently located off Orchard Rd., the Hotel Grand Central is in the heart of the shopping district.

Rooms have air conditioning, color television, IDD telephones, piped-in music, and minirefrigerators. Sichuan Chinese, Italian, and Indonesian food are featured in the hotel restaurants. There is also a coffee house and a Japanese lounge.

Holiday Inn Park View Singapore (320 rooms).

Address: 11 Cavenagh Rd., Singapore 0922
Telephone: 733–8333; US telephone: 212–355–2660
Fax: 734–4593
Telex: RS 55420 HIPV
Rates: Standard—Single S$220; Double S$250; Deluxe—Single S$240, Double S$270

Within walking distance of the shopping and entertainment of the Orchard Rd. district, the hotel faces the parklike grounds of the Presidential Palace. Rooms have air conditioning, color television, IDD telephones, electronic door locks and wall safes, hair driers, massage showers, minibars, refrigerators, large-size beds, and hotel bathrobes and slippers.

Dining attractions are Chinese, Northern Indian, and New Orleans Creole specialties.

King's Hotel (319 rooms).

Address: Havelock Rd., Singapore 0316
Telephone: 733–0011
Fax: 732–5764
Telex: RS 21931 KINGTEL
Rates: Standard—Single S$180, Double S$200; Deluxe—Single S$220, Double S$240

The King's Hotel overlooks the Singapore River and is situated on the edge of Chinatown. Its restaurants offer Chinese and Japanese fare. Snacks and cocktails are available in the 24-hour coffee house and the lounge. Other facilities are a shopping arcade, and convention and banquet rooms.

Hotel Meridien Changi–Singapore (280 rooms).

Address: 1 Netheravon Rd., Singapore 1750
Telephone: 542–7700
Fax: 542–5295
Telex: RS 36042 HOMRA
Rates: Deluxe—Single/Double S$175

This hotel is a 10-minute drive from Changi International Airport, a 5-minute walk from Changi Beach, and 30 minutes from town.

Rooms have air conditioning, color television, IDD telephones, radios, minibars, and refrigerators. French cuisine is served. Live entertainment is featured in the 24-hour coffee house and the Lotus Lounge. Facilities include a health center, swimming pool, business center, and conference and banquet rooms. The hotel also offers complimentary shuttle service.

Ming Court Hotel (300 rooms).
Address: 1 Tanglin Rd., Singapore 1024
Telephone: 737–1133
Fax: 733–0242
Telex: RS 21488 MINGTEL
Rates: Standard—Single S$185, Double S$200; Deluxe—Single
S$215, Double S$230
　　This hotel is situated near the shopping and entertainment district
and is within walking distance of the Botanic Gardens and the Singa-
pore Handicraft Centre.
　　Rooms have air conditioning, color television, telephones,
minibars, radios, and refrigerators. The Ming Court dining facilities
feature Continental, Cantonese, and Japanese specialties. Live entertainment is offered in the hotel lounge. Facilities include a health club,
swimming pool, shopping arcade, executive center, and banquet and
convention rooms.

Hotel Miramar (346 rooms).
Address: 401 Havelock Rd., Singapore 0316
Telephone: 733–0222
Fax: 733–4027
Telex: RS 24709 MIRAMAR
Rates: Standard—Single S$140, Double S$160; Deluxe—Single
S$170, Double S$190
　　The Hotel Miramar is 15 minutes from the train station. Rooms
are equipped with air conditioning, color television, IDD telephones,
piped-in music, radios, and minibars.
　　Dining and refreshment facilities include a Chinese restaurant, a
steakhouse, a 24-hour café, and a cocktail lounge. Additional facili-
ties are two swimming pools, a health club, and a convention hall.

Orchard Hotel Singapore (350 rooms).
Address: 442 Orchard Rd., Singapore 0923
Telephone: 734–7766
Fax: 733–5482
Telex: RS 35228 ORTEL
Rates: Standard—Single S$180, Double S$200; Deluxe—Single
S$200, Double S$220
　　Close to the shopping, entertainment, and business districts, this
hotel is also near the Botanic Gardens and several tourist spots.
　　Rooms have air conditioning, color television, IDD telephones,
minibars, and refrigerators. French, international, and local cuisines

are served. Facilities include a swimming pool, shopping arcade, secretarial services, and meeting and banquet rooms.

Peninsula Hotel (315 rooms).
Address: 3 Coleman St., Singapore 0617
Telephone: 337-2200; US telephone: 800-223-5652
Fax: 339-3580
Telex: RS 21169 PENHOTE SINGAPORE
Rates: Standard — Single S$150, Double S$165; Deluxe — Single S$165, Double S$180

The recently rebuilt Peninsula Hotel is centrally located in the downtown commercial district and a short taxi ride from Orchard Rd. A covered skybridge links the hotel to the People's Park Centre.

Rooms have air conditioning, color television, IDD telephones, minibars, and refrigerators. The restaurants serve Chinese (Cantonese) and Japanese fare. Other facilities include a swimming pool, steambaths, saunas, and three function rooms.

Hotel Phoenix Singapore (300 rooms).
Address: Somerset Rd., Singapore 0923
Telephone: 737-8666
Fax: 732-2024
Telex: RS 23718 FEENIX
Rates: Standard—Single S$160, Double S$180; Deluxe—Single S$200, Double S$220

In addition to its easy access to the shopping and entertainment district, this hotel features a 4-level, 60-shop arcade.

Rooms have air conditioning, color television, IDD telephones, and refrigerators. English, Korean, and local cuisines are served. There are also a coffee house and several function rooms.

Plaza Hotel (353 rooms).
Address: 7500A Beach Rd., Singapore 0719
Telephone: 298-0011
Fax: 296-3600
Telex: RS 22150 HOTLPL
Rates: Standard—Single S$200, Double S$220; Deluxe—Single S$260, Double S$290

The Plaza is conveniently close to the financial district of the city and scenically overlooks Arab St. Its newly renovated rooms have air conditioning, color television, IDD telephones, refrigerators, tea- and coffee-makers, and hair driers.

Cantonese and Thai cuisines are served in the Seafood Theatre-Restaurant. Western and local specialties are also offered in the hotel's café and steakhouse. Live entertainment is provided in the hotel's disco. Recreational facilities include swimming pool, gym, squash, and badminton courts. The hotel also provides a shopping center, several function rooms, and free shuttle service to major shopping areas.

Hotel Royal (331 rooms).
Address: 36 Newton Rd., Singapore 1130
Telephone: 253–4411
Fax: 253–8668
Telex: RS 21644 ROYAL
Rates: Standard—Single S$110, Double S$130; Deluxe—Single S$120, Double S$140
Located in a quiet suburban area, the Hotel Royal is near Orchard Rd. and close to Newton Circus Food Centre.

Rooms have air conditioning, color television, IDD telephones, minibars, and refrigerators. The hotel restaurants serve Japanese, Chinese, and Continental cuisines. Local specialties are served in the 24-hour coffee shop. Facilities include a health club, swimming pool, and function rooms.

York Hotel (400 rooms).
Address: 21 Mount Elizabeth, Singapore 0922
Telephone: 737–0511; US telephone 800–877–2227
Fax: 732–1217
Telex: RS 21683 YOTEL
Rates: Standard—Single S$220, Double S$245; Deluxe—Single S$240, Double S$265
The York Hotel is easily accessible to the Orchard Rd. shopping area. Rooms are furnished with air conditioning, color television, and refrigerators. Rooms in a poolside wing and split-level cabanas are also available. Russian, Western, Asian, and local dishes are served. A shopping arcade, swimming pool, and health club are available to hotel guests, as well as multipurpose function rooms.

HOTELS WITH 50 – 200 ROOMS

Hotel Asia (146 rooms).
Address: 37 Scotts Rd., Singapore 0922
Telephone: 737–8388
Fax: 733–3563
Telex: RS 24313 HOTASIA
Rates: Standard — Single S$110, Double S$130; Deluxe — Single S$130, Double S$150

The Hotel Asia is a short walk from Orchard Rd. and is situated in a residential area. Rooms are air-conditioned and equipped with basic amenities. In addition to a cocktail lounge and 24-hour room service, the hotel features Chinese (Cantonese) cuisine in its notable Tsui Hang Village restaurant. Function rooms are also available.

Hotel Bencoolen (69 rooms).
Address: 47 Bencoolen St., Singapore 0718
Telephone: 336–0822
Telex: RS 42380 HOTBEN
Rates: Standard — Single S$85, Double S$90; Deluxe—Single S$110, Double S$125

The Hotel Bencoolen is located in a commercial area of the city. Rooms are furnished with air conditioning, color television, and piped-in music.

A discount bed and breakfast package is available. Dining is Chinese and Continental.

Broadway Hotel Singapore (62 rooms).
Address: 195 Serangoon Rd., Singapore 0812
Telephone: 292–4661
Fax: 291–6414
Telex: RS 36714 BROADH
Rates: Standard—Single S$75, Double S$85; Deluxe—Single S$85, Double S$95

The Broadway Hotel is about 15 minutes away from the city, near a local shopping area. Rooms are equipped with basic amenities including color television and piped-in music. Chinese and Western fare is served in the hotel's coffee house-restaurant. Other facilities are hotel shops and a pharmacy.

Cockpit Hotel (182 rooms).
Address: 6–7 Oxley Rise, 115 Penang Rd., Singapore 0923
Telephone: 737–9111
Fax: 737–3105
Telex: EA 21366 COCKPIT
Rates: Standard—Single S$140, Double S$160;
    Deluxe—Single S$220, Double S$240

Located within walking distance of the Orchard Rd. shopping district, the Cockpit Hotel dates back to 1941, and a 15-story tower addition was built in 1972.

Rooms are furnished with air conditioning, color television, radio, wall-to-wall carpeting, and refrigerators. Chinese (Sichuan and Cantonese) food is served in the hotel restaurant. A 24-hour coffee house serving Nonya, other Oriental and Western dishes, and a bar are also available.

Duke Hotel (170 rooms).
Address: 42–46 Meyer Rd., Singapore 1543
Telephone: 345–3311
Fax: 345–4025
Telex: RS 25034 DUKE
Rates: Standard—Single S$90, Double S$120; Deluxe—Single S$190, Double S$220

The Duke Hotel is in a suburban area of the city, within walking distance of a park. Rooms are air-conditioned and have color television.

The hotel's Chinese restaurant features live entertainment. A wide selection of Western and local food is served in the 24-hour coffee house. There is also a cocktail lounge and poolside bar.

Great Eastern Hotel (155 rooms).
Address: 401 Macpherson Rd., Singapore 1336
Telephone: 284–8244
Telex: RS 24321 GEHTL
Rates: Standard—Single S$80, Double S$90; Deluxe—Single S$85, Double S$95

The Great Eastern is located in a commercial district, about 10 minutes away from the city. Rooms have color television and piped-in music. Dining facilities include a Chinese restaurant, a nightclub, and a coffee house. A shopping arcade is on the premises as well as massage and sauna facilities.

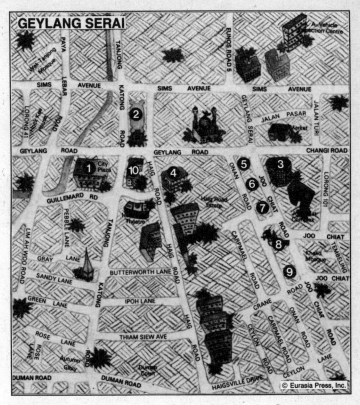

1. City Plaza
2. Tanjong Katong Shopping Centre
3. Joo Chiat Shopping Centre
4. Haig Road Market
5. Shoe Repairmen
6. Textiles, Fans
7. Joss Sticks
8. Birds and Cages
9. Khalid Mosque
10. Lion City Hotel

Ladyhill Hotel (171 rooms).

Address: 1 Ladyhill Rd., Singapore 1025
Telephone: 737-2111; US telephone: 800-877-2227
Fax: 737-4606
Telex: RS 23157 LADYTEL
Rates: Standard—Single S$140, Double S$160; Deluxe—Single S$180, Double S$200

Because of its residential setting and easy access to Orchard Rd., the Ladyhill is popular with locals (on weekend retreats) as well as tourists. Rooms have air conditioning, color television, IDD telephones, minibars, refrigerators, and tea- and coffee-makers. Rooms in the main building were renovated in 1985. In addition to the hotel restaurant's Swiss cuisine, other Western food and local specialties are available in the coffee house. The hotel offers live entertainment in the cocktail lounge. There are also three conference rooms.

Lion City Hotel (163 rooms).

Address: 15 Tanjong Katong Rd., Singapore 1543
Telephone: 744–8111
Fax: 742–5505
Telex: RS 21789 LICITEL
Rates: Standard—Single/Double S$90; Deluxe—Single/Double S$140

Lion City Hotel is five minutes from the center of the city and offers easy access to several shopping, commercial, and tourist areas.

Its air-conditioned rooms are equipped with piped-in music, color television, and telephones. The hotel serves Cantonese cuisine as well as local and international fare. Other facilities are an in-house emporium and supermarket, cocktail lounge, coffee house, conference-function rooms, and hair salon.

Metropole Hotel (54 rooms).

Address: 41 Seah St., Singapore 0718
Telephone: 336–3611
Fax: 339–3610
Telex: RS 21852 METROPO
Rates: Standard—Single S$70, Double S$80; Deluxe—Single/Double S$95

Conveniently located near the downtown area of the city, the Metropole is close to the well-known Raffles Hotel and opposite the Beach Rd. army camp. Rooms have air conditioning and color television. Chinese food is served. There are also a cocktail lounge and coffee house.

Hotel Negara Singapore (104 rooms).

Address: 15 Claymore Drive, Singapore 0922
Telephone: 737–0811
Fax: 737–9075
Telex: RS 34788 NEGARA
Rates: Standard—Single S$95, Double S$110; Deluxe—Single S$125, Double S$140

Hotel Negara is within walking distance of Orchard Rd. A Thai restaurant, a coffee shop, and a swimming pool and roof garden are among its amenities. Room service is provided 24 hours a day.

Raffles Hotel

Raffles Hotel (127 rooms)
Address: 11 Beach Rd., Singapore 0718
Telephone: 535-0627
Fax: 339–1713
Telex: RS 20396 RINTL
Rates: Unavailable at press time.

Dating back to 1887, the Raffles Hotel is one of Singapore's landmarks, comparable in Old-World charm to Shanghai's Peace Hotel. During colonial rule it was the social center for British administrators and visiting notables, and the very name of its Writers' Bar recalls the literary figures, including Somerset Maugham and Noel Coward, who frequented it. One of the hotel's bars is also famous as the place where the gin drink known as the Singapore Sling was created. The Raffles was closed for extensive renovation from March 1989 to mid-1991, during which memorabilia of its palmy days were collected from many sources. Besides restoring the original ambiance, the restoration will also supply innumerable modern comforts, along with a newly developed annex containing additional restaurants, shops, a museum of the hotel's past, and a theater and ballroom.

Hotel Supreme (86 rooms).
Address: 15 Kramat Rd., Singapore 0922
Telephone: 737-8333
Telex: RS 33283 HOTSUP
Rates: Standard—Single S$75,Double S$85
    Conveniently situated near several popular shopping centers, the Hotel Supreme is also within walking distance of Orchard Rd.
    Rooms have air conditioning, color television, telephones, and piped-in music. Western and Chinese food is served. Other facilities are a gift shop–drugstore and a conference room.

JOINT VENTURE HOTELS IN SINGAPORE

HOTEL	US PHONE NUMBER
Dai-Ichi	
Furama	
Goodwood Group	800–877–2227
Goodwood Park	
York	
Boulevard	
Ladyhill	
Hilton	800–HILTONS
Holiday Inn	(212) 355–2660
Hyatt	800–228–9000
Inter-Continental	800–327–0200
New Otani	800–421–8795
Nikko	800–NIKKO-US
Novotel	800–221–4542
Oriental, Mandarin	800–663–0787
Oriental	
Pan Pacific Hotel	800–538–4040
Peninsula	800–223–5652
Marco Polo	
Peninsula	
Ramada	800–228–9898
Shangri-La	800-457-5050
Sheraton	800–325–3535
Westin	800–228–3000

VII
Dining Out in Singapore

Singapore is the perfect place for addressing the issue of whether you live to eat or eat to live. It is said that you could spend one year in Singapore eating three meals a day, each in a different location, and never eat in the same place twice. And if you're a snacker, the possibilities are endless.

The variety of cuisines and dining settings in Singapore will challenge your problem-solving and decision-making skills. Is it sound to follow Indian curry with high tea at the Goodwood Hotel? How much time will it take to get from the Korean barbecue restaurant to the Malay cafeteria? In addition to Chinese, Indian, and Malaysian restaurants, there are French, Italian, Thai, Continental, and Russian restaurants, just to name a few. Prices range from gourmet deluxe to inexpensive fast-food. In general, a low-priced meal does not necessarily mean a low-quality meal. Many of the open-air fast-food stalls serve very tasty food.

If you are an avid gourmet, the *Secret Food Map of Singapore* (on sale in bookstores in Singapore) gives detailed descriptions of the various restaurants and hawker stalls. You can zero in on delicacies you might otherwise miss. Violet Oon, one of Singapore's culinary experts, conducts food tours and cooking classes. The tours include visits to ethnic neighborhoods and markets, a cooking demonstration, and a trip to a restaurant. Specialty food tours can also be arranged (telephone: 250-4712).

Most Singaporeans reserve restaurant eating for more formal occasions or for business entertaining. Local gourmets frequent the food centers or hawker stalls. Hawker stalls are open-air kitchens with vendors selling an amazing variety of dishes, all cooked on the spot in a matter of minutes. Each hawker specializes in one dish. Imagine an open-air restaurant where each of 50 master chefs each prepares his best dish to perfection. That's what makes hawker stalls so special. The hawkers are licensed and health standards are meticulously followed.

Rice and noodle dishes are served at Chinese stalls. Indian dishes are based on a kind of wheat pancake served with curry. *Nasi padang* (vegetable and meat curry) and *satay* are served at Malay stalls.

After you order at a hawker stall, it is customary to take a seat. The hawkers have an uncanny ability to find you, no matter how crowded it is. Drink sellers will come to your table to take your order.

Major hawker centers can be found at Rasa Singapura, Newton Circus, Satay Club, Cuppage Centre, People's Park, Lagoon Food Centre, and the Botanic Gardens.

There are a wide variety of Chinese restaurants in Singapore. Each province of China has its own particular style of cooking. Cantonese cooking is characterized by the stir-fry method, while Sichuan cooking is hot and spicy, as is that of neighboring Hunan. Then there is "Shanghainese," a sweet and mild cuisine far different from the authentic cuisine of Shanghai. Regional dishes such as Hokkien noodles and Teochew porridge are worth trying. If you've never had dim sum (*dian xian*), bite-sized Chinese snacks, you can sample them at the Ming Palace (Ming Court Hotel) or the Tropicana at 9 Scotts Rd. Though dim sum are regarded as a snack, most Chinese consider ordering at least 12 for starters.

Malay food is mostly found in hawker centers, though you may want to stop in at Aziza's (36 Emerald Hill Rd.) for a sit-down dinner. *Satay* is one of the most typical Malaysian specialties. Barbecued kabobs of seasoned beef, chicken, or mutton are served with peanut gravy, cucumber, and onion. *Soto ayam* is also a popular dish. Beansprouts, rice cakes, and chicken in a light broth are served with chili paste. Other traditional Malay dishes are fried soybean curd, curried prawns, and whitebait fish fried with soy, spices, and peanuts.

Although almost everyone thinks of curry when they think of Indian food, in Singapore you can try Indian *rojak* (crab, prawn fritters, beancurd, and cuttlefish). Northern Indian food is mildly spiced. In a southern Indian restaurant, your food will be served on a banana leaf placemat. In Muslim Indian restaurants pork is not served. Beef is not served in any Indian restaurants.

You should have at least one Nonya meal while in Singapore. Nonya cuisine is derived from Peranakan, or "baba" culture, and is a distinctive blending of Chinese and Malay cuisine. Peranakan culture emerged when Chinese immigrants took Malay wives. Nonya cooking is very much home-style cooking, and many of the best Nonya recipes are considered family secrets. *Laksa lemak* is a good example of Nonya fare. Rice noodles and herbs are combined with a spicy coconut soup. *Poh piah* (a roll filled with shredded turnip, bamboo shoots, prawns, and sausage) is another popular Nonya dish.

After sampling Nonya cooking and making the round of your favorite cuisines, if you have overindulged and would like a light meal, you might stop at a hawker stall and then continue on to a fruit stand. There is a huge selection of fruit, including some of the more exotic tropical kinds. Pieces of fruit are sold for about S$0.30. At many of the fruit stands near the hawker stalls, blended fresh fruit drinks are sold.

With the enormous variety of cuisines, atmosphere, and price range available in Singapore, it's easy to see why there may not be a quick, simple answer to "Where should we eat?"

The Inner Game of Chopsticks

Eating with chopsticks can be either challenging or frustrating, depending on how hungry and how dexterous you are. No matter how adept you are with a fork and knife, the first time you use chopsticks is a trial-and-error experience.

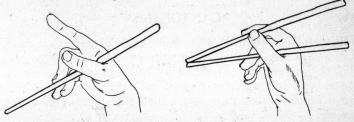

Beginners should aim for the largest, driest, hardest selection on the table, a chunk of beef or a crunchy pea pod. Avoid the slick and saucy items. You'll spend more time watching them slide onto the table than actually eating them. Because of their shape, mushrooms are notoriously slippery and elusive, and you probably won't enjoy very many of these until you reach the intermediate stage of eating with chopsticks. If all this sounds disconcerting, not to worry, you will get the hang of it with a little persistence and practice. Noodles and rice are always dependable. Using the serving spoon, scoop some of the unmanageable mushrooms and savories into your rice or noodle bowl. You can grab a big clump of noodles or rice and the mushrooms and savories all at once in a sweeping motion. Holding your bowl up close to you in one hand and chopsticking with the other really helps. It reduces those moments of anxiety when, just as that morsel was about to meet your palate, it hightailed to the table. This way at least it will fall back into your bowl and you can start over again.

When you have passed through the intermediate stage and feel confident about your skill with chopsticks, you can try the ultimate test. Order a dish of chicken with peanuts. Some say those who can pick up two peanuts at once are true chopstick masters.

Chopstick Etiquette. Some beginners have been known to secretly hone down their chopsticks to a fine point, so as to spear their food rather than pick it up. This method should be considered only in extreme cases of hunger. Always place your chopsticks on a chopstick rest, soy dish, or bone platter. Placing chopsticks on a dinner plate or rice bowl is not customary, as the host may feel he has not offered you enough to eat. Waving or pointing with chopsticks, or placing them upright in a rice bowl, is considered to be in poor taste.

CHINESE RESTAURANTS

CANTONESE

Hillman Restaurant. 159 Cantonment Rd., Telephone: 221–5073. Prices are quite reasonable considering the excellent quality of the food. The Hillman features claypot cooking. Try the pot prawns in tomato sauce and potted pig livers. And, if your budget is limited, you can get an excellent banquet here for moderate prices. Corner coffee shop setting.

Li Bai Restaurant. Sheraton Towers Singapore, 39 Scotts Rd., Telephone: 737–6888. Offering elegant dining on classic cuisine. The average price per meal is S$55. Noted for such seafood delicacies as double boiled shark's fin, fried lobster in black bean paste, and deep-fried scallops (dinner only).

Majestic. 31 Bukit Pasoh Rd., Telephone: 223–5111. Excellent local-style banquet cuisine, averaging S$20–30 per person. The Majestic is known for its shark's fin omelette. A mixture of fin strands, bamboo shoots, crabmeat, and eggs is served eggroll-style, wrapped in crisp lettuce leaves. Also recommended: hand-roasted pork, duck, chicken, and for the adventurous, deep-fried pigeon.

Mayflower Restaurant. DBS Building, Shenton Way, Telephone: 220–3133, and Changi International Airport. Quality cuisine in spacious surroundings at moderate prices. This is a good place to try *dim sum*, delicate Chinese snacks. The Mayflower boasts a variety of 53 different kinds of *dim sum*, ranging from stuffed dumplings, fried vegetables, spring rolls, and soups to sweets.

Shang Palace. Shangri-La Hotel, Orange Grove Rd., Telephone: 737–3644. A variety of Cantonese-style cuisine, from simple to exotic dishes, at moderate prices. Simple dishes such as deep-fried crab claw and braised pork spare-ribs are as tasty as the more exotic fare such as boiled sliced sea whelk and double-boiled superior shark's fin and midriff soup. Chinese courtyard setting.

Other Cantonese restaurants include: **Kelong Thomson Restaurant**, Thomson Plaza, Upper Thomson Rd.; **Tsui Hang Village Restaurant**, Hotel Asia; **Tung Lok Shark's Fin Restaurant**, Liang Court River Valley Rd.; **Union Farm Eating House**, 435 Clementi Rd.

PEKING

Eastern Palace Sureme House. Penang Rd., Telephone: 337–8224. Banquet cuisine at moderate prices. The Eastern Palace's traditional banquet includes such dishes as cold platter, Peking duck, baked fish, steamed chicken with ham and mushrooms, fried dumplings, and shark's fin soup.

Jade Room. Royal Hotel, Newton Rd., Telephone: 254–8603. Recommended more for the quality of the food than for an elegant setting. Prices are moderate.

Pine Court Restaurant. Mandarin Hotel, Orchard Rd., Telephone: 737–4411. Noted for its Peking duck. Its prices are somewhat expensive. Also recommended are baked freshwater tench, served in a sweet vinegar soy sauce, and deep-fried prawns in a sweet chili sauce. The Pine Court also offers a Chinese lunch buffet for S$20.

SHANGHAINESE

Great Shanghai. Mayfair Hotel, Armenian St., Telephone: 337–8240. One of Singapore's most popular restaurants for Shanghainese cuisine.

Prices are moderate. The restaurant features crab, eel, fish, and prawns. Also recommended are drunken chicken (chicken strips boiled in yellow rice wine and garnished with coriander), sweet and sour sliced fish, braised duck with mixed vegetables, and chicken in a basket (sauteed chicken in a basket made of sweet-tasting deep-fried yam noodles).

Temasek Restaurant. Temasek Club, Portsdown Rd., Telephone: 475–2309. Some consider this the best place in Singapore for Shanghainese cuisine at moderate prices. The restaurant offers such typical Shanghainese fare as prawns in curry sauce, shredded chicken in bean noodle and chili sauce, and sliced eel in bean sauce. The Temasek Room is the restaurant for the Army Officers' Club; it is open to the public for lunch from 12 noon to 2:30 PM.

Other Shanghainese restaurants are the **Penthouse**, 4th floor of the Holland Shopping Centre, Holland Rd. (Telephone: 337–8240), and **Esquire Kitchen**, 02-01, Block 231, Bras Basah Complex, North Bridge Rd. (Telephone: 336–1802).

TEOCHEW

Teochew, or Chaozhou, cooking is typified by its variety of porridges cooked in a clear broth. Side dishes of lobster, vegetables, crayfish, and salted eggs are served with the porridge. Flavorings are subtle.

Ban Seng Restaurant. 79 New Bridge Rd., Telephone: 533–1471. Ban Seng is the original Teochen restaurant in Singapore and is still highly recommended. Prices are inexpensive. Seafood and fowl are featured. Some of the more popular dishes are steamed lobster, satay chicken, and fried liver roll. This restaurant is small but popular, so reservations are advised.

Chiu Wah Lin Restaurant. 46 Mosque St., Telephone: 222–3654. Chiu Wah Lin's owners originally cooked for the Teochew Million-aires' Club. Featured dishes are grilled or steamed crayfish; roast mutton served with fungus, shallots, and dates; and liver rolls. Prices are inexpensive.

Guan Hin. Block 34, Whampoa West #01–01, Telephone: 298–3179. Home-style cooking. Steamboat meat or fish is a featured specialty—

a chafing dish of boiling stock is brought to your table and you cook the meat or fish to taste. Other popular dishes are Sambal crayfish with a tomato-garlic sauce, oysters in black bean sauce, and turtle soup.

Other Teochew restaurants include: **Golden Phoenix**, UIC Building Shenton Way; **Hung Kang Restaurant**, 38 North Canal Rd.; **Swatow Restaurants,** located in Centrepoint, on Orchard Rd., in the DBS Building on Shenton Way, and in the Singapore Conference Hall.

HAINAN

Hainanese chefs are most noted for a steamed chicken dish called "chicken rice" and for roast pork.

New Seventh Storey Hotel. 228 Rochor Rd., Telephone: 337–0251. Inexpensive. Both Chinese and Western food are served.

Swee Kee. 51–53 Middle Rd., Telephone: 336–5347. Inexpensive. A good place to try the famous Hainanese chicken rice.

Thien Kee. B-20 Golden Mile Tower, Beach Rd., Telephone: 258–5891. High-quality food at reasonable prices. In addition to traditional Hainanese dishes such as chicken rice and chop suey steamboat, a variety of local Chinese dishes are also available.

HAKKA

Home-style cooking with simple ingredients.

Moi Kong Hakka Restaurant. 22 Murray St. (Food Alley), Telephone: 221–7758. Inexpensive prices. Featured dishes are frog legs in red wine and meat-stuffed bean curd. Also highly recommended is the *Hakka Mee*—homemade egg noodles served with pork, prawns, scallions, and bean sprouts in a sweet and sour chili sauce.

Other Hakka restaurants include the **Plum Village**, 16 Jalah Leban (Telephone: 458–9005).

HOKKIEN

Ben Hiang. 20 Murray St. (Food Alley), Telephone: 221–6684. Simple decor and inexpensive prices. Ben Hiang offers such well-known Hokkien dishes as Hokkien stewed pork with steamed buns, and fried liver rolls. Also recommended is the fried bean vermicelli. Roast suckling pig is available but must be ordered in advance.

Other Hokkien restaurants are **Beng Thin Hoon Kee**, OCBC Centre, Chulia St.; **Hock Beng Restaurant**, 101 Amoy St. (Telephone 222–8777); **Prince Room**, Selegie Complex, Selegie Rd.

SZECHUAN (SICHUAN)

Golden Phoenix. Hotel Equatorial, 2nd floor, 429 Bukit Timah Rd., Telephone: 732–0431. Fairly expensive. The Phoenix offers such Szechuan fare as prawns with dried red chili, deep-fried Chinese pancake stuffed with bean paste, and vegetarian "fish grapes" (fried dough sticks filled with mashed bean curd and served with a sweet and sour sauce). The camphor-and-tea-smoked-duck is also recommended and a Szechuan vegetarian buffet is available here (S$290 for 10 people).

Omei Hotel Grand Central. Cavenagh Rd., Telephone: 737–2735. Reasonable prices. The Omei offers a wide selection of Szechuan dishes: prawns Szechuan-style, diced chicken with red chili, and smoked Szechuan duck.

Crispy rice is an unusual home-style dish worth a try. Crisp rice cakes are served with meat and sauce. The Omei offers a selection of over 250 dishes.

Other Szechuan restaurants are **Cairn Court Peking and Sichuan Restaurant**, Cairnhill Hotel, Cairnhill Circle (Telephone: 734–6622); **Dragon City**, Novotel Orchid Inn Hotel, 214 Dunearn Rd. (Telephone: 254–7070); **Meisan Royal Holiday Inn**, Scotts Rd. (Telephone: 737–7966); **Min Jiang Restaurant**, Goodwood Park Hotel, Scotts Rd. (Telephone 737–7411); **Pin Hsiang**, #02–00 RELC Building, 30 Orange Grove Rd. (Telephone 734–4421).

VEGETARIAN

Buddha's Banquet, 682 Geyland Rd., Telephone: 747–9493.

Fut Sai Kai Restaurant. 147 Kitchener Rd.

Happy Realm Vegetarian Food Centre. 303–16 Pearl's Centre, Eu Tong Sen St.; Telephone: 222–6141.

Kuan Imm Vegetarian Restaurant. 190 Waterloo St. Telephone: 336-2389.

Loke Woh Yuen. 25 Tanjong Pagar Rd., Telephone: 221-2912.

INDIAN RESTAURANTS

Banana Leaf Apollo. 69 Balestier Rd., Telephone: 296-3414. Simple decor and inexpensive prices. This restaurant features southern Indian cuisine served on banana leaves. In addition to such dishes as mutton Mysore, fried chicken, crabs in the shell, and a range of spicy vegetables, the Banana Leaf Apollo is noted for its fish-head curry. As spices run rampant here, a glass of fresh lime juice is highly recommended.

Jubilee Café. 771 North Bridge Rd., Telephone: 298-8714. Muslim restaurant with inexpensive prices. The Jubilee offers a variety of curries, usually served with yellow rice and *noti maryam*—flat fried bread. Notable dishes are fish steak cutlets in curry, chicken *biryani*, and mutton *kuruma*. Side dishes of salad and vegetables are also available.

Komala Vilas. 229 Selegie Rd., Telephone: 293-6980. Cafeteria-style South Indian vegetarian food at inexpensive prices. Located in Singapore's Little India, Komala Vilas has a wide variety of vegetable curries. Rice flour pancakes, whole wheat *chapatis* (bread), and rice accompany the meal.

Mayarani Restaurant. Boulevard Hotel, Cuscaden Wing B-2, Cuscaden Rd., Telephone: 732-6179. Northern Indian cuisine at expensive prices. A broad selection of meat, seafood, vegetable, and rice dishes are available. Tandoori chicken and *chili masala* (prawns in onion, tomato, and chili sauce) are recommended. This is a good place to try *lassi*—a cold, fresh yogurt drink with sugar or salt. There is also a wide selection of desserts.

Moti Mahal. 18 Murray St., Telephone: 221-4338. Northern Indian food at moderate prices. Moti Mahal serves quality food in a casual setting, specializing in tandoor cooking—baked breads, meat, and fish. An extensive variety of curries is served as well as various kinds of rice dishes.

Omar Khayyam. 55 Hill St., Telephone: 336–1505. Kashmiri cuisine at expensive prices. Northern Indian food is served in an old-world setting. The food is only mildly spicy. Such dishes as harem's joy chicken and *shah nauz* marinated lamb are notable. A house specialty is the tandoori chicken served with salad and mint chutney.

Rang Mahal Restaurant. Imperial Hotel, Jalan Rumbia, Telephone: 737–1666. Northern Indian and Moghul cuisine at expensive prices. Fine dining with Indian musicians playing traditional Indian instruments. Featured specialties include prawn korma, tandoori chicken, lobster, and pomfret. A buffet lunch is available at S$25 per person.

Tandoor Holiday Inn Park View, Cuppage and Cavenagh roads, Telephone: 733–8333. Punjabi and northern Indian cuisine at expensive prices. Elegant decor with traditional Indian musicians. Noted for its tandoori dishes, the restaurant also features roast leg of lamb and a variety of curried meats and vegetables.

Zam Zam. 699 North Bridge Rd., Telephone: 298–7011. Southern Indian cuisine at inexpensive prices. Zam Zam is a Muslim-style coffee house. A good place to try *murta baks*, a fried puff pastry filled with spiced meat and onions. The yellow rice with curry is also recommended, as are the mild curries.

MALAY RESTAURANTS

Aziza's Restaurant. 36 Emerald Hill Rd., Telephone: 235–1130. Home-style cooking at expensive prices. Dinner is served in elegant surroundings and a European wine list is available. Though the atmosphere and service are Western, the menu is traditional Malay. The oxtail soup is flavored with cinnamon, anise, and coriander. *Ayam panggang* is a barbecued marinated chicken dish. Also recommended is *tari rendang*, beef with a spicy coconut sauce. Don't forget the Malay custard (*jongkong mutiara*) for dessert.

Bingtang Timur. #02–08 Far East Plaza, Scotts Rd., Telephone: 235–4539. Malay cuisine with an Arab and Indonesian influence at moderate prices. The dishes at Bingtang Timur are cooked to order. Deep-fried *satay* is featured. Rice accompanies such dishes as prawns in spices and tomato, and barbecued chicken.

Satay Club. Elizabeth Walk. Hawker stalls which offer very inexpensive prices. The Satay Club is actually 28 hawker stalls which sell chicken, beef, or mutton *satay* for as little as S$0.25 a stick.

Other Malay restaurants are **Kembar Cafeteria**, #05–119 Far East Plaza (Telephone: 734–4649); **Sate Ria**, #04–22 Far East Plaza; and **Sate Sate Basement**, Forum Galleria, Newton Rd. (Telephone: 254–4357).

NONYA RESTAURANTS

Luna Cafe. 2nd floor, Apollo Hotel, 405–407 Havelock Rd., Telephone: 733–2081. Nonya buffet at inexpensive prices (lunch only). Among the ten dishes and five desserts to choose from, *sayor nangka* (jackfruit stewed in coconut gravy), and *buah keluak* (chicken stewed in hot soup gravy) are recommended.

Other Nonya restaurants are: **Keday Kopi**, Peranakan Place, 180 Orchard Rd. (Telephone: 732–6966); **Rumah Melaka**, Far East Plaza, 14 Scotts Rd. #05–22 (Telephone: 733–2797); **Sin Wah Coffee Shop**, Joc Chiat Place; **Shanghai Restaurant**, 107 East Coast Rd.

JAPANESE RESTAURANTS

Shima. Goodwood Park Hotel, Scotts Rd., Telephone: 734–6281. Authentic Japanese cuisine at expensive prices. At the table, cooking of *teppanyaki*, *shabu-shabu*, and *yakiniku* is offered. A lunch buffet and Japanese-style fondue are also available.

Other Japanese restaurants are: **Gajoen**, Boulevard Hotel, Orchard Rd. (Telephone: 235–6995); **Nadaman**, Shangri-La Hotel (Telephone: 737–3644); **Sushi Koharu**, #02–23 Far East Plaza (Telephone: 235–7172); **Sushiya Tokugawa**, #05–65 Far East Plaza (Telephone: 734–7665); and **Don Japanese Fast Food**, #01–01 Koek Rd. (Telephone: 734–9394).

KOREAN RESTAURANTS

Seoul Garden Korean Restaurant. #02–56 Parkway Parade, Marine Parade Rd., Telephone: 345–1339. Café-style with moderate prices.

Besides the buffet barbecue, there is a wide range of selections in this intimate restaurant. Try the barbecued beef dish (*bulgogi*,) which is cooked at your table, or king oyster fried with egg (*gul jean*). Seoul Garden is one of the least expensive of the Korean restaurants in Singapore.

Other Korean restaurants are: **Han Do**, #05–01 Orchard Shopping Centre, Orchard Rd., Telephone: 235-8451. **Korean Restaurant**, #03–35–Specialist's Centre, Orchard Rd., Telephone: 235-0018; **Go Ryeo Jeong Korean House**, #05–08 Orchard Plaza, Telephone: 734-0903; and **Korean Barbecue and Steamed Bowl Restaurant**, #B6 People's Park Centre.

THAI RESTAURANTS

Siamese Seafood. Cockpit Hotel, Telephone: 737-9111. Authentic Thai fare at expensive prices. Among the exceedingly spicy dishes offered are steamed crab claws and fried prawns with Siamese chili sauce. If your palate prefers something less spicy, your waitress can recommend some of the milder selections.

Other Thai restaurants include the **Café Fontainebleau/Thai Food Centre**, Hotel Tai Pan Ramada, Victoria St. (Telephone: 336-0811), and **Haadyai Beefball**, 467 Joo Chiat Rd. (Telephone: 344-3234).

INDONESIAN RESTAURANTS

Kartini Indonesian Restaurant. 24 Murray St., Telephone: 221-7242. *Nasi padang* and Javanese specialties at moderate prices. Sample the soy chicken and prawns wrapped in a grilled banana leaf. There are also fish, vegetable, and bean curd dishes on display in this cafeteria-style restaurant.

Other Indonesian restaurants are: **Jawa Timur**, #09–00 Chiat Hong Building, Middle Rd. (Telephone: 337-5532); **Kinta Mani**, Level 3 Apollo Hotel, Havelock Rd. (Telephone: 733-2081); **Ramayana Indonesian Restaurant**, #04–17 Centerpoint, Orchard Rd. (Telephone: 734-2249); **Rendevous**, #02–09 Raffles City, Bras Basah Rd. (Telephone: 339-7508); and **Tiong Hoa**, 4 Prinsep St.

WESTERN RESTAURANTS

FRENCH

Le Restaurant de France. Hotel Meridien, Orchard Rd., Telephone: 733–8855. Gourmet dining at deluxe prices. The exquisite dishes served here are under the supervision of Louis Outhier, culinary master of L'Oasis in La Napoule. Twice a year, Outhier makes a special trip to Singapore to cook at special prices. Among the gourmet selections are sautéed veal sweetbreads and wild asparagus in a flaky pastry, and steamed fingers of turbot filled with fresh chives and garnished with oysters.

Maxim's de Paris Pavillion. Inter-Continental Hotel, Tomlinson Rd., Telephone: 733–8888. Elegant dining at deluxe prices. The elegant atmosphere of the original Maxim's has been re-created. *Cuisine classique* and *cuisine du marché* are featured. For lunch, a plat du jour and businessman's luncheon are available.

Brasserie La Rotunde Marco Polo. Tanglin Rd., Telephone: 474–7141. French café fare at expensive prices. This popular restaurant has a Paris bistro setting and an informal atmosphere. Aside from such traditional offerings as French onion soup and fondue, the Brasserie serves *truit aux almondes* (trout with almonds), and *navarin printanier* (lamb and vegetables in red wine). Lemon pancake is a specialty dessert.

Le Pescadou Novotel. Orchid Inn, Dunearn Rd., Telephone: 250–3322. Provençal cuisine at moderate prices. Le Pescadou features Provençal seafood in a rustic setting. An executive buffet is offered and special requests may be ordered in advance.

Other French restaurants include **The Belvedere, Mandarin Hotel**, Orchard Rd. (Telephone: 737–4411); **Blooms, Orchard Hotel**, Orchard Rd. (Telephone: 734–7760); **Chez Bidou, Ming Court Hotel**, Tanglin Rd. (Telephone: 737–1133); **L'Escargot, Imperial Hotel,** Jalan Rumbia (Telephone: 237–1666); **Georges, Hotel Meridien**, Orchard Rd. (Telephone: 733–8855); **Harbour Grill, Hilton International**, Orchard Rd. (Telephone: 737–2233); **Hugo's, Hyatt Regency**, 10-12 Scotts Rd. (Telephone: 737–1188); and **Le Verandah, Hotel Meridien Changi**, Nevarthon Rd. (Telephone: 542–7700).

ITALIAN

Mama Mia Ristorante Italiano. #02–01 Orchard Towers, Orchard Rd., Telephone: 732–0977. Trattoria fare at moderate prices. You can enjoy an authentic Italian soup, pasta or entree, and dessert in this informal setting. There is also a full range of appetizers.

Other Italian restaurants are **Grand' Italia**, 4th level, Glass Hotel, Outram Rd. (Telephone: 733–0188); **Milano Pizza,** #04–26 Orchard Plaza, Orchard Rd. (Telephone: 734–6050); and **Pete's Place**, Hyatt Regency, Scotts Rd. (Telephone: 733–1188).

AMERICAN

Nutmeg's. Hyatt Regency, Orchard Rd., Telephone: 733–1188. Traditional Western fare at expensive prices. Charcoal-grilled meat and spit-roasted duckling are featured in this art-deco–style restaurant. There is also a wide selection of seafood and an irresistable dessert bar.

New Orleans. Holiday Inn Park View, Telephone: 730–0127. Brasserie setting with deluxe and moderate prices. Creole and Cajun specialties can be savored while listening to live Dixieland jazz.

Other American restaurants include the **Ponderosa Steak and Salad**, #02–13 Plaza Singapura (Telephone: 336–0139); **TGIF**, 4th floor, Far East Plaza (Telephone: 235–6181); and **Trader Vic's**, New Otani Hotel, River Valley Rd. (Telephone: 337–2249).

CONTINENTAL

Movenpick Restaurants of Switzerland Pte. Ltd., Scotts Shopping Center, Scotts Rd., #B1–01, Telephone: 235–8700. Gourmet food and snacks at moderate prices. This restaurant has three areas: the Caveau for snacks, the Bistro for an informal meal, and the gourmet bar for specialty items.

Saxophone Bar and Restaurant. 23 Cuppage Rd., Telephone: 235–8385. French food is offered in a Straits Chinese setting for moderate prices. Popular with locals and tourists, the Saxophone Bar offers a unique blend of French food and live jazz.

Other Continental restaurants: **Casablanca Wine Bar and Restaurant**, 7 Emerald Hill Rd. (Telephone: 235–9328);

Chateaubriand, Pan Pacific Hotel, Marina Square (Telephone: 336–8111); **Compass Rose**, Westin Stamford, Raffles City (Telephone: 338–8585); **Domus**, Sheraton Towers, Scotts Rd. (Telephone: 737–6888); **Elizabethan Grill** (English), Raffles Hotel, Beach Rd. (Telephone: 337–8041); **Excelsior Brasserie**, Excelsior Hotel, Coleman St. (Telephone: 338–7733); **Five Continents**, East Wing Changi International Airport (Telephone: 542–0321); **Manhattan Grill**, Boulevard Hotel, Orchard Blvd. (Telephone: 737–2911); **Palm Grill**, Westin Plaza, Raffles City (Telephone: 338–8585); **Restaurant 1819**, B1 Tuan Sing Towers, Robinson Rd. (Telephone: 223–4031); and **Top of the M**, Mandarin Hotel, Orchard Rd. (Telephone: 737–4411).

GRILL ROOMS

The Rotisserie, Marco Polo Hotel, Tanglin Rd. (Telephone: 474–7141); **The Stables**, Mandarin Hotel, Orchard Rd. (Telephone: 737–4411).

STEAK AND CHOP HOUSES

Coachman Inn, Parkway Parade, #03–07 Marine Parade Rd. (Telephone: 348–3237); **Fosters 11**, #02–38 Specialist's Shopping Center (Telephone: 737–8939); **Frisco Restaurant**, B1–02 Hong Kong Bank Building, 21 Collyer Quay (Telephone: 220–3777); **Barn Steakhouse**, #02–15 Coronation Shopping Plaza, Bukit Timah Rd. (Telephone: 468–2914); **The Berkeley-Sloane Court Hotel**, Balmoral Rd. (Telephone: 235–3311); **Bob's Tavern**, 17A Lorong Liput (Telephone: 467–2419); **Emerald Steakhouse**, 115 Emerald Hill (Telephone: 737–7226); **Jack's Place**, Hotel Miramar (Telephone: 732–0001).

COFFEEHOUSES AND SNACK BARS

Café Boulevard, Ming Court Hotel, Tanglin Rd. (Telephone: 737–1133); **Café le Lagon**, 4th level, Hotel Meridien Singapore, Orchard Rd. (Telephone: 733–8855); **Café Vienna**, Royal Holiday Inn, Scotts Rd. (Telephone: 737–7966); **Cascade Garden**, The Orchard, Orchard Rd. (Telephone: 734–7766); **Checkers Health Café and Restaurant**, #01–14 Orchard Point, Orchard Rd. (Telephone: 734–3796); **Good Earth**, #02–10 Shenton House, 3 Shenton Way (Telephone: 223–1763); **Negara Coffeehouse**, Negara Hotel, Claymore Drive (Telephone: 737–0811); **Palms Wine Bar**, 261

Holland Ave. (Telephone: 469–2200); **Plums**, Hyatt Regency, Scotts Rd. (Telephone: 733–1188); **Tanglin Corner**, B2-01 Tanglin Shopping Center (Telephone 734–9863); **Tea Garden**, Pavilion Intercontinental, Tomlinson Rd. (Telephone: 733–8888); **Tiffin Room**, Raffles Hotel, Beach Rd. (Telephone: 337–8041); **Tiffany Coffeehouse**, Furama Hotel, Eu Tong Sen St. (Telephone: 533–3888).

VIII

Cultural Activities, Recreation, and Entertainment

CULTURE AND ENTERTAINMENT

CHINESE OPERA (WAYANG)

Even if you're not familiar with Chinese opera, you should experience the spectacle at least once. These operas are usually performed on open-air stages beside a market area or in temple compounds. Locals bring along stools or low chairs or simply stake out a spot and watch. The performers, portraying maidens, warlords, and various characters from classical legends, are elegantly costumed and dramatically made up. Their highly stylized movements are accompanied by gongs, drums, pipes, and other traditional

Chinese Opera

instruments. Operas are staged in Chinatown throughout the year, but are most frequent from August to September during the Festival of the Hungry Ghosts. Most performances are free. You can also take in a Chinese opera at the Singapore Handicraft Centre on Saturday and Sunday from 7:30 PM to 9:30 PM.

THEATER

The Victoria Theatre on Empress Place and the Drama Centre on Canning Rise are the two main theaters in the city. Each presents traditional drama and English-language drama. The Victoria Theatre also presents musical comedy, dance, and classical music and opera.

The booking office for the Victoria Theatre is open Monday through Saturday to 8 PM and on Sunday from 10 AM to 6 PM. For theater listings check the daily newspaper or the Art Daily brochure available at most hotel reception desks.

Shell Theaterette (Shell Tower Building off Collyer Quay) offers a variety of concerts, plays, and cultural performances.

MUSIC AND CONCERTS

Singapore Symphony. The Singapore Symphony Orchestra, founded in 1979, is composed of 72 musicians. Concerts usually begin at 8:15 PM. Tickets range from S$4 to S$15 and can be obtained from the Victoria Concert Hall Box Office, Tangs, or Cold Storage Centrepoint on Orchard Rd. For program information, call the SSO office at 338–1230 or 338–1239, or check the daily newspaper.

Band Concerts. Free band concerts are given every Sunday evening from 5:30 PM to 6:30 PM in the Botanic Gardens. Most hotels and tourist centers can provide further information.

Chinese Classical Music. Traditional music performances are staged at the Victoria Concert Hall and Victoria Theatre. The Singapore Broadcasting Corporation can provide program details. Telephone 256–0401 (ext. 2732) during office hours or 256–0401 (ext. 2795) on Thursday, Saturday, and Sunday.

Indian Music. Traditional Indian music programs are presented during festivals in temple compounds such as Chettiar Temple on Tank Rd. and Sri Mariamman on North Bridge Rd.

CABARETS AND NIGHT CLUBS

Singapore nightlife includes a number of restaurants with floor shows, some with galleries for non-diners and some with dance hostesses.

The Neptune (Collyer Quay, Mandarin Hotel, Telephone: 737–4411). The Neptune, which serves mandarin cuisine, is the largest theater-restaurant in the city. It is operated by the Mandarin Hotel. Entertainment in English and Chinese is presented by local Taiwanese and Filipino performers.

Lido Palace (Glass Hotel Shopping Centre, 317 Outram Rd., Telephone: 732–8833). The Lido features lavish dining with a Chinese caberet show.

Apollo Theatre Restaurant and Night Club (Apollo Singapore Hotel, Havelock Rd., Telephone: 733–2081). The spicy Hunan cuisine served at the restaurant is accompanied by Chinese singers and a floor show.

Tropicana (Scotts Rd., Telephone: 737–6433). The Tropicana serves up Cantonese cuisine and an international floorshow with live music.

SPECIAL CULTURAL PERFORMANCES

Instant Asia (Raffles Hotel Ballroom, Beach Rd.). Chinese, Malay, and Indian cultures are represented in this 45-minute program which begins with the famous Chinese Lion Dance. The lively introduction is followed by the more serene Lotus Dance and the Dream of the Fairies Dance. Then, Malay dancers with lighted candles perform the traditional Harvest Dance and Indian dancers present a story-dance. Rounding out the program is a python finale. The snake-charmer coaxes the python out, and audience members are invited to drape the python around their necks.

For thrill-seekers and dance enthusiasts, showtime is 11:45 AM daily. Admission S$10 adults; S$5 children.

ASEAN Night (Mandarin Hotel). Enjoy a variety of songs and dances from the Philippines, Malaysia, Thailand, Indonesia, and Singapore. Poolside performances are at 7:45 PM (every night except Monday). Dinner begins at 7:00 PM. Admission S$36 adult diners; S$23 child diners; S$18 adult non-diners; S$14 child non-diners.

Malam Singapura (Hyatt Regency). Malam Singapura is a poolside dinner-culture show, featuring Malay culture. The program begins at 8:00 PM nightly, except on Sunday. Admission S$38 adult diners; S$22 child diners; S$18 adult non-diners; S$12 child non-diners.

Cultural Show (Raffles Hotel). You can order dinner from the à la carte menu in Palm Court or at the Long Bar. The performance, which includes slides and dance, begins at 8:00 PM. Admission is S$30 for dinner and the show; S$14 for the show and one drink.

DISCOS

Black Velvet and Gold (Century Park Sheraton, Nassim Hill, Telephone: 732–1222). This is one of the oldest yet up-to-date discos, noted for its laser light shows.

Caesars Celebrities (Orchard Towers, Orchard Rd., Telephone: 737–7665). Both of these popular discos offer live entertainment from top bands.

Chinoiserie (Hyatt Hotel). One of Singapore's best known discos.

Kasbah (Mandarin Hotel). In contrast to some of the high-tech discos, the house band here plays to a slightly older crowd in a pavilion-style decor.

Peppermint Park (Parkway Parade, Marine Parade Rd., Telephone: 344–5888). The latest on the hit parade is performed by top local groups including Filipino bands.

Rainbow (Ming Arcade, Cuscaden Rd.). Rainbow is a theater-disco lounge, popular with affluent trendies. It offers top bands from the United States and Australia, and also local talent.

Reading Room (Marina Mandarin Hotel). Another popular night spot for Singaporeans, considered one of the premier discos.

Rumours (Forum Galleria, Orchard Rd., Telephone: 732–8181). The main attraction at Rumours is the split-level glass floor combined with mirror and lighting effects.

Studio M (Plaza Hotel, Beach Rd., Telephone: 298–0011). In addition to exciting sights and sounds, this disco is also popular for modeling contests and theme parties.

T.G.I.F. (Far East Plaza, Scotts Rd., Telephone: 235–6181). T.G.I.F. offers a pleasant combination of bistro-style dining and disco dancing. Open daily from 12 noon to 2:00 AM.

Top Ten (Orchard Towers, Orchard Rd., Telephone: 732–3077). Top Ten is probably the most popular disco in Singapore, with the best of local bands, American bands, and an occasional big name performer.

The Warehouse (next to the River View Hotel, Havelock Rd.). Features the largest disco video screen in Singapore and a spacious dance floor. Open daily from 8:00 PM.

COCKTAIL LOUNGES AND PUBS

For jazz, pop music, and easy listening styles, most major hotels have cocktail lounges and increasingly popular piano bars.

Long Bar (Raffles Hotel). Home of the original Singapore Sling.

Europa (Block 5, Upper Changi Rd.). Popular with a younger crowd.

Pavilion (Inter-Continental Hotel, Lower Bar). Sip a cocktail and listen to a string ensemble.

La Vendome Lounge (Dynasty Hotel). Easy listening trio sounds.

British-style pubs, a legacy of the colonial era, abound in Singapore. **Brannigans**, in the basement of the Hyatt Hotel, is one of the newest, and most popular, decorated in authentic English pub style, featuring live music and snacks. Other good pubs include **The Cricketers** at the Marina Mandarin, **Somerset's Bar** at the Western Plaza Hotel, the **Sloane Court** on Balmoral Rd. which serves fish'n'chips, steak and kidney pie and draft beer, and **The Jockey Club** at Shaw Centre.

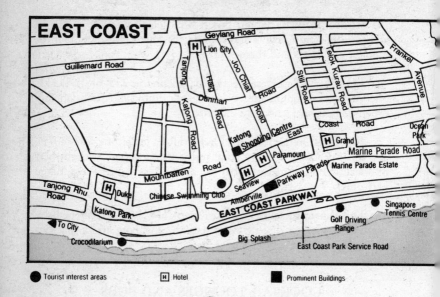

- ● Tourist interest areas
- H Hotel
- ■ Prominent Buildings

MOVIES

There are many movie theaters throughout the city which screen Chinese, Indian, Malay, and English films. Hollywood movies are usually shown in Orchard Rd. theaters. Movie-going is so popular that it is a good idea to buy your ticket an hour before the show. Schedules are listed in the daily newspaper.

SPORTS

SWIMMING

Of the 19 public swimming complexes in Singapore, the ones that are the least crowded and most often recommended are:

CN West Leisure Park (9 Japanese Garden Rd., Telephone: 261–4771). The artificial wave pool has a 164-ft (50-m) slide. Open Tuesday–Friday 10:30 AM–6:00 PM; weekends: 9:00 AM–6:00 PM. Admission S$4 adult, S$2 child.

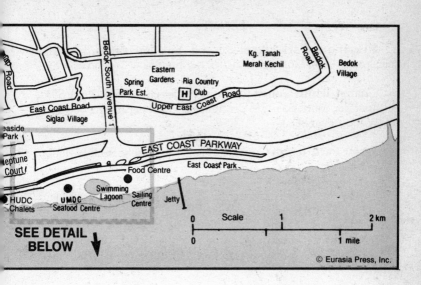

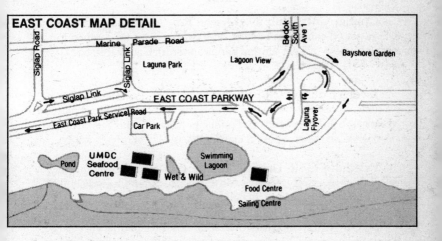

East Coast Park Swimming Lagoon (East Coast Parkway, Telephone: 345–1211). In addition to the longest slides in Southeast Asia, this complex has a wave pool, flow pool, and a children's splash pool. Open 12 noon–6:00 PM weekdays (except Wednesday); weekends and public holidays 9:00 AM–6:00 PM. Admission S$3 adult, S$2 child.

TENNIS

Alexandra Park (Royal Rd., off York and Bedford roads, Telephone: 473–7236). Open til 7:00 PM. Fee S$2.

Changi Tennis Courts (Gosport Rd., Telephone: 545–2941). S$3 per hour per court; S$4–S$5 per hour per court depending on time of day (non-members).

Farrar Park Tennis Courts (Rutland Rd., Telephone: 251–4166). S$3 per hour per court.

Singapore Tennis Center (East Coast Parkway, Telephone: 442–5966). S$14 whole day (unlimited hours).

Sembawang Tennis Center (Deptford Rd., Telephone: 257–1147). S$2-S$4 per hour per court depending on day and time of day.

GOLF

Changi Golf Club (Netheravon Rd., Telephone: 545–1298). 9-hole par 68 course. Green fees: S$40 weekdays (if no competition, with minimum of 3 players and handicap cards). Caddy fees: S$13 (1st class), S$11 (2nd class).

Jurong Country Club (Jurong Town Hall Rd., 9 Science Centre Rd., Telephone: 560–5655). An 18-hole par 71 course. S$50 per player weekdays; S$100 weekends and public holidays. Caddy fee: S$20 (A class), S$17 (B class), S$14 (C class).

Parkland Golf Driving Range (920 East Coast Parkway, Telephone: 440–6726). 48 bays, 656 ft. (200-m) range. Open daily 7:30 AM–10:00 PM. Fee S$5 for 90 balls.

Seletar Country Club (Seletar Airbase, Telephone: 481–7941). 9-hole par 70 course. S$30 per player, Tuesday–Friday. Caddy fee: S$16 (A class), S$12 (B class), S$8 (C class).

Sembawang Country Club (Sembawang Rd., Telephone: 257–0642). 18-hole par 70 course. S$30 per player on weekdays; S$80 on weekends and public holidays. Caddy fee: S$16 (A class), S$14 (B class), S$12 (C class).

Sentosa Golf Club (Sentosa Island, Telephone: 472–2722). 18-hole par 71 course. S$50 per player on weekdays; S$100 per player on weekends and public holidays; S$15 for golf clubs. Caddy fee: S$15.

Singapore Island Country Club (Upper Thompson Rd.). Two 18–hole par 71 courses. S$100 per player weekdays only. Caddy fee: S$18 (1st class), S$15 (2nd class), S$12 (Apprentice).

Warren Golf Club (Folkestone Rd., Telephone: 777–6533). 9-hole par 70 course. S$50 per player weekdays only. Caddy fees: S$15 (A class), S$14 (B class), S$13 (C class).

SAILING

Changi Sailing Club (Netheravon Rd., Telephone: 545–2876).

HORSERACING

Races feature Australian, American, French, English, and Irish horses.

Singapore Turf Club (Bukit Timah Racecourse, Telephone 469–3611). Admission S$5.

JOGGING

MacRitchie Reservoir, East Coast Lagoon, and West Coast Park are the best places for jogging. The Botanic Gardens on Holland Rd. is also recommended.

WINDSURFING

East Coast Sailing Centre (1210 East Coast Parkway, Telephone: 449–5118). 4-hour course (1:00 PM–5:00 PM daily) S$45; 2-day basic course (3 hours per day) S$80. Sailboard rental S$10 per hour. Open 9:30 AM–6:30 PM daily.

IX   Shopping in Singapore

SHOPPING TIPS

Compare Prices. It is worth the effort to compare prices at three or four shops before you make an expensive purchase. You can ask in shops and department stores for a price list for cameras and electrical goods.

Look for the Merlion Emblem. If you see a gold Merlion logo (lion head with fish tale) on a red background displayed where you are shopping, it represents reliability, quality, and reasonable pricing.

Bargaining. Bargaining is acceptable in markets, small shops, street stalls, and souvenir shops. The bargaining style is low-key. Although it is not acceptable at all in department stores, a request for a slightly lower price is sometimes granted in jewelry stores and designer boutiques.

Shipping Packages. Be sure to get written confirmation of instructions given to shops to ship your purchase. Do not rely on street vendors and unlicensed tourist guides who do not have an official Singapore Tourist Board badge.

Voltage. Check for the correct voltage and cycle. Singapore, the United Kingdom, Australia, and Hong Kong use 220–240 volts/50 cycles. The United States, Canada, Japan, Indonesia, and the Philippines use 110–120 volts/60 cycles.

Warranties. Unless you are purchasing something from a small tradesman, you should be able to get a warranty card for cameras, watches, and electrical goods.

Duty-Free Goods. Shoppers can obtain a complete list of duty-free items from the Trade Development Board (Telephone 271–9388) for S$10 per copy.

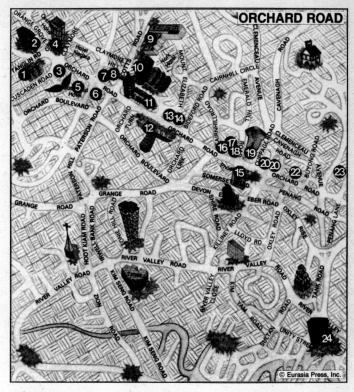

ORCHARD ROAD

© Eurasia Press, Inc.

1. Tanglin Shopping Centre
2. Delfi Orchard
3. Forum Galleria
4. Orchard Towers
5. Far East Shopping Centre
6. Liat Towers
7. International Building
8. Shaw Centre
9. Far East Plaza
10. Scotts Shopping Centre
11. Lucky Plaza
12. Wisma Atria
13. The Promenade
14. The Paragon
15. Specialists' Centre
16. Orchard C & E
17. Midpoint Orchard
18. Orchard Emerald
19. Centrepoint
20. Orchard Plaza
21. Meridien Shopping Centre
22. Plaza Singapura
23. Liang Court

Receipts and Refunds. Most shops and department stores provide receipts. Most department stores will exchange faulty merchandise within three days if you have a receipt and all tags and labels are intact.

Complaints. Written complaints should be sent to: Tourism Services, Singapore Tourist Promotion Board, Raffles City Tower, #36–04, North Bridge Rd., Singapore 0617.

Touting. Avoid touts (street vendors) with offers of discounts or special shopping tours. Touting is illegal in Singapore.

Shop Addresses. Shop addresses indicate the exact location of the shop. For example, if the address reads #03–56, #03 means the third floor, 56 is the shop number.

WHAT TO BUY

ANTIQUES AND CURIOS

Such items as camphorwood chests, lacquer screens, and miniature jade and ivory carvings can be found at Holland Rd. Shopping Centre, Tanglin Shopping Centre, and the Singapore Handicraft Centre.

Nationals of countries that have subscribed to the Convention on International Trade in Endangered Species (CITES) should be aware that they will not be allowed to bring back ivory objects puchased abroad. While it is permitted to import antique ivory, stringent documentary proof of antiquity is required, of a kind that can usually be obtained only by institutions or companies, not by private individuals.

ARTS AND CRAFTS

INDIAN HANDICRAFTS

You can buy handmade Benares silk, souvenirs, artifacts, and papier-maché, beadwork, and filigree handicrafts at the shops in Little India and at the Singapore Handicraft Centre.

JEWELRY

There are many different kinds of jewelry shops in Singapore. Modern jewelry can be found in hotel shops and along Orchard Rd. Gold, jade, pearls, and diamonds can be found on South Bridge Rd., New Bridge Rd., and People's Park Complex. Chinese jewelers sell 22 karat gold ornaments, enamelled pieces, and other traditional kinds of jewelry along South Bridge Rd., Peoples Park, and at Chinese Emporium. Malay jewelry can be found on Arab St., and Indian jewelry is sold on Sarangoon Rd.

WHAT TO BUY

Shopping for Statuettes

CARPETS

Chinese carpets are available at the Peninsula Shopping Centre on Coleman St. and at the Singapore Handicraft Centre, which also has handmade Iranian and Turkish rugs. Persian carpets and rugs are sold on Orchard Rd. and Arab St.

FABRICS AND CLOTHING

For silk garments, Tanglin Shopping Centre, Scotts, Lucky Plaza, and Chinese Emporium are your best bets. You can also find Thai and Malaysian silk at the Singapore Handicraft Centre. Department stores and shops along North Bridge Rd., High St., Arab St., People's Park, and Katong Shopping Centre sell fabrics from Japan, Europe, and the United States.

BATIK

Almost every department store and shopping center sells batik clothing, tablecloths, and paintings. You can also buy batik at the Singapore Handicraft Centre and in the specialty shops on Arab St.

READY-MADE CLOTHING

Designer clothing for men and women can be found in boutiques, hotel shopping arcades, and in shopping complexes on Orchard Rd. and Scott Rd.

TAILORED CLOTHING

Tailoring in Singapore is quick and efficient with a high standard of workmanship. Tailor shops abound in the shopping centers and hotel galleries. Most of them also offer a good range of quality fabrics imported from all over the world.

Another feature of tailoring in Singapore is that you can get a custom-made suit, complete with alterations, within 24 hours.

CLOTHING PRICES

Men's tailored

two–piece suit	between $300–$500	
trousers	between $50–$90	Including
shirt (business)	$35–$75	Material
safari suit	$140–$200	

Men's ready-made

Ermenegildo Zegna — trousers $245–$395
Dunhill —blazer $1,110
Van Heusen — shirts $30–$70

Ladies' tailored

two-piece suit	— $90–$120	
blouse (silk)	— $45 and above	Excluding
trousers	— $60 and above	Material

Ladies' ready-made

Dior — blouse (long sleeved) $250 upwards
Lanvin — two–piece suit—up to $2,000
Gucci — trousers, slacks—$200 upwards

COSMETICS AND PERFUMES

A full range of cosmetics and perfumes is available at cosmetic counters in large department stores or cosmetic houses.

PERFUME AND COSMETIC PRICES

Perfumes

Chanel No. 5 perfume 14 ml	$103.50
Diorissimo eau de toilette 2 oz	$48.00
Private Collection 50 ml	$110.00

Cosmetics

Christian Dior lipstick	$25.00
Christian Dior nail polish	$22.00
Estee Lauder blusher	$36.00
Lancome powder	$22.50
Lancome foundation 40 ml	$23.70

HIGH-TECH PRODUCTS

CAMERAS

Duty-free camera equipment can be found at Tanglin Shopping Centre, Lucky Plaza, Far East Plaza, Wisma Atria, Orchard Towers, and Plaza Singapura.

ELECTRONICS

You can find shops specializing in electronic equipment at the Scotts and Plaza Singapura shopping complexes.

VIDEO-AUDIO

Many different kinds of duty-free audio and video equipment can be found at shopping complexes on North Bridge Rd., Raffles Place, and the Multi-Story Car Park.

WHERE TO SHOP

ORCHARD ROAD

Shopping along Orchard Rd. is comparable to New York's Fifth Avenue as it used to be or London's Oxford St. and Knightsbridge. Its ultra-modern shopping centers offer a wide range of international goods.

Delfi Shopping Centre (top of Orchard Road). Features international brands of fashions.

Far East Shopping Centre (beside the Hilton Hotel). Goods range from silk kimonos, jewelry, and reptile skin goods to electrical appliances.

Chinese Emporium (International Building). An extensive array of Chinese products including clothing, scrolls, figurines, tablecloths, and much more.

Tangs. A veteran department store, famous for over 30 years for its Asian curios and souvenirs. In addition to its Asian merchandise, Tangs sells designer clothing, crockery, jewelry, and furniture.

TANGLIN ROAD

Tanglin Shopping Centre (Tanglin Rd.–end of Orchard Rd.). Specializes in antiques, including antiquarian maps and books, handicrafts, and souvenirs. Designer fashions, silks, sports clothing, and diving gear are also sold here.

Le Classique (opposite the Ming Court Hotel). An Asian souvenir store with a variety of arts and crafts, perfumes, and jewelry.

Singapore Handicraft Centre. This modern Oriental bazaar has crafts from 16 Asian countries. While shopping you can watch carvers, weavers, and many other craftsmen at work. On Wednesday, Saturday and Sunday from 6 to 10 PM the bazaar becomes Pasar Malam, a night market, where you can buy clothing, knickknacks, accessories, and electrical appliances. On Saturday nights, Chinese Opera and cultural and popular programs are staged.

SCOTTS ROAD

Along this street, which runs at right angles to Orchard Rd. near its western end, are two of the city's most modern shopping complexes, Scotts Plaza and the Far East Plaza. The former boasts an "electronic supermarket" and many designer boutiques, while the latter offers sporting wear and other fashions, stamps, and leathers.

CHINATOWN

If you like to browse, you won't be disappointed in Singapore's Chinatown. The streets are full of shops selling a wide variety of goods. A complete stroll through Chinatown includes South Bridge Rd., New Bridge Rd. (between Smith St. and Mosque St.), Ann Siang Hill, and China St.

ALONG SOUTH BRIDGE ROAD

Shops worth browsing in here include goldsmiths, watch shops, herbal medicine shops, and jewelers who specialize in jade and pearls. Be sure to visit the local fortune tellers and palmists for a peek at your future. Chung Hwa Book Store features Chinese paintings and calligraphy, papercuts, and name seals (chops).

Calligraphy Shop

ALONG ANN SIANG HILL, CLUB STREET, AND CHINA STREET

Some of the more unusual items found in shops along Ann Siang Hill are large lion heads (used for the New Year Lion Dance), Chinese dolls, and Chinese opera masks.

At the top of Club St., you can watch woodcarvers making wooden statues of Chinese gods. On **China St.,** you can buy a bottle of Chinese wine or sample some of the traditional pastries and snacks. On **Smith St.,** the best buys are silver, jade, and ivory.

ARAB STREET

Arab St., which begins on Beach Rd., opposite the Plaza Hotel, is known primarily for batik, but there is an assortment of many other Malay and Arab goods in this area.

On Arab St., Muskat Rd., Baghdad St., and throughout this neighborhood, many of the items sold reflect the Muslim influence of their merchants. Copies of the Koran and prayer rugs are sold, as well as worry beads, brassware, and jewelry.

At the Beach Rd. end of Arab St., all kinds of wickerware predominate, from straw hats to hanging lamps. Further up the street are shops which specialize in textiles. Cotton, chiffon, satin, and synthetic fabrics are all sold at very reasonable prices.

The batik sold along Arab St. is from Malaysia and Indonesia, and it is of very good quality. Besides batik clothing, handbags, ties, tablecloths, and wall-hangings are available.

Some of the other shops here specialize in Indian clothing and jewelry. Exotic Malay jewelry and Indian perfume can also be found in this neighborhood.

SERANGOON ROAD

This neighborhood, known as Little India, is one of the most interesting places in Singapore for shopping or just strolling and taking in the sights.

Zhu Jiao Centre, on the corner of Serang and Buffalo roads, has a food market with a variety of Indian, Malay, and Chinese specialties. On the second floor of the center, there are unusual bric-a-brac and household items.

Sari shops and Indian handicrafts are two of the main attractions in Little India. Sari fabric ranges from simple muslin to gold-threaded silk, all of good quality and inexpensive.

The variety of Indian handicrafts includes carved wooden tables, brassware, flower garlands, and incense.

Side lane stalls on Dunlap St. and Campbell Lane have huge assortments of cooking utensils and local groceries such as rice crisps, palm sugar, and dried beans.

If you like to shop and snack, at the top of Serangoon Rd. there is a vegetarian restaurant which sells pancakes and sweetmeats. You can eat them on the spot or have them wrapped and continue strolling.

CHANGE ALLEY

For the more adventurous shopper who enjoys a good buy, Change Alley will either be invigorating or frustrating, depending on how skillful you are at bargaining.

Change Alley covers Collyer Quay and Clifford Pier. It is named after Indian money changers who originally conducted business there. Current money changers are licensed by the government, and they offer the most competitive currency exchange rates in the city.

Perfume, costume jewelry, tee shirts, batik, and light luggage are just a few of the items waiting to be bargained over.

There are also souvenir and specialty shops located in the Clifford Centre and the Arcade, to be found in the Ocean Building Annex.

If all the bargaining is too exhausting, you can relax in the Clifford Pier area and watch the comings and goings of sailors and passengers from nearby ships.

RAFFLES CITY COMPLEX

This complex is composed of the Westin Plaza Hotel, the Westin Stamford Hotel, a convention center, and a shopping complex. Its borders are Bras Basah Rd., North Bridge Rd., and Beach Rd..

Sogo, a Japanese department store, occupies five floors of the shopping complex. Sogo features fashionable clothing, cosmetics, accessories, men's attire, and handbags. Other shops in the complex are noted for audiovisual equipment, cards, books, and clothing. There are also many restaurants and cafés in this complex.

KATONG

For leisurely out-of-the-way shopping, you can take a 15-minute ride on the expressway and try some of the old-fashioned shops which sell antiques, baby clothing, kitchenware, and other household items. This area is not often visited by tourists, so you may find some very good buys here.

Parkway Parade is also worth a visit. There are two large Japanese stores and many small shops dealing in books, electrical goods, shoes, bags, clothes, and jewelry. This complex is popular with the local inhabitants on weekends. On Saturdays many boutiques and shops present cooking demonstrations, fashion shows, or dance programs.

PERANAKAN PLACE

Peranakan Place is located on the corner of Emerald Hill and Orchard Rd. and is open from 9:00 AM daily.

Peranakan culture derives from a blend of Chinese, Malay, and local settlers. Peranakan Place is a series of restored shops selling antiques, gifts, and Peranakan cuisine. Kedai Kopi, a Chinese coffee shop, is open 24 hours. You can be photographed in traditional Peranakan costume or take in one of the cultural programs performed on the open-air stage. A Peranakan tour is available through Tour East at S$45 per person.

X   Doing Business in Singapore

ESTABLISHING YOUR BUSINESS IN SINGAPORE

SINGAPORE'S open-door policy welcomes foreign investment. Individuals or corporations considering doing business in Singapore will find the majority of their needs well met. Singapore offers an efficient working environment and numerous fiscal and income tax incentives.

Since independence in 1965, a stable government and steady economic management have allowed Singapore to become a nation with one of the highest standards of living in Asia. Another factor in Singapore's prosperity is the government's recognition that foreign investment is mutually beneficial. The Minister of Foreign Affairs has said: "It is by plugging into multinationals that Singapore has overcome the handicaps of size, small population, and lack of natural resources. Multinational corporations have brought technological and managerial skills, access to new markets and investment capital to Singapore at a rate far more rapid than it could have achieved on its own. On balance, the presence of these large corporations is advantageous to Singapore and has greatly accelerated its economic growth."

Singapore's status as a free port with no import or export duties on raw materials, equipment, or products, and its location and excellent sea and air transportation, are all highly conducive to business activity.

Singapore's economy is based on free enterprise. There are no foreign exchange controls and no restrictions on foreign ownership of businesses or expatriate employment. Though economic growth has slowed recently, the government continues to develop new economic strategies and solutions to the recession.

More than 3,000 international companies conduct business in Singapore. The electronics industries, precision equipment industries, plastics, garment, and petroleum represent major areas of investment. The United States is the largest foreign investor in Singapore, followed closely by Japan.

Singapore's industrious society reflects the nation's commitment to maintaining its role as an international business center. BERI, a U.S. consultant on international business environment risks, has rated Singapore's workforce as number one in terms of productivity, discipline, technical skills, and labor laws. The work force is primarily English-speaking, and has one of the highest literacy rates in Asia.

Singapore also offers the foreign investor excellent transport and telecommunications. Advanced health care, educational facilities, and quality housing are available for foreign residents.

Dave Reusser, Managing Director of General Motors Singapore, summarized Singapore's benefits for foreign investors in the following way: "The decision to establish a plant in Singapore was the result of an extensive survey which included the southern United States, Mexico, and countries in the Far East. Singapore was the ultimate choice. Contributing factors were a supportive investment climate, an efficient and stable government, excellent communication and shipping facilities, and a skilled and highly motivated work force."

RESIDENCE PERMITS

TEMPORARY RESIDENCE PERMITS

Various types of permits and passes are obtainable by foreigners who wish to work or conduct business in Singapore.

Work Permits, available from the Controller of Immigration under Chapter 8 of the Immigration Act, are required for foreign day workers. Applications should be addressed to the Office of the Commissioner for Employment (Work Permit), 80 Prinsep St., Singapore 0718 (Telephone: 330-9746).

Employment Passes are governed by Regulation 9 of the Immigration Regulations, 1972. These passes are for professional and higher-salaried workers, who should apply by filling out and filing Form 8 and Annex A.

Professional Visit Visas may be obtained by speakers at seminars and conferences and other professionals who need to enter Singapore for short-term assignments.

Applications for Employment Passes and Professional Visit Visas should be addressed to The Controller of Immigration, Immigration

Department, 95 South Bridge Rd. #08—26, South Bridge Centre, Singapore 0718 (Telephone: 532–2877).

PERMANENT RESIDENCE

Professional-technical personnel and skilled workers who have been in Singapore for at least six months may apply for permanent residence for themselves and their spouse and children. Acceptance is based on the applicant's qualifications and expertise, and on the needs of the Singapore economy. In general, experienced technicians and experts in a craft are eligible. They must have proven backgrounds in supplying engineering services or ancillary products to manufacturing enterprises. Applicants should submit requests under this head to the Controller of Immigration. In addition, there are two specialized schemes under which business people may apply for permanent residence.

S$ Million Deposit Scheme. Permanent residence may be applied for by persons with highly regarded entrepreneurial ability and strong financial backing, who deposit S$1 million in cash with the government. The deposit is used for subsequent investment in business activity approved by the government.

Industrial Experts Scheme. To apply under this provision, one should be a highly qualified professional or a well-known industrialist.

Applications under either of these provisions should be addressed to the Secretary, Review Committee (Immigration), c/o Economic Development Board, 250 North Bridge Rd. 24–00, Raffles City Tower, Singapore 0617 (Telephone: 336–2288). If permanent residence is not granted under either scheme, it may be obtainable under the more general provision of "experienced technicians or craft experts," or a temporary pass or permit may be granted.

BUSINESS REGISTRATION

All foreign businesses must register with the Registrar of Businesses or Registrar of Companies. Generally, there is minimal restriction on the kinds of businesses that may be set up. Some types of businesses, such as finance companies and insurance and brokerage companies must obtain a license from the government. It is also necessary to obtain a license from the Registrar of Manufacturers for the manufacture of certain goods. Approval from the Trade Development Board must be obtained if a company has foreign shareholders and intends to carry on the business of shipping. Registration procedures in Singapore are similar to those of the United Kingdom and Australia. It is advisable to engage a firm of solicitors or accountants to facilitate the formalities of registering a company.

Registry of Companies and Businesses
1 Colombo Court #06–06116
Singapore 0617
Telephone: 336–1293

Additional requirements and documents needed for registering a company in Singapore are as follows:

1. The name of the company should not be the same as or similar to that of another company and it should not mislead the public. The applicant must obtain the approval from the Registrar to reserve the name chosen to be the company's name.
2. The following documents must be filed with the Registrar of Companies:
   - The Articles of Association
   - The Memorandum of Association
   - Certificate of Identity of the subscriber-officer to the Memorandum
   - A Statutory Declaration of Compliance with the requirements of the Act
   - A Statutory return of the directors and secretary named in the Article
3. The structure of the authorized capital and the appropriate registration fee payable must be submitted to the Registrar of Companies.
4. Within one month of incorporation all companies must file:
   - Form 24 (return of allotment of shares)
   - Form 44 (notice of situation of registered office)
   - Form 49 (return of particulars of directors, managers and secretaries)
5. A copy of the Memorandum and Articles of Association, Certificate of Incorporation, Forms 24 and 49, and an agreement with a bank must be submitted to the Registrar before a company can open a bank account.
6. Section 199 of the Companies Act requires that directors and officers

must ensure that appropriate accounting and other records are maintained.

7. Every company must hold a general meeting every calendar year. (The Companies Act, Section 175). Audited statements of account and the director's report must be presented at the annual meeting. (The Companies Act, Section 201). The first annual meeting of a new company must be held within 18 months of its incorporation.

8. An annual report must be submitted to the Registrar of Companies within one month following the general meeting. Documents for the Annual Return are specified in the Eighth Schedule of the Companies Act.

Instant Information Service, which provides computerized information on business firms and companies, may be consulted through the Registry of Companies.

TRADEMARKS AND PATENTS

Trademarks can be protected by registration under the Trademarks Act. At present in Singapore there is no protection for the grant of original patents.

COPYRIGHT

Currently, a new copyright law is being drafted which may institute stiffer penalties for offenders and longer periods of copyright protection for original works.

TAXATION

CUSTOMS DUTIES AND EXCISE TAX

Singapore is basically a duty-free port. There are import duties on a limited number of items, but in general, obstacles to industrialization are minimal. Aside from relatively few exceptions, no import licensing is required in Singapore.

IMPORT DUTIES

Imports that require licenses include goods originating from Albania, the Socialist Republic of Vietnam, People's Republic of

Mongolia, and People's Democratic Republic of Laos. Imports of rice, and of air conditioners not exceeding 9,000 kilocalories per hour (except those for motor vehicles), from all countries also require licenses.

Import duties in Singapore include primarily revenue duties applied to three main categories: intoxicating liquors, tobacco, and petroleum products. Duties on a few consumer products such as clothing, non-essential foodstuffs, and motor vehicles are protective in nature. Several free-trade zones have been established to promote trade in dutiable items.

The following is a list of dutiable goods:

- Birds' eggs, egg yolk
- Sugar, confectionery, and chocolate
- Bread, biscuits, pastry, and cakes
- Wines, spirits, beer, brandy, tobacco, and liquors
- Petroleum products
- Hydrocarbons, dulcin, saccharine, and cyclamates
- Clothing of all materials
- Household refrigerators
- Accumulator plates other than nickel-cadmium and fluorescent tubes
- Motor vehicles
- Chairs, other furniture of cane or wood, filing cabinets, mattress supports, and other articles of bedding
- Imitation jewelry
- Headgear and hats
- Leather handbags, purses, wallets, and pochettes

Exemptions. Government policy may determine that certain raw materials and equipment not obtainable locally may be exempt from duty. Exemption may be obtained by applying to the Customs and Excise Department.

Controlled Imports. In accordance with the United Nations resolution, all imports from South Africa are prohibited. Additional items prohibited from entering Singapore are as follows: cigarette lighters shaped like pistols or revolvers, toy currency, toy coins or goods bearing the imprint of any currency note, banknotes or coins which are legal tender in any country or territory, firecrackers, straight-through silencers, multitone horns or sirens of motor vehicles, plants with soil (except from Peninsular Malaysia). Also a number of goods are subject to controls for reasons of health, security, and the personal safety of the users.

EXPORTS

Singapore does not impose export duties on goods from Singapore. However, some goods are restricted quantitatively and others are subject to export licensing. Certain textiles and garments exported to Canada, the European Economic Community, Norway, Sweden, and the United States are restricted quantitatively. Motor vehicles, rubber, and timber are also subject to export control. Granite and sand require export licensing.

Information on Certificate of Origin and import-export documentation is available through a trade documentation service within the Singapore Trade Development Board. Inquiries on publications or documents should be addressed to the STDB or any of its overseas centers.

INCOME TAX

Singapore's income tax is territorial. Both residents and nonresidents must pay tax on income that accrues in, is derived from, or is received in Singapore from any of the following:
- Gains or profits from any trade, business, profession, or vocation
- Gains or profits from any employment
- Dividends, interest, or discounts
- Any pension, charge, or annuity
- Rents, royalties, premiums, or any other profit arising from property
- Gains or profits of an income nature not falling within any of the preceding paragraphs

PERSONAL TAX

Residents must pay tax on income received in Singapore from any of these sources in places outside Singapore, but nonresidents are exempt in this case. Personal income is taxed progressively, at a rate of from 3.5% to 33%, depending on one's income.

Nonresidents employed in Singapore generally need not pay income tax if their period or periods of employment do not exceed 60 days in a single calendar year. Exceptions to this are entertainers and nonresident directors of companies resident in Singapore. Nonresidents employed for more than 60 but less than 183 days in a calendar year pay 15% on the full amount of their earnings, or the amount that a resident would pay under the same circumstances, whichever is larger.

Nonresident directors of Singapore resident companies who are in the Republic for less than an aggregate period of 183 days a calendar year are taxed at the current flat rate of 33% on director's fees and similar remuneration.

COMPANY TAX

A company is considered resident in Singapore for tax purposes if its control and management are exercised in Singapore. If a company's directors' general meeting is held in Singapore, it is considered as resident in Singapore. In general, a nonresident company is subject to the same taxation as a resident company. Currently, the profits of a resident or nonresident company are subject to tax at the rate of 33%.

INVESTMENT INCENTIVES

The government of Singapore offers a number of tax incentives such as:

- Pioneer industries can be considered for complete tax exemption on company profits for periods of 5–10 years (unless they produce products already manufactured locally without incentives).
- Established enterprises incurring new capital expenditure of at least S$1 million for productive equipment can be considered for partial tax exemption for up to five years, depending on the increase of income.
- If a holding company is incorporated and resident in Singapore, is 50% owned by Singapore citizens or permanent residents, and is involved in a new technology project, losses during the first three years, up to 50% of equity invested, can be set off against the holding company's taxable income.

Additional tax and other incentives are available in the following areas: foreign loans for productive equipment, royalties, fees and development contributions, warehousing and servicing incentives, international consultancy services, research and development, antipollution equipment, and product and skills development.

BANKING, FINANCE, AND SECURITIES

AS a leading international financial center, Singapore is highly qualified to serve the business community.

There are no exchange control rates in Singapore, and all Singapore residents, both corporations and individuals, are allowed complete freedom from exchange control for any form of investment and payment.

MONETARY AUTHORITY OF SINGAPORE (MAS)

Although Singapore does not have a central bank, MAS performs all the functions of a central bank, except for currency issuing. MAS is a wholly owned and controlled corporation of the Ministry of Finance and it acts as banker, fiscal agent and financial advisor to the government. It also supervises and regulates matters relating to banks and other financial institutions. All banks are licensed under the Banking Act administered by MAS.

ASIAN DOLLAR MARKET

The Asian Dollar Market was established in 1968. It is basically an international money and capital market where foreign currency funds are traded. The US dollar is the most common currency used in the market. Since rates in the market are closely linked to Eurocurrency market rates, depositors can obtain international deposit rates for their funds in Singapore. Upon approval of the MAS, banks may participate in the Asian Dollar Market through an Asian currency unit, which is a separate accounting unit of the bank concerned. A special concessionary tax rate of 10% is applied to offshore revenue of the Asian currency units.

COMMERCIAL BANKS

Three types of licenses are issued for commercial banks: full license, restricted, or offshore.

Full license banks are permitted to conduct all domestic as well as foreign activities. In general, a restricted bank may engage in the same transactions as a full license bank except that it may not accept fixed and other interest-bearing deposits below S$250,000 from non-bank customers. Also, a restricted bank may not operate more than one banking office in Singapore and may not accept savings deposits.

Offshore banks deal mainly in Asian dollar and foreign exchange transactions. They also are not allowed to operate more than one branch office in Singapore and they may not accept savings deposits.

MERCHANT BANKS

Services provided by the merchant banks include investment and financial advice, portfolio management, underwriting, and loan provision. A number of merchant banks, approved by MAS, deal in interbank foreign exchange transactions.

FINANCE COMPANIES

Licensed finance companies are allowed to accept time and savings deposits but may not deal in foreign exchange or gold, or provide checking facilities. Types of loan financing include housing, real estate construction, commercial, and shipping. Other types of financing provided are factoring, accounts receivable, and hire purchase (consumer credit).

STOCKS AND SECURITIES

STOCK EXCHANGE

The Singapore Stock Exchange (SES) is a self-governing organization. As of 1984, 308 companies were listed on the Exchange. A listed company must meet various disclosure requirements as indicated in the SES Listing Manual and corporate disclosure policy. Companies listed on the Exchange fall into two categories: First Trading and Second Trading. First Trading requires stricter criteria in terms of paid-up capital, dividends, and share turnover. There are 25 member firms in the exchange which provide brokering and underwriting services.

UNLISTED SECURITIES MARKET (USM)

The USM provides an interim point for companies preparing to become listed on the main board of the Stock Exchange. Through USM, upcoming local companies which do not qualify for the main board of the SES may raise capital through the issue of shares.

BUSINESS-RELATED BODIES AND ORGANIZATIONS

GOVERNMENT BODIES

Economic Development Board (EDB). Established in 1961, for the purpose of planning and promoting industrial development in Singapore, the EDB assists investors in obtaining land and factory space, long-term financing, and skilled workers. The EDB evaluates applications for tax and other incentives, provides information to prospective investors, and assists in locating of suppliers, subcontractors, and joint-venture partners.

The Jurong Town Corporation (JTC). The JTC was established in 1968 and is responsible for the development and management of industrial estates. It also provides social amenities for workers and residents of the industrial estates.

National Productivity Board (NPB). The NPB promotes productivity awareness and improvement.

Trade Development Board (TDB). Established in 1983 primarily to promote Singapore's export drive, the TDB has three main functions: expanding Singapore's trade (particularly in export promotion), identifying new markets and expanding existing market share, and providing the business community with up-to-date information on market research and opportunities. The TDB also has extensive services to assist foreign businesses in such areas as trade regulations, trade fairs, and marketing advice.

THE SINGAPORE ECONOMIC DEVELOPMENT BOARD

HEAD OFFICE

1 Maritime Square
#10–40 World Trade Centre (Lobby D)
Singapore 0409
Telephone: 2710844
Cable: INDUSPROMO
Telex: RS 26233
Fax: 2747035

cont...

ECONOMIC DEVELOPMENT BOARD OFFICES *(cont.)*

REGIONAL OFFICES

NORTH AMERICA

New York
55 East 59th Street
New York, New York 10022
Telephone: (212) 421–2203
Fax: (212) 421–2206

Atlanta
234 Peachtree Hollow Court
Atlanta, Georgia 30328
Telephone: (404) 392–9945

Boston
55 Wheeler St.
Cambridge, Massachusetts 02138
Telephone: (617) 497–9392
Fax: 617–491–6150

Chicago
Illinois Center Two
233 North Michigan Ave.
Chicago, Illinois 60601
Telephone: (312) 644–3720
Fax: 312–644–3732

Dallas
Park Central VII
12750 Merit Drive
Dallas, Texas 75251
Telephone: (214) 450–4540
Fax: 214–450–4543

East Windsor (New Jersey)
514 One Mile Rd. South
East Windsor, New Jersey 08520

cont...

ECONOMIC DEVELOPMENT BOARD OFFICES *(cont.)*

Houston (Mailing Address)
6200 Savoy, Regency Square
Houston, Texas 77036
Cable Address: INDUSPROMO
  HOUSTON

Los Angeles
911 Wilshire Boulevard Suite 950
Los Angeles, California 90017
Telephone: (213) 624–7647/8
Cable Address: INDUSPROMO
  LOS ANGELES
Telex: 4720209 TDB LA
Fax: 213–624–4412

New Canaan (Connecticut)
381 Main Street, #13
New Canaan, Connecticut 06840
Telephone: (203) 966–6204

Redwood City (California)
210 Twin Dolphin Drive
Redwood City, California 94587
Telephone: (415) 591–9102

Washington DC
1015 18th Street NW
Washington, DC 20036

EUROPE

Frankfurt
6000 Frankfurt/Main
Untermainanlage 7
Federal Republic of Germany
Telephone: (069) 23–38–38
Cable Address: INDUSPROMO
  FRANKFURTMAIN
Telex: 4189031 SEDB D
Fax: 49–69–252882

cont...

ECONOMIC DEVELOPMENT BOARD OFFICES *(cont.)*

London
Entablature Floor
International House
World Trade Centre
1 St. Katharines Way
London, E1 9UN
England
Telephone: 01-481-4308/01-481-0745
Cable Address: INDUSPROMO LONDON
Telex: 888674 SEDBUK G
Fax: 44-1-481-3809

Paris
c/o Embassy of the Republic of Singapore
12 Square de l'Avenue Foch
75116 Paris
France
Telephone: (33) (1) 4500-3361
Cable Address: SINGAWAKIL PARIS
Telex: 888674 SEDBUK G
Fax: (33) (1) 4414-8138/09

Stockholm
Banergatan 10, 5 Tr
S-115 22 Stockholm
Sweden
Telephone: (08) 63-74-88/67-82-88
Cable Address: INDUSPROMO STOCKHOLM
Telex: 19463 SEDB ST O S
Fax: 46-8-782-3951

AUSTRALASIA
Tokyo
The Imperial Tower 98 Floor
1-1 Uchisaiwaicho 1-Chome
Chiyoda-Ku
Tokyo 100
Japan
Telephone: (03) 501-6041
Telex: J33310 SEDB TYO
Fax: 813-501-6060

cont...

ECONOMIC DEVELOPMENT BOARD OFFICES *(cont.)*

Osaka
c/o Consulate-General of the
    Republic of Singapore
14th Floor Osaka Kokusai Building
30 Azuchi-cho 2-Chome
Higashi–Ku
Osaka City
Japan
Telephone: 06–261–5131/3
Cable Address: SINGAWAKIL OSAKA
Telex: SPORECON J64596
Fax: 816–261–0338

Hong Kong
c/o Singapore Commission in Hong Kong
17th Floor, United Centre
95 Queensway
Hong Kong
Telephone: 5–292131
Cable Address: SINGAWAKIL HONG KONG
Telex: 86630 ETBHYK HX
Fax: 852–5–8610048

Melbourne
2 Peacock St.
Brighton 3186
Melbourne, Victoria
Australia
Telephone: 5929416
Cable Address: HARTOG MELBOURNE
Telex: HART AA 33859
Fax: 61–3–5436603

THE SINGAPORE TRADE DEVELOPMENT BOARD

HEAD OFFICE

1 Maritime Square
#03–01 World Trade Centre
Telok Blangah Rd.
Singapore 0409
Telephone: 2719388
Telex: TRADEV RS 28617/28170
Cable: SINTRADEV
Fax: 2740770

REGIONAL OFFICES

NORTH AMERICA

Los Angeles
Singapore Trade Development Board
Los Angeles World Trade Centre
350 South Figueroa St., Suite 272
Los Angeles, California 90071
Telephone: (213) 617–7358/9
Telex: 4720209 TDB LA
Fax: 005–1–818–241–1721

New York
Singapore Trade Development Board
745 Fifth Avenue, Suite 1601
New York, New York 10022
Telephone: (212) 421–2207
Telex: 421848 TDB NY
Cable Address: SINGAWAKIL NEW YORK

Washington DC
Embassy of the Republic of Singapore
1824 R St., NW
Washington DC 20009–1691
Telephone: (202) 667–7555
Telex: 440024 SINGEMB
Cable Address: SINGAWAKIL WASHINGTON

cont...

TRADE DEVELOPMENT BOARD OFFICES *(cont.)*

EUROPE

Frankfurt
Singapore Trade Development Board
Goethestrasse 5
6000 Frankfurt am Main 1
Germany
Telephone: (069) 281743
Telex: (041)4189605 STCF D
Fax: (069) 285039

Duesseldorf
Singapore Trade Development Board
Kaiserstrasse 42
D-4000 Duesseldorf 30
Postfach 320526
Germany
Telephone: 0211–499–261/5
Telex: 08 584 738 NOLD

London
Singapore Trade Development Board
5 Chesham St.
London SW 1
England
Telephone: (01) 2459707
Telex: 921177 STDBLG

Geneva
Permanent Mission of Singapore
  to the United Nations—
Geneva
6 Bis Rue Antoine-Carteret
1202 Geneva
Switzerland
Telephone: (022) 447330; (022) 447339
Telex: 289067 SINGH CH
Cable Address: SINGAWAKIL GENEVA

cont...

TRADE DEVELOPMENT BOARD OFFICES *(cont.)*

Rome
Singapore Trade Development Board
Via Barberini 11
00187 Rome
Italy
Telephone: 464846
Telex: RS 21241 SIASIN RS 21143 SINSAP

MIDDLE EAST AND AUSTRALASIA

Jeddah
Consulate of the Republic of Singapore
Room 535, 5th Floor
Corniche Commercial Center
PO Box 18294
Jeddah 21415
Kingdom of Saudi Arabia
Telephone: 6435677, 6437267
Telex: 605794 TDBJED SJ

Dubai
Singapore Trade Development Board
Pearl Building
Suite 604, 6th Floor
Bin Yas St., Diera
Box 1385
Dubai
United Arab Emirates
Telephone: 215746
Telex: 46967 STCDX EM

Beijing
Office of the Singapore Commercial Representative
Beijing
4 Liangmahe Rd. South
Sanlitun, Beijing
People's Republic of China
Telephone: 52-3926; 52-3143
Telex: 22578 SINBJ CN
Cable Address: SINGAWAKIL BEIJING

cont...

TRADE DEVELOPMENT BOARD OFFICES *(cont.)*

Shanghai
Office of the Singapore Commercial Representative
Shanghai Branch
400 Walumuqi Rd. Central
Shanghai
People's Republic of China
Telephone: 370776
Telex: 33540 SINSH CN

Tokyo
Singapore Trade Development Board
12–3 Roppongi 5-Chome
Minato-Ku, Tokyo 106
Japan
Telephone: (03) 584–6032
Telex: J26354 TDBTYO
Cable Address: SINGAWAKIL TOKYO

Seoul
Singapore Trade Development Board
8th Floor, Kyobo Building
#1–1 Chong-Ro 1 Ka,
Chongro–Ku
Seoul, 110
Republic of Korea
Telephone: 3133441/5
Telex: K26485 INTBANK

Brunei Darussalam
Singapore Trade Development Board
Singapore High Commission
5th Floor, RBA Plaza
Jalan Sultan
PO Box 2159
Bandar Seri Begawan
Negara Brunei Darussalam
Telephone: (02) 27583–5
Telex: 2385 SINHC BU
Fax: 005–673–2–27583

cont...

TRADE DEVELOPMENT BOARD OFFICES *(cont.)*

Jakarta
Singapore Trade Development Board
23 Jalan Proklamasi
Jakarta, Indonesia
Telephone: (21) 344727; (21) 348761
Telex: 44447 SINGA IA
Cable Address: SINGAWAKIL JAKARTA

Bombay
Singapore Trade Development Board
406 Maker Chamber V
221 Nariman Point
Bombay 400–021
India
Telephone: 232478
Telex: 114925 GKAY IN

Sydney
Singapore Trade Development Board
Suite 3, 1st Floor
Gold Fields House
1 Alfred St.
Sydney Cove NSW 2000
Australia
Telephone: (02)2337015
Telex: AA 71191 NOLAUST

Singapore Institute of Standards and Industrial Research (SISIR). Services provided by SISIR relate primarily to technical assistance and quality improvement. A detailed description of SISIR can be found in the SISIR Act of 1973. Its main functions include standardization and quality assurance, industrial services, research and development, technical information and technology dissemination, and weights and measures.

Small Enterprise Bureau (SEB). SEB assists small and medium-sized local businesses by providing financial assistance and promoting management improvement, technological upgrading, and business development. (Inquiries to SEB should be addressed to the Economic Development Board.)

SELECTED FOREIGN DIPLOMATIC OR COMMERCIAL MISSIONS IN SINGAPORE

Australian High Commission ◼ 25 Napier Rd., Singapore 1025; Telephone 737-9311; Telex RS 21238 AUSTCOM

Belgian Embassy ◼ 09-24 International Plaza; Telehone 220-7677

Brazilian Embassy ◼ Tong Building, 302 Orchard Rd. 15-03/04, Singapore 0923; Telephone 734-3435

Brunei High Commission ◼ 7A Tanglin Hill, Singapore 1024; Telephone 474-3393

Burmese Embassy ◼ 15 St. Martin's Dr.; Telephone 235-8763; Fax 235-5963

Canadian High Commission ◼ 14th and 15th Story, IBM Tower, 80 Anson Rd., 14-00, Singapore 0207; Telephone 225-6363; Fax 225-2450; Telex RS 21277

Danish Embassy ◼ 13-01/02 United Sq.; Telephone 250-3383/8991; Fax 253-3764

French Embassy ◼ 5 Gallop Rd.; Telephone 466-4866

German Embassy ◼ 545 Orchard Rd., 14-01 Far East Shopping Centre; Mailing address Tanglin P.O. Box 94, Singapore 9124; Telephone 737-1355; Fax 737-2653; Telex RS 21312 AASPUR

Hong Kong ◼ Contact the United Kingdom High Commission

Indian High Commission ◼ 31 Grange Rd.; Telephone 737-6777; Fax 732-6909

Indonesian Embassy ◼ 7 Chatsworth Rd., Singapore 1024; Telephone 737-7422

Italian Embassy ◼ 101 Thomson Rd., 27-02; Telephone 250-6492

Japanese Embassy ◼ 16 Nassim Rd.; Telephone 735-8855

Korean Embassy ◼ 101 Thomson Rd., 10-03; Telephone 256-1188

Malaysian High Commission ◼ 301 Jervois Rd.; Telephone 235-0111; Fax 733-6135

cont...

FOREIGN DIPLOMATIC OR COMMERCIAL MISSIONS *(cont.)*

Mexican Honorary Consulate ▣ 50 Raffles Pl. 10–06; Telephone 224–1355

Netherlands Embassy ▣ 13–01 Liat Towers; Telephone 737–1155/4193

New Zealand High Commission ▣ 13 Nassim Rd., Singapore 1025; Telephone 235–9966; Fax 733–9924; Telex RS 21244

Norwegian Embassy ▣ 16 Raffles Quay, 44–01 Hong Leong Building, Singapore 0104; Telephone 220–7122; Telex RS 21225 AMBANVR

Pakistani Embassy ▣ 20A Nassim Rd.; Telephone 737–6988

Philippine Embassy ▣ 20 Nassim Rd.; Telephone 737–3977

Portuguese Consulate ▣ 11/12 Nunes Building; Telephone 535–3278

Spanish Embassy ▣ Commercial Office, Thong Teck Building, 15 Scotts Rd. 05–08/09, Singapore 0922; Telephone 732–9788; Fax 732–9780; Telex RS 55047 OFCOM

Swedish Embassy ▣ 111 Somerset Rd. 05–08; Telephone 734–2771

Taiwan Visitors Association ▣ Singapore Office, 5 Shenton Way 14–07, UIC Building, Singapore 0106; Telephone 223–6546/7; Fax 225–4616; Telex TVA RS 35106

Thai Embassy ▣ 370 Orchard Rd.; Telephone 737–2644; Fax 235–2778

United Kingdom ▣ British High Commission, Tanglin Rd., Singapore 1024; Telephone 473–9333; Fax 475–2320; Telex RS 21218 UKREPSP

United States ▣ American Embassy, 30 Hill St., Singapore 0617; Telephone 338–0251; Fax 338–8472

OTHER BODIES

CHAMBERS OF COMMERCE AND BUSINESS COUNCILS

Companies and individuals of many foreign countries resident in Singapore maintain chambers of commerce, and there are also various other business-related private organizations.

The Singapore Convention Bureau (SCB) assists officials in planning and staging conventions and exhibitions in Singapore. It is a nonprofit organization, and a Convention Facilities Guide, Convention Calendar, and Newsletter are all available through the bureau. Services provided by SCB include: preparation of cost guidelines, provision of films and other audiovisual equipment, and coordination of site-inspection visits for organizers. The SCB is a division of the Singapore Tourist Board. Information on conference facilities and product fairs may be addressed to STPB and the Trade Development Board.

THE SINGAPORE CONVENTION BUREAU

HEAD OFFICE

Singapore Convention Bureau, Singapore Tourist Promotion Board (STPB), Raffles City Tower #36-04, 250 North Bridge Rd., Singapore 0617, Telephone 339-6633; Fax 339-9423; Telex STBSIN RS 33375; Cable TOURISPROM SINGAPORE; Open Mondays-Fridays: 8:30 AM-5:00 PM, Saturdays: 8:30 AM-1:00 PM, closed Sundays and public holidays.

REGIONAL OFFICES

Australia

Mr. Roney Tan, Regional Director, Singapore Tourist Promotion Board, 16th Floor, Westpac Plaza, 60 Margaret St., Sydney, NSW 2000; Telephone (61) (2) 241-3771/2; Fax (61) (2) 232-3658; Telex STBSYD AA 127775; Cable TOURISPROM SYDNEY

Miss Jenny Kramer, Singapore Tourist Promotion Board, c/o Forum Organisation, 55 Saint George's Terrace, Perth, WA 6001; Telephone (61) (9) 325-8033; Fax (61) (9)221-3135; Telex AA 92110

France

Mr. Richard Ng, Regional Director, L'Office National du Tourisme de Singapour, Centre d'Affaires Le Louvre, 2 Place du Palais-Royal, 75044 Paris Cedex 01; Telephone (33) (1 or 6) 429-71616; Fax (33) (1 or 6) 4297-1617; Telex SINGPAR 213593F; Cable TOURISPROM PARIS

cont...

THE SINGAPORE CONVENTION BUREAU *(cont.)*

Germany

Mr. Christopher Khoo, Assistant Regional Manager, Fremden-verkehrsburo von Singapur, Poststrasse 2–4, D–6000–Frankfurt Main; Telephone (49) (69) 2314–5657; Fax (49) (69) 233–924; Telex STBF D4189742; Cable TOURISPROM FRANKFURT

Hong Kong

Mr. Loi Hai Poh, General Manager (North Asia), Singapore Tourist Promotion Board, Suite 1402, Century Square, 1–13 D'Aguilar St., Central; Telephone (852) 5–224–052/3; Fax (852) (5) 810–6694; Telex 86630 ETBHK HX; Cable TOURISPROM HONG KONG

Japan

Mr. Isao Takada, Regional Director, Singapore Tourist Promotion Board, 1st Floor, Yamato Seimei Building, 1 Chrome, 1–7 Uchisaiwai-cho, Chiyoda-ku, Tokyo 100; Telephone (81) (3) 593–3388; Fax (81) (3) 591–1480; Telex STBTYO J25591, Cable TOURISPROM TOKYO

New Zealand

Mr. Rodney Walshe, Singapore Tourist Promotion Board, c/o Walshes World, 2nd Floor, Dingwall Building, 87 Queen St., P.O. Box 279, Auckland 1; Telephone (64) (9) 793–708; Telex WAL-WOR NZ 21437

Taiwan

Mr. Lee Chee Meng, General Manager (Taiwan/Korea), Singapore Tourist Promotion Board, 9th Floor, TFIT Tower, 85 Jenai Rd., Section 4, Taipei; Telephone (886) (2) 721–0664; Fax (886) (2) 781–7648; Telex 24974 STPBTPE; Cable TOURISPROM TAIPEI

United Kingdom

Mr. David Lee, Regional Director, Singapore Tourist Promotion Board, 1st Floor, Carrington House, 126–130 Regent St. London W1R 5FE; Telephone (71) 437–0033; Fax (71) 734–2191; Telex STBLON G 893491; Cable TOURISPROM LONDON

cont...

THE SINGAPORE CONVENTION BUREAU *(cont.)*

United States
Mr. Koh Kay Yew, Senior Vice-President (Americas), Singapore Tourist Promotion Board, Suite 510, 8484 Wilshire Blvd., Beverly Hills, CA 90211; Telephone (1) (213) 852–1901; Fax (1) (213) 852–0129; Telex SING UR 278141

Mr. Dean Victorson, Regional Manager (Central U.S.A.), Suite 818, 333 North Michigan Ave., Chicago, IL 60601; Telephone (1) (312) 704–4200

CULTURAL, SOCIAL, AND SERVICE CLUBS

Various associations in Singapore cater to the needs of foreign residents and people with special interests. International service organizations such as Rotary and the Lions are also represented.

Alliance Française, 4 Draycott Park...................737–8422
American Association, 60 King's Rd................468–6157/8
Australian and New Zealand Association,
    25 Napier Rd.....................................737–9311
British Association of Singapore,
    450/452 Alexandra Rd..........................473–7888
China Society, 190 Keng Lee Rd............256–6310/256–4774
Deutsche Haus, 12 First Ave........................466–3156
Japanese Association of Singapore, 27 Camden Rd.....468–0066
Law Society of Singapore, 1 Colombo Court #307–18.338–3165
Lion's Club of Singapore,
    101 Upper Cross St. #05–40......................535–9022
Masonic Club, Freemasons' Hall, Coleman St.........336–0052
Metropolitan YMCA of Singapore, 70 Palmer Rd......222–4666
Photographic Society of Singapore,
    6A Lorong 7, Geylang...........................743–4835
Rotary Club of Singapore, Mandarin Hotel,
#03–54 Orchard Rd................................737–2504
Singapore Art Society,
    20 Jalan Sedap, Seaview Housing Estate.............344–7791
Singapore Cine Club, 42 Branksome Rd...............344–1348
Singapore Indian Fine Arts Society, 21 Balestier Rd.....252–9618
Singapore Medical Association,
Singapore General Hospital,
    Outram Rd., Houseman's Quarters..................223–1264
Singapore Musical Society, 40 Hemsley Ave...........288–8691
Swiss Club, 36 Swiss Club Rd.............466-3270/466–3233
Toastmasters Club, 38A Hong Kong St................532–2791
YMCA, 6 Fort Canning Rd................336–3150/336–1212

USEFUL TELEPHONE NUMBERS

AA Road Service (24 Hours)........................748–9911

Ambulance.......................................995

American Embassy................................338–0251

Automobile Association of Singapore................737–2444

British High Commission..........................473–9333

Bus Service......................................287–2722

Complaints—Singapore Tourist Promotion Board.......235–6611

Flight Information................................542–5680

Immigration......................................337–4031

International Calls................................104

Long Distance Calls to Malaysia...................109

Police..999

Postal Service...................................533–0234

Railway Administration...........................222–5165

Singapore Tourist Promotion Board.................235–6611

Stolen or Lost Credit Cards

    American Express.............................737–8188

    Diners Club..................................294–4222

    Visa and MasterCard..........................532–3988

Taxi (24 Hours)........................452–5555/250–0700

Time...1711

Weather.......................................542–7788

XI Touring Outside of Singapore

TO MALAYSIA

BUSES

To Butterworth: Departs Lavender St. Terminus 6:30 PM daily. Fare S$30. Journey takes 14 hours, with stops at Muar and Ipoh.

To Johore Bahru: from Banson St. Terminus. Departs every 10 minutes daily. Fare S$1.50.
The No. 170 bus from Queen St. or Bukit Timah Rd. departs every 15 minutes daily. Fare 80 cents.

To Kuala Lumpur: Departs Lavender St. Terminus at 9:00 AM and 9:00 PM daily. Fare S$17 (air-conditioned). Journey takes 7–8 hours, with a stop at Muar.

To Kuantan: Departs Lavender St. Terminus at 9:00 AM, 10:00 AM, and 10:00 PM daily. Fare S$16.00 (air-conditioned). Journey takes 7–8 hours, with a stop at Mersing.

To Malacca: Departs Lavender St. Terminus at 8:00 AM, 9:00 AM, 11:00 AM, 1:00 PM, 2:00 PM, and 3:00 PM daily. Fare S$11.00 (air-conditioned). Journey takes 5 hours, with a stop at Ayer Hitam.

To Mersing: Departs Lavender St. Terminus at 9:00 AM, 10:00 AM, and 10:00 PM daily. Fare S$11.00 (air-conditioned). Journey takes 3–4 hours.

To Penang: Departs Lavender St. Terminus at 6:30 PM daily. Fare S$31. Journey takes 14 hours, with stops at Muar and Ipoh.

TRAINS

To Johore Bahru: Departs daily at 7:00 AM, 7:45 AM, 8:30 AM, 3:00 PM, 3:20 PM, 8:30 PM, and 10:00 PM. Leaves Johore Bahru daily at

5:15 AM, 6:00 AM, 12:34 PM, 1:23 PM, 5:05 PM, 7:32 PM, and 8:40 PM. One-way fare S$1.00 (3rd class); S$1.60 (2nd class) for adults; S$.50 (3rd class); S$.80 (2nd class) for children.

To Kuala Lumpur and Butterworth: Express train ride is 7 hours to Kuala Lumpur, 13 hours to Butterworth. Daily to Kuala Lumpur departs at 7:40 AM and 3:00 PM. Daily to Kuala Lumpur and Butterworth departs at 7:00 AM, stops at Kuala Lumpur and departs again at 1:50 PM (arrives in Butterworth at 8:00 PM). Fare to Kuala Lumpur S$28; to Butterworth S$50. For more information, call the Railway Station on Keppel Rd. at 222-1291.

AIR SHUTTLE SERVICE

Air service to Kuala Lumpur is available from Singapore Airlines and Malaysian Airline System on daily 40–minute shuttles between Singapore and Kuala Lumpur. For schedules and fares, contact SIA (telephone 545–6666) or MAS (telephone 336–6777).

TOURS

There are a wide variety of tours to Malaysia, ranging from four-hour tours to one-week tours. You can make arrangements through a travel agent or at booking desks located in most of the major hotels. Passports are required even for a short trip. Citizens of Albania, Cuba, Israel, North Korea, People's Republic of China, South Africa, and the Socialist Republic of Vietnam are not permitted to enter Malaysia.

DAY TOURS

Plantation Tour. This six-hour tour includes pineapple, coconut, and oil plantations, the Abu Bakrak Mosque, the estate of Ulu Tiram, and a Malaysian-style buffet lunch. Tour begins at 9:00 AM on Wednesday only. Rates S$58 adult, S$29 child. Tour Operator: Tour East.

Kekup Tour (to Johore-Kekup). This eight-hour tour includes stops at rubber, oil, cocoa, coffee, pineapple, and palm plantations, lunch in Kekup, and an optional fishing boat ride to the Kelongs. Tour begins at 8:00 AM on Monday, Wednesday, Friday, and Sunday. Rates S$59 adults, S$29 children. Operators: Tour East, RMG, Siakson, Singapore Sightseeing.

3 TO 9–DAY TOURS

Pulau Tioman Tour. This daily three-day tour to the island of Tioman includes accommodations in a first-class hotel, a tour of a village, swimming, skiing, fishing, and scuba diving. Rates S$360 per person. For more information, contact the Singapore Tour Development Corporation of Malaysia (Telephone: 532–6351).

West Malaysia Tour (by arrangement). Seven-day or shorter sightseeing trips are available to Malacca, Kuala Lumpur, Penang, Cameron Highlands, and Genting Highlands. Rates S$315 per person.

Round Malaysia Tour. This nine-day tour begins in Singapore and stops at Malacca, Kuala Lumpur, Cameron Highlands, Penang, Kota Bahru, Tanjong Jara, and Kuantan, before returning to Singapore. Rates (with twin accommodation) S$1,495. Operator: Tour East.

Exotic Islands and Beaches. A five-day tour from Singapore to Kuantan, a fishing village, Mersing, a ferry to Pulau Tioman and back to Singapore (by air). Rates (twin accommodations) S$817. Operator: Tour East.

There are many other tours to Malaysia which vary in itinerary, price, and activity.

TRAVEL TO CHINA

VISA

In general, it should not be difficult to obtain a visa to travel to China while in Singapore. Application can be made at the Chinese Embassy, and with advance notice, your travel agent can assist you with this procedure. In general, foreigners requesting visas to China must supply proof of a round-trip ticket and hotel reservations and must have valid passports.

CUSTOMS

On entry, visitors will fill out a customs declaration form. Visitors are permitted two bottles of spirits (only one bottle may be taken into

Hong Kong), 400 cigarettes, and 3,000 ft (914 m) of 8 mm movie film. Controversial magazines are not permitted.

CURRENCY

A "declaration of foreign currencies" must be filled out by all visitors upon entry. Visitors must list foreign currencies, traveler's checks, and Bank of China Foreign Exchange Certificates. There is no limit on the amount of foreign currencies, traveler's checks, and Foreign Exchange Certificates that visitors may bring into China. It is illegal to take Chinese currency out of China.

ELECTRICITY

The power supply is 200 volts. Three-prong (flat) plugs are commonly used. Battery-operated razors and hair-driers are recommended, as plugs vary from city to city.

PHOTOGRAPHY

Photographing military installations and photographing from an aircraft are not permitted.

WHAT TO WEAR

Casual dress is appropriate for most restaurants and sightseeing expeditions. Particularly during the very hot and humid summer months, jackets and ties are not required. Women should avoid revealing or flashy clothing. A sturdy pair of walking shoes is essential. Not all buildings are heated in the winter, nor are all buildings air-conditioned in the summer, so visitors may want to consider their tolerance for these situations before discarding extra sweaters or dismissing comfortable shorts from their suitcases.

TRANSPORTATION

Visitors can travel to China by air or by sea. The Singapore Tourist Promotion Board can assist you in making travel arrangements as can the tour operators listed in the sightseeing tour section.

ITINERARIES

Below are some of the itineraries available through Santa Tours and Travel Pte., Ltd.

Five- to Seven-Day Tours. Beijing, Guangzhou, Guilin, Hong Kong; Beijing, Xi'an, Hong Kong; or Beijing, Shanghai, Suzhou, Hangzhou, out via Japan or Hong Kong.

Scenic Harmony Tour (9 days). Shanghai, Suzhou, Wuxi, Nanjing, Beijing, Singapore.

Grandiose China Tour (10 days). Beijing, Xi'an, Shanghai, Guangzhou, Hong Kong, Singapore.

Treasures of China Tour (15 days). Beijing, Xi'an, Shanghai, Suzhou, Hangzhou, Guilin, Guangzhou, Hong Kong, Singapore.

Yangtze River Fantasy Tour (14 days). Beijing, Xi'an, Chongqing, Yichang, Yangtze River cruise, Wuhan, Guangzhou, Hong Kong, Singapore.

Cradle of Civilization Tour (15 days). Beijing, Zhenghou, Kaifeng, Luoyang, Xi'an, Chengdu, Kunming, Guangzhou, Hong Kong, Singapore.

TO OTHER COUNTRIES

INDONESIA

Tours to Indonesia include visiting Jakarta, the capital of the republic, botanic gardens and plantations in such places as Bogor and Puncak, and sightseeing on the islands of Bali and Sumatra.

For tour information contact the Indonesia Tourist Promotion Board at 534–2837.

THAILAND

Tours to Thailand include beach resorts: Pattaya, Koh Samui, Phuket–Hill country, Chiang Mai, Chiang Mai and ancient cities, Sukhothai, Sri Satchanalai.

Contact the Tourism Authority of Thailand (in Singapore) at 235–7901.

PHILIPPINES

For tours to Manila, Pagsanjan Waterfall, and Baguio Resort, contact the Philippine Ministry of Tourism (in Singapore) at 235–2184.

HONG KONG

Tours to Hong Kong include Island City, Lantau Island, Kowloon, Sung Dynasty Village, and Ocean Park.

For more information contact Santa Tours Pte., Ltd.

BRUNEI

Tours to Brunei include Banda Seri, Begawan, Kampong Ayer (Water Village), Sultan Omar Ali Saifuddin Mosque, Brunei Museum, and Churchill Memorial Gallery. For more information contact the Brunei Mission.

XII Singapore Reading List

ARTICLES

Debes, Cheryl. "Will Lee's Tight Rein Slow Singapore's Speedy Pace?" *Business Week* (May 30, 1988).

Hills, Ann. "Singapore's Token Conservation." *Cross Current* (March 1987).

Marshall, Diane P. "Singapore: Shop Place of the World." *Travel Holiday* 168 (August 1987).

Peters, Ann. "The Government as Matchmaker." *Asia Magazine* (February 1987).

BOOKS

Andrews, Ron, and Freestone, Colin. *A Geography of Indonesia, Malaysia, Singapore.* London: George Philip and O'Neil, 1970.

Bloodworth, Dennis. *An Eye for the Dragon: Southeast Asia Observed, 1954–1970.* London: Secker and Warburg, 1970.

Buckley, Charles Burton. *An Anecdotal History of Old Times in Singapore 1819–1867.* Frazer and Neave, Limited, 1902.

Caldwell, Christopher, ed. *Fodor's Singapore 1988.* New York: Fodor's Travel Publications, Inc., 1987.

Chatfield, G. A. *The Religions and Festivals of Singapore.* Singapore: D. Moore for Eastern Universities Press, 1962.

Chia, Felix. *The Babas.* Singapore: Times Books International, 1980.

Collins, Maurice. *Raffles.* New York: Day, 1968.

Comber, Leon. *Chinese Temples in Singapore*. Singapore: Eastern Universities Press, 1958.

Coopers and Lybrand. *Singapore: A Guide for Businessmen and Investors*. Singapore: Coopers and Lybrand, 1986.

Craig, Jo Ann. *Culture Shock: Singapore and Malaysia*. Singapore: Times Books International, 1979.

Doggett, Marjorie. *Characters of Light*. Singapore: Donald Moore, 1957.

Federal Publications. *The Straits Times Bilingual Collection*. Singapore: Federal Publications, 1979.

Guides and Annual Publishers Ltd. *Where to Eat in Singapore*. Singapore: Guides and Annual Publishers Pte. Ltd., 1985.

Hoe, Tan Han, ed. *Singapore 1988*. Singapore: Ministry of Communications and Information, 1988.

Hoefer, Hans Johannes, ed. *Singapore Insight Guide*. Singapore: APA Productions, 1987.

Hooi, James. *The Guide to Singapore Hawker Food*. Singapore: Hospitality Host, 1985.

Hutton, Wendy. *Singapore Food*. Sydney: Ure Smith, Paul Hamlyn Pte. Ltd., 1979.

Jones, Ann. *Antiques, Arts, and Crafts in Singapore*. Singapore: Times Books International, 1988.

Josey, Alex. *Lee Kuan Yew*. Singapore: Donald Moore Press, 1968.

Macaw. *A Bird's Eye View of Singapore*. Singapore: Times Books International, 1985.

Mailaret, Jean-Pierre. *Hinduism in Singapore: A Guide to the Hindu Temples of Singapore*. Singapore: Donald Moore for Asia Pacific Press, 1969.

Moore, Donald and Joanna. *The First 150 Years of Singapore*. Singapore: Donald Moore Press in association with the Singapore Inter national Chamber of Commerce, 1969.

Oey, Eric, et al. *Singapore Feasts*. Singapore: APA Productions, 1980.

Ooi, Jin-Bee, and Chiang, Hai Ding, eds. *Modern Singapore*. Singapore: University of Singapore, 1969.

Oxford University Press. *Organization and Leadership*. Singapore: Oxford University Press, 1971.

Pang, Cheng Lian. *Singapore's People's Action Party; Its History*.

Peat Marwick. *Investment in Singapore*. Singapore: Peat Marwick, 1986.

Singapore International Chamber of Commerce. *Investor's Guide to the Economic Climate of Singapore*. Singapore: Singapore International Chamber of Commerce, 1987.

Singapore Ministry of Culture. *Singapore Street Directory*. Singapore: Ministry of Culture, 1984.

Singapore National Museum. *National Monuments of Singapore*. Singapore National Museum, 1982.

Siong, Ng Poey, ed. *Singapore Facts and Pictures*. Singapore: Ministry of Communications and Information, 1988.

Wilson, Dick. *East Meets West: Singapore*. Singapore: Times Printers Sendirian Berhad, 1971.

Wong, C. S. *A Cycle of Chinese Festivals*. Singapore: Malaysia Publishing House Ltd., 1967.

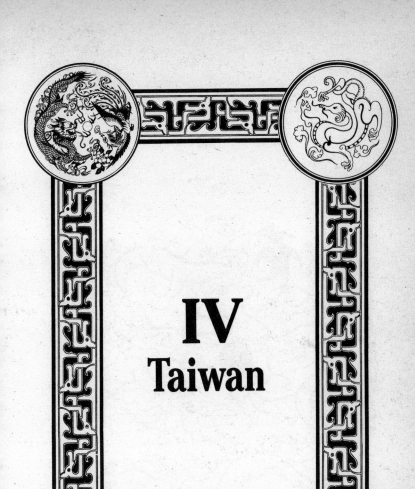

IV
Taiwan

I Taiwan at a Glance

GEOGRAPHY

THE island of Taiwan is located approximately 100 mi (161 km) from the southeastern coast of the Chinese mainland. It is shaped roughly like a leaf and is bisected by the Tropic of Cancer. The island is 245 mi (394 km) long, north to south, and 89.5 mi (144 km) wide at the broadest parts.

The Central Mountain Range runs the length of the island and has numerous peaks greater than 9,800 ft (3,000 m) in height, with Jade Mountain (Yushan) at 12,966 ft (3,952 m) the highest in northeastern Asia. This mountain range occupies approximately two-thirds of the land mass, forcing the population, which numbers some 20 million, to live in a space about one-third the size of the Netherlands. Taiwan is thus one of the most densely populated places in the world.

The island enjoys an annual rainfall greater than 1,500 mm, and has two growing seasons in the north and three in the south. It is one of Asia's leading agricultural producers and, increasingly, a center for seed production.

Besides the main island, Taiwan includes a group of 64 islands known as Penghu or the Pescadores, and 21 other islands located close by.

HISTORY

THE first settlers of Taiwan are thought to have been members of the Miao tribe of southern China. The island was noted in Chinese history prior to the Han Dynasty (206 BC– AD 220), and in 239 AD the emperor was said to have sent a 10,000-man expeditionary force in an attempt to open up the island. Though Chinese settlers may have begun arriving as early as the 12th century, the prohibition of emigration under the Ming Dynasty (1368–1644) slowed the process. Han Chinese are thought to have begun to settle Taiwan in substantial numbers during the 15th century.

The Cross-Island Highway, central Taiwan

Taiwan was seen by the Portuguese in 1517—it was they who named it *Ilha Formosa* ("Beautiful Island"), hence its former name *Formosa*—and was invaded by the Dutch in 1624 and by the Spanish in 1626. The Spanish, however, were driven out by the Dutch, who stayed until 1661. In that year the leader of the Ming resistance to the Manchus, Cheng Ch'eng-kung (Koxinga) defeated and drove out the Dutch. In 1683, the Manchus incorporated the island into Fukien province. Not to be left out, the French, as a result of a disagreement with China, occupied the Pescadores and the northern part of Taiwan proper for a brief three-month period in 1894.

Following the Japanese victory in the Sino-Japanese War, the Treaty of Shimonoseki ceded Taiwan and the Pescadores to Japan in 1895. From that date until the end of World War II in 1945, Taiwan remained under Japanese control. This occupation was to have a dramatic effect on the island, one that is still in evidence today.

In 1949, after the Nationalist Chinese were defeated by the Communists on the mainland of China, Chiang Kai-shek's army retreated to Taiwan and established a provisional capital of the Republic of China in Taipei. Chiang Kai-shek ruled Taiwan as president until his death in 1975, after which his eldest son, Chiang Ching-kuo, took over as president, ruling until his death on January 13, 1988. With the passing of Chiang Ching-kuo, the last of the Chinese de facto ruling dynasties came to an end, and Taiwan is now led by Chiang's vice president, Lee Tung-hui, a native Taiwanese.

POLITICS AND GOVERNMENT

TAIWAN has a democratic form of government based on Dr. Sun Yat-sen's "Three Principles of the People," a document whose underlying concepts resemble Abraham Lincoln's "of the people, by the people, and for the people." The government is composed of five departments (*Yuan*): Executive, Legislative, Judicial, Examination, and Control. It is currently controlled by the ruling Nationalist Party, the Kuomintang (KMT). The process leading to full democratization has been slow, owing to fears of invasion by Communists from the mainland. However, President Chiang Ching-kuo in the last two years of his life added impetus to the democratization movement by bringing more native Taiwanese into the government, abolishing the martial law that had been in effect since the Nationalists arrived, ending restrictions on the press, and allowing, at least unofficially, the formation of other political parties.

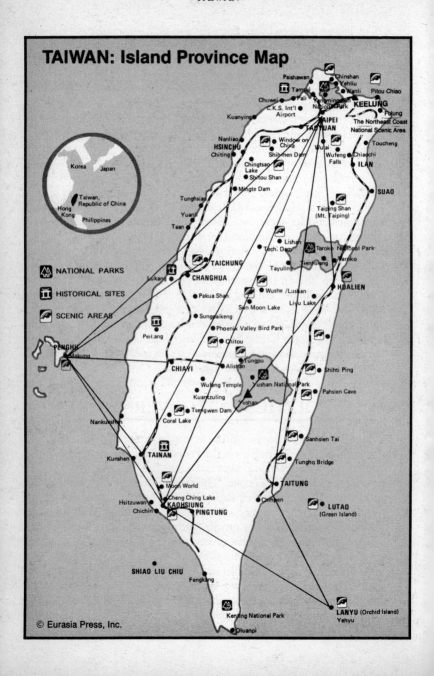

TAIWAN: Island Province Map

Paishawan
Chinshan
Yehliu
Wanli
Pitou Chiao
Tamsui
Chuwei
Pali
Yangmingshan
National Park
KEELUNG
C.K.S. Int'l
Airport
Fulung
Kuanying
The Northeast Coast
National Scenic Area
TAIPEI
TAOYUAN
Nanliao
Window on
China
Toucheng
HSINCHU
Chiting
Shihmen Dam
Wufeng
Falls
Chiaochi
Chingtsao
Lake
Wutai
ILAN
Shitou Shan
Mingte Dam
SUAO
Tunghsiao
Taiping Shan
(Mt. Taiping)
Yuanli
Taan
Lishan
Tech: Dam
Taroko National Park
TAICHUNG
Tayuling
Tienhsiang
Taroko
Lukang
CHANGHUA
Pakua Shan
Wushe /Lushan
HUALIEN
Sun Moon Lake
Liyu Lake
Sunghaikeng
Phoenix Valley Bird Park
Peilang
Chitou
Tungpu
PENGHU
Makung
CHIAYI
Alishan
Shihti Ping
Wufeng Temple
Pahsien Cave
Kuantzuling
Yushan National Park
Coral Lake
Tsengwen Dam
Yushan
Nankunshen
Sanhsien Tai
Tungho Bridge
Kunshen
TAINAN
Moon World
TAITUNG
Cheng Ching Lake
Hsitzuwan
Chimen
LUTAO
KAOHSIUNG
(Green Island)
Chichin
PINGTUNG

NATIONAL PARKS

HISTORICAL SITES

SCENIC AREAS

SHIAO LIU CHIU
Fengkang

LANYU (Orchid Island)
Yehyu

© Eurasia Press, Inc.

Kenting National Park
Oluanpi

Korea
Japan
Taiwan,
Republic of China
Hong
Kong
Philippines

Under President Lee, political reforms are continuing apace, and efforts are being made to retire octogenarian legislators who were elected in mainland China and have been frozen in office since arriving in Taiwan. This move will make room for more indigenous Taiwanese to exercise greater control of the affairs of their country through participation in the law-making body, the Legislative Yuan.

In the past, the only political party of any substance was the KMT, and elections were virtually no more than a show for the rest of the world. Only one candidate was run and the people responsible for electing him were from the same party. All that changed with the implementation of the National Security Law of July 15, 1987. This measure allowed the formation of new political parties and gave the people the right to assemble, petition the government, and demonstrate.

New political parties have come into existence and are beginning to attract many followers. The foremost of these parties is the Democratic Progressive Party (DPP). The DPP is composed mainly of Taiwanese and has had some luck winning seats in the Legislative Yuan. Enough luck apparently to have caused the KMT to consider hiring foreign advertising agencies like Saatchi & Saatchi to burnish its image for the elections at the end of 1989 and in early 1990.

The DPP and the other new parties, which have numbered as many as 14, represent a real threat to the power of the KMT. Some of them have gone so far as to call for the independence of Taiwan (the present government maintains the KMT position that Taiwan is a province of China and that the KMT is the lawful ruler of all of China). Discussion of this subject has been forbidden since the Nationalists arrived on the island: advocating independence is a treasonable offense, punishable by lengthy imprisonment.

ECONOMY

FROM an economic perspective, Taiwan can only be described as an economic miracle. In less than 50 years the island has been transformed from a predominantly agricultural society into one of the most productive countries in the world, ranking 13th in trading power and having a total foreign trade of US$110 billion in 1988. Taiwan holds the world's second largest foreign exchange reserves, amounting to US$74 billion.

Foreign investment by Taiwan citizens during the first 11 months of 1988 was officially put at US$200 million, with unofficial figures increasing that to US$500 million. This represents an increase of 115%

over the same period in 1987. Investments in neighboring Southeast Asian countries jumped 419% to more than US$50 million.

PEOPLE AND LANGUAGE

PEOPLE OF TAIWAN

Taiwan is peopled, apart from approximately 350,000 aborigines, by Chinese whose ancestors migrated from the mainland over the centuries, primarily from Fukien Province. With them came their customs, traditions, and religions. When Chiang Kai-shek's army landed, the island had already developed its own unique identity, and spoke Minanhua, the dialect of Fukien, most often called Taiwanese.

Religions in Taiwan came mainly from the mainland of China and include Buddhism—of Indian origin—and an indigenous combination of shamanism and Taoism. The main divinities worshipped are Kuan Yin, the Buddhist goddess of mercy; Kuang Kung, the Chinese god of war; and Matsu, the Taoist goddess of the sea. The Taiwanese pantheon is also replete with a wealth of gods representing everything from pestilence to agriculture.

Indigenous Chinese religious practices are probably the most widespread, and altars to different gods can be seen in many houses, businesses, and small temples. Buddhism claims the next most followers, with an abundance of temples dedicated to that originally Indian religion.

Freedom of worship has been a long-established practice in Taiwan, provided the religion does not forbid the taking up of arms to protect the country. There are a growing number of converts to Christianity (Mme Chiang Kai-shek was one). Islam is also present, but has only a few adherents.

Taiwan has been described as a citadel of Chinese culture and very much maintains the customs and traditions that have been handed down over the millennia of recorded Chinese history. The main force in the cultural traditions of the island is Confucianism, the thoughts of whose "master teacher" have had a profound effect on the philosophy of not only the Chinese people, but of the Koreans as well.

Confucianism demands virtually blind obedience and respect for parents and authorities, and sets out rules of conduct for daily living-rules that are inculcated into the young people of Taiwan at a very early age, and fostered throughout their formative and adolescent years.

The many traditions that, in addition to Confucianism, have been practiced for centuries by the Chinese have created a people that are very conservative and obedient, and at the same time unusually open and friendly, especially to travelers from abroad. The Chinese spirit of hospitality can best be expressed in the words of Confucius: "There is no greater pleasure than welcoming visitors who have come from afar." This type of thinking makes Taiwan a most appealing place to visit and insures that one leaves with pleasant memories of a friendly, warm people.

Chinese culture is everywhere in evidence in Taiwan. Shops that specialize in reproductions of Chinese artifacts stand shoulder-to-shoulder in the tourist areas, and the National Palace Museum in Taipei boasts the largest collection of Chinese artifacts to be found anywhere outside of the Chinese mainland. The Chiang Kai-shek and the Sun Yat-sen memorials are built along traditional Chinese lines, and the stores, temples, old houses, and restaurants leave no doubt that you are embedded in a Chinese environment. The people, although dressed for the most part in Western-style attire, maintain their love for and devotion to their heritage, as is evident in their mannerisms, conversation, and attitudes.

LANGUAGE

Under Chiang Kai-shek, the dialect of Peking, often called Mandarin, was decided on as the national language because it was the dialect of the capital on the mainland, and the government began taking steps to eradicate the local tongue. Teaching Taiwanese in the schools was forbidden, and all dealings, both business and governmental, had to be conducted in Mandarin. The government's measures, however, have met with little success, and the Taiwanese people (which make up almost 98% of the population) have continued to use Taiwanese in their homes, family businesses, and workplaces. Actually, about the only place where Mandarin is generally heard is in Taipei, the capital city. In the suburbs and especially in the central and southern parts of the island, the main language is Taiwanese. This doesn't mean, though, that people can't speak Mandarin, it simply means that they prefer to conduct their everyday affairs in their native dialect.

Travelers to Taiwan should be aware that the English-language ability of most people they are likely to meet outside of the major hotels and businesses is very low, if not nonexistent, and one should always take the precaution of carrying addresses written in Chinese—written

Chinese is the same, no matter what dialect is spoken—to insure that one arrives at one's chosen destination.

Unless you are very gifted at languages, attempting to speak Mandarin will probably cause more problems than it will solve. Like the other Chinese dialects, Mandarin is tonal, and words are differentiated by the rising, falling, or level tone that the speaker uses. Tones are difficult to master, and it takes much practice before one is able to use the language effectively. Even the Chinese themselves have trouble with the tones and often have to explain the word they are saying by using it in conjunction with another word or by using finger signs, as in the case of counting. The confusion that may arise through mispronunciation is often comical and can result in the speaker saying that he or she is late when what was really meant was that the person had eaten. The word for dumplings, *swei jiao*, if spoken with the wrong tones can mean "sleep" and may elicit howls of laughter from other diners in some restaurants.

The use of Mandarin phrase books when shopping or dining is sometimes helpful, as they usually include the written Chinese characters, which are standard for all dialects, and a person can simply point to the printed phrase if unable to say it. Most large businesses and stores employ people who can speak English, and there is usually someone on hand to help out if a customer gets really stuck.

II

Planning a Trip to Taiwan

TOURIST INFORMATION

INSPIRED by Confucius' saying, "There is no greater pleasure than welcoming visitors who have come from afar," Taiwan is hospitable to tourists. Although Taiwan has few diplomatic offices abroad, it compensates with a large number of trade and tourism offices, at which one can obtain information on places to see and things to do in Taiwan.

TAIWAN TOURISM REPRESENTATIVES ABROAD

HEAD OFFICE

The Tourism Bureau, 9F, 280 Chungsiao East Rd., Sec. 4 (P.O. Box 1490), Taipei; Telephone (02) 721–8541; Fax (02) 773–5487; Telex 26408 ROCTB

Travel Information Service Center, Sungshan Domestic Airport; Telephone (02) 712–1212, Ext. 471

The Tourist Information Hot Line; Telephone (02) 717–3737

FOREIGN OFFICES

Australia

Sydney Office, Far East Trading Co. Pty. Ltd., Suite 2409, Level 24, MLC Center, Martin Place, Sydney NSW 2000; Telephone 231–6942, 231–6973; Fax 233–7752; Telex AA 74625 FAETVA

---

cont...

TOURISM REPRESENTATIVES ABROAD, TAIWAN *(cont.)*

Germany

Asia Trade Center Tourism Bureau, Dreieichstrasse 59, 6000 Frankfurt am Main 70; Telephone (069) 610-743; Fax (069) 624-518; Telex 414460 ASIATD

Japan

Japan Office, Taiwan Visitors Association, A-9, 5F, Imperial Tower, Imperial Hotel, Uchisaiwai-cho 1-1-1, Chiyoda-ku, Tokyo 100; Telephone (03) 501-3591, 501-3592; Fax (03) 501-3586

Singapore

Singapore Office, Taiwan Visitors Association, 5 Shenton Way 14-07, UIC Building, Singapore 0106; Telephone 223-6546, 223-6547; Fax 225-4616; Telex TVA RS 35106

United States

Tourism Representative, Travel Section, Coordination Council for North American Affairs (CCNAA), 166 Geary St., Suite 1605, San Francisco, CA 94108; Telephone (415) 989-8677, 989-8694; Fax (415) 989-7242; Telex 9103722267 LIDD INC SFO

Tourism Representative, Travel Section, CCNAA, 333 North Michigan Ave., Suite 2329, Chicago, IL 60601; Telephone (312) 346-1037, 346-1038; Fax (312) 346-1037

Tourism Representative, Travel Section, CCNAA, 1 World Trade Center, Suite 7953, New York, NY 10048; Telephone (212) 466-0691/2; Fax (212) 432-6436

TAIWAN TRAVEL OPTIONS

FOREIGN visitors to Taiwan can arrive independently or as members of a group tour, which has been prearranged by international travel agencies and tour operators. Group travel, including packaged sightseeing, dining, and hotel arrangements, makes the most efficient use of Taiwan's travel facilities and of the tourist's time and money. Members of group tours generally arrive with the assurance of a hotel room, transportation, dining arrangements, and a bilingual sightseeing program.

In spite of the advantages of group tours, there are some travelers who, for a variety of reasons—time constraints, itinerary requirements, professional interests, or personal choice—prefer to travel independently. Although the costs may be higher, and additional time may be spent in advance planning, independent travel is a popular option in Taiwan. It offers many opportunities for exploration, discovery, and the enjoyment of personal contact with the Taiwanese people.

GROUP TOURS TO TAIWAN

Travelers seeking to visit Taiwan as tourists can purchase space on a tour through travel agents. It is not unusual for group tour participants to save over 50% of what they would have to pay were they to follow the same itinerary on their own. They are also spared all the logistical difficulties: hotel space is booked; sightseeing programs, intercity transfers, and even some meals are prearranged; guides and interpreters are provided. Groups usually consist of 10 to 50 people and follow a fixed itinerary that includes three to six cities; many include stopovers in Tokyo, Hong Kong, or other Asian cities. The costs of tours vary considerably; travelers should be alert to differences in the places of interest included, the quality of the lodgings, and the number of meals provided. Tours may also vary in the trans-Pacific airlines and routes used.

Standard itineraries generally provide for a three-night stay in Taiwan. Usually most of the tour groups have their members stay in hotels in Taipei and visit well-known city sights. In the evenings most tour groups attend a Mongolian Barbecue.

SAMPLE ITINERARIES

Day 1: Depart the U.S., cross the International Date Line
Day 2: Arrive in Tokyo
Days 2–5: Explore Japan
Day 6: Depart Japan, fly to Taipei
Days 6–9: Stay in Taipei
Day 9: Leave Taipei, fly to Hong Kong
Days 9–12: Stay in Hong Kong
Day 12: Depart Hong Kong for return flight back to the U.S.

Day 1: Depart the U.S., cross the International Date Line
Day 2: Arrive in Tokyo
Days 2–5: Explore Tokyo
Day 6: Depart Tokyo, fly to Taipei
Days 6–8: Stay in Taipei
Day 8: Depart Taipei, fly to Bangkok
Days 8–11: Stay in Bangkok
Day 11: Depart Bangkok, fly to Singapore
Days 11–13: Stay in Singapore
Day 13: Depart Singapore, fly to Hong Kong
Days 13–16: Stay in Hong Kong
Day 16: Depart Hong Kong for return flight back to the U.S.

SPECIAL INTEREST TOURS

Some tour operators offer special interest tours, such as shopping tours or opera tours, to Taiwan. Generally these tours stop in Taiwan and other Pacific cities. If you are interested in such tours, it would be advisable to contact the Taiwan Tourist Bureau or your travel agent.

TOURING TAIWAN ON YOUR OWN

The individual visitor to Taiwan can, with prior research and planning, enjoy contemporary city life, see beautiful scenery and historic relics, engage in recreational activities, and pursue special interests. Hotels have been established near locations of special interest. Of course a visit to Taipei is a must for any first-time visitor to Taiwan, as Taipei offers a wealth of sightseeing and cultural attractions. Those who are interested in scenic beauty will want to visit Taichung, the island's third largest city, and perhaps spend at least one or two nights in that area. Southeast of Taichung is the beautiful resort of Sun Moon Lake, which is the favorite honeymoon retreat of the Taiwanese. Many interesting sights surround the lake, and a stay in this area for at least one or two nights is highly recommended. Those who are interested in aboriginal culture will want to visit Hualien, which is located on the east coast of Taiwan, in an area where some 80,000 aboriginals of the Ami and Atayal peoples live. A visit to Hualien will also provide access to the beautiful mountain road of Taroko Gorge, which is the second largest tourist attraction on the island. A stay of at least one or two nights is recommended. Tourists who are interested in visiting temples will want to include the island's second largest city, Kaohsiung, on their tour. A stay in Kaohsiung for at least one or two nights is suggested. Of course, longer stays at all of the foregoing locations are recommended, their actual length depending upon the length of the traveler's trip and the traveler's interests.

Visits to Peitou, Chiayi, Tainan, and the offshore islands of Penghu, Orchid Island, and Green Island are recommended if the traveler has additional time to spend in Taiwan. Those with a particular interest, profession, or specialty can arrange their tours so that part of their time in Taiwan is spent in meetings with professional counterparts and visiting institutions or other appropriate sites.

COSTS

TOUR operators, travel agencies, and airlines that sponsor tours to Taiwan provide listings of their trips for the upcoming year upon request; these include dates and points of departure, a detailed breakdown of itineraries, and prices. Care should be taken to determine the contents of the tour package and the tour policy regarding revision of air fares.

Group Land Costs. The cost of a group tour usually includes most land costs in Taiwan—hotel accommodations, some meals, tour escorts, and all land transportation within Taiwan. It is impossible to estimate the group tour land costs in Taiwan, because most tours to Taiwan include other Asian cities.

Single-Occupancy Supplements. Hotel accommodations are usually based upon a double-occupancy rate. However, hotels are able to provide single-occupancy rooms at a single supplement or surcharge rate. When making hotel reservations, it is important to specify whether the requested accommodations are for single or double occupancy.

Costs for Individual Travel. Individual tour itineraries are of three types: a deluxe package with hotel, all meals, private guide, and car, costing approximately $150 to $200 per person per day. The second individual tour itinerary includes hotel, some meals, and escorted group sightseeing. The third type of individual tour itinerary is an entirely independent one, with only hotel room costs included. As you can ascertain from the hotel guide section, the rates vary depending upon the hotel selection.

AIR FARES

FROM the United States, China Airline (the Republic of China's designated flag carrier) and Northwest Orient Airlines offer direct nonstop service to Taipei. However, when making your reservations, it is important to check that the flights that you are booking are nonstop. Delta Airlines, Korean Airlines, and United Airlines offer direct service (making at least one stop en route) to Taipei from the United States. The direct-service flights usually stop in Tokyo or in Seoul between the United States and Taipei.

Air fare rates vary depending upon the time of the year and day of the week of travel, and how far in advance the tickets are purchased. The least expensive time of the year to travel from the United States to Taipei is from January 1 to March 31. During that time of year, a round trip ticket from San Francisco or Los Angeles to Taipei and back could cost $935.00 plus departure tax, per person if travel takes place in the middle of the week. On the weekends, the air fare during that time period is increased to $1,045.00. The shoulder, or midseason, period runs from April 1 to May 31 and from September 1 to December 13. During that time period, midweek travel would cost $990.00 and weekend travel $1,100.00. Air fares increase during the high season, which runs from June 1 to August 31 and from December 14 to December 31. During that season, midweek air travel costs $1,100 and weekend, $1,210.00. It is important to remember that air fare rates can fluctuate, and though these are the economy rates currently in effect, these rates are subject to change.

WHEN TO GO

CLIMATE

The climate in Taiwan is subtropical, with temperatures ranging from 48° F (9° C) on the colder days of winter to 95° F (35° C) in the summer. The average temperature is 71° F (21.7° C) in the north and 75.3° F (24.1°C) in the south. Winters are short, lasting from December through February. Humidity is high all year round, and a common joke is that there are only two types of weather: hot and wet, and cold and wet.

FESTIVALS

The Chinese in Taiwan are perhaps the luckiest of all people when it comes to holidays, celebrating not only those of the West, but also traditional Chinese festivals.

The year begins with the Western New Year on January 1, which in Taiwan is also kept as a two-day holiday celebrating the founding of the Republic of China. The next national holiday is Youth Day on March 29. April 5 commemorates the passing away of Chiang Kai-shek and is also considered "Tomb Sweeping Day," the time when all households go to their families' graves to pray, offer sacrifices, and generally spruce them up. September 28 is celebrated as the birthday of Confucius and also as Teachers' Day.

October is considered a month of festivals, with October 10, "Double Ten Day"—that is, the tenth day of the tenth month, when the revolution against the Ch'ing Dynasty, in 1911, began—celebrated as Taiwan's national day; October 25, Taiwan Retrocession Day, marking the official return of Taiwan to Chinese control after Japan's defeat in World War II; and October 31, the birthday of Chiang Kai-shek in 1887, observed as Veterans' Day. November 12 is the birthday of Dr. Sun Yat-sen (the father of the Republic of China); and on December 25, Constitution Day is celebrated. (It is interesting to note that Constitution Day just happens to fall on Christmas Day. Rumor has it that Chiang Kai-shek, a devout Christian, wanted the non-Christian Chinese to celebrate Christmas. He therefore waited until Christmas Day to sign the constitution, and so made that day a national holiday.)

Other public holidays that the Chinese on Taiwan observe include several traditional festivals whose dates, determined by the lunar calendar, fall on different days each year. Among them are the Chinese Lunar New Year, a three-day holiday falling on February 15 in 1991; Dragon Boat Festival on June 16 in 1991; and Mid-Autumn "Moon" Festival on September 22 in 1991.

Major Chinese festival days that are not public holidays include the birthday of Kuan Yin, the goddess of mercy; the festival of the god of medicine; the birthday of Matsu, goddess of the sea; the birthday of Kuang Kung, the god of war; the birthday of Cheng Huang, the city god; and the month of "ghosts," or spirits of the deceased.

The best time to be in Taiwan is probably during October and November, when the weather is pleasantly cool and all the cities and towns are decorated for the holidays. The spring months of March, April, and May are also a pleasant time to visit. One should be warned,

Dancers from aboriginal Ami tribe

however, that during October and the Chinese Lunar New Year period it is very difficult not only to get to Taiwan, but, once there, to find a place to stay. In addition, since the entire populace seems to be on the move back to their family homes, on-island transportation, always overcrowded, is jammed beyond belief, and a journey outside of Taipei can be a nightmarish experience.

WHAT TO TAKE—AND WHAT NOT TO TAKE

CLOTHING

Taiwan has very high humidity, and this should be taken into account when packing clothing for a trip. In the spring, summer, and autumn months (March–November), light clothing is advisable. Business travelers should bring light suits and—especially for the summer—short-sleeved shirts. In the winter, heavy sweaters, flannel shirts, and winter suits and jackets are recommended. It is also a good idea to bring a raincoat, as rain is common at any time of the year, especially during the typhoon season, which lasts from June through September.

MEDICINES, PERSONAL HYGIENE, AND GROOMING ITEMS

Taiwan is extremely Westernized, and travelers need anticipate no difficulty in obtaining any of the usual over-the-counter medications or hygiene and grooming products during their stay.

PROHIBITED ITEMS

Besides the usual list of contraband articles (narcotics and hallucinogens, counterfeit currency, obscene materials, real and toy arms, and the like), Taiwan specifically forbids the entry of foreign lottery tickets, any publication promoting communism, and articles produced in or otherwise originating from the mainland of China, the Soviet Union, North Korea, Cuba, and other Communist countries.

III

Getting to Taiwan

VISAS AND HEALTH CERTIFICATES

ALL visitors to Taiwan must have visas. Since there are many countries with which the Republic of China does not exchange diplomatic representatives, you may have to apply for a visa at one of the other offices that the ROC government maintains abroad.

TAIWAN GOVERNMENT REPRESENTATIVES ABROAD

Australia Far East Trading Co. PTY Ltd., D401 International House, World Trade Centre, Melbourne, Victoria 3005; Telephone (03) 223-3207

Belgium ▪ Far East Trade Service, Inc., 16th Floor, World Trade Center, 162 Boulevard Emile Jacqmain, Brussels 1210; Telephone (02) 218-5157/97

Brazil ▪ Centro Comercial de Extremo-Oriente, 2073 Avenida Paulista, Sao Paulo 01311; Telephone (55) (11) 285-6194/6988

Brunei ▪ Far East Trade and Cultural Centre, 5 Simpang 1006, Mile 7 Jalan Tutong, Negara Brunei Darussalam; Telephone (02) 61815

Canada ▪ Far East Trade Service Inc., Branch Office, Suite 3315, 2 Bloor Street East, Toronto, Ontario M4W 1AB; Telephone (416) 922-2412

Denmark ▪ Far East Trade Office, 1st Floor, Ny Ostergade 3, DK 1101, Copenhagen F

cont...

GOVERNMENT REPRESENTATIVES ABROAD, TAIWAN *(cont.)*

France ◙ A.S.P.E.C.T. 9 Avenue Matignon, Paris 75008; Telephone (1) 4299-1688

Germany ◙ Asia Trade Center Tourism Bureau, Dreieich-strasse, Frankfurt/Main 70; Telephone (069) 610-743, 615-534

Hong Kong ◙ Chung Hua Travel Service, 4th Floor, East Tower, No. 89 Bond Centre, Queensway; Telephone (5) 258-315/8

Indonesia ◙ Chinese Chamber of Commerce in Jakarta, 4 Jalan Banyumas, Jakarta; Telephone (21) 351-212/4

Italy ◙ Centro Commerciale per l'Estremo Oriente, 2 Via Errico Petrella, Milan 20124; Telephone (02) 285-3083/3790; or contact Embassy of the ROC to the Holy See, 7 Piazza delle Muse, Rome 00197; Telephone (06) 803-166/278

Japan ◙ Tokyo Office, Association of East Asian Relations, 8-7 Higashi-Azabu, 1-Chome, Minato-ku, Tokyo 106; Telephone (3) 583-2171/5

Malaysia ◙ Far East Trading and Tourism Centre, Lot 202 Wisma Equity, 150 Jalan Ampang, Kuala Lumpur 50450; Telephone (3) 243-5337, 242-5549

Netherlands ◙ Far East Trade Office, 56 Javastraat, The Hague 2585 AR; Telephone (070) 469-438

New Zealand ◙ East Asia Trade Centre, Level 21, Marac House, 105-109 The Terrace, Wellington; Telephone (04) 736-474/5

Norway ◙ Taipei Trade Center, Eilertsundtsgate 4/2 Etg.

Philippines ◙ Pacific Economic and Cultural Center, 8th Floor, BF Homes Condominium Bldg., Aduana St., Intramuros, Manila; Telephone (2) 472-261/5

cont...

GOVERNMENT REPRESENTATIVES ABROAD, TAIWAN *(cont.)*

Singapore ▣ Trade Mission of the Republic of China, #23–00 PSA Bldg., 460 Alexandra Rd., Singapore 0511; Telephone 278-6511

Spain ▣ Centro Sun Yat-sen, 12–4 Paseo de La Habana, Madrid 28036; Telephone (1) 411–3645/3463

Sweden ▣ Taipei Trade, Tourism and Information Office, 4 Tr Wenner-Gren Center, 166 Sveavagen, Stockholm S-113 46; Telephone (8) 728-8533

Thailand ▣ The Far East Trade Office, 10th Floor, Kian Gwan Bldg., 140 Wit Thayu Rd., Bangkok; Telephone (2) 251-9274/6, 251-9393/6

United Kingdom ▣ Free Chinese Centre, 4th Floor, Dorland House, 14–16 Regent St., London SW1Y 4PH; Telephone (71) 930-5767

United States ▣ Coordination Council for North American Affairs, 4201 Wisconsin Ave. NW, Washington, D.C. 20016–2137; Telephone (202) 895-1800; or any of the addresses listed under Tourism Offices

In 1988 the entire visa system was overhauled. However, the new system may not yet be completely ironed out, and problems may occur when applying for a visa. In theory, the old tourist A, tourist B, and business visas have all been supplanted by a single visitor visa. It is issued to foreign nationals holding foreign passports or travel documents with a validity of more than six months, and is issued for purposes of transit, sightseeing, visiting close relatives, special visits, study, specialized training, business, technical assistance, medical treatment, or other legitimate activities.

SINGLE-ENTRY VISA

Business travelers who expect to be entering and leaving Taiwan frequently should consider applying for a multiple-entry visa, discussed in Chapter X of this book. Other visitors can apply for either a two-week visitor visa, for which no extensions can be granted, or a 60-day visa. With the latter, a visitor may, for sufficient reasons, apply for a maximum of two 60-day extensions, for a continuous stay in Taiwan of six months. After that time, he or she must exit Taiwan to acquire additional visas.

To extend your visa while in Taiwan, you can apply in person to the Foreigners' Service Center, Taipei Municipal Police Headquarters, 89 Ninhsia Rd., Taipei; Telephone 537-3680.

RESIDENT VISA

Persons desiring to stay in Taiwan for longer than six months may wish to apply for a resident visa and alien resident card (black book). To do this, you must go to the Ministry of Foreign Affairs (2 Chieh-shou Rd., Taipei; Telephone 311-9292) and present proof that you qualify for resident status, after which a resident visa will be issued. Once you have a resident visa, you must then report to the Foreigners' Service Center (address above), where an alien resident card will be issued for a reasonable charge.

GROUP TOURIST PERMITS

Group tourist permits are issued by the same authorities that issue visitor visas and are valid for groups of at least 15 persons. Group permits are valid for a single visit within three months of the date of issue. They are good for a maximum stay of two weeks and may not be extended or exchanged for other types of visas. Each group must arrive and depart together, and by a common means of transportation.

HEALTH CERTIFICATES

Travelers who have visited cholera-infected areas for more than five days must have valid inoculation certificates. Other than that, there are no health certificates needed.

INTERNATIONAL ROUTINGS TO TAIWAN

SINCE it is an island, you can reach Taiwan only by plane or boat. Apart from that restriction, Taiwan has convenient connections to virtually every location in the world.

BY AIR

Taiwan is served by over 20 international airlines directly; an additional 35 airlines maintain off-line sales offices in Taipei. If a person is coming from a country or area in the world that does not have a direct flight to Taiwan, the easiest way to get there is to fly first to Hong Kong and then on to Taipei.

AIRLINES SERVING TAIPEI

(Numbers are those of Taipei Office; precede with 2 if dialing from outside Taipei, and 886-2 if dialing from outside Taiwan.)

Airborne Express, 757-666
Cargo Lux, 751-1121
Cathay Pacific Airways, 715-2333
China Airlines (International), 715-1212
China Airlines (Local), 715-1122
Delta Airlines, 541-8681
Far Eastern Air Transport, 361-5431/40
Flying Tiger Line, 713-6321
Formosa Airlines, 507-4188
Foshing Airlines, 511-9177
Garuda Indonesia Airways, 561-2311
Japan Asia Airways, 771-3353
KLM—Royal Dutch Airlines, 717-1000
Korean Air, 521-4242
Malaysian Airline System, 716-8384
Martinair Taiwan, 531-1796
Northwest Airlines, 716-1555
Philippine Airlines, 505-1255
Singapore Airlines, 551-6655
South African Airways, 536-6445
Taiwan Airlines, 537-3660
Thai Airways International, 715-4622
United Airlines, 703-7600

OFF-LINE AIRLINES SERVING TAIPEI

Aerolines Argentinas, 773-5422
Air Canada, 581-1133
Air France, 542-7345
Air India, 741-0163
Air Lanka, 595-4201
Air Nauru, 594-8116
Air New Zealand, 521-2311
Air Niugini, 505-3030
Alia Royal Jordanian Airlines, 543-1388
Aliblu Airways, 741-5161
Alitalia, 741-5161
American Airlines, 563-1200
British Airways, 521-2311
British Caledonian Airways, 521-7252
Canadian Airlines International, 503-4111
Continental Airlines, 712-0131/3
Eastern Air Lines, 561-0273
East-West Airlines, 776-6769
EgyptAir, 741-5161
El Al Israel Airlines, 563-1200
Iberia—Airlines of Spain, 773-4992
Lacsa—Airlines of Costa Rica, 773-5428
Lan Chile, 741-5161
Lufthansa German Airlines, 503-4114
Pacific Southwest Airlines, 776-6769
Pan American World Airways, 561-5900
Qantas Airways, 506-2311
Royal Brunei Airlines, 715-3449
Sabena Belgian World Airlines, 563-5121
Saudi Arabian Airlines, 506-3171
Scandinavian Airlines System, 712-0138/9
Swissair, 581-1133
USAIR, 776-6769
UTA, 561-0273
Varig, 712-6892

BY SEA

The only passenger ships serving Taiwan are the Japanese-flag Arimura Line's *Hiryu 2* and *Hiryu 3*, small liners that sail weekly from both Keelung and Kaohsiung to Naha, Okinawa. Sailing dates may change, and it is advisable to check first. Charges one-way run from NT$2,815 for economy class to NT$3,949 for first class. The journey involves one full night at sea. In late 1988, a company started a service from Taiwan to Shanghai via Hong Kong, but it did not prove profitable and was discontinued after only a few voyages.

Taiwan is a major exporting country and is a port of call for shipping companies from most nations. With its five ports (Keelung, Taichung, Kaohsiung, Hualien, Taitung, and Suao), the island is able to ship its goods worldwide and has increasingly become a destination for imported goods.

ENTRANCE AND EXIT PROCEDURES

PLANT AND ANIMAL QUARANTINE

Because Taiwan is an island, it is possible, with rigorous quarantine measures, to keep out plant and animal diseases, and the government makes every effort to do so. Plants with soil attached and all plants whose place of origin is unknown may not be brought in. The importation of fresh fruits and vegetables from any area where the Mediterranean fruit fly (Medfly) is found is forbidden, as is the importation of underground parts of plants from areas where burrowing nematode worms are found.

Dogs and cats may not be brought in from any area where rabies is known to exist (which means pretty much anyplace except the British Isles). Even if the animal comes from a rabies-free zone, an import permit must be obtained from the Bureau of Commodity Inspection and Quarantine. To obtain such a permit, you must submit an application in advance, accompanied by four color photos of the animal, an official certificate of health, and a declaration that the animal has been vaccinated against rabies. Birds may not be imported from any area where fowl plague exists. Anyone who plans to bring in a large number of plants, animals, or plant or animal parts or products should clear the import first with the Bureau of Commodity Inspection and Quarantine. On entering the country with any animal or plant, or animal or plant part or product, you should submit it for inspection by the Animal and Plant Quarantine Station at the airport or seaport.

CUSTOMS

Most imported personal effects are duty-free, but radios, television sets, and tape recorders must be declared. Travelers' checks and bank drafts do not need to be declared. TVs brought into the country for personal use must be modified (by reducing the number of channels to the legal three), and proof of this modification is required. In addition to personal effects, two bottles of alcoholic beverages and 400 cigarettes are allowed in duty-free. Departing travelers are prohibited from carrying out wheat and other grains, as well as genuine antiques or ancient coins. There is also a prohibition against unauthorized reproductions of books, records, and computer programs.

For more detailed customs information, contact the Inspectorate General of Customs, 85 Hsinsheng South Rd., Sec. 1, Taipei.

EXIT FORMALITIES AND AIRPORT TAX

All persons leaving Taiwan through the two international airports, Chiang Kai-shek International in Taoyuan and the Kaohsiung International Airport, must pay a NT$200 airport tax before boarding. It is advisable to pay this amount in New Taiwan dollars so as to prevent delays upon departure.

IV
Traveling in Taiwan

KNOW BEFORE YOU GO

WEIGHTS AND MEASURES

Taiwan uses the metric system, with weights in kilograms, liquid volume in liters, distances and speeds in kilometers, and temperatures in degrees Celsius. Local markets, however, usually weigh in *jin* (a unit of weight approximating 1.3 lb or 0.6 kg). Housing size is measured by the *ping*, equal to two Japanese tatamis, or approximately 36 sq ft (3.2 m²).

ELECTRICITY AND WATER

Electric current in Taiwan is 110 volts, 60 cycles, AC. Most hotels have adapters for those who come from countries using a different voltage.

Tap water everywhere in Taiwan is unsafe to drink and must be boiled first. Most large hotels and restaurants use distilled water or have their own sophisticated water-purification systems, but you should always inquire about the water when checking in.

SAFETY AND HEALTH

It is never pleasant to become ill while traveling, but if you should get sick in Taiwan, rest assured the local doctors and hospitals are equipped to take care of just about any problem. Most hospitals expect a deposit in advance of treatment, so it would be wise to have cash or a credit card handy in case of emergency. The Seventh-Day Adventist hospital, although it too wants some type of security, will usually take a person in without money up front.

Medicine can be bought, usually without the need for a prescription, at any of the many pharmacies in all the towns and cities in Taiwan. However, you must know what you are buying and the dosage required. Few medicines, except for addictive drugs and strong painkillers, are unavailable to the average person.

HOSPITALS IN TAIWAN

TAIPEI (prefix telephone numbers with 02 if calling from outside Taipei)

Adventist Hospital, 424 Pateh Rd., Sec. 2; Telephone 771–8151

Air Force General Hospital, 131 Chienkang Rd.; Telephone 764–2151

Cathay General Hospital, 280 Jenai Rd., Sec. 4; Telephone 708–2121

Central Clinic, 77 Chunghsiao East Rd., Sec. 4; Telephone 751–0221

Chang Gung Memorial Hospital, 199 Tunhua North Rd.; Telephone 713–5211

China Medical Center, 22 Lane 12, Jenai Rd., Sec. 4; Telephone 702–2869, 702–2621

Chungshan Medical Clinic, 11 Lane 112, Jenai Rd., Sec. 4; Telephone 708–1166

Community Services Center (Counseling), 25 Lane 290, Chungshan North Rd., Sec. 6, Tienmou; Telephone 836–8134

Country Hospital, 1 Lane 71, Jenai Rd., Sec. 4; Telephone 771–3161/5; 24–hour emergency, 721–6315

Mackay Memorial Hospital, 92 Chungshan North Rd., Sec. 2; Telephone 543–3535

National Taiwan University Hospital, 1 Changteh St.; Telephone 312–3456

cont...

HOSPITALS IN TAIWAN *(cont.)*

Taipei Municipal Chunghsin Hospital, 145 Chengchou Rd.; Telephone 521–3801

Taipei Municipal Jenai Hospital, 10 Jenai Rd., Sec. 4; Telephone 709–3600

Tri–Service General Hospital, 226 Tingchou Rd.; Telephone 311–7001

Veterans General Hospital, 201 Shihpai Rd., Sec. 2; Telephone 871–2121 (English information, Ext. 3530)

KAOHSIUNG (telephone prefix 07)

Kaohsiung City Tatung Hospital, 68 Chunghua 3rd Rd.; Telephone 261–8131

Kaohsiung City Ming Sheng Hospital, 134 Kaihsuan 2nd Rd.; Telephone 751–1131

Kaohsiung Municipal Women's and Children's Hospital, 82 Kushan 2nd Rd., Lane 37; Telephone 531–1161

Kaohsiung Medical College Hospital, 100 Shihchuan 1st Rd.; Telephone 312–1101

Naval Hospital, 553 Chunhsiao Rd.; Telephone 581–1648

TIME AROUND THE WORLD

When it's 12 noon in Taipei, the standard time in the following cities is:

Amsterdam	5 AM
Bangkok	11 AM
Beirut	6 AM
Cairo	6 AM
Chicago	10 PM previous day
Dallas	10 PM previous day
Frankfurt	5 AM
Hong Kong	12 NOON
Honolulu	6 PM previous day
London	4 AM
Los Angeles	8 PM previous day
Montreal	11 PM previous day
Nairobi	7 AM
New York	11 PM previous day
Paris	5 AM
Rio de Janeiro	1 AM
Rome	5 AM
San Francisco	8 PM previous day
Sydney	2 PM
Tokyo	1 PM
Vancouver	8 PM previous day
Zurich	5 AM

Like Chinese the world over, Taiwan observes the ancient Chinese lunar calendar. This is based on a 12-year cycle, in which each year is named after an animal: rat, ox, tiger, rabbit, dragon, snake, horse, sheep, monkey, chicken, dog, and pig. Like the zodiacal signs of Western astrology, each animal has its own special characteristics, and those born under the different signs are said to be possessed of the nature of that animal. Of all the animals, the dragon is said to be especially good, and Chinese parents try to give birth during dragon years.

RELIGIOUS SERVICES

Besides the temples and shrines of Eastern religions, Taiwan has many houses of worship of the various Western faiths. Hotel reception desks can usually direct you to a place of worship.

HOUSES OF WORSHIP

TAIPEI

Anglican
Church of the Good Shepherd, 509 Chungcheng Rd., Shihlin; Telephone 882–3460

Saint John's Cathedral, 280 Fuhsing South Rd., Sec. 2; Telephone 732–7740

Baha'i Faith
3/F, 149–13 Hsinsheng South Rd., Sec. 1; Telephone 393–6408, 396–7863

Baptist
Calvary Baptist Church, 21 Yangteh Ave., Sec. 2, Yangming–shan; Telephone 831–3458

Grace Baptist Church, 90 Hsinsheng South Rd., Sec. 3; Telephone 701–8197

Christian Science
Christian Science Services, 10 Lane 201, Changan East Rd., Sec. 2; Telephone 711–8212

Church of Christ
Church of Christ (Chinese/English), 1/F, 2 Alley 17, Lane 17, Wolung St.; Telephone 733–7372, 732–4955

Church of Christ, 63 Tyan Yu St., Tienmou; Telephone 871–4742, 871–4834

Islamic
Taipei Grand Mosque, 62 Hsingsheng South Rd., Sec. 2

cont...

HOUSES OF WORSHIP *(cont.)*

Jewish
Taipei Jewish Services, Ritz Hotel, 155 Minchuan East Rd.;
Telephone 597–1234

Taiwan Jewish Community, 6 Alley 11, Lane 186, Hsinyi Rd.,
Peitou; Telephone 871–8228, 861–6303

Latter-Day Saints
Church of Jesus Christ of Latter–Day Saints, 209 Fulin Rd.,
Shihlin; Telephone 836–6185

Reorganized Church of Jesus Christ of Latter–Day Saints,
8/F–1, 699 Pateh Rd., Sec. 4; Telephone 760–6262,
765–0884

Presbyterian
Friendship Presbyterian Church, 5 Lane 269, Roosevelt Rd.,
Sec. 3; Telephone 706–7543

Roman Catholic
Corpus Christi Catholic Church, 2 Shan Tzu Hou Hua Gan
Rd., Yangmingshan; Telephone 861–6185

Holy Family Catholic Church, 50 Hsinsheng South Rd.,
Sec. 2; Telephone 321–2444, 321–2445

Mother of God Church, 171 Chungshan North Rd., Sec. 7,
Tienmou; Telephone 871–5168

Sacred Heart Catholic Church, 22 Hsinhai Rd., Sec. 1; Telephone 321–4205

St. Christopher's Church, 51 Chungshan North Rd., Sec. 3;
Telephone 594–7914

The Salvation Army
1 Lane 208, Szuwei Rd.; Telephone 738–1079, 709–9529,
705–8150

cont...

HOUSES OF WORSHIP *(cont.)*

Seventh-Day Adventist
424 Pateh Rd., Sec. 2; Telephone 771-8151 Ext. 959

Other Christian
Agape International Christian Center (Charismatic Worship), 8/F., 1 Lane 7, Chinan Rd., Sec. 1; Telephone 531-5163

Taipei International Church, Taipei American School Auditorium, 731 Wenlin Rd., Shihlin; Telephone 871-9031, 871-8485

TAICHUNG (telephone prefix 05)

Anglican
St. James' Church, 23 Wuchuang West Rd.

Church of Christ
10 Alley 58, Lane 13, Chungching Rd.; Telephone 232-3346

Lutheran
Chia Yi English Lutheran Congregation, 199 Shantsu Ting; Telephone 222-3051, (05) 223-4430

Roman Catholic
Hsitun Catholic Church, 240 Chunghai Rd., Sec. 2; Telephone 252-8547

Other Christian
Taichung Community Chapel, Morrison Academy Auditorium, 136-1 Shuin Nan Rd.; Telephone 291-4772

cont...

HOUSES OF WORSHIP (cont.)

KAOHSIUNG (telephone prefix 07)

Church of Christ
10 Alley 1, Lane 92, Yungyi St.; Telephone 801-3318

Latter-Day Saints
Church of Jesus Christ of Latter-Day Saints, 292 Shih-chung 1st Rd.; Telephone 334-4186/7

Roman Catholic
Holy Rosary Cathedral, 151 Wufu 3rd Rd.; Telephone 221-4434

St. Mary's Church, 113 Chienkuo 4th Rd.; Telephone 551-4825

Stella Maris International Seamen's Mission, 70 Chihsin 3rd Rd.; Telephone 521-3976

Our Lady of Fatima, 85 Nanhua Rd.; Telephone 231-1753

Other Christian
Kaohsiung Community Church, 54 Tesheng St., Shinhsing District; Telephone 331-8131

TIPPING

Tipping is not yet a universally observed custom in Taiwan, except for bell service at the hotels. To compensate for this, all hotels and almost all restaurants and bars automatically add a 10% service charge to the bill. Should you wish to leave a tip, however, it will definitely be appreciated. The one time of the year when you are expected to tip is during the Chinese Lunar New Year. Some in the service sector, such as hairdressers, barbers, and taxi drivers, expect double their normal fees and charges at that time.

LOCAL MORES AND SENSIBILITIES

Because of Taiwan's traditional ties to the West, the inhabitants are more or less familiar with Western ways. Still, there are certain cultural differences that should be kept in mind. Chinese are sparing of direct physical contact, and back-slapping and indiscriminate touching are not welcome, though a courteous handshake is acceptable. Westerners should also try to spare the inhabitants' sensibilities by refraining from public displays of affection among themselves.

Like all Chinese, those of Taiwan lay great stress on "keeping face." Disagreements should be handled in a way that does not bemean either party. As keeping people waiting is considered humiliating, one should always be on time for appointments and meetings. Loud displays of temper definitely cause a loss of face, and travelers should avoid altercations, not merely with the local inhabitants but also among themselves.

Traditionally, Chinese personal names are given with the surname first: thus Chiang Kai-shek was "General Chiang," and if you are introduced to, say, a Lu Chia-sun, you would address him as "Mr. Lu."

MONEY, CURRENCY, AND BANKING

CURRENCY AND EXCHANGE RATE

An individual may bring unlimited foreign currency into Taiwan and, if the amount is declared, take it out again within one year. Without a declaration, not more than US$5,000 in cash or the equivalent in foreign currencies may be taken out. The basic unit of Taiwan currency is the New Taiwan dollar (NT$). New Taiwan currency may be brought in or taken out of Taiwan up to an amount of NT$8,000, and 20 coins of New Taiwan currency may also be taken out of the country. Not more than 62.5 grams of gold or 625 grams of silver, or both, in ornaments may be taken from Taiwan, and the carrying out of gold and silver bullion or bars is prohibited.

Coins and bills come in denominations of NT$0.5 (not commonly used), NT$1 (a copper coin similar to a U.S. penny), NT$5 (a silver-colored alloy coin slightly larger than the NT$1 coin), NT$10 (a silver-colored alloy coin resembling a U.S. 25-cent piece), NT$10 (a small red bill that is being phased out in favor of the NT$10 coin), NT$50 (a bluish-colored bill, larger than the NT$10 bill but smaller than the NT$100 bill), NT$100 (either of two bills, one green and the other red), NT$500 (a red bill larger than the NT$100), and NT$1,000 (the largest bill issued, and multicolored).

The New Taiwan dollar has appreciated greatly in value against the U.S. dollar. From an exchange rate of NT$40 to US$1, it now stands at approximately NT$26.63 to US$1.

EXCHANGE RATES FOR NEW TAIWAN DOLLAR

Country	Denomination	New Taiwan Dollar*	Country	Denomination	New Taiwan Dollar*
Australia	A$	20.6161	Malaysia	M$	9.8434
Belgium	BF	0.8661	Mexico	P	0.0091
Brazil	Cz$	0.1653	Netherlands	G	15.8581
Canada	CND	23.0337	New Zealand	NZ$	15.7756
China	Yuan	5.0909	Norway	Kr	4.5583
Denmark	KR	4.6435	Pakistan	R	1.2221
France	FF	5.2559	Philippines	Peso	0.9790
Germany	DM	17.8923	Portugal	E	0.2002
Hong Kong	HK$	3.4160	Singapore	S$	15.3203
India	R	1.4719	Spain	P	0.2801
Indonesia	Rp	0.0143	Sweden	Kr	4.7580
Italy	L	0.0238	Thailand	Baht	1.0586
Japan	Yen	0.1980	United Kingdom	£	51.7466
Korea	W	0.0373	United States	US$	26.6255

*Exchange rates provided for reference only; visitors should confirm actual rates at time of exchange.

BANKING FOR TOURISTS

There are over 60 domestic and international banks in Taiwan. However, few of these are able to handle foreign exchange transactions. But as the government continues to open the banking sector, more financial institutions are expected to be able to provide foreign exchange services. It is best to inquire at your hotel for the bank best able to serve you.

CREDIT CARDS AND TRAVELERS' CHECKS

Most major credit cards are honored in Taiwan, especially in the large hotels, restaurants, and stores. Be sure, though, to inquire first before trying to make purchases with credit cards. Travelers' checks are only honored for direct payment in the major hotels and then only when presented by hotel guests; however, they are readily exchanged for New Taiwan currency at most banking outlets.

COMMUNICATIONS AND THE NEWS MEDIA

POSTAL SERVICE

Taiwan has one of the most efficient postal services in the world. Letters and packages mailed locally or coming from abroad are delivered promptly and—remarkably enough, given the often unintelligible romanization of the addresses—to the right party.

A letter to Hong Kong or Macao is charged at NT$9 for the first 20 g and NT$6 for each additional 20 g. An air letter to the same destinations is NT$8, and printed matter is NT$7 for the first 20 g and NT$5 for each additional 20 g. Delivery time for letters is two days. Small parcels sent surface mail are charged at NT$10 if less than 100 g, NT$20 for 100–250 g, NT$35 for 250–500 g, and NT$57 for 500–1,000 g. Air mail rates are NT$7 for a letter weighing less than 20 g, and NT$5 for each additional 20 g.

Rates to Asia and Oceania are NT$14 for letters weighing 10 g, and NT$9 for each additional 10 g. Postcards cost NT$10, air letters are charged at NT$11, and printed matter NT$10 for the first 20 g and NT$7 for an additional 20 g. Delivery takes two to three days. Small parcels sent surface mail are NT$21 if they weigh less than 100 g, NT$38 for 100–250 g, NT$69 for 250–500 g, NT$114 for 500–1,000 g. Airmail charges are NT$10 for less than 20 g, NT$7 for each additional 20 g.

Letters to Europe, the Americas, and Africa cost NT$18 for the first 10 g or less, and NT$14 for an additional 10 g; postcards, NT$12; air letters, NT$14; and printed matter, NT$18 for the first 20 g and NT$10 for an additional 20 g. Delivery takes 7 to 10 days. Small parcel rates to the same destinations are NT$21 for less than 100 g, NT$38 for 100–250 g, NT$69 for 250–500 g, NT$114 for 500–1,000 g. Air mail parcels are charged NT$13 for less than 20 g and NT$10 for each additional 20 g.

TELECOMMUNICATIONS

TELEPHONE

Taiwan's international telephone access code is 886; Taipei's, 02. Overseas calls can be made on private phones either directly or through the overseas operator (dial 100). In most international-standard hotels, international direct dial (IDD) is available. Call the Communications Company at (02) 321–2535 for information on which countries can be dialed directly. Overseas calls can also be made at International Telecommunications Administration (ITA) offices. Discount rates to the United States are in effect from 4 PM to 9 PM, and reduced rates from 1 AM to 7 AM. Rates for direct overseas dialing are calculated every six seconds.

Domestic long distance calls may be made from private phones, from the blue-green public phones, or through the telephone bureau. Local phone calls from public phones are charged at NT$1 for three minutes. Public phones in Taiwan are set to disconnect automatically when three minutes are up, and the caller must then redial.

FACSIMILE

Facsimile service is provided 24 hours a day at the main ITA office. Faxes can be sent to Argentina, Australia, Austria, Bahrain, Canada, Egypt, Fiji, France, Germany, Guam, Hawaii, Hong Kong, Indonesia, Italy, Japan, Korea, Liechtenstein, Luxembourg, Macao, Maldives, the Netherlands, New Zealand, Peru, the Philippines, Puerto Rico, Singapore, Sweden, Switzerland, Thailand, Tonga, Trinidad, the United Kingdom, the United Arab Emirates, and the United States.

CABLE AND TELEX

International cables and in–country telegrams may be sent from the main ITA office at 28 Hangchou South Rd., Sec. 1, Telephone 344–3781 or the following branch offices:

CKS International Airport; Telephone (03) 383–2790 (7 AM–9 PM)

23 Chungshan N. Rd., Sec. 2, Taipei; Telephone 541–7434 (8 AM–10 PM, except Sundays)

118 Chunghsiao West Rd., Sec. 1; Telephone 344–3785 (8 AM–8 PM)

Sungshan Domestic Airport; Telephone (02) 712–6112 (8 AM–8 PM)

Taipei World Trade Center; Telephone (02) 725–1111 (8 AM–5 PM)

RADIO AND TV

Taiwan has one English-language radio station, ICRT, which broadcasts in AM at 1548 KHz in Taipei and 1570 KHz in Taichung and in FM at 100.1 MHz in Taipei and 100.9 MHz in Taichung. News reports are given hourly, and more detailed coverage is given in the mornings and evenings.

The National Broadcasting Corporation of China (BCC) plays English-language music, but all the DJs are Chinese and speak in Chinese. BCC broadcasting is at the following dial locations: AM—657, 954, 1070, and 1460 KHz; FM—103.3, 105.9, and 107.8 MHz.

Taiwan has three national television stations, which, as the title "national" implies, are government-controlled. Very little English-language programing is available. However, many hotels and private individuals have begun to install satellite receiving dishes, and the major Japanese and U.S. networks are now being picked up.

PRINT MEDIA

NEWSPAPERS AND MAGAZINES

There are two English-language daily newspapers in Taiwan, the *China Post* and the *China News*. Both are published in the morning and neither is particularly thorough or reliable.

Many of the world's major magazines, such as *Time* and *Newsweek*, can be found in hotel bookstores or the few English-language bookstores in Taiwan.

BOOKSTORES AND NEWSSTANDS

Although Taiwan has numerous bookstores to satisfy local readers, English-language books are found in only a very few. In Taipei, the two best stores for English-speakers are Caves Books Ltd., located at 103 Chungshan North Rd., Sec. 2, and Lin Kou Books, located at the corner of Chungshan North Rd. and Minchuan East Rd. Both stores have a wide selection of novels, specialty books, and periodicals to choose from. In addition to these two stores, most international-standard hotels have some type of bookstore offering a smattering of novels, travel guides, and newspapers for visitors. Although Taiwan now subscribes to the International Copyright Convention, the illegal "pirating" of foreign-language books—especially expensive reference books and textbooks—is still widely practiced. Buyers beware, however, as importing such books is strictly prohibited by other countries.

The *China Post* and *China News* are available at some of the street kiosks that sell local newspapers.

LOCAL TRANSPORTATION

PUBLIC TRANSPORTATION

TAXIS

In the city of Taipei alone, there are more than 67,000 registered taxis, and the number is growing, thanks to a relaxation of government restrictions on new taxis. As may be imagined, this has added to the already chaotic traffic conditions in Taipei and in all the other major cities on the island as well.

Taxis are a very popular mode of transportation and are quite inexpensive by international standards. Fares are NT$35 for the first 1.5 km and NT$5 for each additional 0.4 km. From 11 PM until 5 AM, an additional 20% is automatically added to the bill. In addition, a waiting-time charge of NT$5 is accrued every five minutes when the taxi is stationary (or moving slower than 5 km per hour!) Be sure you have your destination and return addresses written in Chinese, as most taxi drivers cannot speak English.

BUSES

Buses are the preferred means of transportation for most local residents. Fares are only NT$8 per zone, and buses run quite frequently. A major problem with taking buses is that they are usually very overcrowded. People are packed in as tightly as possible, and there is no way to avoid being pressed against those surrounding you. This does not seem to bother the Chinese, who are used to living in crowded conditions, but it can be claustrophobic for Westerners who sometimes need a certain amount of personal space between themselves and others. In addition to the crowded conditions, buses are generally smaller and have lower roofs than Western buses; tall Westerners find themselves stooping over so that their heads don't hit the ceilings.

TRAINS

Railroad lines, operated by the Taiwan Railway Administration, follow the east and west coasts, connecting Taipei with Kaohsiung and Taitung. The Taipei–Kaohsiung line has two routes, one running through the mountains and another along the coast, and trains run approximately an hour or a half hour apart, depending on the time of day, from early morning until nearly midnight. Sleeper service is available on the night trips. Trains on the Taipei–Taitung line run less frequently, with trips from Taipei concentrated in the morning and evening hours and those from Taitung mostly in the morning and afternoon. Fares vary with distance and class, from NT$22 for a one-way trip from Changhua to Tainan to NT$1088 for a round-trip first-class fare between Taipei and Kaohsiung.

SUBWAY

A mass transit (subway) system for Taipei has been designed, and construction began at the end of 1988. Unfortunately, it isn't scheduled for completion until the 1990s, and the original plans are continually being modified and extended to provide service to more areas. It is thus doubtful whether the system will be in operation within this century.

In the southern Taiwan city of Kaohsiung, the mayor has called for the construction of a subway system, and that project is in the planning stage.

FERRIES

A ferry operates between the small southern port of Fukang and Orchid Island, and another between Kaohsiung and Makung on Penghu Island. There are also public boats serving others of the offshore islands.

RENTAL CARS

There are numerous car rental firms in Taiwan, including Central Auto Service, established and run by an expatriate, Telephone (02) 881–9545, 881–6534; Formosa Rent-a-Car, a division of Hertz, Telephone (02) 717–3673; China Rent-a-Car, Telephone (02) 500–6088; Prestige Limousine Service Co., Ltd., Telephone (02) 783–2166; and Avis Rent a Car, Telephone (02) 500–6633 or toll-free (080) 221–333. Beginning in January 1989, 16 car rental agencies were allowed to offer services at the Chiang Kai-shek International Airport, and cars can now be rented as soon as you arrive in Taiwan, provided you have a valid international driver's license or a Taiwan license.

SIGHTSEEING TOURS

TRAVEL agencies offer regular or special tours to outstanding places of interest such as Taroko Gorge, Sun Moon Lake, and other areas.

These tours are designed to provide adequate time for leisurely sight-seeing. Tour tickets and other travel assistance can be obtained at your hotel reception desk.

Four Taipei travel agencies operate regular daily bus tours for tourists. The buses are air-conditioned, and the crews include bilingual guides. The four travel agencies are:

China Express Transportation Co., 70 Chungshan North Rd., Sec. 2, Taipei; Telephone (02) 541–6466

Pinho Travel Service Co., 3/F, 142–1 Chilin Rd., Taipei; Telephone (02) 551–4136

South East Travel Service Co., 60 Chungshan North Rd., Sec. 2, Taipei; Telephone (02) 571–3001

Taiwan Coach Tours, 8/F, 27 Chungshan North Rd., Sec. 3, Taipei; Telephone (02) 595–5321

The tours listed here offer maximum travel value at minimum cost. Tour fares are given in New Taiwan Dollars (NT$), and are subject to change without notice, so be sure to confirm whether those listed below are still valid.

TAIPEI CITY

Taipei is not only the administrative seat of the government of Taiwan, but also the principal cultural and economic center as well as the island's transportation hub. It is the fastest-growing city in Asia. Like other places in Taiwan, urban and rural, Taipei combines all the best of old and modern China. The city is glamorous at night, and affords the pleasure-seeker a wide choice of diversions.

Half-Day Tour (NT$450). Chiang Kai-shek Memorial Hall, Presidential Square, the Martyrs' Shrine, the National Palace Museum, and the business and theater districts.

Taipei City by Night (NT$750). Mongolian barbecue dinner, the Bazaar area, the Lungshan Temple, the Chinese Opera, and a night market.

WULAI ABORIGINE VILLAGE

Half-Day Tour (NT$650). An hour-long drive into the country-side leads to Wulai, a mountain resort where aborigines in multicolored costumes give special performances. You may, if you wish, participate in the concluding number. The area boasts a waterfall, lake, and picnic facilities. Another exciting experience at Wulai is a ride on a narrow-gauge rail line hugging the hillside.

NORTH COAST

Half-Day Tour (NT$600). First to Keelung, the bustling seaport of Taipei, to view the 72-ft-high (33-m) statue of Kuan Yin, the goddess of mercy, that crowns a hill overlooking the harbor. Next to Yehliu Park, famed for its fantastic rock formations, sculptured through the ages by the elements.

LEOFOO SAFARI PARK AND WINDOW ON CHINA

One-Day Tour (minimum of three persons at NT$2,000 each). The tour includes Tzuhu (Lake Mercy), Shihmen Dam, the Leofoo Safari Park, and Window on China—an assembly of miniature replicas of famous landmarks and architectural wonders from both Taiwan and the mainland.

Yehliu Park, north coast

PENGHU (PESCADORES)

One-Day Tour (NT$3,300, all inclusive). Fly to Penghu in the morning, tour Makung, the county capital, drive along the Penghu Bay Bridge to Hsiyu (West Islet), and back to Makung. Fly back to Taipei at about 5 PM.

TAROKO GORGE

One of the greatest and most awesome natural wonders of the world is the 12-mi (19-km) Taroko Gorge, situated at the eastern end of the 120-mi (193-km) East-West Cross-Island Highway. The towering cliffs of the gorge, some more than 3,000 ft (900 m) high, contain millions of tons of marble deposits, and the area abounds with scenic attractions. No visit to Taiwan is complete without a trip to the gorge.

One-Day Tour (NT$2,700, all inclusive). Fly to Hualien in the morning, drive to and through Taroko Gorge to Tienhsiang for lunch, return to Hualien, see a performance by aborigines of the Ami tribe, and visit a large marble plant and showroom. Fly back to Taipei at about 5 PM.

Sun Moon Lake

SUN MOON LAKE

Sun Moon Lake, in the mountains of central Taiwan, is a truly delightful place for rest and relaxation in beautiful surroundings. The lake, situated at an elevation of 2,500 ft (760 m), is a year-round resort, with luxury hotels fronting it. Besides boating and fishing on the lake itself, the resort is a good base area for hiking excursions and for visiting Taiwan's highest pagoda and its biggest temple, an aborigine settlement, and other places of interest.

Two-Day Tour (NT$3,500, two per room; NT$4,000 single; inclusive except meals). *First day:* Leave Taipei by air-conditioned bus for Taichung, rest and lunch at Taichung, then drive to Sun Moon Lake through scenic rice, sugarcane, banana, tea, pineapple, and other plantations. After check-in at your hotel enjoy a leisurely two-hour motorboat sightseeing cruise. *Second day:* Morning exploration at your leisure. In the afternoon, return to Taipei.

EAST-WEST CROSS-ISLAND HIGHWAY AND SUN MOON LAKE

The Chinese, noted for their graphic descriptions, call the East-West Cross-Island Highway "The Rainbow of Treasure Island." World travelers call it Asia's most beautiful highway. It is an engineering marvel of the first magnitude, a highway of awesome grandeur. Sun Moon Lake is a beautiful, peaceful retreat.

Three-Day Tour (NT$7,000, two in a room; NT$8,000, single; inclusive except meals). *First day:* Fly to Hualien in the morning, drive to and through Taroko Gorge and, after lunch at Tienhsiang, leave for Lishan (Pear Mountain) for an overnight stay. *Second day:* Leave Lishan for Taichung and, after lunch, proceed to Sun Moon Lake for an overnight stay. *Third day:* Morning tour of the lake. Leave for Taipei after lunch.

SUN MOON LAKE AND ALISHAN

Alishan, a range of 18 peaks flanking the great north-south Central Mountain Range, gives its name to a village linked by a 45-mi (72-km) railway to Chiayi, a bustling town in central Taiwan. The three-hour trip on diesel-powered tourist trains traverses one of the most beautiful areas on earth. The railway station at Alishan, at an elevation of 7,185 ft (2,190 m), is among the highest in the Far East. One of the greatest attractions of a visit to Alishan is the beautiful sunrise over the "sea of clouds." A vantage point on nearby Mount Chu affords an enthralling view of one of Taiwan's loveliest sights: as the sun rises, the golden shafts of sunlight begin to paint the clouds and peaks with a variety of hues. The sea of clouds surrounds Yushan (Jade Mountain), 25 mi (40 km) to the east, and the clouds often completely screen the beautiful valley between the two mountains.

Three-Day Tour (NT$7,000, two in a room; NT$8,000, single; inclusive except meals). *First day:* Leave Taipei by bus for Taichung, then proceed to Sun Moon Lake for an overnight stay. *Second day:* Following a morning tour of the lake, leave for Chiayi, then travel from there by alpine train or bus to Alishan for an overnight stay. *Third day:* Morning tour of Alishan, lunch, then return to Taipei via Chiayi.

KENTING NATIONAL PARK

One-Day Tour (NT$3,800, inclusive except meals). Fly to Kaohsiung at about 7:30 AM, then drive to Kenting National Park, visit Chialoshui, noted for its coral limestone formations, and then to Oluanpi Park. After lunch, tour the Kenting Forest Recreation Area. Fly back to Taipei at about 8 PM.

KENTING NATIONAL PARK AND KAOHSIUNG

Two-Day Tour (NT$5,000, two in a room; NT$5,500, single; inclusive except meals). *First day:* Fly to Kaohsiung at about 7:30 AM, drive to Kenting National Park, then back to Kaohsiung in the late afternoon for an overnight stay. *Second day:* Morning, tour Kaohsiung city, Cheng Ching Lake, and Longevity Park. Afternoon, visit Fo Kuang Shan, one of the largest and most complete temple-monastery complexes in Taiwan. Near the summit of the mountain stands an 82-ft-tall (25-m) golden statue of the Buddha flanked by 480 6-ft-tall (180-cm) images of him. Fly back to Taipei in the late afternoon.

ROUND-THE-ISLAND TOURS

Four-Day Tour (NT$9,000, two in a room; NT$10,500, single; inclusive except meals). *First day:* Fly to Hualien in the morning, drive to and through Taroko Gorge, and after lunch at Tienhsiang, leave for Lishan for an overnight stay. *Second day:* Leave Lishan for Taichung; after lunch, tour Taichung City, then drive to Sun Moon Lake for an overnight stay. *Third day:* Tour the lake area in the morning, drive back to Taichung, and entrain for Kaohsiung for an overnight stay. *Fourth day*: Kaohsiung City Tour (Longevity park, Dragon and Tiger Pagodas, Spring and Autumn Pavilions, Cheng Ching Lake); after lunch, entrain for Taipei.

Five-Day Tour (NT$11,000, two in a room; NT$13,000 single; inclusive except meals). *First, second, and third days:* Same as Round-the-Island Four-Day Tour. *Fourth day:* Leave Kaohsiung for Kenting National Park, then return to Kaohsiung for another overnight stay. *Fifth day:* Same as fourth day of Round-the-Island Four-Day Tour.

National Palace Museum, Taipei

V The Taiwan Tour

TAIPEI CITY

TAIPEI is the main city of Taiwan and the designated capital of the Republic of China. It is located in northern Taiwan in an alluvial basin, through which flow the Tamsui (Tanshui), Hsintien, and Keelung rivers. Situated at 25 degrees 6 minutes north latitude, Taipei has a subtropical climate, characterized by a long, warm to hot summer and short, mild winter. Temperatures seldom fall below 59°F (14.8°C).

The population of Taipei, rapidly approaching 3 million, lives in an area of only 41 sq mi (106 km²), which makes Taipei one of the most densely populated cities of its size in the world.

In the late 1980s, Taipei had 274 educational establishments, with a total of 698,941 students. Among them were 24 universities and colleges having an enrollment of 129,240 students, a quarter of the total for the whole island. There were also 116 junior and senior high schools and 134 primary schools. Not counted in the total are 480 kindergartens. The city has 26 municipal hospitals and clinics with 1,979 beds.

Taipei is not only the capital city of Taiwan, but also its entertainment and cultural center. Both an old and a new city, it is continually expanding eastward from the Wanhua District (the original Taipei) toward Keelung, the northernmost city in Taiwan and one of the island's most important seaports. Taipei is rich in both the glamour of an earlier day and the modern accomplishments for which Taiwan is so famous. And because the Chinese infrequently sell their homes, on almost every street visitors to Taipei can see multistory skyscrapers standing side by side with traditional Chinese dwellings. Local color is everywhere in abundance, from the day and night markets, which Chinese housewives still prefer to the modern supermarkets that are beginning to spring up, to roadside peddlers and small restaurants.

Life in Taipei is busy and exciting, and the streets are filled with people virtually 24 hours a day. Traffic is chaotic—motorcycles and cars career down the roads at death-defying speeds and seem to move in five directions at once. Sidewalks, used in the West by pedestrians, are the favorite parking places for all types of conveyances and the

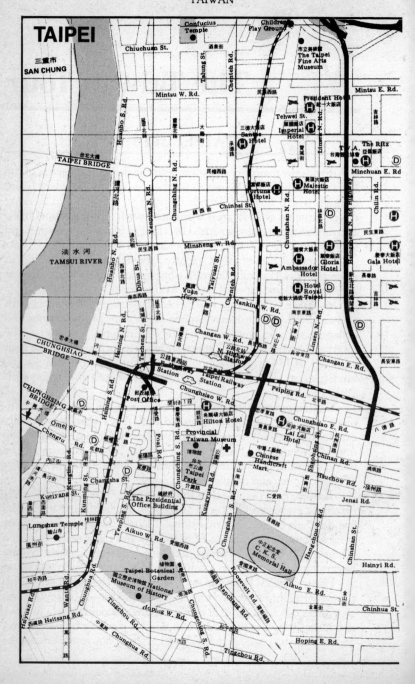

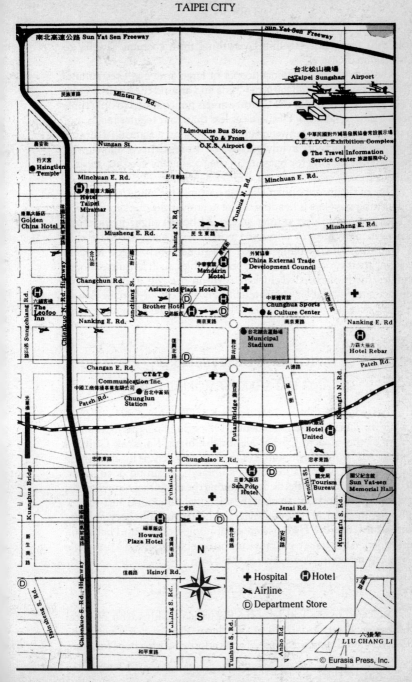

© Eurasia Press, Inc.

storefront for vendors selling everything from costume jewelry to Chinese medicine.

The city possesses a cornucopia of large and small restaurants offering cuisines from all parts of China and around the world. Eating is a continual process for the Chinese and is not confined to only three meals a day. In fact, few Chinese eat less than four regular meals, not to mention constant between-meal snacking. In addition to dining, shopping is an activity avidly pursued by the residents of Taipei, who are often out looking for bargains in the local night markets, located in almost every neighborhood and residential district.

One of the most popular evening pastimes for many local people and visiting travelers is heading to the nearest night market in search of bargains or an after-dinner snack. Although night markets are located in many areas of Taipei, the most famous, and crowded, is that in Wanhua. The Wanhua market is jammed with street vendors hawking their various wares. All types of edibles, such as fruit, seafood, noodles, turtle, barbecued chicken, corn-on-the-cob, and other local delicacies are available. One stretch is Hwahsi St., or "Snake Alley," so called because of the plethora of shops selling snake blood, venom, and meat.

SIGHTS WORTH SEEING

CHIANG KAI-SHEK MEMORIAL HALL

Located at 21 Chungshan South Rd. (Telephone 394–3171), in downtown Taipei near the Presidential Office Building, this monument is part of the 62-acre (25-ha) National Chiang Kai-shek Cultural Center. A 25-ton bronze statue of the late president is located in the main building, which also houses a library containing documents, pictures, and personal effects. Surrounding the monument are gardens, pavilions, and ponds, and within the memorial compound are two new buildings in classical Chinese style: the **National Theater** and the **National Concert Hall,** where symphonies, opera, and ballet are performed. At the main entrance to the complex stands a Ming-style 100-ft (30-m) arch. Open daily 9 AM–5 PM.

SUN YAT-SEN MEMORIAL HALL

Dedicated to the Father of the Republic of China, this classical Chinese-style memorial sits at 505 Jenai Rd., Sec. 4 (Telephone 702–2411), amid a large expanse of grass adorned with a huge fountain and a small man-made lake. Within the hall is an impressive 19-ft-high (580-cm) bronze statue of Dr. Sun, along with exhibition and lecture halls and a research library. Daily half-hour multimedia shows acquaint visitors with the life of Sun Yat-sen. (Sun Yat-sen died on the mainland, where he is also highly revered and where a massive mausoleum in his memory is to be found in Nanking [Nanjing].) Open daily 9 AM–5 PM.

MARTYRS' SHRINE

This example of classical Ming Dynasty architecture, situated at 139 Peian Rd., just east of the Grand Hotel, is dedicated to the nation's fallen war heroes and is modeled after the style of the Forbidden City in Peking. The main building is approached through a triple-arched gateway and a large courtyard. In the main building, the names of the heroes are inscribed next to murals depicting their feats. This shrine was a favorite retreat of the late President Chiang Kai-shek, who often spent afternoons strolling through the grounds. Open daily from 9 AM to 5 PM.

LUNGSHAN TEMPLE

One of the more interesting of Taiwan's 5,000 temples and shrines, this one, at 211 Kuangchou St., has been rebuilt since its original construction in 1740 but is still the oldest Buddhist temple in Taipei. Its name means "dragon mountain," and the temple, though dedicated to Kuan Yin, the Buddhist goddess of mercy, houses many other

Gate to the Martyrs' Shrine, Taipei

Lung Shan (Dragon Mountain) Temple, Taipei

deities, including non-Buddhist ones. Remarkable, ornate decorations and images are to be seen both within the temple and on its exterior. Because it affords visitors an authentic glimpse of traditional Chinese worship, this temple should not be missed. Open daily from 4:30 AM to 10:30 PM

TEMPLE OF CONFUCIUS

Situated at 25 Talung St., in Tatung district, in the northern part of Taipei, this temple, though dedicated to the Chinese philosopher, externally resembles a Buddhist temple. A collection of Chinese ideographs are housed within the temple, and a special ceremony is held at dawn on September 28 each year to celebrate Confucius' birthday.

TAIPEI CITY ZOO

In the Mucha Suburb is one of the largest zoos in Asia, containing a huge butterfly aviary, a petting zoo, a nocturnal animal exhibit, a sea lion aquarium, and Asian, American, desert, Australian, and African animal areas. Delightful for children—and animal lovers of all ages. Open daily 9 AM–5 PM; may be reached by Taipei city buses. Admission NT$40 adult, NT$20 child.

BOTANICAL GARDENS

The palm trees and tropical plants of the gardens (49 Nanhi Rd.) surround not only scenic walks but also the National Science Hall and National Museum of History.

PRESIDENTIAL OFFICE BUILDING

The building itself, on Chungching South Rd., houses the executive offices of the country, and the plaza outside it is the site, every October 10, of large colorful celebrations commemorating the outbreak of Sun Yat-sen's democratic revolution. If you are in Taiwan at this time of year, a visit is recommended.

OTHER MUSEUMS AND SITES

Armed Forces Museum, 243 Kueiyang St., Sec. 1; Telephone 331-5730; open daily except Tuesday 8:30 AM-12 Noon and 1 PM-4 PM.

Butterfly Museum, 71 Chinan Rd., Sec. 1; Telephone 321-6256; open by appointment.

Postal Museum, 45 Chungching South Rd., Sec. 2; Telephone 394-5186; open daily except Monday 9:00 AM-4:30 PM.

Taipei Fine Arts Museum, 181 Chungshan North Rd., Sec. 3; Telephone 595-7656; open Tuesday to Saturday 10 AM-6 PM, Sunday 10 AM-8 PM.

Taiwan Provincial Museum, 2 Hsiangyang Rd.; Telephone 361-3926; open daily 9 AM-5 PM.

KEELUNG

NORTHEAST of Taipei is the city of Keelung, the second largest of Taiwan's five international seaports. Keelung is located on the northern coast overlooking the East China Sea. It is a mid-sized city with a population of over 350,000 and is distinguished by being one of the wettest cities in the world, averaging 214 days of rain annually.

Life in Keelung centers on the waterfront. The main street is filled with shops selling all types of Chinese clothing, handicrafts, pottery, cloisonné, and other traditional Chinese items. In addition, there are many stores that specialize in brassware and ship's articles. Like all Taiwan cities, Keelung has its share of temples and other tourist attractions. Keelung has a well-deserved reputation for fine seafood and is a good jumping-off point for sojourns along the northeast coast.

TAMSUI

THE city of Tamsui is located on the northwest coast of Taiwan, where the Tamsui River meets the Taiwan Strait (both names are sometimes romanized "Tanshui"), and is only a 45-minute drive from Taipei. Tamsui has an interesting history, having been conquered and occupied first by the Spanish and later by the Dutch in the middle of the 17th century.

The most notable attraction in Tamsui is Fort San Domingo, which was built by the Spanish during their three-year rule, was used by the Dutch, and later became the British Consulate. It is now a historical monument, offering a glimpse into Taiwan's colonial past.

Tamsui's restaurants, like those of almost all coastal cities in Taiwan, specialize in seafood dishes and are excellent places for inexpensive fresh lobster, crab, and shrimp. The city also has many fine beaches for summertime relaxation and swimming.

WULAI

ABOUT 12 mi (30 km) south of Taipei is the mountain resort of Wulai, a village inhabited by the aboriginal Atayal people. Wulai is one of the best places in northern Taiwan to witness genuine aboriginal culture. Buses run frequently from Taipei to Wulai, and it is an interesting place to visit, especially for those who have limited time in Taipei and want to glimpse as much of the local color as possible.

EASTERN TAIWAN

THE eastern part of the island is the least populated area and has some of Taiwan's most beautiful scenery. It also contains two of Taiwan's international seaports, Suao and Hualien.

The whole northeastern corner of the island has been specially designated as a tourism area, with efforts concentrated on promoting the area's attractions for nature lovers and outdoor enthusiasts. The fishing village of Pitou Chiao boasts a lighthouse, and nearby the white sandstone Lungtung reef emerges from the sea. White sand beaches offer swimming and other water sports, the foothills of the mountains are clothed with evergreen woods, and the highway offers scenic vistas.

A tour of eastern Taiwan usually begins in Keelung and follows the coastal road down to Taitung. The town of Ilan along the way has several pleasant small hotels. Another popular way to see eastern Taiwan is by train, with stops in the different towns along the way.

HUALIEN

Hualien City is located on the eastern coast of central Taiwan, and is the capital of Hualien County. Although the county is the largest on the island, it is the most sparsely populated, in part because most of it is mountainous.

About 80,000 aborigines of the Ami and Atayal peoples reside in the area, and the city boasts one of the island's international seaports. Hualien is noted for its huge marble deposits, with quarries and marble enterprises providing jobs for more than 20,000 people. Hualien is also the starting point for tours into Taroko Gorge. The city has good accommodations, fine restaurants, and the leisurely atmosphere that predominates in areas of Taiwan removed from the major cities.

EASTERN ISLANDS

LANYU

Lanyu, also known as Orchid Island, is located in the Pacific Ocean about 47 mi (76 km) southeast of the city of Taitung. It is the home of the Yami, Taiwan's smallest and most primitive aboriginal tribe. The Yami number only about 2,600, and their lifestyle is very simple. The Japanese, during their rule of Taiwan, did little to disrupt the Yami, allowing them to maintain their own special culture.

In days past, Lanyu was called Death Island because of the way the inhabitants treated those unfortunate enough to be shipwrecked there, and because of a small mite whose bite was fatal. Those times have passed though, and now the island is named after the numerous orchids that grow in the mountain areas. Despite the Yami's past reputation for ferocity, they were never headhunters, as some of the other aborigine tribes were. They live mainly by fishing, supplementing their diets with cultivated crops such as taro.

Formosa Airlines and Taiwan Airlines operate nearly a dozen daily flights between Taitung and Orchid Island, and there are three daily flights direct from Kaohsiung. There are also three round-trip flights a week direct from Taipei. For anyone wishing to see a remarkable example of unspoiled primitive culture, a trip to Lanyu is a must.

LUTAO

Lutao, or Green Island, is located about 47 mi (75 km) north of Lanyu. With an area of 6.3 sq mi (16.3 km²), Lutao is the fourth-largest of the 85 islands surrounding Taiwan. The present population of Lutao is estimated at about 5,000. Most of the men work as fishermen or breed fish, while the women do the bulk of the farming.

The island has, over the past few years, become a resort, with a comfortable new hostel capable of accommodating 102 people. The hostel, located on the island's southern tip, is the center of a recreational complex offering camping, picnicking, sightseeing, and hiking in the hills. The reefs, waters, and beaches around the island afford opportunities for fishing, swimming, scuba diving, and collecting seashells.

Lutao is well known for another reason: it is the site of Taiwan's most formidable prison. The prison complex, completely isolated from the resort areas, is used mainly for repeat criminals and political prisoners.

There are five daily flights by Formosa Airlines from Taitung to Green Island. The flights take about 15 minutes.

CENTRAL TAIWAN

CENTRAL Taiwan has a great number of excellent attractions and is known best for Taroko Gorge, Alishan, and Sun Moon Lake. The area is blessed with the island's best climate, allowing year-round enjoyment for visitors and locals alike. The city of Taichung, the third largest in Taiwan, possesses another of Taiwan's major seaports.

The east and west coasts of Taiwan are linked by the East-West Cross-Island Highway, many parts of which are hewn through solid marble. In addition to serving the practical purpose of connecting the two sides of the island, the highway's eastern stretch passes through Taroko Gorge, considered by many one of the world's great natural wonders.

TAICHUNG

In 1721, settlers from the Chinese mainland established Tatun village, which was later renamed Taichung, meaning "Central Taiwan." Present-day Taichung covers an area of 63 sq mi (163 km²) and has a population of more than 725,000. The island's third largest city, Taichung has become Central Taiwan's major economic, cultural, and communications center, and is the most convenient starting point for tours to nearby attractions such as the Giant Buddha at Changhua, Sun Moon Lake, Hsitou, the Encore Garden, and the East-West Cross-Island Highway.

LUKANG

Lukang, a small fishing village situated some 13 mi (21 km) from Taichung, is one of Taiwan's most important historical and cultural towns. Established in the 17th century, Lukang was named for the large herds of deer (in Chinese, *lu*) that once roamed the area.

Many years ago, Lukang was one of Taiwan's finest natural harbors and the preferred port of entry for immigrants from the mainland. It was closed during the Japanese occupation, however, and since that time the harbor has silted up, so that it is now useless for anything but small fishing boats. During its golden age, many craftsmen and artisans were hired to construct imposing houses and temples. Their descendants continue to give Lukang a well-deserved reputation for its folk arts and crafts.

SUN MOON LAKE

Taiwan's most popular year-round resort, Sun Moon Lake, is located in the Central Mountain Range, 50 mi (80 km) southwest of Taichung. Besides the beautiful scenery and peaceful surroundings, the lake has other attractions, including temples, the island's highest pagoda, an aborigine village, good hiking trails, a golf course, and boating.

Several hotels and hostels and a youth activity center provide a range of adequate accommodations and dining, and the lake is the most popular Taiwan destination for honeymooners.

ALISHAN

The small village of Alishan is linked to the city of Chiayi by a narrow-gauge railway and a toll highway. There are several hotels in Alishan, and because of the resort's popularity, advance reservations are advisable, especially during holidays.

Taking the train to Alishan is an event in itself. The mountain is so steep that the train goes part of the way forward and then, instead of winding up the mountain, reverses direction and goes up backwards.

Alishan is well known for its spectacular sunrise, and from nearby Mount Chu visitors can, on clear mornings, view one of Taiwan's most enthralling sights: sunrise over the celebrated Sea of Clouds that rings Yushan.

PEIKANG

Peikang, a small town not far from Chiayi, is famous for the most impressive of the island's 383 temples dedicated to Matsu, the goddess

TAICHUNG

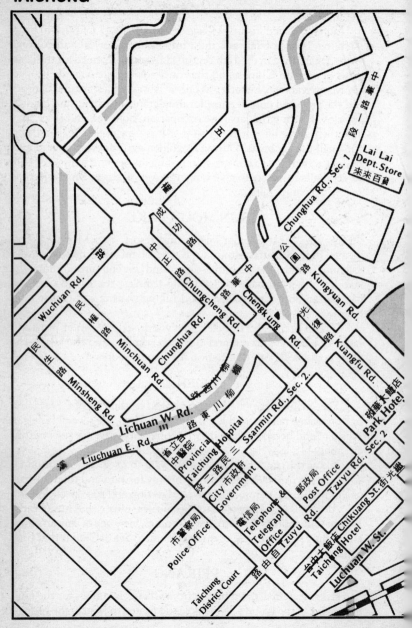

Lai Lai Dept. Store
來來百貨

中華路一段
Chunghua Rd., Sec. 1

成功路

中正路
Chungcheng Rd.

中華路
Chenkung Rd.

公園路

Kungyuan Rd.

Wuchuan Rd.

民權路

光復路

Kuangfu Rd.

Minchuan Rd.

Chunghua Rd.

民生路
Minsheng Rd.

Lichuan W. Rd.

柳川西路

柳川東路
Liuchuan E. Rd.

Ssanmin Rd., Sec. 2

省立台中醫院
Provincial Taichung Hopital

City 市政府 Government

三民路二段

台糖大飯店
Park Hotel

Kuang Rd., Sec. 2

電信局
Telephone & Telegraph Office

郵政局
Post Office

自由路 Tzuyu

市警察局
Police Office

Tzuyu Rd.

自由路 Tzuyu

光街

台中大飯店
Taichang Hotel

Chikuang St.

Luchuan W. St.

Taichung District Court

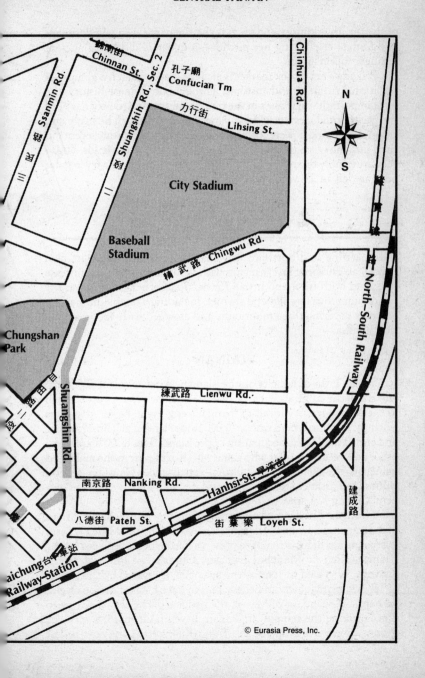

of the sea. In addition, the town is the site of the annual pilgrimage and festival celebrating her birthday, a dynamic display of ancient Chinese folk religion.

Peikang's regular ox market is also the place to catch a glimpse of traditional rural life and customs. Throughout Chinese history, the most important single asset in the traditional agrarian society has been the water buffalo, essential for a variety of farm tasks. The lively and colorful ox markets were for centuries the most important events in rural life, the place to buy and sell and socialize with friends. Today they are rapidly disappearing as Taiwan modernizes; only a few regular ones are left in Taiwan, and the largest is at Peikang.

SOUTHERN TAIWAN

LIKE central and northern Taiwan, southern Taiwan has its own appeal: an enticing, lovely region with verdant green plains, historic sites, and both rural and urban towns. Southern Taiwan is also the site of numerous temples and shrines, including a temple-monastery complex covering three mountains and crowned with 480 images of the Buddha.

TAINAN

Tainan is the oldest city on the island, was its capital for 203 years, and is still the cultural center of Taiwan. The city's history owes much to the Ming Dynasty loyalist Cheng Ch'eng-kung, better known as Koxinga, a national hero whose 30,000 troops landed at Tainan in 1661 and ended the Dutch occupation of the island. The 1,000 literati and other devotees of the arts who came with Koxinga from the mainland launched the island's first cultural renaissance. (Taiwan's second cultural renaissance started 305 years later, initiated by the late President Chiang Kai-shek in 1966.)

The name *Koxinga* is a latinization of the title *Kuo Hsing Yeh* ("Lord of the Imperial Surname") conferred on Cheng by the Ming Dynasty in recognition of his attempt to preserve it from being replaced by the Ch'ing (Qing, or Manchu) Dynasty, China's last imperial rulers. Koxinga, who died in 1662 at the age of 38, is revered by the people of Taiwan, many of whom believe him to have been of divine origin, perhaps a descendant of Matsu, the goddess of the sea. A shrine to him is among the temples in Tainan. It was built in 1875 with the express approval of Emperor Teh Tsung (Kuang Hsü), the next-to-last of the Ch'ing Dynasty's 12 monarchs. This signified that the emperor had forgiven his dynasty's former archenemy and recognized him as a national hero. Also associated with Koxinga are two temples at Deer Ear Gate, where Koxinga's forces landed in Taiwan. One is the Matsu Temple, housing a 1,000-year-old image of the goddess that Koxinga brought with him; the other, the Temple of the Holy Mother, an outstanding complex of buildings, combines Buddhism, Taoism, and the Matsu cult.

Two points that should be visited in Tainan are the Chihkan Towers and the Confucian Temple. After the Dutch surrender in 1661, Koxinga established Taiwan's first Chinese government at Fort Providentia, the former Dutch headquarters. The fort was leveled by an earthquake in 1862, and the Chinese authorities then erected the Chihkan Towers in 1875. Taiwan's oldest Confucian temple, built in 1665, is located three blocks from Koxinga's Shrine in Tainan. Arched gates divide the peaceful garden compound into a series of halls and courtyards. Because of the temple's classical architecture, it is acclaimed as the finest Confucian temple on the island. Another notable building is the Taoist Temple of the Jade Emperor.

Chihkan Tower, built on site of Dutch Fort Providentia

TAINAN

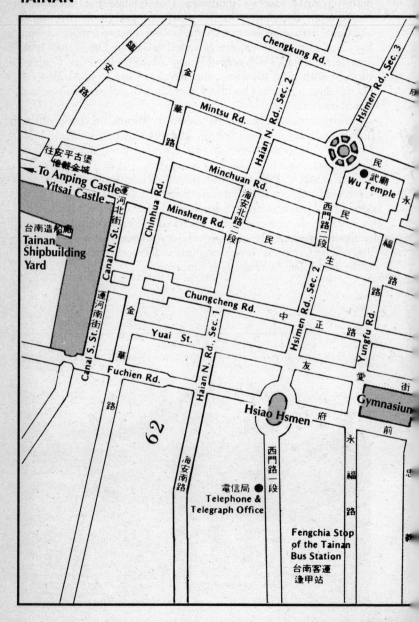

Chengkung Rd.

Hsimen Rd., Sec. 3

Mintsu Rd.

Haian N. Rd., Sec. 2

往安平古堡
憶載金城
← To Anping Castle
Yitsai Castle

武廟
● Wu Temple

Minchuan Rd.

台南造船廠
Tainan Shipbuilding Yard

Chinhua Rd.

Minsheng Rd.

Canal N. St.

海安北路一段

西門路二段

民

生

路

Hsimen Rd., Sec. 2

民

福

路

Yungfu Rd.

Chungcheng Rd.

中

正

路

金

Canal S. St.

Yuai St.

華

路

Fuchien Rd.

Haian N. Rd., Sec. 1

友

62

Gymnasium

愛

街

前

Hsiao Hsmen

西門路一段

府

海安南路

電信局 ●
Telephone & Telegraph Office

永

福

路

街

忠

義

Fengchia Stop of the Tainan Bus Station
台南客運
逢甲站

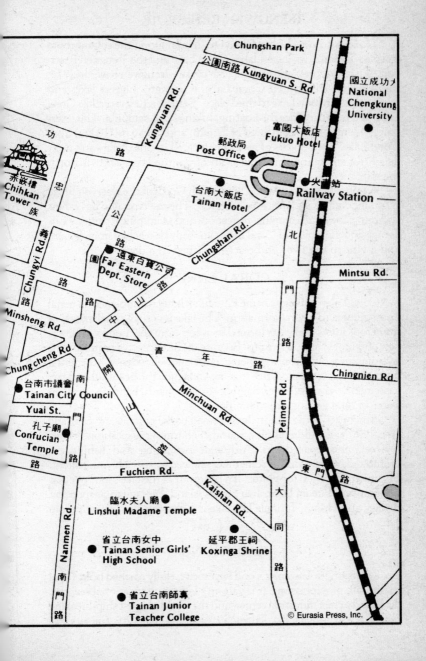

Chungshan Park

公園南路 Kungyuan S. Rd.

Kungyuan Rd.

國立成功大
National Chengkung University

功
路
忠

富國大飯店
Fukuo Hotel

赤嵌樓
Chihkan Tower

郵政局
Post Office

族

火車站
Railway Station

台南大飯店
Tainan Hotel

義

Chungyi Rd

路

公

路

北

門

Chungshan Rd.

遠東百貨公司
Far Eastern Dept. Store

Mintsu Rd.

路

中

山

路

Minsheng Rd.

Chungcheng Rd.

青

年

路

Chingnien Rd.

台南市議會
Tainan City Council

南

門

Minchuan Rd.

Peimen Rd.

Yuai St.

山

孔子廟
Confucian Temple

路

路

Fuchien Rd.

大

Kaishan Rd.

Nanmen Rd.

東

門

路

臨水夫人廟
Linshui Madame Temple

省立台南女中
Tainan Senior Girls' High School

延平郡王祠
Koxinga Shrine

同

路

南

門

省立台南師專
Tainan Junior Teacher College

© Eurasia Press, Inc.

TSENGWEN RESERVOIR

Those who travel from Chiayi to Tainan along the inland route will pass Taiwan's two largest lakes, Coral Lake and the Tsengwen Reservoir. With the completion of the dam on the Tsengwen River in 1973, the reservoir supplanted Coral Lake as Taiwan's biggest lake, and relegated Sun Moon Lake to third place. Tsengwen Reservoir, like Coral Lake, is a popular place for boating, hiking, and camping. The reservoir is 37 mi (60 km) northeast of Tainan, and only 6 mi (10 km) from Coral Lake. Both bodies of water are located in one of Taiwan's most delightful areas, and the drive to and from the lakes alone is worth the trip.

A hostel operated by the China Youth Corps at the reservoir offers accommodations and meals at low prices. The reservoir also has cabins and bungalows and camping, recreation, and swimming facilities. Both Tsengwen Reservoir and Coral Lake can easily be reached from Tainan, and a visit to the two can be accomplished in a day.

CORAL LAKE

Coral Lake derives its name from its striking resemblance, in aerial photographs, to a coral formation. The lake is actually a labyrinth of numerous inlets and islets formed by water from the Tsengwen Reservoir and more than 30 streams. Because of the deceptive nature of this lake of mazes, only licensed operators are allowed to handle the rental boats. This leaves visitors free to relax and enjoy the beautiful scenery: a fascinating world of water, bamboo, fruit orchards, bamboo rafts, and water buffalo grazing or swimming.

Amenities at the lake include a small park, a picnic and camping area, hiking, a children's playground, a charming suspension bridge, a hotel, and boat docks. Although swimming and fishing are prohibited, water-skiing is sometimes allowed by special arrangement. The main attraction for visitors is a boat tour of the lake's four popular destinations: Dream Lake, Two Sisters Island, Paotzuliao Suspension Bridge, and Hsikou Tunnel. The lake is a pleasant half-day trip from Tainan.

KAOHSIUNG

Kaohsiung is Taiwan's second largest city, easily reached from Taipei by air, rail, or expressway. It is Taiwan's largest international seaport, the island's chief industrial center, and the world's largest ship-breaking center. Kaohsiung is, like Taipei, a special municipality: the city has the same status as a province and its mayor the same status as a provincial governor. Kaohsiung is the site of the island's only other international airport besides Taipei's Chiang Kai-shek Airport. The city covers an area of 59 sq mi (153 km²) and has a population of almost 1.5 million. With almost 200 days annually of warm weather, Kaohsiung is a place where winter is more of a concept than a reality.

Differing from Taipei in layout, Kaohsiung is blessed with wide streets and avenues that foster a very friendly and open attitude among its inhabitants. Kaohsiung's charm, like that of the other cities in Taiwan, lies in its number of scenic attractions, many of which are located in the city proper and easily accessible by taxi or bus.

Within easy reach of the city are several popular tourist attractions: Shou Shan, a hill topped by a martyrs' shrine offering impressive views of the city; Lotus Lake, with its Dragon and Tiger Pagodas and Taiwan's newest Confucian Temple; Cheng Ching Lake, a resort area; and Fo Kuang Shan Temple, home to the island's tallest image of the Buddha. For those who want relief from the heat of summer, the beach at Hsi Tzu Bay is located at the city's edge, not far from Shou Shan.

Only a 15-minute drive from downtown Kaohsiung is the beautiful resort known as Cheng Ching Lake, where boating, fishing, hiking, golf, and swimming are available in addition to magnificent scenery. Restaurants, hostels, and the Kaohsiung Grand Hotel provide accommodations and dining for visitors. Kaohsiung is also used as a base for trips to other attractions in the southern part of the island, such as Kenting National Park and Fo Kuang Shan Temple.

FO KUANG SHAN

Fo Kuang Shan—the name means "Light of Buddha Mountain"— is one of Taiwan's largest temple and monastery complexes. The temple is located about an hour's drive northeast of Kaohsiung and is known as Taiwan's center of Buddhist scholarship. The more than 400 monks and nuns who reside in the complex work as counselors in jails, factories, and homes, and the temple offers Buddhist summer camps for students and education classes for primary, secondary, and university level teachers, does charity work with the aged, and runs orphanages for the young.

As one of Taiwan's most active Buddhist monasteries, Fo Kuang Shan is often the scene of Buddhist celebrations, and a 140-room travelers' hostel was built to accommodate people who come from afar. The accommodations are almost up to international standards, with carpeting, television, and refrigerators in most rooms, and a restaurant

KAOHSIUNG

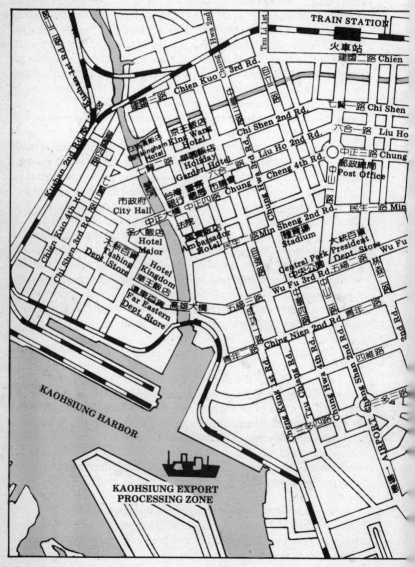

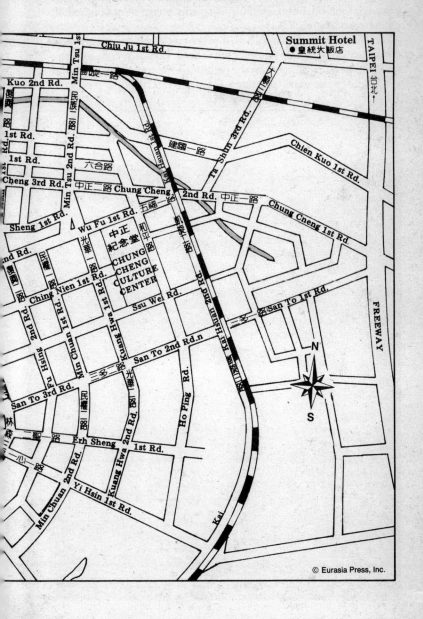

© Eurasia Press, Inc.

that serves excellent Chinese vegetarian cuisine. No fee is charged for rooms or for food, but the temple will gladly accept donations to help defray costs.

In addition to the temples that make up the monastery, there are an orphanage, primary school, high school, Buddhist college, retirement village, and cemetery on the premises. One could literally go from the cradle to the grave without leaving the monastery complex.

Dragon and Tiger pagodas, Kaohsiung

KENTING

The southernmost point of Taiwan is a tropical crescent known as the Hengchun ("Eternal Spring") Peninsula. Two arms, Oluanpi to the east and Maopitou to the west, reach into the sea, and the wide bay between contains some of the island's best beaches, scenic attractions, and lush tropical flora flourishing under a clear, warm sky. Kenting National Park covers a total of 126 sq mi (326 km2), nearly half of which is water. The park includes an ecological protection area, scenic areas, historic sites, and a recreation area.

The unique climate and terrain, from the forested mountains to the coastal plains, nourish abundant plant and animal life. During the fall migration the shallow Lungluan Lake becomes a bird watcher's paradise as ducks, herons, and plovers descend on scenic Kenting. The area's biggest attraction is the sea. The coral reefs off the west coast abound with aquatic life, making the area popular for both scuba diving and snorkeling.

WESTERN ISLANDS

PENGHU

Penghu is an archipelago made up of 64 islands spread over 600 sq mi (1,550 km²) in the Taiwan Strait. The islands were formerly known as the Pescadores ("Fishermen's Isles"), a name bestowed by 16th-century Portuguese mariners. The islands were not formally listed as Chinese territory until the year 1171, during the Southern Sung Dynasty. The islands' natural harbors once served as safe havens for the pirates that ravaged the Chinese coast and, along with Taiwan, the islands were invaded or occupied by the Dutch, French, and Japanese.

Since 1960 the archipelago has been a county of Taiwan Province. Almost half the total population of 120,000 lives on Penghu Island, mainly in Makung, the county capital and the only sizable town in the group, and 21 of the islands are uninhabited. The three largest islands in the group, Penghu, Paisha, and Hsiyu, are linked by causeways and a bridge.

As the islands' former name implies, fishing is the major source of income for their inhabitants, and the day's catch is one of the delights for tourists. The islands are also one of the world's major sources of coral. Farming is difficult because of the strong winds that scour the islands from October through March. The crops (peanuts, sweet potatoes, and melons) are protected from the winds by stone walls, without which it would be impossible to grow anything.

One of the interesting features of the islands is the profusion of temples (147), most erected by fishermen. The Matsu Temple, built in 1592, is Taiwan's oldest and is one of the most interesting temples in honor of the patron deity of fishermen. Another interesting sight is Paisha Island's 300-year-old banyan tree, anchored by 91 trunks and forming the canopy of a small temple. At a place named Fengkuei, typhoon-driven waves force air and water up through small holes in the rock, producing music-like sounds along with the spray.

Another part of the island group that attracts tourists is Chimei Island. During the Ming Dynasty (1368–1644), seven virgins drowned themselves in a well to escape possible violation by raiding pirates. The people were so impressed by their chastity that they erected a tomb in their honor, known as the Tomb of the Seven Virgins. Chimei can be reached from Makung by motorboats (a three-hour trip), or by one of the two round-trip flights a day (15 minutes each way).

Tourists in a hurry can cover the main points of interest in a day trip from Taipei. Public buses, guided tours, or chartered taxis can be taken for the four-hour tour, glass-bottom boats can be hired for a cruise, and other water sports are available. An inexpensive meal of fresh seafood is a must.

Five of Taiwan's domestic airlines fly from major cities to Makung daily. A daily ferry leaves the Kaohsiung pier at 7:30 AM for the four-and-a-half hour voyage. The Alishan liner leaves Putai (near Chiayi) three times a day and costs NT$400 each way; for reservations, call (06) 692–4878 or 223–3969. The *Happy Princess* liner leaves Taichung for Makung at 9:30 each morning. Tickets for the *Happy Princess* cruise are sold at No. 262 Chunghua Rd., Sec. 1, Taichung.

HSIAO LIUCHIU

A small island, Hsiao Liuchiu has only two small villages. But it is a place of lush green beauty and unspoiled charm, offering excellent seafood and an opportunity to snorkel in crystal-clear water. The island is only 12 mi (20 km) from Taiwan and can be reached by boats leaving from the Tungkang fishing harbor. The ride itself is a pleasant experience.

VI

Hotels
and Lodging

There are close to 150 hotels scattered across the length and breadth of Taiwan, and the number is increasing annually. Those that meet international standards are numerous and charge rates close to US$200 per night. Since July 1988, the 5% government tax previously added to every bill has been included in the published prices. However, an additional 10% service tax is standard on rooms and all food and beverage charges. Reservations can be made through international reservation systems such as Utell, Distinguished Hotels of the World, and Delton Reservations, and are necessary, especially during the high season. All international-standard hotels have full amenities, and bilingual staff, speaking either English, Japanese, or some of the European languages.

The Taiwan Tourism Bureau evaluates the country's hotels. While most Western countries award hotels a number of stars to indicate their excellence, in Taiwan hotels are awarded plum blossoms, the Republic of China's national flower. A group of hotel specialists determined the criteria that are used for hotel ratings. The facilities of the hotel, its architectural design, management, sanitation, the quality of the food and service, and other factors are considered by the evaluators in rating hotels. Those that receive the highest ratings—four or five plum blossoms—are considered international tourist hotels, and are usually deluxe properties, offering their guests a wide variety of facilities, services, and amenities. Hotels that receive two- or three-plum-blossom ratings are considered tourist class, and are generally not as deluxe as the four- or five-plum-blossom ones. Taiwan also has hostels and youth activity centers, where budget-minded tourists can stay in inexpensive dormitory-style rooms.

HOTELS IN TAIPEI

LEADING HOTELS

Taipei has approximately 25 hotels classified as international standard, some 13 of which are rated "deluxe." There are roughly the same number classified as tourist hotels and a slightly smaller number not rated. Although it is usually possible to get a room in a deluxe hotel, the Taiwan hotel industry estimates that during the two high-season periods there is a 3,000-room shortage that will not be remedied until 1991 or later. Taipei hotels direct their services primarily to business travelers and are equipped with IDD telephones, fax machines, and complete secretarial services. Group tours are accepted by some of the hotels, but only on a space-available basis. Most of the hotels in Taipei have traditionally been located in the center of the city, close to either the Taipei World Trade Center or the various financial and commercial districts, but Taipei City is expanding eastward, and most newer businesses and hotel properties are being established in that area.

Ambassador Hotel (5 Plum Blossoms—500 rooms)
Address: 63 Chungshan North Rd., Sec. 2
Telephone: (02) 551–1111
Fax: (2) 561–7883
Telex: 11255, 11184
Rates: Single—NT$3,700–5,300; Double—NT$4,300–5,500; Suite—NT$9,900–38,000.

The Ambassador Hotel, newly redecorated at the end of 1988, is in the center of Taipei City on Chungshan North Rd., 40 minutes from CKS International Airport. All the rooms are air-conditioned and completely carpeted, with private baths, IDD, refrigerators, radios, and color TVs. The hotel's restaurants offer French, Japanese, Cantonese, and Szechuan cuisines. Fax and telex service are available at the Ambassador as well as a shopping arcade, swimming pool, and beauty and barber shops.

Asiaworld Plaza Hotel (5 Plum Blossoms—1,057 rooms)
Address: 100 Tunhua North Rd.
Telephone: (02) 715–0077
Fax: (02) 713–4148
Rates: Single—NT$4,840; Double—NT$5,000

The Asiaworld Plaza Hotel was the largest in Taipei at the end of 1988. The hotel is ideally located in the commercial and financial district and boasts a number of fine restaurants. All rooms are equipped with the standard amenities. Because of its size, the Asiaworld is one of the few international-standard hotels that regularly takes groups.

Brother Hotel (5 Plum Blossoms—304 rooms)
Address: 255 Nanking East Rd., Sec. 3
Telephone: (02) 712–3456
Fax: (02) 717–3334
Rates: Singles—NT$2,640-NT$3,300; Doubles—NT$3,300 and up.

The Brother Hotel on Nanking East Rd. in the commercial district is considered one of the better lower-priced hotels. Service at the Brother Hotel is second to none, and the facilities are every bit as good as in those hotels charging considerably more. All rooms are air-conditioned, with private bath, color TV, and refrigerator. Restaurants in the Brother Hotel include Cantonese, Taiwanese, Japanese, and Western. There is a cocktail lounge, shopping arcade, beauty salon and barber shop. The Brother Hotel also has a parking lot and convention rooms seating 500.

Taipei Fortuna Hotel (5 Plum Blossoms—304 rooms)
Address: 122 Chungshan North Rd., Sec. 2
Telephone: (02) 563-1111
Fax: (02) 561-9777
Rates: Singles—NT$3,740-4,180; Double—NT$4,180-4,840
   The Fortuna is located in the commercial district. Each room is complete with all amenities, and in-house facilities include a Cantonese restaurant, coffee shop, health club, jacuzzi, sauna, solarium, business center, and Taipei's only revolving rooftop restaurant.

Fortune Dragon Hotel Taipei (4 Plum Blossoms—312 rooms)
Address: 172 Chunghsiao East Rd., Sec. 4
Telephone: (02) 772-2121
Fax: (02) 721-0302
Rates: Single—NT$3,300-3,850; Double—NT$3,850-4,400
   The Fortune Dragon Hotel Taipei, located in the new eastern business district, was completely remodeled in 1988 and offers personalized service and a wide range of business-oriented facilities, including convention and banquet rooms, a sauna and health center, beauty salon, barber shop, valet service, and an executive business service. The hotel caters primarily to Japanese businessmen.

Grand Hotel (5 Plum Blossoms—575 rooms)
Address: 1 Chungshan North Rd., Sec. 4
Telephone: (02) 596-5565
Fax: (02) 594-8243
Rates: Single—NT$2,695-3,685; Double—NT$3,135-4,125
   The Grand Hotel, traditionally designed to represent the glory of ancient China, sits majestically on a hilltop overlooking the city of Taipei. The rooms are air conditioned and carpeted, with private baths, IDD, radios, refrigerators, and color TVs. There is a Western dining room and a grillroom, as well as a Chinese dining room and a

Cantonese restaurant. The Grand's convention hall can accommodate 1,600 people, which makes the hotel ideal for large conferences. The hotel boasts all the amenities of the other international-standard hotels and is even equipped with its own bowling alley. The main problem with the Grand is that it is government-owned and -operated, and the service leaves much to be desired.

Taipei Hilton International (5 Plum Blossoms—413 rooms)
Address: 38 Chunghsiao West Rd., Sec. 1
Telephone: (02) 311–5151
Fax: (02) 331–9944
Rates: Standard—Single NT$3,800–4,600, Double NT$4,250–5,100;
Executive floor—Single NT$5,500, Double NT$6,000
    The Taipei Hilton Hotel is Taipei's first, and really only, internationally managed property. Each of the Hilton's guest rooms is equipped with all the conveniences of a deluxe hotel. The hotel offers two nonsmoking floors and three executive floors, which provide special amenities to business travelers. The executive floors have separate check-in, a private lounge offering complimentary buffet breakfast and cocktails, and a manager to provide special personalized service. Located in downtown Taipei, almost directly across from the Taipei railway station, the Hilton provides easy access to parks and shopping. For the business traveler, the hotel offers complimentary transportation to and from meetings. Amenities include a rooftop jacuzzi; a health club with sauna, tanning room, fully equipped gymnasium and a beauty salon; function rooms for up to 460 persons; and six excellent restaurants.

Howard Plaza Hotel (5 Plum Blossoms—606 rooms)
Address: 160 Jenai Rd., Sec. 3
Telephone: (02) 700–2323
Fax: (02) 700–0729, 705–2803
Rates: Single—NT$4,400–5,700; Double—NT$4,700–6,000
    Rated the best hotel in Taipei by the *New York Times* in its October 23, 1988, issue, the Howard Plaza Hotel is one of the newest of Taipei's five-star hotels. With guest rooms elegantly furnished in rosewood and authentic art works, the Howard Plaza offers the finest in accommodations for the business or pleasure traveler. The hotel's 10 food and beverage outlets provide European, American, Japanese, Shanghainese, Cantonese, and Taiwanese cuisines. The rooms are deluxe, and their amenities include IDD, satellite television programming from the United States and Japan, refrigerator and mini-bar, and hair drier and

bathrobe. A completely equipped business center, a health center with steam bath and sauna, a beautifully landscaped outdoor swimming pool, banquet and meeting rooms for 10 to 800 persons, a four-floor shopping mall, a doctor on call 24 hours and a dispensary, and parking for 250 cars—all these put the Howard Plaza in a class by itself. Combined with fine service and excellent facilities, the Howard's location (10 minutes from the Taipei World Trade Center) has made it the first choice for business travelers visiting Taipei.

Lai Lai Sheraton Hotel (5 Plum Blossoms—704 rooms)
Address: 12 Chunghsiao East Rd., Sec. 1
Telephone: (02) 321-5511
Fax: (02) 394-4240
Rates: Standard—Single $4,750; Superior — Single/Double NT$5,000; Deluxe—Single/Double NT$5,800; Executive—NT$8,500; Suite—NT$10,500-80,000

The Lai Lai is a landmark in Taipei and one of the best of the deluxe hotels. The second largest of the hotels in existence in January 1989, it attracts mainly a business clientele. Huge banquet and conference areas holding up to 2,000 people make the Lai Lai very convenient for large seminars and cocktail receptions. The hotel's guest rooms are furnished with every amenity including personal safes, mini-bars, refrigerators, IDD, TVs, and radios. Eight restaurants offer French, American, Cantonese, Shanghainese, Taiwanese, Hunan, Italian, and Japanese cuisines to satisfy the most discriminating diner. The Lai Lai also has a complete fitness center, jogging track, rooftop swimming pool, billiard room, and squash court. In addition, the hotel offers 57 shops in its arcade.

Mandarin Hotel (5 Plum Blossoms—350 rooms)
Address: 166 Tunhua North Rd.
Telephone: (02) 712-1201
Fax: (02) 712-2122
Rates: Single—NT$2,970-3,465; Double—NT$3,465-3,905

The Mandarin is located close to Taipei's domestic airport and near the commercial district. The hotel's modern rooms boast all the amenities, Chinese and Western restaurants, a Mongolian barbecue, a beauty parlor and a barber shop, a shopping arcade, a swimming pool, tennis courts, a health center with sauna, a discotheque, and convention halls holding up to 1,500 people.

President Hotel (5 Plum Blossoms—433 rooms)
Address: 9 Tehwei St.
Telephone: (02) 595–1251
Fax: (02) 591–3677
Rates: Single—NT$3,630; Double—NT$3,982–4,427

The President Hotel is one of the first international-class hotels to have opened in Taipei. It is located in the club and bar district and is popular with business travelers who want moderate prices and access to a wide variety of evening entertainment. The hotel is fully air-conditioned and offers complete amenities. Restaurants in the hotel serve American, French, Hunan, and Cantonese cuisines. The President offers Executive Express Service for business travelers, a shopping arcade, and extensive meeting facilities.

Rebar Crown Hotel (5 Plum Blossoms—300 rooms)
Address: 32 Nanking East Rd., Sec. 5
Telephone: (02) 763–5656
Fax: (02) 767–9347
Rates: Single—NT$3,960; Double—NT$4,070–4,290

The Rebar Crown, located in eastern Taipei, has beautifully decorated guest rooms complete with all amenities. The hotel caters primarily to a business clientele and offers French and Cantonese cuisines in its restaurants, a discotheque, lobby and piano bars, a health center with sauna, and a beauty parlor and barber shop. Valet parking is available for guests, and the Rebar Crown has conference facilities and banquet halls for parties or business functions.

Regent Taipei (560 rooms)
Address: 41 Chungshan North Rd., Sec. 2
Telephone: (02) 542–1024
Fax: (02) 543–1643
Rates: Standard—NT$5,200; Deluxe—NT$6,000; Regent—NT$6,800

The Regent Taipei was scheduled to open in 1990 as part of the Regent group and sister to the Regent Hong Kong. Its anticipated clientele is the very top-of-the-line business travelers. The rooms are from 409 to 667 sq ft (38–62 m²) in area and have super-deluxe amenities: three IDD telephones (desk, bedside, and bathroom) with two lines each, 108-sq-ft (10-m²) bathrooms with marble furnishings, and televisions with individual videotape players. Additional services are a videotape library of films and tapes of different businesses in Taiwan, a 24-hour business center, 24-hour butler service, 24-hour room service, health spa and pool, and a 5,380-sq-ft (5,000 m²), two-level shopping arcade. The Regent's four restaurants consist of an all-day dining room serving Continental and California cuisine, and overlooking a beautiful Japanese garden; a steakhouse serving only U.S.D.A. prime; a Chinese restaurant serving the very freshest Cantonese cuisine and using only jade and ivory table settings; and a Chinese restaurant serving dim sum, Peking duck, and other popular dishes. There are two lounges, one in the lobby and one in the four-story atrium, a 400-seat ballroom, six meeting rooms, and parking for 450 cars.

Ritz Taipei (5 Plum Blossoms—204 rooms)
Address: 155 Minchuan East Rd.
Telephone: (02) 597-1234
Fax: (02) 596-9223
Rates: Standard—NT$4,950; Deluxe—NT$6,200
　　　The Ritz Taipei was opened in 1979 and the rooms were completely remodeled in 1987. The hotel, located in the commercial district, is the only Taipei member of Leading Hotels of the World. The Ritz is most famous for its extremely personalized service. There is a central dehumidifying system, and each room has individually controlled air conditioning and temperature control, along with radio, color TV showing English-language movies, large writing desk, alarm clock, full bath and shower, room safe, and other deluxe features. The hotel also offers a nonsmoking floor, same-day laundry and dry cleaning, valet parking, a doctor on call 24 hours a day, secretarial service, gym, sauna, and outdoor jacuzzi. The hotel has 24-hour room service, and its restaurants provide authentic Hunan, Hangchow, French, and Continental cuisines. There are also a lobby cocktail lounge and piano bar, and the banquet hall can accommodate up to 400 guests. No groups are accepted at the Ritz, and its guest makeup is 98%-99% business travelers. The hotel is so popular that it is usually 100% occupied during the high season, and more than a few CEOs plan their trips to Taipei only when they can be assured of a room at the Ritz.

Riverview Hotel Taipei (4 Plum Blossoms—250 rooms)
Address: 77 Huanho South Rd.
Telephone: (02) 311-3131
Fax: (02) 361-3737
Rates: Single—NT$2,400-3,000; Double—NT$3,000-4,000
　　　The Riverview opened only in 1988, and is located in the old part of town, next to the Tamsui River. Rooms come complete with ameni-

ties, and the hotel's restaurants offer Hunan and French cuisines. There is parking for 100 cars, and banquet and conference facilities.

Hotel Royal Taipei (5 Plum Blossoms—203 rooms)
Address: 37-1 Chungshan North Rd., Sec. 2
Telephone: (02) 542-3266
Fax: (02) 543-4897
Rates: Single—NT$3,800-4,500; Double—NT$4,950-5,500

The Hotel Royal Taipei, a member of Nikko Hotels International, is located in the heart of one of the major shopping areas on Chungshan North Rd. The Royal celebrated its fifth birthday in January 1989, which makes it one of the younger of Taipei's deluxe hotels. The hotel offers a full complement of facilities, including French, Japanese, and Cantonese restaurants, a coffee shop, a bar, a swimming pool, a health club, a sauna, beauty and barber shops, and gift shops. The Royal is designed in the European style and its entrance, of Italian marble with Austrian crystal chandeliers, provides a warm and welcoming ambience. Guests at the Royal receive twice-daily maid service and the personalized attention that a smaller hotel can provide. All room amenities are deluxe and designed for the business traveler.

Sherwood Teipei Hotel (335 rooms)
Address: 637 Minsheng East Rd.
Telephone: (02) 718-1188
Fax: (02) 713-0707

The Sherwood is another of the new hotels that opened in late 1989 and early 1990. Located in the financial district, the Sherwood is one of the smaller Taipei properties. The hotel is European style and features super deluxe amenities in the rooms, including two-line IDD phones, kingsize beds, in-room safes, and video tape recorders. The Sherwood's restaurants include ones serving French and Shanghainese cuisine and a coffee shop. Banqueting is very elegant and traditional at the Sherwood with seating for 15, 12-person tables. The hotel's fully equipped business center offers all necessary business services. The hotel also has a complete health center and indoor pool. The only guests accepted by the Sherwood are business travelers and some incentive groups.

OTHER TAIPEI HOTELS

Hotel China Taipei (155 rooms)
Address: 14 Kuanchien Rd.
Telephone: (02) 331-9521/9
Fax: (02) 381-2349

China Hotel Yangmingshan (50 rooms)
Address: 237 Kochi Rd., Yangmingshan
Telephone: (02) 861–6661/5
Fax: (02) 882–0885

Cosmos Hotel (268 rooms)
Address: 43 Chunghsiao West Rd., Sec. 1
Telephone: (02) 361–7856
Fax: (02) 311–8921

Emperor Hotel (97 rooms)
Address: 118 Nanking East Rd., Sec. 1
Telephone: (02) 581–1111
Fax: (02) 531–2586

Empress Hotel (100 rooms)
Address: 14 Tehwei St.
Telephone: (02) 591–3261
Fax: (02) 592–2922

Flowers Hotel (280 rooms)
Address: 19 and 36 Hankow St., Sec. 1
Telephone: (02) 312–3811
Fax: (02) 312–3800

Gala Hotel (200 rooms)
Address: 186 Sungchiang Rd.
Telephone: (02) 541–5511
Fax: (02) 531–3831

Gloria Hotel (220 rooms)
Address: 369 Linsen North Rd.
Telephone: (02) 581–8111
Fax: (02) 581–5811

Golden China Hotel (240 rooms)
Address: 306 Sungchiang Rd.
Telephone: (02) 521–5151
Fax: (02) 531–2914

Imperial Hotel (338 rooms)
Address: 600 Linsen North Rd.
Telephone: (02) 596-5111
Fax: (02) 592-7506

Majestic Hotel (405 rooms)
Address: 2 Minchuan East Rd.
Telephone: (02) 581-7111
Fax: (02) 562-3248

Miramar Hotel (584 rooms)
Address: 420 Minchuan East Rd.
Telephone: (02) 505-3456
Fax: (02) 502-9173

Modern City Hotel (200 rooms)
Address: 1 Chungching North Rd., Sec. 1
Telephone: (02) 531-6101
Fax: (02) 562-8000

New Asia Hotel (120 rooms)
Address: 139 Chungshan North Rd., Sec. 2
Telephone: (02) 511-7181
Fax: (02) 522-4204

Orient Hotel (120 rooms)
Address: 85 Hankow St., Sec. 1
Telephone: (02) 331-7211
Fax: (02) 381-3068

Paradise Hotel (256 rooms)
Address: 24 Hsining South Rd.
Telephone: (02) 314-2121
Fax: (02) 314-7873

Plaza Hotel (180 rooms)
Address: 68 Sungchiang Rd.
Telephone: (02) 551-5251

Santos Hotel (360 rooms)
Address: 439 Chengteh Rd.
Telephone: (02) 596-3111
Fax: (02) 596-3120

Star Hotel (120 rooms)
Address: 11 Hoping West Rd.
Telephone: (02) 394–3121
Fax: (02) 394–3129

United Hotel (400 rooms)
Address: 200 Kuangfu South Rd.
Telephone: (02) 773–1515
Fax: (02) 741–2789

Taipei YMCA International Guest House (90 rooms)
Address: 19 Hsuchang St.
Telephone: (02) 311–3201
Telex: 21308 YMCATPE

HOTELS IN CENTRAL TAIWAN

CHIAYI

Alishan House (3 Plum Blossoms—59 rooms)
Address: 2 West Alishan, Hsianglin Village, Wufeng Township, Chiayi
Telephone: (05) 267–9811
Rates: Single—NT$1,150; Double—NT$1,300 to NT$1,450;
Suite—NT$3,000

The Alishan House is located in the famous Alishan Forest recreation area, near Chayi City. The rooms are air-conditioned and have private baths and telephones. A tennis court, a coffee shop, a restaurant, and a souvenir shop are located on the hotel premises. There is also a parking lot.

Chiayi Farm Guest House (64 rooms)
Address: 3 Community 4, Si-Hsing Town, Ta-Pu Township, Chiayi County
Telephone: (05) 252–1710
Rates: Single or Double—NT$880; Suite for six—NT$990

The Chiayi Farm Guest House is located on the left side of the Chiayi Farm in beautiful, natural surroundings. There are a restaurant, a coffee shop, and a recreation room.

Hotel Country (2 Plum Blossoms—70 rooms)
Address: 678 Kauangtsai St., Chiayi
Telephone: (05) 223-6336
Rates: Single—NT$600 to NT$700; Double—NT$900; Suite—NT$1,100 to NT$3,000
   The Hotel Country has a restaurant and a coffee shop. There is also a parking area.

Crown Hotel (2 Plum Blossoms—60 rooms)
Address: 238-2 She Men St., Chiayi
Telephone: (05) 223-6311
Rates: Single—NT$800; Double—NT$1,000; Suite (six available)—NT$1,400
   The Crown Hotel has a restaurant located on the premises.

Gallant Hotel (4 Plum Blossoms—106 rooms)
Address: 257 Wenhua Rd., Chiayi
Telephone: (05) 223-5366
Fax: (886-5) 223-9522
Rates: Single—NT$1,500; Double—NT$1,700; Suite—NT$2,800 to NT$4,200
   The Gallant Hotel is located three minutes from the Chiayi railway station and five minutes from the Alishan railway station. Rooms are air-conditioned with private bath, telephone, color television, and a refrigerator. The hotel has several restaurants, a coffee shop, a bar, a cocktail lounge, and a nightclub. There is also a swimming pool, a souvenir shop, convention facilities, and a parking lot.

HUALIEN

Astar Hotel (4 Plum Blossoms—170 rooms)
Address: Seaview Ave., Mei-Lun, Hualien
Telephone: (038) 326-111/20
Fax: (038) 324-604
Rates: Single—NT$900 to NT$1,200; Double—NT$1,300 to NT$1,800; Suite—NT$1,800 to NT$5,000
   The Astar Hotel is located on the beach and is ten minutes away from the train station, the ocean terminal, and the airport. The hotel has a swimming pool and a bowling alley. There are Chinese and Western restaurants, a coffee shop, and a bar located on the premises. There are also a shopping arcade and a parking lot.

China Trust Hualien Hotel (5 Plum Blossoms—237 rooms)
Address: 2 Yunghsing Rd., Hualien
Telephone: (038) 221–171
Fax: (038) 221–185
Rates: Single—NT$2,310; Double—NT$3,234; Suite—NT$9,450
   This resort hotel is located in the downtown area, seven minutes away from the airport, seashore, coastal park, and railway station. All rooms are air-conditioned and have private bathrooms, telephones, radios, color televisions, and refrigerators. There are a swimming pool, gift shop, restaurant, and bar. There are also private banquet rooms and a parking lot.

Marshal Hotel (4 Plum Blossoms—350 rooms)
Address: 36 Kung Yuan Rd., Hualien
Telephone: (038) 326–123
Fax: (038) 326–140
Rates: Single—NT$1,600; Double—NT$2,200 and up; Suite—NT$3,000 and up.
   The Marshal Hotel is located in the center of Hualien city, fifteen minutes away from the airport and the beach. All rooms are air-conditioned, with private baths, telephones, radios, and color televisions. The hotel has a swimming pool and a sauna. There are Western and Chinese restaurants, a coffee shop, a bar, a cocktail lounge, and a nightclub. The hotel also has a shopping arcade, a barber shop and beauty salon, an airline desk, and convention facilities.

Tien Hsiang Lodge (40 rooms)
Address: Tien Hsiang, Hualien
Telephone: (038) 691–155
Fax: (038) 563–9755
Rates: Single—NT$1,250 to NT$1,350; Double—NT$1,350 and up; 3- and 4-person rooms also available
   The Tien Hsiang Lodge is located in the well-known Taroko Gorge. Each room has a bath and shower, color television, a telephone, and a private balcony or terrace. There are two restaurants, a bar, a coffee shop, and a swimming pool. There is also a music garden on the roof.

Toyo Hotel (2 Plum Blossoms—70 rooms)
Address: 50 San Min St., Hualien
Telephone: (038) 326–151
Fax: (038) 262–525
Rates: Single—NT$800; Double—NT$1,000; Suite—NT$1,600 to NT$2,000

The Toyo Hotel is a downtown hotel located three minutes away from the train station, five minutes away from the harbor, and eight minutes away from Hualien Airport. Rooms have private baths, color televisions, and telephones. There are a restaurant, bar, coffee shop, and a gift shop located on the premises. There are also a parking lot and meeting facilities.

ILAN

Hill Garden Hotel (3 Plum Blossoms—67 rooms)
Address: 6 Tehyang Rd., Chiaochi, Ilan
Telephone: (039) 882–011
Rates: Single—NT$450 to NT$500; Double—NT$550; Suite (four available)—NT$1,500
The Hill Garden Hotel has a swimming pool, restaurants, and a coffee shop located on the premises.

Lion Hotel (2 Plum Blossoms—47 rooms)
Address: 156 Chung Shan Rd., Lo-Tung, Ilan
Telephone: (039) 551–111
Rates: Single—NT$600 to NT$700; Double—NT$800; Suite (six available)—NT$1,200
The Lion Hotel has a Chinese restaurant, a coffee shop, and a parking lot located on the premises.

KAOHSIUNG

Ambassador Kaohsiung Hotel (5 Plum Blossoms—500 rooms)
Address: 202 Minsheng 2nd Rd.
Telephone: (07) 211–5211
Fax: (07) 281–1115
Rates: Single—NT$3,000 to NT$3,600; Double—NT$3,400 to NT$5,000; Suite—NT$9,000 to NT$30,000
The Ambassador Hotel, which was renovated in 1986, is located in the heart of Kaohsiung, on the banks of the Love River, 15 minutes away from Kaohsiung International Airport. All of the rooms are air-conditioned and each is equipped with a bath, shower, color television, and refrigerator. There are four restaurants offering guests a wide selection of cuisines. There are also a cocktail lounge, a nightclub, a

swimming pool, and a sauna. Other amenities include meeting room facilities, telex service, a shopping arcade, a beauty salon, and a barber shop. Overseas representatives are Utell International, the Tokyo Hotel Chain (Japan), Development Promotions Ltd. (South Africa), and Nikko Hotels.

Buckingham Hotel (3 Plum Blossoms—144 rooms)
Address: 394 Chihsien 2nd Rd.
Telephone: (07) 282-2151
Fax: (07) 281-4540
Rates: Single—NT$1,700 to NT$2,000; Double—NT$1,900 to NT$2,400; Suite—NT$3,000 to NT$5,000

The Buckingham Hotel is located near the Love River, in the center of Kaohsiung city, 15 minutes away from Kaohsiung International Airport and 5 minutes from the railway station. All rooms are air-conditioned and each contains a private bath, telephone, color television, and refrigerator. A Western restaurant, a coffee shop, and a bar are located on the hotel premises. Airport transfer service is available, and there is a large parking lot. The hotel also has meeting and convention facilities.

Grand Hotel (5 Plum Blossoms—108 rooms)
Address: 2 Yuanshan Rd.
Telephone: (07) 383-5911
Fax: (07) 381-4889
Rates: Single—NT$2,000 to NT$2,200; Double—NT$2,300 to NT$2,500; Suite—NT$4,600 to NT$5,000

The Grand Hotel is world-famous. Originally built in 1971, it was renovated in 1988. The hotel resembles an imperial palace and is located on scenic Cheng Ching Lake, 4 mi (6 km) away from Kaohsiung city and 15 minutes away from Kaohsiung International Airport. The rooms are air-conditioned and each room has a private bath, telephone, color television, and refrigerator. Many rooms have a lake view. There are restaurants, a coffee shop, a bar, and a nightclub located on the premises. There are also a swimming pool, a sauna, a gymnasium, and six tennis courts. A golf driving range, convention halls, a beauty salon, a barber shop, and a gift shop are also among the amenities.

Holiday Garden Hotel (5 Plum Blossoms—313 rooms)
Address: 279 Liuho 2nd Rd.
Telephone: (07) 241–0121
Fax: (07) 251–2000
Rates: Single—NT$2,650 to NT$3,460; Double—NT$2,850 to NT$3,460; Suite—NT$4,800 to NT$20,000

The Holiday Garden is a seven-story hotel located in the downtown area. It is 8 minutes away from the train station and 15 minutes away from the airport. All of the rooms are air-conditioned and each has a private bath, telephone, and color television. There are two restaurants, a coffee shop, a cocktail lounge, and a nightclub. There are also a beautiful swimming pool with a floating bar, a complete health center, a beauty salon, a barber shop, and a gift shop.

Hotel Kingdom (5 Plum Blossoms—302 rooms)
Address: 42 Wufu 4th Rd.
Telephone: (07) 551–8211
Fax: (07) 521–0403
Rates: Single—NT$2,200 to NT$2,400; Double—NT$2,600 to NT$2,800; Suite—NT$5,600 to NT$12,000

The Hotel Kingdom is located in the downtown center of the city, 5 minutes from the station and 6.8 mi (11 km) from the airport. The hotel is also 15 minutes away from the beach area. All rooms are air-conditioned, have wall-to-wall carpeting, and are equipped with private baths, radios, telephones, color televisions, and refrigerators. There are two restaurants, a cocktail lounge, and a coffee shop. A barber shop and convention and banquet hall facilities are also located on the premises. The overseas hotel representative is Utell International.

King Wang Hotel (4 Plum Blossoms—150 rooms)
Address: 329 Chihsian 2nd Rd.
Telephone: (07) 281–4141
Fax: (07) 282–0381
Rates: Single—NT$1,500; Double—NT$1,700; Suite—NT$12,000

All rooms in the King Wang Hotel have air-conditioning, telephones, and private baths. The hotel also has a restaurant, coffee shop, bar, sauna, beauty salon, and shopping arcade.

Hotel Major (4 Plum Blossoms—220 rooms)
Address: 7 Tajen Rd.
Telephone: (07) 521-2266
Fax: (07) 531-2211
Rates: Single—NT$2,100 to NT$2,300; Double—NT$2,500 to NT$2,800; Suite—NT$6,000

The Hotel Major is located in the shopping and business center of Kaohsiung, 15 minutes away from the airport. Every room is air-conditioned and is equipped with a bath, telephone, color television, and refrigerator. Two restaurants, a coffee shop, a disco bar, and convention and banquet facilities are located on the premises. Facsimile and telex services are also available.

Summit Hotel (4 Plum Blossoms—220 rooms)
Address: 426 Chiaju 1st Rd.
Telephone: (07) 384-5526
Fax: (07) 384-4739
Rates: Single—NT$2,000; Double—NT$2,200; Suite—NT$4,500 to NT$6,300

Located near Cheng Ching Lake, the Summit Hotel is ten minutes away from the airport and the station. Each hotel room is air-conditioned and has a full bath, a telephone, a color television, and a refrigerator, a coffee shop, a nightclub, and a health center. Convention facilities are also available. The nightly rate is NT$2,000 for a single and NT$2,200 for a double room. Suites can be rented at nightly rates ranging from NT$4,500 to NT$6,300.

KENTING AREA

Caesar Park Hotel (5 Plum Blossoms—250 rooms)
Address: 6 Kenting Rd., Hengchun, Pingtung County
Telephone: (08) 889-5222
Fax: (08) 889-4728
Rates: Single—NT$3,280 to NT$3,680; Double—NT$3,480 to NT$4,480; Suite (five available), NT$6,800 to NT$35,000

The Caesar Park Hotel-Kenting is located in Kenting National Park, which is on Taiwan's southernmost peninsula, and is 56 mi (90 km) from Kaohsiung International Airport. Each room is air-conditioned and has a private bath, telephone, television, and refrigerator. The rooms are furnished with rattan furniture, and each guest room has its own balcony offering splendid views. There are three restaurants at the hotel, offering a wide variety of cuisines. The hotel is located on the beach and has a swimming pool, sauna, a game room, and a gymnasium. Other activities offered by the hotel are tennis, fishing, horseback riding, and scuba diving. A nightclub and several bars are located on the hotel premises. Nikko Hotels International is the overseas representative for the Caesar Park Hotel.

Kenting House (3 Plum Blossoms—204 rooms)
Address: Kenting, Hengchung, Pingtung County
Telephone: (08) 886–1370
Fax: (08) 886–1377
Rates: Single—NT$800; Double—NT$800 to NT$1,200; Triple, Motel, Bungalow, and Suite available

The Kenting House stands on a hilltop, 0.6 mi (1 km) away from Kenting Park. There is a beach annex located on beautiful Kenting Beach. All rooms are air-conditioned with private baths and refrigerators. On the hotel premises are two large swimming pools, recreation rooms, restaurants, a coffee shop, and conference facilities.

South Formosa Hotel (3 Plum Blossoms—104 rooms)
Address: 37 Yuchuan Lane, Szuchung, Checheng Township, Pingtung County
Telephone: (08) 882–2301
Fax: (08) 882–2211
Rates: Single—NT$1,200; Double—NT$1,600; Suite—NT$2,500

The South Formosa Hotel has a hot spring, Chinese and Western restaurants, conference facilities, and a bar.

TAICHUNG

Dragon Valley Hotel (3 Plum Blossoms—193 rooms)
Address: 136 Tungkuan Rd., Sec. 1, Kukuan
Telephone: (045) 951–325, or 951–365
Rates: Single—NT$1,100; Double—NT$1,200 to NT$1,350; Suite—NT$12,000

The Dragon Valley Hotel has a restaurant and a coffee shop.

Formosa Hotel (2 Plum Blossoms—190 rooms)
Address: 27 Chungshan Rd.
Telephone: (04) 222-6701
Rates: Single—NT$500; Double—NT$700 to NT$800;
Suite—NT$1,500 to NT$2,000
    The Formosa Hotel has a Chinese and a Western restaurant, a coffee shop, and a parking lot.

Lucky Hotel (3 Plum Blossoms—113 rooms)
Address: 68 Minchuan Rd.
Telephone: (04) 229-5191
Rates: Single—NT$1,000 to NT$1,100; Double—NT$1,200; Suite—NT$2,000 to NT$2,500
    The Lucky Hotel has a restaurant, a coffee shop, and a parking lot. Conference rooms and meeting facilities are also available.

Hotel National (5 Plum Blossoms—404 rooms)
Address: 257 Taichungkang Rd., Sec. 1
Telephone: (04) 321-3111
Fax: (04) 321-3124
Rates: Single—NT$2,380 to NT$2,580; Double—NT$2,580 to NT$3,000; Suite—NT$3,900 to NT$15,000
    The Hotel National is located outside the city and 2.5 mi (4 km) from the Taichung train station. All rooms are air-conditioned with private bath, telephone, and refrigerator. There is a swimming pool and a sauna bath, and several restaurants are located on the hotel premises. A nightclub, a cocktail lounge, and a lobby bar provide a lively atmosphere. There are convention facilities and a parking lot.

Plaza International Hotel (306 rooms)
Address: 431 Taya Rd.
Telephone: (04) 295-6789
Fax: (04) 293-0099
Rates: Single—NT$2,900; Double—NT$3,200; Suite—NT$5,000
    The Plaza International Hotel is located 10 minutes away from Taichung City and 5 minutes away from the freeway. Each room is air-conditioned and has a color television, refrigerator, private bath, and telephone. There is a rooftop pool as well as a sauna and health center. Several restaurants and a beauty salon and barber shop are also on the premises. Business people will be pleased to see that the hotel offers a business center, international conference facilities, and facsimile services.

Taichung Hotel (180 rooms)
Address: 87 Minchuan Rd.
Telephone: (04) 224-2121
Fax: (04) 224-9946
Rates: Single—NT$1,155 to NT$1,785; Double—NT$1,890; Suite—NT$2,625 to NT$3,675

The Taichung Hotel is situated in the downtown area in a quiet and convenient location. Rooms are air-conditioned with private bath, telephone, refrigerator, and color television. There are several restaurants serving a variety of cuisines, as well as a coffee shop and a lounge.

Taichung Park International Tourist Hotel (4 Plum Blossoms—150 rooms)
Address: 17 Kungyuan Rd.
Telephone: (04) 220-5181
Fax: (04) 222-5757
Rates: Single—NT$1,210 to NT$1,730; Double—NT$1,420 to NT$1,940; Suite—NT$2,680

The Taichung Park International Tourist Hotel is ideally located in the commercial center of Taichung, overlooking Taichung Park. The hotel is a five-minute walk from the railway station and bus terminals. All rooms are air-conditioned, have private full baths, color televisions, refrigerators and mini-bars. There are a Chinese and a Western restaurant, and also a coffee shop, bar, cocktail lounge, nightclub, and souvenir shop. Convention facilities and a parking lot are also located on the premises.

TAITUNG

Jhy Been Hotel (2 Plum Blossoms—20 rooms)
Address: Chihpen
Telephone: (89) 512-220-1
Fax: (89) 513-067
Rates: Single—NT$1,150 to NT$1,380; Double—NT$1,380 to NT$1,725; Suite—NT$2,000 to NT$2,875

The Jhy Been Hotel is a 20-minute car ride from Taitung Railway Station. There is a hot-spring swimming pool at this restful hotel. A variety of cuisines are offered by the hotel restaurants.

TAOYUAN

Hawaii Hotel (2 Plum Blossoms—82 rooms)
Address: 20 Yuloh St.
Telephone: (03) 332–3131
Rates: Single—NT$650 to NT$750; Double—NT$950 to NT$1,500;
Suite—NT$1,000 to NT$1,300

The Hawaii Hotel has a restaurant, a coffee shop, a bar, a gift shop, and a banquet room. There is a also a parking lot.

Taoyuan Holiday Hotel (4 Plum Blossoms—391 rooms)
Address: 269 Tashing Rd.
Telephone: (03) 325–4021
Fax: (03) 325–4021
Rates: Single—NT$1,800; Double—NT$2,000; Suite—NT$3,600

The Taoyuan Holiday Hotel is located 10 minutes away from CKS International Airport and 30 minutes from the Taipei city center. Each air-conditioned room has a private bathroom, color television, a radio, a refrigerator, a mini-bar, and a telephone. There are a swimming pool, a tennis court, and a fishing pond located on the hotel premises. An arcade shop, several restaurants, a nightclub, and a tea house are also located on the premises. Room service and convention facilities are available.

Taoyuan Plaza Hotel (4 Plum Blossoms—300 rooms)
Address: 15 Fushin Rd.
Telephone: (03) 337–9222
Fax: (03) 337–9250
Rates: Single—NT$1,260; Double—NT$1,575; Suite—NT$2,730

The Taoyuan Plaza Hotel is located in the downtown area of Taoyuan city, 9 mi (15 km) from CKS International Airport and 19 mi (30 km) from downtown Taipei. All rooms are air-conditioned and have closed-circuit television, refrigerators, telephones, and bathrooms. There are Western and Chinese restaurants, a cocktail lounge, and a parking lot. Convention facilities are available.

YUNLIN

Tsao Ling Hotel (2 Plum Blossoms—73 rooms)
Address: 36 Tsaoling, Ku Keng Township
Telephone: (55) 831–228
Rates: Single—NT$800; Double—NT$1,200
 The Tsao Ling Hotel has a restaurant.

YOUTH ACTIVITY CENTERS

NORTHERN TAIWAN

Taipei International
Address: 30 Hsinhai Rd., Sec. 3, Taipei
Telephone: (02) 709–1770/9

Chientan
Address: 16 Chungshan North Rd., Sec. 4, Taipei
Telephone: (02) 596–2150/9

Chinshan
Address: 1 Chingnien Rd., Chinsan, Taipei
Telephone: (32) 981–1190/3

CENTRAL TAIWAN

Sun Moon Lake
Address: Sun Moon Lake, Yuchih (Fishing Pond), Nantou County
Telephone: (49) 855–811/2

Hsitou
Address: 15 Senlin Rd., Neihu Village, Luku (Deer Valley),
Nantou County
Telephone: (49) 612–161/3

SOUTH TAIWAN

Tsengwen
Address: 70–1 Michih Village, Nanhsi, Tainan County
Telephone: (06) 575–2772, 575–3164, 575–2575

Cheng Ching Lake
Address: 140 Wenchien Rd., Niaosung Village, Niaosung,
Kaohsiung County
Telephone: (07) 371–7181/4

Chuan Hsi Chai
Address: 32 Taipei Rd., Niaosung, Kaohsiung County
Telephone: (07) 731–2608

Kenting
Address: 17 Kenting Rd., Kenting, Hengchun, Pingtung County
Telephone: (08) 886–1221/4

EASTERN TAIWAN

Tienhsiang
Address: 30 Tienhsiang Rd., Hsiulin, Hualien County
Telephone: (38) 691–111/4

YOUTH HOSTELS

NORTH CROSS–ISLAND HIGHWAY

Fuhsing
Telephone: (33) 332–153/4

Baling
Telephone: (33) 332–153/4

EAST–WEST CROSS–ISLAND HIGHWAY

Wushe
Telephone: (49) 802–209

Chingshan
Telephone: (45) 244–103/5

Tehchi
Telephone: (45) 244–103/5

Tzu-en
Telephone: (38) 691–113

Tayuling
Telephone: (45) 991–009

Loshao
Telephone: (38) 691–111/3

Lushui
Telephone: (38) 691–111/3

Kuanyun
Telephone: (38) 691–111/3

SOUTH CROSS–ISLAND HIGHWAY

Meishan
Telephone: (07) 747–0134/5

Litao
Telephone: (89) 329–891/2

Yakou
Telephone: (89) 329–891/2

Alishan
Telephone: (05) 277–0482/3

VII

Dining Out in Taiwan

W esterners consider eating something that is necessary; will, they hope, be pleasurable; and is usually done three times a day. For the Chinese, though, eating is probably the most important single aspect of their lives, taking up much more time and energy than is accorded it by those in the West. Upon entering a Chinese person's home (at any time of the day or night), the first thing usually asked after greetings have been exchanged is: "Have you eaten?" This expression is almost a greeting in itself and shows the importance Chinese place on food.

It is not surprising, then, that the Chinese have developed the culinary arts to a high degree of sophistication, with Chinese cuisine gaining worldwide recognition for its variety, delicacy of taste, and artful presentation. Chinese cuisine is generally divided into northern, eastern, southern, and western styles. Each major style can in turn be divided into subcategories that reflect the tastes, climate, and foodstuffs of the different provinces and cities.

Northern cuisine derives from the cooking of the capital city, Peking, and the provinces of Hopei, Shantung, Honan, Shanhsi, and Mongolia, and utilizes wheat, millet, sorghum, peanuts, corn, and soybeans as its main ingredients. Instead of rice, which is the basic staple for the southern Chinese, noodles, steamed breads and buns are popular in the north. Food from the north is usually mildly seasoned and includes a lot of meat and poultry dishes.

Eastern cuisine comes from the province of Kiangsu and particularly the cities of Shanghai, Yangchow, Hangchow, Soochow, and Ningpo. This style of cooking employs a great deal of sauces and seafood, and tends to be heavily seasoned.

Southern Chinese cooking, the type best known to Westerners, uses rice as its base and includes Cantonese cuisine, dishes from Chaochow and Foochow, Hakka-style cuisine, and Taiwanese cuisine. Southern Chinese food is lightly seasoned and employs seafood in many of its dishes.

Western-style Chinese cuisine is represented by the styles of Szechuan, Hunan, and Yunnan provinces, and is known for hot, spicy dishes as well heavy reliance on steaming and frying.

When Chiang Kai-shek's army retreated to Taiwan after being

defeated on the mainland, many of China's finest chefs came along and established restaurants offering the best of China's many styles of cooking. Today, restaurants in Taiwan have become world famous for the variety and excellence of their food preparation.

HOTEL CHINESE RESTAURANTS

THE Chinese restaurants in the island's international-standard hotels are among the best in Taiwan. The cooks are, for the most part, well trained in the different styles, and the hotels take pains to keep the food fresh and conditions in the kitchens and restaurant areas sanitary. Some hotel choices are:

Ambassador Hotel—Cantonese and Szechuan cuisines.

Asiaworld Plaza Hotel—Shanghainese, Cantonese, Szechuan, and Hunan cuisines.

Brother Hotel—Cantonese and Taiwanese cuisines.

Taipei Fortuna Hotel—Cantonese cuisine.

Gloria Hotel—Cantonese cuisine.

Grand Hotel—Cantonese cuisine.

Hilton International—Hunan cuisine.

Howard Plaza Hotel—Cantonese, Shanghainese, and Taiwanese cuisines.

Imperial Hotel—Cantonese and Taiwanese cuisines.

Lai Lai Sheraton Hotel—Cantonese, Shanghainese, Taiwanese, and Hunan cuisines.

Mandarin Hotel—Cantonese and Mongolian cuisines.

Miramar Hotel—Taiwanese cuisine.

President Hotel—Cantonese cuisine.

Rebar Crown Hotel—Cantonese cuisine.

Regent Taipei—Cantonese cuisine.

Ritz Taipei—Chaochow cuisine.

Royal Taipei—Cantonese cuisine.

Riverview Hotel—Hunan cuisine.

Santos Hotel—Cantonese cuisine.

United Hotel Taipei—Cantonese cuisine.

CKS Airport Hotel—Shanghainese cuisine.

RECOMMENDED RESTAURANTS

CANTONESE CUISINE

An Lo Yuan, 232 Tunhua North Rd., Taipei; Telephone 715–4929.

Fung Lum, 72 Linsen North Rd., Taipei; Telephone 511–8504.

Jen Hao Cantonese Seafood Restaurant, 7/F, 197 Chunghsiao East Rd., Sec. 4, Taipei; Telephone 752–9227.

King of Kings, 2/F, 646 Linsen North Rd., Taipei; Telephone 591–8128.

Phoenix Restaurant, 3/F, 155 Chunghsiao East Rd., Sec. 4, Taipei; Telephone 741–2657.

Ruby, 2/F, 135 Chungshan North Rd., Sec. 2, Taipei; Telephone 571–1157.

Venice Restaurant, 2/F, 490 Tunhua South Rd., Taipei; Telephone 709–1141.

Ya Yuan, 2/F, 26 Changchun Rd., Taipei; Telephone 543–5513.

CHAOCHOW CUISINE

Chung Hang, 2/F, 39 Nungan St., Taipei; Telephone 594–4155

Golden Island Restaurant, 522 Minchuan East Rd., Taipei; Telephone 500–6878.

Lisboa Chin Chow, 3/F, 26 Changchun Rd., Taipei; Telephone 551–2888.

HUNAN CUISINE

Beautiful Garden, 610 Tunhua South Rd., Taipei; Telephone 715–3921.

Charming Garden, 2–3/F, 16 Nanking East Rd., Sec. 1, Taipei; Telephone 521–4131.

Double Bliss Restaurant, 15/F, 110 Yenping South Rd., Taipei; Telephone 371–6855

Grand Restaurant, 3/F, 206 Nanking East Rd., Sec. 2, Taipei; Telephone 506–8676

Happy Garden, 7/F, 7–6 Lane 14, Chilin Rd., Taipei; Telephone 531–3313.

Hwa Shin Restaurant, 11/F, 20 Pateh Rd., Sec. 3, Taipei, Telephone 752–1331.

Peng Yang Restaurant, 2–3/F, 380 Linsen North Rd., Taipei; Telephone 541–7181.

Treasure House, 3/F, 152 Sungchiang Rd., Taipei; Telephone 581–9151.

Wanhsi Hunan, 5/F, 410 Linsen North Rd., Taipei; Telephone 561–7628.

Yuan Ning Yuan, 6 Lane 111, Chungshan North Rd., Sec. 3, Taipei; Telephone 595–8822.

MONGOLIAN BARBECUE

Genghis Khan, 176 Nanking East Rd., Sec. 3, Taipei; Telephone 711–3655.

Han Chiang Restaurant, B1, 9 Nanking East Rd., Sec. 3, Taipei; Telephone 508–4370.

Mongol, 998 Minsheng East Rd., Taipei; Telephone 762–6645.

Shann Garden, 32 Yuya Rd., Peitou, Taipei; Telephone 894–7185.

Tang Kung, 2/F, 283 Sungchiang Rd., Taipei; Telephone 502–6762.

Yuan Dynasty Restaurant, 131 Sungchiang Rd., Taipei; Telephone 507–5708.

PEKING CUISINE

Bonanza, 4/F, 341 Chunghsiao East Rd., Sec. 4, Taipei; Telephone 731–2720.

Celestial Restaurant, 2/F, 1 Nanking West Rd., Taipei; Telephone 563–2380.

Chinese Muslim, 313 Chunghsiao East Rd., Sec. 4, Taipei; Telephone 771–1004.

Jen Pei Ping Restaurant, 2/F, 37 6th Block, Chunghua Commercial, Taipei; Telephone 312–1002.

Peiking Lou Way Lou, 54 Hoping West Rd., Sec. 1, Taipei; Telephone 396–4536.

Peiping Sung-Chu Restaurant, 96 Chunghsiao East Rd., Sec. 4, Taipei; Telephone 721–0091.

Sheng Nung, 17 Lane 330, Tunhua South Rd., Taipei; Telephone 711–9819.

Tien Tsin Wei Restaurant, 11 Alley 9, Lane 390 Tunhua South Rd., Taipei; Telephone 711–3407.

Yueh Bin Lou, 43–47 Chunghsiao East Rd., Sec. 1, Taipei; Telephone 321–2801.

SEAFOOD RESTAURANTS

Hae Shalan Lou Cantonese Restaurant, 14 Lane 105, Chungshan North Rd., Sec. 1, Taipei; Telephone 521–6188.

Jea Ten Shah, 199 Sungchiang Rd., Taipei; Telephone 502–9130.

Manor Seafood Restaurant, 223 Sungchiang Rd., Taipei; Telephone 505–1195.

Sea King, 59 Chungshan North Rd., Sec. 3, Taipei; Telephone 596–3141.

SHANGHAINESE CUISINE

Fwu Ding, 72 Nanking East Rd., Sec. 2, Taipei; Telephone 531–9174.

Gourmet, 51 Linhsi St., Taipei; Telephone 341–1335.

Hai Chi Chiu Ju, 69 Jenai Rd., Sec. 4, Taipei; Telephone 721–7777.

Hsiang Garden Restaurant, 6 Lane 27, Jenai Rd., Sec. 4, Taipei; Telephone 771–8866.

Hsuchow Hot Pot, 115 6th Block, Chunghua Commercial, Taipei; Telephone 331–9793.

Lung Chih, 1 Lane 101, Yenping South Rd., Taipei; Telephone 381–8823.

Ning Shiang Chuen, 50–1 Hsinsheng South Rd., Sec. 1, Taipei; Telephone 321–8336.

Shanghai Garden, 182 Da-an Rd., Sec. 1, Taipei; Telephone 705–7221.

Silver Wing, 65 Hsinyi Rd., Sec. 2, Taipei; Telephone 341–1600.

Stone House, 663 Tunhua South Rd., Taipei; Telephone 704–4878.

Sunny Garden Restaurant, 3–4/F, 92 Nanking East Rd., Sec. 1, Taipei; Telephone 581–5541.

Tau Tau, 57–1 Chungshan North Rd., Sec. 2, Taipei; Telephone 564–1277.

Yun Fu Lou, 2/F., 59 Chunghsiao East Rd., Sec. 4, Taipei; Telephone 752–8230.

SZECHUAN CUISINE

Chung Hwa Szechuan, 26 Minsheng East Rd., Taipei; Telephone 551–5044.

Rong An Restaurant, 140 Nanking East Rd., Sec. 2, Taipei; Telephone 506–1111.

Rong Shing, 45 Chilin Rd., Taipei; Telephone 521–5340.

Rong Tai, 626 Kuangfu South Rd., Taipei; Telephone 704–9461.

You Ho Yuan, 3/F, 289 Chunghsiao East Rd., Sec. 4, Taipei; Telephone 752–8936.

TAIWANESE CUISINE

Chi-Chia Chuang, 45 Changchun Rd., Taipei; Telephone 581–4360.

Green Leaf Restaurant, 1 Lane 105, Chungshan North Rd., Sec. 1, Taipei; Telephone 551–7957.

Happy Smile, 99–100 Jenai Rd., Sec. 4, Taipei; Telephone 741–0333.

Shin Yeh, 125 Hsinsheng South Rd., Sec. 1, Taipei.

Tainan Tan Tsu Mien, 31 Hwahsi St., Taipei; Telephone 308–1123.

Umeko, 5 Lane 107, Linsen North Rd., Taipei; Telephone 551–6696.

VEGETARIAN RESTAURANTS

Buddhist Vegetarian, 2/F, 30 Minsheng West Rd., Taipei; Telephone 521–3163.

Chyuan Sheeng, 111 Linsen North Rd., Taipei; Telephone 521–7878.

Fa Hua, 576 Minchuan East Rd., Taipei; Telephone 717–5305.

Goddess of Mercy, 139 Minchuan West Rd., Taipei; Telephone 595–5557.

Heavenly Lotus, 47 Tienmou East Rd., Taipei; Telephone 831–5928.

Life Flower Carters, 77 Nanking East Rd., Sec. 2, Taipei; Telephone 543–2666.

Mei Lin Vegetarian, 2/F., 3 Linsen North Rd., Taipei; Telephone 391–0723.

Vegetarian House, 70 Hwaining St., Taipei; Telephone 314–2020.

DINING ETIQUETTE

IT is very likely that on a visit to Taiwan you may be asked out to dinner by either a business associate or newly found friend. If this should happen, there are some things you should know about how to eat Chinese food.

A Chinese meal is served at a round table accommodating 6 to 12 persons and having a large lazy Susan in the middle. The guest of honor will be seated with his or her back to the wall, and the host will sit opposite with his or her back to the door. Each person will have a table setting usually consisting of a small plate, a teacup, a small bowl for soup, a soupspoon, and chopsticks with a chopstick rest. Depending on the type of service provided by the restaurant, the courses may arrive one by one and be served in individual portions by the serving staff; or everything may come almost all at once, and people will just dig in, turning the lazy Susan to the item desired and taking as much as they want with their chopsticks.

The Chinese have their own table manners, and things that would be considered in very bad taste in a Western dining room are perfectly acceptable when eating Chinese food. Many Chinese meat and fish dishes, for example, have a great many bones in them, and removing the bones from your mouth would be very laborious if you had to delicately take each one out with your fingers. Therefore, the Chinese merely suck the meat off the bones and then spit the bones onto their plates. Using both hands when eating Chinese food, your spoon in one and chopsticks in the other, is also quite normal. In addition, making loud slurping sounds when drinking hot soup or eating noodles is considered the best method of cooling the food, and no one gives such sounds a second thought. Not that making noise while eating would matter anyway, because a Chinese restaurant usually consists of a very large room filled with hundreds of happy diners all talking at the same time.

Of course, no Chinese meal can be properly experienced without eating it with chopsticks. They are held in the hand you write with—right for righthanders, left for lefties. Take one chopstick, with its blunt, narrower end near the plate, and place it in the crotch between your thumb and first finger so that the bottom of your thumb presses it against your hand and the tip of your third finger, which should be curved down. Pick up the second stick with your other hand, hold it above the first, and grasp it between the tips of your thumb and forefinger. Remeber to hold both sticks quite close to the blunt end (this will give you leverage). The bottom stick remains motionless, allowing the top stick to do the up-and-down motion necessary to grasp the food. Mastering chopsticks takes some practice, but it can be done relatively easily.

OTHER EASTERN CUISINES

BESIDES the various types of Chinese cuisine, one can also sample other cuisines of the East in Taiwan.

INDIAN

Dazzle Curry House, 84 Jenai Rd., Sec. 3, Taipei; Telephone 706-9504, 702-4279.

Gaylord Restaurant, 328 Sungchiang Rd., Taipei; Telephone 543-4003/4.

INDONESIAN

Pulau Kelapa Restaurant, 718 Tinchou Rd., Taipei; Telephone 391-4717.

JAPANESE

Miyama, Howard Plaza Hotel, 160 Jenai Rd., Sec. 3, Taipei; Telephone 700-2323.

Momoyama, Lai Lai Sheraton Hotel, 12 Chunghsiao East Rd., Sec. 1, Taipei; Telephone 321-5511 Ext. 8085/86.

Tsu-Ten-Kaku Japanese Restaurant, 8 Lane 53, Chungshan North Rd., Sec. 1, Taipei; Telephone 511-7372/3.

TEPPANYAKI

Elite Teppansumi-yaki, Lai Lai Sheraton Hotel, 12 Chunghsiao East Rd., Sec. 1, Taipei; Telephone 321-5511 Ext. 8365.

Island Teppanyaki, 2/F, 22 Tehwei St., Taipei; Telephone 591-6366, 591-6376.

Isshin Teppanyaki Steak House, 181-7 Chungshan North Rd., Sec. 2, Taipei; Telephone 591-9987, 592-7679.

Luckywood Teppanyaki, 18 Lane 14, Chilin Rd., Taipei; Telephone 551-2689.

Manor Teppanyaki, 46-2 Chungshan North Rd., Sec. 2, Taipei; Telephone 542-2691/3.

Matsusaka Teppanyaki, 2/F, 33 Chungshan North Rd., Sec. 2, Taipei; Telephone 581-8232, 581-3284.

Shogun Teppanyaki, 2/F, 32 Nungan St., Taipei; Telephone 596–7204/5.

Sun Dou, 89 Wenlin Rd., Shihlin, Taipei; Telephone 882–2434, 882–2288.

THAI

Ban-Thai Restaurant, 8 Lane 78, Sungkang Rd., Taipei; Telephone 562–2072, 597–3362.

WESTERN CUISINES

IF Chinese or other oriental food is not your forte, Taiwan has a plethora of fine Western restaurants, ranging from such fast-food establishments as McDonald's and Kentucky Fried Chicken to the best in American steakhouses and French and other European cuisines.

AMERICAN

Coffee Shop, Howard Plaza Hotel, 160 Jenai Rd., Sec. 3, Taipei; Telephone 700–2323.

La Brasserie, Ritz Hotel, 155 Minchuan East Rd., Taipei; Telephone 597–1234.

President Steak House, 122 Jenai Rd., Sec. 3, Taipei; Telephone 709–3533.

Traders Grill, Hilton Hotel, 38 Chunghsiao West Rd., Sec. 1, Taipei; Telephone 311–5151.

CONTINENTAL

Chalet Swiss Restaurant, 1/F, 47 Nanking East Rd., Sec. 4, Taipei; Telephone 715–2051, 715–2702.

Hugo's Restaurant, 31 Chungshan North Rd., Sec. 7, Taipei; Telephone 871–9974.

Le Louvre (Executive Chef Chen Ta-ping), Howard Plaza Hotel, 160 Jenai Rd., Sec. 3, Taipei; Telephone 700–2323.

The Ploughman's Cottage, 305 Nanking East Rd., Sec. 3, Taipei; Telephone 713–4942.

GERMAN

Zum Fass, 55 Lane 119, Linsen North Rd., Taipei; Telephone 531–3815.

FRENCH

Antoine Room, Lai Lai Sheraton Hotel, 12 Chunghsiao East Rd., Sec. 1, Taipei; Telephone 321–5511, Ext. 8080/1.

Elysee, 20 Alley 33, Lane 351, Tunhua South Rd., Taipei; Telephone 781–4270.

La Seine, 14 Lane 550, Minchuan East Rd., Taipei; Telephone 713–6084, 716–9669.

Les Celebrites, Hotel Royal Taipei, 37–1 Chungshan North Rd., Taipei; Telephone 542–3266, Ext. 330, 380.

Paris 1930, Ritz Hotel, 155 Minchuan East Rd., Taipei; Telephone 597–1234 Ext. 276, 200.

ITALIAN

Antonio's, 56 Tienmou West Rd., Taipei; Telephone 872–6734.

Casa Mia Restaurant, 628 Linsen North Rd., Taipei; Telephone 591–7478.

La Pizzeria, Hilton International Hotel, 38 Chunghsiao West Rd., Sec. 1, Taipei; Telephone 311–5151 Ext. 2132.

Pizza Pub, Lai Lai Sheraton Hotel, 12 Chunghsiao East Rd., Sec. 1, Taipei; Telephone 321–5511 Ext. 8905.

Round Table Pizza, 60 Nanking East Rd., Sec. 2, Taipei; Telephone 521–4472.

Ruffino Ristorante Italiano, 15 Lane 25, Shuangcheng St., Taipei; Telephone 592–3355, 595–1069.

BARS AND PUBS

IN addition to the culinary offerings in Taiwan, Chinese and Western-style bars and pubs are in abundance. Most visitors to the island have little difficulty in finding a drinking establishment that caters to their particular cultural style.

The most popular watering holes for visitors (at least first-time visitors) are the hotel bars. Every hotel has one convivial bar, if not more, where new friends can be made and business acquaintances entertained. For those who know their way around the city or have traveled to Taiwan before, the establishments on Shuangcheng St. (near the President Hotel) offer an almost infinite variety of pubs and bars. Some of the most famous of these are:

Hsaling Pub, 2/F, 20 Shuangcheng St., Taipei; Telephone 591–8995. The Hsaling has a very pleasant atmosphere and friendly service. It is popular with visitors and foreign residents alike.

Sam's Place, 2–2 Lane 32, Shuangcheng St., Taipei; Telephone 594–2402. Sam's Place is best described as a neighborhood bar. Many of the patrons are American, but representatives of every nationality frequent Sam's, including large segments of Taipei's foreign expatriate community. Sam's is also one of the few places in Taipei to feature Mexican food.

Shakespeare Pub, 6–1 Lane 25, Shuangcheng St., Taipei; Telephone 594–9868. The staff at the Shakespeare Pub are among the most friendly in Taipei, and make a point of learning your name and remembering it when you return the next time (that is, if you return within a reasonable amount of time).

Waltzing Matilda Inn, 3 Lane 25, Shuangcheng St., Taipei, Telephone 712–4965. The Waltzing Matilda provides an authentic Australian atmosphere complete with a wide range of beverages and excellent food.

TEAHOUSES

AS one might expect, drinking tea is a favorite Chinese pastime and one that has been elevated to the status of an art. In addition to drinking tea at home or at the office, lovers of the brew find visiting a local teahouse a refreshing experience. Soothed by light background music, some patrons immerse themselves in contemplation, reading, or writing; others, in groups, engage in conversation that is punctuated at times by soft laughter. This is the scene in Taipei's modern teahouses, where traditional Chinese music and the aroma of the different teas combine to create a relaxing and peaceful ambience.

Teahouses are by no means new to China. They were popular gathering places back in the Sung Dynasty (960–1279 AD). Today, teahouses serve as retreats from the hustle and bustle of modern society. They provide a comfortable place for everything from casual conversation to business negotiations.

Since most teahouses cater mainly to an all-Chinese crowd, it is best to ask at your hotel for directions to one where the staff speak English, and can explain the different types of tea, how it is made, and how to drink it. For those who may choose the Howard Plaza Hotel for their stay in Taipei, the B1 level has an excellent teashop where many types of tea are available, along with finely crafted tea sets.

BUSINESS CLUBS

TAIPEI is a bustling metropolis and possesses a few private clubs where members can go to enjoy everything from drinks and excellent food to a day of tennis or golf. Unfortunately, unless you are a member of an associated club or are invited by a member, access to one of Taipei's better clubs is impossible.

American Club in China, 47 Peian Rd., Taipei; Telephone 594–8260/63. Probably the most popular of the main clubs, the American Club offers on-premises tennis courts, swimming pool, bar, coffee shop, and evening grill room. Membership is difficult to get, especially if you are not an American (U.S. nationals must account for 51% of the membership at all times). However, the American Club does have association with a number of similar clubs worldwide. Please call for the list of associates.

Bankers Club, B1, 685 Minsheng East Rd., Taipei. Located in the financial district, the Bankers is, like many other downtown clubs, primarily used for dining and for entertaining business acquaintances. However, members of the Bankers Club have easy access to swimming pools, tennis courts, and of course, golf courses. Associate clubs are located in 31 U.S. states, Europe, Australia, Hong Kong, Indonesia, Malaysia, Japan, Singapore, and Thailand. The Bankers Club stresses top-of-the-line service and cuisine, and proper dress is required.

VIII

Cultural Activities, Recreation, and Entertainment

CULTURE AND ENTERTAINMENT

TAIWAN has long been known as a bastion of Chinese culture and traditions, and has tried hard to preserve the many Chinese arts and crafts handed down over the millennia of recorded Chinese history. Of this cultural wealth, Chinese dramatic and folk musical performances, which include many uniquely different styles of presentation, have flourished in Taiwan.

CHINESE OPERA

The most popular form of drama in Taiwan is Chinese opera, a type of performance that combines literature, song, music, dance, makeup, and acrobatics, and that has its roots in prehistoric Chinese poetry, dance performances of religious ceremonies, and ancestor worship.

The first set type of dramatic performance in China was recorded in the State of Wei (220–264 AD), during the Three Kingdoms period. By the Yuan Dynasty, the performances had progressed to a fixed form and eventually became what the world today knows as Chinese opera. Although Peking opera, the style that evolved in the capital, is the best-known form, all the different provinces have their own forms of Chinese opera, usually performed in the language of its home province.

In any form of Chinese opera, all actions are performed on the same stage, with few or no background props. The dress and facial makeup of the actors proclaim their characters' position in society and their inner fiber. In addition, acrobatics play an important role in Chinese opera, sometimes being the main feature of the performance. Performers of Chinese opera usually have to spend a minimum of eight years studying their craft.

One can see Chinese opera performed at the Chinese Armed Forces Cultural Activities Center, 69 Chunghua Rd., Sec. 1; Telephone 331–5438 (call to find out performance times), and at Fu Shing Opera School, in Neihu at 177 Neihu Rd., Sec. 2; Telephone 790–9127, on

Tuesdays and Thursdays. It is also possible to observe televised Chinese opera performances on Sunday afternoons.

MUSIC

Music, both Western and Chinese, is very popular in Taiwan and its study is required in primary and secondary schools, many of which have their own orchestras. In addition, Taiwan has two symphony orchestras, the Taiwan Provincial Symphony Orchestra and the Taipei Municipal Symphony Orchestra. Visitors can check *Travel in Taiwan* magazine, published under the auspices of the Tourism Bureau, or *This Month in Taiwan* magazine, published by the China Commercial Service, Inc., in cooperation with the Taiwan Visitors Association (both are available in hotels and restaurants), for a listing of current concerts.

Two cultural landmarks opened in 1987 on the grounds of the Chiang Kai-shek Memorial Hall complex in Taipei. The two buildings, the National Opera House and the National Concert Hall, constitute the National Chiang Kai-shek Cultural Center, and were inaugurated on October 31, 1987, to commemorate the late President's 100th birthday. The two halls, which flank the traditional arch leading to the memorial, have a total seating capacity of 4,296 and cost NT$7.4 billion. During the first six months, artists from Europe, America, Asia, and Australia performed there.

Although the interiors of the buildings are completely modern in every detail, the exterior architecture resembles that of traditional imperial palaces, with vermilion columns and golden roofs. The National Theater is designed for staging Chinese and Western operas, dramas, musicals, ballets, and other types of dance. Typical presenta-tions include performances by mimes, dancers, acrobats, and Western and Chinese operas. The National Concert Hall is a perfect location for holding Chinese and Western instrumental and vocal concerts. In any given month, performances may include a wide range of varying musical offerings.

Modern Western popular music is also avidly listened to in Taiwan, and there are many different night spots around Taipei and Kaohsiung. The favorite places in Taipei to hear rock and roll, country, and jazz are the following members of the Ploughman Group:

The Ploughman Inn, 8 Lane 460, Tunhua South Rd., Taipei; Telephone 773–3268. Live music nightly.

The Ploughman Pub, 9 Lane 25, Shuangcheng St., Taipei; Telephone 594–9648. Live music Wednesday and Saturday nights.

The Ploughman's Farmhouse, 5 Lane 32, Shuangcheng St., Taipei; Telephone 595-1764/5. Live music nightly; jazz session Sundays, 3:00-6:00 PM

MOVIES

There are about 120 movie theaters in Taipei, and Taiwan's residents see perhaps more films each year (an average of 3 full-length movies a week per person) than any other people in the world. Taiwan is one of the world's major markets for foreign films, and all major Hollywood studios have offices there. Most foreign movies shown in Taiwan are in English, with Chinese subtitles, just as most Chinese movies have English subtitles. Local films generally fall into the categories of action-packed drama, romance, semi-historical, or comedy-horror movies. The theaters showing English-language films in Taipei are:

Ambassador, 88 Chengtu Rd.; Telephone 316-1222.

Golden Horse, 6/F, 54 Ehmei St.; Telephone 371-9291.

Golden Lion, Treasure Lion, Silver Lion, 4/F, 75 Wuchang St., Sec. 2; Telephone 314-2214.

Happy, 4/F, 124/2 Wuchang St., Sec. 2; Telephone 381-1085.

Hoover, 91 Wuchang St., Sec. 2; Telephone 331-5067.

Hsin Hsin, 4/F, 247 Linsen North Rd.; Telephone 521/2211.

Hsin Shen, 55 Chunghua Rd.; Telephone 331-4402.

Jade, 5/F, 14 Nanking West Rd.; Telephone 564-1111.

Lolo, 3/F, 124/2 Wuchang St., Sec. 2; Telephone 381-1085.

Lux, 87 Wuchang St., Sec. 2; Telephone 311-8628.

Majestic, 7/F, 13 Chengtu Rd.; Telephone 331-2270.

New World, 1 Chengtu Rd.; Telephone 331-2752.

Oscar, 215 Changan East Rd., Sec. 2; Telephone 711-8298.

Sun, 89 Wuchang St., Sec. 2; Telephone 331-5256.

Ta Shin, 87 Wuchang St., Sec. 2; Telephone 331-5256.

Tung Nan Ya, 3 Lane 136, Roosevelt Rd., Sec. 4; Telephone 341-1640.

MTV

In addition to the theater scene in Taiwan, there are many "MTV shops" about. Taiwan's version of MTV is completely different from the cable TV music videos in the United States that go by that name.

At Taiwan's local MTV centers, one can rent a movie and an individual room, then watch the film in relative privacy and comfort. These centers offer newly released feature films, often before the theaters have them, at very reasonable prices. This proliferation of entertainment facilities showing illegal copies of foreign films was a sore spot between Taiwan and U.S. negotiators trying to work out an acceptable agreement on intellectual property rights in January 1989. MTV owners took to the streets to protest what they felt were unfair demands by the United States. The situation has not been completely resolved and it is expected that MTV shops will continue to operate for the foreseeable future.

DISCO

As it did in many parts of the world, the disco craze swept Taiwan in the mid 1980s, generating a multitude of disco dance halls. Almost every large hotel remodeled one of its banquet facilities to accommodate the crowds of disco dancers, who were willing to pay just about any price for the privilege of dancing the night away to the newest recordings. However, in 1988, the craze began to die down, and many of the hotel discos were changed into piano bars and nightclubs.

Kiss Disco, in the Mandarin Hotel, 166 Tunhua North Rd.; Telephone 712–1201. The most popular disco still remaining in Taipei, KISS is billed as a "super" disco, has three floors of dance areas and state-of-the-art technology and sound systems, and is considered the best place for disco dancing in Taipei. Other popular discos are the **Disco Nightclub** at the Lai Lai Sheraton Hotel; the **Arc de Triomphe** at the Asiaworld Plaza Hotel; and the disco at the Ambassador Hotel. For ballroom dancing, the Imperial Hotel is the ideal place.

NIGHTCLUBS

Nightclubs in Taiwan are of two varieties, those with hostesses and those without. Most nightclubs have a piano bar or some other type of live music. In Taipei, favorite nightclubs are the **Fountain Club** (live entertainment), 2/F, 2 Pateh Rd., Sec. 3; the **High Heel Club,** 23 Lane 18, Shuangcheng St.; the **Pink Lady** (live entertainment), B1-level, 101 Sungchiang Rd.; the **Romeo Club,** 23–3 Shuangcheng St.; the **Utopia Club,** 19 Tehwei St. (basement); the **Mayflower,** 23–1 Shuangcheng St.; the **Blue Star Club,** 615 Linsen North Rd.; and the **Flora Club,** B1-level, 287 Nanking East Rd., Sec. 3.

Pub crawlers should be warned that hostess clubs can be very costly. Guests' drinks are reasonable, but drinks for the young women who chat with you are much more expensive and usually consist of a small glass of water or tea, which can be drunk very quickly. If a guest wishes the woman to accompany him out of the club, a fee of approximately NT$1,600 is charged. Anything further than going to another bar, nightclub, etc., must be negotiated with the woman, and will come to about NT$3,000 for the entire night.

Taiwan doesn't have much in the way of dinner clubs. The ones that are available provide only Chinese or Taiwanese performances that are of limited appeal to Westerners.

SPORTS

TAIWAN is a small island, and the amount of space that can be given over to sporting activities is limited. There is, though, an increasing amount of interest in leisure activities, and such sports as tennis and golf have attracted more and more interest from the local citizenry. In recent years, with increased community athletic activities and competitions, sports have become an important part of life in Taiwan. More than 6,000 athletes take part in the annual National Sports Festival, and Taiwan hosts frequent international sporting events.

TENNIS

Tennis courts are available, but not readily without notice. And unless you are a member of one of the clubs having courts on the premises, it is difficult to find a place to play. Many of the larger hotels, however, can make arrangements for you, and the Howard Plaza Hotel has its own off-premises courts. Visitors can often get playing time at the Sung Kiang Tennis Club, the Taipei Tennis Club, or the Youth Park Tennis Club.

GOLF

Golf is probably the most popular sport in Taiwan, and the island now boasts 36 courses with another 14 under construction. All of the courses are full-sized and currently accommodate over 300,000 golfers. Taiwan's golf courses offer all the usual facilities, services, and amenities, including clubhouses, restaurants, equipment rental, and sales shops. While fees vary, a day's golfing is not cheap, running upwards of US$100. Hotels can usually arrange playing time, and it is seldom that a person doesn't get to play during his or her visit to Taiwan. If you wish to ensure that you will be able to play when you are in Taiwan, contact the secretary general of the Golf Association of the ROC before you arrive on the island:

Golf Association of the ROC, 71 Lane 369, Tunhua South Rd., Taipei; Telephone (02) 711–3046.

SWIMMING

Taiwan, being an island nation, has excellent spots to go swimming, with many fine beaches stretching from Chinshan, Green Bay, and Fulung in the north to Kenting and Oluanpi in the south. A rather interesting aspect of many of the beaches in Taiwan springs from the fact that very few Chinese know how to swim. As a result, swimming areas are sometimes small and very shallow, with strictly controlled swimming times and almost as many lifeguards as bathers.

One of the most beautiful beaches in Taiwan—or, for that matter, anywhere in the world—is Kenting beach, in the southern part of the island. Kenting has white sand and a semitropical climate, and attracts visitors from all over the island. Taiwan's main resort hotel, the Caesar Park, is located there and offers a full range of aquatic activities.

Scuba and skin diving are popular at both Oluanpi, near Kenting, and Yehliu, in the north. For information, equipment rental, and details call the China Diving Association in Taipei; Telephone (02) 596–2341.

Public swimming pools in Taiwan are not recommended for foreign visitors. They are unsanitary, extremely overcrowded, and only about 3 ft (1 m) deep, so that it is virtually impossible to do anything but get wet. But most of the international-standard hotels have swimming pools on the premises or offer access to a private club that has one.

SAILING

Sailing has not been a popular pastime in Taiwan, and has only started gaining real acceptance since the government relaxed restrictions prohibiting it. Now, with more resort properties opening, sailing should start to become a major sporting activity, attracting yachting buffs from Hong Kong, Japan, and Southeast Asian nations as well as Europeans and Americans.

MOUNTAIN CLIMBING AND CAMPING

Mountain climbing is very popular in Taiwan and can take the form of an afternoon hike to a nearby peak or an expedition to the top of one of the numerous peaks over 9,840 ft (3,000 m) high. Mountain trails are good, but caution should be used, as the going can get pretty rugged and it is possible to lose your way. Climbers should also carry sufficient clothing, since Taiwan's weather can change without warning. For some areas special permits are required for reasons of national security. However, these permits can be easily obtained, along with information and guides, from the Alpine Association of the ROC, 3/F., 30 Lanchou St., Taipei.

Camping is a favorite pastime of the Chinese on Taiwan, and the government has provided many excellent campsites. Some are close to the cities, as is the case with the campgrounds in Yangmingshan National Park and Pishan Campground in Neihu, while others are located in the mountain regions. Complete information on camping in Taiwan can be obtained from the Camping Association of the ROC, 179 Fuhsing North Rd., Room 806, Taipei.

FISHING

In early 1988, the Taiwan government lifted its ban on deepsea fishing, and now, with certain exceptions, anglers can fish anywhere within Taiwan's 12-nautical-mile territorial waters.

Shopping

No matter what you may be looking for, whether it be souvenirs, gifts, traditional arts and crafts, modern consumer items, or chic clothing, a few hours of browsing through Taipei's department stores, handicraft shops, boutiques, arcades, and night markets will provide you with almost endless opportunities to see why Taiwan is famed throughout Asia as a shopper's paradise. The biggest problem for shoppers is deciding what not to buy; with a little shrewd comparison shopping, you will find as great a range in prices as in products.

WHAT TO BUY

PRECIOUS AND SEMIPRECIOUS STONES

Taiwan is a manufacturing center for high-quality cubic zirconia and other man-made "precious" and "semiprecious" stones. Prices for these jewelry items are very reasonable, and they can be found almost everywhere. Taiwan has vast resources of both jade and coral, and these semiprecious items are excellent bargains. Other natural precious and semiprecious stones are imported, great care must be exercised when contemplating purchases of such items. For all jewelry items, major purchases should be made only from a reputable jeweler able to provide a guarantee.

For thousands of years the Chinese people have had a special attachment to jade, believing that it could protect against evil and bring good fortune, and they used it for symbols of authority and rank, for worship, and as ritual objects. The price of jade is determined by both quality and color. The Chinese consider the light green Burmese jade the only "real" jade, and all other types, including Taiwan's indigenous dark green, are considered "fake." (Western science distinguishes between the rarer jade, or jadeite, and the more common, less valuable mineral more accurately called nephrite.) Actual jade is cool to the touch and never transparent. It will not scratch, but can be chipped.

Everything from simple jade pendants to intricate carvings and sculptures can be found at roadside stalls and large shops in major cities. In Taipei, inexpensive curios can be found at the Tinghao area

(Chunghsiao East Rd., Sec. 4), on Chungshan North Rd., and in Hsimenting, as well as at the large Holiday Jade Market, open every Sunday in the area around the Kuanghua Market (Pateh Rd., Sec. 1). More intricate or delicate jade items, such as carved dragons, can be purchased at the Chinese Handicraft Mart, hotel shopping arcades, department stores, and jewelry stores.

When buying jade, it is definitely necessary to know what you are purchasing. There are ways to change the color of jade, so either shop with a person familiar with the stone or buy only from authorized jewelry stores.

PORCELAIN

Fine ceramics at attractive prices are a hallmark of Taiwan's modern potters, who combine the latest technological advances with ancient skills and techniques. Good bargains range from modern designs to excellent reproductions of ancient treasures. Many gift shops and stores in major cities carry a selection, and tours of ceramic factories (with bilingual guides) can be easily arranged. Because it is illegal to take genuine antiques (over 100 years old) out of the country, the only items available are reproductions, with prices starting at US$10.

MARBLE

Marble is one of Taiwan's few natural resources, and the only one of which there is an almost inexhaustible supply. The island's biggest marble-processing plant and showroom is in Hualien, near the celebrated Taroko Gorge. The plant, operated by the Ret-Ser Engineering Agency (RSEA), employs hundreds of master craftsmen who produce lamps and lamp stands, checkerboard tabletops, bookends, ashtrays and cigarette boxes, pencil holders, paperweights, and kitchen items. The prices start at just over US$5 for an ashtray and go up to a few hundred dollars for statues and sculptures. RSEA also has a display center at 32 Chungshan North Rd., Sec. 2, Taipei.

BRASS

Many functional and decorative brass items are made in Taiwan, from large solid brass beds and coatracks to pencil holders and trinkets. Larger items are usually packaged disassembled for easier carrying and shipping. There are several brass specialty shops in Taipei located on Chungshan North Rd..

CLOISONNÉ

One of Taiwan's greatest art forms is cloisonné. The items range from inexpensive pendants to costly vases and tea sets, priced from as low as US$4 to over US$150. Most hotel arcades carry cloisonné objects, and many stores specializing in cloisonné are located on Nanking East and Chungshan North roads.

WOOD CARVINGS

The major themes of Chinese handicrafts are religion and nature: mythical figures, historical heroes, landscapes, birds and flowers, intricate miniature pagodas, pavilions, and temples. Bamboo, elm, teak, and camphorwood sculptures and carvings are reasonably priced. Bamboo products, such as musical instruments, canes, flower baskets, lampshades, and ornaments, can be found nearly everywhere at reasonable prices. Taipei and other major cities have shops that sell these items, but at Sanyi, Lukang, and Chushan you can watch the artists at work, and also find excellent prices for wood and bamboo products.

ELECTRICAL AND ELECTRONIC ITEMS

Modern electrical and electronic consumer products manufactured in Taiwan include calculators and watches, kitchen appliances, audiovisual equipment, and computers, among others. For these items, it is best to shop only at government-approved department stores, where the items for sale are generally of export quality, probably UL- and FCC-approved, and safer and more durable than cheaper items purchased from night markets or small stores.

TEA

Quality Taiwan teas are available in bulk, tea bags, or gift containers, and at prices ranging from incredibly low to ridiculously high. Taiwan's three main types of tea are black, green, and oolong, each processed in a different manner. Most stores in the larger cities have at least one clerk who speaks at least a few phrases of English. Because of the many different grades and varieties of tea, prices vary as greatly as does the taste of the tea. After you select some types that appeal to your sense of smell, you can sample them right there in the store, and then purchase whichever you like best.

In addition to tea, most tea shops sell attractive gift packs of tea sets and accessories which make perfect gifts or souvenirs. The larger shops will even show you the steps of the traditional tea ceremony while you sample the teas you're pondering buying.

GARMENTS AND FASHIONS

With a little careful shopping, clothing is another good bargain in Taiwan. Whether you purchase inexpensive casual wear at a night market or designer labels at a department store, the prices are generally very good. Unlike the situation in the West, small boutiques generally have better prices than department stores, so comparison shopping is essential.

Custom-made clothes for men and women are usually a very good buy in Taiwan, both in terms of quality and price. The larger international hotels have tailor shops on the premises, and even better prices can be found at shops outside the hotels. Most tailor shops stock large selections of imported fabrics, and some can complete an order in 24 hours. Many tailor shops are located on Chungshan North and Linsen North roads, and many have clerks who speak some English.

The traditional form-fitting Chinese evening gown, the *chi-pao* or *cheong-sam*, is famous for its feminine allure. Prices range from just over US$50 to more than US$500, depending on the quality of the material and workmanship. Many shops specializing in women's clothing are located on Poai and Hengyang roads in the Hsimenting district, and they can deliver a tailored *chi-pao* to your hotel in anywhere from 24 hours to 3 days.

High-quality, low-priced off-the-rack clothing for men, women, and children can be found at a large number of stores located in the Tinghao district (Chunghsiao East Rd., Sec. 4); on Nanking East Rd., Sec. 4; and on Chingtao West Rd. near the Taipei Train Station.

SPORTING GOODS

Taiwan is one of the world's major exporters of sporting goods, so it is only natural that shoppers can find a wide range of competitively priced sporting goods here. Local manufacturers produce just about every kind of sports equipment, along with a complete range of clothing. Sporting goods shops are scattered throughout Taipei and other cities, and prices of internationally famous brand-name products, made here under license, compare favorably with those in other countries.

WHERE TO BUY

DEPARTMENT STORES

The less modern the shopping facility, the lower the prices usually are. This means night markets and roadside stalls are always cheaper than big, air-conditioned department stores or fancy hotel arcades. Department stores do have some distinct advantages: everything is available in one place, prices (though high) are fixed, they frequently have sales (from 10% to 50% off at the change of seasons and major holidays), and they will accept traveler's checks and credit cards. Furthermore, in department stores and also in hotel arcades, the sales clerks speak some English or Japanese, and unsatisfactory merchandise may be exchanged, provided you remember to keep the receipts from your purchases.

One unique aspect of local department stores is that they rent space in each department to various companies to sell their own brand-name goods. If there are two tables side by side selling men's shirts, they are probably sponsored by two competing shirt companies. Therefore, if you need to exchange unsatisfactory merchandise, not only do you need the receipt, you also have to go to the same counter in the store where you purchased the item.

With the growing number of major and minor department stores in larger cities, competition is becoming very intense, much to the advantage of the consumer. The major categories of items for sale in a typical department store include clothing and fashion accessories, cosmetics, shoes, bags, sporting goods, toys, stationery, housewares, electrical appliances, furniture, and numerous other luxury and daily wares. About 80% of the stores also have Western-style supermarkets.

NIGHT MARKETS AND BAZAARS

If you would like a strong dose of local color, then a visit to a Chinese night market is in order. This is one of the most interesting shopping experiences in Taiwan: bright lights, a carnival atmosphere, tasty snacks, and excited crowds bargaining for everything, with a different selection every day. Vendors in night markets and small stores rarely accept anything other than local currency, so you need enough local cash to be able to take advantage of the lower prices. Relatively few vendors speak English, but with a pen and paper you can still do some good bargaining—which is expected, since there are no fixed prices.

Shopping at the crowded local night markets requires a bit of footwork, and unsatisfactory products can seldom be exchanged. However, open-air bazaars and night markets are the best places to browse for traditional products and casual clothing.

Interesting night markets and bazaars in Taipei include the following: **Shihlin Market,** just north of the Grand Hotel; **Ching Kuang Market,** at the corner of Nungan and Shuangcheng streets; **China Bazaar,** on Chunghua Rd.; **Hwahsi St.** ("Snake Alley") in Wanhua; **Kuanghua Market,** under the bridge; **Hsimenting** ("West Gate," at Chunghua and Hengyang roads), and the **Jaoho St. Night Market,** in Sungshan, eastern Taipei.

Colorful night markets can also be found in Keelung, Taichung, Tainan, and Kaohsiung.

BUSINESS CENTER

The business center of Taipei has been gradually shifting from the Wanhua-Hsimenting District to the Eastern Business District. Hsimenting remains the home of many movie theaters and inexpensive boutiques, and still affords a strong sense of local color, especially at night, but the eastern part of the city is the new business center.

New expansion plans for the city call for the development of eastern Taipei, in part to support the TWTC complex, which is itself the subject of another plan. This area is a virtual wonderland of business and banking institutions, art galleries, bookstores, beauty and barber shops, and stores selling a wide range of jewelry, name brand sporting goods, and fashionable clothing. The area has many of the best Chinese restaurants in Asia, featuring every style of Chinese cuisine. It is also home to many Western fast-food (hamburgers, pizza, fried chicken) establishments and Western restaurants. Also in the eastern district are a concentration of department stores, most on Chunghsiao East Rd., selling top-quality items. Boutiques and stores of all sizes sell imported and locally produced clothing and accessories in a wide range of styles and prices. The area is also an entertainment center, boasting many of the most popular dancing spots (Kiss, Soho, Nasa), movie theaters, and "MTV" centers.

Stores in the northern district, roughly centered along Chungshan North and Linsen North roads, feature Chinese art and antiques, jewelry, Western clothes, restaurants, and the city's night life—bars, pubs, nightclubs, and discos. The Shihlin-Tienmu part of the city is Taipei's expatriate living area, and in addition to many good Western restaurants, the district has a complete range of Chinese furniture, art, and antiques stores. The Shihlin night market is famous for its variety of Chinese-style snacks.

Doing Business in Taiwan

ESTABLISHING YOUR BUSINESS IN TAIWAN

WORK PERMITS

Prior to 1987, the largest groups of overseas workers in Taiwan were executives who headed either the foreign manufacturing enterprises on the island or the companies purchasing Taiwan-made products; native English-speakers (predominantly young travelers) who made a modest income teaching English in the many language schools; and illegals who had overstayed their tourist visas and worked as maids and musicians. However, rising living conditions, the growth of the service sector, and the appreciation of the New Taiwan dollar against the U.S. currency (which lowered the competitiveness of many low-end Taiwan products) have forced the economy away from labor-intensive industries and created a situation in which local Taiwanese are no longer willing to work long hours at low wages in factories or in the construction industry. This has opened the door to illegal workers from less developed countries, who see in Taiwan an opportunity to make a good living. And although many factory owners have opted to hire overseas laborers, the practice is illegal and opposed by the government. To counter this trend a new law was passed that requires all enterprises employing workers from other countries to register them with the government.

BUSINESS VISAS

Besides the single-entry visitor visa discussed earlier, Taiwan issues a multiple-entry visitor visa. It can be applied for by representatives of a foreign company that has purchased a total of more than US$1 million worth of Taiwan products in the preceding 12 months or an annual average of US$1 million over the preceding three years. If issued, it is valid for an unlimited number of visits, not to exceed six-months' duration each, during a period of less than 12 months. To receive a multiple-entry visitor visa, one must apply to the Ministry of Foreign

Affairs, usually through a company agent, representative, or affiliate in Taiwan. In addition to the multiple-entry visitor visa, a person wishing to stay in Taiwan for a period of over six months may request a resident visa from the same Ministry of Foreign Affairs Office.

INVESTMENT IN TAIWAN

For the past 40 years, the government in Taiwan has encouraged foreign investment and has made it attractive by offering such incentives as tax holidays, research and development incentives, duty-free capital imports, deferred income tax, accelerated depreciation, and investment tax credits to foreign investors. Nevertheless, the government does maintain an oversight on foreign investment, chiefly under the Statute for Investment by Foreign Nationals, administered by the Investment Commission of the Ministry of Economic Affairs. Foreign investors will generally have to apply to this body for a certificate of Foreign Investment Approval (FIA).

A number of business alternatives are open to foreign investors. One popular way for foreign investors not overly familiar with the Taiwan market to establish an investment is by means of technical cooperation. Under this alternative, the foreign company licenses technology to a local company and receives royalties. Though there are ways to avoid doing so, an investor intending to enter into a technical cooperation arrangement would usually obtain a Technical Cooperation Approval document (TCA) from the government Investment Commission.

If a company is involved in procurement and similar activities in support of business operations outside Taiwan, a representative office may be set up to facilitate such business. A representative office may not engage in profit-making enterprises, but it can coordinate local business affairs on behalf of its overseas principal. An FIA is not necessary for setting up a representative office, but the office must be registered with the Commercial Division of the Ministry of Economic Affairs.

Foreign companies wishing to engage in substantial profit-making activities in Taiwan might wish to establish a branch office. A branch is part of a foreign company and must be officially recognized by Taiwan under the body of statutes known as Company Law. In seeking this recognition, the parent company agrees to submit itself to the jurisdiction of the Taiwan courts and government agencies in all matters whose value is up to the total paid-in capital of the foreign company. A branch is subject to all Taiwan tax laws and will be treated just like a local company.

Other possible methods of doing business in Taiwan include forming a commercial agency and distributorship (in which a Taiwanese company is appointed to act on behalf of the foreign company), forming a local company as a joint venture with local partners, or forming a local company that is wholly owned by the foreign investors.

BUSINESS PRACTICES AND CONDITIONS

TRADEMARKS

Trademark protection in Taiwan is available to all foreign individuals or entities who register; registration is good for 10 years, and must be renewed every 10 years. It can extend even to nonregistered world-famous marks if the relevant foreign country offers similar rights to citizens of Taiwan. It should be noted, however, that in most instances the right to use a trademark or service mark is granted on the basis of priority of registration, not priority of use. You should, therefore, register your trademark as soon as possible. That said, you should be aware that although the laws exist, enforcement is rather lax, and many counterfeit products such as fake Rolex watches and imitation brand-name clothing abound in the street shops and night markets.

PATENTS

In 1986, the Patent Law was amended to increase the protection available to patent holders, and to expand the number and scope of inventions covered. New inventions are currently protected for 15 years, new designs for 5 years, and new utility models for 10 years. At the same time, many items not included before 1986, such as pharmaceutical products, are now patentable. The burden of proof in infringement cases has been reversed, and it is thus easier for patent holders to protect their rights.

Individuals who are not citizens of Taiwan may apply for patent protection as long as their own countries grant reciprocal protection to Taiwan nationals. They need not be resident in Taiwan to apply for a patent, but they must retain local patent counsel to make the necessary application.

Novelty, usefulness, and nonobviousness are important criteria that help determine whether or not a patent is granted. Therefore, it is advisable to file for patent protection in Taiwan at the same time applications are made abroad in order to preserve the novelty of an invention.

COPYRIGHT

The Copyright Law of the ROC underwent a complete revision in 1986. It now provides wide-ranging protection for authors of almost all original works, including literary, editorial, artistic, graphic, and musical creations as well as recorded, photographic, and design works, translations, and computer programs. Under the law, the copyright holder has the exclusive right to make derivative work and to publicly display and perform, translate, edit, adapt, lease, and reproduce the original work.

The duration of protection afforded by the Copyright Law varies with the nature of the work. Editorial work, motion pictures, videotapes, photographic work, and computer programs are, for example, protected for 30 years; other kinds of works may be protected for terms of up to 30 years plus the life of the author.

The works of Taiwan citizens are granted copyrights upon completion, whereas those of foreign authors must be registered in order to receive protection. The Copyright Law currently requires that the work of a foreign author be published in Taiwan before such registration is sought or that the relevant foreign country grant reciprocal copyright protection to citizens of Taiwan. At present, such reciprocity exists only with the United States, Spain, and the United Kingdom.

SETTLEMENT OF COMMERCIAL DISPUTES

When a trade dispute arises in which it is difficult to reach a satisfactory compromise, the parties involved may ask the Board of Foreign Trade to reconcile their differences or they may seek third-party arbitration.

TAXATION

TAIWAN has various forms of direct taxes (income tax, land tax, land incremental tax, estate tax, house tax, and deed tax) and indirect taxes (customs duties, commodity tax, business tax, entertainment tax, harbor construction dues, and securities transaction tax).

The tax framework is enforced by the Ministry of Finance through the Customs Division of its Department of Taxation, and by the Inspectorate General of Customs. The National Taxation Bureau and various tax offices of the local government are also charged with the responsibility for collecting taxes.

CUSTOMS DUTIES

The government classifies items for possible import as permissible, controlled, or prohibited. At present, there are only 421 controlled items and 18 temporarily prohibited items. All other products are permitted. Importers must have a general license for imports, though for a number of items the license requirement has been waived. A specific import license may also be needed for certain items such as controlled items. Special licenses are issued by the Board of Foreign Trade, while general licenses can be obtained from an authorized foreign exchange bank.

Besides license requirements, there are duties to be paid on imports. The tariff schedule can be obtained from the Department of Customs, Ministry of Finance. Depending on the foreign investor's status and the nature of the imports, it may be possible to obtain an exemption from the duties.

INCOME TAX

Income tax can be divided into profit-seeking business income tax and consolidated income tax. The former, a kind of corporate income tax based on annual net profit, is assessed primarily on local companies and branches of foreign companies. At present, the maximum rate is 25%.

The consolidated income tax is a form of personal income tax, with a maximum rate of 50%. Generally, a person whose stay in Taiwan during a given year is less than 183 days is treated as a nonresident and taxed at a minimum of 20%. After 183 days, the tax rate drops to the level paid by Taiwan residents in the same tax bracket.

COMMODITY TAX

Commodity tax is assessed on certain local products as well as imported goods. The current rates range from 2% to 80%.

BUSINESS TAX

The value-added tax (VAT) is a general sales tax charged as a percentage of the selling price of some goods or services. The business may generally use the VAT it pays for a purchase to offset the VAT levied on the sale of the same item or service. The VAT is currently assessed at 5% of the invoice value. Prior to July 1988, the VAT was added to the charge of any given item. After July, however, the VAT began to be included in the price.

BANKING, FINANCE, AND SECURITIES

BANKING institutions in Taiwan, both domestic and foreign, are controlled by the Ministry of Finance and the Central Bank of China, and are categorized as commercial banks, savings banks, trust and investment companies, and specialized banks.

The banks in Taiwan are strictly controlled and offer limited services; the foreign banks are more limited than the domestic ones. Foreign banks are only allowed two branches, one in Taipei and one in Kaohsiung, and are forbidden to engage in trust and deposit-taking businesses. It is expected, though, that 1989 will see the implementation of a new banking law that will allow foreign banks more latitude. However, as of January 1989, this law had not yet been approved, and only domestic banks were allowed trust departments. Savings in Taiwan are handled by the domestic banks and the more than 1,000 post offices around the island. There are 75 registered credit cooperatives, 284 agricultural credit unions, and 18 fishery credit unions.

International Banks in Taiwan (Taipei)

American Express International Banking Corp., 214 Tunhua North Rd.; Telephone 715–1581

Amsterdam Rotterdam Bank NV, 13/F, Worldwide House, 683 Minsheng East Rd.; Telephone 713–0221

Bangkok Bank, Taipei Branch, 121 Sungchiang Rd.; Telephone 571–3275 (6 lines)

Bank of America, 205 Tunhua North Rd.; Telephone 715–4111

---

cont...

INTERNATIONAL BANKS IN TAIWAN (Taipei) *cont:...*

Bank of Credit & Commerce International S.A., 3/F, Cheng Hsiang Tang Bldg., 146 Sungchiang Rd.; Telephone 542-9456

Bank of Taiwan, 120 Chungching South Rd., Sec. 1; Telephone 314-7377

Bankers Trust Company, 8/F, 205 Tunhua North Rd.; Telephone 715-2888 (10 lines)

Banque Indosuez Taipei, 11/F, 483 Minsheng East Rd.; Telephone 502-9670, 505-8953

Banque Nationale de Paris (BNP), 7/F, Tunhua Financial Bldg., 214 Tunhua North Rd.; Telephone 716-1167

Banque PARIBAS, 11/F, 205 Tunhua North Rd.; Telephone 715-1980

Barclays Bank PLC, 10/F, 205 Tunhua North Rd.; Telephone 713-2040

Chang Hwa Commercial Bank, Ltd., 2/F, 57 Chungshan North Rd., Sec. 2; Telephone 536-2951

Chase Manhattan Bank, 72 Nanking East Rd., Sec. 2; Telephone 537-8100

Chemical Bank, 7/F, Worldwide House, 683 Minsheng East Rd.; Telephone 712-1181

Citibank, 742 Minsheng East Rd.; Telephone 715-5931/49

City Bank of Taipei, 50 Chungshan North Rd., Sec. 2; Telephone 542-5656

Crédit Lyonnais Bank, 15/F, Asia Trust Bldg., 116 Nanking East Rd., Sec. 2; Telephone 562-9475

Dai-ichi Kangyo Bank, 137 Nanking East Rd., Sec. 2; Telephone 561-4371

cont...

INTERNATIONAL BANKS IN TAIWAN (Taipei) *cont...*

Deutsche Bank AG, 10/F, 296 Jenai Rd., Sec. 4; Telephone 755–3838

Development Bank of Singapore Ltd., 214 Tunhua North Rd.; Telephone 713–7711/0

First Commercial Bank of Taiwan, 15 Chungching South Rd., Sec. 1; Telephone 311–1111

First Interstate Bank of California, 221 Nanking East Rd., Sec. 3; Telephone 715–3572

First National Bank of Boston, 5/F United Commercial Bldg., 137 Nanking East Rd., Sec. 2; Telephone 506–3443

Grindlays Bank Ltd., Taipei Branch, 2/F 123 Nanking East Rd., Sec. 2; Telephone 542–7456

Hollandsche Bank-Unie NV, 61–1 Sungchiang Rd.; Telephone 581–8131/5

Hong Kong & Shanghai Banking Corp., 13/F, 14/F, 333 Keelung Rd., Sec. 1; Telephone 738–0088

Hua Nan Commercial Bank, Ltd., 33 Kaifeng St., Sec. 1; Telephone 371–3111

International Bank of Singapore Ltd., Taipei Branch, 178 Nanking East Rd., Sec. 2; Telephone 581–0531

International Commercial Bank of China, 100 Chilin Rd.; Telephone 563–3156

Irving Trust Company, 4/F, 473 Tunhua South Rd.; Telephone 771–6612

Lloyds Bank PLC, Taipei Branch, 3/F, Empire Bldg., 87 Sungchiang Rd.; Telephone 506–8521 (12 lines)

Manufacturers Hanover Trust Co., 10/F, Taipei Financial Center, 62 Tunhua North Rd.; Telephone 721–3150

cont...

INTERNATIONAL BANKS IN TAIWAN (Taipei) *cont...*

Metropolitan Bank & Trust, 107 Chunghsiao East Rd., Sec. 4; Telephone 776–6355

The Morgan Bank, 205 Tunhua North Rd.; Telephone 712–2333

Overseas Chinese Commercial Banking Corp., 8 Hsiangyang Rd.; Telephone 371–5181

Republic National Bank of New York, Suite 606, Bank Tower, 205 Tunhua North Rd.; Telephone 718–2340/2

The Royal Bank of Canada, 8/F Tunhua Financial Bldg., 214 Tunhua North Rd.; Telephone 713–0911

Security Pacific National Bank, Taipei Branch, 2/F, 62 Tunhua North Rd.; Telephone 777–5533

Shanghai Commercial & Savings Bank, Ltd., 28 Kuan—chien Rd.; Telephone 311–0731

Société Générale, 683 Minsheng East Rd.; Telephone 715–5050

Standard Chartered Bank, 337 Fuhsing North Rd.; Telephone 716–6261, 717–2866

Toronto Dominion Bank, 2/F, 337 Fuhsing North Rd.; Telephone 716–2160

United World Chinese Commercial Bank, 65 Kuanchien Rd.; Telephone 312–5555

Westpac Banking Corp., 15/F, 99 Fuhsing North Rd.; Telephone 712–9133

SECURITIES MARKET

The Taiwan Stock Exchange (TAIEX) was established in 1961. The exchange, as well as brokers, dealers, underwriters, and other companies whose activities are related to the exchange, is regulated by the Securities and Exchange Commission (SEC), under the Ministry of Finance.

Although playing the market is popular, only about 10% of the local population invests (foreigners are not allowed to invest), and these are mainly short-term investors. Recent government policy is to expand the market by simplifying public-offering listing requirements, adding at-market issues, asking for more extensive documentation of publicly listed companies, controlling insider trading, creating integrated securities firms, creating tender offers and off-exchange transactions, and expanding the operations of foreign securities firms through their local branches or subsidiaries. An over-the-counter market is also being considered.

Because of the small number of listed companies (only about 170 by the end of 1988), Taiwan's mutual fund market is also small. However, this market is expected to grow rapidly.

BUSINESS CUSTOMS

BUSINESS CARDS

Anyone doing business in Taiwan should be aware that the exchange of business cards is the first thing done after an introduction, and a ready supply of business cards is almost essential. It is a good idea to have cards printed in both English and Chinese. This can be done in just a few days and at reasonable rates. If you know in advance that you are coming, a local contact can order them for you so that they will be ready when you arrive.

BUSINESS HOURS

Most businesses in Taiwan operate on a five-and-a-half-day work week. Banks are open from 9 AM to 3:00 PM during the week and 9 AM 12 noon on Saturday; hours for government offices are from 8:30 AM to 12:30 PM and 1:30 PM to 5:00 PM on weekdays, and 8:30 AM to 12:30 PM on Saturdays. Times for other businesses vary but are usually eight hours a day during the week and four hours on Saturday. Department stores are open from 10 AM to 10 PM daily, and smaller stores and shops open according to their location and clientele. It might be useful to remember that the Chinese take their lunch hour very seriously and are accustomed to eating for part of the time and sleeping for the rest.

It is considered in very bad taste to conduct any business from 12:30 PM to 1:30 PM. This custom is actually quite remarkable. From the time Chinese children begin school, they are taught to fold their arms on the desks, put their heads down, and sleep for 30 minutes. There is nothing stranger for a Westerner than to walk into an office and see all the staff with their heads on their desks, sound asleep.

CONVENTIONS AND EXHIBITIONS

ALTHOUGH Taiwan has been an economic power for some time, its convention and exhibition facilities were sadly lacking. However, with the construction of the Taipei World Trade Center (TWTC), in operation since 1987, and the adjoining Convention Center, which opened in January 1990, the country has taken a giant leap forward and has become an increasingly popular venue for a wide range of exhibitions and product shows.

The TWTC includes a seven-story Exhibition Hall, opened in January 1986. On the ground floor of the 289,000-sq-ft (26,860-m²) hall, about 30 trade shows are held each year. Floors two to seven are occupied by a permanent Trade Mart, with floors two through six reserved for exports, and the seventh floor for imports.

Another part of the trade center complex, opened in 1988, is a 34-story office building, which is the headquarters for the China External Trade and Development Council and other service organizations. Besides the Convention Center, which has a main hall seating 3,300, the facility also includes the Hyatt Regency Hotel, with approximately 1,000 guest rooms.

Conference facilities in Taiwan are mainly located in the large international-standard hotels and can accommodate groups of 10 to 2,000. The main activities are seminars, small-product exhibitions, and cocktail receptions.

BUREAUS AND ORGANIZATIONS

GOVERNMENT ORGANIZATIONS

Whether your visit is for business or pleasure or both, you may need to contact various government bodies, from the local police to the Ministry of Economic Affairs. Following is a list of some of the more useful ones; all addresses are in Taipei unless otherwise noted.

KEY GOVERNMENT SERVICES, TAIPEI *(cont.)*

Taipei Municipal Police Headquarters' Foreign Service Center (for visa extensions), 96 Yenping South Rd.; Telephone 381-8341, 381-7475, 381-7494

Ministry of Economic Affairs, 15 Foochow St.; Telephone 351-7271

Ministry of Finance, 2 Aikuo West Rd.; Telephone 351-1611

Ministry of Foreign Affairs, 2 Chienshou Rd.; Telephone 311-9292

Ministry of the Interior, 107 Roosevelt Rd., Sec. 4; Telephone 341-5241

Anti-Counterfeiting Committee, Ministry of Economic Affairs, 1 Hukou St.; Telephone 396-7667

Council for Economic Planning and Development, 9/F, 87 Nanking East Rd., Sec. 2; Telephone 551-3522

Board of Foreign Trade, Ministry of Economic Affairs, 1 Hukou St.; Telephone 351-0271, 351-0286

Bureau of Commodity Inspection and Quarantine, Ministry of Economic Affairs, 4 Tsinan Rd., Sec. 1; Telephone 351-2141

Government Information Office, 3 Chunghsiao East Rd., Sec. 1; Telephone 341-9211

EMBASSIES AND CONSULATES

Only 23 countries recognize Taiwan, and not all of them maintain embassies or consular offices there. The following is a list of official representatives of foreign governments. Many other nations maintain trade offices or other unofficial contacts, however.

FOREIGN DIPLOMATIC AND CONSULAR OFFICES IN TAIPEI

Embassy of the Republic of Costa Rica, 10 Lane 172, Chungshan North Rd., Sec. 6; Telephone 777–1674

Honorary Consulate of the Republic of Costa Rica, 1/F, 108 Chungcheng Rd., Sec. 2; Telephone 871–2422

Embassy of the Dominican Republic, 110 Chungcheng Rd., Sec. 2; Telephone 871–7939

Embassy of the Republic of Guatemala, 6 Lane 88, Chienkuo North Rd., Sec. 1; Telephone 507–7043

Honorary Consulate of the Republic of Guatemala, 11/F 65–20 Chunghsiao East Rd., Sec. 4; Telephone 721–9463

Embassy of the Republic of Haiti, 3/F, 246 Chungshan North Rd., Sec. 6; Telephone 831–7086

Honorary Consulate of the Ivory Coast, 7/F, 128 Yenping South Rd.; Telephone 381–7042

Embassy of the Republic of Korea, 345 Chunghsiao East Rd., Sec. 4; Telephone 761–9361/5

Consulate of the Republic of Nauru, Room 1B, Chungshan Bldg., 2 Mintsu East Rd.; Telephone 598–1975

Honorary Consulate of the Republic of Nicaragua, 109 Yenchi St.; Telephone 772–5687

Embassy of the Republic of Panama, 5/F, 13 Tehui St.; Telephone 596–8563/4

Embassy of the Republic of Paraguay, 2/F, 20 Lane 38, Tienyu St., Tienmou; Telephone 872–2261

cont...

FOREIGN DIPLOMATIC AND CONSULAR OFFICES *(cont.)*

Embassy of the Republic of El Salvador, 15 Lane 34, Kukung Rd., Shihlin; Telephone 881-9887

Royal Embassy of Saudi Arabia, 11/F, 550 Chunghsiao East Rd., Sec. 4; Telephone 703-5855

Embassy of the Republic of South Africa, 13/F, Bank Tower, 205 Tunhua North Rd.; Telephone 715-3252/4

Honorary Consulate-General of the Kingdom of Swaziland, 12/F, 127 Jenai Rd., Sec. 3; Telephone 751-8257

Vatican: Apostolic Nunciature, 87 Aikuo East Rd.; Telephone 321-6847, 341-5298

Taiwan's own External Trade Development Council maintains branches and offices in many foreign countries. They cooperate with public and private commercial organizations, serving the needs not only of Taiwan's businesses, but also of foreign importers, exporters, and government and foreign organizations.

CHINA EXTERNAL TRADE DEVELOPMENT COUNCIL/FETS
(U.S. Overseas Branches and Representative Offices)

Australia

Far East Trading Co., PTY. Ltd., P. O. Box 148, World Trade Centre, Melbourne, Victoria 3005; Telephone (03) 611-2988; Telex AA 37248 FETR; Cable FETRA MELBOURNE

Far East Trade Service, Inc., Branch Office in Sydney, Suite 1907, Level 19, MLC Centre, King St., Sydney 2000; Telephone (02) 232-6626, 232-6999; Fax (02) 232-7429; Telex 71565 FETRA

cont...

EXTERNAL TRADE DEVELOPMENT COUNCIL/FETS *(cont.)*

Belgium

Far East Trade Service, Inc., Belgian Branch Office, World Trade Center 1, 16e Étage, Boulevard Emile Jacqmain 162, Boite 33, 1210 Brussels; Telephone (02) 218-5157; Fax (02) 218-6835; Telex 25343 FETS B; Cable FAREASTRADE BRUSSE

Brazil

Centro Comercial do Extremo-Oriente, Divisão de Promocão do Comercio, Alameda Jau 1742, Conj. 101, CEP 01420, São Paulo-SP; Telephone (11) 280-0151, 881-0260; Fax (11) 883-7929; Telex 112-5416 CCEO BR ATTN: Mr. Liu Ei-Min

Canada

Far East Trade Service, Inc., Suite 3315, 2 Bloor St. East, Toronto, Ontario M4W 1A8; Telephone (416) 922-2412; Fax (416) 922-2426; Telex 065-28086 TROC TOR; Cable FETSTOR

Far East Trade Service, Inc., Vancouver Office, 650-409 Granville St., Vancouver, BC V6C 1T2; Telephone (604) 682-9501; Fax (604) 682-9775; Telex 04-51162 FETS VCR

FETRA CO. Inc., P.O. Box 349, Place Bonaventure, Montreal, Quebec H5A 1B5; Telephone (514) 866-0598; Fax (514) 866-8325; Telex 055-61456 FETCOR; Cable FETRACO MONTREAL

Denmark

Far East Trade Office, Copenhagen, Ny Ostergade 3, 1st Fl., DK-1101, Copenhagen K; Telex 16600 FOTEX DK; Cable TREPRESENT DK

France

Centre Asiatique de Promotion, Economique et Commerciale, 3, Av. Bertie Albrecht, 5e Étage, 75008 Paris; Telephone (01) 4563-3354, 4563-7900; Fax (01) 4289-1084; Telex 641275 F CAPEC

cont...

EXTERNAL TRADE DEVELOPMENT COUNCIL/FETS *(cont.)*

Far East Trade Service, Inc., Succursale à Paris, 8, Rue de Penthièvre 75008 Paris; Telephone (01) 4266–0512, 4266–0562; Fax (01) 4266–0431; Telex 643786 FETS F

Germany

Far East Trade Service Center, Westendstrasse 8, 6000 Frankfurt/Main; Telephone (69) 727–641/2; Fax (69) 727–553; Telex 416777 FETS D; Cable FETRA FRANKFURTMAIN

Far East Trade Service Center, Hamburg Branch Office, Grosse Bleichen 12, 2000 Hamburg 36; Telephone (40) 351–627, 341–981; Fax (40) 346–601; Telex 403906 FETSHHD

Taiwan Investment Services, Dreiechstrasse 59, 6000 Frankfurt/Main 70; Telephone (69) 610–743, 615–534; Telex 414460 ASIAT D; Cable SINOINVEST

Hong Kong

Hongkong Investment Liaison Office, 415 Central Bldg., 3 Pedder St.; Telephone (05) 243–337; Cable TSINGRICH HONGKONG

Indonesia

Chinese Chamber of Commerce to Jakarta, No. 4, Jl. Banyumas, P.O. Box 2922, Jakarta; Telephone (21) 351–212/4; Fax (21) 380–9063; Telex 45126 SINOCH IA

Italy

Centro Commerciale per L'Estremeo Oriente, Via Errico Petrella, 2, 20124 Milan; Telephone (02) 285–3084; Fax (02) 278–077; Telex 331594 BOFTTFI; Cable FAREASTRADE MILANO

Japan

Far East Trade Service Center, Fukuoka Office, 9–28, Hakata Ekimae 2-Chome, Hakata-ku, Fukuoka, 812; Telephone (92) 472–7461; Fax (92) 472–7463

cont...

EXTERNAL TRADE DEVELOPMENT COUNCIL/FETS *(cont.)*

Association of East Asian Relations, Tokyo Office, 8–7 Higashi-Azabu 1-Chome, Minato-Ku, Tokyo 106; Telephone (03) 583–2171/5

Far East Trade Service Center, Tokyo Office, Nagai International Bldg., 12–19 Shibuya 2-Chome, Shibuya-ku, Tokyo 150; Telephone (03) 407-9711; Fax (03) 407–9715; Telex 242–3591 FETS J

Korea

Office of Economic Counselor, Embassy of the Republic of China in Korea, 83, 2-Ka, Myung-dong, Chung-ku, Seoul; Telephone (02) 776–2889, 757–5567; Fax (02) 757–3859; Telex 27529 MEARO K; Cable SINOECON SEOUL

Malaysia

Far East Trading & Tourism Center, SDN. BHD., Economic Division, Lot 201A 2nd Fl., Wisma Equity, 150 Jalan Ampang, Kuala Lumpur 50450; Telephone (03) 243–5337, 242–5549; Fax (03) 242–3906; Telex FETTC MA 30052

Netherlands

Far East Trade Office, Economic Division, Javastraat 56, 2585 AR, The Hague; Telephone (70) 469–438; Fax (70) 600–105; Telex 34281 ECODINL

FETS Rotterdam Office, Beurs-World Trade Center, Buersplein 37, Room 1269, P.O. Box 30119, 3001 DC Rotterdam; Telephone (10) 405–3388; Fax (10) 404–7409; Telex 24225 FETS NL

New Zealand

East Asia Trade Centre Auckland Office, 3rd Fl., Norwich Union Bldg., C.P.O. Box 4018, Auckland; Telephone (09) 33–903; Telex NZ 60209; Cable EASTRAD AUCKLAND

cont...

EXTERNAL TRADE DEVELOPMENT COUNCIL/FETS *(cont.)*

Philippines

Pacific Economic & Cultural Center, Economic Division, P.O. Box 948, Manila; Telephone (02) 461–880, 461–987; Fax (02) 409–713; Telex 40434 EDPEC PM; Cable SINOECON MANILA

Singapore

Trade Mission of the Republic of China in Singapore, #23–00 PSA Bldg., 460 Alexandra Rd., Singapore 0511, P.O. Box 3428; Telephone 278–6511; Fax 278–9962; Telex RS 25438 SIMISON; Cable SINOMISION

Far East Trade Service Inc., Singapore Representative Office, 5, Shenton Way, 02–01 UIC Bldg., Singapore 0106; Telephone 224–9433; Fax 225–0473; Telex RS 28140 FETS

Spain

Far East Trade Service S.A., Torres de Jerez Planta 12-B, Torre II, Plaza de Colón No. 2, 28046 Madrid; Telephone (01) 410–1414, 410–1513; Fax (01) 410–7314; Telex 41633 FETSS E

Sweden

Taipei Trade, Tourism & Information Office, 4 Tr Wenner-Gren Center, Sveavagen 166, S-113 46 Stockholm; Telephone (08) 728–8533; Fax (08) 728–8584; Telex 15360 SHAMO S

Thailand

Far East Trade Office, Economic Division, 10th Fl., Kian Gwan Bldg., 140 Wit Thayu Rd., Bangkok 10500; Telephone (02) 519–393/6; Fax (02) 535–251; Telex 82184 CHINATA TH; Cable CHINAIRTHA BANGKOK

United Kingdom

Majestic Trading Co., Ltd., 5th Fl., Bewlay House, 2 Swallow Place, London W1R 7AA; Telephone (71) 629–1516; Fax (71) 499–8730; Telex 25397 MAJECO G; Cable MAJESCO LONDON W1

cont...

EXTERNAL TRADE DEVELOPMENT COUNCIL/FETS *(cont.)*

Taiwan Products Promotion Co., Ltd., 4th Fl., Centric House, 390/391 Strand, London WC2R 01 T; Telephone (71) 379-0765; Fax (71) 379-5962; Telex 919744 FETS LG

United States

Economic Division, CCNAA, 4301 Connecticut Ave. NW, Washington, D.C. 20008; Telephone (202) 686-6400; Fax (202) 363-6294; Telex 440292 SINOECO; Cable SINOECO WASHINGTON D.C.

Investment and Trade Office, CCNAA, 8th Fl., 126 E. 56th St., New York, NY 10022; Telephone (212) 752-2340; Fax (212) 826-3615; Telex 426-330 CITO; Cable CITOCABLE

CETDC, Inc., 14th Fl., 41 Madison Ave., New York, NY 10010; Telephone (212) 532-7055; Fax (212) 213-4189; Telex 426299 CETDC NY

Commercial Division, CCNAA Office in Chicago, 8th Fl., 20 North Clark St., Chicago, IL 60602; Telephone (312) 332-2535; Fax (312) 332-0847; Telex 282168 ROCTRADE CGO

Far East Trade Service, Inc., Branch Office in Chicago, Suite 272, The Merchandise Mart, Chicago, IL 60654; Telephone (312) 321-9338; Fax (312) 321-1635; Telex 253726 FAREAST TR CGO

Commercial Division, CCNAA Office in Houston, 1360 Post Oak Blvd., Suite 2150, Houston, TX 77056; Telephone (713) 961-9794; Fax (713) 961-9809; Telex 650-315-9479 ROCTRAUW

Commercial Division, CCNAA Office in Los Angeles, Suite 918, 3660 Wilshire Blvd., Los Angeles, CA 90010; Telephone (213) 380-3644; Fax (213) 380-3407; Telex 910 321 4021 ROCTRADE LSA

Far East Trade Service, Inc., Branch Office in San Francisco, Suite 603, 555 Montgomery St., San Francisco, CA 94111-2564; Telephone (415) 788-4304/5; Fax (415) 788-0468; Telex 4974157 FETS SF

cont...

BUSINESS AND TRADE ASSOCIATIONS

With only 23 countries recognizing the Republic of China, most official and quasi-official dealings, commercial and political, are conducted through the different foreign trade representative offices.

FOREIGN TRADE ASSOCIATIONS IN TAIWAN
(Addresses are Taipei unless otherwise noted)

The Australian Commerce and Industry Office, Suite 2605 International Trade Bldg., 333 Keelung Rd., Sec. 1; Telephone 738-2833/6

Austrian Trade Delegation Taipei Office, Rm. 806, 205 Tunhua North Rd.; Telephone 715-5221

Belgian Trade Association, Taipei, Rm. 901, 685 Minsheng East Rd.; Telephone 715-1215

Bophuthatswana Trade and Tourism Center, 12/F, Formosa Plastics Bldg. B, 201-36 Tunhua North Rd.; Telephone 712-2358, 712-2361

Canadian Trade Office, Suite 707, 204 Tunhua North Rd.; Telephone 713-7268, and

Office of the Alberta Trade Representative in Taipei, Room 7F01, 7/F, 5 Hsinyi Rd., Sec. 5; Telephone 725-2950

Danish Trade Organization Taipei Office, 4/F, 12 Lane 21, Anho Rd.; Telephone 721-3386

Commercial Office of the Republic of Ecuador in Taipei, 7/F, 137 Nanking East Rd., Sec. 2; Telephone 506-1665, 507-1666

European Chamber of Commerce in Taipei, 12/F, 50 Hsinsheng South Rd., Sec. 1; Telephone 395-4572

---

cont...

FOREIGN TRADE ASSOCIATIONS IN TAIWAN *(cont.)*

France Asia Trade Promotion Association, Room 601, 205 Tunhua North Rd.; Telephone 713-3552

German Trade Office Taipei, 4/F, 350 Minsheng East Rd.; Telephone 571-9082

Hellenic Organization for the Promotion of Exports in Taiwan (Greece), Room 2, 6/F, 125 Roosevelt Rd., Sec. 3; Telephone 391-0597

Indonesian Chamber of Commerce to Taipei, Room 802, 289-293 Sungchiang Rd.; Telephone 502-5131

Interchange Association (Japan), 43 Chinan Rd., Sec. 2; Telephone 351-7250/4

Korea Trade Center Taipei, 7/F, 72 Nanking East Rd., Sec. 2; Telephone 581-3030/1

Netherlands Council for Trade Promotion Taipei Office, 11/F, (B) 201-36 Tunhua North Rd.; Telephone 713-6560

Asian Exchange Center, Inc. (Philippines), Room 902, 112 Chunghsiao East Rd., Sec. 1; Telephone 341-1325

Office of the Singapore Trade Representative Taipei, 9/F, 85 Jenai Rd., Sec. 4; Telephone 772-1940

Spanish Chamber of Commerce, Room C, 5/F, 122-4 Chunghsiao East Rd., Sec. 4; Telephone 711-2402, 721-9730

Swedish Industries Trade Representative Office, Room 1503-A, 15/F, 96 Chungshan North Rd., Sec. 2; Telephone 562-7601

Trade Office of Swiss Industries, 4/F, 23 Changan East Rd., Sec. 1; Telephone 551-8276

Anglo-Taiwan Trade Committee, 11/F, 36 Nanking East Rd., Sec. 2; Telephone 521-4116

cont...

FOREIGN TRADE ASSOCIATIONS IN TAIWAN *(cont.)*

UNITED STATES

American Institute in Taiwan, 7 Lane 134, Hsinyi Rd., Sec. 3; Telephone 709–2000, 713–2571

State of Arizona USA Asian-Pacific Trade Office, Room 7E01, 7/F, 5 Hsinyi Rd., Sec. 5; Telephone 725–1134

City of Tucson, Arizona, USA Trade Office, Room 7E10, 7/F, 5 Hsinyi Rd., Sec. 5; Telephone 725–2816

State of Arkansas Taipei Office, Room 7D12, 7/F, 5 Hsinyi Rd., Sec. 5; Telephone 723–2260

Colorado Trade and Investment Office, Room 7D14, 7/F, 5 Hsinyi Rd., Sec. 5; Telephone 725–1941, 725–1946

Indiana Department of Commerce Taipei Office, Room 7D16, 7/F, 5 Hsinyi Rd., Sec. 5; Telephone 725–2060

Minnesota Trade and Investment, Room 7G04, 7/F, 5 Hsinyi Rd.; Telephone

State of Mississippi, USA Taipei Office, Room 7C12, 7/F, 5 Hsinyi Rd., Sec. 5; Telephone 723–1856/7

Oregon Taiwan Trade Office, Room 7C14–15, 7/F, 5 Hsinyi Rd., Sec. 5; Telephone 723–2310/1

State of Utah, USA Taipei Trade Office, Room 7C16, 7/F, 5 Hsinyi Rd., Sec. 5; Telephone 725–2522

Washington State Taiwan Trade Association, Room 7G01, 7/F, 5 Hsinyi Rd., Sec. 5; Telephone 725–2499, 341–5508

USEFUL TELEPHONE NUMBERS

Emergencies:
Fire, 119
Police, 110
Police Broadcasting Network, (02) 351–3610
Foreign Affairs Department of the National Police
    Administration, (02) 396–9781
Foreign Affairs Division, Taipei Police
    Headquarters, (02) 537–3852

Directory Assistance:
Taipei Area, 104
Long Distance, 105
English-speaking Directory Assistance, (02) 311–6796
International Assistance, 100

Others:
Tourism Bureau, (02) 721–8541
Taiwan Visitors Association, (02) 594–3261
China External Trade Development Council
    (CETRA), (02) 715–1515
Ministry of Foreign Affairs, (02) 311–9292
Government Information Office, (02) 341–9211
CKS International Airport Tourist
    Service Center, (03) 383–4631
Travel Information Service Center, Sungshan
    Domestic Airport, (02) 712–1212 Ext. 471
Tourist Information Hot Line, (02) 717–3737

Appendix: Chinese Language

Mandarin Chinese, the official language of both mainland China and Taiwan, in its spoken form is a tonal language. The four tones are the deciding factors in determining the pronunciation and meaning of what is said.

The tones consist of level, rising, falling, and falling then rising. For convenience in pronunciation, this section will use the Yale system of romanization. However, on the mainland of China, *pinyin,* a different system of romanization, with origins in Russian cyrillic, is used.

Some Useful Phrases	
English	**Chinese**
Hello.	Ni hau.
Good morning.	Dzau an.
Good evening.	Wan an.
Good bye.	Dzai jyan.
Thank you.	Sye sye.
You're welcome.	Bu sye.
Yes.	Shr de.
No.	Bu shr.
I, me	Wo
You	Ni
He, she, it	Ta
Right!	Dwei!
Good!	Hau!
Not good!	Bu hau!
Excuse me (I'm sorry)	Dwei bu chi
Welcome!	Hwan ying!
Please	Ching
It doesn't matter.	Mei gwan syi.
Come in.	Ching jin.
Come here.	Lai je li.
Come with me.	Gen wo lai.

cont...

English	Chinese
Wait a minute.	Deng yi sya.
What?	Shem ma?
What is this?	Jei shr shem ma?
What is that?	Nei shr shem ma?
What do you want?	Ni yau shem ma?
Where?	Dzai na li?
When?	Shem ma shr hou?
Why?	Wei shem ma?
What is your name?	Ni gwei sying?
My name (last) is.......	Wo sying..........
My first name is........	Wo de ming dz shr........
Do you speak English?	Ni hui shwo ying wen ma?
Listen!	Ting!
Please speak more slowly.	Ching man yi dyan shwo.
Please repeat.	Ching dzai shwo.
Do you understand?	Ni dung bu dung wo de hua?
I am lost.	Wo mi lu le.
Can you help me?	Ni ke bu ke yi bang wo?

Shopping

English	Chinese
How much?	Dwo shau chyan?
Too expensive!	Tai gwei le!
Inexpensive	Pyan yi
I'm just looking.	Wo jr shr kan-kan.
May I try it on?	Wo ke yi shr chwan ma?
Bigger	Da yi dyan de
Smaller	Syau yi dyan de
Do you have it in......	You mei you.........
Black	Hei se
White	Bai se
Blue	Lan se
Brown	Dzung se
Cream	Nai you se
Gray	Hwei se
Green	Lyu se

cont...

English	Chinese
Yellow	Hwang se
Tan	Hwang he se
Red	Hung se
Pink	Fen hung se
Orange	Sying hwang se
Blouse	Dwan shan
Brassiere	Nai jau
Coat	Da yi
Dress	Yi shang
Handkerchief	Shou jin
Panties	Nyu ku
Shirt	Chen shan
Skirt	Chyun dz
Socks	Dwan wa
Stockings	Chang wa
Man's suit	Syi jwang
Sweater	Mau yi
Trousers (pair)	Yi tyau chang ku
Undershirt	Han shan
Men's underwear	Nan nei yi
Umbrella	Yu san
Wallet	Chyan bau

ILLNESS

English	Chinese
I have........	Wo you..........
Blister	Shwei pau
Burn	Tang shang
Chill	Fa leng
A cold	Shang feng
Constipation	Byan jye
Cough	Ke sou
Diarrhea	Bai li
Fever	Fa shau
Headache	Tou tung
Indigestion	Wei tung
Sore throat	Hou lung tung
Toothache	Ya tung

INDEX

Aberdeen, Hong Kong, 88

Aboriginal culture: Taiwan, Hualien, 538; Lanyu, 581; Wulai, 568, 580

Accounting standards: Hong Kong requirements, 158; Thailand business, 319

Adventure tours, Thailand, 224, costs, 228

Afternoon tea, Hong Kong, 131

Air fares, to Taiwan, 540

Airlines: Bangkok, Thailand, international offices, list, 236; Hong Kong, international offices, list, 48-49; to Singapore, international, 388; Taipei, Taiwan, list, 548-549

Airport: Hong Kong departure lounge, 51, transportation from, 47; Thailand, 228, 247

Airport tax: Hong Kong, 50; Singapore, 390; Taiwan, 551; Thailand, 238

Air shuttle, to Malaysia from Singapore, 517

Air transportation: to China from Hong Kong, 184; to Hong Kong, international, 45-49; to Singapore, international, 388; to Taiwan, 540, 548-549; in Thailand, 247; to Thailand, 235

Alien business law, Thailand, 317-318

Alishan, Taiwan, 570-571, 583

Amah Rock, Shatin, new territories, Hong Kong, 95

American food: Hong Kong restaurants, list, 122-123; Singapore restaurants, list, 466; Taipei, Taiwan, restaurants, list, 629

Amulet Market, Bangkok, Thailand, 259, 314

Amusement parks, Hong Kong, 88, 94, 99-100

Ananda mahidol. See Rama VIII

Animal fighting, Thai sport, cocks and fish, 306

Ann Siang Hill, Singapore, 486

Antiques: Hong Kong, shopping, 144; Singapore, buying of, 480; Thailand shopping, 309

Apartments, Bangkok, 289

Aquarium: Hong Kong, Water World, 88; Singapore, 423

Arab Street, Singapore, 409-411, 486-487

Arbitration: Hong Kong, 158-159; Taiwan, 649

Archaeology: Hong Kong, 25; Thailand, excavations, Bronze Age, 274; Sukhothai ruins, 273

Architecture, Macao, European, 180-181

Armenian Church of Saint Gregory the Illuminator, Singapore, 417

Arts and crafts: Hong Kong shopping, 145, 153; Singapore buying, 480; Taiwan, 641, 642, Lukang, 583; Thailand shopping, 311. See also Handicrafts

ASEAN countries, cultural show, Singapore, 471; visa-free travel, 388

Asian Dollar Market, Singapore, 497

Asian food, Hong Kong, by country, list, 126-129

Asia Television Ltd., Hong Kong, 59

Audio and video equipment: Hong Kong shopping, 150-151; Singapore shopping, 484

Aw Boon Haw Gardens, Hong Kong, 83

Ayutthaya, Thailand, 202; history, 205, 207, 208, 211, 252; town, 263-264

Babywear: Hong Kong shopping, 147

Backpackers, Koh Samui beach, Thailand, 276-277

Baht (Thai currency), 243; exchange rates, 244, 320

Bamboo products, Taiwan, 642

Ban Chiang, Thailand, 274

Bangkok, Thailand: banking, types, lists, 323-327; bus stations, 248; business contacts, private sector, list, 343-344; cooking schools, list, 298-299; cultural activities and entertainment, 304-305; festivals, 230-232; foreign embassies, list, 341-342; handicrafts, 311; hospitals, 311; hotels, 282, types, 228, lists, 283-289; international trade and investment offices and ministries, list, 329-332; jewelry shopping, 310; nightlife, variety, 304-305; pickpockets and con men, protection, 240; population, 215; postal and telegram service, 245; rail services, 247; restaurants, types, list, 300-302; sex-tourist industry reputation, 201; shopping, 313-314; student protests, 210; taxis, negotiated fares, 249; telephone service, 245, 246; tour, inclusive, 252-263; tours, 251; tourist information, 221; trade associations, list, 345-359; travel agencies, list, 227; travelers' checks and credit card acceptances, 243

Bangkok Bank, Thailand, 322

Bangkok International Airport, Thailand, 221

Banglampoo, district, Bangkok, 313

Banking: Hong Kong, 55, 57, 163-164; Singapore, 399; 497-498; Taiwan, 561, international, 651-654; Thailand, 322-328

Ban Na Thon, Kok Samui, Thailand, 278

Banyan tree, Penghu, Taiwan, 596

Bar girls, Bangkok, 304

Bargaining: Singapore shopping tips, 478; Thailand shopping, 308

Bars: Hong Kong, 138; Taiwan, 630-631

Basic Law (draft 1988), China on Hong Kong status, 29

Batik, 482

Bazaars, Taiwan, 644-645

Beaches: Hong Kong, 85-86, 87, 97, 99, 141; Taiwan, 580, 638, Kenting National Park, 595; Thailand, 276-281, Koh Samet, 267-269, Pattaya, 265-267, Phuket, 279-281

Bhumipol. See Rama IX

Bicycle, Macao, 178

Bicycle rental, Chiang Mai, Thailand, 271

Big Wave Bay, beach, Hong Kong, 85-86

Bird sanctuaries, Singapore, 422

Bird watching, Kenting National Park, Taiwan, 595

Boating, Hong Kong sports, 139

Boat people (Vietnamese), in Hong Kong refugee camps, 35

Boat tour: Singapore, 405, 408; Thailand, 251

Boats, Thailand travel, 248-249

Book publishing, Singapore, 401

Bookstores: Hong Kong, 60; Singapore, 401; Taiwan, 564

Boxing, Thailand popularity, 305

Brahmanism, Thailand festivals influence, 219, 230

Branch office, Taiwan investment, 647

Brass, Taiwan shopping, 641

Bridge on the River Kwai (movie), 264

British Crown Colony, Hong Kong as, 27

British East India Company, Singapore, 367, 369

British Forces Broadcasting Service, Hong Kong, 59

British imperial units, Hong Kong measure, 52

Bronze, Thailand items, 309

Bronze Age civilization, Thailand excavations, 274

Brunei, tours from Singapore, 521

Buddha's birthday, Hong Kong, 42;

Buddhism: Singapore, festivals, 382; Taiwan, 532, Fo Kuang Shan temple, 591; Thailand, Theravada, 216, Bangkok temples, 259, Nakhon Pathom monument, 265

Buddhas: Hong Kong, Lantau island, 97, New Territories, 95; Taiwan, multiple images, 586, tallest image, 591; Thailand, Ayutthaya images, 264, Bangkok temples, 256, 257, 258, 259, 260, Chiang Mai temples, 271, festivals, 231, Sukhothai ruins, 273

Buddhist brotherhood, Thailand, 218

Buddhist festivals, Thailand, 230

Buddhist monastary town, Hong Kong, 68

Budget accommodations, Bangkok, Thailand, 288

Bun Festival, Cheung Chow, Hong Kong, 42, 98

Bungalows, Thailand, 282, Koh Samui, 278

Buses: Hong Kong, fares and depots, 61, 62, on arrival, airport, hotel and local, 47; in Macao, 177; to Malaysia from Singapore, 516; Singapore, 404; Taiwan, 565; Thailand, local, 249, long-distance, 248

Business: in Hong Kong, establishment, 156-158; in Singapore, establishment, 489-493; in Taiwan, establishment, 646-648; in Thailand, establishment, 315-318

Business and trade associations, Taiwan, 665-667

Business cards, Taiwan custom, 655

Business clubs, Taipei, Taiwan, 632

Business contacts, private sector, Bangkok, list, 343-344

Business hours, Thailand, 242

Business publications, Hong Kong list, 162

Business service centers, Hong Kong, 159

Business tax: Taiwan, 650-651; Thailand, 321. See also Company tax

Business terms, Cantonese, Hong Kong, 194

Business traveler, Taipei hotels catering to, 598-607

Bus tours, Taiwan, inclusive, 567-572

Buyers' Guide to Thai Gems and Jewelry, A (Hoskins), 310

Buying, from Thailand, export tax, 319

Cabaret: Hong Kong, 138; Singapore, 471

Cable and Wireless Limited, Hong Kong, 57, 58

Cable car, Hong Kong, 62-63

Cable service: Hong Kong, 58; Taiwan, 563

Cameras, Hong Kong shopping, 150

Camping, Taiwan, 639

Canals, Bangkok, Thailand, 253-363

Candle festival, Thailand, 230, 275

Cantonese (language): Hong Kong, 37, examples, 187-195; Macao, 177

Cantonese cuisine, Hong Kong, 117

Cantonese restaurants, Hong Kong, list, 117-119; Singapore, list, 456-457; Taiwan, list, 623

Car rental: Hong Kong, 65-66; Singapore, 404-405; Taiwan, 566; Thailand, 250

Carpets and rugs: Hong Kong shopping, 147; Singapore shopping, 482

Casinos, Macao, 180

Causeway Bay, Hong Kong, hotels, 102; shopping, 143, 150, 151, 153; tour, 84-85

Celadon (stoneware), 309

Cemeteries. See graveyards

Central, district: Hong Kong, hotels, 102; shopping, 143, 144, 145, 151-153; tour, 74-79

Central Market, Hong Kong, 78

Ceramics, Taiwan, 641

Certificates of Origin, Hong Kong items, 159

Chakri Dynasty: Thailand, festival, 230; history, 208, 209, 211; palaces, Bangkok, 257; temples, Bangkok, 258, 259

Chambers of Commerce, Hong Kong, list, 166-167

Change Alley, Singapore, 487-488

Changi Airport, Singapore, 388

Chaochow restaurants, Taiwan, list, 623

Chao Phraya, delta, Thailand, 202

Chao Phraya, river, Thailand, 252, 253

Chaozhow restaurants. See Teochew restaurants

Charter buses, Thailand, 248

Chart Thai party, Thailand, 212

Chatichai Choonhaven (Thailand prime minister), 210, 212

Chaweng, beach, Koh Samui, Thailand, 278; bungalows, 292

Chedi. See towers

Cheng Ch'eng-kung. See Koxinga

Cheng Ching, lake, Taiwan, 591

Cheung Chau, island, Hong Kong, 98; hotel, 115

Cheung Chow Bun Festival, Hong Kong, 42, 989

Chi Chow restaurants, Hong Kong, list, 120

Chiang Ching-kuo (Taiwan president), 529

Chiang Kai-shek (Chinese statesman) Cultural Center: Taiwan, 634; history, Taiwan, 529; holiday, Taiwan, 541; memorial, Taiwan, 576

Chiang Mai, Thailand, 202; festivals, 229; handicrafts, 311; hospitals, 240; hotels and guesthouses, list, 291-292; population, 215; tour, 269-272

Chiang Rai, Thailand, 272-273

Chiayi, Taiwan, hotels, list, 607-608

Children's activities: Hong Kong, 99-100; Singapore, 423, 424

Chimei, island, Taiwan, 596

China: Hong Kong history, 23, 28; from Hong Kong, inclusive, 183-186; Hong Kong status, text of agreement with Great Britain, 195-198; Hong Kong trade, 156; from Singapore, visa, customs, tours, 518-520

China Street, Singapore, 486

Chinatown: Bangkok, Thailand, 253, 261-262; Singapore, 411-413, 485

Chinese (language): Hong Kong, 37; Singapore, 376

Chinese (people): in Hong Kong, 35; Singapore, festivals, 380, 381, 383; Hokkiens, 375; Taiwan, 532-533

Chinese cuisine: regional list, Hong Kong, 116-122; regional variations, Taiwan, 621

Chinese Gold and Silver Exchange Society, 165

Chinese New Year, Hong Kong, 41

Chinese opera, Hong Kong, 134; Singapore, 469-470; Taiwan, history, 633

Chinese restaurants: Hong Kong, regional list, 116-122; Macao, list, 179-180; Singapore, regional, lists, 456-460; Taipei, Taiwan business center, 645; Taiwan, regional types, list, 623-626; Thailand, 301

Chinese script: standard for all dialects, Taiwan, 533, 534; Taiwan, taxi drivers, 565

"Chinglish" (language): Hong Koing, 37

Chi-pao (Cheong-sam) (evening gown), 643

Chopsticks, mastery and etiquette, 455-456, 627

Christie's (auction house), Hong Kong, 144

Chulalongkorn. See Rama V

Chung Yeung Festival, Hong Kong, 43

Churches, Macao, 180-181; Colonial Singapore, 416, 417

Civil War, China (1948-49), refugees to Hong Kong, 25

Clearwater Bay, beach, new territories, Hong Kong, 96

Climate: Hong Kong, 40; Singapore, 379-380; Taiwan, humidity, 540; Thailand, 229

Clock Tower, Tsim Sha Tsui, Kowloon, 89

Cloisonné, Taiwan, 642

Clothing: Hong Kong shopping, 147-149; Singapore shopping, 482; Taiwan shopping, 643; Thailand shopping, 312

Clubs: Deep Water Bay, Hong Kong, 88; Hong Kong Central, 79; Singapore, types, 514-515

Club Street, Singapore, 486

Coach Tours, Singapore, list, 406-407

Coalition government, Thailand, 212

Cocktail lounges: Hong Kong, 138; Singapore, 473

Coffeehouses, Singapore, 467-468

Coffee shops, Hong Kong, list, 130

Coloâne, island, Macao, 183

Colonial powers, Thailand, favorable treaties, history, 209

Colonial rule, Singapore, 369

Colonial style, Singapore government buildings, 416

Commercial banks: Singapore, 497; Thailand, 322, lists, 323-327

Commercial missions, in Singapore, list, 50-51

Commodity tax, Taiwan, 650

Companies, international, in Singapore, 489

Company tax, Singapore, 496

Comparison shopping: Singapore, tips, 478; Thailand, 308, 310

Complaints, Singapore handling of, 479

Computers, Hong Kong shopping, bargain prices, 150; Sham Shui Po, Kowloon discounts, 93-94

Con men, Thailand, avoidance of, 240

Concerts, Singapore, 470

Conference facilities, Taiwan hotels, 656

Confucianism, Taiwan, 532

Confucius, temple of: Kaohsiung, Taiwan, 591; Tainan, Taiwan, 587; Taipei, Taiwan, 578

Confucius' birthday, Hong Kong, 43

Constitutional monarchy, Thailand, 211

Constitution Day, Taiwan, 541

Consular offices. See Diplomatic Missions; Diplomatic offices

Consumer Price Index, Hong Kong, 31

Continental restaurants: Hong Kong list, 124-126; Macao, list, 180; Singapore, list, 466-467; Taiwan, list, 629

Conventions and exhibitions: Hong Kong facilities, 162-163; Taiwan, 656

Cooking classes, Singapore, 453

Cooking schools, Bangkok, list, 298-299

Copyright: Hong Kong, 159; Singapore, 493; Taiwan, 649

Coral: Penghu, Taiwan, 595; Taiwan shopping, 640

Coral, lake, Taiwan, 590

Corporation tax, Thailand, 321-322

Correspondence, incoming, Thailand postal service, 245

Cosmetics, Singapore shopping, prices, 483

Costs: Hong Kong trip, 39; Taiwan tours, 539; Thailand, group tours, types, 227-228

Counterfeit goods. See Fake goods

Country parks, Hong Kong walking, 142

Coup D'etat, Thailand history, 210

Courtesy, Thailand social order, 215-216

Credit cards: Hong Kong, 57; Singapore acceptance, 399; Taiwan, 561; Thailand acceptance, 243

Crocodile farm, Singapore, 422

Cruise ships: to Hong Kong, 50; to Singapore, 389

Cruises: Hong Kong water tours, types, 67; Singapore tours, 408; Thailand, 249, Bangkok luxury, 263. See also Boat tour

Cultural activities: Hong Kong, 134, 136, 137; Singapore, 469-470, 471-472; Taiwan, 633-634; Thailand, 303, 304

Cultural center: Tainan, Taiwan, 586

Cultural clubs: Singapore, 514-515

Cultural Revolution, China (1967), Hong Kong affected by, 25

Cultural societies, Thailand, list, 304

Curios, Singapore, buying, 480

Currency: Hong Kong, 55; Singapore, 398-399; Taiwan, 560; Thailand, 243-244

Custom-made clothing: Hong Kong, 148; Singapore, prices, 483; Taiwan, 643; Thailand, 312

Customs: from China to Hong Kong, 186; Singapore, duty-free, 390; Taiwan, 551; Thailand, buying and selling, 318, 319, restrictions, 237

Customs and Excise Department, Hong Kong, 160

Customs and mores. See Social and cultural mores

Customs duties: Hong Kong, 163; Taiwan, 650

Customs tax, Thailand, 320-321

Dance, Hong Kong, 134

Dance: classical, Thailand, 304; drama, Thailand, 304

Day trips: to China from Hong Kong, 183-184

Deep Water, bay, Hong Kong, 88

Democratic Progressive Party (DPP), Taiwan, 531

Democracy, Taiwan, 529

Democracy, parliamentary, Singapore, 370

Democracy Monument, Thailand, 210

"Democracy period," Thailand history, 210

Department stores: Bangkok, 313, 314; Hong Kong, Causeway Bay's Victoria Park, 84, 153, Hong Kong Central, 79, 152; Japanese, 153, Tsim Sha Tsui 154, 155; Singapore, 484, 488; Taiwan, 642, 644, Taipei business center, 645

Designer labels: clothing, Hong Kong, 148, 152, 154; clothing, Singapore, 482; leather goods, Hong Kong, 149

Development Bank of Singapore, 371

Diety worship. See Divinity worship

Dim Sum (snacks): Cantonese restaurants, Hong Kong, 117, 118, 119; Hong Kong tram tour serving, 69; Singapore restaurants serving, 454, 457

Dining etiquette, Taiwan, 626-627

Dining sampans, Hong Kong, 133

Diplomacy, Thailand history with European powers, 207

Diplomatic missions: in Hong Kong, list, 170-172; in Singapore, list, 509-511; in Taiwan, list, 658-659; Thailand, abroad, list, 234, Bangkok, list, 341-342

Diplomatic offices, Singapore, abroad, list, 385-388

Discos: Bangkok, 305; Hong Kong, 138; Singapore, list, 472-473; Taiwan, 636

Dissipation, Bangkok, 252

Divinity worship, Taiwan, 532, festivals, 541, temples, 577

Dolls, Thai, 311

Domestic animals: Hong Kong entrance requirements, 50; Singapore import permits, 389; Taiwan, restricted entry, 550

Don Muang International Airport, Bangkok, 235

Double Ten Day, Taiwan, 541

Dove Cooing Contest, Thailand, 230

Dragon Boat Festival: Hong Kong, 42; Singapore, 382

Drama, Thai styles, 303-304

Dressmakers, Hong Kong, 148

Drinks: Hong Kong, costs, 40; Singapore Sling, 418, 473

Drugs, Thailand, tourist avoidance, 240

Dusit, Bangkok, 253

Duty-free items: Hong Kong, 50; high-tech products, 484; Singapore, 390, 478

Duty-free post: Macao, 182; Singapore, 493

Dvaravati period, Thailand history, 203, 211

East–West Cross Island Highway, Taiwan, hostels, list, 619-620; tour, 510, 582

Economic Development Board (EDB), Singapore, regional offices, list, 499-503

Economy: Hong Kong, 30-34; Singapore, 371-375; Taiwan, 531; Thailand, 212-214

Education, Hong Kong, 36

Electronics: Singapore shopping, 484; Taiwan items, 642

Elephants, festivals, Thailand, 229, 232, 275

Embassies: See Diplomatic missions; Diplomatic offices

Embroidery, Hong Kong shopping, 147

Emerald Buddha, Bangkok, Thailand, 256, 257

English (language): Hong Kong, 37; Singapore, 376

English Common Law, Hong Kong legal system basis, 29, 162

English food: Hong Kong restaurant, 123; Thailand restaurant, 301

Entertainment: Hong Kong, 134, 136-138, for children, 99-100; Singapore, 471, 472-474; Taiwan, 635-637, Taipei business center, 645; Thailand, 303, 304-305

Entrepreneurship, Hong Kong, 36

Ethnic restaurants, Causeway Bay, Hong Kong, 85

Etiquette, Taiwan dining, 626-627

Eurasians (people), Singapore, 376

Europeans (people), Singapore, 376

Exchange rates; Change Alley, Singapore, 487; Hong Kong dollar, 55; New Taiwan dollar, 560, 561; Singapore dollar, 398; Thai baht, 244; Thailand, Bank of, 320

Excise taxes, Hong Kong, 163; Thailand, 321

Excursion tours, to China from Hong Kong, 185

Exhibitions. See Conventions and exhibitions

Exotic, the, Thailand, 201

Expatriate living area, Taipei, Taiwan, 645

Expatriate professionals, Singapore, 376

Export license: Thailand, arts, 237; business, 319

Export service institutions, overseas, Thailand, list, 339-340

Exports, Hong Kong, 30

External Trade Development Council, Taiwan, list of foreign offices, 659-664

Fabrics: Hong Kong shopping, 147, 152; Singapore shopping, 482

"Face keeping." See "Saving face"

Factory: Kowloon, Hong Kong, 94; Thailand, setting up, 319

Factory outlets: Hong Kong, 149, 152; Hung Hom, Kowloon, 94

Fake goods: antiques, 314; Taiwan, 648; Thailand, 313

Fast food restaurants: Hong Kong, list, Western styles, 132; Taiwan, 629

Fax (facsimiles): Singapore, 400; Taiwan, 563

Females, single, Thailand travel, pitfalls, 241

Fengkuei, Penghu, Taiwan, 596

Ferries: Hong Kong, 50, Hong Kong Central tour, 78, Hong Kong companies, 65, to outlying islands, Hong Kong, 96; to Macao from Hong Kong, 176; Singapore, 404; Taiwan, 566; Thailand, 237, 248

Festival of the Hungry Ghosts, Hong Kong, 43

Festivals and holidays: Hong Kong, 40-44; Singapore, 380-384; Taiwan, 541-542; Thailand, 229-232

Filipino (people), in Hong Kong, 35

Films. See Movies.

Finance, international, Singapore, 497

Finance companies, Singapore, 498

Finance securities firms, Thailand, 328

Firearms, prohibited entry, Hong Kong, 50

Fishing, Taiwan, 639, Penghu, 595

Fishing boats, Thailand, 248

Fishing villages: Hong Kong, 88, 98; seafood restaurants, 85, 133

Fixed-price policy, shopping, Hong Kong, 143

Flight times, to Hong Kong from major cities, 46

Floating market, Bangkok, Thailand, 262

Floating restaurants: Aberdeen, 88, 129; Hong Kong, 133

Flower festival, Thailand, 229

Flower gardens: Chiang Mai, Thailand, 269; Singapore, 420, 422

Fo Kuang Shan Temple, Taiwan, 591

Folk art: Chiang Mai hill tribes, Thailand, 269, 271; Kamthieng House Museum, Bangkok, 260

Folk music, Hong Kong, 136

Food: Hong Kong, Causeway Bay, 84, costs, 39, restaurants, inclusive, 116-133; Singapore restaurants, inclusive, 453-468; Taiwan restaurants, inclusive, 621-632; Thailand, prices, 228, restaurants, inclusive, 297-302

Food stalls: Hong Kong Central tour, 78; Thailand, 299

Food tours, Singapore, 453

Foreign exchange. See International exchange

Foreign films, Taiwan, 635, 636

Foreign investment; in Singapore, 489; in Taiwan, 647; in Thailand, 315. See also International investment

Foreign quarter, Bangkok. See Old Farang

Foreign trade. See International trade

Formosa. See Taiwan

Fort Canning Park, Singapore, 421

Forts, Macao, 182

France, Thailand history, 209

Fraudulent sale practices, Hong Kong, redress, 143

Free-enterprise: Hong Kong, 34, 156; Singapore, 489

Free-market principles, labor market in Hong Kong, 36

Free port: Hong Kong, 30; Singapore, 489, 493

Free trade: Hong Kong, 30, 156; Singapore, 494

French restaurants: Hong Kong, 125, list, 123-124; Singapore, list, 465; Taiwan, list, 630; Thailand, 301

Fruit stand, Singapore, 455

Funicular. See Cable car

Fur, Hong Kong garments, 149

Furniture, Hong Kong shopping, 151

Gaddi's, French restaurant, The Peninsula, Kowloon, Hong Kong, 123

Gambling: legalized, Macao, 175; casinos, 180

Gardens: Chiang Mai, Thailand, 269; Singapore, 420-422

Garments and fashions. See Clothing

GATT. See General Agreement on Tariffs and Trade

Gems, Thai shopping, 310

General Agreement on Tariff and Trade (GATT), Hong Kong, 34

Generalized System of Preferences (GSP), Hong Kong benefit, 34

Geography: Taiwan, 527; Thailand, 202

German restaurant: Taiwan, 629; Thailand, 302

Ghost festivals. See Spirit festivals

Gift-giving, Singapore customs, 397

Girly bars: Bangkok, 305; Hong Kong, 139

Glass-bottom boats, 596

Go-go bars, Pattaya, Thailand, 267

Gold markets, Hong Kong, 34, 165

"Golden Mile," Nathan Rd., Hong Kong, 154

"Golden Mile," Tsim Sha Tsui, Kowloon, Hong Kong, 89

"Golden Mount" (Bangkok Temple), 260

"Golden Triangle": Thailand, 202; Chiang Rai, 272; opium, 213

Golf: Hong Kong, 139-140; Singapore clubs, list, 476-477; Taiwan, 637-638; Thailand, 306-307

Good-luck charms, Bangkok, Amulet Market, 314, shrines, 267

Government banks, Bangkok, list, 323

Government organizations: Hong Kong, business-related, list, 165-166; Singapore, business-related, lists, 499-509; Taipei, Taiwan, list, 657; Thailand, lists, 328-359

Government representation abroad, Taiwan, list, 544-546

Grand Hyatt hotel, Hong Kong, 104

Grand Palace, Bangkok, Thailand, 256-257

Graves: Happy Valley, Hong Kong, 83; sweeping and visiting festivals, Hong Kong, 42, 43; Tomb Sweeping Day, Taiwan, 541

Great Britain: Hong Kong history, 23; Hong Kong status, text of agreement with China, 195-198; Thailand history, 209; Green Island. See Lutao

Green Paper (1984-1987), Hong Kong status, 28

Greetings, in Thai, 215, 220

Grill rooms: Hong Kong, list, 126; Singapore, 467

Gross domestic product (GDP), Hong Kong, 31

Group tours: to China from Hong Kong, 184; Taiwan, 536, 537-538, permits, 547; Thailand, types, 224

Guangzhou, China, day trip from Hong Kong, 183-184; by steamer from Hong Kong, 185

Guesthouses: Kowloon, Hong Kong, 114; Thailand, 282, Bangkok, list, 289

Gurkha brigade in Hong Kong, British broadcasting for, 59

Hainan restaurants, Singapore, list, 459

Hakka restaurants, Singapore, 459

Han Dynasty Tomb, Sham Shui Po, Kowloon, 94

Handicrafts: Hong Kong shopping, 145; Singapore shopping, 419, 480, 482, 485; Taiwan shopping, 641, 642; Thailand shopping, 309, hill tribes, Chiang Mai, 269, 271

Happy Valley Racecourse, Hong Kong, 83

Haw Par Villa, Singapore, 423

Hawker stalls, Singapore, 453, 454

Helicopter, Hong Kong rental, 66

Helicopter tour, Singapore, 405-406

High-tech products, Hong Kong, 150; Singapore, 484

Hiking: Hong Kong, country parks, 142, Stanley, 86; Thailand, Khao Yai National Park, 265

Hill tribes: Thailand, Chiang Mai, 269, 271, 272; handicrafts, metalcrafts, 309, 311; tourist advice on, 240; tours, 251

Hinayana. See Theravada Buddhism

Hindus (people), Singapore, festivals, 380, 383

History: Hong Kong, 23-27; Macao, 175, 180-182; Singapore, 367-370; Taiwan, 527; Thailand, 204-211

Hokkien restaurants, Singapore, 459-460

Hokkiens. See Chinese (people) Singapore

Hong Kong: status, text of agreement between Britain and China, 195-198; tour, inclusive, 74-99; tourist guide, inclusive, 23-198; tours from Singapore, 521

Hong Kong and Shanghai Banking Corporation, 55

Hong Kong and Yaumati Ferry Company Limited, 65, 96

Hong Kong Association of Banks, 31, 164

Hong Kong Club, 79

Hong Kong Commodity Exchange Limited, 34, 165

Hong Kong dollar: 31; exchange rates, 55

Hong Kong Funeral Home, 85

Hong Kong Hotels Directory, 102

Hong Kong Special Administrative Region, 27, 28, 196-198

Hong Kong Telephone Company Limited, 57, 58

Hong Kong Tourist Association (HKTA), offices abroad, list, 38-39

Horse racing: Hong Kong, 83, 140; Singapore, 477; Thailand, Bangkok, 306

Hoskins, John (author), jewelry and gem guide, Thailand, 310

Hospitality, Taiwan, 533, 535

Hospitals: Singapore, 391-392; Taiwan, list, 553-554; Thailand, list, 240

Hostels: Hong Kong, Kowloon, 114; Taiwan, 597, list, 619-620, Fo Kuang Shan Temple, 591, Lutao, 582, Tsengwen Reservoir, 590; Thailand, Bangkok, 288

Hostess clubs: Hong Kong, 139; night clubs, Taiwan, 637

Hostesses, Bangkok nightlife, 304

Hotels: Hong Kong, inclusive, lists, 101-115, restaurants, 116; Macao, list, 178; Singapore, list, by size, 428-452; Taiwan, inclusive, lists, 597-620, bars, 630, Chinese restaurants, types listed, 622; Thailand, inclusive, 282-296, restaurants, 299

Hovercraft, to China from Hong Kong, 184-185

Hsaio Liuchiu, island, Taiwan, 596

Hua Hin, seashore resort, Thailand, 276

Hualien, Taiwan, 538, hotels, list, 608-610; marble, 641; tour, 581

Hucksters, Thailand, protection from, 221

Humidity, Taiwan, 540

Hunan restaurants, Taiwan, list, 623-624

Hung Hom, Kowloon, Hong Kong, 94

Hydrofoil, to Macao from Hong Kong, 176

Ice, Thailand, impurity, 239

Ice skating, Hong Kong, 140

I Ching (fortune telling), 425

Identity card, Hong Kong business, 156

Ilan, Taiwan, hotels, list, 610

Import duties: Singapore, 494; Taiwan, 650

Import permits, domestic animals, Taiwan, 550

Imports, Hong Kong dependence, 30

Income, per capita: Singapore, 370; Thailand, 213

Income taxes: Hong Kong, 163; Singapore, 495; Taiwan, 650; Thailand, 321

Income taxes, personal: Hong Kong, 34; Singapore, 495-496; Taiwan, 650; Thailand, 321

Incorporated companies, Hong Kong, 157

Independent travel: Taiwan, 537, costs, 539; Thailand tours, 226, 228
Indian cuisine, Singapore, 454
Indian restaurants: Hong Kong, list, 127; Singapore, list, 461-462; Taiwan, 628; Thailand, 301
Indians (people), Singapore, 376, festivals, 380
Indonesia, tours from Singapore, 520
Indonesian restaurants: Hong Kong, list, 127; Singapore, 464; Taiwan, 628
Industrial estates, New Territories, Hong Kong, establishment, 30
Industrialization, Singapore, 369, 371
Industry and trade departments, government, Hong Kong, list, 165-166
Insect fighting, Thai sport, beetle and cricket, 306
Insurance, business, Hong Kong, 160
Intercity travel, Thailand, 228-229
International banking: Hong Kong, 31, 55, 57, 156; Taiwan, lists, 651-654; Thailand, 328
International exchange, Hong Kong market, 31, 165; Thailand controls, 319-320
International finance. See Finance, international; International banking
International investment: Hong Kong, 31, 156; Taiwan, 531-532, 647; Thailand, 212, regulations and incentives, 316
International trade: Hong Kong, 156; Taiwan, 531
International trade associations, in Taipei, Taiwan, list, 665-667
International trade and investment, Thailand, offices and ministries, list, 329-332
International Trading Company, Ltd., Singapore, 374
"Iron Buddha" tea, 120
Italian restaurants: Hong Kong, list, 124; Singapore, 466; Taiwan, list, 630; Thailand, 302
Ivory, Hong Kong shopping, 145-146

Jackson, Sir Thomas (Hong Kong banker), statue, 79
Jade, Taiwan shopping, 640, 641
Jade Market, Kowloon, Hong Kong, 93, 146
Jade Museum, Hong Kong, 137
Japan: Hong Kong occupation, World War II, 25; Singapore occupation, World War II, 369; Taiwan occupation, World War II, 529
Japanese occupation (World War II): Hong Kong, 25; Singapore, 369; Taiwan, 529
Japanese restaurants, Hong Kong, list, 127-128; Singapore, 463; Taiwan, 628; Thailand, 301

Jazz, Hong Kong, 136
Jetcat, to Macao from Hong Kong, 176
Jetfoil, to Macao from Hong Kong, 176
Jewelry: Hong Kong shopping, 146; Singapore shopping, 480; Taiwan, 640; Thailand, Bangkok shopping, 310
Jogging: Hong Kong, 84, 140-141; Singapore, 477
Joint venture, Taiwan investment, 648
Jomtien, beach, Thailand, hotels, list, 291
Joss sticks, temple, Kowloon, Hong Kong, 94
Junks (boats): Aberdeen, Hong Kong, 88; Cheung Chau, island, Hong Kong, 98
Jurong Town Corporation (JTC), Singapore, 499

Kai Tak International Airport, Hong Kong, 45, 46, 47
Kampong Glam. See Arab Street
Kanchanaburi, Thailand, 264
Kaohsiung: Taiwan, 538; hospitals, list, 554; hotels, list, 610-613; houses of worship, list, 559; international banks, 651; tour, 571, 590-591
Karon, beach, Phuket, Thailand, 281
Kata, beach, Phuket, Thailand, 281
Katong, Singapore, 488
Keelung, Taiwan, 579
Kenting, beach, Taiwan, 638
Kenting National Park: Taiwan, hotels, 613-614; tours, 571-595
Khao Yoi National Park, Thailand, 265
Khmers (people), Thailand, history, 204, 211
Khon Kaen, Thailand, 274
Khorat. See Nakhon Ratchasima
Khun Sa (opium warlord), 214
Kiosks. See Newsstands
Kite flying, Thailand, 306
Koh Pha Ngan, island, Thailand, 278
Koh Samet, Thailand, beach, 267-269
Koh Samui: Thailand, beach, 276, 277-279; resort hotels and bungalows, list, 292-293
Koh Tao, island, Thailand, 278
Korean restaurants: Hong Kong, list, 128; Singapore, list, 463-464
Kowloon, Hong Kong: history, 25; hotels, list, 106-114; jade market, 93, 146; shopping, 144, 145, 150, 151; tour, inclusive, 89-95; tours, 67, 68
Kowloon-Canton Railway, Hong Kong, 63
Kowloon Park, Tsim Sha Tsui, Hong Kong, 93
Kowloon Walled City, Hong Kong, 94
Koxinga (Chinese leader): 529; Tainan, Taiwan, temples, history, 586
Krabi, province, Thailand, 281
Kuan Yin (Taiwan goddess), 532, 541
Kuang Kung (Taiwan god), 532, 541

Kuomintang (KMT), Taiwan, 529

Kusu, island, Singapore, 426

Kwun tong, area, Kowloon, Hong Kong, 95

Labor force. See Work force

Lacquerware, Thai shopping, 309

Lai Chi Kok, Kowloon, 94

Lamai, beach, Koh Samui, Thailand, 278, bungalow, 292

Lamma, island, Hong Kong, 99

Landmarks, Singapore, 417-419

Lane Crawford, department store, Hong Kong, 79

Languages: Hong Kong, 37; Singapore, 376; Taiwan, 533-534; Thailand, 219-220

Lantao, island, Hong Kong, 97-98, hotels, 115

Lantern Festival. See Mid-autumn festival

Lanyu, island, Taiwan, 581

Lau Fau Shan, New Territories, Hong Kong, 96-133

Leased land: Hong Kong, 161, status, 198; New Territories, 27

Leased property, Hong Kong, prices, 161

Leather goods: Hong Kong, 149; Thailand, 312

Lee Kuan Yew (Singapore Prime Minister), 369, 370-371

Lee Tung-hui (Taiwan President), 529, 531

Legal aid, Hong Kong, 29

Legal system, Hong Kong, basis on English Common Law, 29, 162

Lei Yue Mun, Kowloon, Hong Kong, seafood restaurants, 133

Leisure activites. See Recreation

Leofoo Safari Park and Window on China, tour, Taiwan, 568

Letters patent, United Kingdom, Hong Kong constitution, 27

Licenses: Hong Kong, banks, 163-164, business, 157; Singapore, business registration, 491, 492, imports, 493; Taiwan, investment, 647; Thailand, arts, 237, business, 319

Life expectancy, Thailand, 215

Limited Liability Company, Hong Kong, 157

Lion City. See Singapore

Literacy rate: Singapore work force, 490; Thailand, 213, 215

Little India, Singapore, 414-415, 487

Lodging: Hong Kong, costs, 39; Khao Yai National Park, Thailand, 265; Polin Monastery, Lantau, island, Hong Kong, 133

Loei, Thailand, 274

Lomotil, Thailand, diarrhea guard, 239

Longboat, Thailand, 249

Lukang, Taiwan, 583

Luk Kwok Hotel, Wan Chai, Hong Kong, 82

Lunar calendar: Hong Kong festivals, 43; Singapore Muslim festivals, 380; Taiwan, 555; festivals, 541, 542

Lungshan Temple, Taiwan, 577-578

Lunisolar calendar, Singapore religious festivals, 380

Lu Pan, birthday of, Hong Kong, 42

Lutao, island, Taiwan, 581

Luxury hotels, Kowloon, Hong Kong, 106

Luxury tours, Thailand, costs, 227

Macanese/Portuguese restaurants, Macao, list, 179

Macao, from Hong Kong, inclusive, 175-183

Magazines: Hong Kong, 60; Singapore, 401; Taiwan, 564

Mahjong, Wan Chai, Hong Kong, 82

Maidens' Festival, Hong Kong, 43

Makung, Penghu, Taiwan, 595

Malaria pills, Thailand travel, 233, 239

Malay (language), Singapore, 376

Malay (people), Singapore, 375

Malay cuisine, Singapore, 454

Malay restaurants, Singapore list, 462-463

Malaysia, travel from Singapore, by bus, train, air, and tours, 516-518

Malaysian-Singaporean restaurants, Hong Kong, list, 128

Males, single, Thailand travel tips, 241

Mandarin (language): Hong Kong, 37; Singapore adoption campaign, 376; Taiwan, adoption reluctance, 533; useful phrases, 669-671

Mandarin Oriental Hotel, Hong Kong, 102, 105-106

Marble: Taiwan shopping, 641; temple, Bangkok, Thailand, 259

Marketplaces, New Territories, Hong Kong, open-air, 96. See also individual markets, such as night market, wet market, etc.

Martyrs' Shrine, Taiwan, 577

Masks, Khon, papier-mache, Thailand, 311

Mass Rapid Transit. See Subway

Massage parlors, Bangkok, 305

Matsu (Taiwan goddess): 532; festivals, 541; Peikang temples, 583; Penghu Temple, 596

Medical facilities, Singapore, 391-392

Memorials, Taiwan, 533, list, 576-578

Mens' wear: Hong Kong shopping, 147-148; Temple St. Market, Yaw Ma Tei, Kowloon, 93

Merchant banks, Singapore, 498

Merchant houses, British, Hong Kong history, 30

Merlion logo, Singapore shopping tip, 478

Merlion Park, Singapore, 417

Merlion Week, Singapore, 383

Metalcrafts, Thailand shopping, 309

Metric system: Singapore, 391; Taiwan, 552

Mid-autumn festival, Hong Kong, 43

Military domination, Thailand politics, 211-212

Military government, Thailand history, 210

Minanhua dialect. See Taiwanese (language)

Minibus: Hong Kong, 62; in Macao

Mini car racing, Singapore, 423

Mini-make (Macao transportation), 178

Miu Fat Monastery, New Territories, Hong Kong, 96

Monarchy, Thailand, history, 208

Monasteries, Thailand, 216

Monastery of 10,000 Buddhas, Sha Tin, New Territories, Hong Kong, 95

Monetary Authority of Singapore (MAS), 497

Money belt, 240

Money changers: Hong Kong, 55; Singapore, licensed, 399; Thailand, 243

Mongkok, Kowloon, 35

Mongkut (Thai king). See Rama IV

Mongolian barbecue, Taiwan restaurants, list, 624

Monks: Thailand, 216; Bangkok, 253

Monuments, Singapore, 417-419. See also Memorials; National monuments

Moon festival. See Mid-autumn festival

Mooncakes: Hong Kong festival, 43; Singapore festival, 383

Mosques, Singapore, Arab Street, 410, 420, Chinatown, 413, 419

Motorboats, Hong Kong rental, 66

Mountain climbing: Lamma, island, Hong Kong, 99; Taiwan, 639

Movie theaters, Taipei, Taiwan, list, 635

Movies: Hong Kong, 137; Singapore, 474; Thailand types, 304

MTV shops (Taiwan), illegal copies, 635-636

Muang Sing ruins, Kanchanaburi, Thailand, 264

Multiethnic society, Singapore, 370, 375

Multi-Fibre Arrangement (MFA), Hong Kong, Textiles, 32

Multinational corporations, Singapore, 489

Multiple-entry Visa: Taiwan, 546, 646; Thailand, 233

Murals, temples, Bangkok, 257, 258, 260

Museums: Hong Kong, 137-138; for children, 100; Tsim Sha Tsui, Kowloon, 93; Singapore, 417; Taiwan, 579; Thailand, Ayutthaya, 264; Bangkok, list, 260-261; major attractions, 256

Museums and arts and crafts (pamphlet), Hong Kong, 145

Music: Hong Kong, 136; Singapore, 470; Taiwan, 634

Muslims (people), Singapore, festivals, 380, 383-384

Nai Harn, beach, Phuket, Thailand, 281

Nai Yang National Park, Thailand, 281

Nakhon Panom, Thailand, 274

Nakhon Pathom, Thailand, 265

Nakhon Ratchasima, Thailand, 274

Names, Thailand, and surnames, 216

Nanking, treaty of (1843), Hong Kong ceded to Great Britain, 25

Nanzhao Kingdom, China, Thailand history, 204, 211

Naresuan (Thai king), 207

National Broadcasting Corporation of China (BCC), Taiwan, 564

National Chiang Kai-Shek Cultural Center, Taiwan, 634

National monuments, Chinatown, Singapore, 413

National Museum, Bangkok, Thailand: collections, 261; export license, 237, 308

National Palace Museum, Taipei, Taiwan, 533

National Productivity Board (NPB), Singapore, 504

National Security Law, Taiwan, 531

Nationalist Party. See Kuomintang

Nerai (Thai king), 207

Newly industrialized countries (NIC): Hong Kong, 30; Thailand, 212

Newspapers: Hong Kong, 59; Singapore, 400-401; Taiwan, 564; Thailand, 246

Newsstands: Hong Kong, 60; Taiwan, 564

New Taiwan dollar, 560; exchange rates, 561

New Territories, Hong Kong: history, Great Britain, 25, 27; hotels, 115; tours, 67-68, 95-96

Nielloware, Thai shopping, 309

Nightclub restaurant, Hong Kong, 130

Nightclubs: Hong Kong, 138-139; Singapore, 471; Taiwan, 636-637; music, 634; Thailand, Bangkok hotels, 305

Nightlife: Hong Kong, Wan Chai, district, 82; Singapore, cabaret and night clubs, 471; Taiwan, Taipei, business center, 645; Thailand, Bangkok, variety, 253, 304-305

Night market, Taipei, Taiwan, 576, 644-645

Night tours: Hong Kong, 68-69; Singapore, 407

Nirvana, Thailand Buddhism, 218

Nonya cuisine, Singapore, 454

Nonya restaurants, Singapore, 463

Noon-Day Gun, Tardine's, Causeway Bay, Hong Kong, 84

North Coast, Taiwan, 568

Numbers: Cantonese, Hong Kong, 187-188; Thai, examples, 363

Ocean Park, Hong Kong, children's activities, 99

Office space, lease prices, Hong Kong, 161

Old Farang, quarter: Bangkok, Thailand, 253; The Oriental Hotel, 285

Oon, Violet (culinary expert), 453

Open-door policy, Singapore, investment, 489

Opium: "Golden Triangle," Thailand, 202, 213; Hong Kong history, 24

Opium warlords, Thailand, 214

Opium wars, Hong Kong history, 24

Optical shops, the, Hong Kong, 150

Orchard Road, Singapore, 484

Orchid Islands. See Lanyu

Orchids, Singapore Garden, 422

Oriental, the, hotel, Bangkok, Thailand, 228, 285

Oriental Queen barge, Ayutthaya cruise, 264

Outdoor market. See Wet market

Overseas investment. See International investment

Overseas workers, Taiwan, 646

Ox. See Water buffalo

Oysters, Lau Fau Shan, New Territories, 96, 133

Package rates, Hong Kong hotels, 102

Package tours: Hong Kong 10-day tour, 69-71; to Hong Kong, 45; Macao, 176; Taiwan, 536

Paknam incident (Thailand), 209

Parks: Hong Kong, country parks, 142; Victoria Park, 84; Singapore, 420-422

Passports: Hong Kong, 45; Thailand, 233

Pataca (Macao currency), 177

Patents: Hong Kong, 160; Taiwan, 648

Patong, beach, Phuket, Thailand, hotels and guesthouses, list, 293-296

Pattaya, Thailand: beaches, 265-267; hotels, list, 289-290

Paulkon, Constantine (Greek official), Thailand history, 207

Peace Above Peace, sect, Thailand, 218

Peak, the, Hong Kong, Peak Tram tour, 89, 62-63

Peak tram, Hong Kong cable car, 62-63, 89

Pedicabs (Macao), 177

Peikang, Taiwan, 583-586

Peking, Convention of (1860), Kowloon Peninsula and Stonecutters' Island ceded, 25

Peking cuisine, Hong Kong, 120 Peking duck, Peking restaurants, Hong Kong, 120 Peking opera (Taiwan), 633

Peking restaurants: Hong Kong, list, 120-121; Singapore, list, 457; Taiwan, list, 624

Penghu, islands, Taiwan: 527; tour, 569, 595-596

Peninsula Hotel, Kowloon, Hong Kong, 106, 111-112

People: Hong Kong, 35-36; Macao, 175; Singapore, 375; Taiwan, 532-533; Thailand, 214-215

Peoples' Action Party (PAP), Singapore, 369, 370-371

Peranakan culture: Nonya cuisine, 454; Singapore shopping, 488

Peranakan Place, Singapore, 488

Performing Arts, Thailand, 303-304

Perfumes, Singapore shopping prices, 483

Permits: Singapore, exports and imports, 390; Singapore, work and residence, 490-491; Taiwan, group tours, 547

Pescadores, islands. See Penghu, islands

Pewter, Thailand shopping, 309

Pharmaceuticals: Singapore, 384, 392; Taiwan, 552

Phibul Songkhram (Thai leader), 209, 211

Philippines, tours from Singapore, 520

Phimai ruins, Nakhon Ratchasima, Thailand, 274

Phra Bodhirak (Thai religious leader), 218

Phra Pathom Chedi Buddhist monument, Nakhon Pathom, Thailand, 265

Phrases: Cantonese, Hong Kong, examples, 189-195; Mandarin in Taiwan, 669-671; Thai, examples, 362

Phuket, Thailand: beaches, 279-281; hotels and guesthouses, lists, 293-296

Phukradung National Park, Thailand, 274

Piano bars: Hong Kong, 138; nightclubs, Taiwan, 636

Pickpockets, Thailand, protection from, 240

Pigeon, Sha Tin, Hong Kong, restaurants, 133

Pinyin: mandarin pronunciation in Taiwan, useful phrases, 669; Singapore adoption campaign, 376

Pirated goods: Hong Kong, 160; software, 93-94, 150; Taiwan, books, 564; Thailand, recordings, 313

Pitou Chiao, Taiwan, 580

Place names, Cantonese, Hong Kong, 191

Plants, restricted entry, Taiwan, 550

Plum blossoms, Taiwan hotel ratings, 597

Polin monastery, Lantau, island, Hong Kong: 97; tour, 68; vegetarian food, 133

Politics and government: Hong Kong, 27-29; Singapore, 370-371; Taiwan, 531; Thailand, 211-212

Population, Hong Kong, statistics, 35

Porcelain, Taiwan, 641

Port of call, Taiwan, 550

Portugal, Macao history, 175, 180

Portuguese (language) of Macao, 177

Portuguese cuisine, Macao, 175

Postal service: Hong Kong, rates, 57; Singapore, 399; Taiwan, 562; Thailand, 245

Pottinger, Sir Henry (British governor of Hong Kong), 25

Pousadas (Macao), 178

Prang. See Steeples

Prince of Wales, building, Hong Kong, 79

Private organizations, Thailand, lists, 343-344

Professional visit Visas, Singapore, 490

Prohibitions, legal: Singapore, 395; Taiwan entry, 543; unauthorized reproductions, 551; into Thailand, 237. See also Restrictions

Pronunciation: Cantonese, Hong Kong, 187; mandarin in Taiwan, useful phrases, 669

Property rights, Hong Kong, 159

Property tax, Hong Kong, 163

Provinces, Thailand, 212

Public housing: Hong Kong, 36; Singapore, 370

Public washrooms, Hong Kong, 52

Pubs: Hong Kong, list, 131-132; Singapore, 473

Pulau Hantu, island, Singapore, 427

Pulau Seking, island, Singapore, 427

Punctuality, Taiwan, 560

Puppet shows, Hong Kong, 99

Qing Ming festival, Hong Kong, 42

Quarry Bay, Hong Kong, 85

Rabies control, Singapore, 389; Taiwan, 550

Radio, Hong Kong, 59; Singapore, 400; Taiwan, 563-564; Thailand, 246

Radio-television, Hong Kong (RTHK), 59

Raffles, Sir Thomas Stamford (English colonial administration): Singapore, 367, 369; Saint Andrew's Cathedral window, 420; statue and landing site, 416, 418-419

Raffles city complex, Singapore, 488

Raffles Hotel: Singapore, 418-457; cultural show, 471, 472; long bar, 473

Railroad transportation: to China from Hong Kong, 184; Hong Kong, 60, 63; to Malaysia from Singapore, 516-517; to Singapore, 389; in Taiwan, 565-566; in Thailand, features, 228, 247-248; to Thailand, 236-237

Rains Retreat, Thailand, 216, 230

Rama I (Thai ruler): 208, 211; palaces, 257; shrines, 261

Rama IV (Thai ruler), 208, 211

Rama V (Thai ruler), 209, 211

Rama VII (Thai ruler), 209, 211

Rama VIII (Thai ruler), 209, 211

Rama IX (Thai ruler), 209, 211

Ramkamheng (Thai king), 204

Rawai, Phuket, Thailand, 279

Reading list: Singapore, 522-524; Thailand, 361

Reclamation, land, Hong Kong, 23

Reclining Buddha, Bangkok, Thailand, largest, 256, 259

Recreation: Sports; Hong Kong, 140-142; Singapore, 474-477; Taiwan, 637-639; Thailand, 305-307; "Red light district," Wan Chai, Hong Kong, 82

Regent Hotel, Kowloon, Hong Kong, 106, 113

Registration, business: Hong Kong, 157; Singapore, 491-493; Thailand, 315

Religion, Thailand, 216

Religion, freedom of: Hong Kong, 36; Taiwan, 532; Thailand, 242

Religious services: Hong Kong, 54; Singapore, list, 393-395; Taiwan, 555, list, 556-559; Thailand, tolerance, 242

Remittances, into or out of Thailand, controls, 319-320

Repulse Bay, beach, Hong Kong, 87; indoor-outdoor restaurant, 133

Reservations: Taiwan hotels, 597; Thailand, 283

Residence permits, Singapore schemes, 491

Residential areas, Kowloon Tong, Hong Kong, 94

Resident visa, Taiwan, 547, 647

Restaurant terms, Cantonese, Hong Kong, 191-193

Restaurants: Hong Kong, inclusive, 116-133; Macao, types, list, 178-180; Singapore, inclusive, 453-468; Taiwan, inclusive, 621-632; Thailand, inclusive, 299-302. See also under Hotels

Restrictions: customs, Singapore, 390, exports and imports, 494, 495; into Taiwan, 550; Thailand, foreign business, 318

Reusser, Dave (Singapore businessman), 490

Revolving restaurants: Hong Kong, 82, list, 130; Taipei, Taiwan, Fortuna Hotel, 599

Rickshaws: Hong Kong, 61; Singapore, station, 413

River taxis (Bangkok, Thailand), 262

Roller skating, Hong Kong, 140

Romanization, Yale system, mandarin pronunciation in Taiwan, 669

Royal barges, Bangkok, 256, 262
Royal Cremation Ground, Bangkok, Thailand, 262
Royal family: Thailand, Bangkok museum on belongings, 261; Hua Hin summer residence, 276; Thailand social order, 215
Royal palaces, Bangkok, Thailand, 256-257
Running, Hong Kong, 140-141

Safety precautions: Hong Kong assistance, 54; Thailand, 239, 240-241
Sailing: Hong Kong, 139; Singapore, 477
Saint Andrews Cathedral, Singapore, 419-420
Saint John's, island, Singapore, 427
Sampans: Hong Kong, Aberdeen, 88; Causeway Bay, types, 84
Sangha. See Buddhist brotherhood
Sangkhalok stoneware, Thailand shopping, 309
Sang Nila Utama (Malay prince), Singapore history, 367
Santi Asoke. See Peace above peace
Satellite communications, Taiwan, 564, Taipei, Howard Plaza Hotel, 600
"Saving face": Singapore customs, 396-397; Taiwan, 560
Scotts Road, Singapore, 485
Scuba, skin diving and snorkeling. See water sports
Seafood restaurants, Taiwan, list, 625
Sea gypsies: Singapore, 367; Thailand, 279
Sea town. See Singapore
Secret food map of Singapore, 453
Securities Exchange of Thailand, 328
Security assistance, Thailand, 221, 241
Selling, to Thailand, import restrictions, 318
Semi-precious stones, Taiwan, 640
Sentosa, island, Singapore, 425-426
Serangoon Road, Singapore, 487
Service, Hong Kong restaurants, 116
Service charge: Taiwan, 559; Thailand, 242, hotels, 282
Service clubs, Singapore, 514-515
Service industries, Hong Kong labor force, 36
Seventh-Day Adventist Hospital, Taiwan, 552
Sex shows, Bangkok, 305
Sex-tourist industry, Thailand, Bangkok in particular, 201
Shamanism, Taiwan, 532
Sham Shui Po, Kowloon, Hong Kong, computer discount center, 93-94
Sham Tseng Street, Kowloon, Hong Kong, restaurants, 133

Shanghai, China, by steamer from Hong Kong, 185
Shanghainese cuisine, Hong Kong, 121
Shanghainese restaurants: Hong Kong, list, 121; Singapore, list, 457-458; Taiwan, list, 625
Shangri-La Singapore Hotel, 436-437
Shantou, China, by steamer from Hong Kong, 185
Sha Tin: Hong Kong, region restaurants, 133; sports for children, 100; tour, 95
Shau Kei Wan, Hong Kong, fishing village, restaurants, 85
Shek O, resort, Hong Kong, 86
Shekou, China, day trip from Hong Kong, 183
Shenzhen, China, day tour from Hong Kong, 183
Shipping, Singapore shopping tips, 478
Ships: passenger, to Hong Kong, 50; to Singapore, 389; to Taiwan, 550
Shopping: Hong Kong, inclusive, 143-155; Hong Kong Central, 79; Kowloon, Tsim Sha Tsui, 89; Kowloon, Yau Ma Tei, 93; Wan Chai district, 82; Macao, 182; Singapore, tips, inclusive, 478-487; Taiwan, inclusive, 640-645; Thailand, inclusive, 308-314
Shopping guide: Hong Kong, 143; Thailand, 308
Shopping terms, Cantonese, Hong Kong, 193
Short-term investors, Taiwan, 655
Shortwave radio, Thailand, 246
Shrines: Thailand, Bangkok, 261; Nakhon Panom, 274; spirit houses, 219
Siam. See Thailand
Siam Center Shopping Complex, Bangkok, Thailand, 313
Siam Lodge Group of Hotels, Thailand, 282
Sichuan restaurants: Hong Kong, list, 121-122; Singapore, list, 460; Taiwan, list, 625-626
Sichuanese cuisine, Hong Kong, 121-122
Siddhartha Guatama (Buddha), 218
Sightseeing tours: Hong Kong, inclusive, 66-73; Macao, inclusive, 180-182; Singapore, inclusive, 409-427, list, 406-408; Taiwan, inclusive, 567-572; Thailand, 251, inclusive, 252-281
Silom and Surawong roads, Bangkok, Thailand, 253, 256, 313
Silver, Thailand shopping, 309
Singapore: tour, inclusive, 409-427; tourist guide, inclusive, 367-524; travel outside of, 516-521
Singapore Convention Bureau (SCB), regional offices, list, 511-514

Singapore dollar, exchange rates, 398

Singapore Institute of Standards and Industrial Research (SISIR), 509

Singapore Sling (drink), 418, 473

Singapore Stock Exchange (SES), 498

Singapore tourist promotion board: 374; regional offices, 377-379

Single-entry visa, Taiwan, 546-547

Sino—British Joint Liaison Group, Hong Kong future status, 27, 198

Sino—Portuguese architecture, Phuket, Thailand, 279

Sisters, island, Singapore, 427

Skilled labor, Hong Kong, 161

Sleeper service, Taiwan trains, 565

Small Enterprise Bureau (SEB), Singapore, 509

Smuggling, Thailand restrictions, 237

Snack bars, Singapore, 467-468

"Snake Alley," Taipei, Taiwan, 576

Snake charmer, 471

Social and cultural mores: Singapore, general, 396-398; in mosque or temple, 393; Taiwan, 532-533, 559-560; business, 655-656; Thailand, 215-216, 242-243

Social clubs, Singapore, 514-515

Social Development Unit, Singapore, 370

Song Dynasty Village, Lai Chi Kok, Kowloon, Hong Kong, 94

Song Thaews (Thai pickup truck), 249

Songkhla, Thailand, 281

Songkran (Thai new year) festival, 230

Sotheby's (auction house), Hong Kong, 144

South Bridge Road, Singapore, 485

Space Museum, Tsim Sha Tsui, Kowloon, Hong Kong, 93

Special interest tours, Taiwan, 538

Spectator sports, Macao, 182

Spirit festivals: Hong Kong, 43; Singapore, 383; Taiwan, 541

Spirit houses: Thailand, 219; Bangkok, 261

Sporting goods, Taiwan, 643

Sports: Hong Kong, 140-142; for children, 100; Sha Tin Center, New Territories, 95; Macao, 182; Singapore, list, 474-477; Taiwan, 637-639; Thailand, 305-307

Standard of living: Singapore, 374, 489; Thailand, 276

Stanley, Hong Kong, 86-87

Star Ferry Company Limited, Hong Kong, 65

Star Ferry Concourses, Hong Kong: Hong Kong Central tour, 74; local transportation, 61, 62, 65

Statues, Hong Kong Central tour, 79

Steamers (ships), to China from Hong Kong, 185

Steak and chop houses, Singapore, 467

Steeples: Ayutthaya temple ruins, 264;

Bangkok temples, 256

Stilt houses, Lantau, island, Hong Kong, 98

Stockbrokers, Hong Kong, 164

Stock exchange: Hong Kong, 34, 164; Singapore, 498; Taiwan, 654

Stock Exchange of Hong Kong, Limited, 34, 164

Stock market, Hong Kong, 74, 164-165

Stonecutter's Island, Hong Kong, 25

Stoneware: Celadon, Thai shopping, 309; Sangkhalok, Thai shopping, 309

Street stalls: Hong Kong, 132; Cheung Chau, island, 98

Street vendors, Thailand, safety, 239

Striptease, Bangkok, bars and clubs, 305

Student protests, Thailand history, 210

Subway: Hong Kong, 60, stations and fares, 63; Singapore, 404; Taiwan, under construction, 566

Sukhothai, Thailand: history, 204, 211; ruins, 273

Sultan mosque, Singapore, 410, 420

Summer cottages: Hong Kong, Cheung Chow, island, 98; Shek O, 86

Sun block, Thailand sun protection, 239

Sun Moon Lake: Taiwan, 538; tours, 570, 583

Sun Yatsen (Chinese statesman): China, birthplace, 183; Macao memorial, 182; Taiwan, 529, 541, memorial, 576-577

Supermarkets, in department stores, Taiwan, 644

Surin, beach, Phuket, Thailand, 281

Swimming: Hong Kong, 141; Singapore, 474-475; Taiwan, 638

Swimming pools, Taiwan hotels, 638

Szechuan restaurants. See Sichuan restaurants

Taboos, religious, Thailand, 219

Taichung, Taiwan: 538; hotels, list, 614-616; houses of worship, list, 558; radio, 563; tour, 582

Tailoring: Hong Kong shops, 147-148; Singapore, 482-483; Taiwan, 643; Thailand, 312

Tainan, Taiwan, 586-587

Tai O, Lantau, island, Hong Kong, stilt houses, 98

Taipa, island, Macao, 183

Taipei, Taiwan: airline offices, list, 548-549; Asian restaurants, 628-629; bars and pubs, 630-631; bookstores, 564; business clubs, 632; business center attractions, 645; Chinese restaurants, types listed, 623-626; diplomatic missions, list, 658-659; government organizations, list, 657; group tours, hotels, 537-538; hospitals, list, 553-554; hotels, list, 598-607; houses of worship, list, 556-558; international banks, lists, 651-654; international trade associations, list, 665-667; mandarin, 533; movie theaters, list, 635; music, 634; nightclubs, 636; night markets and bazaars, 645; radio, 563; rail travel, 565-566; shopping, 640; subway construction, 566; taxis, 565; teahouses, 631-632; telephone, 562; tour, inclusive, 573-579; tours, 567; travel agencies, list, 567; western restaurants, 629-630; zoo, 578

Taipei World Trade Center (TWTC), 656

Tai Po, marketplace, New Territories, Hong Kong, 96

Taitung, Taiwan, hotel, 616

Taiwan Retrocession Day, 541

Taiwan Stock Exchange (TAIEX), 654

Taiwan: town, inclusive, 573-596; tourist guide, inclusive, 527-671

Taiwanese (language), 532-533

Taiwanese restaurants, 626

Takraw (sport), Thailand, 306

Taksin (Thai warrior king), 208

Tam Kung Festival, Hong Kong, 42

Tamsui, Taiwan, 580

Tanglin Road, Singapore, 485

Tan Yeok Nee House, Singapore, 417

Taoism, Taiwan, 532

Taoyuan, Taiwan, hotels, list, 617

Ta Pae Road, Chiang Mai, Thailand, 271

Tamil (language), Singapore, 376

Taroko Gorge, Taiwan: 582; tour, 538, 569

Tax, Thailand hotels, 282

Taxation: Hong Kong, 156, 163; Singapore, 493-496; Taiwan, 649-651; Thailand, 320-322

Tax clearance certificate, Thailand, 238, 322

Tax incentives: Singapore business, 496; Thailand business, 316, 321

Taxis: Hong Kong, 60-61; arrival, 47; Macao, 177; Singapore, 401-402; Taiwan, 565; Thailand, 240; negotiated fares, 249

Tea, Taiwan, types, 642

Tea gardens, Lantau, island, Hong Kong, 97

Teahouses, Taiwan, 631-632

Technical cooperation, Taiwan investment, 647

Teenagers, Bangkok shopping centers, 314

Telegram service, Bangkok, 245

Telephone: Hong Kong, rates, area codes, 58; Macao, 177; Singapore, 400; Taiwan, 562-563; Thailand, area codes, 245-246

Telephone numbers: Hong Kong, 173-174; Singapore, 515; medical services, 392; Taiwan, 668; Thailand, 359-360

Television: Hong Kong, 59; Singapore, 400; Taiwan, 564; imported

modifications, 551; Thailand, 246

Telex: Hong Kong, 58; Singapore, 400

Temple of the Heavenly Happiness. See Thian Hock Keng Temple

Temple rubbings (Thailand), 308, 311

Temples: Hong Kong, 36; Hong Kong Central tour, 78; Causeway Bay, 85; Kowloon, 94; Yau Ma Tei, 93; New Territories, 95; outlying islands, 97, 98, 99; Wan Chai tour, 82; Macao, 182; Singapore, landmarks, 419, 420; Chinatown, 412, 413; Little India, 415; Taiwan, 532, 577-578, 591; Peikang, 583; Penghu, 596; Taipan, 586; Thailand, Ayutthaya ruins, 264; Bangkok, major attractions, 256, list, 257-260; numbers of, 253; Chiang Mai, 269-271; Chiang Rai, 272; Sukhothai ruins, 273. See also shrines

Tennis: Hong Kong, 141; Singapore, 476; Taiwan, 637; Thailand, 307

Teochew restaurants, Singapore, list, 458-459

Teppanyaki restaurants, Taiwan, list, 628-629

Textiles. See Fabrics

Thai (language): 219-220; history, Thailand, 204; phrases and numbers, examples, 362-363

Thai (people): culture, Thailand, 214; history, Thailand, 204; Singapore, festivals, 382

Thai Airways: 228; domestic offices, list, 247

Thai cuisine: 297; popular dishes listed, 298

Thai dynasties and kingdoms, chronology, 211

Thai International Airways, 235

Thailand: tour, inclusive, 252-281; tourist guide, inclusive, 201-363; tours from Singapore, 520

Thailand, Bank of, 320

Thailand Phrasebook (Lonely Planet), 362

Thai restaurants: in Bangkok, list, 300; Hong Kong list, 128-129; Singapore, 464; Taiwan, 629

Thai script, 219, 362

Thai silk, 308, 312

Thai sticks (marijuana), 274

Theater: Hong Kong, 136; Singapore, 470

Theater restaurants, Thailand, 302

Theme parks, Singapore, 423

Theravada Buddhism (Thailand): 216; history, 204

Thian Hock Keng Temple, Singapore, 420

Thieves' Market, Bangkok, Thailand, 256, 262, 314

Thompson, Jim (American entrepreneur), Bangkok home, 260

Thonburi, Thailand: canals, 262; history,

208; temples, 257-258

Tickets, to Macao from Hong Kong, 176-177

Tiger Balm Gardens. *See* Aw Boon Haw Gardens, Hong Kong; Haw Par Villa, Singapore

Time zones: Hong Kong and, 52-53; Singapore and, 392-393; Taipei, Taiwan and, 555; Thailand and, 241-242

Tin Haw's birthday, Hong Kong, 42

Tipping: Hong Kong practice, 54; Singapore, 396; Taiwan, uncommon, 559; Thailand, uncommon, 242

Tomb of the Seven Virgins, Chimei, Taiwan, 596

Tonal languages: Cantonese, Hong Kong, 187; mandarin in Taiwan, useful phrases, 669; Thai, 219, 362

Tour bus, in Thailand, 229

Tour companies, Thailand, based in United States and Canada, list, 225-226

Tour operators, Hong Kong, list, 71-73

Tourism Authority of Thailand (TAT), offices at home and abroad, lists, 222-224

Tourism offices, in Taiwan, abroad, list, 535-536

Tourist information: Hong Kong Tourist Association, 38-39; Singapore Tourist Promotion Board, 377-379; Taiwan, inclusive, 535-543; Thailand Tourism Authority, list of offices, 221-224

Tours: to China, from Hong Kong, 184; to China, from Singapore, 519-520; to Malaysia, from Singapore, 517-518

Touts (street vendors): Singapore, avoidance of, 480; Thailand, 308

Towers: Bangkok temples, 257; Chiang Mai temples, 271; Nakhon Panom Shrine, 274. *See also* Steeples

Trade and commercial offices, Thailand overseas, 333-338

Trade and Industrial Promotion International, Hong Kong, representatives overseas, list, 167-170

Trade associations, Bangkok, Thailand, 345-359

Trade Development Board (TDB), Singapore, regional offices, list, 504-509

Trade publications, Hong Kong list, 162

Trade shows, Hong Kong facilities, 162-163

Trademarks: Hong Kong, 160; Singapore protection, 493; Taiwan, 648

Train. *See* Railroad transportation; Subways

Tram tour, Hong Kong, 69

Trams, Hong Kong, 62

Trang, province, Thailand, 281

Transportation: in Hong Kong, costs, 39; to Macao from Hong Kong, 176. *See also* type of, such as Air transportation,

Railroad transportation, etc.

Transportation, public. *See* under type, such as buses, subways, taxis, etc.

Transvestites, Pattaya beach, 267

Travel agencies: Taiwan, 537; Taipei, list, 567; Thailand, 251; hotel reservations, 283; Bangkok, list, 227

Traveler's checks: Hong Kong, 57; Taiwan limited use, 561; Thailand use, 243

Tribal Research Center, Chiang Mai, Thailand, 272

Trishaw (bicycle with sidecar), Singapore, 405

Tropical fruits, Thailand varieties, 297

Tsengwen Reservoir, Taiwan, 590

Tsim Sha Tsui, Kowloon, Hong Kong: 89, 93; shopping, 143, 145, 147, 149, 154

Tuk Tuk (Thai vehicle): 249; Koh Samui, transportation, 278

Typhoons: Hong Kong, 40; Taiwan, 543

Ubon Ratchathani, Thailand, candle festival, 275

Udon Thani, Thailand, 274

Umbrella making, festivals, Thailand, 229

Unlisted Securities Market (USM), Singapore, 498

Urban redevelopment, Singapore, 409

Value-Added Tax (VAT), Taiwan, 650-651

Vegetarian cuisine, Fo Kuang Shan Temple, Taiwan, 594

Vegetarian festival, Thailand, 232

Vegetarian food, Po Lin Monastery, Lantau Island, Hong Kong, 133

Vegetarianism, Buddhism, Thailand, 218

Vegetarian restaurants: Hong Kong, list, 129; Singapore, list, 460-461; Taiwan, list, 626

Victoria Park, Causeway Bay, Hong Kong, 84

Vietnamese (people), boat people in Hong Kong refugee camps, 35

Vietnamese restaurants, Hong Kong, 129

Visas: to China from Hong Kong, 185-186; Hong Kong, 45, 157-158; Macao, 175-176; Singapore, 385; professional visit, 490; Taiwan, 544, 546-547; Thailand, 233

Walking, Hong Kong, 142

Walking tour: peak area, Hong Kong, 89; Singapore, 408

Walla-Wallas. *See* motorboats

Wan Chai, district, Hong Kong, 82

Wan Chai Market, Hong Kong, 82

Wanhua Market, Taipei, Taiwan, 576

Watches, Hong Kong shopping, 146

Water buffalo, Peikang, Taiwan, market, 586

Water skiing, Hong Kong, 142

Water spirits, festival, Thailand, 232
Water sports: Hong Kong, 142; Singapore, 423, 477; Taiwan, 638; Hsiao Liuchiu, island, 596; Kenting National Park, 595; Penghu, 596; Thailand, 307; tours including, 251; Koh Samet, 269; Koh Samui beaches, 278; Pattaya, 267
Water taxis, Aberdeen, Hong Kong, 88
Water tours, Hong Kong Cruises, types, 67
Water World, amusement park, Hong Kong: 88; children's activities, 100
Wat Phra Keo, Bangkok, Thailand, Emerald Buddha, 256-257
Wats. See temples
Wayang. See Chinese opera
Weekend Market, Bangkok, Thailand, 262-314
Western District, Hong Kong, 88
Western hotel management, Singapore hotel list, 452
Wet market, Singapore, 425
White paper (1988), Hong Kong status, 29
Wickerware, Thailand items, 311
Windsurfing: Hong Kong, 142; Singapore, 477
Wine, Chinese, Hong Kong, 117
Wine, Portuguese, Macao, 182
Women, single, Thailand Travel, pitfalls, 241
Wong Tai Sin Temple, Kowloon, Hong Kong, 94
Wood carvings: Taiwan, 642; Thai craft, 311

Work force: Hong Kong, 36, statistics, 160-161; Singapore, 490; Thailand, literacy rate, 213; protection, 319
Work permit: Hong Kong, 157-158; Singapore, 490; Taiwan, 646; Thailand, 315
World War II: Hong Kong, Japanese occupation, 25; Singapore, Japanese occupation, 369; Taiwan, Japanese occupation, 529; Thailand, Kanchanaburi bridge on the river Kwai, 264
Worship, places of: Singapore, landmarks, 419-420, list, 393-395; Taiwan, list, 556-559
Wulai, Taiwan, tour, aboriginal culture, 568-580

Xiamen, China, by steamer from Hong Kong, 185

Yau Ma Tei, Kowloon, Hong Kong, 93
Youth activity centers, Taiwan, 597, list, 618-619
Youth hostels. See hostels
Yunlin, Taiwan, hotel, 618

Zhongshan, China, day trip from Hong Kong, 183
Zirconia, Taiwan, 640
Zoo, Taipei, Taiwan, 578
Zoological Gardens, Singapore, 422

PHOTOGRAPHIC CREDITS